THE NARROW SEA

A History of the English Channel, its Approaches,
and its Immediate Shores

400 B.C. — A.D. 1945

THE NARROW SEAS

By

Reginald Hargreaves

SIDGWICK AND JACKSON LIMITED
LONDON

First printed 1959

© Reginald Hargreaves 1959

Made and printed in Great Britain by
William Clowes and Sons, Limited, London and Beccles

The majority of the early colonists of North America were of British stock; and thus the history of the English Channel is the common heritage of both the British and the American peoples.

Even subsequent to the days of the Founding Fathers and the Declaration of Independence the repercussion of events in the Narrow Seas was felt no less by the people of the United States than by the inhabitants of the Channel's western shore, and Continental Europe generally.

In recent years American and British seamen have fought side by side to keep that narrow strip of salt water inviolate; while British and American soldiers, sailors and airmen have crossed it bearing the boon of liberty to a Continent in bondage.

It is, therefore, to my friends in the Armed Forces of Britain and America, of two world wars, that this book is dedicated.

REGINALD HARGREAVES

Contents

CONTENTS

PART THREE

THE YEARS OF PERIL

Introduction

"PROVIDENCE made man to live ashore," pronounced the seventeenth-century bishop Griffith Williams, "and it is necessity alone which drives him to sea."

Even so, there are few corners of the 141,050,000 square miles of water on the globe's surface to which the adventurous have failed to penetrate. Yet as there are great tracts of wasteland on the 55,214,000 square miles of *terra firma*, so there are oceanic wastes of a desolation almost beyond belief. These persist in sharp contrast to the busy maritime traffic lanes, swarming with freight and passenger transport, and policed by the world's navies.

Certain of these maritime turnpikes, such as the Suez and Panama canals, the Dardanelles and the Straits of the Bosphorus, the Kattegat, the Strait of Messina, and the Gibraltar gateway to the Mediterranean, have acquired a significance, both commercially and strategically, which puts them in a category apart.

But of them all by far the most important is that narrowing strip of waterway whose present limits lie, to the west, between the parallel 48.28 N of the east extreme of Ushant, thence to the Bishop's Rock, the south-west extreme of the Scilly Isles, thence eastward to the Longships, 50.0 N., and on to the Land's End; and, to the east, the line joining the Walde Light House, 1.55 E., and Leathercoat Point, 51.10 N. It is a high-road of the sea which is known to the French as *La Manche*, to bygone mariners as the Narrow Seas, and to the world in general as the English Channel.

Time was when sheep browsing on what are now the Sussex Downs could nibble their way across to the slopes of Picardy dryshod. But some fearful convulsion of Nature brought about a subsidence that admitted the waters of the North Sea and the Atlantic, to submerge the original river flowing east and west and form the Sleeve. Of this the 'forearm' comes where Portland and the Cherbourg peninsula narrow the west channel to half its width; the 'wrist' being formed by the Dover Straits, and the protuberant 'thumb' by the Thames Estuary.

With the wild inrush of the sea a primitive community was totally engulfed. For somewhere beneath the fretted waters tumbling between St. Michael's Mount and the Scillies the Kingdom of Lyonesse, with its forty thriving parishes, lies hidden by the waves. So the story goes; and it well may be that on the Mount itself, as on the Runnelstone and the Wolf rocks, once perched the guardian strongholds of this vanished realm.

At the same period the Wight became separated from the Hampshire coast.

For that matter, time was when an island, a mile and a half in length, extended off the foreshore of St. Leonards, Norden's seventeenth-century map being the last example of cartography to include its contours. Furthermore, if legend is to be believed, the Goodwins—under the name of the Isle of Lomea—once formed part of, and were linked with, the mainland territories of the Eorl Godwin whose son, Harold, fell beneath the on-slaught of Duke William's Normans at the battle of Senlac. Transmogrified into an eleven by four and a half miles' stretch of treacherous sand, they have claimed over fifty thousand human lives and a hundred million pounds' worth of shipping.

Encircled by their salt-water girdle, the British Isles stand within a vast ledge of decreasing soundings. Pounding in with irresistible force, the huge mass of the Atlantic meets the ob-struction of this ledge, to find its progress impeded at the south-west points of Ireland and England. Dividing into three main 'impulses'—of which the middle one may here be ignored—the waters which have passed round the north of Scotland and partly diffused themselves into the North Sea, on their way to the east and south arrive in the Straits of Dover within twenty hours. There they meet the lusty stream that has come directly up Channel and arrived in the Straits within twelve hours. This violent impact, combined with irregularities in the sea-bed, is responsible for the extraordinary variety of currents and eddies, as for the varying times of high water at different places in the same neighbourhood. Compressed between the

Portland and Cherbourg peninsulas, the waters swirl and riot mutinously until, in the neck of the Channel, they find a narrow outlet and race northward, around the remoter coasts of Scotland and Northern Ireland.

Thus the Channel tide table, with its lesser tidal systems, cross-currents, rips, undertows and races, is a law unto itself; with the Solent a wilful law within a law. It can, for instance, be high tide at Portland Bill and low tide at St. Catherine's, Isle of Wight, at one and the same time. Matters are further complicated by the fact that high-water times and the Channel streams go their independent ways. At Dover, for example, the east-going stream has three or four hours still to run *after* high water. Conversely, other places fill up with the west-going stream. There is double tide-water at Southampton and at Poole; while Portsmouth rejoices in two floods and two high waters, during which the level remains constant, with only one low water, and that of short duration.

The Thames Estuary has its own peculiarities, not the least of them being the absence of a wide choice in deep-water channels. There are only two navigable by ships of deep draught: that to the North Sea, running more or less straight and parallel to the Essex shore in a N.E. and S.W. direction, and known as the Barrow Deep; and the Edinburgh Channel on the south side, leading in a south-westerly direction to a point north of the Goodwin Sands. In effect, the Estuary is nothing more nor less than a sunken delta, crowned with a network of sandbanks—the Kentish Knock, The Sunk, the East Barrow, the West Barrow, Gunfleet, the Red Sand, the Margate Sand, and the Longsand—all of them viciously dangerous to shipping.

Yet London takes rank as the Channel's head-port, indissolubly linked to it by the umbilical cord of the Thames. Without the riverway, with its seam of gravel to provide a ford for itinerant merchants, hard-by the site of present-day London Bridge, there is no reason to believe that London would ever have come into existence. From the outset, its importance as a city largely depended upon its value as a waterside entrepôt, whence maritime trade set forth for the ports of entry on the Continental mainland.

One of the most powerful influences on the character and

behaviour of the Channel was defined by the mid-seventeenth-century mariner Richard Gibson. "The wind blowing above three-quarters of the year westerly on the coast of England," he wrote in 1659, "made all our cape-lands and bays very good roads for ships to anchor in." The truth of this is not to be gainsaid. To the eastward, the lack of sanctuary-forming head-lands on the Channel coast of France is patent. There is the Cherbourg peninsula and the Seine Head (*Cap de la Hève*), guarding the estuary of Le Havre, and then nothing but a stretch of low cliff, varying little in height and broken only by Boulogne and Sangatte bays, Calais and Gravelines roads, and Dieppe. Calais and Gravelines, however, suffer the disadvantage of being open roadsteads, with a lee shore—that is to say, a shore on which the wind is blowing—for something over three-quarters of the year.

On the English coast, *per contra*, there are Land's End, the Lizard, Start, Portland, St. Alban's, St. Catherine's, Beachy, Dungeness, and Dover Castle headlands, all offering shelter, as do many small bays and inlets, from the prevailing south-west wind. There was, and mostly remains, safe anchorage to be found in Mount's Bay, Falmouth, Cawsand Bay—now known as Plymouth Sound—Torbay, Dartmouth Range, Lyme Bay, Weymouth, Yarmouth Isle of Wight, Cowes Roads, Stokes Bay, Spithead, St. Helen's Bourne—now merged into East-bourne—Fairlight, Rye Bay, Romney and Hythe Bays, Dover Roads, the Downs, Margate Roads and Birchington Bay, the Swale, the Nore, the Swin, Gunfleet, Hollesley and Aldeburgh Bays, and further north-east, Dunwich, Southwold, Lowestoft and Yarmouth Roads.

For all that, the coast is not without its potent disadvantages. The persistent, unrelenting 'easterly drift' piles up shingle and sand on the westward side of many of these sanctuaries; while erosion is at work on certain other of the beaches, such as those between Brighton and the North Foreland, which face the prevailing wind and the tide. For Purbeck is the last of the rock formations on the mainland, and it is not until the chalk comes down to the sea beyond Brighton that escape is made from low-lying strands of sand and gravel.

The Chesil—or Shingle—beach, with Portland's grim cliffs to the east, and backed by the lowering grey hills of Hardy's

Wessex, offers a deadly, uncompromising lee shore; with the nearest harbour of refuge some miles distant and frequently difficult to make. It is certainly no place in which to find one-self embayed.

In the remote past Selsey—Seolh's Island, where a seal was shot as recently as 1919—was much more of a Bill than it is today; stretching out into the Channel as it did to a point almost level with the Nab Tower, off the Isle of Wight, where the Owen's lightship now stands guard over a welter of shoals and freshets of the Loo stream, that threads its way below. It appears certain that this submerged area was once a settlement, with a great temple and many dwellings. But the newly gouged-out Channel claimed it and the Great Park through which the Loo stream once flowed. Dungeness, on the other hand, is a place which, like 'Topsy', "just growed"—by kind favour of the easterly drift, constantly adding to its substance. For the south-west wind is an on-shore wind, with all that that implies.

The old harbour of Lympne once protected the eastern flank of a great bay, now turned into the 100,000-acre Guildford and Romney Marshes, with their lesser Walland and Denge Marshes. Exactly when and how the metamorphosis came about it is now impossible accurately to determine. Whether the original Rhee Wall, from Appledore to Romney—now a roadway raised above the level of the surrounding marsh—was erected in pre-Roman days or by the Romans them-selves, must remain a matter for speculation. But Roman relics found extensively all over the Marsh make it clear that the sea's recession ante-dated the arrival of Gaius Julius Caesar on the island shores in 55 B.C. Thereafter the process of 'inning' the marshlands with the shingle driven in by the easterly drift —to create the St. Thomas 'innings' between 1162 and 1174, the Baldwin's 'innings' between 1184 and 1194, and the Boniface 'innings' between 1240 and 1270—has continued steadily, progressively choking the pristine waterways.

It is an extraordinary experience to set out—leaving Hythe musketry range behind you—to cross the Marsh to Rye and Winchelsea. For mile after mile you drive over what, an aeon ago, was the sea bed. Incredibly desolate—for the few houses scattered about scarcely impinge on the attention—with here and there a wary clump of trees and an occasional field of kale or clover, the whole great land-bay is given over to a myriad of industriously munching sheep, battening on the tough but nutritious grass that somehow has established itself in the shallow crust of earth that time has formed over the sub-stratum of barren shingle. In 1939 over two hundred thousand sheep fattened on the Marsh, and during the war years, when the flock had diminished by half, arrangements were made to evacuate over twenty thousand of the creatures when 'Opera-tion Sealion' really looked as though it were to be attempted. Surveying the scene under its own variety of aqueous, wind-raked sky, it is easy to understand why it has been termed "the Fifth Quarter of the Globe".

From the axis of the low-lying terrain, far away on the hori-zon can be seen the rolling, thickly wooded hills that swing round from Hythe to Appledore, in a demi-lune whose curve is completed by the miniature promontory on which Rye nestles like a slightly truncated Mont St. Michel. It is that line of hills which defines the coastline of primordial Albion. All that lies about you has been piled up by the irresistible thrust of the easterly drift, sweeping its endless store of shingle before it. It is true that the activities of the easterly drift have been aided by the violent storms that blow up so easily in the narrow seas; their surge and fury have demonstrably affected the huge saucer of marshland over which they have swept. Somewhere about 1287, for example, a tempest of unprecedented violence and magnitude caused the river Rother—which threads the Marsh—to alter its course and abandon Romney in favour of Rye; destroying the former's usefulness as a harbour first by flooding and then by silting up the haven. In another fierce storm Old Winchelsea—Gwent-chesel-ey, "the Shingle Island on the Level"—disappeared completely, only a sandbank remaining to mark its probable site. But Rye was not destined for long to enjoy its pre-eminence. With New Winchelsea, it suffered invasion by the endless drifts of shingle; and by the time of the Spanish Armada its maritime eclipse was as pro-found as that of its neighbour.

To see the easterly drift at work in all its tireless malignancy it is only necessary to cross the Denge Marsh—'inned' as early as A.D. 774 by a generation of ruthlessly acquisitive Church-men—and traverse the dreary waste beyond Lydd to Dungeness,

perched precariously on a great wind-swept expanse of virtually
naked shingle. Here and there a sparse patch of marram
struggles obstinately to expand; a clump of gorse valiantly
defies uprooting; a tuft of sea thistles or catmint bends in the
stiff breeze that blows almost eternally from the south-west.
Behind you, across ten miles and more of featureless flat to
Appledore, the Marsh crouches in its sinister, brooding still-
ness, where once dancing waves shifted and sparkled under the
summer sky.

*   *   *

But it is not only about Hythe, Lympne, Romney, Winchelsea and Rye that the sea has receded in face of the ever-advanc-
ing shingle. To the north-east, beyond Dover, Rutupiae
(Richborough) Castle, on its mound, was once surrounded not
by meadow land but by salt water. Indeed, the whole Isle of
Thanet—the Isle of Tanatus, or Isle of Fire—to the east of the
ancient stronghold was cut off from the Kentish mainland by a
wide estuary, into which flowed the waters of the Greater and
Lesser Stour, the Wantsum and the Genlade. In its days of
yore this great arm of the sea formed a most convenient salt-
water highway to the Thames, affording direct approach to
the head-port of London. It was a fact of geography which
accounted for the erstwhile importance of Stonor and Sandwich as the capital's principal out-ports.

The Isle of Thanet, being separated from the mainland by
a channel three-eighths of a mile across at its widest, formed a
natural stronghold very difficult of approach; a state of
affairs of which the Vikings, in their many efforts to invade the
country, were quick to take advantage, turning it into a
virtually impregnable *point d'appui*.

The tiny hamlet of Sandwich was reconstituted and enlarged on reclaimed land by Canute; and in its heyday it was
used as the port of embarkation for royal personages bound
for the Continent. It reached its zenith of activity under
Henry IV (1399–1413), and at one time took pride of place as
the leading member of the Cinque Ports. But it was no more
immune from the effect of the easterly drift than its neighbours
further west. With the steady silting up of its harbour its maritime traffic sensibly declined. Nowadays it stands as helplessly

marooned on its shingle bed as Romney, Rye or Winchel-sea; while the once thriving out-port of Stonor boasts little more than a ballast undertaking and the quarters of a Royal Air Force installation.

All in all, the Sandwich littoral differs from the Romney Marsh only in scale. Sandwich, with its huddle of narrow streets, is Rye and its cobbled alleys all over again. Somnolent but dignified, like veteran warriors sunning themselves in an ale-house porch, they seem alike to be brooding on glories long since departed.

In effect, the Cinque Ports—Hastings, Romney, Hythe, Dover and, with the Conquest, Sandwich; to which, in 1247, were added the 'antient towns' of Winchelsea and Rye—fought a long but losing battle with the unremittent easterly drift of silt and shingle, and the steady 'inning' of the Marsh. In time of storm the loss of their respective harbours was, and remains, particularly grievous, since between Portsmouth and the mouth of the Thames no safe anchorage offers which is accessible at all tides, save Newhaven. For the facilities at Folkestone are negligible, while Dover is neither a natural haven nor a good one, invaluable as may be the purpose it has been brought to serve. In effect, its usefulness as a harbour has fluctuated with the success or failure of the authorities to cope with the effects of the easterly drift. During the Napoleonic wars, for example, its accessibility was seriously in jeopardy; and it was not until the Admiralty pier on the west side of the bay—begun in 1897—had succeeded in stopping the easterly drift of shingle from Shakespeare beach, that the haven's full-scale utility was finally established.

There was one effect of "the wind blowing above three-quarters of the year westerly" upon which Master Richard Gibson did not enlarge. To beat down Channel in the teeth of bitterly contrary winds, in the days of sail, was often a matter of sheer impossibility. Supports and supplies for Buckingham's 1627 expedition to the *Ile de Rhé*, for example, were held up by unfavourable winds for weeks on end, and in consequence the whole enterprise foundered miserably. Indeed, the tale of transports and their escorts held up or forced to run for shelter in Torbay or Plymouth, forms one of the most persistent records of frustration ever to be compiled. It was a state of

affairs which only underwent remedy when steam power came
to provide the energy that could propel a vessel in any
direction, irrespective of the quarter in which the wind might
happen to be blowing. Up to that time the mariner all too
often found himself

> *To be imprisoned in the viewless winds*
> *And blown with restless violence round about*
> *The pendant world.*

And never more so than in the Narrow Seas.

*   *   *

If Jove occasionally nodded, it still remains extraordinary
that Shakespeare, with his vast fund of general knowledge and
his real understanding of shipmen and the sea, should ever have
been guilty of such bathetic nonsense as that spouted by one of
the King's counsellors in *Cymbeline*:

> *. . . Remember, sir, my liege,*
> *The kings your ancestors! together with*
> *The natural bravery of your isle, which stands*
> *At Neptune's park, ribbed and paled in*
> *With rocks unscaleable and roaring waters,*
> *With sands that will not bear your enemies' boats,*
> *But suck them up to the topmast.*

Now as that eminent naval historian Sir Geoffrey Callender
pointed out, this is so much high-sounding blatter—or, at
best, a sly dig at the manifest want of sagacity so characteristic
of the politician when animadverting on matters of warfare.
In point of fact, England's natural defences, her "rocks
unscaleable", are all strewn along her western coastline; where,
in early days, no invaders were to be expected. On the other
hand, the whole sweep of the Channel, in the bleak words of
the seventeenth-century author of *The Sussex Breviary*, "lyeth
open and ready for foreign invasion, since there be so many
havens, harbours, creeks and other places of ready descent".
Indeed, the east and south coasts of "this fortress, built by
Nature for herself, against infection and the hand of war"
offers vantage point after vantage point, including the requisite
harbours, for an enemy landing force, sweeping in across a
sea which so far from being "a fence impregnable" is an open

waterway over which any competent seaman can journey at will—providing there be no opposition. As Admiral Fisher briskly summed it up, "The last places to defend England are the shores of England. The frontiers of England are the coasts of the enemy." If command of the Channel is lost, England cannot survive. For as Alfred the Great was at pains to emphasise, "There is no advantage in living on an island unless your navy rides in undisputed sway over the waters that surround it"; and, in these days, lords it in the skies above those waters.

It was the want of proper naval defence that rendered possible the landing of Gaius Julius Caesar, Aulus Plautius, Julius Agricola, Hengist and Horsa, Canute, Harald Hadrada, Norman William, Henry of Anjou, Bolingbroke, Warwick the King-maker, Edward IV, Henry Earl of Richmond (Henry VII), and that crafty, wheezing opportunist, William of Orange.

Yet when England has borne it steadily in mind to

> . . . *Chiefly keep the sharp narrow sea*
> *Between Dover and Calais, and as thus*
> *That foes pass none without goodwill of us,*[1]

her enemies have ever assailed her in vain. Philip II of Spain, Louis XIV of France, Napoleon, the Kaiser's Germany and Hitler's Third Reich—in all their cases their military efforts prospered mightily until it came to making the passage of those narrow seas where British Naval strength—and latterly the sea-eagles in their darting 'planes—kept unremitting watch and ward.

Even if the Channel waters, in these days, have been transmogrified from England's first line of defence into a glorified tank ditch, it still behoves us to

> . . . *keep the amyralte*
> *That we may be masters of the narrow sea.*

A country is never conquered until it has been physically occupied by its adversary's forces.

Unquestionably the proximity of the Continental mainland constitutes a perpetual menace in time of war; and Antwerp in

[1] *A Libelle of English Policy*, attributed to Adam de Moleyns, Bishop of Chichester (*circa* 1450).

hostile hands is "a pistol pointing straight at England's heart". For all that, Britain's position dominating the only seaway linking the two ocean zones of the Mediterranean and the Baltic turns the Straits of Dover into a marine toll gate through which must pass all the naval strength and water-borne commerce on passage between North and South. This was a consideration by no means overlooked by the shrewd mind of that selfsame Henry VII; although it was shamefully lost sight of by the shambling, pusillanimous James I; the one man who had the opportunity to end what has become known as the Thirty Years' War, by denying passage through the Straits to the Spanish mercenaries who principally fought it.

The British, facing Holland and the Northern Powers on the one hand, and on the other confronting France and the Atlantic, can always operate on interior lines, even when threatened by a coalition between Hollander, Gaul and Scandinavian. Thus they are, as Alfred Thayer Mahan put it, "readily able to interpose their united forces against either one of the enemies which should seek to pass the Channel to effect a junction with its ally". Furthermore, with the Dover Straits under their control, no nation is in a better position to transfer and subsequently support an expeditionary force operating on the Continental mainland. Since, however, the British are never prepared for war, at the outset of hostilities their primary obligation is to concentrate on maintaining their sea communications—to keep the larder filled and the factory wheels turning. At least partial command of the Channel must be assured; and the emphasis is on the Navy and the Fleet Air Arm. There follows the struggle for supremacy in the skies; when the emphasis is transferred to the Air Force. (Even were there atomic or hydrogenic bombing, these obligations would still pertain with the survivors of the initial 'terror' onslaught.) It is only during the final but decisive land battles that the emphasis shifts to the expeditionary force of all arms, and even then command of the Channel remains a *sine qua non* of victory.

As a magnet and an entrepôt for trade, England's position is equally advantageous; while the configuration of her coastline along the Channel made her, in days gone by, a profitable Tom-Tiddler's-ground for those smugglers who so cheerfully helped a very large proportion of the populace to set the draconic Customs laws at commendable defiance.

All in all, the English Channel, and particularly the narrow Straits of Dover, may fairly claim to have played a more important part in history than any other waterway in the world. For here history has been made more often than can readily be calculated.

*   *   *

Modern cartographers have defined the limits of the Narrow Seas with great exactitude. Their present-day bounds, however, are a good deal more restricted than those which found acceptance in the past. The Elizabethans, for example, regarded the eastern extremity of *La Manche* as extending far beyond a line drawn from 1.55 E. to 51.10 N. Again, in the peace treaty which terminated the third Anglo-Dutch war— that of 1674—it was decreed that the English Flag should be entitled to salute "within the English Sea", which was defined as extending from "the meridian of Cape Finisterre to the middle point of the land Van Staten in Norway". Another definition referred to "all the seas between Cape Finisterre and the Naze"; an area which the seventeenth-century diplomatist Sir Philip Meadows described as "too wide for dominion and too narrow for respect". Small wonder that Richard Cromwell confessed his inability to determine exactly "how far the British seas extended". It is a problem that has puzzled wiser heads than his.

It is obvious, however, that the description of past events must be related to the Narrow Seas' contemporary bounds. Otherwise the account of the Armada fight, for one, could not be brought to a conclusion, since in its later stages it passed well beyond the limit set by a line drawn from Leathercoat Point to the Walde lighthouse. The same is true of the Dutch wars of the Commonwealth and the Restoration. Equally, the story of England's innumerable transactions with the Hansa towns, in peace and war, and with the thriving entry-ports of the Netherlands, would be but a half-told tale were erstwhile latitude of definition denied its full meed of recognition.

*   *   *

No people can hope to expand and prosper if they confine their activities to taking in each other's washing. To flourish they must trade with their neighbours. This is a stubborn fact which even the most unlikely quarters have been compelled to recognise. When the Inquisition was introduced into the Netherlands in 1550, for example, the bustling port of Antwerp remained immune from its attentions. For any interference with the swarm of English Protestant merchants resident in the city would have led to their prompt departure, and the loss of the handsome revenue the authorities derived from the 'merchant-strangers'' taxation.

Where an island race is concerned, mercantile prosperity is very largely a matter of the transhipment of goods by sea; those of indigenous manufacture, or those of foreign origin consigned to native vessels exclusively devoted to the carrying trade. It follows that the story of the English Channel is concerned as much with maritime commerce as with the fighting for which its waters so frequently furnished the arena. As often as not, indeed, it was some point of dispute over trade, some irreconcilable commercial rivalry, that rendered warfare ineludible. The thrice-renewed conflict between the Dutch and the English for predominance in the lucrative carrying trade and the sole right to exploit the riches of the Spice Islands was characterised by a persistence and resolution in battle that reflected the immense value of the issues at stake.

It was, *au fond*, the multiplicity of the demands of maritime commerce that gave impetus to the improvements in shipbuilding, in navigational aids, and in armaments; to the emergence of the Admiralty Courts and the administration of the laws of wreck, piracy and 'reprisal'; to the evolution of the system of pilotage and the installation of lights and buoys; to the building of docks, wharves, moulding lofts, rope walks and repair yards; to the institution of the Customs service, and to the incidence of smuggling. Even the pirate was inspired by an ever-increasing flow of water-borne trade to demand a better trimmed and speedier vessel, in which to outstrip the maritime forces of law and order sent forth for his suppression.

"Naval strategy", quoth Morogues, "has for its end to found, support, and increase, as well in peace as in war, the sea power of a country." And sea power represents a country's ability to trade, under the protection of its armed naval strength.

Actually, England's appearance as a competitor in the world's markets was somewhat belated. But with the tremendous asset of her native-grown wool, she very speedily became a Power with which the Continental manufacturing countries had seriously to reckon. So solid was her progress, indeed, that towards the end of the seventeenth century de Witt, in his penetrating study, *The Interest of Holland*, could justifiably observe: "This mighty island . . . seated in the midst of Europe, having a clear, deep coast, with good havens and bays, in so narrow a sea that all foreign ships that sail to the eastward or westward are necessitated, even in fair weather, to shun the dangerous French coast, and sail along that of England, and in stormy weather to run in and preserve their lives, ships and merchandise in its bays, so that now England . . . being much increased in strength, as well by manufactures as by navigation, will in all respects be formidable to all Europe. For according to the proverb, a master at sea is a lord at land, and more especially a King of England, seeing he is able, both by whole fleets and private ships of war, at all times to seize on ships sailing by that coast. . . ."

The Royal Navy was another belated arrival, being the lineal descendant of the self-defensive medieval trading vessel and the formidably armed mercantile marine of the first Tudor; as it was the logical outcome of the improvement in weapon design. The gun-deck imposed radical changes in ship construction, which had the effect of usurping what heretofore had been valuable cargo space. Thus the fighting ship became, at long last, a thing apart, in effect a floating gun platform; although in war-time the Royal Navy continued to be supplemented by armed merchant vessels, and looked to the Officers and men of the mercantile marine for the immediate augmentation of its personnel. In short, "A successful mercantile marine", as Admiral Fisher took every occasion to point out, "leads to a successful war Navy." It follows that a comprehensive account of the way of life and fluctuating conditions of employment, both in the Royal Navy and its elder-sister Service, must form an integral part of the general theme.

*　　　*　　　*

The activities of the sea being inextricably bound up with the life of the land, it has throughout been necessary to extend the narrative to include events transpiring on the Channel's immediate shore, and even further afield. For men originated on the land, and mostly cross the sea to fight or traffic on the land. For that matter, the very ships that give them passage originate on the land, are built, rigged and provisioned by land-based establishments: a fleet without a base is soon rendered impotent. In the same way, merchandise is freighted from land-based warehouses; Customs dues paid in land-based sheds; insurance rates and the terms of charter parties agreed in land-based offices. Even "brandy for the parson and 'baccy for the clerk" involved the closest collaboration between ship and shore. The story of the Channel, therefore, would be partial and incomplete were insufficient attention paid to events that transpired along the shores that bound it. Indeed, a proper appreciation of developments at sea is frequently dependent on a prior knowledge of what has taken place on land. In short, the story of the Narrow Seas must be unfolded, to some degree, against a background of general history, lest the narrative lack all causation and perspective and events take place in a bewildering vacuum.

This, however, being a work primarily concerned with the English and their activities, it is on home waters and the English shore that attention has principally been concentrated. Doubtless an enthralling book could be written on the Hansa fleet, the Breton corsairs, or the Salee rovers who once roamed at will in the mouth of the Thames. But here they qualify for mention only in so far as their destinies intermingled with those of the English shipmen with whom they so often warred.

*   *   *

In traversing the considerable span of history covered by the Channel story I have, inevitably, been driven to a certain amount of that over-simplification which so infuriates the warts-and-all, every-time-the-clock-ticks school of literary pedants. But in dealing with over two thousand eventful years a certain amount of short-circuiting has been ineludible. Doubtless I have been equally guilty, here and there, of that wisdom after the event which lends to posterity its insufferably smug air of superiority. Yet it is not only the duty of the striving historian to record what *happened*, it is also his obligation, in some sort, to point out what *mattered*.

This leads to the vexed question of footnotes. Diligent enquiry over a period of years has forced home the conclusion that many readers dislike them intensely. As many others appear to be animated by sufficient intellectual curiosity to appreciate them as a means of authenticating—and occasionally elaborating—statements of fact and sources of information. It is in the hope of satisfying the more enquiring mind that a certain number of them have been introduced in this work. To those who find them vexatious it might respectfully be pointed out that it is in no way incumbent upon them to read them.

It is realised, of course, that if he is to attain the ideal of impartiality the would-be historian, at work at his desk, should have no country, no politics, and no one religion. On the other hand, one of our most distinguished literary critics has affirmed that, "No man can write history—at least history which is readable—without a certain bias." To which may be added Taine's comment, that "Prejudice is a sort of reason operating unconsciously. It has claims as well as reason, but it is unable to advance them.... It issues from a long accumulation of experience." Perhaps we had better leave it at that!

Finally, Alfred the Great concluded a foreword to the works of Boethius in these terms: "I would pray and beseech every man that careth to read this book ... not to blame it on me if he understand more rightly than I could. For every man must, according to the measure of his understanding, speak what he speaks, and do what he does."

I can think of no better words with which to introduce the narrative that follows.

REGINALD HARGREAVES

Acknowledgments

FIRSTLY, my most sincere thanks must go to Miss Kathleen Withy, B.A., for her ungrudging and invaluable labours in preparing the typescript and the Index. I am most grateful to Mrs. Elmo Lascelles for the loan of maps, and to Dr. Marion Siney for the opportunity of reading her *Allied Blockade of Germany* in proof and for her permission, together with that of the University of Michigan, to quote from this work. I am greatly indebted to H. M. Sherry, Hampshire's resourceful County Librarian, for his unfailing help in securing the loan of many obscure and remotely accessible books; to Commander P. K. Kemp, R.N., Admiralty Archivist, for assistance and advice; to Wing-Commander E. Bentley-Beauman, R.A.F., and his successor as Librarian of the Royal United Service Institution, Brigadier John Stephenson, O.B.E.; to T. J. Holland, O.B.E., Assistant Librarian; to F. C. Tighe, B.A., County Librarian, Nottinghamshire; to W. Best Harris, F.L.A., City Librarian of Plymouth; to P. H. Coe, M.B.E., F.I.M.E.M., also of Plymouth; to H. K. G. Bearman, F.L.A., County Librarian, Sussex; to Miss F. A. E. Davies, M.A., F.L.A., County Librarian, Kent; to Edward J. Coombe, F.L.A., County Librarian, Devon; to Alfred E. Blackwell, Librarian, North Devon Athenaeum; to Percy Russell, F.S.A., Hon. Curator, Friends of Dartmouth Borough Museum; to J. Blanchard, L.L.M., Town Clerk, Portsmouth; to H. Jackson Seed of Southampton; to C. F. A. Tomlinson, of the Port of London Authority; and to the officials of the Admiralty Record Office, the Public Record Office, and Trinity House Corporation.

I am most grateful to the following authors and publishers for permission to quote from the respective works cited: to Admiral Sir William James, G.C.B., D.L., and Messrs. Macmillan, for extracts from *The Portsmouth Letters*, and to the same distinguished author and Messrs. Longmans, Green, for an extract from *The British Navy in Adversity*; to Major-General Sir Edward Spears, K.B.E., C.B., M.C., and Messrs. William

Heinemann, for an extract from *Assignment to Catastrophe*; to Dr. C. V. Wedgwood, C.B.E., and Messrs. William Collins, for an extract from *The King's Peace*; to Professor Christopher Lloyd and the Cresset Press, for an extract from *The Nation and the Navy*; to F. W. Brooks, M.A., and Messrs. A. Brown & Sons, for an extract from *The English Naval Forces, 1199–1272*; to G. E. Mainwaring and Bonamy Dobrée, and Messrs. Geoffrey Bles, for an extract from *The Floating Republic*; to Messrs. Constable for an extract from George Dangerfield's *Victoria's Heir*; to Messrs. Christopher, for extracts from Sir Geoffrey Callender's *The Naval Side of British History*; to Messrs. Macmillan for an extract from Sir John Fortescue's *History of the British Army*; to Messrs. Eyre & Spottiswoode, for an extract from *The Private Papers of Sir Douglas Haig* (edited by Robert Blake); to Messrs. John Murray, for an extract from *The King's Customs*, by Henry Atton and Henry Hurst Holland; and to the Managing Editor, Commander Roy de S. Horn, U.S. Navy (Ret.), and the Board of the United States Naval Institute, for permission to quote from the article *The German Side of the Channel Dash* by Captain H. J. Reinicke, published in the United States Naval Institute *Proceedings*.

Finally, my especial thanks are due to Commander F. J. Guppy, R.N., who so diligently scoured my narrative for those errors of naval history and maritime terminology of which the mere landlubber writing of the sea can so easily be guilty.

R. H.

"Rejoice, O Albion, severed from the world by Nature's wise indulgence."

JOHN PHILIPS (1676–1708)

PART ONE

In Time's Eye

"Cities and Thrones and Powers
Stand in Time's eye
Almost as long as flowers,
Which daily die."

RUDYARD KIPLING

CHAPTER I

The Beckoning Main

"... A span of waters; yet what power is there!
What mightiness of evil and for good."
                                    WILLIAM WORDSWORTH

THEY were desolate and lonely as a star, the narrow seas that separated Gaul from the glimmering white cliffs of Clas Merdin—the 'sea-defended green spot'—beyond the strait. Nothing moved across their surface, tranquil and sparkling under the summer sun or whipped to fury by the winter storm.

Whatever the activity on the eastern seaboard, on the westward shore it was only in sheltered creeks and estuaries and in the shallows under the lee of the land that a frail coracle of plaited, hide-covered withies ventured out into the shoal water, daring the waves in search of the sea food that everywhere abounded.

There was only a scattering of these fishermen, and they had little in common with the people of the forty tribes, descendants of the primitive Goidals and Brythons, who roamed the uplands. But even with the coastal folk the great land-mass of Europe was *terra incognita*, something glimpsed occasionally across a water-barrier that they accepted as impassable.

It was not until the fourth century B.C. that the Greeks acquired their scanty knowledge of the dim, mist-shrouded domain that lay beyond the Cassiterides, the islands off the north-western coast of the Iberian peninsula, which they had explored successfully in their search for tin.[1] It is possible that some of the more enterprising shipmen from the thriving port of Massilia (Marseilles) had ventured out across the western approaches to visit Clas Merdin in the early days of the Celtic penetration. But the first voyage to its shores of which there is

[1] Believed by some, however, to be the Scilly Islands. Vide works of Eratosthenes, Pliny, Polybius and Strabo.

3

actual record was that undertaken somewhere about 324 B.C.
by the Greek mathematician and astronomer Pytheas.

Taking ship at Massilia, Pytheas and his companions sailed
up the Gallic coast to Brittany and thence across the narrow
seas to Kent, skirting the island's southern and eastern shores
as far as the mouth of the Thames. What particularly astonished
the voyagers from the tideless Mediterranean was the ebb and
flow of the waters on these northern shores, which Pytheas put
at a maximum of 28 cubits. They were profoundly relieved,
however, to discover that the local inhabitants, once they had
recovered from their astonishment at the strangers' appearance,
were quite disposed to be friendly. In his investigation of the
local living conditions, Pytheas was particularly interested to
observe the indigenous method of threshing, and not a little
astounded at the potency of the native brew of methaglin and
beer. But his main purpose was to open negotiations for the
regular export of tin; and with this mission accomplished the
Channel waterway witnessed the first trickle of that stupendous stream of commerce which has since flowed across it
in ever-increasing volume.

For good or ill, the Island peoples' 'glorious isolation' was
at an end.

About two centuries after the appearance of Pytheas another
Greek voyager, Posidonius the Stoic, included Clas Merdin in
an extensive tour of north and north-western Europe. Landing
in the West, he was quick to observe the civilising influence
that contact with the outer world had already exerted on the
local tribesmen. Their mining methods had improved, as had
their standard of living; even their boat-building was noticeably
less primitive. For a small but steady two-way trade had come
into being across the narrow seas; corn and cattle, tin, lead,
hides and slaves being bartered for salt, brass and domestic
earthenware. It was rough but useful stuff, this early pottery,
as was made clear by the specimens retrieved off Marseilles,
early in 1953, by Commander Jacques Cousteau, in the
research ship *Calypso*, from the oldest wreck known to exist—
that of a Greek trading vessel of the third century B.C.

So far, however, the sea-traffic was exclusively in the hands
of those who sought out the island for purposes of barter. The
Bretanii, or Brythons, as they were called, had not taken so

kindly to salt water as their cross-Channel neighbours, the Gaulish tribe of the Veneti. With their mines, their fishing, and their grain crops to occupy their attention, the Islanders were content to chaffer with the occasional stranger who came their way, bringing goods to a restricted but mutually profitable market. But none save merchants were welcome to enter the island's havens, and even they were not encouraged to roam far from their vessels. Insularity is not a characteristic peculiar to the mid-Victorians.[1]

The Veneti, on the other hand, were not above a hardy attempt to turn the narrow strait off the north-west extremity of Gaul into a toll-gate exacting tribute from such shipping as ventured down from Scandinavia or up the narrowing Channel. They even sought to harry the Roman vessels supporting the Legions' advance through the seaboard provinces of Gaul. With their stout ships, whose seams were strongly bolted and securely caulked with seaweed, they resolutely contested the passage of the narrow seas with the triremes sent to guard the Roman flank. Constructed with high counters of seasoned timbers, the Venetan craft proved quite impenetrable to the Roman *rostra*, or beaked prows, while the lofty counters rendered it impossible to ply the usual missile weapons with any hope of success. It was only when the Mediterranean shipmen improvised sharp-bladed *rochets* to cut their opponents' running tackle and bring their leathern sails down with a run, that the Venetans were forced to haul off as best they could, and accept defeat.

With these obstinate adversaries swept aside, the Roman Legions were free to proceed with their work of conquering the territories of the Moroni and Menappi which occupied the area of present-day Picardy.

* * *

By the turn of the year 56 B.C. Gaius Julius Caesar, that middle-aged voluptuary turned successful soldier, had completed the nine years' campaign which had brought the whole of Gaul under the Roman Eagles. With the final drive, to hustle the intrusive Germanic tribes back across the Rhine, the

---

[1] *Lives of the British Admirals*, Vol. I, Robert Southey.

Legions had made good their hold on the coastal provinces facing out towards the narrow seas.

It is difficult for any victorious General to find himself confronted by a water obstacle without immediately yearning to establish a bridgehead beyond it. In this particular instance there were additional inducements to attempt the passage of the Channel. To begin with, the Islanders had shown the temerity to intervene on behalf of the pro-consul's recent adversaries; and such insolent defiance merited heavier punishment than the destruction of their pitiful little fleet, already accomplished. Furthermore, it was necessary, for political reasons, that Caesar's warlike activities should be made to yield a handsome dividend; while cupidity was inevitably aroused by merchant-venturers' tales of tribal hoards of gold and silver and rich stores of pearls. In any case there should be captives who could profitably be sold into slavery. Nor was it to be overlooked that the further triumph of adding Brython to his earlier conquests would entitle the conqueror to a *supplicatio* of public feasting and applause of at least twenty days' duration. Lastly, a hitherto unguarded flank would have been prudently secured.

Still weighing the advantages and disadvantages of the venture, Caesar was so deluded by the over-sanguine reports of conditions just across the Straits, rendered by Caius Volusenus, his principal spy, that orders were given to put the enterprise in hand forthwith. And this despite the vociferous protests of loyalty offered the pro-consul by certain tribal envoys, who had hurriedly crossed the Channel hoping that a little timely show of deference to Rome would suffice to preserve the inviolability of their territories.

It was just before midnight on August 25th that the men of the 7th and 10th Legions were embarked in eighty ships; crossing the Channel at its narrowest on a course laid from Gessoriacum (Boulogne) to a point near what is now the town of Dover. A first-class cavalry contingent embarked further up the coast in eighteen craft had orders to follow in support of the initial assault.[1]

[1] *De Bello Gallico* (Duncan's translation), Lib. IV; *History of the Royal Navy*, Vol. I, Sir Nicholas Harris Nicolas; *England before the Norman Conquest*, Sir Charles Oman. The whole force was under 10,000 strong.

Caesar's first landfall was a rockbound strip of coast, whose bordering cliffs were crowned with a swarm of tribal warriors who watched his every movement lynx-eyed. Probing for a more favourable beach-head, the pro-consul finally gave orders to force a landing near the site of the present-day town of Deal.[1]

As the galleys neared the shore, a swarm of charioteers in their scythed warcarts streamed on to the beach, heading a press of tribesmen who yelled defiance and brandished their weapons with such unbridled ferocity that even the veteran Legionaries quailed a little at the prospect of going in to the assault. It was not until the Standard-bearer of the 10th Legion leaped boldly into the shoal water that his comrades tumbled from their boats to form up in the shallows. At the same time some of the lighter galleys pushed forward on the flanks, whence they could bring the converging fire of their missile weapons—darts, slings, catapults and carrabalistas—to bear on the massed forces of the defence. With their Standard-bearer still in the lead, the *maniples* of the Legion splashed doggedly forward to engage their opponents breast to breast.

The struggle was fierce and bloody, but as the Roman swordsmen gained a footing their discipline and trained skill in arms slowly won the advantage, and their adversaries fell back in considerable confusion. Had the cavalry been promptly landed, the tribesmen's retreat could have been turned into a rout. As it was, Caesar was content to establish his camp hard by the shore, and to receive the submission of those of the natives who came forward with offers of surrender.

It was then that the narrow seas themselves took a hand in events that were to prove decisive. The voyagers had already suffered considerably from the 'chops of the Channel'[2]—those plunging, rolling, vicious seas that differed so demoralisingly from the short seas and even swell of their own familiar waters—but even worse things lay in store for them. Accustomed, like Pytheas, to the tideless shores of the Mediterranean, the Roman shipmen had casually secured their craft without thought of the

[1] There is a tablet on Deal beach commemorating Caesar's landing; but such has been the effect of the easterly drift in piling up shingle that the actual spot may well have been as much as half a mile further inland.

[2] The term is also applied to the 'chops' or 'jaw' of the Channel—i.e. the entrance to the Channel from the Atlantic.

vagaries of wind and tide for which the narrow seas are so
justly notorious. On the fourth night ashore a violent gale
aggravated the normal swell to such an extent that the vessels
that had been hauled up on to the shingle were filled with
water, while many of the anchored transports parted their
cables and were wrecked along the shore. The craft transporting the cavalry were driven back to the coast of Gaul; and
all hope of making use of the Horse to forage and help in
extending the bridge-head had perforce to be abandoned.
Drenched with rain, hungry and disheartened, the troops
were driven to 'cannibalise' twelve of the wrecks to patch up
such ships as could still be rendered seaworthy.

The expedition had been disrupted at its most sensitive
point—its line of communications.

All this was by no means lost on the local chieftains, who
speedily persuaded their followers once more to take up arms.
The successful ambushing of a foraging party of the 7th Legion
was followed by a mass assault on their would-be rescuers.
Despite the fact that his men succeeded in holding their own,
Caesar was only too thankful to accept a specious promise of
submission from some of the less pugnacious of the chieftains,
as an excuse to end the fighting. On an unfamiliar and tricky
shore, with worsening weather a constant threat to its line of
communications, the expedition confronted the unwelcome
prospect of being penned within a narrow bridgehead throughout the vilely inclement months of winter. Most serious problem
of all was the shortage of provisions, for no one knew better than
Caesar that the soldier becomes hungry, with the greatest
punctuality, three times a day. The only thing to do was to
pull out and make his way back across the capricious narrow
seas while opportunity still offered.

Embarking the remnant of his forces in such ships as were
still serviceable, the conqueror of the Helvetii, of Gallia
Cisalpina, Gallia Transalpina, of Illyricum and of Gaul,
dejectedly recrossed the narrow seas he had breasted with such
high hopes a mere three weeks before.

*   *   *

Brython had proved a harder nut to crack than Caesar
had anticipated. Through overconfidence, based on faulty

intelligence, he had badly underestimated the means required to ensure the stubborn islanders' conquest. It was a mistake he was determined should not be repeated with the second venture.

For this, far more careful preparations were put in hand. Vessels of smaller draft and with lower freeboard, to facilitate 'up-and-over' loading and unloading, were especially constructed to ensure speedy debarkation on the shallow, shingly beaches. They were also made commodious enough to accommodate a number of horses. For a contingent of 2,000 cavalry were considered essential to the success of the forthcoming enterprise. Six hundred of these transports were to be accompanied by tenders and an escort of twenty-eight powerfully-armed galleys.

With the Spring a force of five Legions, with their supporting Horse, set forth from Portus Itius in Gaul,[1] in an armada that stretched across the Channel almost from coast to coast. Borne forward by a gentle southerly wind and, in the later stages, greatly helped by the tide, after an untroubled night, landfall was made about noon. Gaining a footing, without much opposition, at a point on the coast not far from the Wantsum inlet, Caesar proceeded to establish a strong camp to guard the ample supply of provisions with which he had been careful to come provided.

Once again, however, the pro-consul had forgotten that he no longer had to deal with tranquil, tideless seas. A sudden storm totally destroyed forty of the vessels anchored in the roads and drove many of the remainder ashore. It was only by ordering the undamaged craft to be manhandled to safety above the water line, and by surrounding them with make-shift fortifications, that the invader could regard his base as reasonably secure.

Free, after ten days of incessant toil, to press on with the country's subjugation, the Legions fought their way resolutely into the interior. It was hard slogging; for the tribesmen, led by the courageous but ruthless Cassivelaunus, King of the Catauvellauni, fought with rare tenacity; relentlessly laying waste the countryside over which they retreated, in the

[1] M. D'Auville, an expert in the early history of Gaul, considers Portus Itius to have been Wissand Bay, between Cape Griznez and Blanchnez.

desperate hope of retarding the invaders' determined advance. So pitiless, indeed, were the methods employed by Cassivelaunus to impede his enemies' movements that it became a question whether submission to Rome would be fraught with less evil consequences than obstinately sustained resistance. The fervour had gone out of the fight and many were eager to come to terms.

At length Cassivelaunus was persuaded to sue for peace. Caesar, who feared the approach of the equinox and all its arrival portended, willingly subscribed to a treaty as insubstantial as the show of goodwill with which it was concluded. The mighty pro-consul had scored a sufficient military success to 'save face'; beyond that a few hostages and an empty promise of annual tribute was all that he took back with him across the narrow seas, so calm in the September sunshine that their recent fury was almost impossible to recall.

Such were the petty results of this formidable enterprise. Caesar had discovered—as many were to find after him—that it was one thing to land on the island's soil, and quite another thing to stay there; that its defenders have no stouter ally than the narrow seas that wash its shores.

*   *   *

For nearly a hundred years the island folk retained their freedom. But when the Emperor Claudius sent the experienced Aulus Plautius, at the head of four Legions, for the outland's reconquest, the Foot were accompanied by a strong body of *auxilia*. Light troops, accustomed to the shifts and hazards of fighting in enclosed country and across rivers and morasses, these hardy *ferentarri* bore the brunt of the long and sanguinary conflict which ended in the island's transformation into a Roman province.

There had been no attempt to bar the passage of the narrow seas; the Brythons were still very largely a shore-bound people. But Caractacus, at the head of the Catauvellauni tribe and the Silures, fought stubbornly to the end. Defeated in the last of thirty pitched battles, he crossed the Channel a captive weighed down with chains.

Boadicea's revolt flamed into temporary prosperity, only to be quelled by the superior fighting quality of the Legions, the batteries of catapults, and the Emperor's own Praetorian Guard. With the government of Cucuis Julius Agricola (A.D. 78–84) the last embers of resistance were methodically trodden out.

With Brython securely in their hands, the conquerors lost no time in creating a strong chain of defensive works at all the more commanding points along the Channel shore. At Dubris (Dover) the natural harbour formed by the estuary of the Dour, or Dwr, was still comparatively free from the encroaching shingle. On this score and because it was the place of passage nearest to the Continent, it was selected as the victualling port for the Navy and the headquarters of the *Comes Littoris Saxonici*—the Count of the Saxon Shore, responsible for the defence of the whole south-eastern coastline. Guarding the haven, a formidable fortress was constructed which served as the bulwark of Kent; with a lofty *pharos* on either cliff to cast their warning beams out over the waters. Across the shallow half-moon of beach passed the main stream of reinforcements and military stores required for the upkeep of the garrisons further north.

Overlooking the broad waters of the Wantsum[1] and the flats where Sandwich was one day to arise, stood the twin strongholds of Rutupiae (Richborough) and Regulbium (Reculver),[2] the guardians of the most direct and convenient waterway to the Thames. The *castrum* of Rutupiae boasted flint walls from eleven to twelve feet thick, which were further strengthened by stout bastions, and external towers, with circular turrets capping the corners. From these, converging fire could be brought to bear on any assailants temerarious enough to try and scale the walls or batter down the gates. Within the seven acres enclosed by the battlements there was ample room to provide ancillary quarters for the *Comes Littoris Saxonici* and barracks for the Officers and men of the Second Legion of Augustus, with spare chambers for distinguished guests *en route* for London, or awaiting passage across the narrow seas. In the western face of the walls the main gate—Portus Decumanus—gave access to Watling Street, that splendid highway which slashed its way across country to Wroxeter and the river Severn.

[1] The Nethergong of the Saxons.
[2] Celtic, *Reg-ol-ium*, i.e. Point-against-the-waves.

To and fro along the waters of the Wantsum passed the laden
dromons and darting galleys, bound for a resurgent London,
risen phoenix-like from the ashes to which it had been reduced
by Boadicea, to become a burgeoning port and the country's
commercial capital. For despite capricious weather, puzzling
tides, and the incidence of pirates, an expanding maritime
trade plied briskly hither and thence across the Channel.
Against tax-yielding imports of brassware, salt and Samian
pottery, the Island exported tin, lead, a little gold and silver,
many oysters and a few pearls,[1] hides, grain, and sacks of those
fabulous beans which led the Romans to name their place of
origin Barton-in-Fabis, or Barton-in-the-Beans. There was
also a certain traffic in slaves; while both native bears and
dogs—the former for baiting—found ready purchasers; the
latter being "of various species, all excellent in their kind,
which were highly valued by the Roman connoisseurs in
hunting".[2]

To the north, and guarding the arm of the Wantsum where
it reached up to the Thames, stood Regulbium (Reculver[3]),
garrisoned by a cohort of Gaulish *auxilia*, known as the Velasii.

To the west, beyond what is now Rye Bay, frowned Anderida
(Pevensey Castle), named after the Forest of Andred, which
stretched inland for over a hundred and twenty miles. In this
instance the *castrum*, overlooking the quay, was egg-shaped and
designed for all-round 'hedgehog' defence. For there were still
bands of rebellious Brythons lurking in the impenetrable
woodlands, and in times of shortage a raid was an ever-likely
possibility. In such event, reinforcements could speedily be
summoned from the Roman camp on the East Hill overlooking
the settlement that later went by the name of Hastings.

Portus Lemanae—now marked on the map as Stutfall
Castle—stood guard over the area to the south-west which
forms the fringe of Romney Marsh. A subsidiary port of embarkation for Gaul, its garrison consisted of the Turnacensian
Band of *auxilia*, housed in a *castrum* covering ten acres of ground.

[1] Seutonius affirms that Caesar collected a large quantity of British pearls
and dedicated a breastplate made up of them to the Goddess Venus. Since
Mommsen asserts that above all things Caesar valued his victories over
women, the tribute would have been singularly appropriate.

[2] *Annals of Commerce*, Vol. 2, David Macpherson.

[3] In the Saxon vernacular, Reculfcestre.

Further west again stood Portus Adurni (Porchester Castle), the last stronghold on the Saxon Shore. Like the strongholds at Rutupiae and Lemanae, the walls of the fortress were strengthened by many stout bastions. Set squarely at the head of the inlet on whose banks Gosport and Portsmouth[1] were one day to arise, it was built during the third and early fourth centuries by a Roman Pioneer Corps known as the Exploratoris; and so admirable was their work that neither neglect nor outright abandonment of the structure brought appreciable deterioration to its sturdy fabric.

Apart from these well-sited shoreward defences, escort vessels accompanied all ships bearing personages of importance or cargoes of especial value, on passage across the narrow seas. And notwithstanding the fact that the Romans approached salt water—especially in Northern latitudes—rather with awe and respect than with confidence, patrols took the sea whenever the Channel's vagarious meteorological conditions allowed. For the audacious raids of the Scandinavian and Germanic corsairs, or "the Saxons, who might come with any wind",[2] constituted a perpetual menace to the regular flow of commerce. The Imperial flotillas, however, although established by the Emperor Claudius at the time of Brython's invasion by Aulus Plautius, had never enjoyed the care lavished on the Legions, and their efficiency steadily declined.

If Brython was no more than the Cinderella among Rome's many conquests, the need to guard the seaward flank of the Continental mainland rendered the Island's permanent occupation a matter of elementary precaution. And difficult as conquest might be to stomach, it was not entirely without advantages. A firm, centralised government ensured for many of the natives a life well above the mere subsistence level to which they had hitherto been accustomed; and under the rule of law, the man who so wished could live in peace. The more even tenor of the country's way of life was only threatened, indeed, by the steady deterioration of the coinage and the parasitic growth of officialdom.

The first sign that the Imperial grip was slackening came

[1] *Port's Mutha*, named after Port, the Saxon chief who landed there.
[2] *Germania*, Tacitus.

2*

when the upstart Carausius, the Netherlander corsair turned temporary watch-dog, impudently reneged the bargain he had struck with the Emperor Maximilian. Abandoning his task of scourging the Frankish pirates in the Channel, he dared to endow himself with the purple of the Emperor; and his reign in Brython continued, without penalty or reproof, until he was struck down by the hand of an assassin.

Thereafter, the in-gathering of the Legions for the defence of the Empire's inner bailiwick saw the beginning of the end. Word came from Rome that Brython must shift for itself. No longer were there Legionaries' burnished shields to flash their message from the Wall down country and across the Channel, and thence on to the capital itself. The *pharos* on Dover cliffs had ceased to cast their warning beams out over the waters. The *Comes Littoris Saxonici* no longer kept watch and ward over the Straits from Dubris or his stronghold on the East Hill above Hastings. The Eagles had marched down the splendid Roman roads and vanished across the narrow seas. In their place a rabble of petty kings were left to wrangle over their rival claims of inheritance. It was not so much that a civilisation had died as that a civilising alien government had ended.

With the midsummer of A.D. 406 the last of the Imperial war-galleys had passed down the Channel, never to reappear. The sun of Rome was setting, and over Brython the twilight was deepening into night.

*   *   *

With the collapse of classic Roman civilisation the soil of Brython came slowly but steadily under the sway of successive waves of migrants from the infertile territories lying between Schleswig and the Rhine; sailing in across the north-eastern approaches of the narrow seas. There was fighting at first, of course, but the inroads of the Anglo-Saxon newcomers, who flowed in, literally, with the tides, could only be contained in Wales and what is now the Duchy of Cornwall. Greedy for the rich, fertile land their ruthless vigour won for them, they established settlements which swiftly expanded into Northumbria, in the north, the boundary 'march' of Mercia, in the west, East Anglia, covering Norfolk and Suffolk, and Wessex,

embodying Essex, Kent, Sussex, Surrey, Hampshire, Dorset,
and Devon. Of these domains Wessex gave early promise of
becoming the strongest and most stable.

First over the seas had been Ella and his sons. Then—if the
chroniclers are to be credited—came Hengist and Horsa,[1]
who, somewhere about A.D. 450, "sailed from the land of
robbers" in "three long ships" that went by the name of
ceols. Invited by the confiding Vortigern, King of the Demetae,
to join him as allies, they made the alleged need for reinforcements an excuse to bring over a swarm of predatory ruffians,
as loot-hungry and unscrupulous as themselves. Ravaging
Kent with fire and sword, the newcomers virtually emptied
the south-east corner of the Island of its original inhabitants.
Many of those who managed to escape capture or death fled
across the Channel to Gaul, where they settled in the Gaulish
coastal area of Armorica, or Brittany. It was from this stock
that there arose a race of hardy sea-rovers destined to rank
amongst the English shipman's most bitter foes. In A.D. 495
came Cerdic and his son Cynric, to found the Kingdom of
Wessex.[2] Port and his followers were hard on their heels,
making a landing on the Hampshire coast opposite the Isle of
Wight. Sporadic raids had developed into a steady process of
invasion, of which the partial assimilation of Celt and Saxon
was an inevitable outcome.

The only uncontested landing was that of Augustine and his
fellow missionaries, sent in A.D. 596 by Pope Gregory the
Great not only to seek the conversion of the heathen, but to
attempt the spiritual recovery to the Roman See of a province
that had once formed part of the Roman Empire. Welcomed
by Æthelbert of Kent—whose authority was acknowledged by
all the Saxon Princes south of the Humber—it was only upon
London that the evangelist failed to make any impression.
Rebuffed in the commercial capital, Augustine chose Canterbury as the centre of his archiepiscopal see. To Canterbury's
convent of Christ Church went a generous grant of land which
included Romney, Lydd and Hudonfleot (West Hythe), and

---

[1] *Anglo-Saxon Chronicle*. Palgrave accepts the fact of Hengist and Horsa's
existence, although Kemble commits himself no further than to affirm that
"the expeditions known to tradition may have some foundation in fact."

[2] I,e, the Kingdom of the West Saxons.

further territory along the banks of the Wantsum, where a
cluster of fishermen's huts formed the nucleus of Sandwich.
It was to Sandwich—Sandwicke, or "the town within the
salts"[1]—that Wilfred, Bishop of Northumberland, returned in
A.D. 664, after his consecration in France at the hands of the
saintly Agilbert.[2]

The Romney area was already sparsely populated by a race
of Mersewara, or marshmen. Hardy and industrious, they were
fishermen as well as fowlers; and from their loins sprang that
turbulent breed of Portsmen which was destined to play so significant a part in the development of the Channel seaboard and
the emergence of the Island as a first-class naval Power.

With the passing of the years it became the turn of the
invaders to undergo invasion. For in A.D. 787 'the heathens'
—Norsemen out of Haere-tha-land—splashed ashore from
their ships, burning and pillaging and killing the King's
Reeve, ere departing into the Northern mists whence they had
come. It was the first comprehensive foray the Viking freebooters had attempted, and only too typical of the many
piratical descents that were to follow.

The Isle of Sheppey was successfully raided in A.D. 832, and
the following year a Danish and Norwegian fleet of some
strength sailed down to ravage the southern coast of England;
King Egbert being badly trounced in a sanguinary battle with
the crews of thirty-five hostile ships at Charmouth, in Dorset.
It was a disaster he retrieved a couple of years later when he
beat back a raiding force that had landed at Hengston, in
Cornwall. With such varying fortunes the struggle was
bitterly pursued.

The raids of these *Fin-Gaill*, or White Strangers from Norway, were solely for the purpose of pillage. Their 'long ships'
—seventy-five feet in length, with a beam of seventeen feet
amidships—were manned, on average, by forty men, steered
by oar, and propelled by sixteen sweeps a side, helped out,
when scudding before the wind, by a single sail. Possessing
neither compass nor any other nautical instrument, the
Norsemen navigated by the stars and their intimate knowledge
of the coastline down which they passed. Whether in their

---

[1] I.e. salt sands.
[2] *Collections for a History of Sandwich*, W. Boys.

eols or in their lighter twenty-oar *snekkers* (water-serpents) they were led by 'sea kings', for the most part petty chieftains, whose only concern was booty. In this they differed from the *Dubh-Gaill*, or Dark Strangers, of Denmark, many of whom, owing to disturbed conditions in their homeland, were anxious to acquire fresh territory in which to found new settlements. To both types of invader the Channel and its approaches offered a sea-highway to their destination rather than an arena of conflict. It is true that with oar propulsion, their vessels were highly manœuvrable for short periods, irrespective of the wind. But the motive power of the long ship, being of human sinew, was soon exhausted under the demands of battle-action. Furthermore there were no long-range offensive weapons available; and the hand-to-hand *mêlée* to which combat was largely confined demanded a more stable platform than was afforded by a long, narrow craft of shallow draught. The Norsemen, therefore, regarded their vessels much as the mounted infantryman regards his troop horse—as a convenient means of transporting them to the scene of action, the battle on land. Since this *modus operandi* also characterised the Anglo-Saxons, the first purely naval engagement between them and their Danish opponents did not occur until A.D. 851, when "King Athelstan and Ealchere, the eoldorman, fought on shipboard, and slew a great number of the enemy at Sandwich in Kent, and took nine ships and put others to flight; and the Heathen-men remained over-winter in Thanet."[1]

Thanet, with a sea-channel three-eighths of a mile wide to isolate it from the mainland, offered a perfect lodgment area for the Danish invaders. It also provided a stout flank defence, when, in that same year, a formidable fleet of no less than three hundred and fifty ships arrived safely in the mouth of the Thames. Swarming ashore, the crews to the number of close on 14,000 proceeded swiftly to the sack of Canterbury. Flushed with success, the marauders crossed into Surrey. There they were defeated "with greater slaughter than ever before, or for many years after, was heard of in this island".[2]

---

[1] *Anglo-Saxon Chronicle.* This Athelstan was the son of King Egbert (800–836), and is not to be confused with that Athelstan who was the son of Alfred the Great. Egbert was the first English Monarch to command a fleet in action.

[2] *Anglo-Saxon Chronicle.*

None the less the invaders were left in sufficient strength to retire to their winter quarters in the Isle of Thanet; where their bridgehead had been so strengthened that it was beyond the Saxons' power to expel them. Raids on Winbury and Sandwich might fail, but there was always a secure base upon which to fall back and reorganise.

With Thanet firmly secured, the Danish hold on the eastern territories was greatly strengthened when, in A.D. 866, a great fleet, transporting a host of warriors under the two chieftains Ivar and Ubba, found anchorage on the coast of East Anglia.

The arrival of this formidable force came at a moment which found the country singularly ill-prepared to defend itself. With their conversion to Christianity many of the hardiest warriors had been persuaded to abandon their arms in favour of a slothful, emasculate life of retirement within the confines of a monastery, until "there were in the kingdom more monks than military men".[1] Furthermore the respective Anglo-Saxon kingdoms were entirely without plans for co-operation and mutual support in times of stress. But with the invaders in possession of all the eastern territories between the Tyne and the Thames, on the appeal of the King of Mercia for succour King Æthelred—eldest surviving son of King Æthelwulf—readily took the field at the head of his West Saxons.

By Æthelred's side marched his younger brother Alfred. Still under twenty, the maturing influence of his sojourn in Rome and at the Frankish Court of Charles the Bald had endowed the youth with a poise, sagacity and resolution far beyond his years. The battle of Ashdown, on the Ridgeway hard by Lowbury Hill, gave him an early chance to demonstrate his innate capacity for leadership in action; and the outcome of the contest did not falsify the expectations he had aroused.

It was not until A.D. 872, however, when his brother's death officially invested him with leadership, that Alfred was forced to recognise that the only way to secure a lasting peace for the people of his kingdom was to meet and overthrow his enemies before they could effect a landing and consolidate their forces.

Since his own followers were as sadly lacking in experience

[1] *History of Music*, V, 11, Sir John Hawkins (1719–89).

of blue water and the crafts associated with it as they were of the technique of sea-fighting, Alfred did not hesitate to call in friendly foreign aid to help in the construction of the "long ships, . . . full nigh twice as long as the others", of which "some had sixty oars and some had more", eked out with a single mast, on which his hopes were founded. Clincher-built, "their heads and sterns very erect",[1] they were neither Danish nor Frisian in their lines, but—less crank and apt to roll— owed something to the Mediterranean galley and a very great deal more to the Saxon King's own forethought and ingenuity.

It was not long before Alfred's far-sighted measures were rewarded with success. A small Danish flotilla, hovering off the coast, was surprised by the appearance of an armada, of which no previous word had reached them. The Saxon leader closed to the attack, his missile weapons hurling their darts and heavy stones, and his steersman seeking a chance to ram. But there was little manœuvring, both sides moving in to grapple and board, and fight it out with sword, barbed spear, scamase axe, and double-headed bipennis. It was a short, fiercely con- tested struggle from which the Danes, leaving one vessel in Alfred's hands, were only too glad to escape with the remaining six.

A Danish landing at Thornseata (Wareham) was brought to nought by Alfred's application of sea power to cut off supplies; while a fleet bringing numerous reinforcements to the Norse- men fell victim to the temperamental Channel weather; half the vessels being cast away on the Hampshire coast. The battered remainder was met by Alfred's strengthened flotillas, which had been blockading the mouth of the Exe, and virtually annihilated. As at Thornseata, the garrison in Exeter had been cut off from all hope of succour by the proper application of naval pressure. Too numerous to be victualled for a siege out of local supplies, yet not strong enough to meet the West Saxons in open fight, the Danes capitulated. Solemnly pledged to keep the peace, they were allowed to march away under their leader, Guthrum, to the sanctuary awaiting them in a

[1] *Anglo-Saxon Chronicle*, Florence of Worcester, Simeon of Durham, the *Chronicle of Melros*. Henry of Huntingdon and Bromton say forty or more oars. The transposition of L and X accounts for the difference.

persistently supine Mercia—where appeasement was only concerned to find sufficient cheeks to turn.

*   *   *

With Guthrum false to his oath, by the January of A.D. 878 Alfred had once more been driven on to the defensive and forced to seek a final refuge in a two-acre patch of solid ground known as the Isle of Athelney, amidst the marshes that extend between the Parret and the Tone. It was a last-ditch stronghold such as Hereward the Wake was one day to organise in the fenlands of the Isle of Ely—and Francis Marion, the 'Swamp Fox', to study and seek inspiration from during the American War of Independence.

Never were the Saxon King's fortunes at lower ebb. Yet Athelney was a clear case of *reculement pour mieux sauter*. By prodigious efforts all the lost ground was steadily won back; and in the outcome Guthrum was left with no option but to surrender at discretion. By the terms of the subsequent Treaty of Wedmore it really seemed as though a genuine *modus vivendi* had been worked out whereby, in accepting the Danes as his neighbours, Alfred insured himself against their further encroachment on his Wessex homelands. To this end he fixed the boundary of the Danish territory so that it reached right up to London without including it. Within the city itself he carefully restored and added to the stout Roman walls, so that the headport of the Thames barred all easy passage across the river and served as a gateway excluding unauthorised entry into his kingdom.

Despite these precautions, however, the Saxon King's severest ordeal was yet to come.

In A.D. 880 a fleet of two hundred and fifty ships put out from Boulogne under the leadership of the predatory Norseman, Hasting (Hæsten), bent on nothing less than the conquest of the whole of England.

Crossing the Channel at its narrowest, the freebooter made his landfall at the mouth of the Lymene (or Rother) in East Kent. Part of his force proceeded upstream to the capture of Apuldre (Appledore), while Hasting, with eighty ships, swept round to Thames-mouth, and, navigating the river Swale, landed at Milton. It was a pincer movement which brought a large area of Kent under the invaders' control, while leaving their sea lines of communication and reinforcement reasonably secure.

None the less, where Alfred was concerned the Danes had learnt caution; and their inactivity throughout the ensuing winter enabled the Saxon leader to reorganise his fleet and land forces; and this despite the distraction of enemy squadrons that threatened first one point and then another, up and down the coast. Committed to war at sea and on land, Alfred thrust a force between Milton and the Danish host at Apuldre; maintaining such close blockade as to cut off all supplies for either stronghold. Hasting, recognising that he was cornered, took to his shipping and actually made sail for the narrow seas. But putting about, he crossed the Thames to Benfleet. At the same time the Apuldre contingent struck out in search of a ford whereby to cross the river; harried and hotly pursued across Essex and over the river Colne into the Isle of Mersea. There Alfred had to leave them securely invested, since his presence was urgently needed in the West.

A fleet of one hundred enemy ships had passed down the Channel to land their crews at the mouth of the Exe; their arrival timed to coincide with the appearance of another forty vessels brought round from Bristol. Alfred's swift and unlooked-for intervention speedily persuaded the Norsemen to raise the siege of Exeter and take to their boats. The costly failure of the raid on Chichester, on their way up Channel, was another setback that Hasting determined to retrieve by launching a vigorous offensive. It was a course to which he was the more easily persuaded in view of the vexatious success which had rewarded the London watermen's assault on his Benfleet camp.

But if the initiative was still with the Norseman, it was the initiative of the goaded bull charging wildly about the arena. Hounded from pillar to post, he eventually took refuge in South Shoebury, where the arrival of winter gave him time to recuperate and marshal his strength.

Early in the following year the sea rover sailed for the mouth of the deep-running river Lea, ascending the waterway as far as Ware, about twenty miles north of London, where he speedily erected a strong fieldwork. With equal promptitude

Alfred built two *burhs*, or stockaded strongpoints, on either side of the river mouth, joining them so effectually with booms that the Danes found themselves sealed up. Alfred then proceeded to dig two deep channels from the Lea to the Thames. It was an ingenious device which had the effect of so lowering the level of the tributary stream that "when a ship might sail in times afore passed, then a little boat might scarcely row".[1] With all their craft aground, the Danes were left no option but to abandon their shipping; many of them seeking refuge in accommodating Mercia. Defied and frustrated at every turn, the Scandinavian Hannibal broke up the remnant of his forces; and a small flotilla, headed by his galley wearing the banner of the raven drooping dejectedly at the masthead, sailed out across the narrow seas *sine lucro et sine honore*.

*   *   *

Alfred's fleet of well over a hundred sail was now divided into squadrons, each charged with the guardianship of its own particular area of the Channel and based on its own port. For if the township of Hastings was only just coming into its own, the Richborough haven, Dover, Hythe and Romney were easily accessible in almost any weather, while Winchelsea and Rye, though no more than fishing hamlets, could be made reasonable use of at a pinch. Such an organisation was of vital importance, for there were still sporadic Viking raids to be dealt with, when bands of immigrant Northumbrian and East Anglian sea rovers sought to harry the coast of Wessex in their nimble *æses*. But the West Saxon King had learned to handle his fleet tactically; as the crews of six Danish vessels speedily discovered when they came marauding to the Isle of Wight. Discovered embayed, with only three vessels capable of putting to sea, two of the water-borne craft were pursued and captured, while the men of the grounded ships were defeated in a stiff fight at the water's edge. Such of them as survived were taken to Winchester and there hanged as common pirates.

In the same year no less than twenty of these raiding craft were captured in the narrow seas, their crews falling in open fight or suffering summary execution.

[1] *A. S. Chronicle.*

The Channel was not yet inviolate, but Alfred's unflagging exertions had rendered its hostile penetration a matter of increasing hazard. At the same time, by ensuring that its passage was a good deal less precarious for maritime commerce, he had done much to stimulate overseas trade. This had increased appreciably since the pact of A.D. 796 between the Emperor Charlemagne and Offa, King of Mercia, which legislated for the rights and responsibilities of merchants domiciled overseas, and the safe passage of pilgrims journeying "to visit the precincts of the Apostles".[1] London, relieved from the menace that had overshadowed it for so many a weary year, became once more "the mart of many nations resorting to it by land and sea".[2] Its port facilities were extended by Archbishop Ethelred's construction of a useful hithe, or quay, on a river frontage given him by the King. Vessels from Normandy, France and Flanders regularly paid toll at Billingsgate, hard by the cross-river ferry. If Dover served the devout, London's outports of Stonor and Reculver dealt with the modest flow of maritime trade; which now included, among the imports, furs from the North and wine and a certain number of weapons from Gaul and Germany. The smaller havens along the Kentish and Sussex shores acted as entrepots for the narrow seas' generous yield of fish, without which the winter board would have indeed been lean.

But it required more than the endeavours of a single monarch to transform a people of tilth and pasture into a race that thought instinctively of the sea as the biggest single factor in the development of their future destiny.

[1] Macpherson, *op. cit.* This compact takes rank as the first commercial treaty to be negotiated by an English King.
[2] The Venerable Bede.

CHAPTER II

Sea-way to Conquest

"Life itself is essentially appropriation, injury, conquest of the strange and the weak."
FRIEDRICH WILHELM NIETZSCHE

ONCE it has started, migration is like an avalanche that gains in power and impetus with every forward leap.

Alfred had done much to stem the Danish inroads; had perceived and in some degree had organised the only means by which they could be held at bay. But the corsairs' urge to return to the land their forebears had so profitably pillaged was not to be suppressed. Raiding was vigorously renewed until Athelstan, who came to the throne in A.D. 925, succeeded in subduing the Anglo-Danes in East Anglia, and assumed the rank and title of King of all England.

Athelstan's aim was stability, based upon peace and increasing plenty. Shrewdly aware that there is no sounder basis of national well-being than successful commerce, he decreed that the dignity of Thegnhood should be awarded to any merchant who thrice fared forth across the narrow seas in his own ship, freighted with a cargo purchased out of his own resources. It was a reward for enterprise which not only reflected the high estimate in which the exploit was held, but demonstrated to what lengths the Monarch was prepared to go to encourage maritime trade. The measure was amply justified, for under Athelstan and his immediate successors sea-borne commerce increased sufficiently to warrant the imposition of a graduated tax on home and alien shipping. At Billingsgate, for example, ruddy-faced mariners searched their pokes for dues that ranged from one halfpenny to fourpence, according to the size of their craft. The voluble men of Rouen who came to the aliens' moorings at Ethelred's hithe with their 'great ships' weighed down with 'wine and grampus', reluctantly doled out six shillings toll and the twentieth part of the said grampus. For the skins of whales and walrus were highly esteemed for making ships' cables. Merchants of Flanders and of Poitou, as those of Normandy and France, were under obligation to declare their goods and pay the statutory tolls. The men of the Hague, Liège and Nivelles 'did scavage'[1] and rendered fixed dues. Only 'the men of the Emperor', Easterlings who were the forerunners of the Hanseatic League, were accorded especial treatment. Providing these men of Dantzic, Lubeck and Brunswick refrained from any attempt to forestall[2] the market, they were absolved from all taxation other than a Noeltide and Easter tribute of two grey cloths and one brown cloth, 10 lb of pepper, five pairs of men's gloves, and two vessels of vinegar.[3] Greasemongers and lardners, as the traffickers in cheese and butter were termed, paid one penny tax fourteen days before Christmas and a similar sum seven days after the festival. Other dues were mostly settled in kind, for coin was scarce and often so outrageously 'clipped' as to be virtually worthless. Sometimes purchases were paid for in little coils of silver wire; but as many of these, on investigation, were found to be no more than spirals of copper thinly coated with silver, barter was often preferred as furnishing a safer basis for a transaction.

What passed for a fighting fleet was found and manned by the cities and towns according to an established rate, such as the sixpence a hearth paid by Colchester, Dover and Sandwich. Even inland Warwick was liable for four seamen, or a fine of £4 in lieu thereof. But the naval strength available was in no way commensurate with the amount of money raised for its upkeep.

To the traditional, and now Customed, articles of export—lead, tin, and hides—was presently to be added a small quantity of raw wool. For about A.D. 960 or a little earlier, many districts of Flanders had taken to the manufacture of woollen goods; and with the progressive increase in this activity there arose a demand for raw wool and wool fells that was to

[1] In effect, opened their goods for inspection.
[2] A forestaller was one who bought up commodities in bulk from the improvident, at a cut price, to sell again at a handsome profit.
[3] *Die Gesetze der Angelsachsen*, F. Liebermann.

encourage an export trade in these commodities out of England, destined to develop into a stupendous traffic, bringing unparalleled prosperity to native pasture owners, if at the increasing expense of agriculture.

It was King Athelstan who created the precedent of confederation with a foreign ruler against a rival overlord; his fleet, in A.D. 939, crossing the narrow seas to the support of Louis à Outremer of France against Otho of Germany. Not only did the English vessels maintain a close blockade of the enemy coast, but a moiety of their crews formed a landing party to penetrate the hostile shore.

It was the first of England's many entanglements with the Continent, and the earliest of the country's attempts to ensure a balance of power by the employment of her naval forces.

Personal leadership was the lynch pin of the realm's successful defence under Athelstan. But that inestimable quality was sadly wanting in his immediate successors. Under progressively weak administrations Thanet was reoccupied by the Danes, who also landed in Hampshire, defeating the raw levies of the *fyrd* and killing the two high-reeves who were their leaders. Next came a descent on Exmouth, whereafter the raiders went on to ravage the borders of Wilts and Dorset; once more inflicting defeat on the *fyrd* at Penselwood. Thence they marched east, quite unopposed, to Southampton Water, burning Bishop's Waltham on their way. "This was in every wise a heavy time", the chronicler ruefully records, "because they never ceased from their evil doings"; as King Ethelred 'No Council'—more familiarly known as Ethelred the Unready—never ceased to prevaricate and seek to secure by money tribute the peace that only well-organised defence could have ensured.

In the Spring of A.D. 1002 came the final gesture of defeatist appeasement, when Ethelred sought to buy off the invaders by the payment of Danegeld amounting to £24,000. Danegeld, originally designed as an especial ship geld for the maintenance of war vessels, and subsequently stabilised as a tax to provide the means of repelling invasion, by Ethelred's pusillanimous decree was degraded into a bribe that in any case purchased no more than temporary immunity. For within a year of its payment King Sweyn of Denmark headed an invasion force intent not only on pillage but on settlement by conquest. Having ravaged Sandwich and the Kentish shore, he landed on the Hampshire coast; his followers securing their first victory at Aethlin-ga-dene (Alton). Thence they proceeded westward to join hands with another body of freebooters, eager to pile loot on top of their recent bribe.

Once again gold prevailed, for the nonce, where steel was wanting to strike a sterner bargain; and for a further sum of £24,000 the raiders agreed to return whence they had come. But the egregious folly of Ethelred the Redeless in seeking to avoid payment of another instalment of Danegeld by authorising the St. Brice's Day massacre of every Dane left in the kingdom, brought Sweyn hotfoot across the sea to avenge the outrage.

Bought off temporarily by the surrender of the tremendous sum of £30,000,[1] the Danish Monarch eventually returned to the charge with a great fleet, that swung down the Channel approaches to land its crews, virtually unopposed, at Sandwich; where the hostages taken by the Danes were also set ashore, horribly mutilated in reprisal for St. Brice's Day. The whole man-power of Wessex was ordered out to oppose the swarm of invaders, and "even lay under arms during the harvest".[2] But an ill-ordered rabble of foot is of little avail against trained warriors. Nothing less than a bribe of £48,000[3] sufficed to purchase a truce, that continued precariously for the next two years.

For once borrowed time was not wasted. The building of war craft on a lavish scale was subsidised by a special fiscal measure, which decreed that the owner of every 310 hides of land subject to tax should undertake the construction and upkeep of one war vessel. It was an impost designed to support national defence by nation-wide rather than purely local taxation, in which the precedent for 'Charles the Martyr's' 'ship money' can clearly be discerned.

---

[1] Ethelred had already paid large money bribes to be left in peace; £10,000 in silver in A.D. 991, £15,000 in A.D. 994. To gain some idea of the contemporary spending value of money, multiply by fifteen.

[2] A. S. Chronicle.

[3] The figure given in the A. S. Chronicle is £8,000. But as Macpherson points out, "Florence, Simeon, etc., have transcribed from copies wherein the number stood at £48,000, which accords with the progressive augmentation of the extortion."

Within the year the craft were ready, and "there were so many of them as never before had been among the English nation in any King's days".[1] Some 800 ships and 30,000 armed men were the outcome of the national 'war effort'; and orders were given for *all* vessels to rendezvous at Sandwich. Since no patrols were established to keep watch and ward in the Channel, it was an imprudent concentration of force which left much of the coast unguarded. In the outcome, all Ethelred's elaborate preparations foundered in disaster. Twenty of his ships were enticed away to piracy by the treacherous Wulfnoth, Eorl Godwin's father; while the force of twenty vessels sent to take the renegade dead or alive was driven ashore in one of the Channel's sudden storms. The wrecked craft were subsequently burned by Wulfnoth where they lay stranded. Ethelred and his noblemen having fled in despair, what was left of the fleet was rowed back to London, and "they let the whole nation's toil thus lightly pass away".[2]

England lay at the mercy of the Danes, soundly based on the Isle of Wight, and free to pillage and burn the coastal settlements at will. Only London,[3] guarded by the remnants of Ethelred's fleet and the strong sword-arms of its citizens, remained an island of resistance in a sea of plundered submission. What was lacking was co-ordination for the purpose of defence; and Ethelred's successor, Edmund Ironside, was given no time to reorganise before he was called upon to take the field. For Sweyn's son Canute had arrived at Sandwich intent on completing the task his father had put in train in the midsummer of 1013. Reinforced by a contingent of renegade Saxons, the invader sailed up the Thames estuary to blockade London by land and water. Brisk and resolute as it was at first, all the spirit went out of the citizens' resistance with the news of Edmund Ironside's untimely death.

There was little opposition when Canute was vociferously acclaimed conqueror and King by the men of his fleet, the first Monarch to be elevated to the Throne by the navy he had led into action; about as peculiar a manifestation of 'sea power' as any yet recorded!

Once its task has been accomplished, a mercenary army is

---

[1] *A. S. Chronicle.*   [2]*Ibid.*
[3] Rebuilt after its almost total destruction by fire in A.D. 982.

best broken up before it can be beguiled into taking sides against the individual who originally employed it. Canute therefore, retaining only a picked bodyguard, rid himself of his Danish hirelings by levying an indemnity of £72,000 of silver on the country at large, of which £11,000 was furnished by London. Having regard for the swingeing tribute exacted no great time before by Ethelred the Redeless, the ability of the land to meet this further impost speaks remarkably well for its latent resources. With this handsome solatium to console them, Canute's erstwhile Praetorian Guard disappeared into their northern mists. It was mainly with English ships, therefore, manned in large part by English crews, that Norway was conquered and united with England and Denmark in a triple kingdom.

Although the sanguinary means by which it had been brought about may be deplored, the fact remains that the Danish conquest of England was the most important event in the early history of the country's commerce. The Danes were not only skilful navigators and stout swordsmen, but indefatigable traders—at once corsairs and merchants, in whose graves a pair of scales would keep harmonious company with a battle-axe.[1] Through Scandinavia they were in touch with the fabulous wares of the East, particularly the spices required to render tainted meat and rancid fats reasonably palatable. These wares reached the northern ports along the great rivers that traversed Muscovy; while Danish vessels themselves were not unknown even in the distant waters of the Black Sea and the Caspian.

Canute in uniting the three kingdoms was quick to appreciate that nothing gives the vanquished a more convincing impression of good government than a feeling of security and national prosperity. To ensure it he took many measures to encourage trade; at the same time strengthening the coastline defences. Since the castle of Richborough had fallen into decay and the encroaching shingle had already brought decline to Stonor, Sandwich was rehabilitated and enlarged, "inriched with great and large privileges and liberties", and turned into a strongly fortified base for the guardian vessels kept on patrol

[1] *Norway and the Norwegians*, C. F. Keary. A pair of scales has been found in a Viking burial ground in the Hebrides.

in the narrow seas. Their presence made possible a steady growth of trade with the North and across the Channel; a fact reflected in the increase in the mints authorised to stamp out coinage.[1] At the same time Canute "spoke with the Emperor and the Pope himself, and the Princes . . . as to the wants of the people, English and Danes, that there should be granted to them more equal justice and greater security in their journeys . . . that they should not be hindred by so many barriers on the road nor harassed by unjust tolls". Furthermore, the members of the Danish seafaring community—with their shore-going settlements established in the area now occupied by the Law Courts and the Temple, and still known as St. Clement Danes—were always cheerfully prepared to pass on their knowledge of navigation and the lore of the sea to the less experienced mariners of English stock.[2]

Had the regime continued untroubled something might have been done even to revive agriculture, fallen into such woeful neglect since the days of the Romans that not a single bushel of grain had been exported since the collapse of their overlordship. But like his more ambitious predecessors, Canute soon discovered the impossibility of controlling a large, scattered domain without delegating power; and in those days to delegate power was tantamount to losing it. The division of England into four great eorldoms, for example, left Wessex to the virtually autonomous rule of the shifty, avaricious Eorl Godwin; a typical specimen of those profligate, hectoring and unscrupulous petty tyrants who invariably abound in times of lawlessness and confusion.

Hardicanute, who came to the throne following the death of Canute's son, Harald Harefoot, arrived at Sandwich to take up the succession at the head of a fleet of sixty war vessels, which were very welcome. But he speedily alienated such good-will as awaited him by clapping on a shipgeld for the construction of a further sixty war-craft; an impost that was assessed at the old high rate, previously yielding some £21,099. Since he was very widely held to have more than a sufficient

---

[1] The coinage was made of silver which came from the East by way of Russia and Scandinavia.

[2] St. Clement was the patron Saint of Danish sailors, as may be seen at St. Clement's Church at Aarhus in Denmark.

fleet at command, resentment at the tax was general, and the tax gatherers met with a good deal of rough handling, some of them suffering death at the hands of the mob despite their having sought sanctuary at the foot of the Cross. It was a defiance of authority that was not allowed to go unpunished.

At the outset, relations between Godwin and the King were darkened by the suspicion that, among other things, the former had contrived the murder of Hardicanute's brother, Alfred. In a hasty attempt to anticipate reprisals the Eorl of Wessex presented his Sovereign with a vessel of such surpassing beauty that the royal ire was mollified. For the craft was roomy enough to accommodate eighty warriors in addition to the crew; its prow was sumptuously gilded; while the equipment of mariners and soldiery alike was ornamented with gilt and silver inlay, each man displaying on either arm a bracelet of finest gold sixteen ounces in weight. It was a judicious bribe which effectually averted the retribution which might otherwise have been exacted.

Hardicanute's death from apoplexy occurred in the second year of his reign; and with it Canute's grandiose triple-kingdom fell apart, its components reverting to their original status. It has to be recognised, however, that had Canute's great Anglo-Scandinavian empire persisted, England might have adhered permanently to Northern Europe, and for many generations remained isolated and without benefit of contact with the Mediterranean littoral and the astute and enterprising mercantile and seafaring people of southern Europe, to whom the future of the western world so obviously belonged.

As successor to Hardicanute the choice of the London merchants and shipmen fell on Edward 'the Confessor', despite the fact that this rather monkish individual had been a voluntary expatriate in Normandy and was thought too fondly to favour Norman ways and interests. Edward evinced sufficient manhood, however, in the face of threatened invasion by the Norwegian Pretender, Magnus, to assemble an armada as powerful as any that had sailed the narrow seas. Unfortunately this fleet was not kept together long enough to suppress the piratical raids of a pair of hardy sea rovers named Lothin and Yrling. Their most successful swoop was on 'the Confessor's' favourite coastal resort of Sandwich, whence they bore off great booty in gold and silver, and many captives. For the township had speedily become a place of considerable importance, "a hundred in itself", held in gift by the Archbishop of Canterbury "for the clothing of the monks", and yielding a yearly rent of £50 in addition to the 40,000 herrings it contributed for the sustenance of the holy men of Christ Church. With over three hundred houses, it was well worth any raider's close attention.

Lothin and Yrling next descended upon Thanet; but meeting with considerable opposition, they thrust across to the Essex shore, where their inroads met with unvarying success. A market for their loot was provided by Baldwin, Earl of Flanders; and with rare impudence they returned once more to Sandwich; thoroughly ravaging the Isle of Wight into the bargain.

A modest effort had been made to organise the defences of the *fif-burgas* of Dover, Hastings, Hythe, Romney and, ultimately, Sandwich, together with the 'antient towns' of Winchelsea and Rye.[1] But their obligation, at forty days' notice and in return for the grant of sac and soc,[2] to furnish ships and men for the King's service on a scale in accord with their individual resources, in no sense established a standing force on an organised war footing. It followed that like all pseudo-warlike make-shifts, it failed to meet the demands made upon it. Many generations were to pass, indeed, before it was brought home to the English people and their rulers that to be of real service a fleet must be kept permanently in commission; that the one thing that cannot hastily be improvised is a competent fighting marine.

The want of proper means of national defence was grimly emphasised by the revolt of Eorl Godwin, and the appearance off the coast of a fleet manned by his followers. First putting into Sandwich, the renegade led his men along the Kentish

---

[1] As emphasised by Samuel Jeakes, in his *Charters of the Cinque Ports*, the implications embodied in the *Liber de Wintonia* (Doomsday Book) and the earliest Charter of the Cinque Ports still extant (that of Edward I, dated 1278), make it clear that these havens were under obligation to furnish ships and men for the King's service so early as the reign of Edward the Confessor.

[2] The right of jurisdiction over their own communal affairs, normally vested in the King.

coast to commandeer all the shipping that could be found in
Romney, Hythe and Folkestone. Mustering his amplified force
at Sandwich, Godwin sailed through the harbour's 'north
mouth' heading for the Thames. With ravaged Sheppey and
burning Milton behind it, the fleet eventually dropped anchor
off Southwark. The quarrel between the King and his rebellious subject, supported by his sons Swain and Harold Godwinson and many of the lesser Thanes, might well have led to
civil war. But the commendable reluctance of the rank and
file of either party to come to handstrokes with men of their
own race led to a patched-up peace; and for a time the affairs
of the kingdom wore an aspect of unaccustomed, if precarious,
tranquillity.

*   *   *

On January 5th, 1066, the childless Edward died. Since
Anglo-Saxon custom did not assent in the exclusive claims of
kinship, the country was immediately thrown into a turmoil
over the respective pretensions to the succession of Eorl
Harold Godwinson and William Duke of Normandy.

Declaring that the dying King had named him heir, Harold
proclaimed himself Monarch and hurried through the coronation ceremonies before his predecessor had been two hours in
his shroud. But the protest of Duke William that a testa-
mentary declaration of 'the Confessor's' had specifically
nominated him as his successor was powerfully reinforced by
the disclosure that Harold himself had sworn to support the
Norman's claim to the Throne.

In 1064, as Duke William took occasion to recall, Eorl
Harold, together with his brother Wulfnoth and his sister
Ælfgifu, had set out from Bosham in Hampshire on a little
party of pleasure. Unfortunately the Channel weather had
proved unkind and their vessel had been cast away on the
coast of Ponthieu. Exercising his 'right of wreck', Count Guy
of Ponthieu had imprisoned the whole party. But at Duke
William's insistent demand—sweetened by the offer of a
substantial ransom—Harold had been handed over to the
protection of the bastard son of Robert of Normandy and the
tanner's daughter of Falaise. As his stay at the Court of Rouen
lengthened, however, the distinguished guest had been sharply

brought to realise that being entertained by William of Normandy differed little in essentials from being the captive of Guy of Ponthieu. In no position to protest, Harold had yielded to his host's demand and sworn to support his regal pretensions. That was an established fact; and whatever the condition of duress under which the vow had been extorted, no man could lightly forswear such an oath in an age wherein all the forces of superstition could be marshalled to give weighty endorsement to its sanctity.[1]

Having sufficiently committed himself, Harold had been permitted to return to England.

In the outcome, the breach of the Saxon leader's personal pledge to support him became Duke William's prime excuse for his attempt to seize the Crown of England by force of arms. Denouncing his rival's hasty enthronement as an unscrupulous *coup d'état*, the Duke successfully appealed for Papal support for an expedition against 'the usurper'. Having thus tactfully regularised affairs with the supreme ecclesiastical authority, William threw himself into preparations for the invasion of England with characteristic energy and competence.

In Normandy, at first, there was a certain reluctance to further the Duke's design with the necessary contributions. But William was so lavish with his promises that the avaricious Baron FitzOsbert came forward with the offer of sixty ships, with a full complement of soldiery. Then Bishop Odo promised forty; the Bishop of Mans a further thirty, with crews and pilots. Money, armour, provisions and warlike stores began to pour in as fast as the greedy adventurers, *enfants perdus* and loot-hungry soldiers of fortune that flocked to the ducal banner. At one end of the scale were the neighbouring overlords, such as Baldwin of Flanders, only too eager to encourage the predatory Norman in any adventure that promised to remove him permanently overseas; at the other, Remi the grasping priest of Fécamp, who guaranteed to furnish a ship and twenty men-at-arms in return for the promise of an English bishopric. Small wonder that the Spring and Summer of that momentous year saw every haven and harbour along the Norman coast the scene of busy preparations.

[1] *Roman de Rou*, Wace.

In England the news of William of Normandy's high-pressure activities spurred Harold into the organisation of large-scale measures of defence. In great haste he called out his butse-carls (shipmen), the mariners of the fif-burgas and the hus-carls (household troops), supporting them with the raw levies of the *fyrd*. Sandwich was nominated as general headquarters, with a forward command-post in the Isle of Wight; and in due course a fleet was mustered totalling 700 vessels.[1]

The Bastard of Falaise had appointed the mouth of the Dive, a small river between the Seine and the Orne, as a first rendezvous for his ships and land forces; and there the whole armament duly assembled. But owing to contrary winds it was not until the approach of the equinox that a further move could cautiously be attempted. At length, with the wind at last in the right quarter, the word was given and, in the wake of the Papal banner, the fleet set out. But the breeze freshened to gale force, driving the clincher-built, hastily carpentered vessels helplessly along the coast, on which many were wrecked in trying to make the shelter offered by the harbour of St. Valery. There were many losses and much damage, which the Bastard of Falaise hastened to make good. But the breeze had veered again; and with everyone chafing at the delay, morale in the extemporised camp sank so low that the furious, baffled William deemed it time to call in the aid of the supernatural. The mouldering bones of Saint Valery were hastily disinterred and paraded through the streets, with everyone on his knees, praying for a change of wind. And a little after midnight on September 27th the breeze began to blow encouragingly from the south-west. At last the Norman Agamemnon was free to quit his Aulis.

*   *   *

The delay which William had inveighed against as likely to prove his undoing in point of fact worked out to his immeasurable advantage. The price of safety is not intermittent, but eternal, vigilance, since vigilance, like peace, is indivisible.

[1] *Histoire de la Conquête de l'Angleterre*, Augustin Thierry; Nicolas, *op. cit.*; Oman, *op. cit.*; Macpherson, *op. cit.*; *Fifteen decisive Battles of the World*, Sir Edward Creasy; *Decisive Battles*, Major-General J. F. C. Fuller.

Yet by the Feast of the Nativity of Our Lady (September 8th) Harold's guardian fleet[1] had totally abandoned its watch and ward over the narrow seas, "for the season of provisioning had begun, and no man could keep them there any longer".[2] In effect, for want of the proper feed to carry them over the winter, all but the sturdiest beef cattle were customarily slaughtered off in the Autumn and salted down; work of such urgent importance that even the demands of a state of emergency were not permitted to interfere with it.

Then, in the wake of a flaming comet, out of the North came the dire news of a hostile landing, headed by Harold's own rebellious brother, Tostig, supported by all the resources at the disposal of his ally, Harald Hadrada, King of Norway. Leaving the South entirely unprotected, Eorl Harold raced North, passing through Tadcaster on September 24th and York the day following. Coming up with the invaders at Stamford Brig, Harold inflicted defeat on them in a furious *mêlée* in which both Tostig and 'the last of the Vikings' were slain.

But the weathercock on the steeple of the little church of St. Valery had steadied to a south by south-westerly wind; and William of Normandy gave the signal for the invasion force to up-anchor and make sail. His own vessel, *Mora*—a gift from his wife, Matilda—led the way, with the consecrated gonfanon signalising the Pope's approval of the venture a-flutter at the masthead. At the ship's prow was "the figure of a child in brass, bearing an arrow with a bended bow" pointing towards the land it was hoped to conquer. The single sail was striped red-yellow-red, and the *rector*, Stephen Fitz-Erard, held the sheet in one hand and manipulated the *clavus* with the other. Around the thwarts were clamped six and twenty shields, thirteen a side, while above the silken banner the masthead was crowned by a gilt weathervane and a great lantern, on whose light the fleet was to rally after the fall of darkness. For there was no standardised signal code for the purpose of inter-communication. Once the armament had taken to the high seas everyone had to rely on the prescience of orders that had been cried round the camp just prior to departure.

[1] It is unlikely that any of them was over 30 tons burthen.
[2] *A. S. Chronicle.*

The strength of the Duke's fleet has been variously estimated, but the figure of a little under seven hundred transports,
with perhaps a couple of hundred smaller craft to act as
tenders, would be approximately accurate. The raw-timbered,
hurriedly constructed vessels were not decked over, nor fitted
with warlike superstructures in the shape of fore- and aft-
castles. They were in no sense warships; they were transports,
only required to hold together long enough to give passage to
an army. Had they been intercepted by anything like a competent naval force, or met with anything but good weather,
the expedition would have foundered in ruin ere it had crossed
the narrow seas.

But the Channel was calm, the gentle, steady wind could
not have been more helpful. William, forging ahead of his
fleet and meeting no opposition, was the first to make a landfall. Coming ashore, still unhindered, at Bulverhithe, between
Pevensey and Hastings, he set about the immediate occupation
of Pevensey Castle. There, while certain of his troops dis-
tracted attention by foraging inland, three wooden forts were
speedily erected with materials brought over in sections all
ready to fit together. These *points d'appui* lent a certain strength
to his shallow bridge-head; while the deliberate destruction
of his already warped and leaky craft served as a grim reminder
that there would be no turning back.

With the news of the Bastard's landing Harold raced south
to confront the intruder at such a pace that many of his troops
were straggling after him through the tangled forest country
of the Weald right up to the moment when the pretensions
of the rival claimants to the Throne were put to the test of
battle. On the ridge of the hoar apple tree hard by the little
Sandlake stream, the Saxon host, outmanœuvred by the very
same ruse of feigned flight that had proved the Norseman's
downfall at Stamford Brig, and utterly demoralised by their
leader's death, fell apart in precipitate retreat. Elements of the
fleet, hastily reconstituted, arrived far too late to menace an
army firmly established ashore and living comfortably at
free quarter on the surrounding countryside.

With Harold slain and his army routed, the Saxon-English
had found their masters—and their saviours. The Normans,
coming from an undeveloped and war-ravaged territory they

3+

had wrested from a degenerate Frankish *noblesse* so recently as A.D. 912, brought the boon of a centralised system of government, and a carefully stratified social structure based on a clear-sighted recognition of the fact that class distinctions form the only foundation of sound national discipline. Where hitherto there had been no more than an impotent simulacrum of authority and interminable internecine strife, the hard-headed and dynamic Bastard of Falaise established order and such respect for the law that, as Wace affirmed, "a man that was worth aught might travel over the kingdom with his bosom full of gold unhurt. And no man durst slay another man, though he suffered never so mickle evil from the other."[1] Slavery was abolished; and all the land brought under the King's dominion, since he realised that the wealth it represented was both an instrument of government and an essential to national expansion.

All in all, never has conflict of such modest dimensions as the Hastings battle been fraught with greater consequences. From sharing in the gradual decline that overtook the North, England was brought within the ambit of the Mediterranean and all the pulsing life it fostered. And if thereby its people were dragged into the maelstrom of European politics, it was only by this selfsame enlargement of responsibility that they acquired those qualities which enabled them ultimately to found the great overseas empire over which, for so many years, they were to exercise firm but benevolent sway. As Campbell boldly affirmed, "the Normans high-mettled the blood in our veins". Only in their bleak unawareness of the overriding importance of the sea in the future destiny of the land they had conquered can the Normans be made the target of warrantable criticism.

[1] *Master Wace His Chronicle of the Norman Conquest, from the Roman de Rou*, translated by Edgar Taylor (1837).

CHAPTER III

'The Ditch'

"To have an opportunity is one thing, to recognise its value is another."

VAUVENARGUES

THE Norman *petit noblesse* who had helped their Duke to win a throne were men whose interests were purely military and latifundian. They understood the art of combat and the means whereby law and order could be maintained in the territories they had acquired as spoil of war. But of the sea and its boundless possibilities they knew nothing and cared nothing: if they or their Sovereign were aware of the fact that the balance of Harold's fleet had been carried off by his fugitive sons, it was quite beyond their capacity to envisage the probable consequences of its removal. In their estimation the narrow seas constituted no more than a tedious ditch separating one part of their domains from the other. Thus it continued to be regarded for some hundred and thirty-eight years. To all intents and purposes, "the English Channel dried up. Richard Lionheart could ride from the Trent to the Pyrenees, and his horse's hooves need tread no ground that was not his own."[1]

The urgent need for a standing naval force was sharply demonstrated, however, in 1069, when Swain, King of Denmark, swept into the Channel at the head of a fleet of two hundred and forty vessels. His earlier successes, in company with the many unreconciled Saxons who flocked to his banner, enabled him to winter in England undisturbed. In no case to take any active steps to expel him, William resorted to the flaccid expedient of a heavy bribe to persuade him to return whence he had come.

In 1071 sufficient shipping was drummed up to help in the blockade of the defiant Saxons, Hereward and Morcar, in

[1] *The Naval Side of English History*, Geoffrey Callender.

their Isle of Ely "fortress of reeds"; and to support an extremely modest enterprise against Scotland.

In 1073, again, the need to put down insurrection in the Conqueror's province of Maine—close neighbour to his sea-girt Duchy of Normandy—called for the improvisation of a considerable fleet, which could only be got together by the wholesale 'arrest' of shipping for the King's service. Then in 1077 the Channel havens had once more to be scoured to furnish another armament, when William's eldest son, Robert *Courte-heuse*, sought to secure the untrammelled overlordship of his father's Norman duchy.

It would be inaccurate to term the fleet which eventually took the sea anything but a makeshift; although it appeared formidable enough to deter King Knud of Denmark from pressing home his attempted invasion of England, even at the head of some seven hundred vessels. For all that, it was clear that the country stood in urgent need of something more readily available in the way of a reliable marine fighting force.

As the source most likely to furnish it, the King turned to the hardy shipmen of the Cinque Ports, who had so resolutely beaten back such venturesome Danes as had recently appeared along their shores. In return for extended privileges, responsibility for the guardianship of the Kentish coast and coastal waters was taken out of the hands of Bishop Odo, the Conqueror's slippery and untrustworthy brother, and confided to John Fiennes, as Constable of Dover Castle and the first *de facto* Warden of the Cinque Ports. In effect, Fiennes was entrusted with similar responsibilities to those undertaken in the days of the Roman occupation by the *Comes Littoris Saxonicci*.[1]

In return for the grant of its additional 'liberties', Dover was required, upon forty days' notice, to furnish twenty ships for the King's service, at the town's own charge, for fifteen days. Should they be called upon to keep the sea for a longer period, the cost of their maintenance was to be assumed by the Sovereign. Each craft was to be manned by twenty men "and a grommet",[2] under the command of a *rector* or master;

[1] The Lord Wardenship was hereditary until the reign of Richard I.
[2] Ship's boy.

and the terms of the obligation were duly entered in Dooms-day Book. Sandwich, Romney and other havens were under bond to provide vessels in proportion; but the whole armament never totalled more than fifty-seven craft.

Sandwich, nominated as the port of embarkation for royalty bound for the Continent, paid an annual tribute to the King of £18,[1] while Dover tendered £15; as against the modest £6 4s. 1¼d. rendered by Lewes and the "100 shillings wanting one penny" found by Chichester.

Apart from his other duties, Fiennes was responsible for the lights and buoys in his particular area; enjoying in return the exclusive rights to "flotsam, jetsam and lagan".[2]

To supplement the Cinque Ports' fleet, a further array of shipping was to be ensured by the imposition of a ship geld throughout the country of two and seventy pence on every non-exempted hide of land. But although the tax—subse-quently reduced to 4s. *per* hide—was sedulously collected, it led to no appreciable increase in naval strength. Much of the money was diverted to the repair of Dover Castle and the extension of the Cinque Ports' landward defences. This mis-application of funds which should have been devoted to rendering the narrow seas safe for the passage of trading vessels and passenger transport may have discouraged the swarming sea rovers from raiding a well-guarded coast, but left them entirely free to pursue their nefarious activities on the open waters.

Yet the King's Customs, like the ship geld itself, were paid on the understanding that in return the Sovereign would protect "such as pass on the sea upon their lawful occasions".

The 'Ancient Custom', which the Conqueror had secured by swearing to abide by the laws formulated by his predecessors on the Throne, consisted of a 'subsidy' levied on all exported wool, wool-fells, hides, tin and lead, as on imported fine-cloth and wax; in all of which there was a lively cross-Channel traffic. A tax on wine, given the name of prisage, was taken in kind; a certain proportion of the cargo being set aside, before landing, for the use of the King and his Court. The

---

[1] About £270 in terms of the present-day spending value of money.
[2] Goods deliberately sunk and buoyed, to be retrieved surreptitiously at some future date.

Monarch also enjoyed the privilege of purveyance, that is of purchasing wine at cost, thereafter retailing it at the market price and pocketing the profit. As time went on, however, the tendency arose to commute a large proportion of this prise on wine for a fixed money payment. To this revenue were added the few pence levied on every tun of wine entering the country.

Since every English household produced a sufficient supply of necessaries for its daily needs, virtually all 'dry' imports fell into the category of luxuries or near-luxuries, the taxes on which made no demands on the funds of any but the relatively well-to-do. In the same way, the members of the poorer classes, being ale drinkers by preference, experienced no inconvenience from the tax on wine, which they ungrudgingly regarded as the tipple appropriate to their betters.

One of the few free imports was building stone from Caen; already acclaimed, and destined to increase in popularity until superseded by Portland stone in mid-seventeenth century.[1] Folkestone stone, which was in great demand for paving market squares, city gateways and waterside wharves, as a local product was exempt from all but certain town tolls.[2]

It was the Sheriff's responsibility to appoint bailiffs to collect the Customs at the ports; but he had himself to account to his Sovereign Lord the King for the monies accruing from their activities. And there was no laxity about the collection of the dues, or in the regal scrutiny of the totals paid into the Exchequer. The hard-headed Norman monarchs may not have been interested in the actual conduct of trade, but they were in no need of an abacus to arrive at what was due to 'the King's hoard' at Winchester as the outcome of other men's pursuit of it.

It was to the Customs revenue that the Sovereign looked to meet some of his more regular and pressing disbursements. For according to the contemporary ethic, whatever circumstances might arise, the King was required to 'live in his own'. That is to say, he was expected to support the dignity of his position and fulfil all the obligations that fell to him as the

---

[1] In 1086 the Bishop of London began the reconstruction of his cathedral with stone from Caen (*A. S. Chronicle*, William of Malmesbury).
[2] *Street Life in Medieval England*, G. T. Salusbury.

head of State, on the extremely modest income he derived from his rents, his mining royalties, and such other small revenues as were annexed to the Crown; of which that derived from the Customs was not the least considerable. For any extraordinary expenditure—such as war or the fitting out of a fleet—he had to resort either to some extraneous and restricted fiscal measure, to the temporary 'farm' of one of his standard sources of income, or to an outright loan. Personal taxation, being founded upon the payment of scutage, or shield money, in lieu of knight service in the field, was indissolubly associated in the popular mind with a nation-wide call to arms. To try to convince the ordinary mass of the people that the administration of the country in times of peace also called for the expenditure of a certain amount of public money, was to cut right across the Englishman's perennial belief in public economy and private self-indulgence. It was a state of affairs which was to become progressively more unsatisfactory, and was the source of increasing friction between the Monarch on the one hand and, on the other, all those laid under contribution to supply his pecuniary needs.

*　　　*　　　*

Henry 'Beauclerc' was the next to be given a sharp reminder of the fact that an English Sovereign lacking the support of a loyal and powerful fleet stands in perennial danger of losing his throne. For in 1101, almost before he had fitted the Crown comfortably to his brow, his elder brother came surging across the narrow seas to dispute the succession.

Even with such armament as Henry contrived to muster, want of enthusiasm soon led to many desertions and the drastic diminution of what in any case was an entirely inadequate force.

With *Courte-heuse* brought safely into Portsmouth harbour through the treachery of certain local pilots, Henry hastily put about and hurried ashore, to place himself at the head of a makeshift army brought up from Pevensey. Confronting his brother at Alton, on the road from Portsmouth to London, 'Beauclerc' was fortunate in finding his fundamentally indolent elder more inclined to negotiate than to fight. With Robert bought off with promises the incumbent of the throne had no real intention of redeeming, the momentary alarm died down.

It was obvious, however, that the whole problem of defence and maritime jurisdiction along the Channel coast was in pressing need of attention.

The first measure of reform was the establishment of an embryo Admiralty Court; not a Naval Court in the modern sense of the term, but a purely civilian assize concerned with the outlawry and banishment of those attainted of certain maritime offences; with the administration of the ports; with the collection of murrage—the dues for the construction of harbour works, sea walls, and coastal fortifications—and with the dispensation of the law of wreck.

On a coast-line where to the natural hazards of capricious weather conditions were added the activities of wreckers and looters, the law of wreck was of necessity on the side of severity. As it stood, a wreck was said to have occurred when a ship was cast away, no matter how many the survivors. Its hull and everything in it, in addition to flotsam, became the absolute property of the monarch on whose shores the catastrophe had occurred, or of the local lord of the manor should the terms of his tenure include 'rights of wreck'.

But more often than not such rights could not be exacted, owing to the speed with which the wreck was plundered by the predatory rascals who had deliberately brought the disaster about. The men of Portland had a particularly unsavoury reputation in this respect, as had the coastal folk of Devon and Cornwall. For example (to anticipate a little), in 1363 four great ships, deliberately brought to wreck off Plymouth, were pillaged of cargo worth more than a million in terms of present-day currency; while in 1454 a gang of Cornishmen deliberately cut the cables of a Genoese carrack to ensure that she should drift to ruin on the rocks. Nor were conditions any better under 'Beauclerc'.

Henry therefore gained considerable popularity, both with the maritime and commercial classes, when he ordained that even if there were no more than one survivor of the disaster, the vessel should not be esteemed a wreck, while property in her and her contents should not be held to have passed away from the original owner. Claims had to be rendered within a year and a day, and it was customary to make some payment for salvage.[1] It was a shrewd move in the Sovereign's general scheme to encourage his own mercantile class and at the same time conciliate his Saxon subjects, since it was amongst the last-named that he found the most reliable of his shipmen. Experienced mariners were obviously worthy of every possible consideration; for profitable maritime traffic was on the increase.

On the heels of Duke William's victorious army there had swarmed into the country a whole horde of hard-headed Norman merchants; astute and bustling 'huckers' who had speedily installed themselves in London and the coastal towns of Kent, Sussex and Hampshire.

At the outset, with a native population sullenly resentful of the energetic aliens that conquest had brought to settle in their midst, it was only natural for the newcomers to band themselves together in a trade association organised for their mutual benefit and support. In the beginning, these Merchant Guilds enjoyed no trade monopolies; there was no compulsion with regard to membership, while craftsmen were as freely admitted to the fraternity as their employers. For the separation between the man who took the risks and the man who took the wages was yet to come. On the other hand, in their day-to-day transactions the *Gildeins* were under oath not to outbid each other, while any *Burgeis de la Gilde* could claim a share in another's purchase, at the original selling price.

At first, Guild membership was almost wholly restricted to men of Norman blood; although Englishmen were frequently called upon to act as brokers for the retail disposal of merchandise, on the score of their intimate acquaintance with local requirements and marketing facilities.

As mutual antipathy diminished, more and more English merchants paid their fees and were admitted to the brotherhood of the Guilds; the regulation of which, however, the Normans were careful to retain in their own hands. For Guild traditions were unquestionably Continental, as—with

[1] *Commentaries on the Laws of England*, Sir William Blackstone; Nicolas, *op. cit.* Some commentators have attributed to Henry I and Henry II a further modification in the law of wreck for which the credit should go to Henry III. See page 54.

one exception, that of Alderman—were the titles of office usually adopted. It followed that Norman-French was the language employed in the Guilds' written transactions and in the records they kept of their business dealings.

As time went on and the Guilds increased in solidarity and wealth—as occurred at Southampton in particular—the tendency arose for the same men as headed the trade associations to assume the direction of municipal affairs. The Saxon townmoote, presided over by a town reeve, gave place to a mayor and council of prominent burgesses—Guildsmen all. With local government in the hands of the leading *Gildeins*, it may be taken for granted that their own personal interests were not allowed to suffer neglect, any more than those of the Guild itself. Indeed, the tendency was for a strong local autonomy to supervene, with monopolistic practices and local rules and regulations designed to conserve and enlarge the town's prosperity at the expense of its neighbours. This trend— originating during the general turbulence which had characterised the land in the early days of the Conquest—encouraged communities "to be nowhere but within walled towns, castles and safe places".[1] Thereafter, isolation and the lack of free intercourse invariably tended to harden into restrictive local legislation. As a result, it became highly necessary for all towns, especially those on the coast, to keep a careful record of the Charters of other burghs, so that the bailiffs of any given place could determine who amongst the traders passing through their gates were entitled to claim exemption from toll. For reciprocal arrangements often existed between towns— as, for instance, Winchester and Southampton—to relieve their respective citizens from the dues normally exacted from all doing business within each other's boundaries. The production of a 'letter of credit'—the contemporary equivalent of the modern *carte d'identité*—absolved its owner from all tolls on goods passing through the gates, as well as pavage—the contribution exacted from all strangers towards paving places of public resort.[2]

Charters securing a town's 'liberties' were granted by royal patent; and since the attendant fees—found by the *Gildeins*— brought in a useful sum of hard cash to the monarch invariably

---

[1] Macpherson, *op. cit.*   [2] Salusbury, *op. cit.*

at his wit's end for ready money, the increase in their award had almost the inevitability of a mathematical progression.[1]

At the outset, alien merchants were rather encouraged than forbidden to frequent and trade in the English ports. For until an adequate native mercantile marine could be organised to ply in the carrying trade, it was only through the activities of such foreign intermediaries that the exchange of English and foreign merchandise could be assured. But the activities of merchant-strangers were restricted to wholesale dealings with enfranchised traders. They were not allowed to chaffer amongst themselves, or to sell retail to the general body of consumers. In effect, the *Gildeins* were determined to retain the internal trade of the country in their own hands; a bias in favour of monopoly which was to characterise both mercantile and fiscal practice for centuries to come.

To ensure some sort of surveillance over the activities of the merchant-stranger, it became customary to limit his stay in England to forty days, during which period he was under the control of the native *Gildein* upon whom he was billeted. The hosteller accepted full responsibility for his involuntary guest; subjecting all his commercial transactions to the closest scrutiny. Indeed, hostellers took oath "to be privy and oversee all manner of merchandise that any merchant-alien, being under your said hostage, hath".[2]

There soon arose considerable diversity of approach between the policy of the Guilds and the aims of the Monarch and the nobility, who as consumers and, in many instances, exporters of vendible commodities, such as wool, would have preferred to trade with the Continental merchants directly. For thus they would have secured for themselves that proportion of the profit which, under the Guild system, had to be surrendered to the middleman. It was a virtually irreconcilable ambivalence which was to bedevil the whole complicated pattern of cross-Channel trade as vexatiously as the competing claims to especial consideration advanced by burgesses and aliens.

*   *   *

[1] London's Charter, granted by William I and confirmed by Magna Carta, decreed that "the city of London shall have all its ancient liberties and free customs as well by land as by water" (Letter Book, A 80).

[2] Letter Book (Southampton), D 194.

With the early years of the twelfth century the pattern of commercial activity was beginning to take shape. London, having been relieved from paying tolls, the lastage elsewhere charged on all goods—such as herrings—sold by the last, and the dues, known as passage, normally imposed on travellers by sea, was steadily rising in prosperity. This happy state of affairs was clearly reflected in the handsome total of £1,043,[1] representing the city's involuntary 'gift' to the King at a moment of acute pecuniary embarrassment; a contribution which far exceeded the joint offering of Lincolnshire, Somerset, Essex and Kent. There was ample money too for the construction of a stone bridge on the west side of the old wooden London Bridge; while Queenshithe was established on the site of the erstwhile Ethelred's hithe, for the discharge of corn, fish, salt and fuel. It was a wharf particularly patronised by the ships of the Cinque Ports, whose crews were eager customers of the taverns and cook-shops of the adjacent waterfront. A burly, blustering, lubricious fraternity, the money they could invariably jingle in their pokes ensured a ready welcome for them from the bawds whose stews in Southwark and Cokkes Lane were all too handy to the riverside.

Southampton, the principal port of entry for the wine trade, was also beginning to attract a number of Italian merchants. Already enriched by the vast sums earned in the transportation of pilgrims and Crusaders to the Holy Land, they were prepared to incur the risks involved in directly extending their traffic in silks and spices to the markets of the North. Thus, with a flourishing Guild-merchant and jurisdiction—immune from interference by the Admiralty Courts—that extended from Hurst to Langstone and included Portsmouth harbour, the Hampshire haven enjoyed a turnover far exceeding that of any of the Cinque Ports. The wealth of the Kent and Sussex coastal settlements lay in their extensive fishing grounds—and in a little surreptitious piracy and wrecking!—although a certain amount of wine was discharged at Sandwich; whose streets were now so spruce and well paved that at certain times of the year it even permitted the passage of wine carts through them whose wheels had been rimmed with iron fellies, a most unusual

---

[1] In spending value the equivalent of £90,000 in present-day currency.

concession.[1] For iron-shod wheels were the ruination of the primitive paving of mediaeval days and were usually forbidden the town. But municipally, Sandwich was extremely well run. It even rejoiced in a water-bailiff to ensure that washerwomen did not pollute its stream by rinsing their clothes and tubs in it; for to some extent it was a show place, since it shared with Dover the passenger traffic across the Channel.[2]

Despite lurking corsairs and the hazards of dangerously unpredictable weather, men were learning to pass to and fro across the narrow seas with a certain degree of confidence; although the seaworthiness of their craft had undergone little substantial betterment.

This was cruelly brought home to the King by the disaster which overtook the *White Ship*—the nef *Blanche*—in the November of 1120.

She was a new vessel, rigged with every device known to contemporary seamanship; and her passengers included the eighteen-year-old Prince William, his sister, the Countess Maria—none the less cherished for having been born *de la main gauche*—several men of title, and half the royal household. With the King speeding on ahead of them, it was a merry company aboard the *Blanche*, and there is no disguising the fact that everyone was a little flown with wine—including the crew. But Thomas Fitz-Stephen, whose father had sailed with the Conqueror's armada, was the trusted ship-master; and he laughed to scorn any suggestion that the main fleet could not be overtaken. So with the turn of the tide the *White Ship* hoisted sail and set off on her course. There was music and dancing as the sun declined and the lanthorns came to light up the scene of revelry. With a following wind, Fitz-Stephen's promise to overtake the King's ship seemed in a fair way of redemption. Then as the frail craft reached a reef then called the *Raz de Catte*[3] disaster overtook it; it struck hard, starting a number of larboard planks, and immediately began to founder. Only Fitz-Stephen kept his head. Lowering Prince William into a boat—in all probability the only boat—he bade him make for land. But in the general panic the Countess Maria

---

[1] Salusbury, *op. cit.*
[2] *Collections for a History of Sandwich*, W. Boys.
[3] Now the *Raz de Catteville*.

was heard crying out to her brother to save her. As the Prince
turned back there was a swirl of courtiers and their womenfolk
seeking madly to crowd into the fragile boat. Overladen and
swamped, it sank immediately beneath the waters; the *Blanche*
herself being engulfed with all the ship's complement save one
survivor.[1]

Although the legend that Henry consoled himself for the
news of his son's demise by a fatal gorge of peaches and lam-
preys is more picturesque than accurate—he survived another
fifteen years—Prince William's untimely death undoubtedly
complicated the issue of the succession. Striving to achieve a
balance of power amongst his followers, Henry proceeded to
wed his only other child, Maud, to the fond hope of the
Angevins, Geoffrey, nicknamed Plantagenet, much to the
vexation of his 'die-hard' Norman barons. With her father's
death in 1135 the Princess, supported by her natural brother,
Robert of Gloucester, contrived to cross the Channel and land,
unopposed, at Portsmouth. There had been no time to call
out the Cinque Portsmen; in any case there was considerable
dubiety as to which way their sympathies might incline. Un-
ashamed opportunists to a man, they preferred to wait and see
which way the cat jumped before declaring their allegiance.
But Maud's bid for the throne was frustrated by the opposition
of the powerful barons; whose choice had fallen upon Stephen
of Blois and Boulogne, the Conqueror's eldest male descendant.

Stephen's lukewarm interest in things maritime is reflected
in the single entry in the Treasury accounts, recording the
purchase of a couple of ships. Their insignificant dimensions
are sufficiently indicated by the modesty of their price—forty
shillings the pair!

It did not take Henry II, of the quick mind and ungovern-
able temper, very long to realise that in the absence of a standing
naval force, it was necessary that the pick of the mercantile
marine should remain always available for requisition. But it
was not until 1181 that he secured assent to an ordinance
which forbade, under the heaviest penalties, the sale of any
ship for permanent removal out of England. By the same law
it was rendered an offence to entice any English shipman to

[1] According to *Ordericus Vitalis*, passengers and crew totalled three
hundred.

take service in a foreign craft. These measures ensured that if it
came to the improvisation of a fighting force, the best ships
would not be sold to avoid 'arrest' and transfer to the King's
service, nor the best men seduced into enemy employ. In effect,
an enactment was brought into service which very largely
anticipated the provisions of the subsequent Navigation Acts.

Stout ships and lusty men to sail them were a crying need,
lest commerce in the narrow seas should suffer serious hurt.
For the lurking corsairs were ever ready to pounce upon and
overwhelm the craft incapable of offering a stout resistance.
Time and time again, however, the men of the Channel havens
so vigorously showered their adversaries with stone shot from
their fustables[1] that the pirate craft was beaten off without
chance to board and enter.

The Portsmen could scarcely employ such summary methods
with the Dutch, in their squat *slabbaerts*, whose infiltration of
the fishing grounds in the Channel's eastern approaches
coincided with one of those shifts in the herrings' spawning
grounds which have led to the rise and fall of whole cities,
and even of nations. But there were the makings of a very
pretty quarrel in this encroachment on waters the English
shipmen had long regarded as exclusively their own; and the
years were to witness its culmination in scenes of violence and
bloodshed which ranked little short of open battle.

The Portsmen, as sturdy individualists, were always cheerfully prepared to take their own line in any political quarrel.
So it was to them that Thomas à Becket turned for succour
when he had fallen under the King's displeasure. If the first
attempt by the Romney Marsh freebooters to smuggle him
across the Channel turned out a failure, its frustration must be
attributed to the refusal of the storm-tossed narrow seas to
assist his flight. Forced to put back, the unhappy Archbishop
returned to Canterbury, sneezing his head off with a violent
cold.

When he was forced to flee for the second time, it was the
men of Sandwich who cunningly concealed him for over a
week; eventually transporting him safely across the Channel in
a cockleshell of a boat, that landed him high, but very far from
dry, on Gravelines beach.

---

[1] A kind of sling.

The helpfulness of these rough and ready shipmen was in sharp contrast to the dastardly behaviour of another Marshman, Hugh of Horsea. A renegade clerk who was known throughout Kent as the 'Evil Deacon', this predatory ruffian did not scruple to pillage the vessel bearing the fugitive Archbishop's personal baggage overseas; returning ashore to ravage the lands that Becket held by right of his episcopal preferment.

*   *   *

Save for the illicit toll levied by Hugh of Horsea and other sea-rovers of equally elastic conscience, the merchant-venturers had remarkably few grounds for legitimate complaint. In many ways they were extremely favourably placed. For their Sovereign, by his coldly calculated marriage with the divorced wife of Louis VII of France—the flighty Eleanor of Aquitaine —had acquired suzerainty over the flourishing provinces of Saintonge, Auvergne, Perigord, Angoumois, Guienne, and Gascony; about a third of France, including the finest wine-producing territory in the land. Since the merchants in this area were subjects to the same monarch as the 'occupiers of wares' on the English side of the Channel, trade across the narrow seas substantially increased.

It was given further encouragement by the conclusion in 1157 of an agreement between Henry and the Emperor Frederick Barbarossa of Germany for "friendly traffike between the Merchants of the Empire and England". As an outcome, the *Kontor* of the thriving Guild of German Merchants, of Cologne, Bruges, Lübeck, Bremen, Hamburg, and other important trading centres in Flanders, on the Rhine, and in the Baltic, was established in Dowgate, a little above London Bridge, and taken under the Sovereign's especial protection. In this manner the way was smoothed for the establishment, in a key position, of that enterprising confederation of Teutonic traders which was presently to adopt the style and title of the Hanseatic League.

At the outset, German transactions were primarily concerned with the purchase and transhipment of uncarded wool. For "the worthiest and richest commodity in the kingdom", product of the 'Cotswold lion'[1] and the sheep-walks of

---

[1] As the sheep was proudly termed in Gloucestershire.

Yorkshire, Lincoln, Norfolk, Somerset and Hampshire, was in perpetual demand in all the cloth manufacturing centres of Europe. A commerce was in process of rapid expansion whose importance, both financial and political, it would be impossible to overestimate.[1] The great Flemish cloth merchants assiduously cultivated the favour of the English Kings, lent them money, and consulted with them on matters of policy. The pecuniary risk was one they could well afford to take, since they had the capital to invest, and saw to it that their stake was covered by substantial collateral. Whereafter, if their activities lend colour to the belief that money knows no frontier, and rejoices in an extremely elastic conscience, at least they saw to it that their coinage was always worth its face value and was therefore regarded as entirely trustworthy. Indeed, the Osterling pound—of 20 shillings of 20 groats to the shilling—set a pattern of financial probity and stability which the present-day term of sterling still reflects.

Naturally, as a plain matter of business, the Easterlings saw to it that they got the better of most bargains; and they were at pains to ensure that it was almost exclusively in foreign bottoms that wool and the lesser exports crossed the narrow seas to Bruges, Ghent, Ypres, Arras and St. Omer, and their many satellites.

For in addition to wool there was a modest outgoing trade in lead, tin, silversmith's ware, embroidery, cattle, fish, and a certain amount of dairy produce. But there was no grain to spare, the ever-expanding sheep-walks saw to that.

In return, the great overland trade routes, from the Black Sea and the Bosphorus by way of Novgorod to the Baltic, or over the Alps and along the Rhine, brought gold and silver work, precious stones, silks, velvets, and tissued cloth from the East, and on the way picked up stamped leather work from Spain, linen from Lorraine and coats of mail from Mainz—precious cargoes that crossed the Channel bound for the great mart of London. All through the late Spring, Summer and early Autumn the Thames and its approaches were crowded with shipping; and the Pool was so thronged with vessels as to call for the services of a river police for their protection—three men and one boat!

[1] It was a heavily punishable offence to mix inferior imported Spanish wool with native English.

In their respective ways, Southampton, Portsmouth and the Cinque Ports were flourishing. For most imports, being high-priced luxury goods, commanded sales amongst a limited clientele, whereas exports, "being adapted to the wants of all classes of mankind", were in great and general demand. The balance of trade, therefore, was comfortably in England's favour.

But prosperity had not yet reached out to the West, where Poole was accounted no more than a coasting haven; while a contemporary scribe termed Southtown, or Sutton—as Plymouth was then called—"a mene thing as an inhabitation for fishers".

It was for the most part in backward Devon and Cornwall, and on the Portland peninsula—long notorious for wreckers —that muttered criticism was levelled at Henry's revision of the law of wreck. As amended, it abolished the claim hitherto enjoyed by the Sovereign and certain landed proprietors with foreshore rights, to *all* vessels wrecked on their strands. The decree laid it down that should any craft be cast away on the coast of England, Poitou, Gascony, or the Isle of Oléron, and any living thing survive the catastrophe, even a dog or cat belonging to the ship, then the said vessel should be preserved for the owners. Three months would be allowed them to render their claim, and failing its presentation within this period, the wreck should belong to the King.[1]

The loss of a ship had become a matter of very serious importance. For not only had the call on their services increased, and the vessels themselves grown in size—this is witnessed by the recorded loss of a vessel in the Channel in 1170 with a complement of four hundred—but they had undergone a striking development. The galley had never been the appropriate craft for Northern waters. Such rough weather as characterises the Mediterranean gives rise to a *short* sea, with which the galley could deal well enough. But it was a very different story with the rolling pitch and toss to be found so often in the Channel. Unless especially strengthened, the Venetian and Genoan cargo galleys could only venture these unpredictable

[1] *Foedera Anglia*, Thomas Rymer; Nicolas, *op. cit.*; Macpherson, *op. cit.* This was a piece of legislation inspired by Rhodian law, the law of the Roman Emperor Andronicus, and that of the Pontiff, Alexander III.

waters during the middle months of the year. In any case the galley offered too little stores and cargo space to permit of lengthy voyages in uncertain, obstructive weather. Lastly, the galley, with its complement of deck hands amplified by as many as a hundred and fifty oarsmen toiling at the sweeps, was hopelessly uneconomic from a commercial point of view, even had such a labour force been available elsewhere than in the 'Middle Sea'.

The vessel which emerged after considerable trial and error was the English round ship, or buss, which the learned chronicler Holinshed termed *navis oneraria*. Tactically it was nowhere in the same category as the galley or the even more nimble galliones. But strategically, as from a mercantile point of view, it was infinitely their superior. In length a little more then twice its beam, with bluff bows, a firm stem and a blunted stern, this round, pot-bellied craft had a capacious cargo deck, with a roomy hold beneath. Propelled not by oar but by a single sail, its progress was maddeningly slow; but it could stand up sturdily to dirty weather. Being unable to sail more than three points off the wind at most, the vessel was entirely at the mercy of the breeze; and at its unhandiest on a lee shore. Otherwise it was solid, it was sure, and it was remarkably cheap to run. In due course out of its loins was born that most admirable of craft—the ship of the line.

Mathew Paris affirms that the armament mustered in England's havens for the Third Crusade included thirteen buccas rigged with 'triple sails'.[1] But it was with a fleet of busses, "vessels of great capacity, very strongly and compactly built", that Richard Lionheart designed to support his squadron of war galleys, when he set out from Dartmouth to give life and impetus to yet another attempt at the redemption of the Holy Land . . . and the extension of trade with the Levant, especially in the import of spices and the wines of Tyre, Cyprus and Rhodes.

Doubtless there were men from Kent, Sussex and Hampshire in Richard's Crusader fleet; but Southampton and the Cinque Ports as such had little concern with the exalted

[1] Whether they were three-*masted* ships is not clear, but Brooks, in his *English Naval Forces, 1199–1272*, affirms that "the larger Mediterranean galleys often carried two or even three masts".

enterprise against the 'Infidels'. They had, however, borne a conspicuous part in the expedition of 1147, to redeem Lisbon from the Moors. Indeed, the grateful Alphonso, first King of Portugal, had elevated the priest accompanying the Hastings contingent to the dignity of the city's episcopal throne. But with the Third Crusade in train, it was the responsibility of the Cinque Ports' mariners to guard the narrow seas during the absence of their Sovereign abroad. They were his 'free men', as the special Charter granted to the 'antient towns' of Rye and Winchelsea—'limbs' of the veritable Cinque Ports—specifically affirmed; and his confidence in their prowess and loyalty was unbounded.

For that matter, the seven-and-fifty vessels of the Cinque Ports' fleet were not designed for long ocean-going voyages. They were primarily fishing craft, at need capable of adaptation to the purposes of war. But it is doubtful if any of them exceeded a burden of fifty tons; the normal burden of the Hastings' ships, for example, being no more than twenty tons. For all their modest size, however, they were stout enough in construction; with the bow and the stern in a great curve to support the fore- and aft-castles, erected on temporary stanchions, for the accommodation of the military who swarmed aboard at the call to active service. The strong, girthy mast— easily furnished, like the rest of the timbers, from the neighbouring Weald—carried a third and smaller top-castle, the prototype of the later fighting-top; while the great strength of the prow facilitated the tactic, so dear to the Englishman's heart, of running down an enemy. The firm stem was particularly adapted to beaching and hauling up, a manœuvre in which the crew was thoroughly practised.

But in rough weather, with a single sail, no proper nautical instruments, no better rudder than an oar worked over the quarter, and further endangered by a top-heavy superstructure, the hazards encountered by such a vessel were numerous and menacing. Hence the numberless wrecks, the wholesale disasters which sent scores of men and ships to the bottom, when the smiling waters of the Channel were lashed to fury, and the cross-tides and boiling races added to the perils of the angry sea.

*   *   *

If Cœur de Lion had not been so fantastically obsessed with his fancied obligation to slaughter 'Infidels', and had spent a little more time in his own kingdom, his influence and encouragement would have materially benefited both the expansion of maritime commerce and the advancement of nautical skill. Infinitely more sea-minded than the majority of his predecessors, he understood the shipmen and their ways, and had more than an amateur's comprehension of their professional problems. Not only did he take a keen interest in such charts and pilots' rutters as then existed, but he boasted some acquaintance with that Arab device, "the needle mounted on a pivot", which was the embryo of the nautical compass.[1]

Richard's name will always be associated with the sponsorship of the Rolls of Oléron; that symposium of a series of judgments arrived at by the maritime Court of Oléron, which was codified, according to Cleirac, by Queen Eleanor, on her return from the Holy Land with her first husband, Louis VII of France. Promulgated at Chinon somewhere about 1190, the Rolls constitute a synthesis of the Sea Laws of Rhodes and Barcelona, together with the best of the *Tabula Amalfitana*, on which had been grafted a number of well-designed additional regulations.[2]

In all, the Rolls of Oléron comprised forty-seven Articles. Among the most important provisions was the clause which decreed that if a ship were wind- or weather-bound, the master was under obligation to consult his crew as to the advisability of putting to sea, and thereafter abide by the decision of the

---

[1] Mentioned at the time of the Third Crusade by Alexander Neckham. Hughes de Bercy (also called Guiot de Provens) a writer of *circa* 1190, set it down that "They [the seamen] have an art which cannot deceive, by virtue of the manete [magnet], an ill-looking brownish stone, to which iron spontaneously adheres. They search for the right point, and when they have touched a needle on it, and fixed it on a bit of straw, they lay it on the water and the straw keeps it afloat. Then the point infallibly turns towards the star. . . ." (*Receuil de la Langue et Poesie Française*.) The Chinese claimed to have directed their ships "south by the needle" so early as the third century (*Ships and Men*, W. J. Bassett-Lowke and George Holland). Christopher Lloyd affirms that "the compass was known in England as early as the twelfth century" (*The Navy and the Nation*).

[2] As Sir Travers Twiss points out, the cardinal difference between the ancient and modern systems of maritime law is, that under the latter the mariner is a free man; the slave can no longer be thrown overboard to lighten ship.

majority. If he failed to pursue this course and any disaster occurred in consequence, the damage had to be made good by himself. The master was empowered, with the crew's concurrence, to pledge the ship, but not the hull, in return for necessary provisions. If the crew failed to make adequate attempt to save their craft from wreck, they were to forfeit their wages. Should it become imperative to jettison some of the cargo during a storm, the master was required to consult with such merchants as might be aboard as to what should be sacrificed. The master could override dissent to his own ruling only if he were prepared to pay compensation. In case of real danger during a storm, should the master insist on lightening the vessel despite the protests of his merchant-passengers, on arrival in port he and at least a third of his crew were under obligation to make oath that the action taken had been for the preservation of the ship. The loss was then to be borne equally by the merchants concerned.

Before the goods were shipped, the master had to satisfy the consignors as to the reliability of his ropes and tackle. Should he fail to do so, or should he be neglectful when requested to make repairs, he was to be held responsible for any damage that resulted. To furnish justly awarded compensation, everything in the ship could be seized save the running tackle, provisions, cooking utensils, the master's private money, girdle, ring, and silver cup—were he the proud possessor of such an article.

The arrangement by which a merchant, or group of merchants, hired a vessel to freight cargo was known as a Charter Party. One copy of the agreement was retained by the ship-owner and one by the merchant. But contracts made at sea were not regarded as valid; since, with profound human understanding, it was held of individuals suffering from *mal de mer* that "if they had a thousand marks of silver, they would promise it all to anyone who would ask it to put them ashore"!

In the case of a collision by a ship under sail running on board another at anchor, if the former were damaged the cost of repair was to be equally divided, providing the master and crew of the latter were prepared to take oath that the collision was accidental. For it was not unknown for the owner of an old and decayed craft deliberately to court an accident and then claim damages.

If they were not in a position to make full reparation, pilots who ran their ships aground through negligence or incompetence were liable to lose the right hand and left eye. In extreme cases they could, by majority vote of the crew, be summarily beheaded. The rule was drastic, but it was aimed at the rascally type of pilot who purposely ran vessels ashore at a point where, by custom, a moiety of the wrecked ships' cargoes fell to the local lord of the manor; with whom, of course, the untrustworthy lodesman had an understanding. If apprehended, the pilot who had conspired to 'procure' a wreck was hanged on a gibbet erected near the spot where the calamity had taken place. Nor were the wrecking lords and their minions overlooked. A plunderer of wrecks was chained to a post in the middle of his own dwelling, and his house was then set ablaze over his head. Thereafter, its walls were demolished, and the site turned into a market for swine; while all the malefactor's goods were confiscated for the benefit of those he had robbed. Desperadoes who, "more barbarous, cruel and inhuman than mad dogs", took the lives of the shipwrecked, were ducked in the sea and then stoned to death.

Flotsam and jetsam were to be kept for a year and a day, and if not then claimed were to be sold to provide marriage portions for plain and dowerless maids, or for other charitable purposes.

All this forethought and prevision reflected the striking increase in maritime activity which was fast turning the narrow seas into a commercial waterway to vie with the Mediterranean itself.

Rules governing the welfare of the shipmen received as great attention as the regulations designed to ensure his good behaviour.

With the aim of maintaining discipline it was decreed that should a man slay another aboard ship, he was to be fastened to the dead body and cast into the sea. If reliable testimony convicted a man of unsheathing his knife, or of drawing blood in any manner whatsoever, he was to lose his hand. For brawling, the offender was to be plunged three times into the sea—"to abate his choler". If anyone reviled or insulted another, he was to pay the offended party an ounce of silver. A thief was to have his head shaven and boiling pitch, mixed with feathers, poured over it "as a mark by which he might be known". Thereafter, he was to be put ashore at the first opportunity. In general, obedience to the lawful commands of those in authority was to be esteemed a first condition of service.

Should a man fall sick he was to be sent ashore, and lodging, candles and a grommet provided for him; the last-named to act as attendant and nurse. On the other hand, should a seaman suffer any hurt through drunkenness or quarrelling, it was not obligatory to provide for his cure, and he could be summarily turned off the ship. In port, no man was permitted to leave his ship without the master's consent. In the event of his desertion, the delinquent could be branded in the face with a hot iron.

The wages of the crew were a first charge on the vessel's earnings; and if no other means of honouring the debt remained, the ship itself could be sold to meet it. In certain circumstances wages were commuted, in part, in return for permission to ship a certain amount of cargo, which the sailor was free to sell for his own profit. Crews that entered into partnership with the master shared both risks and profits; but were not held liable were the vessel to be lost. Derogatory work, such as "carrying bundles on the neck", could be refused without penalty.

All in all, a working code had been evolved from the jumble of ancient customs and rules of conduct embodied in the early *Jugements de la mer* which served not only to impose a standard of behaviour on the English seaman, but was taken as a model by the Hansa merchants when they came to devise a set of laws for their own *negociants*[1] and mariners. If some of its provisions were sanguinary and draconic, they were harsh only with the harshness of the times. At all events, the ordinances gave full consideration to the peculiar circumstances to which an ocean-going community would find itself committed, cooped up for long periods in cramped, uncomfortable vessels, under conditions of considerable strain and

[1] The agent of a commercial house resident in a foreign port. Among other things, he acted as "ship's husband".

exacerbation. If it was a severely strict code, it was no less a fair one; and under its terms a man of goodwill was better treated than at any other period in the history of the sea. It follows that desertion was far from frequent, and a popular ship-master could be sure of retaining the same crew from voyage to voyage. Slowly but surely the experience gained in mastering the navigation of *La Manche* was breeding a race of men whose pride it was to wear upon their breasts the medallion of St. Nicholas, the patron Saint of "all that go down to the sea in ships and do business in great waters".

Indeed, the conditions of the shipman's service were at their prime from the reign of Richard *Cœur de Lion* to the end of the sixteenth century; whereafter their decline was sharp and progressively more wretched until the mid-nineteenth century witnessed the slow swing back of the pendulum.

*   *   *

Under Richard, crews were predominantly English rather than Norman; although the gradual assimilation of the two peoples tended to dissolve racial differentiation and blend them in a common type, which experienced

> *. . . a sea change*
> *Into something rich and strange.*

Pride of place in this emergent brotherhood of the sea must go to the ship-master, or *rector*. Responsible for the navigation, for handling his ship and his crew, as for all arrangements regarding the cargo, he was the forebear of the mercantile marine skipper of more recent times. He was assisted by a *contremaître*, or mate, as later days learned to term him. One of the larger craft, such as the great Crusader dromon, *The World*, would carry in addition to a crew of fifty to sixty *marinelli*, or deck hands, a carpenter, a *calfat*, or caulker, a *sturmanni*,[1] or steersman, a barber-surgeon—candidly entered in the ship's book as 'Tormentor'—an *escrivain*, or writer, and a boatswain. The bo'sun, responsible for all masts, sails, ropes and rigging, was a very old rating indeed, the ancient Saxon butescarles having been headed by a butsnen.

Wages ranged from 3*d.* a day, with all found, for the ordinary

---

[1] Also known as a lodesman.

foremast hands, to 7d. a day for the *sturmanni*; who, like
the boatswain and the carpenter, ranked as what would now
be termed a petty officer. Sometimes a bonus or weekly 'reward'
of sixpence brought the pay of the ordinary *marinelli* up to
9s. a month; but even so his emoluments compared very unfavourably with the 2s. 6d. to 5s. 6d. a week demanded, and
obtained, by Gallic crews less inclined to the sea service than
the men of the island race. Gambling aboard ship was strictly
controlled; 'knights and clerks' *en voyage* could incur a loss of
20s. "in any one day and night", but no more. For men of
lesser degree all gaming was forbidden, although there was a
good deal of surreptitious dicing.

Very often the larger type of vessel would carry, in addition
to several grommets at 2½d. a day, a number of *campani*,
youths come aboard to learn the way of the sea and ships.
Galleys demanded a hundred and more oarsmen, prisoners
condemned to slave at the benches to which they were chained
until exhaustion put an end to their miseries. Vessels carrying
royalty or persons of distinction would invariably ship two or
more trumpeters "with good sufficient trumpets", a tamburle
player and a couple of drummers. They not only provided
"a concourse of sweet notes" in times of leisure, but sounded
off the rudimentary signals when battle-fighting was toward.

The subsistence provided, with its emphasis on salted fish
and pickled meat, biscuit, dried pease and lentils, was monotonous but ample enough in content. But the absence of all
anti-scorbutic foodstuffs tended rather to aggravate than to
diminish the seasonal affliction of scurvy—due to an improperly
balanced dietary—of which the contemporary landsman and
mariner alike were victims. It was not until the lengthy
voyages of the Elizabethans, however, that the shipman's
vitality was so undermined by this dreadful scourge that it
exacted a greater toll than the wounds inflicted by sword and
musket.

Originating more often than not in one of the havens along
the Channel coast, the English seaman was everywhere
acknowledged to be hardy, enterprising and resourceful. If
engaged in the coastal or cross-Channel traffic his garb would
consist of stout woollen hose and a 'sea-gown' of falding with a
knife in the girdle about his waist and his tousled mane crowned

by a round cap of *cuir bouilly*.[1] But if his voyage was to Levantine waters his surcoat would bear the red cross of St. George—the livery of the Crusader.

Not that fighting was the mariner's primary work aboard a ship rigged for war. That was largely left to the soldiery, under their own military leaders, who so appreciably swelled the ship's company when the vessel was 'arrested' for the King's service in time of conflict. It was the sailor's business to 'work' the ship, as it was the soldier's task to 'fight' it. It was a different matter, of course, with a ship plying in merchandise, which had come under piratical attack. Then all hands joined in the fight with a will, led by the *retenue de poupe*, or poop guard. Especially recruited from among the *rector's* dependants and relatives, it was the responsibility of this devoted band to take station at the break of the poop and should their craft be successfully boarded and entered, to defend this last stronghold against all comers. All merchant ships went fully armed, since piracy was rife, not only in broader waters but even in the narrow seas.

As the century drew to a close English maritime enterprise was everywhere expanding. With the Crusades to encourage voyaging to more distant shores, the island shipman, to his infinite benefit, was brought into contact with foreign rig and alien sailing ways; and from the general exchange of ideas and experience he rarely failed to profit. But if Lionheart had introduced his shipmen to wider oceans, they had learned the rudiments of their business in the fishing grounds of the Channel's easterly approaches and more particularly in the 'Ditch' that washed their native shores. Their proving ground had been their own familiar narrow seas.

*　　　*　　　*

Passing the twelfth century's final decade in review, it is impossible to discern more than a hint of the shape of things to come.

Possibly because the process lacked the impetus born of a nation-wide call to arms, the assimilation of the Scandinavian, Anglo-Saxon and Norman strains exhibited little progress; the last-named still ruled the roost both at the Court and in the

---

[1] Leather hardened by being boiled.

world of commerce.[1] The Guilds-merchants, although their
hold on local government had appreciably strengthened, were
not yet the oligarchies into which they bid fair to harden. The
Angevin connection, while certain sooner or later to em-
broil the Island people in Continental politics, in the meantime
had significantly increased the volume of trade with the
Continental markets; as had the growing demand for raw wool
and wool fells on the part of the Hansa merchants. Wool,
indeed, had already proved itself to be England's most substantial and profitable export: the heavy ransom of 100,000
marks which had secured Lionheart's release from the clutches
of Leopold of Austria had come, it was said, "off the back of
the English sheep".

But what Main, the Victorian jurist, termed the advance
from status to contract—i.e. from a position of servility to one
of freedom of choice and equality in bargaining—had barely
got under way. It followed that as yet there was no firm, long-
term commercial or fiscal policy; nor any sustained attempt to
deal with the vicious piracy in home waters which exacted so
heavy and continuous a toll from maritime trade.

England, in effect, was still in the melting pot; and organisation on truly national lines would have to await the consolidation of a heterogeneous population into a homogeneous
people.

[1] At the Battle of the Standard the Yorkshire barons were addressed by their
leader as "unconquerable Normans" and bidden to remember Senlac;
the writs of Henry I and Stephen were usually addressed to their subjects
"French and English", while the contemptuous retort of Richard's Chancellor, the ungainly, simian William Longchamp, when pressed to take some
action against his will, was that rather than agree he would "turn Englishman". On the other hand, an Italian Archbishop of Canterbury could
write of "we English" and "our island".

CHAPTER IV

Salt-water Barrier

". . . as rich in having such a jewel
As twenty seas, if all their sand were pearls,
The water nectar, and the rocks pure gold."
SHAKESPEARE

IT invariably requires a major military disaster on their own doorstep to arouse the majority of the English people to a realisation of the fact that they inhabit a land entirely surrounded by water.

During the last years of Richard Lionheart and throughout most of the reign of his younger brother and successor, John, the salt-water barrier which separated England from France assumed an importance it had not held for over a century and a quarter, and one the meanest intelligence could not fail to grasp.

The aim of Philippe Augustus of France to enlarge and unify his territories had always been reinforced by his distaste for Angevins in ermine. It was a prejudice he knew to be shared by a number of Richard's Norman barons, who exhibited little enthusiasm for Angevins in general and even less for absentee Angevin Sovereigns in particular.[1]

With Richard's return to the command of his armies in France, Philippe's attempt to overrun the English Monarch's overseas territories had momentarily been checked. But with Lionheart's obscure death before the walls of a minor Limousin castle, Philippe's crafty espousal of the cause of John's rival for the throne—Arthur, son of John's elder brother Geoffrey —in due course enabled the Frenchman to pouch all the English Continental possessions save Gascony, which Henry II had acquired by way of the marriage bed of Eleanor of Aquitaine.

[1] Richard was in England for about four months in 1189, thereafter departing for the Holy Land. He returned to his kingdom early in 1194, leaving it for good later in that same year.

In a political sense, the Channel once more filled up with salt water; and the newly-crowned John found himself confronted with the pregnant question—to whom should go the mastery of the narrow seas, and with it the opportunity to carry the war into the enemy's camp?

Few kings have been more headstrong, shifty and self-centred than John 'Lackland'. The spoilt child of elderly parents, in later years this violent, restless but intermittently slothful little man—he was under five feet five inches in height —was quite unable to discipline himself and therefore to control others. Unpredictable and unbalanced, he lacked the stability to exploit even such success as came his way. But he was not without drive or administrative ability; and although morally colour blind, to one thing at least he remained passionately constant—the recovery of his stolen heritage. To that end all else was unflinchingly subordinated, and there were no means he scrupled to employ to further his abiding purpose. If in pursuing it he laid the foundations for the Hundred Years' War and the centuries of conflict between France and England for command of the Channel, in any case the struggle, sooner or later, would have been bound to arise. No country which ignores the seas that wash its shores can aspire to the status of a Great Power. And it is almost a law of Nature that the French should head the list of Britain's rivals for mastery of the Channel: psychologically too remote for friendship, geographically too near for safety, "France is, and must always remain, England's greatest danger." [1]

In the days when John had plotted with Philippe Augustus against a royal brother persistently absent in the Holy Land, 'Lackland' had been given every opportunity to take his fellow-conspirator's measure. An abler politician than soldier, the Frenchman could none the less muster a military force of such magnitude as to render him an exceedingly dangerous opponent.

Intent from the first on seizing the initiative, John bent all his considerable energy on the task of mobilising a fleet, the nucleus of which was furnished by some fifty 'King's ships'. It is possible that these vessels were the *cursoria* built to the order of Richard Lionheart, and referred to by Guillaume le Breton as suitable for both sea and river work; for it should be

[1] Third Marquess of Salisbury.

borne in mind that *Cœur de Lion* had penetrated a considerable way up the Seine. Falling into the galley category, they were propelled by oar but also stepped a single mast, rigged with a single sail. There was no bowsprit, despite the evidence of the Seal of Sandwich of (approximately) 1238; for the attachment thereon depicted is in fact no more than a piece of scantling to which ropes could be made fast. Two centuries were to elapse before the genuine bowsprit, carrying its own sail, made its appearance in Northern waters[1]; and the 'King's ships' embodied many elements of the traditional Mediterranean galley, with a slightly higher freeboard in deference to the more turbulent local waters.

There is also mention of certain cogs[2] retained for the King's service; short vessels of great breadth, like the cockleshell from which they are said to derive their name. They were employed on occasion as small passenger craft or for the transport of horses and stores, and were frequently used as ship's boats by the more substantial busses. As general purpose craft they came in time almost entirely to supersede the Northern variant of the Mediterranean galley.

For immediate supplement to his own inadequate flotilla the King had recourse to the fleet of fifty-seven vessels, of an average burden of eighty tons, maintained by the hardy and experienced shipmen of the Cinque Ports; whose support he was at considerable pains to woo. The relevant Charters were re-enacted confirming their right to "Honours in the Court",[3] freedom from toll, lastage, tallage, passage, quayage, rivage and portage, as of market charges, "on both sides of the sea", and equally from the jurisdiction of shires and hundreds; while the burgesses were to take rank as barons. A moiety of these privileges was extended to the 'limbs' which the authentic Cinque Ports were in process of acquiring for their support.[4]

---

[1] The Romans had made use of a small sloping mast over the bows, known as an artemon, but it disappeared from ship construction after the fall of Rome.

[2] Also rendered kogge, gogga, kogghe, coca, cogna, cohha, and cocco; and the name survives in the term cock-boat.

[3] At his (or her) Coronation the Sovereign walked in procession beneath a canopy (*umbraculum*) "supported by four long lances" held by four barons of the Cinque Ports.

[4] See Appendix A.

All in all, these Sussex and Kentish havens could ventilate few legitimate grievances. Not being ports of merchandise on the scale of London and Southampton, national taxation, through the medium of the Customs and other State charges, pressed upon them lightly. As the Assize of Winchester revealed, the Exchequer derived a mere £32 6s. 1d. from Dover, £16 from Sandwich, and £1 13s. 5d. from Rye, as against South-ampton's heavy contribution of £912 15s. 0½d. Inter-port tolls, for the upkeep of harbour works and the like, worked out at the modest impost of a fish and a farthing or a fish and a halfpenny a boat. A voracious and enduring market was provided for all the fish surplus to their own requirements by the demands of the innumerable religious houses in and about Canterbury. Once Rouen and Caen as the ports of debarkation for overseas expeditions had given place to the more distant Bordeaux, it proved cheaper for the King to 'arrest' bigger ships elsewhere for the transport of his troops and warlike stores, than expensively to extend the Portsmen's annual period of service with their smaller craft; and they were thus very largely free to busy themselves with their own concerns. The guardianship of the narrow seas—with every opportunity for a little profitable piracy—and of the Kent and Sussex shores, rather than the transhipment of an army through the Channel, became increasingly the Cinque Ports' obligation. They were, of course, aided in their task of policing *La Manche* by the 'King's ships'; which also relieved them of the duty of guarding the convoys of trading vessels on passage through these danger-ous waters. It is clear, however, that the English convoy system did not compare in efficiency with that organised by the authorities of Genoa and Venice.

Time was to show, however, that the increase in the Cinque Ports' consequence which followed on the loss of Normandy was based on factors that equally ensured their decline before the fifteenth century had reached its climacteric.

*   *   *

With an attempt at invasion a very lively possibility, 'Lack-land', with the approval of his Council, ordered a nation-wide *levée-en-masse*, which rendered every male over sixteen and under sixty liable for service upon notification by the shire, hundred, or parish constable. The King's authority to 'arrest' ships for the purposes of war was reaffirmed, while an interdict was placed on the removal of vessels abroad save under rarely awarded licence. A temporary ban was imposed on the export of wheat; while a tax was sanctioned of one-fifteenth on all goods imported or exported—that is, on all merchandise entering into foreign trade. At the same time care was taken to distinguish between foreign and coasting trade, the latter being recorded but exempted from all but local tolls; the possession of a document known as a transire safeguarding the coastal trader from any demand on the part of the Customs at the port of discharge. To prevent coastal vessels from surreptitiously slipping across to a foreign port and there disposing of uncustomed goods, a system of bonds and certificates —or cockets, as they were termed—was inaugurated, of which the record was entered in the Port Books.

When the whole range of imposts on foreign goods was regularised by the 1204 Assize of Customs, a real advance was made towards establishing this source of national revenue on that sound and systematic basis which came to maturity under Edward I.

These preliminary acts were no more than prudent measures of precaution.

Of far greater significance was the appointment of William de Wrotham as one of a tribunal—completed by William de Formell and Reginald de Cornhille, an erstwhile Sheriff of Kent—to carry the new legislation into effect, and at the same time to act as Keepers of the 'King's ships'.

William de Wrotham, Archdeacon of Taunton and a member of the exclusive circle of intimates and counsellors about the King that went by the name of the *Curia Regis*, was a typical specimen of that variety of medieval cleric who never permitted his spiritual obligations to interfere with the profoundly relished discharge of those purely secular tasks which added so immeasurably to his authority. Brisk, bustling and unquestionably efficient, he brought a boundless store of energy to a highly responsible position, which combined something of the duties of a First Lord of the Admiralty with those of a Supervisor of Embargo—with a dash of Master-General of the Ordnance thrown in for good measure. His sway, although not grounded, like that of the Admirals of the following century, on a judicial basis, functioned in perfect harmony with the common law of the land; which at this period was based upon regional judicatures whose authority either lacked local application—as in the Cinque Ports' enclave—or halted abruptly at the water's edge.

Wrotham's first step was to subdivide his area of control into districts, each embracing four or five havens, under a trusted subordinate. He then proceeded to turn Portsmouth into a naval base, furnishing it with store houses and the best that contemporary skill could contrive in the way of a dock. In addition, the indefatigable fellow undertook the supervision of the Customs, ensured that the Assize of Weights and Measures[1] was observed, purchased stores, enforced the embargo on would-be fugitive shipping, dealt with the disbursements to ship-owners whose craft had been 'arrested', forcefully operated the law of impressment to swell the ranks of the seamen, and distributed the prize money for which certain of the more enterprising of their number had qualified. He also kept a sharp eye lifted to check the traffic in smuggled wheat to which the ban on the export of this commodity had immediately given rise. Fines ranging from 300 to 1,000 marks were sternly exacted from "free-traders" caught in the act.

In effect, with de Wrotham's appointment the first effective steps had been taken to found an administrative personnel solely concerned with the sea and the ships that sailed it. Since, in broad terms, the difference between the fighting marine and the mercantile marine was largely a matter of adding a few men and weapons to the latter to turn it into the former, the same organisation served for the administrative control of both, without detriment to either.

The welding together of the 'King's ships', the Cinque Ports' fleet, and the vessels 'arrested' "to go on the King's service", into a well-disciplined, swiftly responsive and fully integrated fighting force must have been a task of very considerable difficulty. None the less, in anticipation of a naval assault from the direction of Flanders, by the midsummer of

---

[1] Standard or King's Weight had been made universal by Richard's Chancellor, Hubert Walter.

1205 John had assembled a serviceable armament with which to launch a counter-offensive for the recovery of Normandy. So large a force was concentrated at Portsmouth "that it was believed so many ships had never been brought together before"; while the number of mariners was said to total 1,400.[1] Provisions and warlike stores had been gathered in plenty; for once there was actually enough to pay an advance on wages and leave enough over to establish a small pension fund for the wounded. Furthermore, while it was accepted that all prizes taken at sea became the property of the Sovereign, it was known that the royal bounty never failed to award prize money to the ship's captors. So far as sound organisation and capable administration could make for success, the venture seemed assured of it.

Yet there were not wanting querulous voices to complain of the King, "*cet animal est méchant, quand on attaque il se défend*"; while the idea of seriously carrying the fight to the enemy found such lukewarm support that John was beguiled into subscribing to an armistice which he privately resolved should be devoted to furthering preparations for a second bout.

Most people have their madness, but they hug it close to them. John flaunted his like a banner, and never more flagrantly than in his plunge into matrimony with Isabel of Angoulême. Since she was already betrothed to a scion of the one clan he could not afford to offend, 'Lackland's' heady impetuosity speedily brought about his ears a veritable hornet's nest of frustrated relatives-to-be and political sympathisers with the jilted swain. Scorning the wiles of diplomacy and wilfully forgetting how wonderfully "the jingling of the guinea helps the hurt that Honour feels", John chose the path of defiance. From the war on two fronts—those of Aquitaine and Normandy—which was the outcome of his intransigence may be traced the decline of the Plantagenets and the progressive ruin of 'Lackland's' personal fortunes.

Heedless of the generally unfavourable portents, however, as of a hostile Church and a baronage sourly divided in its loyalties, the King doggedly set about his preparations for war.

---

[1] So affirm the contemporary chroniclers. But these gentry are prone to exaggeration save when underestimation of the total of the English personnel would add reclame to the victory achieved.

As a preliminary, a small expedition of "five galleys and five great ships" set out to reaffirm the regal claim to the Channel Islands; and to ensure—as is recorded by the chronicler, John Selden—that all vessels rendered homage to the King's ships, on passage in *La Manche*, by striking and lowering their sails, in accordance with a rescript promulgated by John 'Lackland' at Hastings in the second year of his reign.[1]

Meanwhile in the home ports the ship-masters were gathering; including the notorious privateer known as Eustace the Monk, an experienced shipman and sea-fighter, but as false as a quicksand. As a hireling in John's service, he is credited with the ransoming of Barfleur and the capture of five ships and a "*très bon et riche nef*".[2] But the occasion arose when he had to be called sharply to account for having neglected to obey the King's order to hand back the vessel belonging to a certain William le Petit, of which he had possessed himself by means that smacked a little too nakedly of piracy even for contemporary standards to condone. He was retained in the royal service, however, despite the fact that he appears to have founded something indistinguishable from a pirate community in one of the Channel Islands, which faithfully anticipated the nest of rogues established on Okerere Inlet by Captain Edward ('Blackbeard') Teach, of infamous memory.

But Eustace the Fleming was not the only dubious character to make his way to the ports; where the cartels—scrolls fastened to a post or the tip of a spear—were on display in every gateway, nominating the vessels required for the King's service. And woe betide any ship-owner or *rector* who dared to disregard the command given him by the Sergeant-at-Arms to rendezvous at the place appointed for the fleet's assembly. For the law decreed "that he that hath broken the arrest of his ship arrested for the King's service . . . he shall loose [lose] his ship,

---

[1] John Selden (1584–1654), in his *Mare Clausum*, supports his belief in this pretension by citing as his authority an early copy of *The Black Book of the Admiralty*, no longer to be found. He is supported by Sir John Borough in his work the *Sovereignty of the British Seas*, written in 1633 and first published in 1651. Sir Travers Twiss has drawn attention to the fact that a fuller rendering of this rescript than that transcribed by Selden is to be found in the Cottonian MS. A thorough review of the whole matter is to be found in Vol. III of the *Naval Miscellany* (Navy Records Society, 1928).

[2] *Li Roman de Wistasses le Moine* (W. Foerster, 1891).

unless he obtaineth pardon of the King". This ensured that every ship 'arrested' would duly report; and as further supplement John hired vessels on contract from such widely separated ports as those of Flanders and La Rochelle.

While the ships were mustering and re-fitting, the scriveners were busy registering the names of mariners and craftsmen, both volunteers and those brought in by impressment, settling the terms of their engagement, and sternly warning the half-hearted that desertion brought a sentence to a year's imprisonment for the first offence, to two years' were it repeated.

Wherever space could be found for them the womenfolk were busy at the task of fabricating sails, mostly of silk backed, at points of particular strain, with strips of stout Oléron canvas.

Wide-eyed but wary, swarthy Genoese cross-bowmen mingled with the jostling crowd, gazing about them with all a homeless mercenary's aimless curiosity. For warfare was becoming more and more 'professionalised', demanding men of exceptional military skill and experience to fight it. It was necessary, therefore, to supplement holders of Knight's fees and their followers, called upon to serve under the terms of their land tenure, by mercenary troops hired for the period of the campaign. It was a costly process, the expense of which was met, in part, by the payments accruing to the King from the yield of scutage, or shield money. This was forthcoming from those liable for service who found themselves unable or unwilling to take the field in person, and from such persons as minors and ecclesiastical tenants unwishful to emulate the example set by Bishop Odo, the Conqueror's half-brother, and sally forth to battle mace in hand. Like all indigent medieval Monarchs, John was hoping for a short campaign, since after his two months' self-supporting service the Knight and his retainers became a charge on the Crown. With mercenaries to pay in addition, the strain on the Sovereign's limited resources became proportionately more acute. It was, therefore, in the hope of speedily reducing his rebellious vassals in Poitou to a more obedient frame of mind that 'Lackland' passed down the Channel at the head of his fleet.

From the outset of operations, however, the King's activities led to nothing but frustration. Even when one of his characteristic bursts of energy led to the capture of his would-be supplanter, the death of Arthur followed in circumstances so sinister that every finger pointed to the uncle as the nephew's murderer. Whatever the truth of the accusation, the results were catastrophic. One after another John's new-forged but tenuous ties with his overseas dominions were severed. All the Angevin territories were occupied by Philippe or his henchmen, and by Midsummer Day the Channel Islands represented all of the Norman Duchy to remain in English hands.

A second attempt by 'Lackland' to recover what had slipped through his fingers was so feebly supported by a disgruntled baronage that although an improvised fleet put out from Portsmouth, once on the high seas its inadequacy was so nakedly apparent that orders were given to put about and return to harbour.

John's fatal gift of alienating his own supporters had never been in greater evidence; nor was the general atmosphere of dissatisfaction sweetened when he proceeded to levy fines on all those who had failed to respond to his call to arms.

The shadow of *Magna Carta* was already discernible on the horizon.

*   *   *

Macaulay pontifically pronounced that England's loss of Normandy and her other Continental possessions was an unqualified benefit to the nation. If this be accepted as just another example of this writer's tendency to indulge in rhetorical extravagance, the fact remains that England's rising commercial prosperity was scarcely affected either by the incidence of warfare or by its outcome. Trade knows no frontiers; and traffic with France had continued almost without interruption throughout the whole course of the struggle.

Wine was regularly shipped from Poitou, Gascony and Auxerre—John himself was partial to a goblet of good St. Emilion—and sold at from 26s. to 34s. a cask, or tun, of sixty-three gallons, the heaviest bulk it was possible conveniently to man-handle at a time when the wharves were without ramps. There was also a brisk trade in Rhenish from Cologne. Cloth rivalled wine as an import; although an indigenous cloth-making industry had come into being which pre-empted a certain proportion of the wool-crop. By far the greater quantity of this, however, whether marketed by the great religious foundations of the Cistercians, Gilbertines and Premonstratensians, or by private flock-owners, still went overseas to the insatiable looms of Flanders. Furthermore, the densely packed and mainly urbanised population of the Low Countries was in perennial need of those foodstuffs without whose steady inflow it would soon have found itself on remarkably short commons. Any political wavering on the part of such hunger-driven customers could invariably be resolved in England's favour by a threat to cut off supplies—of wool or aliments, or both.

'Lackland' was always short of ready money, and his pressing need for it led him not only to farm the Customs in many ports against a flat annual payment, rendered in advance, but in return for a money consideration to grant Charters to a number of ambitious craft-guilds and to boroughs aspirant of emancipation. Equally, there were shekels to be raked in for the suppression of those selfsame associations of craftsmen. The London guild of weavers, for example, was swept away "at the petition of the mayor and citizens"; but not, of course, without a guarantee that the civic authorities would pay into the Treasury far more than the equivalent of the sum the weavers had rendered up in return for the regal recognition of their guild. It was an unconscionably murky bargain, but one that clearly reflected the detestation in which the craft-guilds—particularly the weavers'—were held by the municipal authorities whose determined rise to the exclusive exercise of power within their own burghs could brook no challenge to their authority. The "law of the fullers and weavers", which openly avowed its derivation from "the franchise and custom of London", and which operated in Winchester and several other centres, forbade weavers to sell cloth save to merchants of their own city—and virtually on those worthy's terms. It also debarred weavers from becoming freemen of their own city unless they renounced their craft. It was equally unlawful for them to attaint or bear witness against a freeman, and in general they were isolated and made to feel inferior even to the franchisers, who enjoyed but a tithe of the privileges reserved for a full-blown *Burgeis de la Gilde*.

These arbitrary regulations clearly reflected the Guild-

Merchants' determination to retain all local government in their own hands. In effect, the old latitudinarian Saxon Burghmote[1], headed by its town reeve, had yielded place to an authoritarian mayor and council, resolved that no *imperium in imperio*, in the shape of a powerful craft-guild, should interfere in the administration of the community primarily in the interest of the *Gildeins*.

The privileges reserved by the Guild-Merchant for its members were, of course, as fruitful in profit as they were high-handed. In Southampton, for example, once it had secured its Charter, the *Gildein* imported and exported his goods free of all Customs dues and town tolls. Only one of the elect would receive permission to keep a wine house, or qualify for such rewarding Guild offices as that of bailiff, eschevin, and usher.[2] Although the town largely owed its prosperity to goods brought in by merchant-strangers, in foreign-owned craft, the duration of the stay of these aliens within its walls was still limited—with very few exceptions—to forty days. During this period they still remained under constant surveillance, and were under bond not to sell by retail save on certain specified market and fair days. Exemption from certain of these prohibitions could, however, be obtained on the payment of a substantial *gildagium*, or fine.

All these vexatious restraints were rigorously insisted upon, despite the "general safe conduct granted to all forreine Marchants" by the King, with its specific proviso that "they be vouchsafed the same favour in England, that is granted to the English marchants in those places from whence they come".

For a time the burgesses of Southampton even contrived to substantiate their claim to farm the Customs of Portsmouth; over whose harbour they continued to exercise jurisdiction until well into the thirteenth century. They were, of course, in a very strong position since their town contribution to the *quinzième*, at £712 3s. 7d., was second only to that of London at £836 12s. 10d. But the fact remains that at Southampton, as elsewhere, the *Gildeins* sought in all things to exercise local autonomy, and to operate a monopolistic trade policy designed

[1] Sometimes termed Court Leete or portmote.
[2] *Oak Book of Southampton.*

to benefit their own burgh at the expense of its neighbours; wilfully blind to the fact that prosperity can only batten fruitfully on prosperity.

In the prevailing circumstances it is scarcely surprising that the promising native cloth-making industry should have failed to expand as it undoubtedly would have done had it been free from the artificial restraints that so grievously hampered it. Even as it was, more home-made cloth was manufactured in John's short reign than in any previous period; the Assize of Measures of 1196 having given foreign buyers the assurance that a standard width to the ell would characterise all English fabrics.[1]

However, such was the power of the *Gildeins*—swag-bellied men with wary eyes, lean, vulpine men with round Norman heads and tight lips like a crack in a chunk of granite—that it was only in certain purely maritime matters that William de Wrotham could assert his authority. Owing to his resolution and energy, however, the work of walling-in the Portsmouth dockyard went steadily forward; while he was at pains to keep Southampton Water free of obstructions. The erection of stankes (water dams), weres, and kiddles (wicker fish weirs), in the fairway was sternly discouraged; the offender who sought to emulate the industry of the beaver being fined for having "appropriated salt water and taken to himselfe the benefitt". At the same time the charges for ships' anchorages were stabilised at 4*d*. for any craft of over 50 tons, and 2*d*. for a vessel of 50 tons and less.

In general, however, the money-power wielded by the *Gildeins* could successfully challenge many deeply-entrenched vested interests hitherto regarded as immune from attempted encroachment.

For the absolutism which had characterised the Conqueror's reign, with his successors had yielded to government based on dualism. On the one hand stood the Monarch and his *Curia Regis*, on the other the baronage, supported by the Knights of the Shire, representing county interests and what was termed the "mesne gent". When in accord they epitomised the will of the nation as a whole. But when agreement failed

---

[1] According to William of Malmesbury, the length of the ell was that of the right forearm of Henry I.

4*

them, and particularly when adherents of the barons' party took sides with a Monarch and *Curia Regis* which had lost some of its members to a baronage temporarily at odds with their Sovereign, it was a plain case of "confusion worse confounded"; with a powerful Church intervening to advantage its own interests as opportunism might dictate.

A new element was introduced into this complicated, shifting pattern of government when the towns, encouraged by Lionheart's one-time Justiciar, Hubert Walter, sought successfully to emulate what many regarded as the dangerous independence of the city communes of Flanders and Northern Italy. This emancipatory process had been sharply accelerated by 'Lackland's' own money-raising award of over seventy Charters endowing communities—which for all practical purposes meant the *Burgeis de la Gilde*—with the right to elect mayors, formulate regulations governing their own trade, and assess their individual contributions to national taxation. Furthermore, John's endeavour to play off the new bourgeoisie against elements hostile to him only put another rod in pickle for the eventual castigation of his own shoulders.

For good or ill, it was under John's erratic rule that mercantilism established itself as a permanent factor in the apparatus of government. Its influence was automatically to increase in power as the fluctuating tide of commerce came slowly to the flood.

*   *   *

'Lackland's' quarrel with the Pontiff, Innocent III, over the right of appointment to the See of Canterbury, brought Philippe of France cantering into the lists in the unlikely role of Champion of Christendom. For such an opportunity to strike a blow at his erstwhile crony was far too good to be missed. But John's nicely timed submission to the Pope, in the Spring of 1213, although forcing him to exchange the role of religious freedom's guardian for that of the most submissive son of the Church, at least left him at liberty to enter into negotiations with the Emperor Otto for a coalition against the French; who were reported to be overrunning Flanders as a preliminary to a descent on England.

Yet again the ports hummed with activity, as William de

Longuespée, Earl of Salisbury, assembled the fleet and army for an assault on Damme, the port of Bruges,[1] where the main invasion force had been ordered to keep its rendezvous.

As a foretaste of what was to come, a small flotilla of Cinque Ports' vessels bustled briskly across the narrow seas to raid and burn Dieppe; going on to play havoc with the Gallic shipping assembled at Fécamp and in the Seine.

While this vigorous foray was in progress an army was mustering on Barham Down, between Canterbury and Dover; while at Portsmouth William de Wrotham and the staff of secretaries and technicians he had recruited from the versatile Templars were busy ensuring that all vessels capable of carrying six or more horses, or their equivalent in men and warlike stores, were fully manned with "good and proper mariners".

Then on a day of bright Spring sunshine, and helped by a kindly wind, five hundred sail streamed out from the shelter of Dover Roads, crammed with seven hundred English and Flemish Knights and a strong body of arbalestiers and men-at-arms. At any moment they expected to encounter and join combat with the hostile fleet. But the French ships were all riding at anchor in the muddy estuary of the Zwyn, or beached along the adjacent coast; some of the Knights having repaired to the siege of Ghent, while many of the crews had deserted their craft to pillage the wealthy citizens of Damme.

As the English fleet sailed in to make its landfall the look-outs espied a number of vessels lying without the haven, which, capacious as it might be, lacked room to accommodate an armament whose total strength some chroniclers have put as high as 1,700 craft. Without loss of time swift shallops were sent out to ascertain whether the anchored ships were friends or foes, and if enemies, what their strength might be and in what order they lay. These scouts, approaching as though they had been fishermen, were allowed near enough to learn that many of the hostile vessels had been left with the minimum of hands for their defence. Hastening back, they assured Longuespée and his lieutenant, William Count of Holland, that victory lay in their hands if only they would make good speed.

---

[1] It ceased to be a port in the fifteenth century owing to the silting up of the Zwyn estuary, another victim of the easterly drift.

There was no hesitation among the English leaders. Crisp orders were given for the whole force to take to the ships' boats; and the assault went in with a rush that swamped such spasmodic, inchoate defence as it encountered.

But far sterner work lay ahead, where the main fleet swung calmly at its moorings in the harbour; and "here was hard hold for a time", since the crowded state of the narrow arena of conflict left little room for manœuvre and allowed no advantage to superior numbers. It was at this juncture that "those Frenchmen that were gone abroad into the country, perceiving that their enemies were come, by the running away of their mariners, returned with all speed to their ships to aid their fellows, and so made a violent resistance for a time. Then the Englishmen, getting on board, and ranging themselves on either side of the haven, beat the French so on the sides, and the ships grappling together in front, that they fought as it had been in a pitched battle, till that, finally, the Frenchmen were not able to sustain the force of the Englishmen, but were constrained, after long fight and great slaughter, to yield themselves prisoners."

A few of the more stout-hearted of Philippe's men-at-arms rallied on the beach, where they continued to defend themselves with the hysterical courage of despair. For it was clear that the English had secured an overwhelming victory. Three hundred vessels laden with corn, bacon, wine and arms were taken as prize, their cables cut and their sails hoisted to catch the off-shore wind that sent them speeding on their way to England. A further hundred of the bigger ships were added to the English fleet; while so many of the remainder were set on fire that "it seemed as though the sea were ablaze". What had been planned had been well and truly executed. So as the opposition against them strengthened, the beach-head rearguard fought their way back to their boats and succeeded—not without loss—in gaining the fleet, which thereupon put to sea.[1]

Although scarcely ranking as a veritable naval action—it was more in the nature of an attack on what Mahan disdainfully terms a "fortress fleet"—the enterprise to Damme

[1] *Histoire de Guillaume le Maréchal. De Gestis Philippi Augusti,* Rigord and le Breton; *Foedera,* Rymer; *Flores Historiarum,* Wendover; *Philippide,* William le Breton.

unquestionably destroyed any immediate fear of an enemy descent on England. Moreover, it had demonstrated that, at a pinch, the English could arm, man, and fight a better fleet than the French could put into the water; and this very largely with 'arrested' ships that could be returned to commerce the moment the conflict had ended.

All in all, the nation had every reason to be satisfied with the first naval victory it had won since the days of Alfred the Great.

Furthermore, the rout of the French at Damme furnished the opportunity for a two-pronged drive on Paris, from Flanders and Poitou, which John immediately sought to animate. But the effort was insufficiently co-ordinated. In Poitou there was fumbling and craven hesitation amongst John's own disgruntled followers and his allies; while at Bouvines Otto met with so crushing a defeat that the English King had no option but to abandon an enterprise ill-starred from the very outset.

John's tenacious but costly struggle with the French—never popular with the short-sighted majority of his subjects—had committed him to many exactions which even the worthiness of his cause could barely extenuate. The years of war had no less fostered a combustible discontent among the baronage—which 'Lackland' himself had debased in search of funds—whose loyalty, such as it was, was very largely founded on a lively expectation of favours still to come. Since 'gratifications' were not forthcoming on the scale expected, an interim instalment was assured when the King, yielding to his vassals' importunities, set his seal to *Magna Carta*—"the grand charter of English liberties", or "the consecration of feudal anarchy", according to the manner in which it is interpreted.

What is not to be questioned is the fact that the field of Runnymede witnessed John 'Lackland's' final surrender of the power to reanimate the fight for the redemption of the territories filched so brazenly from his realm. For "increase of appetite had grown by what it fed on": both the baronage and the new 'aristocracy of the counting-house' had enjoyed a taste of the rich diet of power and were determined to demand a second and larger helping. A situation arose which the French resolved to exploit to the full. Amongst other things, they hastened to suborn the venal Eustace the Monk, who blithely entered his late enemy's service; while it became increasingly apparent that the men of the Cinque Ports proposed to requite past favours by siding with the gathering forces of rebellion.

With the country divided into two camps, a large force raised in Flanders for John's succour by Hugh de Boves was wrecked in one of the Channel's sudden storms, and "lay in heaps of rotting corpses on the beach round Dunwich".[1] The final blow fell when Prince Louis of France, at the rebellious barons' invitation, succeeded in mustering a fleet of which the first echelon contrived to cross from Calais to the Kentish coast. Why the considerable armament left to John, even after the defection of the Cinque Ports' vessels, failed to challenge the Frenchman's passage is inexplicable. That nothing was done subsequently to intercept the bulk of the Gallic fleet must be attributed in part to losses suffered in the violent tempest which had so gravely imperilled Louis and his advance guard, and partly to the fatal apathy which overtook his opponent at the very moment when he should have exhibited the utmost vigour and resolution.

John's golden moment went for nothing. Entirely unimpeded, the Frenchman put ashore at Stonor in sufficient strength to capture Sandwich, which he promptly proceeded to loot and burn. But even this demonstration of what might be expected of Gallic allies failed to shake the Portsmen's allegiance to the rebel cause; and with the initiative in his hands, Louis proceeded to occupy an ill-defended London, and lay siege to such strongholds—as Winchester and Dover—as continued to hold out in the King's name. In the narrow seas and at Portsmouth, Ryde and Hastings, Eustace the Monk, supported by elements of Louis's fleet, played the pirate with such ferocious industry that the Portsmen were driven to doubt the wisdom of their recent departure into apostasy.

For the country as a whole the turning point came with John's death in the October of 1216. All but a minority of the barons had endured about as much as they could stomach of their rapacious Gallic allies; members of a race that invariably wants to win the lottery without going to the expense of paying

[1] *The English Naval Forces, 1199–1272*, F. W. Brooks.

for a ticket. And although the rebel leaders would never have been prepared to come to terms with a King they had wronged almost as much as he had injured them, they were quite prepared to accept the olive branch held out to them by the venerable William Marshal, Earl of Pembroke, the *rector regis et regni* for John's successor, the nine-year-old Henry III.

Welded together in a new unity of purpose, the Royalists' first task was to rid the land of Louis; whose hold on the narrow seas, on Sandwich, and on the Kentish coast generally, goaded the Portsmen into a wary reconciliation with the Regent and the popular party.

Dover had resisted Gallic assault throughout; and Cinque Ports' vessels undoubtedly played their part in turning back the fleet of forty ships whose purpose was to strengthen Louis's attack on the obstinately resistant stronghold. Unquestionably, the Lord Warden's men joined in the congenial task of harassing the craft which Blanche of Castile was gathering together to send to her husband's support. With Rye, Winchelsea and Romney reclaimed and held, it became a question whether the Frenchman would make use of any momentary command of the Channel to attempt a surprise landing with the large body of reinforcements he had collected at Calais—a stroke which the Royalists might be hard put to it to counter.

All through June the Gallic armament lay inactive in its haven, repeatedly raided by the regenerated Portsmen and a mosquito fleet under Philip d'Albigny. But by the end of August the French were ready for the final throw, and set off in a great armada for the English coast. It was a move that Pembroke had anticipated, and he promptly marched from Canterbury to Sandwich, to marshal such defence forces as could immediately be concentrated.

At Pembroke's urgent command, a few of the local vessels hoisted sail and put out to sea; promptly turning tail, however, the moment they sighted the Gallic fleet. It may have been a case of *reculer pour mieux sauter*, it may not. The Frenchmen, steering for the North Foreland, the mouth of the Thames, and the relief of Louis and the rump of the rebellious baronage mewed up in London, may well have looked too formidable to tackle.

Fortunately, the alarm had speedily reached Hubert de

Burgh in Dover, and he lost no time in going into action. Swearing the men of his garrison never to yield their fortress, the key of England, even if he fell into the hands of the foreigners and was hanged before their eyes, he gathered such ships as lay in harbour and sallied out to intercept the hostile fleet. His craft were few in number—something under thirty [1] —since a little earlier on the English had suffered an unusually serious reverse, with the loss of close on 140 ships, in an ill-organised assault on Calais. But de Burgh was not to be deterred.

The French were sailing on a course which gave them the full advantage of a strong south-easterly wind; with Eustace the Monk in the van and the balance of the fleet crowding close on his heels. But some of their craft were so crammed with stone-throwing *trébuchets* and *mangonels*, men and stores, as to be riding low and sluggish in the water. De Burgh, reinforced by the revitalised men of Sandwich, stood out with a good wind and rising sea, but tacking [2] on a course as though bent on counter-raiding Calais; a procedure which aroused the French to ribald laughter, since they knew the stronghold to be powerfully garrisoned.

But in "keeping the luff" de Burgh was deliberately executing a manœuvre that would give him the weather gage of his opponents. Having gained the advantage of position, he eased his helm and swept down large before the wind on to the French, who turned to meet him, but with the sun and wind in their faces. Riding high in the water, the English were enormously advantaged by the favourable breeze, which gave added length to the blizzard of sling-shot and *quarrells* with which they deluged their opponents' decks. It also whipped down-wind a blinding cloud of unslaked quicklime, the deadly alternative to the Eastern shipman's Greek fire. There was no need to spray the enemy planking with a film of soft soap, so that he might slip and impale himself on the three-pronged *triboli* thrown down to imbed themselves in the deck. Grappling the hostile craft, the billmen—like the Roman mariners in their encounter with the Veneti—set to work with

[1] Brooks, *op. cit.*

[2] This is no more than surmise, but unless the wind changed between the first and second encounter between the fleets, the English must have worked into it to approach the French shore.

their long-handled *rochets*, slashing the stays to bring down masts and sails with a run, to envelop the French sailors and men-at-arms in the heavy canvas-backed silken folds "like a net upon ensnared small birds".[1] Before they could free themselves from the hampering gear they were cut to ribbons by the hard-smiting boarding parties.

The whole thing was quickly over, with most of the French ships taken and a poor remainder limping unhappily for home. Dragged from the bilge of his ship, Eustace the Monk was given the choice of having his head lopped off on the bulwark of his own vessel or on the butt of the *trébuchet* which had so weighed it down in the water. "He had little desire for either," the contemporary chronicler dryly comments, "but anyhow they cut it off,"[2] the actual operation being enthusiastically performed by one of John's old ship-masters, Etienne Trabe.[3] The severed head was subsequently exhibited, impaled on a pole, throughout the length and breadth of the land.

England had won the first of her purely naval actions against the French; a battle in which, almost for the first time, the sea had been turned from a hindrance into a servant of the tactical design; a combat in which, at last, maritime manœuvre was recognised as something entirely different from the devices to be employed on land. Without in any way amounting to a concerted fleet action, the encounter of August 24th, 1217, saw the foundation of that doctrine of sea-warfare—to gain the weather gage—upon which, throughout the days of sail, all our subsequent victories were based.

Neither were the political consequences of the Dover battle without profound and far-reaching significance. Cut off from reinforcement and blockaded by the victorious fleet, Louis's once prosperous venture had clearly run its course. Realising that "there is a time to go fishing and a time to take in the nets", he hurriedly concluded terms of peace and withdrew to France. No one could better have demonstrated that any enterprise against England is doomed to failure unless command of the narrow seas be first achieved and then steadfastly maintained.

---

[1] Matthew Paris.   [2] *Histoire de Guillaume le Maréchal.*

[3] He may well have been the Stephen Crabb mentioned in the Close Rolls; orthoepy, like orthography, was largely a matter of individual choice in those days.

CHAPTER V

'The English Sea'

"There are always ships putting into, or sailing out of these harbours."

ARISTIDES

FROM 1194 to 1815 the Englishman had to accustom himself to a factor in his day-to-day existence as constant as hunger and the need for sleep—war with France. At times it was desultory, no more than an intermittent rumble of thunder on the horizon. There were even interludes of shallow amity and queachy alliance. But far more frequently the conflict was open, and waged with a bitterness which revealed how impossible was the hope of its permanent reconciliation.

It is unlikely that those hard-headed realists, Pembroke and de Burgh, ever gave the thought of a lasting peace between the two peoples a moment's consideration. If, on the heels of the Dover fight, France desired a breathing space, it suited England's current policy to grant one—on terms.

With Porchester Castle crammed with Knights and shipmen taken captive on St. Bartholomew's Day, and another haul of privateers and *marinelli* held in Sark,[1] the English were in a position to demand the return of Normandy, Anjou and Maine as the price of suspending hostilities. Agreement on this proviso was reached in the September of 1217; although the French exhibited no eagerness to carry the restoration into effect. With Louis's accession to the throne in the July of 1223, the concessions to which a failing Philippe Augustus had perforce agreed were promptly repudiated; and on both sides of the Channel preparations were pushed steadily forward for a resumption of the struggle.

[1] In the Dover battle the English had captured 125 Knights and over 1,000 soldiers and mariners, including Eustace the Monk's brother, James, and one of his uncles.

Louis having seized La Rochelle and advanced to the gates
of Bordeaux, an expedition was organised, under the Earl of
Salisbury, to cross into Poitou. The King's 'great ship', the
Cardinal,[1] together with several others, was ordered round from
Southampton to Portsmouth; the ship-masters being directed
to place themselves under the orders of Frater Roger de Temple,
another of those bustling, worldly clerics in the tradition of
William de Wrotham, with as great partiality for the reek of
bilge-water as for the odour of sanctity. The barons of the
Cinque Ports were instructed to assemble in Shepway to concert measures for the protection of the sea-coast against the
King's enemies, and to ensure that all persons still living who
had seen service in the time of King John should take oath to
arm themselves. The Ports were also to provide five craft for the
Poitou venture, in addition to those scheduled for coastal defence and the patrol of the narrow seas; all of which was duly
done. For the Portsmen were in somewhat chastened mood.
Memory of their temporising and intransigence during 'Lackland's' struggle with his rebellious barons and their Gallic
supporters, had not been sweetened by the acts of unblushing
piracy they had perpetrated against the shipmen of Calais
during a period of truce. There had also been the tiresome
business of their feud with the Bayonnais, in which the King
had been forced personally to intervene. On de Burgh's urgent
recommendation, a thorough reconsideration of their several
Charters had been accompanied by an intimation, couched in
no mincing terms, that in future they would be required to
display considerably more restraint. They were also reminded
that only the strict fulfilment of their obligations would ensure
the perpetuation of their privileges.

These matters satisfactorily settled, orders were issued to
restrain any vessel, large or small, from quitting Dover, or any
other port, unless security was first given that no cargoes would
be shipped to any haven other than on the coast of England.
Letters from the bailiff at the port of discharge were to be
brought back by way of assurance that the order had been
obeyed. The wholesale 'arrest' of merchant craft for the King's
service went steadily forward; and the supplementary docks
built under Wrotham's direction at Southampton, Winchelsea

[1] Captured from the Portuguese.

and Rye—the last-named big enough to accommodate seven hulls—were kept hard at work on refits and repairs.

The shipwright's skill had more than kept pace with the steady improvement in ship design. Vessels of anything up to 200 tons burden, and stepping two masts each carrying a single sail, had become a commonplace; while reasonable cabin accommodation was now taken as a matter of course. Space was allotted to travelling merchants in proportion to the quantity of wares they freighted; the more goods under hatch, the greater the share of the cabin set aside for their use; and the better the 'kitchen'—i.e. meals provided. Indeed, the day was not far distant when the King and his Consort would voyage in "convenient cabins" elaborately wainscotted. It was with vessels of this quality that the King's ships and the vessels of the Cinque Ports were supplemented in time of war.

Yet for all the impressive array of force that Henry's lieutenants continued to muster, in 1225 and again in 1230, "nothing was done in France", as Roger of Wendover dourly lamented, "but expending immense treasure".

The boy-King who had succeeded to the throne in 1216, the "little pretty Knight" who had ridden pick-a-back on de Burgh's broad shoulders, had won everybody's delighted approval. With young manhood, however, he had degenerated into a flighty dilettante, whose emotional piety was strangely interlarded with wholly unrealisable dreams of military glory. As unwise as he was ungrateful—he even dismissed the solid, steadfast de Burgh—his marriage with Eleanor of Provence brought a swarm of needy Savoyards and Provençals hurrying across the seas in search of lucrative sinecures and those "unconsidered trifles" that represent wealth without any corresponding burden of responsibility. Their numbers were swollen by the rabble that clung to the heels of Henry's own grasping Poitevin half-brothers and sisters.

With such a rackety crew distracting so irresponsible a helmsman, it is small wonder that the course pursued by the Ship of State was erratic and prone to run on the shoals. Dame Fortune, moreover, was consistently perverse. In 1242 what should have been a full-scale encounter between the English and Gallic fleets—in which the former would undoubtedly have had the advantage—was frustrated by a sudden storm, which blew up at the very moment at which contact had been made. Driven helplessly before the wind, the crews scarcely knew friends from foes, and consulted only their own safety, "fearing alike", as one onlooker recorded, "the elements and the French".

To revenge himself for this humiliating fiasco, the King, from his refuge in Gascony, gave orders for the Portsmen to ravage the coasts of Brittany, Normandy and the *Pas de Calais* with fire and sword, sparing only Churches and men of proven English blood. A thoughtful addendum to the royal decree reserved a fifth part of any prize that should be captured for the benefit of the Exchequer. With an entourage exclusively made up of harpies, the King had every encouragement to keep a sharp eye on the till.

A very different technique had characterised the campaign of 1225, when Salisbury, in his solicitude for maritime commerce, had insisted on waging 'limited' warfare, with the armed forces' energies confined to operations on land. In those days, the bailiffs in all the ports had been instructed to permit any Gallic vessel laden with wine, corn and provisions to enter their havens and discharge its cargo. Equally, French vessels had been free from molestation on the high seas; and although word had gone forth to expel all merchant-strangers of Gallic origin from the country, the decree had not been too hurriedly or too rigorously enforced.

Unquestionably, this policy of restraint had returned a worthwhile dividend. For although the first forty years of Henry's reign had witnessed the standstill imposed on the towns' unwearying efforts to extend their immunities and consolidate their constitutional advance, they had also seen a steady increase in the volume of maritime trade. This was particularly true of the first two decades.[1]

The clauses in the Great Charter[2] which guaranteed that "all merchants shall have safety in coming to, or going out of England, and in travelling through it by land and water", had

[1] It was not until Henry accepted the Crown of Sicily for his son in 1255 that he was driven to resort to every variety of expedient to raise money; a state of affairs of which the towns were swift to take advantage.

[2] The term 'Great Charter' was employed to distinguish the main covenant—which was re-issued in 1217—from a lesser deed dealing with the laws of the forest.

been reaffirmed; and a treaty of commercial intercourse was concluded between England and Norway. Wine merchants were offered a safe conduct to bring their wares to any English port upon payment of the "old and accustomed" duties; the King promising not to take their liquor for his own use or permit others to do so; an abrogation of the regal right to a prise on wine which must have left the importers considerably better off in pocket.[1] By 1220 the amount of business transacted by the Merchants of Cologne had been sufficient to warrant their establishment of a *Kontor*, or Guild hall, in London, for which privilege they were only too ready to pay an annual tribute to the King of thirty marks. It was known as the *Gildhalla Teutonicorium*, and in many ways it was the forerunner of the even more powerful *Staelhoef*, or steelyard, which came into existence in 1475.

On the other hand by 1248 an association of English merchants known as the Brotherhood of St. Thomas à Becket, had come tentatively into being, and gaining strength eventually as the association of Merchant Adventurers, was to provide a powerful counter-balance not only to the merchant-strangers established in England, but to the indigenous Merchants of the Staple. For there is every indication that the institution of the Staple, or Mart, with its guaranteed standard for the wares it had passed for sale, originated in mid-thirteenth century, although the details of its organisation were not fully worked out till the fourteenth.

In the circumstances, it was only natural that the weavers and all those connected with the most steadily prosperous industry in the land, as with the new trade in home-manufactured coarse linens, should again have banded themselves together for mutual support; since the detestation in which they were held by the *Gildeins* was scarcely mitigated by the knowledge that it was extended to two other classes of tradesmen. For the Assize of Bread and Ale, although fixing the weight and cost of the former and the price and quality of the latter, had done nothing to dispel the odium in which both brewers

---

[1] By 1258, however, the King was again insisting on his right to take one tun before and one tun behind the mast—i.e. one tun of the best and one of inferior liquor—at lower than market price, from any cargo of over 19 tuns (Madox).

and bakers were held by the populace in general and by the *Burgeis de la Gilde* in particular. Tradesmen who are accused, with more than a tincture of truth, of habitually trying to 'short-weight' their customers, cannot hope to bask in the sun of popular esteem. Sharp practice the *Gildeins* looked upon as their exclusive privilege; and notwithstanding the temporary check to their political ambitions, in local matters they were still all-powerful. It had been on their insistence, for example, that the ban on Sunday fairs and markets, introduced after a whirlwind evangelising campaign, by the puritanical Abbot of Fleix, had been withdrawn. For as the burgesses had been at pains to point out, fairs and markets were fundamentally religious rather than commercial institutions, originating in the assembly of pious worshippers at famous shrines on the feast days of the Saints. The fact that the pilgrim was frequently also a trader, and therefore a source of profit to the town—i.e. the Guild-Merchant—was not unduly stressed!

*   *   *

In the natural order of things, ports differ with regard to their *raison d'être*. It is the port which makes the shipping, and not the shipping that makes the port. The population may be *of* the port, as with London and Southampton, and deal primarily with the reshipment of goods, or it may be *behind* the port, as with the Kent and Sussex havens, which lived very largely by supplying the perennial demand of the nearby inland towns for fish. Sandwich sold vast quantities of herring in addition to rendering an annual tribute of 40,000 of them to the religious fraternities of Canterbury. The monks of Christchurch even owned their own quay in the town, catering for their needs by purchasing the whole catch as it was landed; while tonsured bursars were a common sight on every Cinque Port waterfront. The standard of contemporary commercial morality is reflected, incidentally, in the regulation which forbade the sale of fish, beans, peas or salt "when the sun was down", thus ensuring that the customer had sufficient daylight to see what he was buying!

The sea yielded an ample harvest for everyone, although the Portsmen never ceased to wrangle violently with the fisher-folk of Yarmouth over what they were pleased to regard as

encroachment on their rights. The quarrel was, indeed, inveterate, and flared up on the flimsiest pretext. On one occasion,
for example, when the men of Yarmouth had fitted out a ship to
carry Prince Edward to France, and the Winchelsea mariners
had rigged another craft to transport the Queen, the two parties
fell to fighting as to which was the better vessel; and some of the
Portsmen received fatal injuries.[1] But they were always ready,
temporarily, to sink their differences to turn on such a ravening
sea-wolf as Savary de Mauleon, whose activities in the Channel's
western approaches seriously threatened the lines of communication between England and Bordeaux.

The Cinque Ports had benefited substantially by adopting,
under licence and at an annual payment of 20 marks, the improved method of curing fish perfected about A.D. 1200 by
Peter Chivaliar. The new technique was equally effective when
applied to pilchard; and once the Cornishman, Peter de Perars,
had secured the right to operate it, a steady stream of salted
pilchard swelled the cargoes of salted herring that found so
ready a market throughout Germany. At the same time pack-
trains, loaded with consignments of salted pilchard and herring,
penetrated even the loneliest of England's own rural areas.

A subsidiary, but highly profitable, activity with the Portsmen was the transport of pilgrims from Dover to the Continent,
on the first stage of their journey to Jerusalem or to visit the
shrine of St. James of Compostella in Spain. For years Simon of
Wastlegray headed the list of burgesses seeking permission to
continue the traffic which brought them in a very comfortable
return.

London still welcomed many Cinque Ports' vessels, to discharge their fish and corn at Queenhithe; while the neighbouring wharves were crowded with foreign craft breaking out
their cargoes of masts, pitch, tar, hemp, cables, cordage, wains-
cot, wax, and steel, and the rye and other grains that England's
concentration on pasture—i.e. sheep-walks—at the expense of
arable, had rendered it necessary to import.

With the King's impulsive and pettish order to the Cinque
Ports, the whole aspect of affairs underwent an instant and
violent change. In peace or war, the Sussex and Kentish
mariners never missed an opportunity to harry their *bêtes-noirs*

[1] Matthew Paris.

from the other side of the Channel. Relieved of all restraint, the Portsmen sallied forth across the narrow seas intent on taking the very fullest advantage of the generous licence they had been accorded. Afloat, as along the Gallic shore, they slew and burned and pillaged with a large-hearted latitude that rarely paused to discriminate between friend and foe.

The effect of their unbridled activities was only what might have been anticipated. The whole French coast, from Calais to Rochelle, was mobilised against a mosquito fleet, without discipline, integration or over-all control. Since the French squadrons were strong and well organised, the Portsmen soon found themselves penned within their harbours; and in a trice *La Manche* became the barely disputed highway of the Gallic fleet. With pained indignation, the Portsmen protested that "the Count of Brittany, with all the shipping of Brittany and Poitou, well armed and equipped, was waiting to intercept vessels passing between England and the King"; that to increase their distress, the Normans and sailors of Whitsand [1] and Calais scarcely permitted them to fish; that the pirates who guarded the high seas with their galleys "would not suffer even pilgrims to return home"; and that "such was the position of the King, that Bordeaux might be considered his prison". [2]

Henry, who in military matters rarely needed much persuasion to take the line of least resistance, speedily concluded a five-year truce with France; and his relief at having made the passage to England without interference is reflected in his gift of 20s. apiece to his ship-master, Roger Tresor, and to three of the ship's officers, Robert Garderebeure, Thomas Tumair, and Robert Alard.

As a consequence of all this turmoil in the narrow seas, the free flow of commerce was gravely impeded, while steeply rising prices brought it home to the most isolated landsman that a plenteous larder is ever dependent upon the Englishman's command of the waters that surround his island.

Not that efforts were wanting to keep the stream of trade flowing: the spirit of mercantilism thrives on obstruction. Infuriated by the freebooters who preyed upon their vessels, the merchants of Hamburg and Lübeck formed an association subsequently to be known as the Hanseatic League, which was

---

[1] Wissant. [2] Nicolas, *op. cit.*

destined to become the most important and powerful trading corporation of the Middle Ages, with influential regional head-quarters in Lübeck, Bremen, Hamburg, Bergen and Brunswick. Even at its outset it easily contrived to furnish heavily-armed escort vessels to protect its seaboard commerce; craft that both English and Gallic sea-rovers learned to eye with wary respect.[1] Escorts were also provided for the ships carrying the wool, lead and tin exported by the newly formed association of the Mer-chants of the Staple of England; whose faith in the protection afforded by the squadron of King's galleys allocated to coastal defence was noticeably lukewarm. Somehow the wine fleet from Bordeaux and Bayonne still managed to break out its welcome cargo on the West and Castle quays of Southampton, at Win-chelsea and Sandwich, and in London Pool. Vessels in trade from the Levant ran the gauntlet in the Channel's western approaches, hoping to reach the sanctuary of Southampton, and the cosy taverns in the lee of frowning Bar Gate, without molestation. But the merchant-strangers suffered many losses on the way.

For it was a period in which virtually all cargoes, whether imports or exports—including wool—were freighted in foreign bottoms, even the stone from Caen, which was in such universal request for building. It is true that a certain amount of coasting trade, in consumer goods and the transhipment of imports, was carried on in English vessels. For sea-carriage was twenty times cheaper than wheeled carriage, fifteen times less costly than pack transport, and seven times less expensive than passage by river.[2] Apart from this question of unfailing demand, the Eng-lish ship-owners' concentration on the coasting trade, to the exclusion of deep-sea commerce, can in part be attributed to the fact that the Germans and Italians had already skimmed the cream off the international market, and partly to the absence in the West of any scheme for insuring cargoes, such as the system, known as bottomry, which was in full operation in the Mediterranean. Even so, the usefulness of such coastal havens as Hythe, Romney, Dunwich and Melcome was already seriously threatened by the steady, irresistible easterly drift of silt and shingle; while the more westerly havens of Poole,

[1] Lambrecius, Struvius, Pfeffel.
[2] *A History of the Royal Society*, T. Birch (4 vols., London, 1786–7).

Weymouth, Dartmouth, Exmouth and Plymouth were yet to undergo real development.

* * *

As the year 1258 drew to a close, attempts on the part of a Baronial Council to curb Henry's feckless extravagance and check the horse-leech methods by which his entourage of rapacious popinjays contrived to fill their coffers, were frustrated on almost every count. So long as the cost of the King's ships and the King's shirts was carried on the same account by the same set of scriveners, the evasion of control was ridiculously simple. Infuriated by the Monarch's incurable shuffling and prevarication, the party of opposition eventually found a leader in Simon de Montfort, an individual whose English title of Earl of Leicester could not disguise the fact that he was the scion of a family whose roots were deeply embedded in the soil of France. Neither could it be entirely forgotten that at one time the contemporary Simon-pure had unashamedly revelled in the King's extravagant favour.

As the leading advocate of the liberalisation of the Constitution, like all reformers in a hurry de Montfort was totally blind to the virtues of gradualism; completely oblivious of the fact that "you always have to give the English time; they realise things slowly".[1] Time could not be spared to cozen obstinate profligacy with sweet reason; it must be converted instantly with the sword.

The ensuing "Barons' War", as it has come to be termed, in a naval sense was a struggle in which only the coastal waters of Kent and Sussex played any significant part.

Like the Londoners, the Portsmen, with their usual genius for backing the wrong horse, declared for Montfort. But the support of Pope Urban IV for so ductile a son of the Church as Henry, was a foregone conclusion; and the earlier activities of the Cinque Ports' shipmen were primarily directed to the interception and destruction of Papal bulls, which placed them, among others, under Interdict. With equal diligence they succeeded in blockading the loyalist reinforcements concentrated on the Flemish coast; an activity the temporarily captive Monarch dolefully witnessed from the heights of Dover. The

[1] John Galsworthy.

opportunity to prey on all and sundry craft plying in the narrow seas was, of course, one of which they took the most liberal advantage. In consequence, the flow of imports was so interfered with that wine from 40s. a tun rose to the abnormal price of 10 marks,[1] pepper increased from 6d. to 3s. a pound, and for want of cloth dyed on the Continent, men and women went about in garments of the natural colour of the wool.

Then at Lewes, on May 13th, 1264, de Montfort's army, strengthened by a contingent of 15,000 Londoners, scored a victory which served to introduce that era of democratic Caesarism which soon brought realisation to the country at large that it is better to "bear those ills we have than to fly to others that we know not of". The gilt with which it was so lavishly decorated could not disguise the fact that de Montfort's gingerbread was remarkably unpalatable.

With the rebel leader's death at the battle of Evesham, on August 4th, 1265, the way was left clear for Prince Edward to bring London and Dover to submission. Ironically enough, it was to the Portsmen's East Anglian rivals that the Heir to the Throne appealed for ships; the King—like his father—having failed to maintain a fleet that could operate efficiently without augmentation by the Cinque Ports' vessels. It was a lesson that was not lost on his son.

In considerable alarm, many of the Portsmen bundled their families aboard ship and sought to escape the consequences of having opposed their Sovereign, by taking to the open sea— having first burnt Portsmouth in a final gesture of rather futile defiance. Proud and prosperous Winchelsea—stoically unheedful of the breaches the eroding sea had made in its defences[2]—was the last Cinque Port stronghold to fall, after a lengthy resistance which only crumpled under the weight of a full-scale assault led by Prince Edward in person. The struggle ended with a great but discriminating slaughter, the 'multitude'

---

[1] In 1769 Lord Lyttleton, in his biography of Henry II, assessed the value of the mark as fluctuating between £10 and £15 in terms of the contemporary spending value of money, which was, of course, much higher than that prevailing today.

[2] In 1212 Winchelsea had been partially inundated; in 1250 a series of tremendous storms had destroyed several of the town's walls and 300 houses, and in 1254 further substantial damage had been done to defence works and private property.

being spared as scrupulously as the rebel barons were put to
the sword.

With the country still unsettled by the backwash of rebellion,
Prince Edward succeeded his father in the November of 1272.

*   *   *

In many respects Edward I can be regarded as the first truly
representative Monarch of a race no longer polymorphous, but
so conscious of its individualism that plain, vigorous English
was steadily replacing the Anglo-French argot which had
hitherto been in general use with all but the lowest classes of the
community.[1] Furthermore, Edward was a warrior-king who
combined personal intrepidity with a remarkably shrewd sense
of business; an irresistible combination to the English, with
whom patriotism is far more estimable if it can be made to
yield a profit.

Unquestionably, 'Longshanks', as he was dubbed, was a
competent statesman and an accomplished jurist. But his appreciation of the supreme importance of sea-power, like his
interest in all that concerned his marine, was no more than
intermittent, and far more lively when mercantile rather than
purely defence measures were involved. He found it easy
enough, for example, to deal with the Countess of Flanders who,
when her preposterous claim to an English pension was refused,
retaliated by seizing all the merchandise of English traders then
in her domain. Edward's *riposte* was to expel all the Flemings
from his territory, ban the export of wool, and empower the
delighted Cinque Ports' shipmen to seize all ships freighting
wool or woolfells to Flanders. With her country's principal
industry brought to a standstill, the Countess was forced to
abandon a pretension as maladroit as it was frivolous.

The King was less successful in suppressing the Zeeland
pirates, who had made the merchant vessels plying between
London and the Continent their particular prey; while the
Portsmen had to be severely reprimanded and the Bayonnais

[1] Latin was still employed for legal documents, and was preferred to
French as the language for diplomatic and legal letters. Pleadings in the
Law Courts were still in French; and even in the fourteenth century the
pious founder of an Oxford College, seeking to make his scholars gentlemen,
forbade the use of English at the common table.

placated with the gift of £100, to bring the petty war between these testy irreconcilables to a precarious suspension.

Edward's business acumen was again well to the fore when, in 1275, the First Statute of Westminster was framed to include a new system of Customs for the King's support. Designed very largely on the method of taxation operative in Gascony— particularly at Bordeaux—the Statute, while legislating against the arbitrary regal and seigniorial exactions hitherto imposed at will, granted the King a 'subsidy' of half a mark on every sack of wool and every three hundred wool-fells, and a mark on every last of leather exported. In effect, the impost levied on commerce to enable the Sovereign to discharge his obligations became subject to strict control, having been concerted, not by the King-in-Council, but by the King-in-Parliament; that is, by the consent of the Third Estate. Novel in kind as taxes, as they were in the authority which established them, these new im-posts immediately gave rise to what was virtually a civil service for their ingathering. In place of the erstwhile port bailiffs, who too often were no more than the pliant creatures of the *Gildeins*, independent Collectors were appointed, who were responsible for the issue of cockets—receipts for the dues paid—and for keeping the books. The Collectors were under the supervision of Controllers; while Searchers checked the cockets with the cargoes to which they referred. Searchers drew no stipends, but were allowed to levy certain fees; although not permitted—at least in theory—to accept 'welcome' or 'farewell' money, nor the uproarious hospitality which they had hitherto regarded as amongst the less venal of their perquisites. Ultimately, a fourth official, the Surveyor, was appointed as "a King's clerk to examine and survey the business of the Customs". A vessel passing safely through the hands of these assorted myrmidons could obtain its discharge for a payment varying, according to the size of the craft, from twenty pence to six shillings.[1]

The reframed *Magna et Antiqua Custuma*, although a distinct concession by authoritarianism to parliamentary control, at

---

[1] Among notables who served at one time or another in the Customs must be counted Geoffrey Chaucer, Joseph Addison, Daniel Defoe, William Congreve, Matthew Prior, Adam Smith, Horace Walpole and W. W. Jacobs. Tom Paine was also a Customs official, although twice dismissed for shameless peculation.

least tended to do away with those great officials of the Customs
—mostly clerics and invariably sinecurists—responsible only to
the King's Treasurer and the barons of the Exchequer; complaints against whom were treated as complaints against the
Treasury. And to complain against the Treasury was to run into
a blank wall; the final court of appeal in all instances being
furnished by—the Treasury; and Caesar does not reprobate
Caesar!

The new system equally served to provide the Sovereign with
a stabilised asset upon which cash advances could be raised by
farming the Customs to an association rich enough to oblige
with an immediate pre-payment. Such resources were mostly
to be found at the disposal of the wealthy Spini or Frescobaldi
of Florence or the equally prosperous Bardi, or maybe the Ricci
or Ballardi of Lucca; men as well regarded and respected as the
Venetians were disliked and distrusted. In the main, however,
King Edward's preference was for dealing with the Hanseatic
League or the merchants of Brabant; although it was to the
opulent Italians that he turned to finance his successful Welsh
campaigns; the farm of the Customs recompensing the lenders
for the cash they had so obligingly advanced. The Monarch's
recourse to these alien sources of supply was, of course, part of
a settled policy designed to destroy the cramping monopoly of
the privileged boroughs; where the *Burgeis de la Gilde* were ever
ready to queer their own long-term prosperity for the sake of
inflicting injury on their neighbours' immediate well-being. In
effect, the old inter-municipal trading arrangements were
undergoing supersession by an imperial policy formulated by
treaties or statutes of Parliament.

Since, theoretically, usury was forbidden to Christians, when
in need of ready money the normal practice, both for King and
commoner, was to resort to the Jews. Their rates of interest rose
so steeply, however, that riots were provoked in which 700
Semites perished in London alone. By the King's intervention,
the charge on a loan was restricted to 2*d.* a week on every
20*s.* borrowed. Eventually, the Jews were expelled from the
country *en bloc*; some 16,500 of them departing with no more
than the movable property they could carry. Bonds for the
money owing them were impounded and encashed by the
King; a piece of sharp practice which tickled the popular

fancy as much as it was lamented by its victims—lender and debtor alike.

In both Edward's Welsh campaigns the Cinque Ports' fleet played a notably useful part; and the Portsmen's reward came in the form of a new and even more generously framed Charter. Not only were the barons and Portsmen generally confirmed in all their ancient privileges, but the towns were freed from the prise on wine purchased for their own use and exempted from all taxation on hulls and rigging. Furthermore, the whole community was relieved from 'wardship and marriage', that long-standing and much resented medieval custom which gave the Sovereign guardianship over all well-dowered orphans, with the right to dispose of them in wedlock as best suited his own book.

In return for these and other minor benefactions, all that was demanded of the Ports was the normal service of fifty-seven ships, at their own cost, for fifteen days, when summoned. The Charter was accompanied by a *Dite*, or declaration, which, while dealing with the Portsmen's right to "denne and strond" at Yarmouth, sought—however vainly—to reconcile the age-old animosity between the Cinque Ports and their East Anglian rivals, which in the first four years of the reign cost the lives of 206 Yarmouth shipmen.

At the same time Edward relinquished the office of Lord Warden, which he had held temporarily, appointing Stephen Pencestre, his erstwhile Lieutenant, in his place, and Gervase Allard to command the Cinque Ports' fleet.

The Charter of 1278[1] was unquestionably the palladium of Cinque Ports' liberties; nor did the Monarch's local benefactions end with its award. The Great Storm of 1287, which entirely altered the course of the river Rother—to Romney's progressive ruin as a port—and dammed out the tides from a large portion of the already shrunken lagoon, also swept Winchelsea, on its shingle islet, right out of existence. Very wisely, the King decided not to try and re-erect the town on its original site, but to start work afresh on the tableland of the peninsula-promontory of Iham (or Higham). Here, crowning the steep

---

[1] The document of 1278 is the oldest Cinque Ports' Charter to have survived; but it is clear from its phraseology that it was preceded by several others.

banks that overlooked the sea on three sides, the new town of Winchelsea, with its thirty-nine 'quarters', was speedily erected; the stronghold of Monsegur, near Bordeaux, serving as a model for this early exercise in town-planning, designed to furnish an additional port of embarkation for any enterprise against France. From a friend's house at nearby Udemore, the King kept a benevolent eye on proceedings, as the work went swiftly forward. The pity is that neither Edward nor any of his contemporaries in any way grasped the implications of the steady, irresistible easterly drift. Thus, as a port, Winchelsea the Second was predestined to extinction by the ever-encroaching shingle, as Winchelsea the First had been doomed to submergence under the Channel's pounding seas.

Edward had dealt with the Cinque Ports with rare generosity, but he was far too shrewd a man not to tincture benevolence with precaution. For memory of the Portsmen's rebellious conduct in 1217 and again at the time of the Montfort uprising was not easily to be obliterated. To forestall any further backsliding he appointed an Admiral [1] with overriding control of the Ports, who combined the administrative duties of the Keeper of the King's ships with the executive and command responsibilities of the Captain of the King's mariners. Moreover, in his choice of William de Leybourne for the office, he was careful to select someone with no invidious local interests or obligations. Among his other functions, Leybourne supervised the activities of the local Keepers of the Coast—answerable for defence in their respective regions—selected the most likely man to act as Wafter of the Wool Fleet, the official responsible for the freighting of this invaluable cargo across the narrow seas, and ensured that the provisions of the revitalised Law of Wreck were faithfully observed. Since the term 'Admiral', when first employed, had a purely administrative connotation, and the King's representative, his *Admirallus Maris Angliae*, was also a fighting Officer, he was speedily renamed "Captain *and* Admiral of the Fleet of the Cinque Ports and all other Ports from the Port of Dover by the sea-coast westwards as far as Cornwall". As leader in battle *and* administrator of the fleet— in effect, virtually combining the functions of First Lord, First

---

[1] The word is from the Arabic, *Amir-al-Bahr*—Chieftain of the Sea.

5+

Sea Lord, and Commander-in-Chief—he was remunerated at the scarcely excessive rate of 2s. a day.[1]

Edward 'Longshanks' was financier enough to appreciate that too exuberant a system of taxation fails in the very object it sets out to achieve—the production of a healthy revenue. It was with this salutary consideration firmly in mind that he introduced the far-reaching *Carta Mercatoria*, in which the principles laid down in *Magna Carta* with regard to the privileges conceded to all merchants were for the first time fully recognised. To begin with, wine was absolved from prisage, the importer paying the standardised 'butlerage' of 2s. a cask, afterwards stabilised at 2s. per tun. The impost, however, was to be paid in 'pence' within forty days of the consignment being landed.[2] In consideration of the Bordeaux wine-importers' complaint of lack of cellarage in London, some old cook-houses on the river bank were pulled down and replaced by commodious store-houses; the area covered by them acquiring the name of the Vintry. At the same time the unpopular additional tax—of Henry III—of 1d. on a tun of wine, known as the Gauge, was abolished. There was a small tax on imported cloth and wax; although the detested exaction of 'purveyance' was abolished, to everyone's jubilant satisfaction. Aliens were required to pay a special *ad valorem* duty of 3d. in the £1 on all the goods they imported, and especially high rates on exported hides and wool; for the latter roughly 10s. as against the 'denizen's' 6s. 8d.[3] For all that, the traffic in this commodity, despite a bad outbreak of murrain consequent on the importation into England of Spanish sheep, was so huge and at the same time so profitable that, grumble as they might, the foreign-born exporters were fain to abide by what amounted to an early experiment in 'protection'. More legitimate grounds for complaint could be found in Edward's ban on the export of money, foreign or English, or bullion, save under rarely-awarded licence. On the other hand, merchant-strangers were free to traffic, wholesale,

---

[1] As always, it is extremely difficult to determine the exact spending value of money at any given time. But in *circa* 1265, 20 pence of silver weighed a full ounce, whereas by 1465 the number had dropped to 30, and by 1480 to 40; an obvious decline. [2] In other words, in coin of the realm.

[3] Twelve sacks of wool made up a last, 2 weyes a sack. The pound of 12 oz. was used only for money, spices and electuaries; the pound of 15 oz. for all else.

with other aliens or with natives—another blow to the restrictions hitherto imposed by the *Gildeins*—and they could reside where they pleased for as long as they pleased; privileges which quickly brought Hollanders seeking a share of the cross-Channel traffic. Whereafter, by making debts recoverable by process of law, the Charter rendered the extension of credit, hitherto unknown, a practical proposition, to the infinite benefit of legitimate commercial expansion. In the hope of curbing lawlessness at sea, all ship-owners and masters of ocean-going vessels were required to find security for the good behaviour of themselves and their mariners. But the profits of freebooting often made it very well worth while to sacrifice the bail lodged with the authorities.[1]

In the outcome, the provisions of the Charter undoubtedly brought about a steady increase in the trade flowing into London, Southampton and the lesser ports, across the narrow seas; a traffic whose safety was guarded, with varying success, by vessels kept on permanent station in the Channel for its protection.

Despite war with Scotland and a mutinous Wales, Edward could survey his realm and its growing prosperity with considerable satisfaction. There were pirates still lording it in the Channel, of course; while the Portsmen's genius for putting the cat among the pigeons had by no means diminished. But despite handicaps the outlook was far from discouraging.

In the event, it was the Portsmen who were responsible for the maritime Donnybrook Fair which touched off the smouldering French; never spiritually at ease when restrained by an interlude of fictitious amity from rapturous dreams of slitting English throats.

The whole preposterous business started when two of the crew of an English ship, landing in an officially friendly Norman port, were obstructed in their search for water. The dispute led to an exchange of blows; one of the Englishmen being killed and the other hounded to his ship by a yowling pack of assailants. Shortly after, a powerful Gallic squadron fell in with six English ships which they promptly attacked, capturing two of them. Strangling such of the crews as had not been killed or

---

[1] Southampton, ever prone to defy authority and go its own way, was disciplined by having the prise of wine exacted from it until 1308.

mortally wounded, they strung them up to the yards, with the
carcase of a dead cur dangling between each corpse. Then,
passing up the Channel, they indulged themselves in an orgy
of rapine and outrage "that made no distinction between an
Englishman and a dog."[1]

This was the signal for the infuriated Portsmen to throw off
every last semblance of restraint. Mustering a large fleet, they
set sail, under the leadership of Sir Robert Tiptoft, in search of
the enemy. But with singular circumspection the French had
sought the shelter of their harbours. Failing to find trace of
them at sea, the Portsmen thrust into Seine-mouth, where they
discovered a number of the enemy vessels at anchor. These they
instantly attacked, slaughtering many of their hated foes and
making off with half a dozen of their ships. On the heels of this
enterprise ensued a period of running fights, "great slaughter
on both sides, shipwreck and rapine—both thirsting for blood",[2]
and "all being done rashly between the Normans, without any
commission of their princes". But as Mathew of Westminster
bleakly commented, "there is neither King nor law for sailors".
The final trial of strength came in response to the Portsmen's
challenge to their enemies to meet them in pitched battle, at a
spot in mid-Channel to be indicated by an empty, anchored
ship. Taking up the gage, the French duly appeared at the
rendezvous accompanied by their Norman, Flemish and
Genoese supporters; the English cause being strengthened by
the accretion of certain Dutch, Gascon and Irish sympathisers.

In a tempest of howling wind and pelting rain and snow—a
vile day even by April standards—the rival fleets set to work
with the utmost venom, despite the fact that the English and
their supporting armament were considerably outnumbered.
There was little attempt to manœuvre, bar an effort to ram.
But such was the resolution with which the smaller force
pressed the attack that its victory was scarcely in question even
at the outset. Leaving a few useless hulks, crammed with dead
and dying, to swing idly between tide and current, the victors
triumphantly bore off their spoils; having in their indurated
way first dealt with the wounded among their enemies by

[1] *Chronicon de Eventibus Angliae*, by Henry Knyghton.
[2] Knyghton, *op. cit.*

casting them into the sea.[1] It was only in Eastern waters that prisoners of war were spared to keep the galley benches filled. The attitude of the European sailor towards his captives was best summed up by Chaucer:

> *Of nyce conscience took he no keep*
> *If that he sought and hadde the higher hand,*
> *By water he sent him hoom to every land.*

Although in the beginning the French had been the aggressors, the opportunity to exploit the latest situation was too good for Philippe IV to reject. Demanding redress in hectoring terms, by a particularly sleazy artifice the French monarch went on to possess himself of Aquitaine, and thence marched into Gascony; and war was inevitable.

In the early stages of the ensuing conflict the English cause prospered; the Gascons readily joining in to help defeat the execrated French. But with the hostile fleet fully mustered, Sir Thomas Turbeville, held captive by the French, treacherously suggested to Philippe that he should be sent to England, ostensibly as an escaped prisoner, to persuade Edward to place him in charge of the Kent and Sussex coast. Then "having obtained from his Sovereign the custody of the sea and of the ports, he promised to join the French, who, on seeing his own banner hoisted above that of the King, were to land and he would deliver the place into their hands. Philippe agreed to the plot, promised him large rewards, and took two of his sons as hostages. Turbeville arrived in England; and though he was kindly received, the King refused to entrust the sea or the ports to him. The King of France having collected above three hundred ships from Marseilles, Genoa and other places, he sent them to cruise off the English coast, and wait for the promised signal. After the French ships had waited for some time for Turbeville's signal, they sent five of their best galleys to examine the coast, and, one of them preceding the others, landed at Hythe. To induce the French to come further inland, the King's

---

[1] With the usual tendency to concur in exaggeration, Nicholas Trevet, in his *Annales Regum Angliae*, does not question Knyghton's extravagant estimate of 240 vessels captured.

forces at that place pretended to retreat. The stratagem completely succeeded; and suddenly turning upon the enemy, the whole of them, to the number of two hundred and forty, were slain. The English then captured and burnt the French galley, and her four consorts hastily rejoined their fleet." Turbeville's treachery being subsequently exposed, he met the traitor's death that was his due.

Raid and counter-raid across the narrow seas—in the course of which Dover was burned to the ground—preceded a meeting between Edward and Count Guy of Flanders, to conclude an alliance against their mutual enemy.

Among other clauses, the pact included a proviso that "All the ships of England and Bayonne . . . going to Flanders, shall carry the signal of the arms of the King of England, and that the ships of the Count of Flanders, going by sea, shall have the signal of the said Count, and also letters patent sealed with the common seal of the city to which such ship might belong, certifying that it did belong to that town, and was subject to the Count of Flanders, which was agreed to in order that the enemies of England and Flanders might not falsely hoist the Count's signal." This constitutes the first instance of the use of ship's papers as a means of identification, and created an invaluable precedent.

It was to Flanders that Edward repaired, as the flank from which to launch his campaign against the French; John de Botetourt commanding the Yarmouth division of the fleet, William de Leybourne that made up of the Cinque Ports and Portsmouth ships, and an Irish shipmaster those from his own country and the West. In the home ports the *rectors* of all neutral vessels were under bond not to sail to France; no distinction having been made between contraband of war and lawful goods.

Edward landed at Sluys on August 27th, and no sooner had he taken up his quarters than a furious quarrel broke out between the Portsmen and the *marinelli* from Yarmouth, in which the former were undoubtedly the aggressors. Boarding and entering their rivals' vessels, they set about the systematic slaughter of every East Anglian that came their way. Edward did his utmost to quell the riot, but it did not subside until twenty of the Yarmouth craft had been burnt out; only three of the contingent contriving to make good their escape by featly putting to sea.[1]

With his naval force openly mutinous and his Welsh troops more concerned to plunder Ghent's citizenry than strike a blow for their overlord, it was with considerable relief that Edward agreed to the truce proposed by the Pontiff, Boniface VIII. The fruits of the enterprise were nil; for the region about Bayonne was all that was left of England's Continental territories to acknowledge 'Longshanks' as its overlord.

What followed furnished a dish the English Monarch found hard to digest; but it was the inevitable outcome of the fact that the resources of Philippe had gained in strength as Edward's had become more enfeebled, and his diplomacy less effective. With nothing to bar their passage across the narrow seas the French, landing at Hythe and brushing the local defence aside, moved on and boldly raided Dover, once more reducing the town to cinders; while Winchelsea was only saved in the nick of time from sharing a similar fate. Then, when with difficulty the French had been driven off, trouble broke out in Scotland, claiming so much of the royal attention that in Gascony the attenuated English forces barely succeeded in holding their own.

It was the Scottish defeat at Falkirk, foreshadowing Edward's release to fight elsewhere, that persuaded Philippe to agree to a grudging truce; which in 1303 was expanded into a peace treaty which, among other things, formally restored Gascony to English rule.

With matrimonial alliances negotiating with the Court of France, Edward grudgingly agreed to support King Philippe's expedition against Guy of Flanders with twenty of the best ships to be found between London and the Isle of Wight— Dover alone being exempted from the requisition. At the same time he reluctantly expelled all the Flemish merchants from the country; to the immediate ruin of the wool trade, said, at this juncture, "to be equal to half the land in value".

Philippe having encountered far more stubborn resistance from the Flemings than he had anticipated—"*Mon Dieu*," he was heard to exclaim, "it rains Flemings!"—was glad enough

---

[1] After A.D. 1300 a similar state of hostility grew up between the mariners of Lyme and Dartmouth.

to conclude a truce which, among other things, reopened empty warehouses to the inflow of those wool consignments of which they had too long been starved. Patriotic indignation is difficult to maintain with hungry faces around the table.

In many things Edward 'Longshanks' had been successful. He had done much to regulate trade and the system by which the national revenue was derived from it; his measures had helped it appreciably to expand. He had broken up the dangerous coalition between the baronage and the clergy that threatened the equilibrium of the nation as a whole. He had shown the acumen to encourage the use of the Welsh long-bow, which, expertly wielded, was to prove the master-weapon of the age.[1] He had realised the necessity of delegating his authority in naval matters, and had chosen a deputy to whom posterity owes the concept of an efficiently organised Admiralty. He had done his best, with inadequate means, to ensure that maritime commerce passed in safety through the narrow seas. But he died only too well aware that the main problem—a final, definitive settlement with France—formed a burdensome legacy for his successor.

[1] It also put an end to chivalric combat as waged hitherto, and permanently proletarianised warfare, since the arrow-shaft, like the bullet that succeeded it, "made all men alike tall".

CHAPTER VI

Variations on a Traditional Theme

"Princes are like heavenly bodies, which cause good
and evil times."

FRANCIS BACON

If ever a man must have felt

> . . . *his title*
> *Hang loose about him like a giant's robe*
> *Upon some dwarfish chief,*

that individual must have been England's flighty, inconsequent
Edward II. Yet it was this "slight unmeritable man" who was
acclaimed as heir to the proud and puissant title of Sovereign
of the English Seas; first acknowledged in an undated Anglo-
French agreement drawn up between the formulation of the
peace treaty with France and the death of Edward I. In its
preamble the Kings of England were unequivocally recognised
as having been "in peaceable possession of the sovereign lordship of the Sea of England, and of the isles within the same",
and of "ordering all things necessary for the maintaining of
peace, right and equity among all manner of people . . .
passing through the said seas". Nor were the French alone in
acknowledging the oft-asserted claim. Another parchment, submitted by certain Flemings, petitioned for redress for alleged
injuries inflicted by "the men of England, on the sea of
England".

It was a tribute that no one insisted upon with greater
severity than the Portsmen, who demanded that it should be
rendered to all Cinque Ports vessels, as "the King's ships",
even by fellow fisherfolk from further along the coast. When
the mariners of Fowey neglected to "veil their bonnets"[1] on

---

[1] The bonnet was an extra strip of canvas attached to the mainsail, which
could be hauled up and dipped in salute.

one occasion, out stormed the Portsmen in strength, intent on administering sharp rebuke. For once they had taken on more than they could accomplish and, soundly trounced, they retired to their havens to nurse their hurts. So far as the stalwarts from the West Country were concerned, the Portsmen were never 'complimented' again. On the contrary, from that time onwards craft out of Fowey flaunted their burgee, with the town's armorial bearings prominently displayed on it, *above* the distinctive pennant of the Cinque Ports!

In any case, the dominion of the seas so boldly protested by the English King, was a good deal more imaginary than real. The unbridled piracy[1] that disgraced 'the Sea of England' offered sufficient proof of that. Twenty-two rascals out of Calais, for example, attacked and captured four English vessels laden with wool for the Staple at Antwerp; the contents of one hold alone being worth 2,000 marks. The same sea-wolves even had the audacity to cut out a vessel lying in low water off Margate; the owner-master, John Brand, a merchant of London, being spirited away into captivity, in company with his crew and three merchants of the Hansa travelling as passengers.[2] For that matter, in John Lambot the Cinque Ports themselves had sired one of the most unconscionable ruffians ever to roam the narrow seas on his indubitably unlawful occasions. A son of Winchelsea, he was twice outlawed "for all manner of trespass and felonies committed by him". Pardoned for having rendered a notable service at Bannockburn, he again returned to his evil ways. At length it became necessary to appoint a Commission to deal with the complaints of the merchants of Brabant whose ships he had rifled with every circumstance of barbarity. Lambot was again outlawed, but cared so little for the law's displeasure that he seized the anchored vessel of a merchant of Bremen named Albridus, and having pitched the crew overboard, coolly made away with the cargo. This was his last exploit in Channel waters; but it was well matched by the

[1] Up to the fourteenth century all men aboard a vessel—*myoparo*—capable of warlike action were known as pirates; sea-robbers being termed felons, trespassers, malefactors, and the like. From the time of Edward II onward we find the designation 'pirate' applied specifically to the maritime freebooter.

[2] *Foedera*, Rymer. This entry makes it clear that the term Merchant of the Hansa was now in general use.

capture, at Plymouth, by Jack Paulyn and Benedict Semen, of the vessel belonging to Robert Wyche and William de Stokesby of Yarmouth; and the cutting out of the Yarmouth buss belonging to William de Colkyrk by Henry de Hatheland, another desperado who claimed Winchelsea as his port of origin.

In plain terms, it made no matter whether England was at peace or at war with France, Holland, or Flanders; the shipmen of the respective countries carried on their own private conflicts, quite indiscriminately, virtually without pause, and "heedless of the laws of God and man". The situation was realistically summed up by the Earl of Flanders when, in answer to Edward's protest that the Fleming had given aid and comfort to his enemies, the Scots, that wily funambulist had pointed out that Flanders, "being a country common to all mankind", it was impossible to deny free access to it to merchants of *any* race, "agreeable to ancient custom". And 'merchant' was an elastic term that could be stretched to cover virtually anyone who brought goods to the market that were in popular demand. Stolen goods, in short, found a ready sale on both shores of the narrow seas; while the spate of claims and counter-claims, petitions and cross-petitions kept the lawyers in a happily lucrative state of ferment.

Yet for all the impediments it had to overcome, the flow of ordinary trade was steadily maintained; with Sandwich an enterprising rival to the far bigger haven of Southampton. For Sandwich was in growing favour as a port of discharge for wine shipments, which were then taken on to London in coasting craft. Not that Winchelsea was easily to be outdone. Between September 17th, 1306, and May 19th, 1307—a typical trading period—six hundred and five vessels left the German ports laden with wine. Of these three hundred and six sailed for England, thirteen heading for Winchelsea. Amongst this flotilla *La Faucon* could carry $143\frac{1}{2}$ tuns of liquor, *La Godyere* 136, *La Wallifar* 181, *La Bonagon* $100\frac{1}{2}$, and *St. Bartholomew* 152 tuns. Sharing the relief from the prise on wine enjoyed by all the Cinque Ports, in a good year Winchelsea imported 2,900 tuns of Gascon and a comparable quantity of Rhenish. Wine had come to supplement the Englishman's stoup of ale to no inconsiderable degree. None the less, fishing remained the principal source of the Cinque Ports' wealth. For the catch brought in showed so little sign of diminution that the monks of Christchurch esteemed it well worth their while to undertake the construction of a new quay at a cost of £26 16s. 6d. Sandwich had become so prosperous a centre, indeed, that Ralph St. Lawrence was considered exceptionally fortunate to have had the ferry rights between the town and the Isle of Thanet deeded to him for life. Southampton's rising prosperity, on the other hand, owed a great deal to the fact that it had become the port of discharge for the three to five merchant galleys chartered annually by the Doge; whose example had set the pace for the rapidly expanding Venetian trade. As such, this new commerce was undoubtedly welcome; but the Venetians proved remarkably touchy gentry, as was witnessed by the sanguinary affray between certain visiting "patrons, merchants, masters and sailors" and the household of Sir John de Lisle. Knives were drawn and quickly fleshed, passers-by were brought, not unwillingly, into the fray, and by the time the town-sergeants had put in a belated appearance to restore order, the whole affair had taken an ugly turn, with a number of the combatants severely pinked, many broken heads, and much damage to property. But good customers are never long in ill-odour; and the matter was compounded by the payment of an agreed sum to de Lisle by way of damages.

Gallic respect for Edward's sovereignty over "the English Sea", however speciously protested, did not preclude an assault on the wool fleet off Margate, or the capture, by the French privateer, Birenger Banck, of a large Genoese, laden with corn, oil and honey, lying peacefully at anchor in the Downs. Nor was this nefarious work in any way confined to shipmen of foreign blood. So lawless were the times that an English vessel, driven into the mouth of the Thames on passage from Flanders to Scotland, was ruthlessly pillaged by the Thanet islanders of Cliffe, who then proceeded to kill off their surviving countrymen without a qualm. But although there were one hundred and seventeen attacks on shipping in the narrow seas of sufficient gravity to find record in the contemporary Close Rolls, Edward was in no case to do anything but fulminate and protest. For the exhausting war with Scotland demanded all the resources in men, arms and shipping he could scrape together.

A few Cinque Ports' vessels were left to guard the Channel coast, as best they might; but they could do little to stem the raids in which the French were exuberantly joined by the Flemings and their kinsmen owning a somewhat sketchy allegiance to the Count of Hainault and Holland. One way and another, the 'Sovereign of the English Sea' seemed to have mislaid his trident.

'Rule by favourites' inevitably breeds contempt for all regal authority. Thus Edward's obsession with his *mignons*, the insolent, primping Piers Gaveston, and his successor, the scheming opportunist, Hugh de Despenser, so weakened his hold on the country that he was powerless to deal with the formidable opposition headed by his own Consort, the steely but dissolute Queen Isabella. Having earlier repaired to France, ostensibly to conclude a peace treaty with Charles IV, but actually to secure the interests of her youthful son, Isabella, with her leman, Roger Mortimer, in her train, set out in force for England, ostensibly "to deliver her husband from the hands of the Despensers". There was nothing with which the 'Sovereign of the English Sea' could oppose her passage, so he was left no alternative but to seek safety in flight.

With Isabella in control of affairs, the hue and cry for the fugitive was pursued with the utmost vigour. Betrayed by the Welsh familiars with whom he had sought refuge, Edward was hurried away to close confinement at Kenilworth. Even before his capture his son had been proclaimed King; and it only remained to ensure that the late incumbent did not linger on embarrassingly to overcrowd the scene. He departed from it in the September of 1327, in circumstances as obscure as they were suspiciously timely. Shovelled into a casual grave, there were few "to mourn the passing of a man whom they in no wise would have had alive again".

*   *   *

The reign of Edward III cannot be said to have got fairly into its stride until he reached an age to deal firmly with his hectoring, raffish mother, the 'She-wolf of France', and dispose of her boorish paramour. With the former relegated to the permanent enjoyment of such amenities as Castle Rising could offer, Mortimer was hustled off to the elms of Tyburn: and

Edward was free to deal with their political legacy. This consisted of a shabby, pie-crust peace with Scotland and a treaty with France that left much of Gascony and Aquitaine at the mercy of its Gallic neighbours. But with the breath temporarily knocked out of the Scots at Halidon Hill, the King was free to turn and deal with the French, and thus secure his rear as a preliminary to a final effort to settle matters north of the Border.

There were grounds enough for a quarrel with the newly-crowned Philip of Valois. Not only had he openly supported the Scots, but his gross interference with the Anglo-Flemish trade had been accompanied by unforgivable encroachments on England's cherished overseas territories. Since they included such invaluable cross-Channel trading areas as Gascony, Poitou, Saintonge, Aunis, Agendis, Perigord, the Limousin, Quercy, Rouergue and Augumois, Edward's urge to retain his heritage inviolate is easily to be comprehended.

The King's resources for an enterprise against France included a number of old but repairable ships and a sturdy, steadily increasing mercantile marine with which to supplement them. Two-masted craft of 200 tons burden were by no means uncommon; one vessel, the *Christopher of Exmouth*, running to 300 tons. Most of the ships were now fitted with a reliable stern rudder, affixed with proper pintles and gudgeons, and an embryonic bowsprit, and yards and shrouds. In the more progressive craft there was even an elementary 'bilakyll', or binnacle, to house a compass of similar design to the instrument devised by Florio Gioja of Amalfi. The chief trouble lay in the necessity to import so many of the articles required for a ship's rig; although the consequences of the reckless, inconsequent cutting of timber had yet to make themselves seriously felt.

For purposes of war the merchantman could easily be rigged with *bellatoria*, or elevated stages, fore and aft, which together with the fighting tops, or 'towers', housed the hundred and thirty-odd bowmen and infantry who supplemented, to the point of congestion, a crew of about the same number. The names of all shipmen were now carefully registered; a preliminary step towards the eventual registration of all shipping, and the appointment of three Admirals with the power of "chusing, either within the liberties or without, as many men as they might think necessary to manning the fleet, and seizing and impressing them, if they were unwilling to go aboard". They were also endowed with authority to punish all those proved guilty of evasion or desertion.

The days of the non-combatant seaman content just to 'work' his vessel were long since past, such was the prevalence of piracy and the licence allowed themselves by craft sailing 'in reprisals' under Letters of Marque. Originally, the law of 'reprisals' had been enacted to enable English merchants who had suffered loss at the hands of foreigners, or were unable to recover debts from them, to seize goods of commensurate value from *any* trader of the defaulter's State whose ship happened to be in an English port. It was a maritime version of the long-established law which empowered the *Burgeis de la Gilde* to distrain on the merchandise of those traders, temporarily domiciled in their midst, who were natives of a town which had exacted illegal toll on the *Gildeins'* wares.[1] Theoretically, maritime 'reprisals' were carried out by authorised officials and not by the injured party. The latter could, however, be issued with Letters of Marque which empowered him legally to adjust his claim at sea by force of arms. In 1243, for example, Henry III had granted a licence to Adam Robernolt and William le Sauvage "to annoy our enemies by sea, and by land wheresoever they are able, so that they share with us one half of all their gain", while in the reign of Edward I formal Letters of Marque were issued by the King's Lieutenant in Gascony to Bernard d'Ongressill, whose ship had been captured on the high seas, taken to Lisbon, and there sold. The trouble arose when a merchant continued to operate "on the plundering account" long after he had reimbursed his original loss to the full, embarking on a career which was tantamount to that of an out-and-out pirate. To preserve their own, master and shipman had to be ready to fight to the death. For the system of insuring both craft and cargo inaugurated by the Bruges Chamber of Assurance was very rarely at the disposal of merchants or ship-owners not of Flemish birth. It is true that the enactments collected together—and constantly added to—in what came to be known as the *Black Book of the Admiralty*, sought to establish

---

[1] The law remained in operation until 1353, when Edward annulled it; the law of reprisals at sea remaining operative.

certain 'laws of the sea' by which everyone would abide, and which would afford protection to all. But it was only in such matters as the liability between merchant and *rector* that these well-meant regulations were observed to any serious degree; although the 'laws of the sea' were sufficiently comprehensive to legislate for a cat to be housed aboard ship to keep down the rats, failing which the shipmaster became liable for any damage to cargo attributable to the rodents! When afloat, however, men very largely took the law into their own hands, and were cheerfully prepared to abide the consequences. For there were good profits to be made by the shipmaster who succeeded in coming scatheless into port. Wine sold cheaply and well at from $2\frac{1}{2}d.$ to $4d.$ a gallon; currants, raisins, rice and figs commanded a steady $2\frac{3}{4}d.$ a pound, sugar changed hands at as much as $2s.$ a pound, while the well-to-do were prepared to pay as much as $4s.$ for a box of ginger. To Southampton's busy wharves came cargoes that included woad, littinus, grain, brazil, orpiment and copperas, for dyeing woollens, and shipped from Amiens, Corby and Nesle. There were haberdashery, cotton yarns and mercery. There were dates, apples, pears, 'French nuts' (walnuts) and almonds, and such welcome spices and condiments as pepper, aniseed, zedoary, cinnamon, galingale, mace, cubibs, cloves, saffron, cummin and peony. Garlic and onions came from France, as did olive oil and an increasing quantity of soap; while alum—virtually a Papal monopoly— was in constant transit to the apothecaries, who used it extensively in the preparation of their nostrums.

In a worthy attempt to improve the breed of rather stunted native horses, a number of sturdy mares were bought from the Flemings and transhipped in cogs to England. The King alone spent 25,000 florins on the purchase of horseflesh from the Low Countries, and a further 1,000 marks on fifty Spanish barbs.

Wool, although rigorously taxed, was as always a thriving export whose turnover was barely halted by a temporary interdict on its shipment to Flanders, whose insouciant flirtation with France demanded discouragement that could not for long be ignored with safety. Meanwhile, what Flanders was denied, Brabant, in its own small way, was ready to welcome eagerly; while the concern of the Flemish wool-importers for their continuing prosperity could be relied upon speedily to persuade their overlord where his—and their—best interests really lay. In the interim, however, conditions were such that so many merchant-strangers left England, taking their capital with them in specie, that the community suffered from a serious dearth of coinage. This was only remedied when a limit was set upon the amount of money travellers could take overseas. But the temporary suspension of wool exports to Flanders helped materially to encourage the indigenous cloth industry. Hitherto, on a good year, wool exports had totalled 30,000 sacks, bringing in over £60,000 to the Exchequer. Within a century and a half this number was to fall to a quarter and then to a sixth. Nor was this extraordinary diminution due to any curtailment in the area devoted to the growth of wool. On the contrary, sheep-walks continued to increase in number and dimension. It was the progressive demand for wool on the part of the native cloth manufacturing industry that had wrought the change. By 1355 England was sending abroad between five and six thousand cloths a year; by the end of the fifteenth century the Merchant Adventurers alone would be exporting 60,000 cloths annually.

This progress was materially helped forward by the steady trickle of Flemish refugees—nearly all expert weavers and fullers —who took up permanent residence in England from 1231 onwards. It also gave rise to a new manufacturing class of the community, whose steady growth added enormously to the wealth and influence of the towns; although the insulation and self-sufficiency of the weaving industry constituted a constant threat to the monopoly of power the *Gildeins* still sought so tenaciously to exercise.

Not that the weavers refrained from the imposition of restrictions quite as irksome and shortsighted as those enforced by the *Burgeis de la Gilde*. It was a common practice, for example, for a Guild of Weavers to deny to any weaver not of their fraternity the right to work at his trade within twelve leagues of their town. So the stultifying policy of grab continued until this and all other restrictive practices were done away with by the Statute of Cloths of 1351.

During the temporary decline in wool exports, such shipmen as had lost employment in the carrying trade turned to fishing as a profitable alternative. Herrings for daily consumption and to salt or pickle, to tide over the winter, were in huge and constant demand, and they could be bought at twenty for a penny. During the war years the demand for them rose even higher. For a series of bad winters and murrain amongst the cattle necessitated a strict system of 'rationing'. Save on certain specified holidays, no man could be served with more than one meat dish, and salted fish filled such aching void as still persisted. So lucrative was Yarmouth's and the Cinque Ports' commerce in this bountiful harvest of the sea that the King found it necessary to frame no less than half a dozen enactments for its regulation.

With the Flemings wearied of coquetting with the French, wool exports to the Low Countries were resumed, and soon reached a new high level. There was money enough to support a war, providing it was not too protracted. In the meantime, however, with many of the King's forces and much of his shipping still in the north, the sketchy defences organised by the Keepers of the Coast, like the nebulous watch and ward maintained in the Channel, left a very great deal to be desired. For the Portsmen were far too immersed in their perennial quarrel with the fishermen of Yarmouth to have time or inclination for the fulfilment of the duty to which they were pledged. Without a finger being raised to stay them, the French dashed across to attack a muster of shipping at anchor off the Isle of Wight, slaughtering the crews and incontinently throwing the wounded overboard. They were careful, however, to preserve such vessels as were worth sailing back to Normandy.

In a letter rebuking the unruly Portsmen, Edward took occasion to reaffirm his claim to the Sovereignty of the Sea, asseverating that, "As our progenitors, the Kings of England, in such contests between themselves and the Sovereigns of foreign countries, were the lords of the sea and of the passage to the continent at all times, it would grieve us exceedingly if our royal honour should in the smallest degree be impaired in our times."

To more practical purpose, the King directed that all ships on passage between Gascony and England should travel in convoy. The instruction was accompanied by an order for the 'arrest' of all shipping likely to prove of service in the impending operations. Thereafter, Southampton was nominated as the victualling port, Portsmouth as the place of assembly for ships of war.

Edward's preparations, however, proved to have been most vexatiously delayed by the intractable vendetta between the Portsmen and the Yarmouth fisherfolk, who had even turned a deaf ear on the remonstrances of so august and awe-inspiring an individual as the Archbishop of Canterbury. So the French—deceitfully flying English banners—were free to land a force at Portsmouth, led by Sieur Nicholas Bahuchet, and having in their array the exiled Scottish champion, David Bruce. Before a sufficient defence could be mustered the town was in ashes, with only the parish church and the hospital left to brood over the smouldering rubble and the pitiful huddle of the slain. A belated rally by the townsfolk exacted a considerable toll from the raiders as they made for their boats; but it was a poor retaliation for a haven so ravished that the King hastened to relieve it of the taxes of the tenth and the fifteenth until such time as life should flow again through its bravely refashioned streets.

Raids on Jersey and Guernsey as well as the Hampshire coast, spurred Edward to hasten preparations to carry the war to the enemy. As a preliminary, it was necessary to clear a flank threat to any major operation by subduing the island of Cadsant, hard by Sluys, where some 5,000 troops formed the garrison under the redoubtable Guy, Bastard of Flanders.

The English force that approached the windswept stronghold on a sullen morning of November consisted of five hundred experienced men-at-arms, a couple of thousand bowmen, and the hardy crews of the ships transporting them. At their head were Henry Plantagenet, Earl of Derby, and the chivalrous, war-scarred veteran, Sir Walter Manny, "whose memory", Froissart avers, "the very worms dare not assault".

The converging host found the garrison well entrenched; but the slow-firing cross-bows of the defence were no match for the long-bows of the English archers, in whose speedy rate of discharge and deadly accuracy of aim the triumph of Creçy was patently foreshadowed. At the head of the assault, which was immediately thrust home, Henry Plantagenet was beaten down in the press and only saved from disaster by the vigorous sweep of Sir Walter Manny's battle-axe. Both sides engaged hotly in a furious *mêlée*; but stout as was the garrison's resistance "the English resolved not to part stakes by any means", while the dreaded *ballisteros Ingleses*, very expertly flanking their men-at-arms, "shot with such violence and so wholly together, that they were not to be endured".[1] With the doughty, hard-fighting Bastard brought to his knees and taken prisoner, the heart went out of the resistance; with the last few resolute defenders hunted through the streets of the town and there cut down.

It was a small thing well done, but at no inconsiderable cost; and the *riposte* came swiftly in savage raids on Hastings, Dover, Folkestone, Southampton and a burgeoning Plymouth. The westerly haven was, indeed, raided twice, with many ships fired in the Catwater and the houses on the foreshore set furiously ablaze. Only the strenuous efforts and rousing example of Hugh de Courtenaye, a veteran of nigh four-score years, served to rally the demoralised townsfolk in a successful counter-attack which "chased the residue of impudent varletry back to their ships". At Southampton, likewise, the raiders paid dearly for their temerity; great execution being done among them by a country chawbacon whose dexterity with a flail was positively inspired. None the less, such terrible damage had been inflicted all up and down the coast that orders were given that no church within seven leagues of the sea should toll more than a single bell, save when danger threatened, when the whole peal was to be rung to summon the countryside to arms.

The final blow came with the loss of two of the King's ships, the *Great Christopher* and the *Edward*, captured after a desperate fight against a squadron of enemy vessels thirteen strong.

As in the days of the Scottish war, the King had failed to realise that a fleet is no more than a mobile extension of the offensive power of its base; that to leave that base exposed to hostile assault is fatally to cripple the offensive potential of the fleet itself.

Having reorganised his disarrayed coastal defences and negotiated certain precautionary Continental alliances, Edward's renewed preparations for carrying on the war were seen to have imposed so heavy a toll on merchant shipping as seriously to affect trade, and, of course, the inflow of much-needed revenue. In addition, he had alienated the sympathies of the Lombards and other merchant-strangers by seizing their

[1] *Life of Edward III*, Joshua Barnes.

goods and chattels and threatening all but the powerful Bardi and Peruchi with imprisonment when they complained. Lastly, he had courted the invasion of his regal authority by borrowing money from the Church. But his prime purpose of mobilising all the available resources of the country went steadily, inexorably forward; nor was the home-front overlooked. The ports' defence works were overhauled and repaired, while substantial forces were stationed in the Isle of Sheppey, the banks of the Thames fortified, and large piles driven into the waterway to impede the approach of hostile ships.

At the same time the right to search neutral shipping for contraband of war was fearlessly affirmed and put vigorously into practice—that 'right of search' which remains a matter of acrimonious international controversy to this day.

With half the King's armament assembled at Winchelsea and the balance gradually mustering at Dartmouth, the Portsmen proceeded to exact a partial revenge for the recent damage done to their havens by thrusting across to Boulogne, in wild, wintry, 'smuggler's' weather, to raid the hostile shipping there enharboured. Firing the lower town, a naval blockhouse full of stores, nineteen galleys, four 'great ships', and twenty boats, they paused only long enough to string up a dozen enemy shipmasters ere bidding the blazing township "farewell for that time".

It was an enheartening prelude to the principal enterprise, whose aim was to encounter and defeat the enemy fleet of four hundred sail—of which two hundred were 'great ships'—to clear the way for an invasion of the Gallic mainland.

Having staked everything by boldly assuming the arms and title of King of France, on June 20th, "about the first hour of the day, in the name of God and St. George", Edward set out at the head of an armament of two hundred vessels, steering for the coast of Flanders. Before the van made its landfall it was joined by a further fifty ships of the Northern squadron; and as the coastline hardened orders were given for a reconnaissance of the forest of masts and streamers that appeared to be concentrated in the mouth of the Zwijn.

Nothing could be more typical of the mentality of these soldiers afloat, however, than the manner in which this reconnaissance was conducted. Instead of sending a couple of swift

galleys to investigate and report back, three knights, their
horses, their squires, and a mounted escort, were laboriously
landed and sent across country "to view the countenance of
the enemy".

The intelligence they brought back made it clear that the
entire Gallic fleet was concentrated off Sluys, in the estuary of
the Scheldt. In command was the Breton knight, the Sieur de
Kiriet, and the truculent, sadistic coast-harrier, Bahuchet; with
the veteran Mediterranean sea-fighter, Barbareva,[1] as Captain-
and-Admiral of the Genoan and Spanish auxiliaries.

Despite the fairly heavy odds against him, Edward was
determined to attack while the enemy were still in process of
forming their line of battle. Drawing off a little, he proceeded
to manœuvre for position. But it seemed that the very last thing
the French proposed to do was to up-anchor and seek combat in
the open sea. Barbareva had urged the folly of waiting supinely
on the defensive; but with the English approach held up by an
ebbing tide, the Frenchmen preferred to utilise the respite
afforded them to draw up their armament in three divisions,[2]
one behind the other; with the captured *Great Christopher* on the
extreme left of the front line. All the craft were lashed together
so that they could only be boarded and entered at the high,
narrow bows; while barricades of heavy spars and planking
were erected inboard, to form a barrier across the forecastle,
behind which the Genoese cross-bowmen could take post. High
on the masts small boats were hoisted, full of heavy stones for
the men in the fighting-tops to hurl at any boarding party that
came within range. Balks of timber were triced to the masts
themselves, to be smashed down on those coming over the side.

Barbareva might protest, but the Frenchmen had turned
their fleet into a series of long, narrow, floating forts; and as one
assailing a fortress Edward was borne in by a strong wind to the
attack. Glowing with richly-tinted sails and gleaming banners—
the Cross of St. George, the lions of England, and the heraldic devices of the English Chivalry—they sailed in like a great
flock of seabirds streaming towards the shore. As they drew

[1] Nicolas, following Froissart, names him Barbenoire, Southey prefers
Bocanegra.
[2] Hemingford's *Chronicle* affirms that there were four divisions, but the
point is not particularly material.

within bowshot the trumpets sounded their piercing challenge, and the archers thrust purposefully into their lissom staves, sending flight after flight of slender arrows arching over, to deal injury and death behind the crowded enemy barricades. Handicapped by their weapons' slow rate of discharge, the stolid Genoese arbalestiers sought vainly to return shot for shot.

The spearhead of the assault steered straight for the left of the line, where the recovery of the *Great Christopher* was the aim of a dozen eager knights, vying with each other for the honour of being first over her bows. Pressing close behind, the other ships of the English van swung in bow to bow with the next in line, threw out their grapples and fought like wildcats to make good an entry; Edward in the forefront of the fray and his gleaming sword the centre about which the tussle swayed and eddied.

With the fighting-tops cleared by the deadly shafts of the English bowmen, the assailants' plan was to take each line *en enfilade*—as a flank is rolled up in war on land—a device that virtually paralysed the defence. For as ship after ship was cleared from the left inward, the vessels beyond were powerless to intervene lest their fire wrought as much damage to friend as foe. Fighting with desperate courage, the French were forced slowly but inexorably back along the line. Quarter was neither asked nor given; the crews of the captured ships were cut down where they stood or driven over the stern into the water, where their heavy battle-harness dragged them to their death.

With noon but a little sped, Kiriet's and Bahuchet's squadrons of the left and centre were all in their assailants' hands, and the fight raged about the tall Genoan vessels of the right. But the tide had turned, and fearing that his 'great ships' would ground in the shallowing upper waters of the estuary, Edward bade the trumpets sound to break off the attack. By sheer hard fighting, allied to accomplished seamanship, the gallant but thwarted Barbareva managed to get clear, at the head of a draggle of his battered Genoese; his escape materially aided by the English shipmen's joy in the recapture of the cherished *Christopher*, and their preoccupation with hanging the execrated Bahuchet from the main yard of his own vessel.

It had been an action of unusual ferocity, prolonged for over nine hours, and its cost was exceptionally heavy. One ship, the

St. Jacques of Dieppe, no harder stricken than any other, had four hundred dead on board, all that was left of her crew, the rest having gone overboard to drown. On the English side a Hull galley and a 'great ship' had been sunk outright, while from another craft belonging to the King's wardrobe,[1] the sole survivors were two men and one woman. There was, of course, the consolation of prize money for the survivors, awarded by the Admiralty Court in the proportion of one-fourth to the Sovereign, one-fourth to the owners of vessels 'arrested', and the remainder to the men responsible for the captures, "if in the King's wages".

Sluys added little to the lore of sea-fighting, for too much weight should not be attached to the rhyme, written nearly a century later, which avers of the gold noble struck in 1344

> *For foure things our noble sheweth to me,*
> *King, Ship, and Sword, and power of the Sea.*[2]

But the victory at least ensured that the impending conflict with France would be fought rather on Gallic than on English soil. It also paved the way for the establishment of the invaluable bridgehead of Calais.

The siege of Calais itself was rendered possible by Edward's temporary command of the sea—at least, so far as local waters were concerned—by which he was in a ·position not only to supply his own necessities, but to deny them to the besieged. This state of affairs could only be brought about by a considerable sacrifice of trade, for as is revealed by the first roll of shipping ever to be engrossed, a good half of the country's mercantile marine had been 'arrested' for the King's service.[3] Fortunately the marked decline suffered by commerce was not

---

[1] The King's ships included a 'Hall', or *Salle du roi*, in which the Sovereign made his voyage, a 'Wardrobe', to carry spare armour, artillery engines and all kinds of warlike stores, and a 'Larder', in which was a reserve stock of provisions and liquor.

[2] The gold noble was struck simply and solely to have a currency common to England and Flanders; where marks, sols, florins, ecus, and 'moutons'—the latter stamped with the Pascal lamb—although accepted, were subject to fluctuations in the rate of exchange.

[3] The totals of Edward's fleet at Calais given from an MS. list by Macpherson and that quoted by Hakluyt, do not agree; but it would appear that between 738 and 748 vessels, of various sizes, were mustered, with crews totalling approximately 15,000.

endured in vain. Philip of Valois, coming up at the head of an army of relief, measured his chances of dislodging his enemy with dispiriting memories of Creçy, and speedily gave orders to strike camp and abandon the seaport to its doom. It met a fate that might well have been more draconic. Retaining only twenty of the leading burghers as hostages, Edward forcibly evacuated the remainder; filling the town with carefully selected colonists, housing them at very moderate rentals, and providing for its guardianship by a reliable garrison.

With Calais in his hands, Edward not only possessed an invaluable *point d'appui* from which to launch his ventures against France, but held the key to the Straits of Dover. The years were to reveal, however, how scant was his appreciation of what could be achieved by the exercise of the dominant sea-power that was his.

*   *   *

Creçy marked the zenith of Edward's success, severely as the victory may have strained his own and the country's resources. But there was a lively hope that the truce with France which ensued would modulate into a definite peace treaty. Trade was reviving, the Venetians had even thought it worth their while to appoint a Consul of Merchants to negotiate on behalf of their traders; while the establishment of the Staple in Bruges, with all goods not properly cleared thereto liable to seizure, had done much to stamp out the smuggling of wool, wool-fells, hides, and other dutiable commodities across the narrow seas.

Then as the crops began to ripen with the steamy, breathless summer of 1348, news came out of Dorset's Melcombe Regis of a malignant sickness that struck with the rapidity of lightning, and from which recovery was as rare as the spread of the plague was swift. The Black Death was abroad in the land; the pestilence that within a year was to reduce England's population of five millions by nearly half.

Like all other classes of the community, the seafaring population were hard hit by the epidemic sickness; and as the ravaged country emerged from the shadow of disaster, ships lay idle for want of crews to man them. Neither were the much-sought-after survivors among the shipmen any more averse to profiteer out of calamity than the workers in agriculture. Wage demands, theoretically based on the depreciation in the value of the currency, rose to such preposterous heights that regal intervention was required to curb their soaring cupidity.

One thing remained constant, however—Gallic reluctance to conclude peace; and even if major operations languished, the war of raid and counter-raid persisted with all its accustomed venom.

With the aim of reducing his war expenditure, the King devised a new impost in the form of convoy duty, at 1s. a sack on all wool exports. The proceeds of this tax were to be handed to a select body of merchant shipowners in return for their provision of a sufficient maritime force to convoy the wool ships safely to their destination. Needless to say, the experiment was a failure; only a national organisation can successfully undertake the task of policing the seas. But petitions to repeal the new impost were firmly resisted; and in slightly modified form, and under the name of tunnage and poundage, it took its place as one of the standard sources of national income.[1]

France and Spain still being technically in hostile association against England, a number of Spanish privateers appeared in the English Channel and proceeded to prey with alarming success on English shipping and the craft of neutral origin bound for English havens. Emboldened by the success which attended their daring efforts, these Spanish sea-wolves even had the impudence to dub themselves the 'Lords of the English Sea'. Matters were not bettered—particularly for the proprietors of English sheep-walks—by Edward's placatory gift of a flock of prime English sheep to Alonzo XI of Spain. In breaking one of the strictest laws imposed on his subjects, the King did the economy of the country a lasting injury. For the gift-sheep speedily became acclimatised, and soon were producing the finest wool in Europe.

*　　　*　　　*

The loss of Calais had always been a barbed thorn in the Gallic flesh; and force having consistently failed to retrieve it, in the January of 1350 resort was made to a nice admixture of

---

[1] A similar tax, for "the protection of the merchant navy", had been voted in 1303. It became the practice to vote this particular impost to the King "for life".

guile and attempted corruption. At this period responsibility for the town's defence was in the hands of an Italian mercenary, the supple, wily Amerigo de Pavia. Like all soldiers of fortune, Pavia was in arms for what he could get out of it; but he was not the man to betray his paymaster. So when Geoffrey de Chargny, the Captain of St. Omer, gently insinuated that 20,000 gold crowns would reward the man who stealthily admitted a body of French troops within the fortifications, the Italian appeared to fall in with the suggestion—and promptly revealed the whole plot to his royal patron. The opportunity to set a trap for the French was far too good to be missed. So the King, the Black Prince, and a select handful of followers hastily crossed the narrow seas, disguised as fishermen, and smuggled themselves into Calais.

At the given hour the agreed postern was duly opened— *after* the astute Amerigo had pouched the last instalment of his bribe!—and the swarm of incoming French found themselves confronted by such an overwhelming display of force that speedy surrender offered the only hope of survival.

In the event, Edward treated his prisoners with extraordinary magnanimity, seating them at a right royal feast and, with the exalted chivalry demanded by the tenets of the newly-created Order of the Garter, personally waiting on them as though they had been veritable guests of honour.

The succession of Philip of Valois by John II did nothing to further the cause of peace; neither did prosperity attend the English King's reanimation of a war he found it increasingly difficult to finance. With rapidly expanding powers, Parliament's tendency was to insist that the Monarch should 'live in his own', regardless of the fact that the cost of maintaining paid fighting forces, as against the erstwhile relatively cheap feudal levies, far exceeded the royal income. A number of the Crown jewels were already pledged to Italian usurers; and even the impost of tunnage and poundage, now established at 2s. on the tun of wine and 6d. in the £ on *all* merchandise, imported or exported, failed to expand revenue sufficiently to meet expenditure. In any case the impost, although inaugurated by Order in Council, in 1373 became subject to pinch-purse Parliamentary control.

With his war effort very largely financed by those Italian

usurers who had learned their business handling the Pope's affairs, and were determined therefore to have the last shred of their pound of flesh, the King was committed to an enterprise that lacked proper monetary resources as badly as it wanted popular support. For the average fourteenth-century Englishman cared as little about the fate of Guyenne as his Georgian descendant worried about that of Hanover. The defeats inflicted on the French were always severe but never decisive.[1] To achieve them—although they led nowhere—Edward, both economically and nautically, was compelled to live beyond his means; and the dire results of this impoverishing practice added appreciably to his difficulties in contending with a resurgent Scotland.

None the less, the King and his fleet were still capable of striking a remarkably shrewd blow, as Don Carlos de la Cerda discovered when, forgetful of the fact that he had treacherously attacked a number of English ships during a period of truce, he left the sanctuary of Sluys and headed down Channel, homeward bound.

Edward embarked at Sandwich, accompanied by the Black Prince, John of Gaunt—a stripling of ten—Henry of Lancaster, the Earls of Arundel, Warwick, Salisbury and Huntingdon, William Bohun of Northampton, fiery Walter Manny, Reginald Cobham, and the young John Chandos. Putting to sea with a fleet of fifty ships, including pinnaces, the King and his followers awaited the Spaniards off Dover. The Dons, with a north-easterly wind to help them, could have avoided the English squadrons had they so chosen. But "by pride and presumption they designed not to pass them by without speaking".

The King, who had hoisted his flag in the *Thomas*, "posted himself in the forepart of his own ship; he was dressed in black velvet and wore on his head a small hat of beaver which became him much. He was that day as joyous as ever he was in his life, and ordered his minstrels to play before him a German dance, *Sir John Chandos*, which delighted him greatly."

About 4 p.m. the English fleet had dropped down wind about forty miles, and was opposite Dungeness, and there drew near

---

[1] In effect, while the English can be said to have 'won' the Hundred Years' War, they failed to gain the objects for which it was fought.

the Spanish armament; Admiral Morley so manœuvring his ships that they lay dead across the path of the Dons. Had the English put their helms down and lain up into the wind, the enemy would have passed them at too great a speed for it to have been feasible to grapple them. The only possible alternative was to put their helms up and run on a parallel course to their opponents, shortening sail the while in order to be overtaken. The Captain of the *Thomas*, showing insufficient judgment, closed with the nearest Spanish ship as it passed, ramming her "with so much force that it seemed a tempest falling; and in the rebound that they made the tower of the King of England's ship struck the tower of the Spanish ship in such wise that the force of the blow broke it off where it was, high up on the mast, and overthrew it in the sea; and they within were drowned and lost."[1]

The timbers of Edward's ship were badly sprung and she was taking in water fast. The only thing to do was to grapple the nearest enemy carrack and carry her by boarding and entering. Clinging like leeches to the towering sides of the next in line, the knights and men-at-arms doggedly fought their way inboard. Meanwhile, the Black Prince's cog, heavily rammed, was awash beneath his feet; and although the whole ship's company "fought right bitterly to win the Spanish ship, they could not, for she was strongly kept and defended". The moment was critical, and it might have gone ill with the Prince and his followers had not the Earl of Lancaster, with a shout of "Derby to the rescue!", sailed in to attack the Spaniard on the other quarter. Vigorously pressed both port and starboard, the Dons went down in swathes, their dead littering the deck, their wounded tossed incontinently into the sea. In the heat of the fray the Black Prince was ever to the fore, his ardent valour a splendid spur to his fledgling brother.

On every hand the great height of the Spanish vessels gave them the advantage of an elevated firing-platform; and when the gallant little *Salle du Roi* manfully grappled her towering opponent the Dons, thinking to deal with her at leisure, simply made all sail to leave the scene of battle, with the helpless English craft caught up alongside. They would certainly have accomplished their design had it not been for the

[1] Froissart.

matchless gallantry of a body-servant of Sir Robert de Namur, called Hannekin. A man of giant strength and amazing agility, with one sweep of his blade he "cut the rope that held the sail, so that the ship slackened and had no force; and with this, by a great feat of his body, he cut four principal ropes that governed the mast and sail, insomuch that the said sail fell down upon the ship, and stayed the ship quite, that she could go no further".[1] With half the defenders struggling to free themselves from the *trief's* clinging folds, the men from the *Salle du Roi* contrived to hack their way inboard, "with their swords naked in their hands, and sought out and attacked whom they found in her so that they were all slain and put overboard, and the ship was won".

While the fight was in progress both fleets perforce continued to sail before the prevailing wind, and so passed within sight of Winchelsea. There was tremendous excitement in the little harbour as on the bluffs beyond, with the multitude cheering wildly as ship after ship wearing the Spanish colours struck and surrendered. It was some small recompense for the grievous injury that Winchelsea had suffered in the past, and "the musk and amber of revenge" was savoured with noisy relish.

There is no gainsaying Froissart's dry comment, however, that the Spanish armament had "given the King of England and his people plenty to do". But a fleet smaller in size and less substantially armed had contrived, for small loss, to capture a number of enemy vessels, sink several more, and put the remainder to flight. Although resembling nothing so much as the escalade of a number of detached fortresses, the action of *Espagnols-sur-mer* must be rated as a very considerable achievement. It was also the swan-song of Edward III as 'Sovereign of the English Sea'.

*   *   *

Despite trouble on the Scottish Border, the struggle with France continued on its desultory course; but with pilgrims setting out hopefully from Dover and students, under safe conduct, passing between Oxford and the Sorbonne; the fare across the Channel standing at the 'controlled' price of 2s. for every horseman and 6d. a head for every passenger travelling

[1] Froissart.

afoot. Although there were many complaints regarding the progressive decay of the country's maritime resources, there was no lack of foreign shipping coming into the home ports; in 1350 no less than 1,350 shiploads of wine left Bordeaux for delivery at English havens; to be paid for in currency that had depreciated from 256 pennies in the £ to 270. But trade, generally, was wilting badly under the prevailing penal system of taxation; and it was even considered advisable to remove the Staple from overseas and establish it in England; while Englishmen were no longer permitted to export goods, but had to sell them to foreigners for cash, thus keeping the money in the country. As always in times of shortage and financial strain, a 'black market' arose in many commodities; and to prevent 'forestalling' in the purchase of fish, a Statute of Herrings was enacted which decreed that none might be sold until the craft had been "made fast to the land". Even so, inflation had sent up the price of herring to 40s. a last of 10,000 fish.

With the Spring of 1356, however, while the King departed on a wasteful and abortive expedition into Scotland, tremendous effort went to the assembly of a fleet to transport a great army under the Black Prince for yet another attempt to inflict final defeat on France. It was a fleet that now fell under the jurisdiction of a Lord High Admiral, to which exalted post Sir John de Beauchamp was the first man to be appointed.

It was to Sandwich that the Heir to the Throne returned in triumph, with King John, Philip the Hardy, James of Bourbon, and many other distinguished Gallic captives in his train. But the military victory of Poictiers—won by an army almost prostrated by dysentery—only served to emphasise the fact that although humiliating defeats could be inflicted on the French, it was impossible to conquer them to the extent of occupying their country and exercising the powers of government. What might have been within the nation's power in the days of Richard Lionheart was no longer feasible at the turn of the fourteenth century. All that emerged from this particular attempt was the thoroughly unsatisfactory Treaty of Calais.[1]

Treaties, even when honestly concerted, are worth no more

[1] More commonly known, from its preliminaries, as the Treaty of Brétigny.

than their own consequences: and the outcome of the Calais pact was unwearying Gallic evasion of its obligations.

Its rupture, however, and the military activities which ensued, only served to demonstrate the extremity of exhaustion to which Edward's resources had been reduced. Once again the Channel coasts lived in such terror of hostile raids that the humiliating order was given for vessels to be drawn up high on shore at a considerable distance from the water, to "spare them from the French".

Edward's removal of the Staple to Calais, as a check to wool smuggling and an encouragement to merchants to freight their cargoes in English bottoms, would have had more beneficial results had the narrow seas not been given over to incessant guerrilla warfare, which kept the waterway and its adjacent coasts in perpetual ferment. With Edward himself thrashing about France in an attempt to avenge the virtual repudiation of the Calais pact, one hundred and twenty sail, under the Count of St. Pol, brought fire and sword to Rye, Hastings and Winchelsea, "spoiled the towns, slew the people, and did much harm to the poor fishers".[1] By way of reprisal, "an expedition scoured the sea from Boulogne to Harfleur, and wasted all that part of Normandy lying between the Seine and the Bresle".[2]

As Edward's painfully erected Continental alliance fell apart, the new coalition between Charles V of France and Henrique II of Castile and Leon endowed their combined fleets with virtual command of the Bay of Biscay and of the narrow seas. Edward's shipmen could still deal out sharp punishment to a band of upstart Flemish adventurers who had sought to lay a trap for them; but the Earl of Pembroke's major expedition for the relief of Rochelle met with so crushing a defeat that the subsequent loss of thirty-nine merchant vessels to the Spaniards seemed a trifle by comparison. The best that could be pleaded in extenuation of the Rochelle fiasco was that for the first time the English encountered naval gunfire, the Castilian vessels being armed with cannon which, however uncertain in their action, contrived to work a deal of mischief and, in addition, gravely demoralised those to whom their intimidating bark and whistling missiles came as a stunning novelty.

Infuriated by these humiliating reverses, as by the perpetual

[1] Barnes, *op. cit.*   [2] Fabyan's *Chronicles*.

chevauchées descending on his coastal havens, the King bent all his dwindling energies to the task of organising a powerful force for the succour of beleaguered Thaours, under pledge to surrender if not relieved by Michaelmas. It was then that the treacherous weather conditions in the Channel took a hand in affairs that was to prove decisive. Setting out from Sandwich on August 30th, for five weary weeks the unhappy King with his 400 sail sought to beat his way down Channel. But uniformly unfavourable winds persistently headed him back to his point of departure; and with its time limit overshot the enterprise had perforce to be abandoned.

With his proud pretensions crumbled in ruin all about him, and with his last days saddened by the death of the heir on whom his fond hopes had been fixed, only the splendid memories of Sluys and Creçy and *Espagnols-sur-mer* remained to console the man whose claim to be 'Sovereign of the English Sea' was mocked, in the very year of his death, by venomous enemy raids on Gravesend, Yarmouth, Lewes, Hastings, Folkestone, Rye, Portsmouth, Dartmouth, Plymouth, and the oft-assaulted Isle of Wight. Only Sandwich contrived to beat off the swarm of Frenchmen that sailed in to try and carry it as in days of yore.[1]

Throughout the course of his reign Edward had done much to foster English trade; although the expenses of his interminable war with the French had almost bled it white; while his shortsightedness in 'arresting' shipping long before it was wanted not only cost the owners dear in day-to-day charges they were unable to recoup, but witheld the vessels from participation in the regular cycle of trade. Nonetheless, merchant-strangers conducted their business under the safeguards of the Statute of the Staple; the expatriate Flemish weavers enjoyed the Crown's especial favour and protection, while the quality of English wares was guaranteed when the Staple for exports was brought under direct gubernatorial control. Only in the narrow seas had the King failed to provide his commerce with consistent safe-conduct, since he was content to employ sea-power to brush aside opposition to the transhipment of troops. It was Edward's salient defect that he saw 'his' Channel as little more than an ante-chamber to the battlefields of France.

[1] Lambart, Walsingham, Holinshed.

CHAPTER VII

Waters of Conflict

"St. George he was for England,
St. Denis was for France;
Sing *Honi Soit Qui Mal y Pense!*"
Black Letter Ballade,
London 1512

I T was an unenviable heritage that was handed on to the Black
Prince's ten-year-old son, Richard of Bordeaux. For he came
to the throne—as Richard II—when the direction of affairs
was divided between Edward's self-centred son, John of Gaunt,
and a corrupt clique of office-seekers who had been manœuvred
into power by the late King's mistress, Alice Perrers. Furthermore, the Exchequer had been so drained that, with the
country lying under the menace of an Hispano-Gallic invasion,
it could do no more than stand weakly on the defensive. Since,
once more, there was no adequate fleet to patrol the narrow
seas, marauders could harry the Channel ports with little fear
of hindrance. With Rottingdean and Lewes hard put to it to
hold their own, Rye and Hastings blazing as fiercely as the
ineffectual warning beacons strung along the coast, Winchelsea
twice threatened and the Isle of Wight ruthlessly plundered,
only Dover and Southampton contrived to keep the raiders at
bay. Plymouth's recovery from its many and grievous injuries
had been so remarkable that with a population of over 7,000—
the fourth largest in the kingdom—it might well have been
thought too strong to assail. But the lure of the riches amassed
by its successful commerce in tin and wool proved irresistible,
and it was twice heavily assaulted by a force of Bretons; descendants of those refugees who had fled from Sandwich in the days
of Hengist and Horsa—men as daring and skilled in seamanship
as the consanguineous seafarers on whom they preyed. On the
second occasion the raiders surprised the defence, scaled the

Castle and succeeded in battering down the Old Town gate before yielding to the onslaught of a swarm of infuriated towns-folk, rallied to the fight by a descendant of stout old Hugh de Courtenaye, who had saved the day in 1339. Fowey and Poole were not so fortunate, however, and suffered bitterly from forays they were unable to repel. Not even the Thames tide-water area was immune from hostile attention. In 1380 four French galleys, having again brought fire and sword to the South Coast, boldly penetrated London's river as far as Gravesend, plundering and burning many houses in the township and carrying off their captives and booty without a hand being raised to stay them.

Attempts to counter-raid were naturally not wanting. Sir Hugh Calverley led a successful thrust round Bayonne; while a London merchant, John Philpott, wearying of the procrastina-tion and delay attendant on John of Gaunt's assumption of command at sea, fitted out a fleet at his own expense, with which—to the Government's pettish indignation—he captured a pirate who had long been preying on Channel shipping. When John of Gaunt at last ventured forth, he accomplished nothing. Reinforcements under Sir John Arundel, sent to his aid in 1379, fell victim to just such a storm as had scattered the fleet detailed to harry the Spaniards at Sluys. And this despite the fact that Arundel callously 'lightened the load' by casting overboard some sixty women—including girls of barely nubile age—acquired by violating a nunnery on the eve of sailing.[1]

The depths of humiliation were reached in 1382, when Anne of Bohemia, on her way to England to wed its youthful Sove-reign, was delayed for a solid month in fear of a privateer squadron cruising the narrow seas to intercept her. For there was no naval force at the King's command to scour it off the face of the waters. It was, indeed, only by favour of a safe conduct given her by the French Council that England's Queen-designate was able to complete her passage. Yet tunnage and poundage were still exacted ostensibly for the maintenance of ships "to keep the English Sea"!

It was only when the Governor of Calais and the men of the Cinque Ports combined to take action that success against the enemy was temporarily achieved. Acting in concert and based in the complementary strongholds of Calais and Dover, in one

[1] *Historia Anglicana*, Vol. I, Walsingham.

year the combined fleets took 800 Gallic vessels of varying size. One ship belonging to Clisson, the Constable of France, was valued at 3,000 francs; another, with her holds packed with valuable cargo, at 20,000.

The Frenchmen's immediate *riposte* was to raid and plunder Stonor, which was put to the torch despite the gallant efforts of the Abbot of St. Augustine's Priory, Canterbury, who marched to meet the invaders in full panoply of battle. One consequence of this bloodthirsty foray was a tax of 3*d.* on every boatload of fish caught by the men of Kent and Sussex, to restore the battered fortifications of Rye; where a special watch was always stationed in the Ypres Tower to give warning of an impending assault across the narrow seas by tolling the great bell that hung in Watchbell Street. At the first alarm the defenders hastened to prepare a device they termed the *machicoulis*, heating up the molten lead and boiling oil, and preparing the flaming tow and powdered quicklime, which they would pour down through holes in the Ypres Tower's first storey floor-boards on any assailants hardy enough to attempt the strongpoint's capture.

In essence, Richard's earlier years witnessed Aquitaine's steady shrinkage and England's sullen acceptance of the fact that, almost at will, the French could invade a homeland hopelessly divided by asp-like theological wrangling and the bitter feuds begot of faction.

Yet for all the restriction on enterprise brought about by the ban on the removal of coin and bullion out of the country, and despite the sea-wolves swarming off every coast, trade contrived to flourish to a remarkable degree. The retention of Calais and its continued use as the home of the Wool Staple was found to be well worth the heavy cost of its garrisoning and upkeep, which averaged £20,000 a year. The value of the outpost was further enhanced when the King introduced a revolutionary Navigation Act,[1] which for the first time ensured that native wool and wool-fells crossed the Channel *exclusively* in English ships, manned by predominantly English crews. Direct trade was also opened up with Scandinavia and the Baltic, hitherto a market preserved to the merchants of the Hansa.

Richard's Navigation Act was the first of a series of enactments whose repercussions were markedly to affect the course

[1] 5 Rich. II, Stat. V., Cap. 3.

of events on both shores of the narrow seas for the ensuing two and three-quarter centuries. In design it was an unequivocal measure of 'protection', aimed at the substitution of a native monopoly in the carrying-trade for that hitherto enjoyed by alien ship-owners. But the 'permissive amendments' introduced a year or two later went far to stultify its efficacy. The trouble was that under Richard's haphazard regime there were not enough English bottoms to carry the freight in transit; so permission had to be given to employ foreign craft where no native vessels were available.

Taxation remained inordinately high; and to encourage home sales foreign merchants were required to give security to the Customs that at least half their gains would be expended on English commodities—which must have added considerably to the labours of good Master Geoffrey Chaucer, Controller of Petty and Aliens' Customs in the Port of London.

As the inevitable counterpoint to fiscal extortion there arose a remarkably brisk trade in contraband; mostly Hampshire, Isle of Wight, Devonshire and Cornish wool, which was smuggled over to the Staple at Middelburg. But the wool so insistently demanded by the weavers of Flanders and Brabant was not for the manufacture of finished cloth for return to England. In that commodity the country was now not only comfortably self-supporting, but had become a burgeoning rival to the Low Countries as an exporter of expertly-finished fabrics. It is true that this satisfactory advance had largely to be attributed to the skilled work of the expatriate weavers and fullers from Flanders and Brabant; a fact which signally failed to enhance their popularity with their fellow workers of English birth. Indeed, there was considerable ill-feeling between the native and immigrant weavers, the former foolishly refusing to learn the finer points of their trade from men whom they resented not only as master-craftsmen, but as individuals who set a standard of slogging hard work which—since they were required to emulate it—they resented with all the outraged indignation of the fundamentally indolent.

Yet in technical superiority, as in numbers, these expatriate craftsmen, banded together in their own craft-guild, wielded such potent influence that it was deemed expedient to set aside the churchyard of St Lawrence Pulteney for the deliberations of the Flemings, while the men of Brabant were allotted that of St. Mary Somerset.

Wool was king; with Blackwell—originally Bakewell—Hall, with its weekly market, the thriving centre where the country clothiers came to dispose of their wares; and where the Merchant-Adventurers, who exported made-up cloths, carried considerably more weight than their close rivals, the Merchants of the Staple, who dealt solely in the raw material. Officialdom was represented by the aulnagers, who kept a sharp eye lifted to ensure that no "disorderly and deceitful bargains against the franchise and liberties of the city" were surreptitiously concluded—such as the sale of cloth by aliens either in retail or to non-burgesses. 'Monopoly' was a practice it had not taken the weavers and wool-merchants long to assimilate. But whatever its menace for the future, if and when the 'seller's market' came to an end, there is no gainsaying that at the moment it paid the individual right handsomely. As one wealthy wool-merchant engraved on the lintels of his new house:

> *I praise God and ever shall*
> *It is the sheep hath paid for all.*

The standard of living had unquestionably risen; but wealth as a means to an end was in increasing danger of becoming wealth as an end in itself; and with that trend went the tendency for industry to harden into mercantilism.

In the prevailing circumstances, however, it is scarcely surprising that Richard, in a feverish search for loans, should prefer to approach his own wealthy wool merchants rather than the Bardi and the Lombards, or even the Church, which was only willing to part with money in return for an enlargement of its temporal powers.

But with commerce flourishing, there were constant grumbles at the rate of hire for ships 'arrested' for the King's service. For this had arbitrarily been reduced from 3s. 4d. a 'ton-tight' to a mere 2s. Equally, resentment was universal at the continued exaction of ship-geld—at 6d. a ton on cargo, 6d. a month on the infrequent collier, 6d. a week on herring boats, and 2d. for other fishing vessels—without commensurate official protection. Men such as the enterprising John Philpott added some of the new-fangled cannon to their ships' armament—somewhat elementary weapons designed rather as man-killers than ship-killers—and thus ensured that their own maritime commerce should be well equipped to protect itself. Philpott even contrived to carry the war to the enemy, capturing the fleet of a certain John Mercer, a Scot openly in trade with France and therefore fair game. If the London merchant's social betters—the great City magnates and their friends at Court—were filled with jealous envy at this successful *coup*, the humbler folk among the small shopkeepers and guild craftsmen were delighted, and at the next municipal election they manifested their approval of worthy Master Philpott by electing him their Lord Mayor.[1]

Guns—hand-guns and small cannon—which may have appeared on the field of Crecy,[2] constituted a new feature in naval armament, but they were certainly in use by 1372, possibly so early as 1338. A list of stores for the *Christopher of the Tower*,[3] made out in the June of that year, included three iron cannon, five chambers (breech blocks), and a hand-gun.

Yet commendable as were the activities of men such as Philpott, personal enterprise in the form of a private fleet can never furnish a satisfactory substitute for a national fighting marine, directed by a central administration. But as things stood, while Parliament could expand or reduce the sources of taxation, it exercised virtually no control over the way in which the money raised by taxation was spent. The tendency arose, therefore, to restrict the flow of funds which, although raised ostensibly for the purpose of national defence, were destined to be frittered away in private extravagance. The corollary of this procedure was an unreadiness for war *at its outset* which was, unhappily, to become traditional.

* * *

With Charles VI building up a strong fighting marine, based on the excellent new dockyard at Rouen, fear of Gallic invasion, in combination with a fresh stroke by the Scots, gained new

[1] The prefix 'Lord' and the style of 'Right Honourable' had been granted by Edward III in 1354.

[2] Nowhere is this controversial point examined with greater authority than in *The Crecy War* by Lieutenant-Colonel Alfred H. Burne, D.S.O.

[3] The suffix 'of the Tower' had virtually the same meaning as the present-day prefix 'H.M.S.'.

intensity. The situation was not improved by the absence of many ships and a large army under John of Gaunt, grimly intent upon substantiating by force of arms a distinctly shadowy claim on the throne of Castile, based on his marriage to the daughter of Pedro the Cruel. With 1,200 enemy vessels mustering between Rouen and Sluys, the Earl of Arundel sallied forth at the head of a well-ordered fleet to offer battle. In the lengthy running fight that ensued no less than 126 enemy craft were either sunk or captured, though not without serious loss to the English forces.

When Arundel's booty-laden armament returned to the Thames, it was received with great joy on account of the quantity of superior wines it brought with it, which were quickly sold off at 4d. a gallon. Amongst other captures was "a wooden wall 20 feet high, 3,000 paces long, and with towers to hold ten men every 12 feet". This curiosity was acquired by Sandwich and promptly incorporated in its defences, to the infinite chagrin of Oliver de Clisson. For it had been to his order that the contraption had been constructed, in sections, at Treguier in Brittany, as a portable fort in which 'the Butcher' and his comrades could sleep safe and sound at night—once they had succeeded in landing on English soil.

It was not until Richard assumed full regal authority in 1389 that the atmosphere of tension lightened. By personal negotiation the King secured an interval of peace and quiet which lasted until 1397. But the widowed Sovereign's design to consolidate the truce by contracting a marriage of state with the infant Isabella of France aroused an immediate clamour of opposition. Yet the 'war party' was as empty of resource as it was big with words. For it was useless any longer to rely on the Cinque Ports as the prime source of auxiliary naval strength. Their power had declined as much through the deterioration of their harbours as by the injuries inflicted on them by the French. Hythe, for example, had been so ruined by pestilence, enemy raids, and the silting of its haven that it took regal intervention to prevent its total abandonment. In any case, the increasing size of deep-water craft rendered the harbour facilities of the Ports progressively more inadequate, irrespective of the effects wrought by the implacable easterly drift; while Portsmouth, Southampton and the westerly havens were in no position as yet to make good the lacuna thus created in the dispositions for defence.

It was an odd moment to appoint Edward of York to the new and honorific post of Admiral of England![1]

The King's feckless extravagance and perpetual demands for money—such as the additional tax of 2s. on a tun of wine and 6d. a pound on woollen cloth, imposed for the upkeep of a virtually non-existent fighting marine—had already alienated popular sympathy. Then, hard on the death of John of Gaunt in 1399, he committed the incredible folly of seizing the Lancastrian domains that should have passed to the temporarily banished Henry of Derby and Hereford. By contemporary standards it was a bold, piratical stroke that would have been understood and condoned if perpetrated by a man of granite ruthlessness and determination. But Richard's parade of strength amounted to little more than a petulant outburst of hysteria; and in challenging the scion of the House of Lancaster he was signing his own death warrant.

With nothing afloat on the narrow seas to oppose his passage, Henry hurried back to England, and from the outset experienced little difficulty in arousing almost universal support for his cause. With Richard a helpless captive whose only hope was abdication, Henry's formal claim to the throne was endorsed with boisterous acclamation.

From the very outset Richard's unhappy reign had been bedevilled by threats from without, "made sick with civil blows", rent with faction and torn by the envenomed bickering of ecclesiastics. His obscure end was as mysterious as his life had been heavy with folly and frustration.

*   *   *

Henry IV could advance the claim that he assumed the Crown by right of conquest and by popular election as the nation's nominee. But his pressing need to consolidate his titubant position on the Throne left him little time to devote to external affairs. It is true that for the moment France and England were not officially at war. None the less English and

---

[1] John de Beauchamp, brother of the Earl of Warwick, had been appointed to what was virtually the same post in 1360, but without the honorific title.

Gallic shipmen continued to attack each other at every opportunity. Quite obviously it behoved the King to improvise
some sort of fleet to police the narrow seas. But without proper
monetary resources and in fear of jeopardising his shallow
popularity by clapping on the necessary taxes, he resorted to a
score of humiliating expedients to scratch together an armament which in the long run not only proved quite inadequate
for its responsibilities, but did much, by the revelation of its
impotence, to alienate the sympathies of that rich merchant
class to which the new incumbent looked both for moral and
financial support. In the event, the long-familiar interchange of
raid and counter raid continued almost without intermission;
a state of affairs by no means bettered by Henry's preoccupation with military ventures in Scotland and Wales.

"The English pirates", as the Monk of St. Denys bluntly
termed them, "discontented with the truce and unwilling to
abandon their profitable pursuits, determined to infest the seas
and attack merchant ships. Three thousand of the most skilful
sailors of England and Bayonne had confederated for that
purpose . . . and incessantly harassed the French coast." They
ravaged the isle of Rhé with fire and sword, burnt a famous
abbey, exacted heavy ransom to spare the neighbouring township, and carried as prisoners to Thanet a hundred fishermen
of Picardy; which, the Monk adds mournfully, "made fish
extremely dear during Advent and Lent".

The English sustained heavy defeat off Brittany, however,
when they were intercepted on their way home from a
raid by a strong force out of Chastel Pol, near Morlaix,
under the command of Sir John de Penhoet, Admiral of
Brittany, his father, the Sire de Penhoet, and Sir William de
Chatel.

So the struggle swayed to and fro, with varying fortune for
either side. When Waleran Count de St. Pol, at the head of a
thousand men, landed to pillage the Isle of Wight on the eve of
Christmas, "a sensible priest of the island came to the Count to
treat for the ransom and security of the island, for which he
gave the Count to understand a very large sum of money
would be paid to him and his captains. He too readily listened
to this proposal; for it was a deception on the part of the priest
to delay their operations, and amuse them with words until the

English should arrive to fight with them".[1] The ruse succeeded, for the islanders, having won time to rally, gave so spirited an account of themselves that the raiders were beaten into retreat, having acquired more punishment than booty. When the Island was raided again the year following, the natives were so sure of themselves that they actually invited the enemy to land, and promised them six hours in which to rest and refresh themselves before they set about them. At Dartmouth the women fought at the side of their men with an inspired fury against which nothing could prevail.

Headed by the Admiral of England, Thomas of Lancaster— still in his 'teens—a strictly unofficial expedition raided Sluys, and survived a subsequent encounter in the open sea in sufficient strength to land and burn La Hogue, Harfleur, and thirty-eight towns, some of them thirty miles inland. So the long tale of cross-Channel forays continued, with profit and loss about evenly balanced. For if the French gained spoil worth £100,000, the sum of English loot can scarcely have been smaller. But it was obvious that had the vessels allocated to these raids been concentrated for an organised defensive-offensive, much injury to the coastal towns would have been prevented—but at the sacrifice of many opportunities for profitable pillage. And for the chance of swiftly-won fortune many a man was prepared to risk returning home to find his habitation a heap of smouldering ruins.

Among the most successful freebooters plying the narrow seas were Henry Spicer of Portsmouth and the even more notorious Harry Paye (or Page) of Poole. So indiscriminate was their industry, indeed, that they were summoned before the Council for having made a good deal too free with the craft of certain friendly Powers. But after the singular fashion of the contemporary judicature, the charge was not pressed; and within a few months Paye was chaperoning a handsome Brittany ship into Portsmouth, having also taken under his wing, off the Isle of Wight, a Spanish vessel laden with a particularly valuable cargo.

Throughout the whole period strife between the English shipmen and the crews of the Hansa vessels fell little short of organised warfare; and it is clear that the latter were deliberately

[1] *Chronicles of England, France and Spain*, Book I, Monstrelet.

egged on by the Hansa merchants themselves. For the Easter-
ling magnates, like those of Genoa, were resentfully alarmed at
the steady enlargement of English commerce, despite the many
handicaps under which it laboured, and were determined to
take action to embarrass it. Vessels and cargoes to the value of
£24,000 were impudently seized by the Genoans in their own
harbour, a *fait accompli* to which the English ship-owners retorted by taking out Letters of Marque for a like sum, plus
£10,000 damages. In effect, a handful of English merchants
cheerfully embarked on a private war with the whole of the
Republic of Genoa; nor did they rest content until they had
recouped their losses—and a little over for good measure! As
for the tussle between the English and Hansa shipmen, it is
patent that the former had by far the better of it. For when the
authorities stepped in to impose a temporary composition of
differences, the sum paid to the Flemings by way of compensation came to 32,326 nobles, as against a contra-account of 766!

Small wonder that the Bordeaux wine fleet voyaged in close
convoy; that the 'subsidy' on such wool as the Customers
could contrive to check rose to 50s. for denizens and 60s. for
aliens. For wool smuggling continued almost without diminution, despite the decree that all merchant vessels should discharge their cargoes at recognised ports, eschewing the quiet
creeks where no official eye could be kept on them. Irrespective
of the rule that all Customs' officials must henceforth be of
native birth and possessed of some knowledge of the locality
in which they were stationed, they were as helpless to deal with
the determined contrabandist as was the King to safeguard the
incoming vessels of the wealthy Venetian importers—from
whom he fondly hoped to raise a loan. For the increasing power
of Parliament to withold or deny finance had the effect of
sending the Sovereign cap in hand to any source wherefrom he
could hope to wheedle a sum of money without reference to the
Lords and Commons. Not that the London exporters were in
any better case than the merchant-strangers. Protests were loud
and long from the Merchant-Adventurers, who, in desperation,
revived the proposal for a contract fleet, to be maintained out of
the payments for tunnage and poundage, to 'keep the sea' from
May 1st to September 29th, the period which saw the greatest
flow of traffic through the Channel.

With a gap between public expenditure and his means of meeting it of approximately £76,000—a gap which Parliament evinced no readiness to fill—the King had no option but to hand over to private enterprise one of the first things that should always remain a public responsibility. It was characteristic of this substitute armament, incidentally, that prominent among its captains was "that whoreson mad fellow" the ubiquitous Harry Paye of Poole; like the Henry Morgan of later days, a remarkable example of the poacher turned gamekeeper. But the "guard of the sea" by the contract fleet having proved no more efficacious than that maintained by Henry's improvised armaments, "the duty was resumed by the King, who ought not to have delegated it to other hands", as Nicolas so rightly comments.

In the prevailing circumstances, remarkable commonsense characterised the agreement reached by the masters and mariners living between Southampton and Thanet and those dwelling on the French shore from Harfleur to 'Hardrenesce', whereby a fixed tariff governed the ransom of *rectors* and shipmen, and the terms of their weekly board while prisoners. Fishing boats, whatever their size, were redeemable at 3s. 4d., while all matters of dispute were settled by arbitration. But the compact did not apply to merchant craft, which continued to ·ply the seas at their constant peril.

The ailing Sovereign's last attempt to "busy giddy minds with foreign quarrels" sent an expeditionary force to assist the warring Dukes of Berry, Orléans and Bourbon; who agreed, in return, to deliver up the Duchy of Guienne "as loyal vassals and lieges ought". But the enterprise to regain lordship over the whole of Aquitaine was one whose inglorious outcome Henry was not to witness. For on March 20th, 1413, this unhappy, haunted, distrustful, and distrusted man resignedly breathed his last.

*   *   *

Henry V leaps from Shakespeare's heroic pages as the *beau ideal* of the chivalrous Warrior-King. Unquestionably, the rackety Prince Hal had matured into a man whose soldierly austerity almost bordered on the self-righteous. With a flair for diplomacy as marked as his aptitude for war, it is only in his failure to grasp the need to achieve permanent dominance of the narrow seas that his appreciation of the situation which confronted him can seriously be faulted.

Unaffected by the Dauphin's mocking gift of a basketful of tennis balls, Henry was coolly determined to press his claim to the Throne of France either by negotiation—with the bargain sealed by marriage to Katherine of Valois or Katherine of Burgundy, it mattered little which—or by force, should the French resort, as so often before, to trickery and time-wasting evasion.

Negotiation having proved abortive, the King turned to the ships a-building at Deptford and Smallhythe, and on the Hamble. In the Hampshire yards the master-shipwright and ex-Collector of Customs, William Soper of Southampton, was putting the finishing touches to the 400-ton *Gabriel*, the 540 *Trinity Royal*, and the 760 *Holigost*, mounting six cannon manu- factured by the foundries of Sussex and the Weald of Kent,[1] and costing in all £496. The balance of the thirty-eight royal vessels was headed by William Catton's splendid *Grâce Dieu*. Though not so big as the Mediterranean caracks, these English ships, fitted with a 'bilakyll' and proper pumps, were staunch and handy craft, even if rarely employed as more than armed transports. Moreover, their crews were based on a hard core of experienced shipmen, retained on a yearly wage running from £3 6s. 8d. to £6 13s. 4d.; the Navy's first 'Standing Officers'.

Another step in the right direction was the election by the masters and men of the Bordeaux wine fleet of one of the former to act as commodore of the convoy on the homeward voyage. In the event, although all hands had taken oath to "remain by" their leader, when his ship was attacked by pirates, she was basely deserted by her companions. But the original idea was sound, and subsequently proved effective.

Since Henry's primary objective was the reclamation of the ancient fief of Normandy, Southampton—"the best port in the royaume"—was nominated as the concentration area for the store ships; the new South or Watergate quay being fitted with

---

[1] Williams, a brazier of Aldgate, was casting guns of latten (a brass mixture) and copper before 1353, and by 1411 English cannon had become articles of export; although the shipment of gunpowder abroad was for- bidden. The first casting of *iron* cannon was at Banstead, in the Weald of Kent, in 1543.

an elementary crane for hoisting-in stores. Not that Portsmouth was neglected, additional fortifications being put in hand which ultimately cost over £3,500; while the Porchester basin was nominated as the rendezvous for the ships of war.

To supplement the royal vessels Henry had perforce once more to fall back on the traditional 'arrest' of merchant shipping; to be recompensed at the old rate of 3s. 4d. a quarter per 'ton-tight'; a payment, however, which was far too often permitted to fall into arrear; as was that of the 'bounty' for the masters with which the King had sought to sugar the pill of impressment. In any case 'arrest' was a method of augmentation which militated with increasing severity against the normal flow of trade, and thus struck at the very sinews of war on which the King relied for the prosecution of his enterprise. With the provisions of *Carta Mercatoria* in full operation and trade with Holland steadily developing, with the Venetian traffic a steady source of fiscal revenue, and with English merchandise penetrating to Lisbon and, despite the jealous hindrances put in its way, even into the Mediterranean, had commerce been unhindered the Customs' yield—the 'subsidy' from which provided the bulk of the King's income—would soon have passed the £40,000 it averaged.[1] For even the grave differences with the Easterlings had been composed, after a turbulent period in which the Flemings had carried things with a remarkably high hand, demanding especial privileges in England to offset the effects of the Navigation Act, while refusing reciprocal treatment for the English merchants domiciled in Flanders or any of the two hundred 'free cities' of Germany. Matters were adjusted with the decree that all importers of merchandise, denizens or merchant-strangers, should invest the whole proceeds from the sale of their cargoes in English wares, reserving only sufficient cash in hand for their necessary expenses. By such means a degree of equilibrium was attained; and if there was no real feeling of stability, its absence can be attributed to the lack of anything comparable to the Roman *ius gentium* or common law of contract, of universal application.

It can scarcely be in question, however, that the main handicap to the free flow of trade was the continued 'arrest' of

[1] *The King's Customs*, Henry Atton and Henry Hurst Holland.

shipping for the purposes of war, which swept in craft even of 20-tons' burden. Since they were so commodious, it even interfered with the passage of the thirty-two ships a year engaged in transporting pilgrims from Dover to Corunna, the nearest port to the favoured shrine of St. James of Compostella. This was a serious matter for the Dover authorities, who enjoyed a monopoly in the pilgrim traffic; none of the devout being permitted —unless specially licensed—to sail from any other haven, under penalty of a year's imprisonment.

As a check on the menace of trade embodied in the freebooter, Harry of Monmouth not only decreed that the pirating of friendly neutrals should be penalised as high treason, but appointed a number of Conservators of Truces with plenary powers of enquiry and punishment with regard to all illegal acts at sea. At the same time care was taken to ensure that Letters of Marque were issued only to shipmen of reasonable probity and standing.

Aided by the 43s. 4d. 'subsidy' granted him on wool, in addition to the usual tenth and fifteenth, and some timely help from the City of London and the Counties, the King was able to concentrate some 1,400 vessels of varying size; some having been hired from Holland and Zeeland. Having observed that the Castilian and Genoan vessels consistently outmatched his in size, he was careful to include some heavy dromons of impressive proportions "such as were never seen in the world before"[1]; and somewhat unwieldy they proved. The King's design was to establish a bridgehead in depth at the mouth of the Seine; a secure base from which to launch the operations which would seat him on the throne of France.

Having brought forward and embarked the stores accumulated in the huge dumps at Windsor and London, on Saturday, August 10th, the King gave orders for the sail-yard of the *Trinity Royal* to be hoisted to the middle of the mast as a signal for the armament assembled in the lee of Porchester Castle to put to sea.

With her mast-head adorned by the lion of England and a gilded crown and sceptre, and with the royal banner fluttering above twin streamers bearing the emblems of the Trinity and Our Lady, and half a dozen gitons gleaming with the badges of

---

[1] *Fragment and Lybell of English Policy*, Hakluyt, V.

chivalry, the King's ship led the way. As squadron after squadron fell into line a roar of cheering went up from the nine thousand men-at-arms, bowmen, armourers, artillators, bowyers, fletchers, farriers and assorted 'rude mechanicals', swarming on the crowded decks, that fairly drowned out the gay music of the 'pypes, trompes, nakers and clarionnes' played by the musicians in the bows.

As the glittering, bright-hued flotillas passed the Isle of Wight, swans seen swimming in the midst of the fleet were hailed as a happy augury. Then with the whole air bright with the multi-coloured blazonry whipping in the breeze, the huge armada plunged purposefully on towards the enemy shore. Far to the rear the four 'great ships' and their attendant barges and ballingers took up their task of guarding the army's lines of communication.

Henry made his landfall at Kidecaus, three miles from Harfleur; and with the troops safely ashore siege operations were promptly put in train. Almost immediately there was a violent outbreak of dysentery, which laid low the Earls of March and Suffolk and swept off Michael de la Pole, Bishop Courtenay, eight knights, and close on 2,000 of the rank and file; the surviving sick making their miserable way back to Southampton.

The surrender of the fortress on September 18th was the prelude to the overwhelming victory gained on the rain-sodden sward of Agincourt, which left the English Monarch master of the field. On the morrow of Agincourt the English column, herding 2,000 prisoners in its midst, set out to complete the forty-five miles to Calais. It took four days' march to reach the stronghold, so heavily had the exhausted men laden themselves with the booty that victory had brought them. Within the walls, instead of the townsmen exhibiting that instinctive charity and hospitality so characteristic of medieval days, fearing for their food supplies they abruptly turned the sick and weary men away from their doors. Only those prepared to part with a moiety of their valuable loot could be assured of grudging shelter and a minimum of victuals. It was an unworthy addendum to one of the greatest military triumphs of the age.

The habit of mind which persuaded Henry to regard his marine primarily as an armed transport service rather than as a fighting force, had omitted to take any real steps to retain dominion of the Channel save in the narrow gut between Calais and the Downs. As a result a strong enemy armament under Robert de Braquemont was free to make its appearance off Harfleur, intent on blockading the garrison; while another powerful squadron roamed *La Manche* "where none dared oppose them"[1]. Southampton was threatened and, despite valiant work on the part of the women slingers for which it was famous, Portland was roughly handled ere the Duke of Bedford could muster sufficient craft to sally forth and challenge the intruders.

As it fell out, contrary winds dispersed the rival fleets before they could get to grips. It was not, indeed, until the August of 1416 that the Earl of Huntingdon took an armament to sea which, after a swift passage, dropped anchor in the mouth of the Seine estuary. The French fleet, strengthened by a number of powerful Genoese carracks, was found to be at its moorings further inshore. The Gallic vessels were massed but in no definite formation, and upon this huddle of shipping the English craft bore down impetuously, aided by a strong following wind. What followed was in the nature of a scrambling, inchoate *mêlée*; and after a severe hand-to-hand encounter lasting over seven hours the assailants put to flight all of the Gallic squadron that had not been sunk or captured. The largest of the enemy carracks, the *Mountnegrie*, in her eagerness to escape, struck a sandbank off Harfleur and foundered; and for days the corpses of the slain were to be seen floating on the sea "as if they were seeking for other burial than that of the fishes".[2]

With Harfleur once more safely linked with England, Henry was free to pursue his unrelenting campaign against the Dauphinists. His sinews of war included a loan of £17,000 somewhat reluctantly forthcoming from the immensely wealthy Bishop Beaufort, and secured on the Customs at Southampton, and the involuntary gift of six wing feathers from every goose throughout the land—save breeders—to flight arrow shafts.

The King's success in battle, leading to the Treaty of Troyes, brought a breathing space—and a wife for Henry in the enchanting Katherine of Valois. But hostilities were presently resumed and they only came to a temporary halt when, with

[1] St. Remy.
[2] *Vita et Gesta Henrici Quinti Anglorum Regis*, Elmham.

the Whitsuntide of 1422, an obsequious throng saw the English King installed in the Louvre as Regent and Heir Presumptive to the Throne of France. In cold fact, he had arrived there some two hundred and thirty years too late.

In any case death had already scrawled its signature on Henry's handsome, wasted features. There was a severe outbreak of dysentery during the long siege of Meux, and Henry himself had started out for the relief of Cosne—on the Loire and under investment by the Dauphinists—so sick a man that he had been forced to hand over the command to Duke Philip of Burgundy. In the last day of August, 1422, this commanding warrior-King came to his untimely end in the castle of Bois de Vincennes.

Although few perceived it, the star of Lancaster was on the wane.

CHAPTER VIII

Roses Red and Roses White

"A plague o' both your houses."
WILLIAM SHAKESPEARE

WITH the death of Harry of Agincourt, the English leaders exhibited greater determination to quarrel amongst themselves than to administer the triangular wedge of territory—with the Somme basin and Brittany forming the base, and Paris the apex—which represented the fruits of the late King's success in arms. John Duke of Bedford did his best to settle and govern the domain; but at home the dangerous bickering between the rival supporters of the Royal Houses of York and Lancaster gave grim promise of the thirty years of internecine strife that were to come. During the whole of the boy-King Henry's minority the Regents, truculent, indeterminate and mutually distrustful, exercised a feeble direction of affairs that was the very antithesis of the wise, strong government of which the country stood so urgently in need. And this at a time when the mildly conciliatory Charles VI had been succeeded by that Dauphin (Charles VII) whose derisive present of tennis balls to Monmouth Harry had epitomised the enmity he nourished for everything that bore the stamp of England.

In the prevailing circumstances, it showed incredible lack of foresight for the Regents to seize the very first opportunity to rid themselves of the King's ships, so laboriously acquired by Henry V. In all, thirty-four vessels were disposed of by public auction; and such few craft as were left were laid up 'in ordinary', unrigged and with no care and maintenance parties to look after them. The parlous condition to which the country's naval defence was thus reduced is witnessed by the fact that the guardianship of the whole of the Hampshire coast was confided to 'the ballinger of Clifton', known as *The Jacket*, whose crew totalled a modest forty.

With the wholesale dispersal of the fleet all continuity of naval policy ceased; just at the moment when the increasing incidence of forays and skirmishers clearly presaged the resumption of full-scale military operations; activities from which it was glaringly apparent that England's shuffling ally, the Duke of Burgundy, would adroitly withdraw at the very first opportunity. Yet in 1425 Parliament had the effrontery to confirm the rate for tunnage and poundage at 3s. on the tun of wine and 1s. in the £ on merchandise, *not* for the support of its fighting marine, but for the upkeep of an army whose quality showed grave signs of deterioration. As a natural consequence piracy ran riot all up and down the Channel; Danish freebooters alone accounting for the loss of merchandise to the value of £20,000 in one year.

Despite the decree reaffirming that the abrogation of a safe conduct, or 'truce', would be punished as high treason—with Conservators of Safe Conducts appointed to every port to enforce the edict—attempts to clear the narrow seas of the corsairs infesting them far more closely resembled lawless 'reprisals' than punitive naval action. William Morfote, the Honourable Member for Winchelsea, for one, played the pirate in the Channel with all the ferocity of a Teach or an Avery. The rascally Abbot of St. Augustine's, Canterbury, at the head of a band of cut-throat wharf-rats, openly seized a harmless Brittany vessel off the Isle of Thanet and made away with craft, cargo and crew. Cornish freebooters from Fowey acquired an unenviable reputation for ruthlessness and rapacity, which outmatched even that of the Breton desperadoes with whom they were so often at loggerheads. Indeed, such was the lawlessness which characterised the narrow seas and their adjacent coasts that many of the local gentry, charged to aid in the suppression of piracy and wrecking, deliberately connived at their practice and were themselves industrious traffickers in stolen goods.

The best that the Regency could do to check this rampageous illegality was to resort to the old device of an indenture fleet to 'keep the sea' for a specified period—usually between February and mid-November. These squadrons were founded on a nucleus of the three or four royal ships still in commission, including the veteran *Nicholas of the Tower*. Service in this contract fleet was remunerated at the rate of 1s. 6d. a week pay and a further 6d. a day 'subsistence". For with most of the King's ships paid off, shipmen were more plentiful than jobs, with the natural consequence that wage-rates, in relation to the current cost of living, had fallen steadily.

Since the French Channel coast was still under English or allied control, the indenture vessels were free to devote all their attention to the suppression of the freebooters. But with twelve ships moving in company and manned by crews totalling 1,200, the temptation to plunder that which should have been protected was not always resisted; and many of the activities of this so-called guardian flotilla amounted to little more than piracy legalised by success.

It was the crew of the *Nicholas of the Tower*, violently Lancastrian in sympathy, who lawlessly seized the 'Yorkist' Duke of Suffolk, who had been impeached and was on his way to five years' banishment in Calais. Greeted with the sneer, "Welcome, traitor!", the unfortunate fugitive was subjected to an irregular trial and speedily found guilty of treason. Then, "the men of his own ship readily assenting", he was "drawn out of the great ship into the boat, and there was an axe, and a stock. One of the lewdest of the ship bade him lay down his head, 'and he should be fairly dealt with and die on a sword'; and took a rusty sword and smote off his head within half a dozen strokes; and took away his gown of russet, and his doublet of velvet mailed, and laid his body on the sands of Dover."[1]

Partisan feeling was rising, and another stage had been reached on the road towards the anarchy of civil war.

Yet in the teeth of mounting turmoil at home and constant menace at sea, the nation's trade fought hard to maintain the prosperity it had won. The wine fleets, now consisting of English vessels out of Bordeaux and Bayonne, if still made up of foreign bottoms out of the Levant, vied in prosperity with that Genoan and Venetian trade which enabled many of the wealthy alien merchants to maintain their country estates in the pleasant woodlands about Winchester. Some of these gentry, however, were a little too spry, and legislation had to be passed against 'forestallers', whose enterprising habit it was to ride around the remoter countryside buying up wool from the improvident at knock-out prices, for cash down; which was then profitably

[1] *The Paston Letters.*

disposed of at full market price. But law or no law, they experienced little difficulty in continuing their lucrative excursions; ready money spoke, as ever, with a remarkably persuasive tongue!

Yet with exports of leather carrying a tax of 100s. the last for denizens and 106s. for aliens, and wool exports bearing a 'subsidy' of 33s. 4d. and 53s. 4d., the country's commerce was weighed down with a heavy fiscal burden; and that at a time when there had been a noticeable drop in English wool sales at the Calais Staple. With a view to restoring the Staple's prosperity an Act was passed prohibiting the export of live sheep to Flanders, where they had been in great demand to improve the strain of the Flemish flocks. An exception was made in favour of supplies for the troops of the Calais garrison—to ship carcase meat to them seems to have occurred to no one—and this loophole, of course, afforded ample opportunity for the smuggling of a great number of live sheep to purchasers on the other side of the Channel, under the pretext of furnishing the soldiery with their necessities.

The evasion of their obligation to carry their goods to the Calais Staple and there pay the Customs due on them, practised so extensively by the merchants of Flanders, Holland and Brabant, also led to a serious drop in the national revenue. Nor were matters bettered by the alien merchants' demand that their imports should privily be settled for in gold, which they subsequently contrived to smuggle out of the country.

The allowance in coin of the realm permitted to pilgrims journeying to Compostella was no more than offset by the money spent in the country by the devout from overseas, who came to pay their pious homage at the Canterbury shrine of the beatified Thomas à Becket.

Experience had shown that the best Spanish wool mixed well with the English variety. Indeed, as de Moleyns had pointed out:

> It is of little value, trust unto me,
> With English wool but if mingled it be.[1]

Unfortunately, certain foxy English weavers had taken to mixing inferior—but cheaper—Spanish yarn with the native product; and while maintaining and even increasing their

[1] *Libelle of Englysche Polycye.*

prices, they were turning out indifferently satisfactory cloth. The inevitable consequence was a considerable falling off of trade, with a consequent loss of prestige in the vital foreign markets. This was doubly shortsighted since Flanders was becoming more of a central mart for the exchange of merchandise —on which that honest broker, the Fleming, drew his middleman's profit—than the home of manufactures.

This generally unsatisfactory state of affairs was only too painfully reflected in the returns from the Calais Staple. In the days of Edward III they had reached £68,000. Halfway through Henry's reign they had diminished to £12,000.

By 1436, therefore, the public finances had reached so deflated a condition that the first Income Tax made its unwelcomed appearance. The impost was levied on all incomes derived from land, rents, annuities, and offices of profit; the rate being graduated from 6d. in the £ on incomes between £5 and £100, to 2s. in the £ on incomes over £400.[1] Folk fretted and grumbled—but paid. Indeed, many of them could well afford to; for the luxurious tastes alike of the wealthy landowning nobility and the still opulent members of the trader class were clearly reflected in the exotic incoming cargoes from distant lands. Pouring across the narrow seas came argosies crammed with rich velvets and brocades from Italy, shimmering damasks from the Levant, gorgeous furs from Russia, 'red Gascoine wine', 'white Alsace', Romany, Malmsey, Piment, Clarry, Hippocras, Sherrisack, Tyre, Rhodes and Cyprus wines, and an amazing range of sundries, which now included mastic, grains of paradise for the dyer, euphorbium, senna, scammony, cassia and worm-seed for the apothecary, frankincense and spikenard for the perfumier, stavesacre "for to kill vermin", and the gastronomic novelty of rhubarb from distant Muscovy.

London and Southampton were the principal ports of entry for these fabulous shipments; but in addition to its other activities Southampton had become the great centre for the coasting trade. Sulphur, cordwain and basan leather, wood, alum and spices, brought by the "Flanders galleys"[2] from

---

[1] Cal. of Letter Book K, 72–75, 195–197.
[2] So called because they continued their voyage to the Flemish trading centres before returning to their home ports.

Genoa and Venice, were transhipped for distribution up and down the coast. For the return trip, Cornwall yielded its tin and lead, and the pasture counties their endless bales of wool.

With the bailiffs of the port always on the spot to ensure that the port regulations were faithfully observed, the work of loading or breaking out cargo went forward smoothly and in good order. No short-tempered master could take the law into his own hands and do violence to a member of his crew. If the man was guilty of an offence, the remedy was to arraign him before the Admiral or his representative; who could adjudicate in both civil and criminal causes. Brawling could be dealt with summarily, and punished with a fine up to a maximum of 100s. But petty theft—of oars, nets, buoys, anchors, and the like—and trespass,[1] could only be tried by a jury, since the penalty, on conviction, ranged from forty days' imprisonment to loss of liberty "for half a year". Disputes over the terms of fulfilment of a charter party could be settled by the Admiral's Court directly; and the Court itself could be convened, if necessary, on the quayside "close to the flux and reflux of the tide". Deodands—the personal chattels of an individual slain or drowned at sea, or killed in a vessel at anchor within the port—did not become the property of the finder, at least in theory, but had to be rendered up to the authorities, to be administered for the benefit of the dependents of the deceased. The same was true of flotsam, jetsam and lagan; although in these particulars the law was more honoured in the breach than in the observance. But there was no evading the penalty for arson, which was death.[2]

In times when provisions were especially costly, the shipman was safeguarded against short commons by the payment of a weekly 'regard'—an extra-ordinary bounty in addition to his wages. These stood at 6d. a day for the master and gunner—sometimes referred to as 'constable'—for shipmen 3½d. a day, plus 6d. a week 'regard', and for the ship's boy, 1½d. a day, rising to 2½d., and a 'regard'. Furthermore, the restrictive regulation against "carrying bundles on the neck" having wisely been abrogated, ships' crews joined in the work of

---

[1] As a term 'trespass' could also mean misdemeanour, as distinguished from felony.

[2] *Black Book of the Admiralty.*

stevedoring, with extra pay for portage to reward their labours.

The Admiralty Court was supported by a scale of fees that ranged from 12*d*. for the sealing of a "lesser Warrant" to 6*s*. 8*d*. for affixing the official seal to a contract.

*   *   *

With a Regency Council whose policy was little more than the glorification of its own power, the want of central direction was nowhere more painfully reflected than in the ebbing fortunes of the armies overseas. The French had been aroused to a veritable frenzy of resistance by the gawky but inspiring little sibyl whom men knew variously as Jeanne d'Arc and *La Pucelle*, and whom acute theopathy seemed to have turned into a remarkably effective military leader. Their efforts had been equally fortified by the patriotic generosity of the opulent merchant, Jacques Cœur, who, when the Treasurer had revealed that the contents of his coffers totalled a mere four crown pieces, had come forward with the offer of 200,000 more.[1] The combination of religious ecstasy and hard cash has invariably worked wonders; and led by the Maid, the French had gone on from strength to strength. With Charles VII crowned in Rheims Cathedral, *La Pucelle* had experienced the misfortune to fall captive to the Burgundians, who promptly sold her to the English. After a trial that was not only a battle of obstinacies but a masterpiece of casuistry and polemics, Jeanne had been brought to the stake. But her death in the flames "was more than a crime, it was a blunder". For the impetus given by the Maid to Gallic arms did not expire with her oblation to organised religious bigotry. On the contrary, the French set so vigorously about the task of driving the perfidious English into the sea that even the long-established bastion of Calais was seriously imperilled. Only the prompt reaction of the veteran garrison sufficed to save it when it was surprised and rushed by a force which, recalling the ruse employed by Edward III in 1349, stole into the harbour in a myriad innocent-looking fishing boats.

[1] Almost needless to say, Jacques Cœur was requited by having false charges brought against him; suffering the confiscation of his property and imprisonment, before escaping from captivity to take service with the Pope, who appointed him commander of a division of his fleet. He died in the Papal service in 1456.

"Our enemies laugh at us, and say 'take off the ship from your precious money and stamp a sheep on it, to signify your sheepish minds'. We who used to be conquerers of all peoples are now conquered by all."[1] Such was the rumbling comment as the English saw the waning of their power in France; and sometimes discontent took on more violent form. When Bishop Moleyns repaired to Portsmouth to try and placate the riotous shipmen and soldiery who had turned the town into a hellish bear garden, he was set upon and incontinently slaughtered, as "the traitor who had sold Normandy".[2] A nation in defeat invariably looks round for a scapegoat on whom to vent its furious sense of shame and frustration; and the higher the rank of the victim, the greater the satisfaction in exacting retribution.

To try and restore a rapidly deteriorating situation, Henry— now four and twenty—opened negotiations for the hand of the strong-willed but shrewish Margaret of Anjou; a measure of desperation not necessarily attributable to the mental in-stability which was to dog the King's whole life. But the marriage did nothing to placate the French, while materially helping to precipitate an open rupture between Lancastrian Henry and Richard Duke of York, supported by his wealthy jackal, Richard Neville, Earl of Warwick. Kin to royalty and husband of the Earl of Warwick's heiress, Neville was not content to assume his late father-in-law's title and enjoy his riches, but pictured himself in the grandiose role of king-maker and the power behind the Throne controlling the country's destiny—with Richard the first puppet dancing to his mani-pulation of the strings.

The Wars of the Roses, as the strife between the rival branches of the Royal House came to be termed,[3] can be regarded either in the light of a contemporary outbreak of gang warfare, or as the medieval method of holding a general elec-tion. In a large measure, the conflict was a repercussion of the setbacks suffered abroad; in the same way that those aforesaid defeats had been, in part, the consequence of violent discord at home.

[1] *De Illustribus Henricis,* John Capgrave.
[2] William of Worcester, *Annales Rerum Anglicarum.*
[3] The term was not employed until Tudor times. The Yorkist badge was the heraldic white rose; the Lancastrian red rose was far less common.

When the quarrel between the rival factions broke into open violence, despite the prevalence of the plague, neither Yorkists nor Lancastrians experienced any difficulty in raising a 'Falstaff's army' out of the horde of vagrants and 'poor masterless men' whom a declining agriculture had rendered destitute. And if one body of ragged followers melted away overnight, the hedgerows would readily produce another. With both parties the forces lacked trained skill, as they were entirely without discipline, and their numbers never exceeded five thousand a side.

The first clash between the White Rose and the Red, at St. Albans, ended in a victory which elevated Richard Duke of York to the dignity of Lord Protector. For his support of the temporarily triumphant cause Warwick was rewarded by being appointed Lord Warden of the Cinque Ports and Constable of Calais; and it was to this Yorkist stronghold that he fled when a turn in fortune's wheel brought a setback to his party, with the renewal of the struggle in 1459.

At Calais Warwick was well placed to command the Channel and a South coast bitterly resentful of the King's open bias in favour of the Flemings and Italians. In any case, while Plymouth and the West were largely in sympathy with the Lancastrians, the men of the Cinque Ports and the Hampshire littoral inclined towards the Yorkists. Indeed, they had little choice in the matter since they were in no position to defend themselves even from marauders, let alone defy so powerful an outlaw as Warwick, almost within hailing distance across the narrow seas, and in command of a pliant garrison and a strong fleet. An improvised armament it might be, but it was sufficiently new-found to offer proof that the transition from the slow, cumbersome and unsightly 'round ship' to the comely, sharp-prowed and 'answerable' ship of the line was well on its way.

Warwick's own flagship was clincher-built, with a roofed cabin, or round house, with shrouds to a mainmast fitted with a top and a single square sail, and with a smaller mizzen. Along the bulwarks were cannon placed *en barbette*, so that the bowmen were free to fire over them; while in the waist, apertures—not gun-ports—permitted other cannon to be trained forward on their targets. From the mainmast floated a forty-yard streamer adorned with the Cross of St. George, next the staff, and "a grete Bear and Gryfon holding a ragged staff, poudrid full of ragged staves", in the fly. Altogether, a very formidable but eye-taking ship of war.

In command of what was virtually a private armada, Warwick soundly thrashed a Spanish fleet of double his numbers, capturing six of the hostile craft to add to his strength. Then when the Lancastrians sought to provide for coastal defence by Commissions to array the *posse comitatus*, the 'King-maker' showed his contempt for their futile efforts by twice raiding Sandwich; already enfeebled by a recent outbreak of plague. The price of failure to realise that the first line of defence is the coastline of the enemy was again exacted of Sandwich, when it was later raided by Sieur Pierre de Brézé, Senechal of Poitou; as contemporary opinion held, with the complicity of Margaret of Anjou. In the year following, however, a timely word of warning from a well-wisher in Calais found the Portsmen better prepared. With guns in position on the Ness and the men of Lydd so carefully divided into watches that surprise was out of the question, the French were sent to the rightabouts in remarkably short order.

Pestilence, hunger, and the fury of its Gallic raiders were not the only afflictions from which Sandwich sought manfully to achieve recovery. The silting of its harbour had become a serious problem, and one that had wantonly been aggravated by the greed of Cardinal Morton, the principal owner of land in the town's vicinity. "For his singular advantage and commoditie [he] stopped up and muryd[1] and infitted in such sort the said haven at a place called Sarre, that by means thereof, and also by like evill doing of the other land adjoining unto the saide haven, the said haven is at present utterly destroyed and lost."[2] In effect, an 'inning' had been carried out as detrimental to local interests as those in course of completion at Rye and between Appledore and Romney.

*   *   *

York's outright claim to the throne was closely followed by his death at the battle of Wakefield (December 1460); and his pretensions passed to his son, Edward Earl of March. By

1 I.e., enwalled.   2 Sandwich Public Records.

identifying himself with that type of popular reform that looks no further than the day when "seven ha'penny loaves sold for a penny, and the three-hooped pot shall have ten hoops", the Pretender experienced little difficulty in winning support. Success at the battle of Towton enhanced his appeal, so it was as Sovereign that the Fourth Edward was welcomed in the metropolis after his victory over the Lancastrians.

It was an uneasy and diminished Throne to which Edward had fought his way. Of all the Crown's proud cross-Channel heritage little remained but the bridgehead of Calais. A hundred years of dynastic war with France had ended in defeat when Charles VII made a conqueror's entrance into Bordeaux in the October of 1453.

Set against this sombre background of failure and loss, the futile raid on the coast of Brittany undertaken by the Earls of Kent and Essex, was no more than an empty gesture of defiance at the irrepressible Margaret of Anjou, busy weaving her plots on the other side of the narrow seas. For despite Warwick's appointment to control the Navy—at an annual stipend of £1,000—a great deal had still to be done to bring the fighting marine up to strength. No new ships had been laid down as yet, although a few vessels had been bought here and there and 'anglicised' by renaming them the *Trinity*, the *Grâce Dieu*, the *Martin Grasia* and the *Mary of the Tower*. Equally, no attempt had been made to form a centre for naval equipment such as had existed under Henry V at Southampton and Bursledon. The King had every intention of restoring his fleet but neither time nor events were on his side.

Sandwich, having made its peace with the winning party, quickly recovered something of its erstwhile prosperity; commerce worth over £14,000 passing through the Customs annually. Plymouth, despite having backed the wrong horse politically, had too lucrative a trade in silver from the Tamar and other valuable ores—not to mention wool—for commerce not to regain its steady flow, despite the widespread piracy which still exacted its toll from all water-borne trade.

At the outset of his reign, Edward's fiscal policy was cautiously designed to defend native industry against foreign competition. To this end he kept aliens' rates on the export of wool fairly high, while increasing the tunnage on sweet wines imported by foreigners. At the same time a double tax was clapped on all tin exported by aliens, the commodity's principal customers. As under Henry VI, merchant-strangers were forbidden to buy and sell with each other; were again placed under the surveillance of a 'hoste'; restricted to an eight months' period of residence in which to complete their business, and obliged to lay out the proceeds of their sales in English wares. Thereafter, since Cyprus yew had been found to furnish better bow-staves than the indigenous variety, it was decreed that, in addition to the normal tax, every cargo of Tyre, Rhodes and Cyprus wine should be mulcted at the rate of four true butts of Cyprus yew per tun of liquor. It was an ingenious method of maintaining the archer, whose days of usefulness had by no means passed, despite the arrival of the arquebusier.

The mounting flow of commerce added appreciably to the labours of the Customs. It also proffered considerable scope for malfeasance on the part of the Customs' officers themselves. This was especially noticeable at Fowey, Plymouth, Dartmouth and Poole. In some instances the erstwhile tallies[1] had been superseded by 'warrants'; and the manipulation and issue of these to cover the landing of a far larger cargo than had been officially 'cocketed' was subject to so steeply rising a tariff of bribery that the Venetian merchants came to a mutual agreement not to resort to corruption at a heavier rate than £20 a ship. But it was the discovery, by the newly-appointed Controllers of the Scrutiny, of a purely personal tax exacted by the Customers on ships' fittings, that called down the King's wrath and put a period to the more nefandous of their activities.

With native cloth-making a thriving industry, the craft-guilds were increasing not only in prosperity but in power, to the swelling resentment of the *Gildeins*. The tailors of Exeter, for example, became an independent body, with its own Seal, given —for a consideration!—by the King. With some justice, the association was accused of "dividing the mayor's authority",

---

[1] Tallies were received in the office of the Tellers of the Exchequer; in London known as Tally Court. Tallies were two to three inches in width and three and a half feet in length. Cloven asunder, one half—the stock—was retained by the payee, the other half—the counter-stock—by the office. The destruction of the Houses of Parliament in 1839 is said to have been occasioned by the overheating of flues caused by the burning of old Exchequer tallies.

for it was at bitter enmity with the civic authorities, who condemned its Charter as "prejudicial and against the liberties of the city". But it was as idle to try and curb the advancement of the craft-guilds in the fifteenth century as it was to seek to retard that of their lineal descendants, the trades-unions, in the twentieth.[1]

Edward, realising that wealth is a form of strength, was assiduous in the garnering of riches. But he was shrewd enough to remit a portion of the Calais 'subsidy', to be devoted to the repair of the stronghold's defences and the upkeep of the garrison. In general, however, the national finances were in so parlous a condition that in Warwick's loud-voiced opinion, affairs could only be remedied by a marriage which would restore amicable relations with France.

Edward, however, would not be baulked of wedlock with "the golden wood nymph" Elizabeth Woodville, regardless of the consideration that she was not only a commoner but the widow of a notorious Lancastrian supporter. Warwick, with all a thwarted paranoic's boiling fury, immediately made preparations to avenge defiance by challenging Edward's Throne itself. All personal efforts at rebellion having gone off at half-cock, the 'King-maker' experienced no difficulty in coming to terms with his erstwhile enemy, Margaret of Anjou. A common object is a great solvent of differences, and the purpose which Margaret and the serpentine Warwick soon found they had in common was the restoration of the captive Henry at least to nominal authority.

Warwick's command of the Channel enabled him to transport a strong landing force where he listed. Adverse winds, however, while enabling the 'King-maker's' armies to avoid the handful of war-craft with which Edward designed to oppose it, drove the rebel leader and his followers into Dartmouth and Plymouth; where the streets suddenly blossomed with the red roses of Lancaster, long held prudently in reserve.

Moving on London, the 'King-maker' snatched the feeble Henry from captivity and proclaimed his re-ascension of the Throne. For the moment Edward's cause seemed lost, and he hastily took refuge in the Low Countries.

---

[1] Edward prohibited the import of silk made up into garments; so it is implicit that the pleated silken tunics so fashionable at this period were tailored in England from imported lengths of silk.

But the Lancastrian—or rather, the Neville—rule hung by a thread; so Edward speedily set about organising a counter-stroke; an enterprise to which the merchants of the Staple of Calais contributed handsomely.

At the second battle of Barnet fortune was with the White Rose; Warwick being slain together with many of his principal supporters. This success was followed by the crushing victory of Tewkesbury, in which Margaret's son was killed; she herself being subsequently made captive. Within less than a month the wretched Henry was reported to have died "of pure displeasure and melancholy", as smooth a euphemism for political assassination as well could be desired.

In his hour of triumph Edward could afford to ignore the belated raid on the South Coast and the mouth of the Thames staged by Warwick's supporter, the Bastard of Fauconbridge, who had come several days too late to the fair.

Re-installed in the purple, Edward settled down to a steady strengthening of his position. Every possible step was taken to cultivate friendly trade relations with other Powers. There was even reconciliation with the Hansa League, whose members, following defection from the English cause in 1436 by their overlord, the Duke of Burgundy,[1] had been cut off from all trade with England. Hustled back to their own country, they had rigorously been denied those precious consignments of wool on which their continued prosperity so patently depended; the Lord Warden of the Cinque Ports and the mayors of Chichester, Southampton and Poole being especially enjoined to ensure that no vessel cleared their ports with Flanders as its destination. The prohibition proved a two-edged blade, however, which injured England almost as much as it damaged Flanders. So there was no great difficulty in agreeing terms that would include the resumption of trade relations. The Easterlings were encouraged to establish their *Staelhoef* in Thames Street, hard by Blackfriars[2]; and there was even talk of the property passing permanently into their possession. But even if their timely loans had helped to restore Edward to the throne, it was still forbidden for merchant-strangers

---

[1] Margaret of Burgundy, who survived her ducal husband, was Edward's sister.

[2] Approximately where Cannon Street railway station stands today.

7+

to bring dogs into the country, to catch rabbits on the Downs!

Relations having also been resumed with Brittany, all masters of vessels, on both sides of the Channel, were obliged to find security, prior to departure, that they would refrain from committing depredations on the subjects of the other realm. Officials were appointed in all the ports, again on both sides of the Channel, to mete out summary justice to offenders or their guarantors, or, failing them, to the inhabitants of the delinquents' haven.

Holland, which had almost been ruined by that adherence to the Gallic cause it had been unable to evade, was also encouraged to resume the useful trade that previously had helped to swell the turnover of the Calais Staple.

The English merchants, and particularly the Merchant-Adventurers,[1] viewed this cosseting of individuals they could only regard as interlopers, with mounting indignation. Rising in prosperity as they were, and with an increasing mercantile marine of their own, which rendered them largely independent of foreign craft, they bitterly resented the favour shown to commercial rivals still all-too-capable of getting the best of any bargain that might be concluded with them. Their sense of injury was further inflamed by Edward's gift to his sister, the Duchess of Burgundy, of 1,000 oxen and 2,000 rams, duty free, "for every year for as long as she should live". For no more grievous blow to England's monopoly in high-grade wool could very well have been conceived. There were protests and petitions, and in London serious riots broke out against the 'Jannayes',[2] as all merchant-strangers were termed, whatever their country of origin.

In effect, Edward, a master of expediency, was no longer bound by his erstwhile policy of 'protection'. All 'occupiers of wares' were welcome to trade, providing they paid their dues honestly and punctually. It was only where France was concerned, it seemed, that the King nursed the desire to exact vengeance for Gallic support of Warwick. But a realignment of

---

[1] The Merchant-Adventurers offer an early example of a regulated company—i.e. a company in which membership was open to all who were willing to pay the admission fees and acquiesce in its authority.

[2] I.e. Genoans.

interests on the Continent persuaded the wily Louis that it would be more profitable to bribe the English Sovereign into exercising restraint. So successfully did he accomplish his task that Edward virtually became the Frenchmen's pensioner. This at least permitted him to accomplish the unusual regal feat of dying without debts.

As for the ordinary people, for all that straggling war had persisted all about them for year after weary year, on the testimony of the eminent jurist, Sir John Fortescue, the English seagoing, artisan and mercantile classes were still "the beste fedde and also the best cledde of any nation, crystin or heathen".

*　　　*　　　*

With the Fourth Edward's death and a lad of twelve called to the Throne in the person of Edward V, it could only be a matter of time before somebody secured the post of Lord Protector as a step towards seizing the Crown. That individual duly emerged in the malformed person of Richard Duke of Gloucester. By the June of 1483 he had taken over the reins of power.[1]

For the two years of his reign Richard III can scarcely have known a moment's peace.[2] For there was no escape from the haunting fear of what fate might have in store for him through the agency of the expatriate but powerful Henry of Richmond. Descended from John of Gaunt and that Owen Tudor who had married Katherine of Valois, the widow of Henry V, as a boy Henry had prudently been removed to safety in Brittany by his uncle, Jaspar Tudor, Earl of Pembroke. Grown to man's estate, his pretensions to the Throne were supported by every Lancastrian with a grudge to repay or expropriated lands to reclaim.

In the outcome, 'Henry Tydder', as his contemporaries called him, made an entirely unimpeded crossing of the narrow seas, to decide the issue on Bosworth Field past any peradventure.

[1] What fate befell the wretched little Edward and his brother—the two little Princes in the Tower—whether they were done away with by Richard or by his successor, is still a matter of controversy.

[2] It is notable that of the fifteen Acts passed by Richard's one Parliament, seven were for the regulation of trade; legislation that in the main was ungenerous, impolitic and unavailingly restrictive.

With 'Crookback's' dead body slung across a pack-horse saddle and trundled off to obscure and unhonoured burial at Leicester, the Wars of the Roses ended. The Age of Chivalry was dead. The old feudal aristocracy, having forfeited its rightful authority through preoccupation with its imbecile factional quarrels, had virtually committed suicide. The island people was without a navy, and had scarce a thought for the sea power that lay well within their grasp. But they had found a ruler who would give them the one as he would steadfastly teach them the meaning of the other.

PART II

The Sea-People

"If either the honour of a nation, commerce or trade with other nations, peace at home, grounded upon our enemies' fear or love of us . . . if these things be things worthy of esteem, then next to God and the King give thanks for the same to the Navy, as the principal instrument whereby God works these good things to thee."

JOHN HOLLOND, *Discourses of the Navy* (1638)

CHAPTER IX

New Horizons

"The sea alone is capable of creating a world power."
FRIEDERICH RATZEL

THE England of 1485 was a land whose tremendous potentialities had been temporarily overlaid by its immediate distress. Impoverished and weakened by conflict with France extending over two and three-quarter centuries, it was further debilitated by the years of civil strife brought tentatively to a head on Bosworth Field. What it required was a firm hand to re-knit its ravelled fabric and revitalise its energies, infusing them with a fresh impetus and guiding them in a new direction. By great good fortune, the hour brought forth the man in the person of the new Sovereign.

Henry VII, the first of the 'moderns', applied himself to the task of kingship much as some especially hired high-pressure executive would set about the job of restoring prosperity to a sound but rather sluggish and old-fashioned business house. Astute, patient and thrifty, and with a frigidly realist distaste for profitless military adventures on the blood-soaked fields of France, it was his abiding hope that the English people "might turn their backs on the Continent and point their prowess towards the setting sun and the Fortunate Isles of the Blest".

Enthralled by all that had to do with salt water, he rejoiced as heartily in the unpretentious charts and rutters, or 'manuals of the sea', compiled by his own pilots, as he delighted in the geographical globes constructed by the illustrious Martin Behaim. Exploration had his enthusiastic support; and it was through no fault of his that Christopher Columbus failed to enjoy a similar patronage to that which, from 1497 onwards, he extended to John and Sebastian Cabot, Hugh Ellyot and Thomas Ashurst, and John Gonzalez and Francis Fernandez.

Henry's unwearying efforts to keep on good terms both with
Spain and France, so long as the latter accepted English control
of the Breton Channel ports, were actuated by the same motive
as inspired his marriage of conciliation with Elizabeth of York—
the desire to avoid conflict abroad and the turmoil of faction at
home. In foreign affairs his aim, by cultivating Spain, was to
achieve a balance of power to offset the growing might of
France. In domestic matters his purpose was to placate or
suppress those elements whose resolve to put a Yorkist on the
Throne had rather been fortified than discouraged by the setback undergone at Bosworth. Above all, his resolve was to
secure those conquests that are the spoils of successful commerce,
rather than accumulate the unrewarding gains which are the
Dead Sea fruits of war.

To ensure the protection and expansion of English trade the
King's prime need was ships—ships of such superb construction
that, once they had been seen and made use of, would leave no
one content with anything inferior. In the form of a fighting
marine, Henry inherited little more than the battered *Grâce
Dieu*. So orders were promptly given for the Smallhythe shipyard to set to work on the construction of the *Regent*; in the
framework of whose sister-ship, the *Sovereign*, some of the timbers
of the broken-up *Grâce Dieu* were frugally incorporated. The
Regent was fitted with a big foremast with a topmast crowning
it, a huge mainmast with a main topmast and main topgallant,
and two mizzen masts, while her aftermost mizzen, or bonaventure, was neatly sheeted to an outlicker which balanced
the bowsprit. In place of the erstwhile relatively flimsy *bellatoria*
there was a high, built-in, double-decked forecastle, and a poop
in the stern embodying an equally solid, triple-tiered somer-
castle, or quarter-deck, constructed one stage lower than the
poop itself. Both forecastle and somer-castle were pierced with
embrasures for cannon. With this great weight of ordnance the
vessel's sides had to be sloped sharply inwards from the water
line, and this 'tumbledown', by retracting the deck by several
feet, added appreciably to the difficulty of boarding and entering. The more accessible waist was defended by netting and by
three hundredweight 'serpentines', so sited in the fore- and
somer-castles as to be capable of sweeping the whole of the
area amidships with hail-shot, the lightweight forerunner of

grape and canister. The ship's square sails were no longer reduced by reef-points, but by strips of canvas, called 'bonnets', which could be unlaced or replaced as the wind decreased or strengthened. Three boats and no less than eight anchors attest the size of a vessel which, like the *Sovereign*, laid down in 1488, easily eclipsed even the Gallic 'great ship' *Caronne*, which in 1475 had put to flight a whole squadron of Hollanders. But both the *Sovereign* and the *Regent*, with their built-up 'castles' acting as unwieldy fixed sails, must have been as difficult to handle as the old round ships which, in many respects, they undoubtedly resembled.

Both craft could accommodate a ship's company of well over a thousand men; men who were presently to adopt a semi-uniform garb in the Tudor colours of white and green; in cut not unlike the 'jackettes' of standard pattern first issued to the crews of the Crown ships by Edward IV.

The improvement in the spending value of money was reflected in the current rates of pay. These ran from 1s. a week, 'with vittels', for foremast hands when in harbour—rising to 1s. 3d. when actually at sea—to 10s. a day for an Admiral. The ship-master received a basic 3s. 4d. a week; the lodesman, or pilot, 20s. a month. Subordinate officers drew a monthly 5s., with 5s. victualling money and a certain proportion of 'dead shares'. The growing importance of the cannoneer was recognised in the wage of 20s. a month for the master-gunner, with the quarter-gunner qualifying for 15s. 3d. Pursers and boatswain were paid a weekly 1s. 8d., with subsistence; the quartermaster 1s. 6d. and the steward and cook 1s. 3d., with fluctuating increases when afloat. The basic rate for all shipwrights, sawyers and ship's labourers was 1s. a week. In certain circumstances up to three months' wages could be drawn in advance, with 'conduct money' at 6d. a day to cover the journey to the port of embarkation.

The smaller three-masted *Sweepstake* and *Mary Fortune*, completed in 1497 and costing no more than £120 and £110, respectively, to build, set the limit to Henry's immediate construction programme. But, as in Spain, there was a standing offer of a bounty of from 4s. to 5s. a ton for anyone prepared to build up to the standard of the royal ships and, in times of emergency, charter them to the Crown at the rate of 3d. a ton

7*

per week. Equally prepared to hire out his own craft as occasion offered, Henry aimed at getting the best of both worlds by making his own ships self-supporting, while having a number of sizeable, well-armed vessels, constructed to his specification but very largely at his subjects' expense, ready and waiting in the event of war.[1] All things considered, there can be little wonder that the Seventh Henry was dubbed the 'Huckster King'!

As part of the general plan Robert Brygandine—appointed head of naval administration in 1495—was instructed to build at Portsmouth the first dry dock in the kingdom. Save for the reinforced dockhead, it was constructed of wood, at a total cost of £193 0s. 6¾d. What is more, so stoutly was it put together that it continued in service right up to modern times. Concurrently, Portsmouth's protective works were strengthened by twin towers at the harbour mouth, and with a chain across its entrance. But all the emphasis was on passive defence.

Yorkist attempts to stage a revolt and to pass off Lambert Simnel—the son of an Oxford baker—as Richard Duke of York,[2] were frustrated in a manner entirely Henry's own. The rebel lords were dealt with by the sword; the captured pretender contemptuously pardoned and relegated to the swill tubs in the royal kitchens.

The next crisis to be sprung upon him put Henry in something of a dilemma. In the days of his exile he had been afforded generous shelter by the Duke of Brittany. With the Duke's death his twelve-year-old daughter, Anne, appealed to England for help against a predatory France; and for once the 'Huckster King' was compelled to abandon evasion and cautious half-promises and commit himself to something definite. A force of 6,000 bowmen, therefore, was safely shipped to the scene of action—and as carefully kept *out* of action. For 'Henry Tydder' had no intention of embroiling himself more closely than he could help with a France which had been transmogrified from a mere geographical area into a firmly consolidated kingdom, boasting a far more numerous population than that of its traditional rival across the Channel.

---

[1] The custom arose at this period of passing on the name of an old, worn-out vessel to her successor. Thus the *Grâce Dieu* in due course handed on her name to her replacement, the *Henri Grâce à Dieu*; the new craft costing, it was alleged, a cool £14,000.

[2] The younger of the two Princes in the Tower.

As a gesture, Boulogne was half-heartedly blockaded; but a handsome bribe of £100,000 not only ensured the abandonment of the enterprise, but paved the way for Henry's surrender of Brittany to the Gallic maw. Recalling the heavy 'subsidy' demanded to support their abortive operations, the disgusted soldiery and shipmen openly complained that the King had not scrupled "to plume his nobility and people to feather himself".

Henry had certainly lived up to his principle that "war once begun should pay itself". Even so, the brief period of desultory strife had clearly demonstrated that if the coastal towns and ever-turbulent narrow seas were to be made safe for commerce, the dual-purpose King's ships would often be compelled to exchange the pursuit of profitable trade for less rewarding conflict. For the traditional 'service' of the Cinque Ports now went little beyond the cross-Channel transport of travellers of distinction and occasional bodies of troops; although their shipmen had consoled their indubitable decline in consequence by adopting as a uniform "a cote of white cotyn with a red Crosse and the Arms of the Portis, that is to say, the halfe lyon and the halfe shippe".

The Portsmen dealt drastically enough with yet another pinchbeck Yorkist pretender, Perkin Warbeck, when he landed on the sands of Deal. But the plausible rogue openly ranged the narrow seas without challenge by a single local squadron.[1] The coastal waters were, indeed, still the scene of unbridled lawlessness. When certain of the 'Flanders galleys', on passage from Antwerp to Southampton, fell in with three English ships off St. Helen's they were utterly confounded by a peremptory order to strike sail. Wonderingly, they hove to and explained that they were friends; "but finding mischief meant, went to quarters". In the ensuing fight eighteen of the English marauders were slain. Making their way to Southampton with their tenacious assailants still on their heels, the only response the 'Jennayes'' justifiable complaint evoked was Henry's evasive comment, that "they had nothing to fear", as "those that had been killed must bear their own loss, and a pottle of wine would settle any other matter outstanding". Quite obviously, the local

[1] Certain Tudor chroniclers maintained that Perkin was either the natural son of Margaret of Burgundy and a Prince of the Church or the fruit of a liaison pursued by Edward IV while in exile. Actually, he was the offspring of a Jew of Tournay, who settled in London during the reign of Edward IV.

authorities were without control over their immediate waterways. For on one occasion the Venetian Consul and the Captain of the visiting 'Flanders galleys' were snatched out of the very harbour itself, and had to be ransomed at 500 ducats apiece.

Normally, terms were a little less extortionate; the customary ransom for a ship-master taken by privateers being 40s.; that of an ordinary seaman standing at half as much.

The Western approaches were a death trap; the whole fleet of 'Flanders galleys', bound for Antwerp, having been captured in these waters by an adventurer in the French King's service, after a twenty-four-hour fight in which 400 Venetian *marinelli* had been slain. Rates to cover the risks involved in the voyage to England were so high in Barcelona, the contemporary centre for marine insurance, as to be virtually prohibitive. Not unnaturally, therefore, many Italian merchants came to favour the longer, but safer, overland route across the Alps and down the Rhine valley, which spared them the cost of the hundred extra hands and score of additional gunners required to render the sea-passage reasonably safe.

Henry, of course, still maintained the fiction of English dominance in the narrow seas, nor did his contemporaries ever think to challenge it. In this particular perhaps more than in any other, history must be regarded horizontally and not perpendicularly. Otherwise it is impossible to appreciate the fact that rampant lawlessness at sea did not excite the same alarm and discouragement as it aroused in later and more law-abiding times. In effect, most people realised that the increase of commerce had not been accomplished by a comparable growth in the organised forces of defence; that the incidence of piracy had to be faced up to, and the implicit risks of trafficking across the Channel waters boldly accepted.

The Tudor merchant class included many men of great shrewdness, industry and accomplishment. They were, of necessity, reasonably at home in two or three languages, while they mastered Latin as a matter of course, as a *lingua franca* when all else failed.[1] They were proficient in book-keeping by single and double entry and did their figuring in both Roman

---

[1] Even so late as the Stuarts, Latin was considered essential for "gentlemen who go to travel, factors for merchants and the like" (*The Boke of Gouvenour*, Sir Thomas Elyot).

and Arabic cyphers. They could cast up their accounts in Flemish pounds, ducats, pistolets, crowns of the sun, francs, sous, postulates, horiadores, crusadores, philippus, carolus and lewes gildons. For the most part they philosophically accepted the occasional loss of a ship and valuable cargo as a concomitant in an irremediable pattern of commerce, to be balanced by the high charges exacted for the wares that did come safely into port. But there were some among their number who preferred paying higher duty and turning a smaller profit at a lesser risk by disposing of the merchandise ventured across the narrow seas in foreign bottoms. It was by legislation such as the Navigation Act of Richard II and the shipbuilding bounties offered by 'Henry Tydder' that the more hardy and intrepid were induced to freight their own cargoes, and in so doing swell the number of vessels plying in native ownership, and increase thereby the total of the deep-water seafaring population. It was upon their shoulders that England's future rested in the Oceanic Age just dawning.

*   *   *

The one military enterprise that Henry did push through with a reasonable show of resolution was that aimed at the extermination of a band of corsairs—long a plague to English shipping—under the command of the Flemish rebel, Philip of Ravensteyn, who had established a strong base at Sluys. After some delay, a combined operation against the fastness was put in train; with troops mustered by Maximilian, King of the Romans, closing in on the land side, and a naval armament, under Sir Edward Poynings, blocking all avenues of escape by sea. With Maximilian's contingent thrusting hard at the nearer of the stronghold's twin towers, and the Englishmen put ashore to carry the other, the assault was vigorously pressed home. The end came when a daring party of English men-at-arms and shipmen set fire to the bridge of boats by which communication was maintained between the two complementary outworks. Surrendering at discretion, Ravensteyn handed over the town to Maximilian's representative, Duke Albert of Saxony, while the keys of the fortress were ceremoniously surrendered to the simple English sea-captain. He was, however, resourceful enough to foil any attempt on the part of the wily Albert to debit Henry's treasure chest with the German mercenaries' wages!

With Anne of Brittany forced into wedlock with Charles VIII of France, the eventual loss of the Breton Channel ports was a foregone conclusion, with the consequence that Gallic strength in the narrow seas was doubled. But Henry declined to make the havens' annexation a *casus belli*; and a definitive peace treaty was concluded which left the 'Huckster King' free to work for that expansion of trade on which his heart was set.

The cherished aim of Henry's fiscal policy was universal free trade. To that end he concluded reciprocal commercial treaties with Spain, the Empire, Friesland, Denmark and Florence; although strict Navigation Laws required that all merchandise shipped to and from the South of France should be freighted in English vessels manned by English crews. It was only where the Netherlands were concerned that the King pursued a system that adopted progressively more stringent methods of protection. Margaret of Burgundy's obstinate support of Perkin Warbeck's preposterous claim to be the younger of the two Princes in the Tower had offended 'Henry Tydder' mortally. Moreover, the foining 'Easterlings' themselves, by their insistence on the literal interpretation of clauses in their outdated Charters which were entirely at variance with contemporary trading practice, had presumed too much on their traditionally privileged standing. Furthermore, they had lent themselves far too freely to the cheat of 'colouring' a non-privileged alien's wares, passing them off as their own and thus putting them through the Customs at a reduced rate of impost.

It was, therefore, with the enthusiastic support of his own Merchant-Adventurers[1]—who had come virtually to monopolise the carrying-trade to Flanders—that the King decreed that the strict enforcement of a comprehensive Navigation Act should be accompanied by the withdrawal of all the licences issued to the Hansa merchants. For by their terms they had been able to evade the more crippling regulations applying to foreigners. Furthermore, the 'Easterlings' were forced to deposit the enormous sum of £20,000 as security for their strict observance of the new enactment. This tightening of the reins

[1] The association was rewarded in 1505 by the grant of a Charter.

was shortly followed by orders from the Merchant-Adventurers to remove their Staple from Antwerp to Calais.

But for his prudent disinclination to commit himself to a position from which there was no retreat, Henry would probably have closed the 'Easterlings' London *Staelhoef* into the bargain; and in any case, for a period of several years, all trade with the Flemings virtually came to an end. At the same time the embargo on the import of silken garments was reaffirmed in the interest of the native tailoring industry; the export of *all* English wares was to be exclusive to English ships manned by English crews; it was forbidden to freight raw, unfulled cloth "in order that the King's Customs might be increased, and the weavers and fullers of the realm well occupied"; while the 'fine' of £40 exacted by the Merchant-Adventurers from anyone desirous of trading with their Staples was reduced by royal decree, to the modest sum of £6 13s. 4d. Whereafter, if the more monopolistic tendencies of the *Burgeis de la Gilde* and the Craft Guilds were firmly restrained, the 'Huckster King' himself profited to so pretty a tune out of the business of money-changing—*cambii, excambii, et recambii*—for individuals going to, or forwarding coin to, foreign parts, that the royal coffers were positively bulging.

England might be no more than a broken-off fragment of the Continental mainland, lost in its eternal rain-mist and approachable only at the risk of violent *mal-de-mer*; 'Henry Tydder's' claim to its Throne might rest on the most dubious of premisses. But the Powers in general had been brought to realise that quite small puddles sometimes contain quite sizeable frogs; and the rest would follow.

Perkin Warbeck's ill-advised appearance at the head of a mob of disgruntled Cornish tax-payers, somewhat belatedly garnished with the White Rose of political partisanship, led to the Pretender's capture and his incarceration in the Tower. With this obstacle of reconciliation out of the way, Henry could afford to relax his unrelenting attitude towards the Flemings. A treaty was signed, known as the *Intercursus Magnus*, by whose terms freedom of trade was guaranteed between Flanders, Brabant, Hainault, Holland and Mechlin on the one hand, and England, Ireland and Calais on the other. Merchants of either party might own houses in the domains of the other; a free market was assured for the disposal, wholesale, of English cloth; save in Flanders itself[1]; only customary duties were to be imposed; while neither nation was to allow corsairs or privateers within its harbours; merchants being required to deposit double the value of their vessels as a security against their masters and shipmen engaging in piracy. The trade in precious metals and foreign bullion—already flooding into Europe from the mines of South America, to the serious embarrassment of its economy—was also to be free.

As Bacon was to write of him, Henry Tudor was "ever in strife, but ever coming out victorious".

*   *   *

The Papal Bull issued by Alexander VI, which awarded to Spain and Portugal "all land and water" on either side of a line drawn between the 41st and 44th meridian west of Greenwich, and denounced all who intruded on this preserve as 'pirates', left England's Sovereign to all appearance unperturbed; although it was clear that the heyday of Genoa and Venice was over, that the Spanish, Portuguese and Gallic ports on the Atlantic seaboard now held the world in fee. But English trade was booming, and the 'Huckster King' restrained any immediate urge to challenge Portuguese and Spanish enterprise in the Indies, on the Guinea Coast, or in Calicut, where the Iberians were strongly established. For an alliance with Spain, through the usual medium of the marriage bed, was the keystone of his policy—a policy obviously designed to curb any tendency towards further expansion on the part of France.[2]

Spain and Portugal were indubitably ahead in the quest for new sources of national wealth. But there was so much spadework still to be done at home that it must be left to others to do the pioneering in "the Fortunate Isles of the Blest". A prosperous commerce took time to consolidate; in the immediate present something had to be done to arrest the dangerous decay of agriculture—the outcome of the wholesale change-over from

[1] A subsequent agreement, the *Intercursus Malus*, established the English merchants' freedom to sell English cloth retail throughout all the Netherlands save Flanders. At the same time standard Weights and Measures were universally adopted.

[2] Katherine of Aragon was wed first to Arthur, Prince of Wales, and then, on his premature death, by special dispensation, to Henry, heir to the Throne and the "Bluff King Hal" of the succeeding reign.

tillage to sheep-pasture—and the consequent drift to the towns of a redundant rural population in desperate need of employment. There was no great need to worry about the narrow seas. Although no more than half a dozen vessels had been added to those built originally, and expenditure on the Crown fleet had rarely exceeded £2,000 a year, the mercantile marine had been enlarged substantially with fine, powerfully armed craft. As an absolutist who never indulged in bloodshed when punishment could take the form of an exemplary fine, Henry's coffers were crammed with a sum not far short of £2,000,000 sterling. And under the tutelage of a penurious 'Huckster King' the English people had been brought back to prosperity, and to a lively awareness of the overriding importance of the seas that washed their shores.

*   *   *

Holbein's portrait of a sullen, gouty, domineering, middle-aged sensualist tends to obscure the fact that the Henry VIII who succeeded to the Throne in 1509 was a comely young man of astonishing vigour and many sterling qualities. More romantic and impulsive, and less tight-fisted than his predecessor, he was exactly the sort of thrusting Head of State to suit the new aristocracy of the counting-house that was steadily replacing the old nobility, whose members now rather enjoyed prestige than power. As the centre of social and economic authority, the manor had yielded place to the *bourse*. For the real power in the land was swiftly passing to the *noves homines*, men such as Thomas Gresham, who gave London its Royal Exchange, and reached such eminence in the world of commerce as to challenge the powerful Fuggers of Augsburg; or Lawrence Washington who, in 1539, could well afford to purchase Sulgrave Manor from the Priory of St. Andrew, and there found a family that one day was to give the United States its first and greatest President.

Bluff King Hal boasted far wider interests than his royal Sire; but it was fortunate for his country's destiny that he had inherited his father's concern for all things maritime. For with the death of Anne of Brittany the sovereignty of her Duchy had been merged with the Crown of France; and England's strong position on the flank of her ancient enemy was no more.

Her best policy, therefore, was to try and act as makeweight in the balance of power in Europe; a possibility that grew in promise with the mounting rivalry between France and Spain.

With the Gallic Monarch ostentatiously bringing vessels round from the Mediterranean to supplement those just off the stocks, Henry entered into an alliance with Ferdinand of Aragon against France. By its terms each party was to furnish three thousand men "armed and equipped for naval war", while the Spanish contribution to the combined fleet was to be 40 vessels of 100 to 300 tons burden.

Mustering such craft as could be made seaworthy, Henry gave orders for the immediate construction of victualling and shipbuilding yards at Deptford and Woolwich, and for work to be put in hand on the Crown ship *Mary Rose*.

This trim, sturdy craft was the first vessel especially constructed to carry heavy ordnance; in other words, the first ship to be specifically designed for the purposes of war and war only. For heavy cannon demanded a far firmer and more solid platform than had been provided by the built-up fore- and somer-castles, which in any case were too high above the water line for effective fire to be directed on an enemy vessel's hull with cannon of flat trajectory. The only way out of the difficulty was to mount the pieces on what had hitherto been the main cargo deck.

Apertures had to be cut in the ship's side fairly close to the water line through which to run out the gun when in action. Equally, it was necessary to close the openings at other times lest in bad weather the vessel shipped a sea and swamped. On the available evidence, it was James Baker, Henry's Yeoman of the Crown, who solved the problem; devising a stoutly under-pinned gun-deck and transforming the entry-port introduced by the Breton shipwright Descharges, into a watertight gun-port. In general, the policy pursued was that of reducing the number of guns and increasing the weight of those retained. This had the effect of ridding the craft of a lot of top hamper and getting nearer the flush-deck type of vessel, which was not only easier to handle but presented a far smaller target to an enemy. With ordnance having taken the place of cargo, the warship had become, as it was to remain, a floating gun-platform.

What was not immediately appreciated, was that broadside fire demanded a complete change of tactics. Hitherto ships had gone into action in line abreast—rather like infantry charging in close order—their object being either to ram the enemy or to close him, ship to ship, grapple, board and enter, and fight out the issue breast to breast. But with man-killing slowly yielding precedence to ship-killing, *the direction of attack could no longer be that of the line of advance, but operated at right angles to it, so that the full weight of the broadside could be brought to bear.* It was some considerable time, however, before this elemental principle was assimilated; before line abreast gave place to line ahead, and the 'off-fighting' this method of combat involved. Throughout all three of Henry's maritime campaigns with France, indeed, there was no true realisation—on either side—of what 'off-fighting' and the new gun-deck really involved; nothing more than a fumbling towards a technique which was not to reach perfection till well into the eighteenth century. Admittedly, the principle was established of first getting the weather gauge and then sending a fleet into action in three divisions of 'Van', 'Battle' and 'Wing'; with the 'Wing' always to windward "the better to beat off the gallies from the great ships". Furthermore, boarding and entering was forbidden "in smoake" or until the enemy's deck had been cleared by small shot; and there were some rudimentary flag signals. But ships were still handled much as if they were troops of Cavalry or companies of Infantry.

*   *   *

By the terms of a treaty concluded in 1511 between Henry and the King of Aragon, the first-named had agreed to hold the Channel between the Thames and Ushant. To ensure the fulfilment of his obligation King Hal entered into an indenture with his Lord High Admiral, Sir Edward Howard, to furnish 3,000 seamen, gunners and soldiers. The terms of the warrant decreed that:

"I. The Admiral to have for the maintenance of himself in diet, 10s. daily pay during the voyage; and each captain 1s. 6d. a day.

II. The soldiers, mariners and gunners to have per month of 28 days, 5s. wages and 5s. more for victuals.

III. The Admiral undertakes to manage this armament for those allowances, he receiving three months' expenses always beforehand.

Item: for the coat of every captain and soldier 4s., and of every mariner and gunner 1s. 8d.

IV. For the dead shares of the said 18 English ships, the Admiral is to have as follows:—

For the *Regent*, being of 1,000 tons burden, 4 pilots & 50 dead shares.

For the *Mary*, 500 tons, 34½ dead shares.

{
John Hopton's ship, 400 tons,
The *Nicholas Read*, 400 tons. Dead shares needless to be named.
The *Mary George*, 300 tons.
}

The rest of the ships were, one of 200 tons, three of 160 tons, one of 180 tons, two of 140 tons, three of 110 tons, one of 100 tons, and one of 70 tons.

For re-victualling and re-watering, there are at disposal two crayers, one of 65 tons and the other of 55; in the former 12 mariners and a boy, in the latter 10 and a boy, beside their commanders. Each of the masters and mariners to have 10s. a month for wages and victuals.

All the soldiers and mariners to have 6d. a day conduct money, allowing a day's journey to be twelve miles only.

It is further agreed that:

Forasmuch as our Sovereign lord at his costs and charges victualled the said army and navy, the said Admiral shall reserve for the King one half of all the gains and winnings of the war which he and the fleet, or any of them, shall have fortune to obtain in the voyage, either on land or water; and also all prisoners being chieftains, and one ship-royal of 200 tons or upwards, with the ordnance and apparel [1] of every prize taken by them." [2]

Sir Edward Howard had already shown his mettle in fitting out an armament for the destruction of the notorious freebooter Andrew Barton, who had long sailed the seas with great

[1] I.e. sails and running gear.

[2] Quoted in *Foedera*. This is a very early instance of ships being described in terms of tonnage and gun-capacity.

profit to himself, under Letters of Marque issued by England's implacable enemy, James IV of Scotland. Accompanied by his brother Thomas, Howard had sailed from Thames-mouth in search of the freebooter, his force made up of two well-manned craft. Barton, in the *Lion*, had eventually been sighted in the Downs, in company with the pinnace *Jenny Pirwin*.

Actually, it was Thomas Howard[1] who had sighted the *Lion*, having become separated from his brother by the prevailing foul weather; as had Barton from his pinnace.

In heavy seas the two vessels had gradually closed, exchanging shots from their cannon as rapidly as they could be loaded and fired; while a hail of *quarrells* and solid shot had been maintained by the crossbowmen and arquebusiers, that had speedily strewn the decks with dead and injured. Again and again Howard had brought his vessel alongside the *Lion*, seeking to board and enter, only to be beaten off. At length the English leader had gained a footing on his opponent's deck, and a furious hand-to-hand fight had ensued which had only ended when the mortally wounded sea-wolf had ceased to encourage his shipmen's stubborn resistance.

Sir Edward meanwhile had overcome the captain and crew of the *Jenny Pirwin*; and the two captured vessels had been brought back in triumph and added to the nucleus of the Crown fleet.

In command of the main fleet, a few months later, Sir Edward lost no time in ravaging the Breton coast, landing near Conquet and Brest to lay waste the countryside with fire and sword. The French response was to muster a fleet of 29 sail in Brest harbour. The first clash between the rival armaments, off Bertheaume Bay, led to a furious exchange of shot; whereupon a rearguard consisting of the *Nef de Dieppe* and the *Cordelière* put about, seeking to lure their opponents under the guns of their main 'Battle'. In the ensuing *mêlée* the *Cordelière*, grappled by the *Mary James*, the *Sovereign* and the *Regent*, suddenly burst into flame. The *Regent*, tightly interlocked with her foe, was unable to break free; and the two mightiest French and English ships yet built plunged beneath the waves in a smother of flying sparks and whirling smoke. Of the seven hundred men aboard

---

[1] Sir Thomas Howard succeeded his brother as Lord High Admiral, and lived to become the fourth Duke of Norfolk.

the *Regent* only one hundred and eighty were saved; of the numerically superior Gallic crew no more than six.

On the day's work, however, the English had suffered the greater loss. To replace the *Regent* the King gave prompt orders for the construction of the *Henri Grâce à Dieu*. The 'Great Harry', as this striking craft was more commonly termed, was truly a vessel "such as was never before seen in England". Costing, together with three barks built at the same time, the exceptional sum of £8,708 5s. 3d., she was the work of Robert Brygandine and William Bond. A four-masted two-decker, carvel built, of something well over 1,000 tons burden, some 3,739 tons of timber were required for her construction—of which 1,987 were the gift of private individuals—together with 56 tons of iron, 565 stones of oakum, and 1,711 pounds of flax. In her armament of 182 guns the pieces ranged from heavy brass cannon and demi-cannon to 5-inch 15-pounder 'basilisks'. With a crew consisting of 300 shipmen and gunners and 250 soldiers, she was a towering and impressive, if pot-bellied and clumsy, floating fortress. But being nowhere near long enough for her beam she was extremely difficult to handle; while tactically no one had the slightest idea of what to do with her—or, indeed, with any of the new floating fortresses which now constituted the hard core of the fleet.

Sir Edward Howard had taken oath that he would never more see the King until he had avenged the death of Sir Thomas Knyvet, who had perished in the flames of the *Regent*. Sailing in March from Portsmouth, at the head of a fleet of 42 vessels, the Lord High Admiral made straight for Brest; anchoring in sight of the enharboured Gallic squadrons.

Faithful to his maxim that temerity at sea becomes a virtue, the English leader determined to assault the enemy armament in its haven; and "so in good order of battle they sailed forward". Being unacquainted with the peculiarities of local navigation, however, the lodesman conning the vessel commanded by Arthur Plantagenet put it on the rocks, and "it burst asunder". Thereupon, with the exchange of a few shots, the English drew off.

Command of the French fleet having been transferred to the Gascon soldier of fortune Pierre Jean le Bidoux, the Mediterranean galleys which had accompanied the new arrival, finding it impossible to penetrate the English blockade and join the Gallic squadrons in harbour, took refuge in Conquet bay; having sunk one patrolling English craft by gunfire—the first ship to suffer such a fate—and seriously disabled another. Snugged down in Conquet, the Gascon "set his basilisks and other ordnance at the mouth of the bay, which was so bulwarked on every side, that by water it was not possible to be won". From this base le Bidoux "sent out his small foists, upon every fair occasion, to annoy the English, in the hope of provoking them to some fresh enterprise". In this he was only too successful, Howard promptly organising a cutting-out expedition of row-barges and galleys; while an independent force put ashore further down the coast, with the object of assaulting the Gascon's land defences.

Howard entered the bay in a small row-barge; but so hot a fire was opened on him, both from the bulwarks and the enemy craft, that "those who should have supported him were afraid", and failed to follow up closely. Undaunted by the desertion of most of his followers, Howard dashed for le Bidoux's personal galley, boarding and entering it at the head of a mere handful of faithful stalwarts. The end was inevitable. Seventeen out of the eighteen henchmen who had clung to his wake were struck down. Howard himself realising that escape was impossible, plucked from his breast the silver whistle that was the badge of his exalted rank and cast it into the sea, before he himself was borne overboard by pike thrusts that drove at him from every point.

Badly demoralised by the loss of its intrepid leader, the fleet bore away and made for Plymouth; its banners flying dismally at half-mast. Disease and lawlessness completed the demoralisation of the crews, who swore that they would "as lief go to purgatory as against the French".

Bidoux was scarcely the man not to follow up success, and his raids on the Sussex coast ended with the substantial village of Brighthelmstone (Brighton) in flames. But the marauder was not destined to escape unscathed. Pressed back on his boats by a handful of hardy bowmen, he only won free at the cost of an eye; an injury from which his recovery was so miraculous that "he had his image in wax, with the English arrow in his face, and offered it as a memorial at the shrine of Our Lady of Boulogne".

With the English naval forces temporarily demoralised and out of hand, the Channel coast lay invitingly open to hostile raids; and Henry hastened to strengthen its defences. Hurst Castle and the forts opposite at Cowes were erected to guard the western approach to the Solent. Camber Castle was the watch-dog for Winchelsea and Rye; Southsea Castle and its outworks protected Portsmouth. Castles were also thrown up at Walmer, Deal, Sandgate, Queensborough and Sandown, while the mouth of the Fal was shielded by the stronghold of St. Mawes and Pendennis Castle on the bluff above Falmouth town. Since the French and Bretons, by reason of their fishing off the Devon and Cornish shores, knew every creek, haven and landing place "as well as any of the King's subjects", a chain of earthworks was dug which covered every vulnerable point. These supplementary defences might be made "upon any man's ground, of what estate or degree soever, and stones, turf and heath taken for the purpose without compensation" [1] The Thames was accorded particular attention. Tilbury fort was built, the gun-battery at Gravesend strengthened, and a block-house frowned across Thames-mouth at Sheerness. Dover, the traditional 'Key of England', was given further security by an additional fort at Archcliff, and the construction of the Moat Battery and the Black Bulwark.

For gunpowder had appreciably narrowed the Channel waters, since the coast now lay at the mercy of off-shore bombardment.

A period of rest and recuperation was all that was required to restore morale in the navy; and Henry presently discovered that he had at disposal 23 'King's ships', 21 hired and re-fitted merchantmen, and 15 victuallers; manned by 3,982 sea-men and 447 gunners. Indeed, the time was not far distant when regular patrols would be established between the Thames and Rye, and Rye and the Channel Islands. The craft were manned by a set of rough, hardy and turbulent shipmen, very difficult to control, and quite capable of echoing the sentiments of one of their number, who informed an Admiralty Court that "If his blood and the King's were both in a dish, there could be no difference between them; and if the Grand Turk would give him a penny a day more, he would serve him." However, as

[1] 4 Hen. VIII, Stat. I, Cap. I.

contemporary punishments included lashing to the bowsprit, with a biscuit, a can of beer and a knife, with the delinquent left to starve or cut himself into the sea, a certain grip on the unruly could generally be maintained. Yet so slack was discipline normally that when the French attacked Dover in 1514, the Crown ships lay idly at their anchorage, their crews having endowed themselves with leave to go ashore in a body.

With the King in personal command, however, they showed a more orderly spirit. Sailing unchallenged past Boulogne to land at his Calais bridgehead, Henry led his expeditionary force to the support of the English troops already besieging the French in Thérouanne. Efforts to raise the siege by the Count of Angoulême[1] culminated in an action in which the Gallic forces panicked so wildly that only the chivalrous Bayard and a few of his more immediate followers refrained from ramming home their prickers and galloping headlong from the field.

Victory in the "Battle of the Spurs"[2]—as Bayard ironically termed it—and the possession of Tournay and Thérouanne might well have raised the traditional hope of crushing France finally, in a breast as sanguine as Bluff King Hal's. But Henry quickly discovered that his shifty allies had left him to carry on the war alone; a feat quite beyond his limited resources. It was the first contact of the youthful Sovereign's romanticism with the facts of life as translated in terms of Continental diplomacy; and the outcome was his shocked agreement to a suspension of hostilities that was destined to last for seven years. Some consolation for the frustration suffered on the Continent might be derived, however, from the fact that Scotland's ability to disturb her neighbour's tranquillity had been thoroughly sterilised by her overwhelming defeat at Flodden Field.

A conspicuous part in the diplomatic negotiations leading to the settlement with France had been played by the King's Almoner, Thomas Wolsey. Another of those pushing clerics who perceived that intervention in secular matters opened the likeliest road to clerical preferment, his reward for sparing the

[1] Subsequently Francis I of France.
[2] In an allusion to the tragic battle of Courtrai of 1302, so called because of the great number of gold spurs found where the nobility of France had fallen under the swords of the victorious Flemings.

French further military humiliation had been a pension from King Louis and Gallic support for the immediate award of a Cardinal's hat. Eventual candidature for the Throne of St. Peter's could doubtless form the basis of some future diplomatic skulduggery. If the ploughboy Henry Chichele could be elevated to the See of Canterbury, there seemed no reason why the butcher's son from Ipswich should not aspire to the Papacy.

* * *

The peaceful interlude that ensued was not allowed to lull Bluff King Hal into neglect of his navy. Between 1514 and 1519 the 'Great Harry' was completed, the *Mary Imperial* and the *Trinity Henry* were built, and the *Gloria*, the *Katherine Pleasance* and the 900-ton *Great Elizabeth* purchased, while the *Mary and John* was put on the stocks at the end of 1520.

At the outset Henry obtained the heavy pieces which now formed the warships' basic armament from the celebrated Hans Popenruyter of Mechlin; although the foundries of the Frenchman, Pierre Bawd, and the Dutchman, Peter van Collen, also made their contribution. For notwithstanding that 1516 had seen the payment of £33 6s. 8d. to John Rutter "for hurts and damages by him sustained in a tenement to him belonging wherein the King's great gonne called the Basilicus was cast", it was not until 1543 that the first iron cannon were fabricated at Braxstead, in the Weald of Kent, where fuel was still obtainable. But the Owen brothers were already busy in the foundry hard by the Church of St. Botolph in Aldgate; Cornelius Johnson, Tyler, and Humphrey Walker on the threshold of their great repute as gun-founders; while negotiations were in train which would bring the Arcanus brothers, Raphael, Francis and Archangel, all the way from Cesana to serve as the King's munition experts.

The provision of ordnance posed far less difficult a problem, indeed, than that of maintaining the supply of wood for ships' timbers. The reckless cutting in Bere Forest and the Weald of Kent, for domestic fuel and to fire the many foundry furnaces, threatened an acute shortage within the forseeable future. England was still a tremendously wooded country; but the abominable condition of the roads rendered it impossible to transport timber in bulk over any considerable distance; yet it was not until 1544 that an Act[1] was passed for conserving the woodlands of England—particularly near the coast—and the first fumbling attempts were made at systematic reafforestation.

The effect of many centuries of steadily persistent silting was beginning very seriously to diminish the Cinque Ports' harbour facilities. Hythe and Romney were virtually out of action, Sandwich yielding helplessly to the encroaching shingle. At Dover the King had given orders for the port to be dredged and for a new mole to be constructed—a continuation of Archcliff Point. In practice, however, this had the contrary effect to that intended, the shingle speedily piling up across the bay as far as Castle Cliff; and contemporary engineers lacked the technical knowledge to suggest a remedy.

Responsibility for lights and beacons, as for pilotage, had been assumed by "the Master, Warden and Assistants of the Guild, Fraternity, or Brotherhood of the Most Glorious and undivided Trinity of St. Clements in the Parish of Deptford in the County of Kent"; based by Sir Thomas Spert on a constitution similar to that in use by the Cinque Ports' Court of Lodemanage.[2] The association was granted its Charter in 1514, and busied itself in erecting almshouses for aged shipmasters and mariners, and in seeking to improve the seafarer's rates of pay and working conditions. Amongst its other responsibilities was the clearance of the Thames for shipping and the supply of the needful ballast-hoys. Its Elder Brethren also undertook the exmination of the "forty mathematical boys of Christ's Hospital" who aspired to become pilots.

With the improved techniques of commerce had come a rising demand for better means of communication. The Strangers' Post between Antwerp and the Netherlands, and London, had been established by the Flemings in 1514. The Dover Post—a Crown service—took only two days to deliver a London letter in Calais, sending it by boat to Gravesend and

[1] 35 Hen. VIII, Stat. I, Cap. 17. The statute was made perpetual under Elizabeth.

[2] Hakluyt maintains that Trinity House was an imitation of the association formed at Seville for the purpose of examining pilots and organising lectures on navigation. Since Henry did no more than confirm the Society in "all its ancient rights and privileges &c", it had obviously been in existence for some time.

thence by the Pilgrims' Way, Sittingbourne and Canterbury, to shipment at Dover. The Merchant-Adventurers were licensed to carry private letters out of England; and big business firms ran their own courier service to Calais, or to Antwerp—an *entrepôt* whose constant extension bore eloquent witness to its ever-increasing consequence.[1]

But with the prevailing south-westerly wind in the narrow seas, it took anything up to four times as long for missives to make the return trip to England.

With the King's ships on constant patrol and the appointment of Vice-Admirals to administer the laws of piracy and wreck on much the same lines as the erstwhile Keepers of the Coast and Conservators of Truces, outrages such as that which occurred in the August of 1546, when a friendly vessel was openly pillaged in Plymouth roads, could be punished if not always averted. The peace treaty between England and France had decreed, *inter alia*, that no privateer, of either nation, should set sail without giving security not to injure the subjects of the other contracting party. Neither should a privateer sell his goods, or restock with supplies, in any of the contracting parties' ports. For all that, special courts had to be established in Rouen and London to deal with the many cases of piracy that still occurred; since a sufficient standing naval force completely to suppress the corsairs, was still wanting. Much of the incoming commerce, therefore, still voyaged prudently in convoy; with substantial importers, like the enterprising George Lazenby, under bond to employ English shipping exclusively. The steadily increasing volume of trade is reflected in the Customs payments (less the wool duty) for the Port of London, which rose from an average of £12,000 for the last five years of Henry VII to over £17,000 *per annum* for the period 1533–8. Unhappily, as London's prosperity expanded that of Southampton declined, very largely owing to the waning trade with Venice; the outcome of the penetration of the Mediterranean by English shipping, not all of it from the Hampshire havens. Bridport—then known as Burport—had long been renowned for its cable, rope and hawser-making; and its industry was materially aided when an Act[2] was passed decreeing that all hemp grown within five

[1] The foundations of Antwerp's magnificent *bourse* were laid in 1531
[2] 21 Hen. VIII, Stat. I, Cap. 12.

miles of the town should be sold nowhere but in Bridport itself. Exeter, Dartmouth and Plymouth all maintained a comfortable turnover; the last-named not only fitting out the long-ranging voyages of William Hawkins the elder, but qualifying in its own right as a subsidiary naval base. And this despite the rival activities at Gillingham, on the Medway, and at Portsmouth; now rejoicing in an enlarged dock, a fine new brewhouse and a commodious victualling storehouse.

In effect, notwithstanding the diminished sales of wool and cloth, and a persistent imbalance between pasture and arable, Henry's predominantly 'protectionist' fiscal policy did a great deal to offset the mischief wrought by his incredibly ill-advised debasement of the currency.[1]

*   *   *

By 1522, partly through political miscalculation and partly because of his eagerness to secure the support of the newly-enthroned Emperor, Charles V, for his candidature for the Papacy, Wolsey adopted a policy undisguisedly anti-Gallic.

In a tense and inflammable atmosphere events were touched off when a Spanish vessel, whose holds contained a consignment of English merchandise, was captured in Thames-mouth by a French privateer. A condition of quasi-war ensued, "a state of things as favourable for the freebooters as it was injurious to the peaceable merchant".[2]

Eventually, the Earl of Surrey led the fleet to an attack on Morlaix, which was thoroughly pillaged before being sent up in flames. Brest was also raided; but an attempt on Boulogne was frustrated by one of the Channel's sudden, violent storms. So much loss and damage was inflicted on the fleet, indeed, that Benjamin Gonson, Senior,[3] was constrained to assemble such small craft as Calais and the Cinque Ports could render

---

[1] Price Contrasts

	Circa 1512	Circa 1554
Biscuit	3s. 6d. to 5s. a cwt.	7s. a cwt.
Salt beef	£1 11s. 0d. a pipe	£3 12s. 0d. a pipe
Beer	13s. 4d. a tun	16s. to 21s. a tun
Red herring	5s. a cade	9s. 6d. to 11s. 6d. a cade
White herring	10s. a barrel	21s. a barrel

[2] Southey.   [3] Subsequently Surveyor of the Navy.

seaworthy, to form some sort of coastal defence and furnish a degree of protection for the fishing fleet.

A French attempt to block Calais harbour with a ship loaded with Caen stone failed miserably when the craft drove on to the sands towards Risebank. Set afire, her unusual cargo was revealed to the astonished onlookers who lost no time in forwarding an ironical letter of thanks to the Captain of Dieppe for this unexpected gift of first-class building material!

A raid on Tréport resulted in the destruction of five enemy ships and the capture of several pieces of ordnance, though not without heavy casualties. A few days later a squadron of twelve Gallic vessels were chased into harbour with the loss of two of their number. The 40-ton *Katherine* galley, on the other hand, fell a victim to six well-appointed French corsairs; as did Captain Markham's *Bark of Sandwich* when it sought to come to its sister-ship's rescue.

By 1527 Wolsey's unstable, opportunist policy had once more veered in favour of the French, and the consequence of this realignment was an open conflict with the Emperor, that took the form of a trade war conducted on the tit-for-tat principle by both sides. English property was seized in the Netherlands and Flemish ships detained in English harbours; with rigorous application of the Navigation Act to give a turn to the screw. It was a struggle in which the principal victim was the commerce on which the two parties to it depended for their prosperity; for the English trade with Denmark in no way made good the losses incurred with the cessation of all traffic with the traditional Hansa market.

It was of minor consolation that, in agreement with France, the principle of territorial waters was established; for their extent not being clearly indicated, very little regard was paid to such limitations as had rather been the subject of legalistic straw-splitting than the basis of precise and practical definition.

Both countries were retrieved from a condition of sullen, costly stalemate by the intervention of Margaret of Burgundy; amicable relations were restored, and with them the free flow of trade.

*　　　*　　　*

Henry's matrimonial tangles and his defiance of the Pope, although they relieved the country of Wolsey's mischievous

handling of foreign policy, led to a *rapprochement* between France
and Spain, and to the threat of a joint attempt at invasion.
Bluff King Hal's reply took the form of industrious shipbuilding and a minatory demonstration of his mastery of the
narrow seas, even with a fleet suffering from considerable
neglect. A pirate squadron was caught and destroyed in
Mount's Bay; while Flemish privateers venturing into the
Downs saw their leader taken prisoner ere they themselves
were sent incontinently to the bottom. With 150 sail concentrated at Sandwich and more on the way, Hispano-Gallic
ardour cooled, and all thoughts of attempting invasion were
abandoned.

The third and final maritime war of Henry's reign opened in
1546 with hostilities against Scotland; whereafter Gallic intervention led to a successful amphibious operation against
Boulogne. Notwithstanding this reverse, when Henry was
abandoned by his ally, the Emperor Charles V, the French
concentrated all their energies on assembling 150 "*gros vaisseaux
ronds*", 60 auxiliary craft, and 25 Mediterranean galleys; all
under the command of Admiral Claude d'Annebaut. To oppose
this formidable force Henry could muster some 80 vessels of
varying size.

The French plan was to sweep the Channel and use the Isle
of Wight as a base from which to blockade and destroy Portsmouth, and with it the English fleet. Whereafter Boulogne, cut
off from succour, should fall like a ripe mulberry. Contact
between the two armaments was made within the enclosed
waters off Spithead; the initial attack coming from the galley
squadron, under Antoine Paulin, which went in and valiantly
sprayed the English fleet with such small pieces as could be
brought to bear. Since Lord Lisle, in command, had no clear
idea how best to reply, he withdrew his heavy craft to gain the
support of the land batteries and a new fort recently completed.
But with incredible folly *he anchored his vessels in line abreast, so
that the cannon along their gun-decks were quite unable to give fire.* For
a time the galleys kept up an ineffectual peppering from their
light-weight ordnance, until, an off-shore breeze springing up,
Lisle's towering squadrons could slip their cables and swan
forward on their tormentors.

Fearing to be rammed—by lumbering 'great ships'!—

Paulin's swift galleys promptly turned tail; and Henry's 'roo-barges', miniature galleys, fitted with sails and sweeps, bored in to complete the rout by briskly cannonading the runaways, until they eventually found the shelter of their main fleet. It was an action without any hint of true sail tactics, in which the mosquito craft were the only ones to acquit themselves with anything like credit, albeit on outmoded traditional lines. More-over, the day had been saddened by the loss of the *Mary Rose*, with her Captain and most of her crew of four hundred. Discipline being the shaky thing it was, through gross negligence her lower gun-ports—a mere sixteen inches above the water-line—had not been closed, and she shipped a heavy sea which sank her in a matter of minutes.

Later in the same year there was another confused and in-determinate encounter off Shoreham; the crews in both fleets being weakened with dysentery and plague. In due course, the pestilence spread to Portsmouth, which suffered severely.

Disappointed with the sluggish performance of his 'great ships' in the recent fight, Henry issued the reactionary order for as many as possible to be furnished with sweeps; but the armada is also notable for having included craft whose rig foreshadowed that of the later galleon.

The English fleet had gone into action with a 'Vantward' and a 'Main Battle', supported by a 'Wing' to windward, composed exclusively of 'oared pieces'. It was its especial duty to ward off the attacks of the enemy galleys on the cherished big ships. Tactically, the action had been indecisive, but strategically the French suffered lasting defeat, since their project of invasion was frustrated. Apart from this, however, the encounter was notable for a significant development, which Lisle recorded in his despatch to the King in the following terms:

"... the *Anne Gallant* and the *Greyhound*, with all your High-ness's shallops and rowing pieces, did their part well, but especially the *Mistress* and the *Anne Gallant* did so handle the galleys as well with their sides as with their prows, that your great ships in a manner had little to do."

In other words, it was the smaller 'oared pieces' that, in-advertently or with full intent, set the example of using their sides—i.e. bringing their broadsides to bear—with the maximum of effect, and in the only way in which a gun-deck can profitably be fought. It only remained—it long remained—for the big ships to follow the admirable example given them by their smaller brethren.

*　　*　　*

The Reformation—set in motion by a sordid wrangle over the proceeds of the trade in Papal 'indulgences'—and King Henry's break with Rome wrought many changes in men's outlook as in the pattern of society. The old feudal nobility found itself very largely ousted in favour of the rather brash new aristocracy made rich on the spoils of the Church—men such as the Russells, Cavendishes, Parrs, Dudleys, Pagets and Seymours; names destined increasingly to figure in the record of the nation's affairs.

With primogeniture in force, many cadets of the impoverished older families had 'gone into trade', and had proved worthy pupils of 'the great cobs of Lombard Street': wealthy merchants such as Sir Andrew Judd, Sir William Chester, Richard Lambert, Thomas Lodge, the Offleys and the Lewisons, whose roots were firmly embedded in international commerce.

They found formidable rivals, however, amongst the adherents of Luther, Bucer and Calvin. For the Puritans, as they were dubbed, conveniently identified material success with Divine favour, and firmly believed that although money might not be regarded as a means to reprehensible happiness, there was no harm in it helping you to be nice and miserable in comfort.

The commercial prosperity built up so carefully by Henry VII had undoubtedly been gravely diminished by the costs of four expensive conflicts, and the heavy toll taken of maritime commerce by the pirates and privateers who infested the narrow seas in times of pseudo-peace as in days of war.[1] But trade exhibited wonderful resilience; "the struggle to grow rich waxed more intense. Men would not submit to the old

[1] The Emperor's sea communications with the Netherlands, for example, had been ravaged, blithely and continuously, both by the English and the French, irrespective of their current alliances.

8+

restrictions, or be content with the old ways of doing business. Custom was more and more replaced by competition"[1]; although the would-be monopolist remained as blind as ever he had been to the fact that commerce is a two-way street.

Where maritime matters were concerned, at least the principle had been accepted that a nation's water-borne commerce has the right to protection by a standing fighting-marine, devoted primarily to its guardianship; although far from sufficient had been done to put teeth into the concept. But a small Crown fleet of 53 ships—of which six were over 500-ton burden—and 37 auxiliary craft, had definitely come into being. Furthermore, two years before his death the King had established a Navy Board which, under the Lieutenant of the Admiralty, the Treasurer of the Navy, the Master of the (Naval) Ordnance, and the Controller, Surveyor, and Clerk of the Ships, gave the sea-service a fixed system of administration and a reasonable continuity of policy. There was also a useful nucleus of 'Standing Officers'; and there were the 'great gonnes', and something more than an inkling of how best to handle them.[2]

Above all, the English mariner had demonstrated the superiority of the ship over the galley; while a certain Master Fletcher of Rye was hard at work perfecting a new fore-and-aft rig which was to exert as revolutionary an influence on seafaring and maritime warfare as had the introduction into conflict of cannon, powder and shot.

[1] J. E. Symes.
[2] Henry VIII loved his 'great gonnes', particularly the 'Twelve Apostles', which he took with him on all his later expeditions. To test their effect he had part of Houndsditch cleared of its inhabitants and used as a proving ground. The area selected was knocked to pieces, and Henry expressed himself delighted with the result of the experiment.

CHAPTER X

'The Sick Man of Europe'

"When discords and quarrels and factions are carried
on openly and audaciously, it is a sign that the rever-
ence for government is lost."

FRANCIS BACON

HENRY VIII broke the bonds that clamped England to
Rome, successfully defied France, and taught the 'Easterlings' temporarily to bear themselves with a becoming humility.
The secret of his strength had lain in his possession of the
nucleus of a standing fleet. Within five years of his death that
fleet had been reduced to half its tonnage, while losing nearly
one-third of its numbers.[1] Fortunately, the personnel of the
Navy suffered no marked deterioration, although all hands
had to endure some remarkably scurvy treatment.

Such were the consequences of confiding the destinies of the
sickly nine-year-old Edward VI to a Regency Council, of which
Edward Seymour, Lord Hertford, was the self-appointed
leader. Brazenly assuming the title of Lord Protector, he proceeded to demonstrate the quality of his political integrity by
elevating himself to the Dukedom of Somerset. At the same
time he ennobled his brother, the Lord High Admiral, and
sought to forestall opposition from John Dudley, Lord Lisle,
by placating him with the lapsed Earldom of Warwick.

Religious differences characterised the whole of Edward's
short reign; and serious affrays between Catholics and Protestants, at their worst in Plymouth, were not unknown in the
fleet. Indeed, the whole period parades a gallimaufry of in-
capables, rogues, zealots and hypocrites, with only two
characteristics in common—self-righteous intolerance, and a
lust to fill their coffers that boggled at no scheme for their
further enrichment.

[1] Report of the Commission on the Navy, 1618.

One of the Lord Protector's first acts was to try and implement the old King's cherished design to reconcile Anglo-
Scottish differences by a marriage between Edward and Mary,
daughter of Caledonia's James V. With the imbecile idea of
furthering the project by a display of force, he marched north
at the head of a powerful army, and, with exquisite tact, proceeded to inflict defeat on the Scots at Pinkie. At one blow, all
the effect of Henry's years of firm but patient diplomacy was
undone. Gallic influence was immediately in the ascendant;
and a French flotilla embarked the Princess and, eluding the
Crown vessels keeping watch and ward in the Channel's
eastern approaches, by sailing round the Orkneys, bore her to
France and the eventual embraces of the Dauphin.

The delicate balance between peace and war with the French
was further jeopardised by the local garrison's attempts to
strengthen the defences of Boulogne; retained as surety for an
unpaid war indemnity of 800,000 crowns. Not that there was
any immediate cause for alarm. The call of emergency still
could summon ten well-armed 'great ships' and up to forty
galleys, pinnaces and smaller craft to the stronghold's support.
Thus when news came through that Leone Strozzi, a mercenary in Gallic pay, was concentrating troops and galleys for
an assault on Boulogneberg, a naval force under Captain
William Winter, sent out to "traverse the seas", carried
through its task so effectually that in due course it was able to
repulse a covert Gallic attempt on the Channel Islands;
which were thereupon re-provisioned and stocked with munitions on a scale that rendered them immune from anything but
full-fledged assault. Thereafter the fleet hung in the offing to
keep a watchful eye on Brest.

Muttering, but not yet ready for an open trial of arms, the
French subsided—much to the relief of London's epicures,
for whose delicate palates live quails were shipped direct from
Calais, in great openwork baskets thoughtfully furnished with
water and hempseed for the journey.

But the general spirit of unease was reflected in the appointment of a Rowt Watch to ride the Sussex Downs and super-
intend the coast watchers, at a wage of 12d. a night for himself
and followers, plus a fine of "2d. out of every sleeper that
watcheth not".

In a naval sense, the Lord Protector and his opportunist brother, Seymour of Sudely, were, of course, living on capital; with the result that in 1552 four 'great ships' were unavailable, being in need of major repairs, while of the ten on service at least five required extensive overhaul.

Contemporary wooden vessels demanded constant attention and a complete 'make-over' at least once in every twenty years. The Spaniards had introduced lead sheathing, to keep the toredo worm and the barnacle at bay, as early as 1514, but the device was not adopted by English shipyards until 1553. The need for overhaul, therefore, was constant. Yet without the authorisation of the Navy Board even so reliable a shipwright as James Baker could not effect the repairs that were patently necessary. Moreover, not all shipwrights were men of Baker's unimpugnable probity. There were plenty of shiftless craftsmen to warrant complaints similar to that penned by Sir Edward Howard, who had protested that one of his ships "had many leaks by reason of Bedyll, the carpenter that worked in her, hath bored a hundred auger holes and left [them] unstopt". Indiscriminate cutting over many centuries had, of course, resulted in a shortage of readily accessible timber, while increasing its price; for attempts at reafforestation were too recent to have yielded fruitful result. Thus Bere Forest and New Forest oak commanded 1s. a ton 'rough and unhewed', 1s. 8d. a ton 'seasoned', and 3s. 4d. a ton 'ready squared'. Bridport and Lynn cordage, on the other hand, had largely replaced the store of rope hitherto brought in from the Baltic; and since the Hansa no longer enjoyed a monopoly in freighting them, Dantzic spars and Stockholm tar were now transhipped in English bottoms at more economical rates. Dantzic also furnished excellent cable up to 17 inches in circumference; while Oléron canvas, at 14s. 4d. to 15s. a bolt, vied with that from Vitré, at £4 13s. 4d. the *balet*—28 French ells. Another variety could be obtained from Poldevys, in Brittany, at 18s. the bolt.

If the tendency to develop the Medway—or Gillingham Water, as it was termed—at the expense of Portsmouth persisted, that was attributable in part to the latter's vulnerability, and partly to the rising costs of transporting everything but timber all the way from London to the Hampshire port.

It had become customary to allot men to specific stations
in the ship—so many to the forecastle, so many to the second
deck, so many to the tryn, the dryngs and the strykes,[1] and so
on. Not that crews always kept their stations obediently,
despite the fact that Standing Orders were nailed to the mainmast for all who could to read. Discipline still left a good deal
to be desired. Only a boat from the flagship, for example, was
entitled to board a strange vessel "for enquiry". Otherwise
all and sundry "would pilfer things from oure nation as well
as the King's dere friends". The general ruling was that with
legitimately captured craft all plunder between the upper and
the lower decks—save treasure—was for division amongst the
foremast hands. The real trouble lay with the shipmen's
remarkably generous interpretation as to what qualified as
legitimate 'prize'. For privateering on lines virtually indistinguishable from sheer piracy still characterised the narrow
seas. With France momentarily not an official belligerent, a
certain John Grynfyld thrust into a fleet of twenty-seven sail
of Normans and Bretons, drove three ashore—to be pillaged
at leisure—and captured a fourth vessel after killing her
captain in a hand-to-hand fight. And Grynfyld was no exception. So blandly unheedful of such unwarrantable activities
was the Admiral Commanding in the Channel, however, that
he had sharply to be exhorted to attend to his business and
"not lye in the haven of Dover idlyie". One of the counts in
the Writ of Attainder which eventually brought the *farouche*
Seymour of Sudely to the block was to the effect that he
had "maintained, aided and comforted sundry pirates, and
taken to his own use goods pyratuslye taken against the
laws".

By 1553 Somerset's policy—if such it can be termed—had
succeeded in thoroughly antagonising Scotland; while Boulogne was so menaced that it was eventually surrendered in
return for the airy promise of an additional tribute of 400,000
gold "crowns of the sun"; a deal which rather betokened
English weakness than reflected Gallic strength. Since the
likelihood of collecting either this sum or the former indemnity
seemed remote in the extreme, the Lord Protector had obviously gone too far on his erratic course to be borne with any

---

[1] Helm, halliards and ropes.

longer. The block on Tower Hill saw his unlamented end; with Warwick hastening to step into his shoes.

To remedy the situation that confronted him on assuming power would have taxed wits far readier than Warwick boasted. Commerce was dwindling, since throughout the Continent there was a growing tendency to refuse to trade with the English heretics on any terms. For apart from they themselves being brands that only the most optimistic could hope to snatch from the burning, they had given refuge to many hundreds of Protestants—Walloons, Germans, French, Italians, Poles, and Switzers—who had fled to England to escape the attentions of a Holy Inquisition that was all-powerful through-out the Continent—save at Antwerp. In this great mart even the disciples of Torquemada were forced to stay their hands, since it had been made plain to the Emperor that "should the Inquisition come, the English most assuredly will go"; to the progressive decline of the city's bounding prosperity, for want of the wool that only England could supply.

Wool in great quantity still passed over Antwerp's many wharves, out of the holds of vessels exclusively in English ownership. But when it came to the export of cloths manu-factured in England, the position was nowhere near so satis-factory. Taking full advantage of their trading privileges, the 'Easterlings', on average, shipped three times as many lengths as their English rivals.[1] Moreover, they consistently offended by the brazen fashion in which they 'coloured' the wares of merchant-strangers not of their Association; at an annual loss to the Customs, it was alleged, of £20,000. In six years the price of raw English wool increased threefold; and the practice arose of debasing it by mixing in inferior Spanish yarn. This dubious device, plus the abnormally high cost of native manu-facture, combined with the general inflationary tendency of the economy to flood the market with English cloth so grossly 'falsified' that foreign competitors could challenge the home industry with nonchalant confidence; the inevitable outcome of a policy that sought to favour the trader at the expense of the producer.

With the prevailing shortage of shipping, and with the cost

[1] In 1552, for example, the Hanseatics exported 44,000 full cloths, as against the 11,000 shipped by the Merchant-Adventurers.

of living spiralling as the steady depreciation of the coinage continued, the Navigation Act was suspended, as a temporary measure, between February and October, to permit the transport of wine and woad from Bordeaux in foreign bottoms.

With their commerce shrinking steadily, the Merchant-Adventurers appealed to the Privy Council; whose members were persuaded to clap a heavy additional duty on all merchandise imported and exported by the *Staelhof*; in the case of some commodities, 20 per cent in lieu of standard 1 per cent paid since the days of Henry III.

It was a game of international beggar-my-neighbour in which the last state was, if anything, worse than the first. 'Monopoly' had run riot, and not only in international trade. For in England itself towns and cities still fought for the exclusive right to manufacture a particular commodity—as when York sought to exclude everyone else from the fabrication of felt hats, thrummed caps, coverlets and dornocks,[1] and wool-manufacturing centres like Winchester and Exeter strove to prohibit the weaving of wool in the hamlets and villages adjacent to them. As always, the industrious piece-worker was anathema to those banded together not only to support artificial prices, but to ensure that the naturally diligent refrained from setting a pace unacceptable to the less energetic majority.[2]

In the outcome, devaluation having involved the Administration in the very difficulty it had been designed to remedy, the whole country was plunged into a condition of financial and economic chaos. With the humbler folk "not able to keep a cow for the comfort of them and their poor family",[3] and with English grain demanding 20s. a quarter, food was in such short supply that, save under special licence, the export of corn, cattle, pigs and sheep was forbidden; subsistence for the Calais garrison providing the only exception to the rule. There was even a scheme propounded to import 40,000 quarters of wheat

[1] Diaper linen.

[2] The guilds which had been developed out of religious brotherhoods—such as that at York for the performance of a morality play—were largely swept away by the Reformist legislation of Henry VIII and Edward VI. But the purely craft guilds were little affected even by enactments aimed at the control of their restrictive practices. A class had come into existence which invariably fought hard, and often successfully, to resist any policy it did not condescend to approve.

[3] *History of the Reformation*, Gilbert Burnet, Bishop of Salisbury.

from Dantzic; while especial efforts were made to reinvigorate
the fishing industry, which had fallen into something of a
decline. The dissolution of the great religious foundations had,
of course, greatly diminished all-the-year-round demands; and
the tendency of the herring and pilchard to migrate south-
westwards had seriously affected the bulk of the catch normally
trawled—and this all the way from the languishing Cinque
Ports to the once prosperous huthes of Fowey and Dartmouth
—the last-named still struggling with the debts incurred in the
erection of its guardian castle and outer batteries. In general,
the out-ports were in sore need of sympathetic consideration,
since the loss of the English possessions in Gascony had permanently reduced the volume of trade passing through them;
as had the tendency to concentrate the handling of as much
overseas commerce as possible in the port of London. For there
Customs dues could be more easily checked and collected; and,
for that matter, farmed.

With the prevailing food shortage, an enactment[1] was passed
which was designed not only as a measure for conserving carcase
meat, but as a means of stimulating the consumption of fish
and at the same time swelling the ranks of fisherfolk, among
whom the Crown ships and the merchantmen found by far
their best recruits. This Act decreed that "No person or
persons . . . shall . . . willingly or wittingly eat any manner of
flesh . . . upon Friday or Saturday, or the Embring Days, or
in any day in the time commonly called Lent, nor at any such
other as is or shall be at any time hereafter commonly reputed
and accepted as a Fish Day", under penalty of heavy fines.

Having regard for the widespread 'Reformist' prejudice
against the Romish practice of fasting, the desperation of the
measure only too clearly reflects the sorry state into which
affairs had fallen.

The joint venture of Sir Hugh Willoughby and Robert
Chancellor to try and find the North-West passage, like the
voyage of Plymouth's William Hawkyns to the Guinea Coast,
opened up potential new avenues of trade, as they added
appreciably to the English mariners' store of oceangoing experience. But their beneficial effect was long-term rather than
immediate. The Russia Company, for example, founded to

[1] 2–3 Edw. VI, Stat. I, Cap. XIX.

8*

develop trade with Muscovy, did not receive its Charter till 1554.

The unfortunate Edward furnishes a grim example of the sins of the fathers being visited on their children. Born of a sire foully diseased and prematurely aged, his bright promise quickly dimmed with the development of pulmonary tuberculosis. With puberty the spirochaetes that had been lying latent became violently active. Racked with an incurable cough, in his last moments he managed to gasp out, "O Lord God, free me, I beseech you, from this calamitous world". And for Edward Tudor the individual, as for Edward VI the country's nominal ruler, a calamitous world it had been indeed.

With the boy-King in his death-throes, and as the members of the Privy Council left their deliberations in Greenwich Palace to cheer Willoughby and Chancellor's ships on their way, Warwick—now elevated to the Dukedom of Northumberland—was busy plotting to oust the Sovereign's named successor, Mary, the Catholic daughter of Bluff King Hal and Katherine of Aragon, in favour of the Protestant granddaughter of Henry's younger sister, the sixteen-year-old Lady Jane Grey.[1]

* * *

Seeking to flee the country, Mary found her first supporters in the very shipmen sent by Northumberland to detain her. They were far from being alone in their readiness rather to bear with a half-Spanish Queen of dubitable legitimacy, than again accept the detested combination of a Monarch under age, swayed by a dictatorial Lord Protector. With her mother, Mary had passed through years of hideous suffering and humiliation; and with her plain face and frightened ways she was, at thirty-seven, a typical old maid—but one smouldering with damped-down fires whose molten heat could only find an outlet in a religious fervour barely distinguished from rabid bigotry. Welcomed to London with the traditional pomp and circumstance, it was not without significance that the pageants of the merchant-strangers—the Easterlings, Genoans and Florentines—"were the mightiest".[2] For the unfortunate

---

[1] She was an heiress of the Suffolk line, but had been expressly excluded from the succession by the terms of the will drawn up by Henry VIII.

[2] *Chronicles of London*, C. L. Kingsford.

Queen was to be the focus of a seesaw struggle between these alien merchants and her own thrusting waresmen, that was to bedevil her whole brief reign. In the general turmoil of hoisting the lonely, friendless woman on to the throne it was very largely overlooked, however, that a sworn enemy of the Reformation had been elevated into the one position wherefrom a counter-Reformation movement could best be engineered. For that matter, equally little thought was spared for the possible fate of the Queen's Protestant half-sister, Elizabeth.

During the years of their abasement both Katherine of Aragon and her daughter had been buoyed up by the moral support of the Emperor, the magnificent and romantic Charles V. It was to him, therefore, that Mary turned on ascending her uneasy Throne, even—and right eagerly—offering herself in marriage to the widower-monarch. But solicitous as Charles might be for the Catholic cause, this was one sacrifice that he preferred his son to make. Philip, who was already betrothed to the Infanta of Portugal, "sighed as a lover, but obeyed as a son";[1] although it was clear that the Queen of England's marriage to the future King of Spain would not only unleash the forces of religious persecution, but put a premium on war with France.

With conflict in the offing, naval stocktaking offered scant ground for satisfaction. The venerable *Grâce à Dieu* had been accidentally destroyed by fire; and of the 23 vessels optimistically classed as great ships, at least three were no more than pinnaces; a craft out of which had been evolved the more substantial barque, which in its turn was the forebear of the frigate. None the less, the stalwarts who manned and commanded the craft were still capable of a magnificently arrogant gesture. The fleet of 160 sail escorting Philip of Spain to the celebration of his marriage with England's Queen was met in the Channel by a tiny squadron under William Lord Howard of Effingham. Philip's Admiral was wearing the Spanish flag at the main, and showed no inclination to render that traditional

[1] To quote Gibbon's immortal phrase when confronted by similar parental commands. The House of Austria was always famous for the skill with which it arranged its matrimonial alliances; and a pasquinade summed it up thus:

Bella gerunt alii—tu, felix Austria, nube!

(Others wage war for a throne—you, happy Austria, marry!)

tribute to the 'Sovereign of the English Sea' her shipmen
regarded as her due. This insolent neglect Howard bluntly
refused to countenance; and when the Spaniard exhibited a
disposition to argue the matter, a shot was put across his bows
with exemplary promptitude. It was a hint scarcely to be
ignored, and the offending Colours were dipped and the topsails struck with a speed that exhibited the authentic note of
apology. Salty and audacious, the whole gesture was redolent
of that gusty self-satisfaction to which the English shipman,
not without warrant, was beginning to deem himself entitled.
Men who had taken their cockleshell craft to the distant fishing
grounds of Iceland and Newfoundland, and brought their
catch safely back to harbour, could be pardoned a little
touch of self-assertion. Plymouth, ever the home of aggressive
Nonconformity, was far from diffident in its approval of "an
action highly meritorious and worthy imitation"; nor were
words of approbation in any way confined to the West Country.

Philip lost no time in trying to influence the Council in
favour of the Spanish Netherlands; deliberately jettisoning the
policy laid down in the days of Mary's predecessor, and as
flagrantly cutting across those measures—such as concessions
to a wilting Southampton—the Queen herself had authorised
for the resuscitation of trade. "This," commented Borough[1]
drily, "was the first effect of this Queen's alliance with the
Emperor." Since their Russian and Danish markets had virtually closed down on them, the three-year suspension of the
legislation, devised to restrain their activities in England,
proved the Hansa merchants' absolute salvation. The Merchant-
Adventurers were immediately in arms, protesting that
preferential treatment for the 'Easterlings' could only result
in injustice to the homeland trading community. Since the
London waremongers could support their contention by pointing to the decay of the cloth industry, the diminished wool
sales at Blackwell Hall, and the consistently unfavourable rate
of exchange prevailing on the great Antwerp Bourse, they
could scarcely be ignored. Perhaps the most telling argument
advanced was to the effect that the Flemish merchants resident

[1] Sir John Borough, Keeper of the Records in the Tower of London, and
author of the treatise, previously referred to, on *The Sovereignty of the English
Sea*.

in London, by the rules of the *Staelhoef*, were bachelors every man, and thus with far fewer calls on their coffers, in a domestic sense, than their Benedict English competitors. In the outcome, the Council's quiet, deferential but unwavering defiance of the Spanish interloper's attempt to influence policy culminated in an edict—that of 1555—as comprehensively 'protectionist' as the Edward VI enactment of 1552. The days of the 'Easterlings' were numbered.

As was only to be expected, the Hansa League immediately resorted to reprisals. English ships in such ports as the Flemings controlled were put under arrest and their cargoes forcibly broken out under extortionate rates of duty. The next step was to banish all English vessels, men and goods from the Hansa towns; an embargo which threatened consequences of some seriousness with the outbreak of the Anglo-Spanish war with France.

The opening of hostilities found the Crown fleet quite unprepared for any major operation. The measure of its general unreadiness to act as guardian of the narrow seas had long since been painfully demonstrated by the lawlessness which prevailed in the Channel, even within sight of the naval centre and victualling station at Dover—the transmogrified *Maison Dieu*. For a number of the vessels had been sold, including the *Primrose*—which rated as a 'great ship'—and certain smaller craft; some of which had been knocked down for as little as £8 and £10 apiece, so decayed was their condition. The most considerable vessel in Lord Howard's fleet escorting the army to France was the 700-ton *Jesus of Lübeck*. Of her sister ships only five were over 200 tons.

It was not an armament upon which to rely with any particular confidence when news came of intensive preparations to invest the Calais outpost by land and water; and this despite the fact that, without the formality of Parliamentary consent, a stiff export duty had been clapped on cloths and an import duty exacted from wines, specifically to strengthen the means of national defence. In the event, Howard made no move, although considerable precedent existed for taking the fleet to sea even during the winter months.

The war was not generally popular, however; the malcontents, forgetful of Gallic enmity for all things British, grumbling that the Queen, "contrary to promise, had tangled herself in her husband's quarrels". It was a sentiment which better expressed distrust for the Spaniard than a clear appreciation of French intentions. So there was no one of sufficient influence to point out that, although the Anglo-Spanish forces had scored a victory at St. Quentin, the Calais garrison, reduced in numbers by two-thirds during the winter months, as a measure of pinch-penny economy, had not been restored to full strength with the outbreak of hostilities.

On New Year's Day the French, under the duc de Guise, entered the English pale in overwhelming force; the Calais outworks at Risebank and Nieulay Bridge being overborne in the first rush. The town itself was then brought under close siege, and subjected to heavy bombardment. For a solid week the Lord Deputy, Wentworth, and his five hundred followers, repulsed every assault made on the crumbling defences; hoping against hope that succour would arrive from England. But even if a relieving force could have been scraped together, the criminally negligent authorities lacked the vessels in which to transport them. In the prevailing spirit of lethargy and pessimism, little or nothing had been done to arouse the 'great ships' from their winter hibernation and get them speedily into commission.

On the eighth day of the siege, therefore, a stronghold which it had cost Edward III eleven months to reduce surrendered on terms the French should have been more ashamed to offer than the English to accept. Futile sailing orders for the sluggard fleet were issued on the very day that England relinquished its grip on a fortress-city it had held firmly in its hands for two hundred and eleven years.

The loss of Calais was a blow right to the country's heart. Emerging from their numbed bewilderment, the authorities again gave agitated orders for the fleet to make ready to put to sea. By hastily re-equipping the Crown ships and fitting out some substantial hired merchantmen, Howard's successor, Edward Lord Clinton, contrived to assemble a reasonably formidable armament by the midsummer of 1558. But a storm struck Clinton's armada off the Channel Islands "the licke of which was never syn, ffor there were many ships that halfe the men were thrown down sick at once". For all that, a squadron was detached from the main fleet which intervened successfully on the flank of a tussle between the French and some of Philip's Netherlanders, fought out on the shore at Gravelines. Caught between two fires, the Gallic forces were given so thorough a trouncing that the recapture of Calais would not have been beyond the power of a courageous and resolute commander. But Clinton preferred to pursue the less risky course of launching futile raids on Brittany. The wretched haven of Conquet was "put to saccage, with a great abbey and many pretty towns and villages thereabout"; which was little enough to set against the loss of Calais and all that it entailed. Small wonder that the noted traveller and Orientalist Sir Henry Blount could refer despondently to England as "the sick man of Europe",[1] a country that, so far as the prevailing competition in oceanic expansion was concerned, appeared to have dropped clean out of the race.

Absorbed in the horrid interplay of persecution and martyrdom, the ever-forgetful English had failed to bear faithfully in mind that a house divided against itself is an open invitation to aggression from outside. The best that can be said of the Calais *débâcle* is, that it served as a painfully sharp reminder that without a strong standing fleet an island race is condemned to live in a state of perpetual humiliation and alarm.

[1] Just prior to the Crimean War the term was employed again, in reference to Abdul Medjid, Sultan of Turkey, by the Tsar Nicholas, in conversation with Metternich. That mordacious diplomat immediately replied, "Do you speak, Sire, as physician or as heir?"

CHAPTER XI

The Long Haul

"Man's foot is chained to the path, but the prow of a
ship opens its way where it will."

Arab Proverb

THE Elizabethan age did not burst into full flower overnight.
Starting slowly, its floriation was as gradual as it can now be
seen to have been inevitable. The Queen herself had emerged
from a seclusion that had about it all the characteristics of
political house arrest; it took some time for her to accustom
herself to the feeling that her head was fixed securely on her
shoulders. As for her people, they were still numbed by the
loss of Calais. Even the revealing eagerness with which the
French concluded peace, on the understanding that the
stronghold should remain in their possession, for a maximum
period of eight years, brought insufficient consolation. There
had been too many instances of Gallic perfidy for much faith
to be reposed in promises of the outpost's eventual return. A
carking sense of frustration persisted; and the fact that Sark
was won back from enemy hands by a party of Flemings only
added to the general feeling of inadequacy. There was so much
stirring in the world; and so much from which the English
began to realise that they had been excluded. This state of
affairs they speedily discovered to be entirely unacceptable.
For institutional religion—a technique for enabling a certain
dogma to survive—was swiftly giving place to a strong sense
of nationalism. "The World, not the Church, called the tune
to which the Elizabethan age danced and sang"[1]—and, be it
added, was ever ready to draw a sword never rammed home
too tightly in its scabbard.

Of all the people on the fairway to the fabulous New World
the island people were by far the slowest off the mark; a

[1] Professor Walter Raleigh,

tardiness mainly attributable to their lingering Continental commitments and the empty Treasury which was the outcome of their unsuccessful pursuit of them. With Papal blessing, Spain and Portugal had long since carved out stupendous overseas dominions, which they clearly intended to exploit as an inviolable monopoly—for France had virtually dropped out of the race. The Dutch, on the other hand, had so materially improved their port of Amsterdam that it bid fair to attract more trade than Antwerp.

So far as Protestant England was concerned, the Papal ban on enterprise was regarded as an open challenge by seamen-traders of the quality of John Hawkins, Martin Frobisher and Francis Drake. Futile, profitless warfare on the Continental mainland, it was hoped, was over and done with: if sanction was denied to the adventurous peacefully to make trade wheresoe'r they listed, then the only thing to do was to set forth boldly to take trade by force of arms—preferably in those "Fortunate Isles of the Blest" of which Henry, the Huckster King, had thought so fondly, and which the Dons had the temerity to look upon as their own exclusive dependencies.

The first process called for the discovery of a market and the route to it, the planting of a settlement and its subsequent protection; the second involved the intrusion into someone else's monopoly, and victory in the warfare that inevitably would ensue. Trade might be established with Russia and even with Persia and India by the methods of peaceful penetration. It would be far otherwise in the vast territories that the Iberian Catholic Powers claimed as exclusively their own. Philip II was the ruler of Spain, Naples and Sicily, the Milanese territory of Northern Italy, the province of Franche-Compté, the Netherlands, and the new colonies of America. Portugal held sway in Brazil, the islands of the Atlantic, Guinea, Angola and Mozambique in Africa, in Macon and the Philippines; and had organised a vast system of trade with the Far East. The Catholic sister-nations bestrode the world like a Colossus; but that was not a prospect to affright the men who had resolved that England should take her place amongst the world's great Oceanic Powers.

Nor did they lack the support of "the great cobs of Lombard

Street", *entrepreneurs* such as Sir Lionel Ducket, Sir Thomas Smythe, Sir Andrew Judd, and William Chester; men with the wealth to support such venturesome enterprises. Above all, there was practical encouragement forthcoming from the Court, with Francis Walsingham—ever a good friend to seamen—and Sir Edward Dyer as eager to sponsor profitable adventuring as Christopher Hatton, the great Leicester, and, on occasion, the Queen's Majesty herself; although when the political situation demanded it, she would brazenly disavow in public an interest that privately she watched with the very closest of attention. For there was much of her grandsire's parsimony about 'Gloriana', and she was ever careful of the pieces. More rarely, even the Queen's most influential counsellor, William Cecil—born with the gift of perpetual old age —might be persuaded to support a venture that gave reasonably fair promise of returning *cent per cent*; for the man's natural propensity for temporising and holding back was ever at odds with the rashness born of an avarice to which only a Molière could render proper justice.

But there was a tremendous leeway to make up; and for the remarkably long haul that lay ahead the first need was ships —ships to ensure the protection of the homeland; ships for the ventures into far-off seas as yet unpenetrated.

Some 22 effective vessels of 100 tons and upwards, with a further 12 sail deemed "of no continuance and not worth repair", were listed by a committee appointed to ascertain what naval resources, other than merchant ships on charter, were immediately available. Endorsed by Edward Bashe (General Surveyor of the Victuals) and Benjamin Gonson (Treasurer of the Navy), the committee's admirable report, entitled *The Book of Sea Causes*, clearly envisaged a future when not the army, but the navy, would take pride of place as the principal factor in the country's defence.

The growing tendency was to classify vessels in categories: the first rates of 600 tons and upwards; the second-rates of 400 to 600 tons; the third-rates of 200 to 400 tons; the fourth-rates of 100 to 200 tons; the fifth-rates of 50 to 100 tons, and the sixth-rates of anything under 50 tons.[1] The marked preference

[1] This did not become an official method of classification until the time of the Commonwealth.

of both Bashe and Gonson, as of Hawkins and Drake, was for ships of the middle class, of 400 to 500 tons, which were termed race-built galleons. They were fore-and-aft rigged, mobile and, by contemporary standards, remarkably seaworthy, with a keel three times that of the beam, and a beakhead with a pronounced forward rake to slice the seas and prevent them from breaking inboard. Although still handicapped with an amount of top hamper that made for erratic sailing, as a warship the medium-rater, with its speed, weatherliness and manœuvrability, was far superior to the high-charged, unwieldy Spanish galleon or the traditional Mediterranean 'oared pieces.'[1]

In support of the lighter vessels a ship such as the *Triumph*—into whose structure John Hawkins introduced such improvements as the chain pump and topmasts that could be struck—possessed a weight of ordnance to out-gun any adversary it was likely to encounter. For disregarding its lighter man-killing pieces, the total weight of cannon carried by the *Triumph* was 148,000 lb., as against the 83,720 lb. mounted in earlier days by the *Henri Grâce à Dieu*; giving a broadside of 374 lb. as against one of 275 lb. for the older craft.

The exaction of ship-money from the ports and coastal counties was offset, to some degree, by the offer of a bounty of 5s. a ton for all craft of 100 tons and over. But when it came to the naval measures to be generally pursued, there was a fundamental dichotomy between the advocates of a bold 'forward' policy and those who preferred to evade rather than defy the stranglehold on trade with South America and the Indies that Spain and Portugal sought to maintain by every means in their power. It was typical of the Queen's evasiveness and opportunism, as of the continued influence exercised by the hebetudinous Cecil, that neither party could be sure of her lasting favour, which was bestowed or withdrawn as caprice or the tortuous arabesques of her own personal diplomacy might dictate.

Elizabeth cannot altogether be blamed, however, for blowing

[1] The Spanish galleon was constructed to bring large non-perishable cargoes over a long sea-passage to the home port. The smaller, faster craft had been developed to carry 'perishable' cargoes of fruit and slaves. 'Galleon built' implied strong upper works, but not so high-charged as those of the galleon proper.

hot and cold as expediency demanded, for hers was a particularly difficult row to hoe. Mary Queen of Scots was an
abiding menace, whether enthroned in Edinburgh or seeking
by flight to England to escape the extremist fervour of the
'Reformists' north of the Border. For wherever she abode she
became the focus of every plot to restore the 'Old Religion' and
a Catholic Queen on England's throne. In addition, Elizabeth
constantly found herself embroiled in the backwash of trouble
occasioned by those whose efforts to take trade where forbidden
to make trade, aroused Spain and Portugal to indignant protest
and sanguinary reprisal.

The matter was first brought sharply into focus by the far-
ranging voyage of John Hawkins, of 1562-3. Hawkins was a
Plymouth man, the son of that tough old tarpaulin-captain,
William Hawkins. Possessed of remarkable seafaring qualities
and an exceptionally robust sense of business, his naive love of
ostentation was balanced by a pronounced streak of Puritanism,
which forbade "oaths and swearing" and mustered his crew
"to serve God daily" at morning and evening prayers. For all
that, he did not baulk at conducting a lucrative traffic in the
slaves so desperately required as manual labourers by the
Spanish colonists in South America—an enterprise reprobated,
on moral grounds, by neither Catholic nor Puritan. But
politically the Devon Captain's spirited penetration of a
jealously cherished Hispano-Portuguese preserve—defiantly repeated in 1564 and 1567—had consequences out of all proportion to the relatively modest scope of his activities.

Officially, Spain and England were at peace. But the length
to which unofficial hostilities could be pushed without leading
to an open rupture was a peculiarity of that "unsolemn war"—
as legal jargon terms strife lacking official countenance—which
raged as furiously in European waters as in the Caribbean.
Apart from Hawkins, the Huguenots, with Rochelle as their
base, harried the 'Idolators' ' shipping right into the chops of the
Channel; vastly enriching Plymouth, incidentally, by turning it
into a mart for the disposal of their booty. Philip's army of
occupation in the Netherlands, short of replacements, money
and supplies, were almost entirely cut off from succour by way
of the narrow seas through the activities of the 'Beggars of the
Sea'. For this fraternity of banished Flemish lords, ruined

merchants and exiled seamen waged incessant war on the Spaniard under Letters of Marque distributed by the Prince of Orange, although legally he had no admiralty jurisdiction.[1] Dunkirkers and Englishmen, such as Champernowne, Killigrew, Carey, Horsey and Oglander, shared with the 'Sea Beggars' the hospitality and trading facilities of Southampton and the Cinque Ports. The Orange Admiral, Count de la Mark, actually lived ashore at Dover when not preying on such Spanish shipping as ventured into *La Manche*. Remonstrances from Castile were loud and frequent; and every so often Elizabeth would make a great parade of reproving the offenders. She would even send a small squadron to 'scour the seas' as a gesture of conciliation. But Sir Henry Palmer, in command of three of the Queen's ships, was visited with no more than a mild reprimand for "lyeing at ease" in Dover harbour while the freebooters worked their will right under his nose. As everyone was comfortably aware, the Queen's display of ire was no more than a piece of play-acting demanded by the exigencies of *la haute politique*. Her anger was real enough, however, when informed of the looting of a friendly Dutch ship, cast ashore off Romney and promptly despoiled of a cargo worth £2,600. The Vice-Admiral of Kent was also sharply reminded of his duty when the news came that, with a Danish vessel wrecked off Dungeness, "the inhabitants there, coming aboard the said ship under colour to yield assistance, fell a-spoiling and hewing the ship"; the Bailiff of Lydd himself being "a principal instrument" in the outrage.

Gillingham and Chatham, supported by the capacious dockyards and ropewalks of Deptford and Woolwich, had become the principal bases for the Queen's ships; while a dockyard was projected for the Medway haven. These yards, with a little help from Portsmouth, gave steady employment to over 500 men, working under the eye of the master-shipwrights Peter Pett and Matthew Baker. The ordinary run of shipwrights drew a basic rate of pay of 8*d.* to 1*s.* a day—rising in 1588 to 1*s.* and 1*s.* 6*d*—with victualling, "as much beer as would suffice", and lodging—although they still had to sleep two in a bed.

A register compiled in 1573 revealed that there were 135

---

[1] For this reason, the "Sea Beggars" were for some time treated by the Spaniards as pirates.

merchant craft—many of 500 tons and upwards—plying from English ports; with London well in the lead for the number of its ship-owners.[1] Elsewhere, the tendency was to desert a south coast lacking in really good harbours and dangerously exposed in time of war, and concentrate more on the westward havens. Over the years, however, Dartmouth and Fowey had reluctantly yielded pride of place to Plymouth; which owed its increasing consequence to its sheltered anchorage, its more populous hinterland, and to the presence on St. Nicholas Island of the Vice-Admiral of Devon. The growing importance of the West was clearly reflected in the register of shipmen, which showed 342 as belonging to Hampshire as against Devonshire's 1,100. "To encourage ship-building and increase the breed of mariners", Elizabeth went even further than Edward's Regency Council, and decreed that "every Wednesday of every week" should be observed as a Fish Day additional to the many already incorporated in the calendar. Furthermore, Customs dues were remitted for English fishermen trading in English vessels, and heavy restrictions were placed on the importation of fish by aliens. This last measure was particularly approved along the coasts, and was vigorously supported by the pamphleteer, John Nashe, in his widely read *Lenten Stuff: The Praise of the Red Herring.*

Elizabeth was far too long-headed to repose any faith in the Gallic pledge to restore Calais, in due course, to English occupation. She had the less compunction, therefore, in acceding to the appeal of Condé to go to the support of his Huguenot forces, holding on somewhat precariously against the duc de Guise in Normandy. It was a move which not only would put her in possession of the commanding port of Havre de Grâce, but would win the enthusiastic support of the Puritan element amongst her own subjects; determined as they were to clear the ground of the last remnants of Papal tyranny the better to erect one of their own.

Under the command of the Earl of Warwick, 6,000 troops were sent across the narrow seas, Havre de Grâce was garrisoned, and Rouen prepared to resist assault. As it transpired, the latter outpost was speedily captured by de Guise, after desperate

[1] *Complete History of the Most Remarkable Transactions at Sea*, Peter Burchet.

fighting. With Condé treacherously entering into a separate peace with his enemies, the undernourished, plague-ridden English troops in Havre were forced to capitulate. Actually, the articles of surrender were signed on the very day that Clinton appeared off the port with a reinforcement of 3,000 men. He had been delayed by the prevailing and persistent south-westerly wind, which, as so often before, had proved an ally to England's enemies.

This setback was followed by the military occupation of the Netherlands by the Duke of Alva; with the rack and thumb-screw of the Inquisition to hasten the process of forcible con-version. Elizabeth's plan to encourage the Flemish Protestants and French Huguenots to pull the Catholic Monarch's teeth for her and at the same time hasten the return of Calais, had not only misfired but been guilty of the enormity of leaving her with seriously depleted coffers. The only consolation to be derived from the venture was to be found in the arrival of a fresh swarm of Protestant refugees. For nearly all of them were skilled woollen, linen or silk manufacturers or craftsmen—weavers, dyers, cloth-dressers and silk-throfters. Under their instruction the English workers greatly improved the quality of their products, and in addition learned to fabricate stockings, damasks, linen bays and sayes, the famous Flemish black-and-white chequered cloth, and many light materials, to their sub-stantial profit.[1] Sandwich, for example, was licensed to receive twenty-five master-craftsmen, clothworkers, and fishers, in the hope of reviving, or instituting, industries in a town suffering from sad decay owing to the persistent silting of its harbour. So important was the position the Flemings quickly made for themselves in the community that the Church of St. Peter was set aside for their exclusive use. German workers bent an equal skill to the mining of the West Country's copper, zinc and silver. The technical accomplishment these newcomers introduced was undoubtedly welcome. In addition, however, they brought with them a variety of glum, acrid Calvinism that was destined to proliferate in an anarchy of rancorous subdivision. Its incidence drove the thin end of the wedge of schism into the country's vitals, and religious intolerance was presently to

---

[1] It was the Dutch immigrants who introduced the new industry of market gardening.

harden into political bigotry, with consequences that split the realm in twain.

*   *   *

Hawkins' third voyage to the West Indies, of 1567, ended with his escape by the narrowest of margins from the snare laid for him by the Spaniards at San Juan de Uloa. Among his subordinates in the venture had been his cousin, the Tavistock-born Francis Drake; at this period well under thirty years of age. Sanguine, dynamic, and infused with a double dose of vitality, in an era of outstanding seamen-warriors he was to show himself the most daring and accomplished of them all. As yet, however, he had to prove himself; for his conduct in sailing clear from San Juan in his ship the *Judith*, before Hawkins had made good his own escape, undoubtedly exposed him to criticism. In any case, the venture could hardly be accounted a success; while the provocation it afforded was out of all proportion to the profits in trade and 'black ivory' made on the voyage.

Philip of Spain, however, was soon to be given even more serious grounds for complaint. A squadron of five Biscay ships, carrying stores and money for the payment of Alva's army in the Netherlands, fled before a fleet of Huguenot corsairs from La Rochelle, to seek refuge in Falmouth, Plymouth and Southampton. Espès de Guerau, the Spanish Ambassador in London, immediately lodged a protest, averring that the pirate fleet had included two English ships. But the matter was amicably settled with arrangements for the million ducats on board the Spanish *nao* at Southampton to be landed, taken by road to Dover, and thence conveyed to Flanders under the English flag. In the outcome the temptation of 159 barrels of glittering specie was too strong to be resisted, and the treasure was seized on the somewhat tenuous pretext that, in truth, it did not as yet belong to the King of Spain, but was a loan put up by certain Genoan bankers and money-lenders, from whom Elizabeth was quite prepared to borrow it at the usual rates of interest![1]

Protests from Madrid were immediate; but with Alva took the more practical form of seizing the goods and imprisoning the persons of all the English merchants on whom he could lay

[1] State Papers, Foreign, 1569–71.

his hands.[1] English warships having openly landed arms and munitions for the use of the Huguenot insurgents in La Rochelle, the French joined in by impounding all the English merchandise in Rouen. Elizabeth, who was in no mind for a double war with France and Spain, was full of excuses and apologies; while with France pacified, Spain was unwilling to enter on a conflict with England that would weaken the front she esteemed it necessary to maintain against her Gallic neighbour.

Alva's rough handling of the English Merchant-Adventurers was accorded the heartiest of approval by their rivals of the Hansa. Driven from Antwerp by the suspension of commerce with the Netherlands, the members of the Association took up their residence in Emden; moving on to Hamburg and thence to Staden and Middelburg as the machinations of the Hanseats increasingly hampered their trading operations and deprived them of the privileges they had so long enjoyed. Reprisals were not wanting on the part of the Administration in England; and the war between these two monopolistic corporations persisted well into the following century.

If gubernatorial support for the Merchant-Adventurers was not always as uncompromising as the members of the Association might have wished, the reason was to be found in the consideration that it was only through the *Staelhoef* that certain essential imports, such as gunpowder and naval stores, could be regularly procured.

Despite the trading difficulties experienced by the Merchant-Adventurers, however, the yearly profit of the Kingdom—other than the wards of the Duchy of Lancaster—averaged £118,000[2]; yearly payments and assignments averaging £110,000, of which the Admiralty's share was between twenty-five and thirty per cent.[3]

*   *   *

Drake's first individual voyage to Spanish-American waters plenished his holds with a reasonable store of treasure, and fired him with a resolve to find his way to that Pacific Ocean he had glimpsed from the ridge above Darien. When he sailed into

---

[1] The wares were valued at £100,000 sterling.
[2] Cotton MS., *Cottoni Postuma*, 1851.
[3] In 1570, for example, £30,000.

Plymouth again, on a Sabbath morning in the August of 1576, the congregation in the parish church gladly fled its droning parson to give him welcome, "all hastening to see the evidence of God's love and blessing towards our gracious Queen and country".

The Spaniards took a somewhat less sublimated view of the Devon shipmaster's activities, bluntly terming him a pirate; and there were not wanting those to counsel the immediate organisation of an expedition to mete out punishment to the insolent English heretics and the evasive, smooth-tongued Queen who had failed so signally to restrain their damnable propensity for filibustering.

But the Spanish King was not yet ready to deal with England. Flanders had still to be pacified, France to be muzzled, and victory secured over Turkey—and little as he could foresee it, the defeat of the Infidels was on the way, with the triumph of Don Alvaro de Bazan, Marquis of Santa Cruz, at Lepanto. For the nonce, however, Philip was prepared to trade humiliation for time; as Elizabeth used equivocation to win time to prepare for the trial of strength that, deep down, they both knew to be inevitable.

In 1577 Drake, eating his sumptuous meals off gold and silver plate to "a concourse of sweet sounds" furnished by certain members of the Norwich Musical Association, set out on a voyage that before its end was to circumnavigate the globe. It was not until the September of 1580 that he sailed into Plymouth Sound with his ships fairly ballasted with silver, gold and precious stones—"a little comforting dew from heaven", as he termed it, forcibly acquired from the Dons in the course of his travels.

In a strategic sense, the haul was of no mean value. It helped to fill Elizabeth's coffers and to deny replenishment to Philip's. And "the sword of Spain was forged in the gold mines of Peru",[1] so that only the regular inflow of wealth from overseas could preserve the Duke of Parma's army in the Netherlands from galloping disintegration.

After a little havering and a specious show of contrition in the face of renewed protests from Madrid, Elizabeth crowned the outrage to Spanish susceptibilities by proceeding in procession

[1] *English Seamen*, J. A. Froude.

down the Thames to Deptford, to knight Drake aboard his 'pirate' flagship—having first assured the presence on the scene of Philip's fuming Ambassador.

Once again, however, the Spanish Monarch was too pre-occupied to do more than register complaint, over Drake's activities as over the presence of English volunteers in the forces deployed against the Duke of Parma by the United Nether-lands.[1] Philip was busy making good his claim to Portugal and her overseas dominions; a task that was only concluded with the double victory won by Santa Cruz at Terceira, in the Azores.

Meanwhile Drake, in command of a powerful squadron of 25 ships, had once more set out for the Spanish Indies. Sacking Puerto Rico, San Domingo and Cartagena, he returned home with a wealth of treasure—and 160 dispirited colonists who had failed to establish themselves in Virginia.

During Drake's absence Parma had brought Antwerp under close siege. To cut the garrison off from the sea a fortified bridge had been constructed across the Scheldt below the city. No sooner had the structure been completed than a ship crammed with gunpowder packed in stone chambers had been sent floating down the river, slow matches burning in her hold. The explosion had been timed perfectly, and had torn a breach 200 yards wide in the bridge and hurled nearly a thousand Span-iards to their death. Although Parma had eventually succeeded in subduing Antwerp, the horrors of this terrible explosion had haunted the memory of every Spaniard who had heard of it; and recollection of it was to exercise a potent influence on Philip's attempt, three years later, to bring England to her knees.

With the return of Santa Cruz to Spain, after Terceira, "this valiant and unconquered leader"[2] settled down to formulate a plan for the invasion and conquest of heretic England. His scheme envisaged the employment of 596 vessels, of all kinds, with a complement of 94,222 seamen, gunners and soldiers, whose aim would be to put a strong landing force ashore some-where on the south-west coast—thus eliminating the passage of

[1] The original United Provinces were Guelderland, Holland, Zeeland, Frieseland and Utrecht, to which were added Overyssel and Groningen.
[2] *La Armada Invencible*, Fernandez Duro.

the narrowing part of the Channel—to proceed with the military subjugation of the country.

The less grandiose plan finally adopted predicated the passage of a smaller Armada through the narrow seas, to link up with Parma's army in the Netherlands. From this force a body of 30,000 Infantry and 1,800 picked Cavalry was to be shepherded to a landing place—preferably in Thames-mouth—within easy marching distance of London. Since a hostile garrison still held Flushing, Antwerp could not be used as the point of junction, and Dunkirk was named in its stead.

Philip's own memory of the territory over which operations would be conducted had been supplemented by the reports of agents—sharp-eyed men such as the chart-collecting Bautista Pauli, and Hortense Spinoli, who had made an extensive tour of the Dartmouth–Plymouth area—and by the correspondence of Catholic enemies of the regime. With his plans finally matured, Philip gave the word to hasten preparations for a venture whose real objective he sought his utmost to keep a secret.

To strengthen the existent Spanish armament, shipyards all along the Mediterranean were given orders to hasten the construction of the *urcas*, or armed transports, and the 'tall ships' that would bear the brunt of the fighting. At the same time, all the resources of Portugal were impressed to swell the Armada destined to undertake the "Enterprise of England"; while troops and stores were brought in from places as far apart as Germany and Peru.

Walsingham and Cecil were not, however, without their own intelligence service; so Philip's were not the only shipyards where work went forward with unabated vigour. In 1577 John Hawkins, having held the reversion of the office of Clerk of the Ships for ten years, had been appointed to the highly responsible post of Treasurer of the Navy. Immediately and with characteristic energy he had set about a thoroughgoing reform of the sordid welter of peculation and corruption for which the royal dockyards had long been notorious. Overcharging was ruthlessly checked; shifty pursers, boatswains and cooks who had bought their billets intending to recoup their outlay by the sale of the stores entrusted to their charge, were summarily dismissed; while impressed seamen found it impossible any longer to bribe their way to surreptitious discharge. But Hawkins'

greatest difficulty had been to secure agreement for the substitution of a fleet of strong, ocean-going medium-raters for an
armament consisting principally of the outmoded 'great ships'
still favoured by the veteran William Wynter and the equally
reactionary William Borough. There was also the vexed
question of expense, always a difficult and even a dangerous
matter to raise with a Sovereign in whom an inherited parsimony had developed into a miserliness whose intensity was
almost pathological. On top of all else, the need persisted to
confute the flabby, shortsighted contention that the Navy's true
function was to remain on the defensive, hugging the country's
shores, and to substitute the bolder plan, so strongly favoured by
Drake, of seeking the adversary in the open sea and there
inflicting decisive defeat on him in open battle. For only
through outright victory over an antagonist as powerful as
Philip of Spain could a balance of power be struck that would
maintain Western Europe—and world trade—in a reasonable
state of equilibrium.

Tension was already acute when it was further heightened by
the exposure of the Babbington plot to assassinate Elizabeth,
which led in turn to the execution of Mary Queen of Scots—
urged on by Cecil, whose head could never feel safe on its
shoulders so long as she remained alive.

From Philip's point of view, to have overthrown Elizabeth so
that Mary might step into her shoes would have been a move
singularly lacking in attraction; since Mary's succession would
have seen England and Scotland in alliance with France; a
Power whose influence and might it was the Spaniard's aim to
weaken. But with Mary conveniently martyred, nothing could
better become her co-religionist than a punitive stroke to
avenge her execution. The ample robes of pious loyalty would
serve to obscure the real intent—consolidation of a trading
monopoly and an empire.

For Spain, as for England, the writing was on the wall. But
still Elizabeth equivocated and babbled of peace as if it
remained in her gift. Drake, once more in England, shared
none of his Sovereign's fond delusions, and was only too ready
to undertake a reconnaissance of the Spanish and Portuguese
havens to ascertain how far Philip's warlike preparations had
progressed.

With the April of 1557, therefore, he slipped out of Plymouth at the head of a squadron of 30 ships fitted out, respectively, by the Crown, the Lord High Admiral, and the City of London. Before his vessels were hull down a Queen's messenger arrived at the port with orders forbidding Sir Francis to "do hurt" to any Spanish subject. In effect, had the Admiral been worsted and taken captive, the Queen's revocation of her original instructions would have delivered him over to the fate of a common pirate. Self-preservation may be the first law of Nature, but to win the respect of their subjects it behoves Sovereigns to learn when to abjure it.

Drake was supported by a number of men who had made the sea-service their lifelong career. For the day of the professional Sea-Officer—with his undisguised contempt for gentlemen-adventurers who volunteered for a voyage or so with little knowledge of the sea and its ways and less of its technical lingo —had indubitably arrived. Naturally enough, the appearance of the full-time Naval Officer had been followed by the production of certain rudimentary Articles of War, Queen's Regulations, and Admiralty Instructions, which embodied but enlarged upon the old Rolls of Oléron, and were primarily designed to maintain and enforce discipline. With the details of these regulations Drake was speedily to demonstrate his close familiarity.

Approaching the Spanish coast, the Admiral found that the great naval base of Cadiz was without so much as a guardship for the protection of the swarm of vessels in its basin. Interpreting his instructions with characteristic latitude, he promptly thrust into the harbour; and in the fight that followed he proceeded to demonstrate past all peradventure that against the broadsides of the medium-raters, galleys—which had won virtually every sea-victory since Salamis—were so many lambs for the slaughter. In an hour the whole history of the world was revolutionised: the gun-deck had come into its own.

With thousands of pounds worth of military stores destroyed, the Devon Captain put about; his raids along the enemy coast-line completing a spectacular voyage which is also noteworthy as having witnessed the first official naval Court Martial of which there is a record.[1] The offence was one of mutiny,

---

[1] Caesar Papers, British Museum.

permitting no other verdict than that of Guilty. Execution of the sentence pronounced by the Admiral was suspended, however, until the Queen's pleasure should be known; although Drake did not fail to voice his hope of seeing the delinquents "come to the court gate with halters about their necks, as an example to all such offenders".

On the homeward trick Drake had the great good fortune to snap up "the King's own East Indiaman, the greatest ship in all Portugal", the bulging treasure craft *San Felipe*. Flushed with triumph, he made for Plymouth, all eagerness to refit. So far he had only "singed the King of Spain's beard"; another swift, shrewd blow and the "Enterprise of England" would be frustrated ere ever it set forth.[1]

But the Queen was still procrastinating, still deaf to Charles Lord Howard of Effingham's blunt pronouncement, "We have to choose either a dishonourable and uncertain peace, or put on virtuous and valiant minds to make a way through with such a settled war as may bring and command a quiet peace." She was still lending far too eager an ear to the subversive mammerings of Sir James Crofts and others of the 'Spanish party' among her advisers; still nodding agreement when the more puling counselled caution. Drake's high-hearted, urgent plea, "Prepare in England strongly and most by sea. Stop him now and stop him ever", was meat too strong to be entirely palatable. The only hesitation not evinced by Majesty was in pouching the £40,000 which represented the royal share in the captured *San Felipe*.

While Spanish guitars twanged to the lilt of the popular ditty

> *My brother Don Juan*
> *To England has gone,*
> *To kill Drake*
> *And the Queen to take,*
> *And the heretic all to destroy,*

and as the shipwrights of Lisbon, Vigo and Corunna toiled to complete their work by the light of blazing flares and cressets,

---

[1] Drake's raid did much to postpone the Armada venture, but so did Gresham's and Walsingham's shrewd stroke of protesting all Spanish bills of exchange drawn on the merchants of Genoa—the very men on whom Philip was relying to victual and supply his fleet.

the air about the English Court was rancid with the sour stench of appeasement.

With the unlooked-for death of the valiant Santa Cruz, the command of the "Enterprise of England" had been conferred on the thirty-eight-year-old Don Alonzo Perez de Guzman, 7th Duke of Medina Sidonia. A wealthy land-owner, a Grandee of Spain, and the Captain-General of the Coast of Andalusia, the Duke openly protested that he "knew nothing of the sea or of war", and indeed his sole experience of active service had been confined to a distant view of the smoke-wreathed shipping fired by Drake in Cadiz bay. But the King's fiat had gone forth, and as a loyal subject he could only obey, relying thereafter on the skilled professional advice of his lieutenants—Recalde, Diego de Valdez, Orquendo, and de Leyva, in command of the troops— to help him to carry the venture to success.

With Medina Sidonia confusedly trying to get to grips with the task entrusted to him, Drake's bold but valid plan to "seek God's enemies and Her Majesty's where they are to be found" and destroy them piecemeal as they emerged from harbour, was forced to yield to the weakening compromise that split the English fleet into two contingents. One squadron, based on the Thames and including the Cinque Ports' meagre contribution of five ships and one pinnace, was to blockade Parma's port of embarkation. The other armament was scheduled to concentrate at Plymouth. Of this latter force the Lord Admiral, Howard of Effingham, took over the supreme command. A practical sailor who, eighteen years earlier, had exacted the traditional 'Salute of the Flag' from a powerful Spanish fleet encountered in mid-Channel,[1] Howard was supported by Drake as his Vice-Admiral, and Hawkins, Frobisher and Thomas Fenner of Chichester as his Flag Officers. But the division of forces—urged by the egregious William Cecil, Lord Burghley—was a typical example of landsman's amateur strategy, and openly invited defeat in detail. Appeasement when stung at last to action invariably worsens the dilemma its own invertebracy has brought about.

It was with sunrise on May 30th that the Grand Armada, with Medina Sidonia leading in the *San Martin*, cleared the

[1] The Spanish fleet had been conveying the youthful Anne of Austria from Flanders to Spain, for her marriage with the widowed Philip.

headlands of the Tagus and breasted the Atlantic billows. But it was not until July 5th that Gilbert Lee, master of the *Rat of Wight*, brought the news that a violent storm had scattered the enemy fleet in all directions. Most of the vessels took refuge in Corunna, though some were driven into Vivero, Ferol and Gijon, and a few had been hustled as far as the Scillies; whence they beat their way back to rejoin the main concentration. Many of the craft had suffered damage; provisions were giving out and water becoming putrid, while sickness was already exacting a heavy toll amongst the troops and shipmen.

With the news of Medina Sidonia's setback, Howard, Drake and Hawkins were insistent that this was the moment to take the fleet to the Spanish coast and destroy the crippled Armada in its harbours. So bold a policy, however, met with nothing but discouragement from Whitehall, where the authorities preferred that the English ships should do no more than maintain a defensive watch on the Channel approaches. Thereafter, Drake's attempted reconnaissance as far as Corunna was largely frustrated by bitterly contrary winds.

His disgruntled return to port was scarcely consoled by his Sovereign's letter rebuking him for having wasted powder and shot on mere target practice!

In Plymouth, Howard, courageously disregarding the reckless, pinch-penny order to cut expense by demobilising 50 per cent of his crews, kept his men together on reduced rations, eked out by such additional supplies as he could purchase out of his own pocket. In the absence of all replenishments, provisions had to be jealously husbanded against the inevitable time of action; although the crews were already suffering from the ineludible sickness bred of undernourishment and long confinement under insalubrious shipboard conditions. Pay, of course, was long in arrears, and there was no reserve of powder and shot. With some acerbity Howard wrote to London, "If the Queen's Majesty would not spare her purse, I have men with me who will not spare their lives." But for over a fortnight the English seamen standing by in their cramped shipboard quarters fed on rumour and, in a literal sense, on very little else.

It was not until Saturday, July 30th, that, as Medina Sidonia noted in his diary, "at dawn the Armada was near the land, so that we were seen therefrom, whereupon they made fire and

9+

smokes". In the rain-sodden air the warning beacons, long
since prepared, sent up their coils of heavy vapour, the danger
signal passing swiftly from height to height; while Plymouth's
narrow streets rang with the news that the whole great armament of 130 enemy vessels, crammed with 30,000 men, was off
the Lizard and ploughing steadily up-Channel.[1]

A comparison between the Spanish and English fleets reveals
that the former included seven vessels of 1,000 tons and upwards; while of the 197 vessels manned by the latter the
Triumph and the *White Bear* were the only craft topping 1,000
tons; the *Ark Royal* and one other being of 800 tons. But sheer
size was not the only criterion, since in armaments an English
ship of 800 tons far outweighed a typical enemy craft of 1,150
tons, while one of 300 tons could bring a concentration of fire
to bear of nearly double the power of that mounted by a
Spanish vessel of twice her size. Moreover, the English flotillas,
with their lower freeboard, were less conspicuous targets than
were their opponents, were more 'answerable', and infinitely
better suited to Northern waters. Best of all, they were manned
by crews that went into the fight full of confidence and the will
to victory; shipmen such as swarmed aboard Dartmouth's
300-ton *Roebuck*—which acted as powder ship to Drake's
Revenge—or the scratch crew of local worthies that took out the
250-ton *Samaritan*. Not all the ports had responded so readily
to the call to supplement the 34 Queen's ships that constituted
the hard core of the fleet. Poole, the Isle of Wight, once-
proud Southampton, and Lyme, had been generous with
nothing but excuses. The great port of London, on the other
hand, had swiftly equipped 30 'ships and barks', manned with
2,160 seamen and gunners.

Moving up the Cornish coast, Medina Sidonia rejected all
advice to carry the fight to the English fleet, held to their
anchorage in Plymouth Sound by adverse winds. His first duty,
as he saw it, was to make straight for his rendezvous with Parma,
and from this course he would not be deflected even if, by
pursuing it, he threw away the chance of catching his adversaries at a disadvantage.

[1] The rough seas encountered in 48° 30′ had proved too much for the
four Portuguese galleys, with their low freeboard, and they had put about
and run for home.

Immune, as was believed, from all fear of assault, *La Armada Invencible* (as some of its more boastful young Officers termed it) spread its gorgeous sails and, with the fitful sun glittering on its bright paint and elaborate gilding, ploughed on up-Channel in what was little less than military formation. Nosing ahead, like a cavalry advance guard, went the galeasses. Next came the main body, like an infantry brigade moving on a three-battalion front; while the rear was brought up by 45 weakly armed victualling ships and tenders, partly covered by the fleet's back-swept wings.

'Way ahead, a few English vessels that had managed to work out of the Sound seemed too flimsy a barrier to impede the Grand Armada's stately progress.

Sunday morning revealed a very different posture of affairs. Despite their shortage of ammunition and provisions, a strong force of English ships had beat out, with the wind abeam, and passed astern of the Armada, with the object of getting the weather gage. Reaching its turning point, the powerful squadron cast about and under easy sail steered for the enemy's left flank, which was the furthest from the chance of immediate support.

Closing the Spanish ships, the English gunners got happily to work with their pieces—cannon, demi-cannon and culverins. Their weapons, although lighter shotted than those of their opponents, were of longer range. So each vessel as it reached the point of aim let loose a devastating broadside into craft rashly overcrowded with men; whose return cannon and musket fire fell far short of their adversaries' decks. In any case the Spaniards had neglected their artillery practice, regarding the gun as 'an ignoble weapon'; while the English had never forgotten its shattering effect at San Juan de Uloa and, more recently, at Cadiz.

The English vessels made no attempt to form true line ahead, with every ship meticulously keeping station. It was rather a case of follow-my-leader, with each craft belching forth her broadside and then swinging round to take station astern while she reloaded—with the gunners wiping the sweat from their powder-blackened faces and hitching up their coarse tyrtene breeches, as they toiled cheerfully to prepare their reeking pieces once more for action.

Momentarily, the vigorous, rapid fire of the Englishmen's long-range culverins, which could loose off five shots to the Spaniards' one, threw their enemies into confusion. Sailing orders went unheeded; the damage to spars was considerable, and there were several collisions. Two fine vessels, one of them de Leyva's magnificent *Rata Coronada*, were so badly battered that their total loss could only be a matter of time. But under the inspiration of the flagship's great Banner, emblazoned with the figures of the Saviour and the Holy Mother, the towering galleons furled their sails and paused to await the Englishmen's next onset, hoping to close, run them aboard and overwhelm them by sheer weight of numbers. That was the last thing their nimble opponents purposed, and they drew off smartly to the westward. They were not turning tail, as the Spaniards gleefully concluded. They were momentarily drawing out of the fight for sheer want of that powder and shot they had so often pleaded for in vain.

With night falling, the Grand Armada, struggling to regain sailing formation, swept up-Channel, Drake abandoning his responsibility of leading the pursuit to turn back and snap up the crippled *Nuestra Senora del Rosario*, on the principle, as he put it, of "plucking their feathers one by one". His capture included, in addition to 50,000 ducats and a box of jewel-hilted swords, a very useful quantity of powder.

Having helped in her capture, it was the ubiquitous *Roebuck* that was told off to tow the helpless flagship of Don Pedro de Valdez into Tor bay; its crew being confined in the great barn of Torre Abbey.[1] Subsequently, a swarm of Brixham boats shepherded the great craft round to Dartmouth; but not before the game little *Roebuck* had thoughtfully increased her armament with twelve of the Spaniard's cannon.

The first clash had been inconclusive; the main force of the Armada was as yet untouched, and held steadily on its way.

Throughout Monday there was no fighting. But before noon the *San Salvador*, badly shattered by an internal explosion, reported to Medina Sidonia that she was sinking. While her

---

[1] Disgusted at having so many prisoners to feed, the Sheriff expressed a wish that "the Spaniards had been made into water spaniels"; but Sir John Gilbert, a local magnate of Greenway, eagerly availed himself of some cheap labour to improve his grounds.

Captain was doing his best to obey the order to get "the King's money and the people out of her", she was made captive by Hawkins in the *Victory*, when on the point of scuttling herself. Miraculously kept afloat, she was taken into Weymouth; where the Queen's Commissioners bitterly complained that she had been well and truly pillaged before they could get their hands on her. Subsequently, she was lost in Studland bay, while on passage from Weymouth to Portland, 23 of her prize crew being drowned.

From his flagship Howard wrote off urgently to beseech supplies from Weymouth, Poole and Portsmouth. Then, while Cardinal Allen, with a disloyalty foreign to the majority of English Catholics, was on his knees praying for the success of his country's enemies, the Lord Admiral penned the confident postscript, "We mean so to course the enemy that they shall have no leisure to land".[1]

On Tuesday morning the Grand Armada was off Portland, with some detached English vessels between the Spaniards and the shore, and Howard badly placed to come to their support. For a time it looked as though Frobisher and his few companions would be "caught between the sword and the wall". But the galleasses were slow in getting into action, and with the breeze shifting the English craft found room to back and fill. Frobisher sent his shot ripping amongst the galleasses' long sweeps, inflicting many casualties on the rowing benches; and with Howard coming up to intervene, the fire-fight gained rapidly in intensity; being renewed later when an attempt was made to capture the straggling *San Luis*. As the Isle of Wight's Governor, Sir George Carey, wrote that night from Carisbrooke:

"This morning began a great fight between both fleets south of the island, which continued from five o'clock until ten, with so great expense of powder and bullet that during the said time the shot continued so thick together that it might rather have been judged a skirmish with small shot on land than a fight with great shot at sea. . . . The fleets kept the direct trade,[2] and shot into the sea out of our sight by three

---

[1] It was at about this juncture that the Officer commanding the troops in Sandwich was forced to borrow £20 from the town authorities "to satisfy the wants of his men" (Records of Sandwich).

[2] i.e. in the fairway of the Channel.

of the clock of this afternoon; whereupon we have dissolved our camp wherein we have continued since Monday."

The English had not broken off the contest from lack of will but for want of powder. In the fury of the fight the small supply picked up at Poole and Weymouth had been expended. But at least Medina Sidonia had been prevented from landing to establish a stronghold on the Isle of Wight, wherefrom to effect contact with Parma. With his Holy Banner split in twain, his double timbers pierced and splintered, and his magazines nine-tenths empty, the Duke doggedly pursued his way up-Channel. Howard followed faithfully on his enemy's heels; his men weak and sickly by reason of the foul, starvecrow rations and putrid water to which they had been reduced, but still full of fight; and cheered by a reinforcement of five craft from the Isle of Wight. The guns on both sides were silent, however, and for identical reason. While the Trained Bands mustered and a rabble of half-starved militia drifted into Tilbury, it occurred to no one to ransack the Thames-side depots, where a certain amount of powder and shot and a few provisions could have been found for a fleet fairly famished for both.[1] A well-intentioned consignment of plough shares "for to make shott" can have added little to such satisfaction as Hawkins and Frobisher experienced in the knighthoods bestowed upon them by Howard at Her Majesty's express command.

Dividing his force into four squadrons, the Lord Admiral doggedly held on to the pursuit.

*   *   *

On direct orders from the Court, Lord Henry Seymour and his Eastern Squadron had abandoned the strong tactical position it had taken up in Thames-mouth and the Downs, to institute a close blockade of Dunkirk and Gravelines. There was nothing, therefore, to hinder Medina Sidonia from reaching such shelter as was offered by Calais roads—which, of course,

[1] Much of the store of arms in the Tower and the Minories remained unissued; while "four thousand men who had marched, pursuant to orders, twenty miles into Tilbury, found they must go that distance from the camp again before they could find a loaf of bread or a barrel of beer. A thousand Londoners who were likewise on the march, were ordered to halt unless they could bring their own provisions with them" (*History of the British Army*, Vol. I, Hon. Sir John Fortescue).

he would never have dared to approach had the French not recanted on their pledge to return the town to English occupation.

At anchor in the shallow roadstead, in touch with Parma, seven leagues away—from whom he hoped to receive an immediate supply of munitions—the Spanish Admiral plumed himself that his task had virtually been accomplished. But de Leyva and Recalde realised only too clearly that until the English fleet had been swept from the seas it would be impossible to transport Parma's army of invasion across the Channel. And at any moment Howard's armament and Seymour's inshore squadron might join hands, thus increasing the odds against them.

Sunday was a day of rest for the Spaniards, with plenty of time to peer across the water and wonder what the English heretics, anchored out to sea and taking in a modicum of victuals and munitions, might have in store for them. The answer came with the fall of darkness, when the tide had turned and was setting strongly towards the anchorage. Soon after midnight the uneasy watchers picked out eight black shapes, each defined by a flicker of light, that speedily rose in a roaring mass of flame. As the metal of their armament heated, gun after gun went off with a roaring flash. Remembering the flaming bridge and the terrible explosion at Antwerp, there were no volunteers to row out and tow off the fireships so that they could burn to the waterline well away from the anchorage. The sole idea was to shake out the sails and get clear of the advancing line of flame—which might be something even more deadly. With their particular dread of 'floating volcanoes', for the first time the Dons gave way to panic. Otherwise, good seamen as many of them were, they would never have cut their cables and broken sailing orders by making individually for the open sea.

With daylight at least two-thirds of the scattered Grand Armada was discovered to have drifted to leeward, near Gravelines, on a dangerous shore, and with one 800-ton galleon —Moncada's splendid *capitana*, the *San Lorenzo*—already cast away. Finding their enemies already fatally dispersed, Drake and Hawkins lost no time in going into close action; the former heading the *Revenge* straight for Medina Sidonia and the forty vessels he had gathered about him—the cream of his fighting craft. With very little ammunition, it was no longer a case of long-range off-fighting. Using their speed and nimbleness to obviate any chance of being boarded and entered, the English ships pressed home their attacks at close range; pouring in the fire of their bow guns and then that of their broadsides, to hole the enemy gun-decks, while their fighting tops flailed the crowding arquebusiers with a steady pelt of musket shot. It was less of a formal battle than a general *mêlée* in which the initiative was always with the English.

Despite the fact that the Dunkirk banks were dangerously close under their lee, the Spaniards had no thought of yielding, but fought back with a resolution undiminished by the spectacle of the *San Felipe* and the *San Mateo* drifting helplessly on to the Dutch coast. Drake's own cabin had been twice wrecked by gunfire; but by noon the *San Martin* had lost half her ship's company, and the scuttle-holes of many another shot-torn hulk ran red with blood.

Had the fight continued there is no doubt that several of the galleons would have been destroyed by gunfire or forced to strike. But a sudden change of weather put an end to the contest, as a violent squall beat in from the north-west, accompanied by blinding showers of rain. In the midst of a wild burst of wind and a torrential downpour, a large Spanish vessel which proved to be the 665-ton *Maria Juan*, heeled over and sank beneath the waves.

As the rain squall subsided and with the wind in such a point that the enemy vessels were in dire peril of being driven on the Zeeland shoals, Howard made no attempt to take up the fight anew. Virtually all his ammunition had been expended, and fully aware that the Queen "had a saving mind", he could entertain few hopes of it being speedily replenished.[1]

As the night closed down the battered Armada contrived to claw off the yawning lee shore, close up, and make sail to the north-east with the wind abeam. Howard, leaving Seymour's squadron to continue the blockade of Parma, "set on a brag countenance and gave chase". It was pure bluff on the Lord Admiral's part, for he was entirely without means to clinch the

[1] Over 100,000 'great shot' had been fired, all told, yet not a single English vessel had foundered or struck.

victory. None the less he was determined to intervene should the Spaniard evince any inclination to put about and try to beat his way back to the Channel and a helpless Parma, cooped up in his blockaded port of embarkation. But if any such thought entered Medina Sidonia's mind, it was never translated into action. With the English watch-dogs still hounding them, all that was left for the leaking, splintering galleons was to take the long road home.

Lost in the grey mists that shrouded the Orkneys and the Faroes, cast away on the iron-toothed rocks of Fair Isle and Lochaline, or strewn along the unwelcoming shores of Ireland, it was not until the last days of September that the surviving ships of the ill-fated Grand Armada limped into the northern ports of Spain. Five powerful craft had been lost in action, over sixty cast away on the passage home. One vessel, the hospital ship *San Pedro el Mayor*, was driven so far off course as to find itself once more in the English Channel. In the last week of October the waterlogged craft was wrecked on the rocks within Bolt Head, near the Devonshire village of Hope. By the time the Commissioners arrived to claim the hulk in the Queen's name, "great pilfering and spoils" on the part of the local inhabitants had stripped it of everything of the remotest negotiable value.

Howard had followed up Medina Sidonia's shattered armament for three days, condemned to do no more than shadow a force he was without means of bringing to action. For when his Officers were summoned by council flag to the *Revenge* it was to learn that enquiry throughout the fleet had revealed that "there was not munition enough to make half a fight". Helpless to do more, the Admiral put about to land his sick and wounded and repair the damage his own vessels had sustained.

To those uninformed in the principles of strategy, Parma still constituted a serious menace; although it was characteristic of the cheese-paring methods of the authorities that even before the Spaniard was authoritatively reported as having gone to Brussels, many ships and men had been summarily paid off. Meanwhile, the ailing and injured landed at Deal and Margate were in such a sorry plight that Howard was constrained to write to London: "Sickness and mortality begin to grow wonderfully amongst us; and it is a most pitiful sight to see,

9*

here in Margate, how the men, having no place to receive them into here, die in the street. I am driven myself, of force, to come a-land, to see them bestowed in some lodging; the best I can get is barns and outhouses. It would grieve any man's heart to see them that have served so valiantly to die so miserably."

The men were not dying of their hurts—all told, there had scarce been a hundred casualties to the Spaniards' 10,000[1]— but of scurvy, typhus, and a scandalous neglect on the part of the Administration which was all too faithfully reproduced by the inhabitants of the coastal havens wherein the sufferers had been dumped.

Yet for all the shameful neglect to which they were subjected, nothing could rob the seamen and their leaders of their sturdy satisfaction in a victory which, had it been properly supported, might well have proved as decisive as Trafalgar. As it was, in the first great campaign in which gun and sail had taken the place of boarding pike and oar, the English shipman had demonstrated those sterling qualities of courage, tenacity and fortitude which were to distinguish him through every succeeding generation. If the final triumph was denied to Howard and his followers, it was for want of the very means that would have ensured it. When Elizabeth whimpered at having to foot a bill for £161,000 it was because she lacked the wit to realise that double that expenditure would have quadrupled her sailors' chances of vanquishing her enemy once and for all.

When good Master Sutcliffe sat down, in 1593, to indite his *Laws of Arms*, the circumstances in which the Armada had been fought must have been very vividly in his mind when he wrote: "Whosoever for envy or feare or other cause goeth about to persuade Princes to pare their Generall's authoritie and to binde them to strait conditions, hath an evil mind himself, and as much as in him lyeth, ruinateth the affairs of his Prince. For what service can they do that are not onlie pinched in their provisions, but also bound by their commissions[2]? *Nothing is more hurtful to the proceedings of warres than miserable niggardise.*"

*   *   *

The reverse inflicted on the Grand Armada had impaired Spain's formidable might but had failed permanently to injure

[1] Including the many sick.   [2] I.e. "appropriations" or "estimates".

it. Another attempt to cripple it took the form of an expedition to restore Don Antonio to the Throne of Portugal. Unfortunately, the venture proved a failure, despite the fact that it was led by Drake and the veteran John Norreys, who had learned his business as a Colonel-General in the service of the Prince of Orange. Since the Queen—like the Devon Captain and his partners—had invested £20,000 in the enterprise, it was fortunate for all concerned, and particularly for Drake himself, that he was able to recoup the joint losses by snapping up a Hansa fleet of 60 sail, on the passage home.

This somewhat piratical stroke was excused as a reparation against the Hansa League, whose members, throughout the recent hostilities, had persisted in transhipping necessities to Spain. In effect, the war of monopolies between the Merchant-Adventurers and the Hanseats had reached a point, on both sides, at which all desire to arrive at a reasonable *modus operandi* had been swallowed up in a splenetic urge to inflict injury on the detested rival. It was not until 1598, however, that matters came to a head, with the Queen—enraged by a further attempt on the part of the Hansa to interfere with the trade between England and Holland—issuing a peremptory order for the closure of the *Staelhoef*. The erstwhile pupils at last had outdistanced the masters who had tyrannised over them for generations; and the 'Easterlings'—still permitted to trade but shorn of all their privileges—were evicted from the commercial stronghold they had occupied for centuries "with no more stir than would have accompanied the seizure by bailiffs of a private debtor's house". Burghley and Gresham had had their way; although they lacked the vision to perceive that in sterilising the activities of the Hanseats they gave impetus to a rivalry on the part of the Dutch which the future was to make the occasion of prolonged and bloody strife.

The Administration could afford to flout the Hansa League simply and solely because commerce was everywhere expanding, as the vast increase in the size and population of the head-port of London in itself bore eloquent witness.[1] Customs revenue which in 1586 had totalled £24,000, by 1590 rose to £50,000, and by the end of the century was to touch £127,000,

---

[1] There was even an attempt to restrain suburban building and create what would now be termed a Green Belt.

London contributing 50 per cent of the whole; while shipping returns reveal that whereas in 1559 there had been no more than 55 merchant vessels of 100 tons upwards, by 1603 the number had risen to close on 300. Between 1563 and 1576 the fishing fleet, with craft of between 10 and 30 tons, increased by 140 sail, and proportionately thereafter. Moreover, the majority of the large ocean-going vessels were safeguarded by an elaborate system of insurance, as were their cargoes; and this at a time when it was virtually impossible for any Spanish ship to obtain similar cover.[1]

The contemporary trend was for the capitalist to contribute towards an enterprise wherein his risk did not extend beyond the possible loss of his limited investment. Hence the tendency of the old outmoded regulated company—almost as inelastic and demanding in its working methods as the still medieval-minded craft guilds—to give place to the joint stock company, with its far more flexible organisation. At the same time, if, in an age of hardening mercantilism, there were still a few who realised that money is rather a means to wealth than wealth itself, there was complete unanimity of agreement that the acquisition of wealth virtually amounted to a moral obligation. "Profit to the English", reported Don Bernardo de Mendoza, "is like nutriment to savage beasts"; and no one drove a harder bargain, incidentally, than the members of the Puritan faction who had not scrupled surreptitiously to ship Mendip lead to Spain "to find its ultimate billet in Englishman or Netherlander".[2]

Expansion in overseas commerce had been accompanied by a minor industrial revolution at home, with the printing press, the new blast furnaces for using coal in glass-making and for separating silver from copper ore, the stocking-knitting frame and the Dutch loom, the horse and water-driven engines for draining mines, and the new methods of refining sugar. In producing nearly all these useful innovations a conspicuous part had been played by the refugees from religious persecution on the Continental mainland.

The influx into Europe of silver from the Peruvian mines had been followed by a sharp rise in prices. But if the island realm was not immune from the prevalent wave of inflation, English

---

[1] Fugger News-Letters.   [2] Victoria County History, Somerset.

cloth "made all Europe England's servant", since it wore "our livery".[1]

Usury was widespread, and although an Act was passed to establish the rate of interest at 10 per cent,[2] folk continued to make their own private bargains at far stiffer rates. Timber conservation brought about a ban on the erection of any new iron works within 22 miles of London which would have been more efficacious had the embargo applied to districts adjacent to the coast.

Trade between Southampton and Venice had come virtually to an end when a large Venetian argosy, with a rich cargo and many passengers, was lost off the Isle of Wight in 1587. The Turkey Company was therefore formed to enter into direct trade with the entrepôts of the Levant. In the outcome supplies were marketed at a price considerably below that hitherto prevailing. At the same time agriculture underwent sufficient revival again to permit the export of grain.

In the prevailing circumstances, the fact that the early abrogation of the Navigation Acts had been followed by stringent measures for the protection of home trade from foreign competition, must be regarded rather as a manifestation of flexibility than of wanton inconsistency. Since the days when England first appreciated the folly of selling its raw wool abroad only to buy back the manufactured article at seven times the price of the material it was made of, protective fiscal measures had always been employed to help establish any struggling industry; being subsequently modified when it had found its feet. The method may have been no more than empirical, but it had served to spare the country—surrounded as it was by powerful neighbours—from becoming a mere dependant, a Cinderella amongst nations, by enabling it to find the means for its own defence. With many of its indigenous industries firmly established, the general rule was to discourage alike the importation of manufactured goods and the exportation of raw materials, while encouraging by every possible means the sale abroad of native products, fabricated, processed, and finished off by native labour.

[1] Historical Manuscripts Commission, Various, II.
[2] 13 Eliz. Stat. I, Cap. 8. Concurrently, the interest on loans in France stood at $6\frac{1}{2}$ per cent.

Naval doctrine and practice engaged the attention of more than one Elizabethan writer experienced in the ways of the sea. William Borough produced his *Discourses of the Magnet and Lodestone*, Martin Cortes his *Brief Compendium of the Sphere*, John Davis his *The Seaman's Secrets*, and William Bourne his *Regiment of the Sea*. In a more practical sense, cables had been appreciably lengthened to permit the ship to ride with greater ease and safety; studding sails, spritsails and topgallant sails had come into general use, while the cross-staff had been superseded by the backstaff, the invention of the aforesaid navigator, John Davis. In 1590 or thereabouts the telescope was devised by Jansen, a spectacle-maker of Middelburg, and improvements were speedily devised for the instrument by Galileo and Baptista Porta. Mercator completed his famous chart of the world, and William Bourne conducted his experiments with the first submersible.

Renewed Spanish maritime activity took the form of savage galley raids on the Scillies and the English west coast. In the July of 1595 two fishermen reported from St. Keverne that "there is sixty sail of ships within the Manacles in our bay, turning off and on all this day". Shortly after, four galleys landed two hundred men at Mousehole, who fired the hamlet and neighbouring villages before pushing on to Newlyn and Penzance. The resistance they met with was negligible, and both these latter townships were set ablaze; the raiders returning to their craft unhindered. In the outcome, with the aid of a grant out of the local Customs and an impost of 1s. 6d. on every hogshead of pilchards exported by foreigners, the fortifications at Plymouth were strengthened at a cost of £5,000, while work on those at Scilly was urgently pressed forward.

It was not until 1597 that Philip launched his second Grand Armada, which was promptly blown back to its harbour by a violent storm. This perhaps was fortunate, since those two stout pillars of defence, Francis Drake and John Hawkins, had perished miserably in the expedition to the West Indies in 1595. There was no further attempt to get the Armada to sea, Spain resting content thereafter to work her mischief against England by sustained and vigorous activity in Ireland.

Little had been done for the mariner fallen upon evil times, other than by the Brethren of Trinity House, until the foundation by Drake and Hawkins, in 1588, of what was known as the Chatham Chest "for the relief of the maimed and superannuated mariner".[1] To this endowment fund all serving seamen contributed 6*d*. a month. Hawkins, to whom the welfare of the shipman was an abiding concern, had also been instrumental in raising wage rates from 6*s*. 5*d*. a month to 10*s*., with subsistence; and it had been at his instance that the foremast hands were given sleeping hammocks.

The decay of Antwerp and the rise of Amsterdam had seen the Dutch filch much of the trade hitherto monopolised by the Hansa; who had no option but to sell some of their larger ships to the Italians. As Wheeler, the historian of the Merchant-Adventurers jubilantly commented of their rivals, "Most of their teeth are out and the rest are loose."

The Dutch, on the other hand, were clearly resolved to fasten their teeth on all the profitable trade their indestructible digestion could cope with; and their enterprise and industry bid fair to turn them into rivals for the world's marts as formidable as the 'Easterlings' in the heyday of their good fortune. But the papers captured in the *San Felipe* had revealed the long-kept secret of the East India trade, and the struggle between the Hollanders and the English for predominance in this vastly profitable commerce was taken a long stride forward with the turn of the year 1600. For on December 31st a Charter was granted to George Earl of Cumberland "and twenty-five knights, aldermen and merchants" to exploit at their own charges "the territories of the East Indies". The original shares in what was shortly to be turned into a typical joint stock company, cost £50 apiece; and the association was given freedom from the payment of Customs dues for the first four voyages—in effect, until it had got on its feet.

The first East India fleet set sail in 1601, with Captain James Lancaster as commodore of one ship of 600 tons, one of 300, two of 200, and a victualler of 130 tons. The convoy made the Downs again in the September of 1603, after a voyage of two years and seven months. The cargoes included 1,030,000 pounds of eagerly awaited pepper, which was marketed at 3*s*. a pound, as against 8*s*. a pound the Dutch had demanded for it in 1599.

As for the shipmen who brought these richly-laden argosies

[1] The Chest itself was kept at Hill House, Chatham.

back not only from the Indies, but from every known quarter of the globe, to their home ports in the narrow seas, the Venetian Agent wrote frankly that they were of a different quality from all other seamen, "bearing a name above all the West for being expert and enterprising in all maritime affairs, and the finest fighters upon the oceans". Through their exertions England could no longer be dismissed as a negligible island on the fringe of the great Mediterranean trading community; through their prowess she had become a formidable maritime Power, so placed strategically that she could dominate the sea-routes to the fabulous New World as easily as she could control the narrow seas that linked Italy, Spain and France with the thriving marts of the United Provinces, Germany, Scandinavia and the Baltic.

CHAPTER XII

Recession

"Behold . . . with how little wisdom the world is
governed."

COUNT AXEL OXENSTIERNA

In 1602 Queen Elizabeth, tongue in cheek, had authorised a
proclamation exhorting her subjects to refrain from pirating the
ships and merchandise of those countries with which she was in
amity, under pretence that they belonged to Spain or Portugal.
This little piece of play-acting for the benefit of Philip III had
speedily been followed by an unsuccessful stroke on the part of
Sir Richard Leverson and Sir William Monson against a
treasure-laden Spanish flotilla, and by their far more fruitful
raid on Cezimbra. In the latter enterprise two enemy vessels
had been destroyed and a rich prize brought home in the shape
of a carrack which, with its cargo, had been valued at a million
ducats. On the heels of this exploit seven of the eight ships that
had escaped from Cezimbra had been destroyed near Dover by
a squadron commanded by Sir Richard Mansell.

Amongst other things inherited by James I, therefore, was a
hit-and-run war with Spain, in which one shrewd blow would
have consolidated all that the Elizabethans had toiled and
suffered to achieve, and left England free to deal with the Dutch,
whose rivalry had intensified as that of the Spaniards had
declined.

In days when the personal policy of the Sovereign largely
influenced a country's destiny, it would almost seem that James
I was Mary Queen of Scots' revenge on England. Slobbery,
lurching, and with a weakness for liquor and demonology, he was
that rare thing, a garrulous Scot, than which there is no more
relentlessly loquacious creature on this earth. "Few talkers are
good doers", his son Charles was one day to scribble in the
margin of a book, and certainly the comment applied with rare

cogency to the Prince's own father. Erudite, but prone to mistake ponderous sententiousness for wisdom. Henry of France's description of him as "the wisest fool in Christendom" implies that in the eyes of the Gallic Sovereign timidity rated as a rarified form of sagacity. For James lost no time in declaring himself to be "at peace with all the world"; thereafter concluding a spiritless treaty with Spain which accepted an absolute embargo on trade with Philip's colonies in Central and South America, and left it to private enterprise presently to institute three nests of pirates in the Caribbean which sought to combine buccaneering against the Dons with "the behaviour and morals of a Calvinist theological seminary".[1]

The King even went to the length of making the practice of privateering by English shipmasters a penal offence. Thus "virtually all the Powers of the world were invited to prey on British shipping, and the British shipping alone upon the sea was forbidden to hit back".[2] Nor did this furnish the only cause for uneasiness with regard to the future of the country's commerce and its languishing shipbuilding industry. In Elizabeth's days twenty 'legal quays' had been instituted in London's dockland, the better to facilitate the collection of Customs dues. Three years after her death most of the vessels taking on cargo at these wharves wore a foreign flag. For the highly profitable carrying trade was progressively falling into the hands of a Dutch marine that consistently undercut its rivals in the matter of freightage. Possessing far more knowledge of anti-scorbutics than the British, the Hollanders could sail bigger ships with fewer hands than their rivals, who invariably overcrowded their vessels with extra seamen taken on to replace the casualties that were bound to arise from scurvy. This was particularly true of the craft owned by the Dutch East India Company, an amalgamation, with a joint capital of 6,600,000 guilders, of all the Hollander commercial interests trading in the Spice Islands.

From his Tower prison, into which he had been thrown on suspicion of complicity in the plot to dethrone James in favour

---

[1] *The King's Peace*, C. V. Wedgwood. The Providence Company, of which the Puritan John Pym was secretary and in which the anti-monarchist John Hampden was a shareholder, was founded to populate three godly settlements in the Caribbean. Their prime business, however, was to keep watch for Spanish shipping and prey upon it whenever possible.

[2] Callender, *op. cit.*

of Arabella Stuart, Sir Walter Raleigh penned a remarkably penetrating survey of contemporary commercial conditions. In the course of it he pointed out that between 500 and 600 Dutch vessels traded all the year round with England, as against a mere 50 English ships plying regularly to Amsterdam. Furthermore, the Dutch deliberately encouraged foreign merchants to settle in the United Provinces, kept their Customs low, and cannily stored incoming commodities to sell them back again to their country of origin in times of shortage. In short, having regard to the fact that Rochelle and Brittany imposed no Customs, that the Danes and the French exacted them only between Bartholomew-tide and Michaelmas, and that the Hansa towns and the Dutch exempted all "new trade" from them entirely, it was clear that the heavy scale of imposts levied in England constituted a serious handicap on enterprise. "Low duties", Raleigh soberly emphasised, "draw all traffic to the Dutch, and the great liberty allowed to strangers makes a continuous mart." Where English exports were concerned, moreover, with the cost of living still climbing steeply, a tendency had arisen for native manufacturers and exporters either to price themselves out of the market or to proffer wares of inferior quality in an endeavour to keep their prices down to an acceptable level. Finally the survey drew particular attention to the fact that with Continental Europe annually consuming 100,000 lasts[1] of fish and herring, worth approximately £1,759,000, the English share of this lucrative trade had declined to a little over 100 lasts. Indeed, the industry had fallen into such decay that even fish for home consumption was netted off English shores by alien fishermen and sold by them in English markets.

Perhaps the most serious manifestation of all was the tendency of the cream of the English shipmen—privateers all!—to take service in foreign vessels, where their hardihood and wide seagoing experience ensured them a ready welcome. It was idle for the King to boast that the increasing number of colliers constituted "the especial nursery and school of seamen": the blunt fact remained that the key county of Kent could register no more than 442 mariners to serve in English bottoms.

[1] A last was reckoned at 10,000 fish.

The ban imposed by the Emperor on the Merchant-Adventurers had not been lifted, although negotiations on the part of the 'Easterlings' to regain possession of their London *Staelhoef* offered an obvious opportunity to bargain for the embargo's removal. Under interdict in one direction, harried and obstructed in another, the Merchant-Adventurers still clung to their traditional but outmoded way of doing business; and it was rather the small independent waresmonger than the old Company that took advantage of the improved letter service that the Postmaster for Foreign Ports had organised for the trading community's convenience.[1] Attempts on the part of individual merchants not of the Association—known as interlopers or freetraders—to break into the markets where the Merchant-Adventurers still clung precariously to their monopoly, were, however, fiercely contested. Yet competition, combined with a lowering of tariffs, offered the only means of consolidating the prosperity of a commerce in which the old restrictive ways of doing business had obviously outlived their usefulness.

In the general picture of commercial uneasiness and confusion the activities of the East India Company provided the only encouraging feature. Having abandoned the system of terminable stocks—i.e. money provided for a single undertaking and returnable, with any profit accruing, at its termination—in favour of a joint stock of permanent capital, its representatives bent all their energies to the cultivation of a steady traffic with the Spice Islands; and the Company's 1,100-ton vessel, the *Trade Increase*, was perhaps the most impressive craft to leave the stocks during the whole of James's reign. For the Company's shipbuilding yards at Deptford were stocked with ample supplies of seasoned timber, first-class canvas and cordage, and all the materials for fabricating its own cannon and munitions. Moreover, the management treated their 500 workmen with real sympathy and consideration, paying pensions to the widows and orphans of their veteran employees, and maintaining an excellent canteen where their shipwrights could

---

[1] An internal postal service took letters as far afield as Scotland and Plymouth. The charge was 2*d*. a letter up to 80 miles, 4*d*. between 80 and 140 miles, and 6*d*. if above 140 miles. For the remoter Scottish addresses a charge of 8*d*. was made.

purchase bread, milk, butter, cheese, eggs and 'pease', with ale on tap at a maximum price of three pints for a penny. The Association was equally attentive to the welfare of its ships' companies, who were better fed than most, and were assured, should the need arise, of the services of a medical man. For a chirurgeon was appointed to every vessel in the Company's service.

It was not long, however, before the directors of the concern were complaining that they had "patiently endured sundry notorious wrongs and injuries at the hands of the Hollanders" who sought "wholly to deter the English from the trade".[1] And this at a moment when the Dutch jurist, Hugo Grotius, in his treatise *Mare Liberum*, was extolling the virtues of universal free trade!

It was not, indeed, until 1619 that the Dutch consented to conclude a treaty by whose terms it was agreed that "commerce and traffic shall be free in the East Indies both to the English Company and that of the United Provinces". It was a covenant that the Hollanders, four years later, honoured by arresting, torturing, and finally executing Captain Towerson and nine other Englishmen of Amboyna,[2] on a trumped-up charge of conspiracy.

*   *   *

Raleigh's plea for low tariffs could have little appeal for a Monarch who, even had he been endowed with the parsimony of an Elizabeth, commanded insufficient personal revenue to "live in his own". For an individual who possessed all the Stuarts' innate genius for squandering money with virtually nothing to show for it, any appeal for economy was, of course, absolutely meaningless. Defying Parliament by exercising the Royal Prerogative to award himself tonnage and poundage for life, his original exactions stood at the swingeing rate of a £3 impost on every tun of wine, with poundage at £1 on every £20 worth of goods exported or imported, save for woollens handled by British subjects. In addition, there was a slightly more

[1] First Letter Book of the East India Company, 429.
[2] An island of the Molucca group, in the Banda Sea, where the natives, resentful of the highhanded methods of the Dutch, had voluntarily put themselves under British protection.

justifiable aliens' tax of £1 13s. 4d. on every sack of wool exported, and a like sum on every 240 wool fells taken out of the country.[1] Although the scale of dues obviously verged on the prohibitive, James's right, under his Prerogative, to increase them was upheld by a subservient Court of Exchequer in 1606. When this orange had temporarily been sucked dry, the King turned to the sale of peerages and baronetages, and to sordid transactions over the grant or renewal of patents and monopolies.

Although the "guard of the sea" was the legal foundation upon which rested the Sovereign's claim to the revenues accruing from taxation, James paid the responsibility scant regard. It is true that during his reign the number of Crown ships increased from the 13 in existence at its outset to a total of 24. But the additions were made not so much to enhance the country's naval might as to enable the King's *mignons* and *privatos* to feather their nests out of public funds. For having recalled, by a Proclamation of June 1603, "all vessels sent out with hostile intent", James went on to ensure the progressive deterioration of his fighting marine by appointing Sir Robert Mansell as Treasurer of the Navy. Mansell had played a minor part in the later stages of the Anglo-Spanish war; but his claim on the tremendously responsible post of Treasurer rested upon nothing more estimable than an eclectic taste in finery, a handsome presence, and a sympathy with his Sovereign's peculiar amorous whims which did not boggle at submission to them. Regarding his Treasurership purely as a remunerative sinecure, under his complacent sway corruption, embezzlement and peculation positively ran riot, as everyone from the highest to the lowest proceeded with uninhibited enthusiasm to loot the public till. Places were bought and sold in every degree and at every level. Worn-out vessels were re-commissioned—on paper —for the sole purpose of providing sinecurists with appointments, and apocryphal posts were created as an excuse to pay an Admiral's salary to favourites who "were so contented on land that they could not brook the seas".

One ship still shown on the Navy List had been broken up for seven years, but each year £63 had been paid out for the

---

[1] The object of the tax was to discourage the export of raw materials in favour of manufactured goods.

craft's upkeep. Two other non-existent vessels cost £104 9s. 5d. and £60 16s. 10d. respectively "for keeping". Another outrageous swindle was worked over lodemanage, for the charge for piloting the 13 vessels transporting the Princess Elizabeth and her entourage to Flushing[1] came to £208, as against £198 for the pilotage of the 286 ships at sea throughout the *last five years* of the reign of Queen Elizabeth. At the other end of the scale, a storekeeper was appointed at Woolwich at £54 a year, "and the store not worth forty shillings". A subsequent report recorded that "great workes are taken in hand, and a multitude kept in pay", with nothing to show for it, and that "when provisions are made, the best are not chosen, nor the worst refused . . . yet his Maty's provisions of all kindes are wasted without measure". In nine years, it was revealed, £108,000 was paid for cordage; two thirds more than the standing value of the material in hand. Anchors costing £1 13s. 0d. were entered at £3; oil at £16 a ton was charged at £20; tar at £18 a ton actually cost £7 10s. 0d. The admirable cannon turned out by the English gunfounders, on the other hand, could find no purchasers save among foreigners.

Mansell not only sold to himself, as Treasurer of the Navy, the requisite stores at a usurious price that was passed without demur, but having duly mulcted the seamen of their 6d. a month for the Chatham Chest, "falls presently into raging passions and pangs when they call for it". The Customs presented a similar picture of corruption and unabashed thievery; the State being robbed of something like 75 per cent of its just dues.

This welter of eleemosynary malfeasance was accompanied by a progressive deterioration in the shipman's status and treatment. Though tardily paid and vilely fed—on a diet that alternated 'salt horse' (salted beef) with stockfish, 'Poor John' (salted hake) and haberdine (salted cod), with a handful of fried peas by way of relish—the man before the mast was visited with savage punishments that regularly included ducking, keel-hauling, tongue-scraping, and tying up with weights hung round the neck "until the heart and back were ready to break".

[1] She married the Elector Palatine, Frederick V, and lived to become the beloved 'Winter Queen', Elizabeth of Bohemia. It was through descent from her that the first four Georges came to occupy the Throne of England.

Although divine service was held aboardship twice a day, at the King's particular behest, flogging was so common that "some sailors believed in good earnest that they should never have a fair wind until the poor boys be duly . . . whipped every Monday morning". Small wonder that so early as 1609 it was said that the Navy was "manned with aged, impotent, vagrant, lewd and disorderly companies, a ragged regiment of common rogues"; or that the ship-keepers at Chatham included such unlikely marine-creatures as barbers, weavers, shoemakers and bakers.

James affected a great interest in his shipmen, yet when persuaded to visit them at Rochester he deliberately neglected their inspection in favour of a day's hunting. Small wonder that the sailor came to be held in remarkably scant esteem both by his Officers and by the community in general. Yet with the sea-soldier temporarily eliminated from naval warfare, and the fighting as well as the working of the ship confided exclusively to the mariner and the seaman-gunner, a magnificent opportunity had arisen to give practical expression to Drake's fond dream of a ship's company of Officers and men that should "haul together" as a single unit. Instead, naval morale suffered further deflation when, in 1613, James' policy of fawning conciliation reached its nadir with his consent to forgo the traditional right to the Salute of the Flag.[1]

*   *   *

The last prize taken, under authority, by English privateers had been the Portuguese carrack *St. Valentine*, with a cargo valued at £26,000. But with the 'Sovereign of the English Sea' exercising scarcely a vestige of control over 'his' Channel, Dunkirk and Algerine pirates lorded it in the narrow seas unchecked. A favourite anchorage of the Algerines was Torbay, recommended to them by their renegade English pilots, whose intimate acquaintanceship with these home waters dated from their apprenticeship. In this sheltered roadstead the sea-rovers were quite immune from interference. For Plymouth lacked the docks to accommodate big ships, so that the whole protection

[1] Only a few years earlier a vessel carrying the French Minister, the Duke of Sully, had lowered her flag at the command of a mere despatch-boat, commanded by an English Captain of considerably stouter heart than his Royal master (Richelieu, quoted by Mahan).

of the West had been turned over to the pinnace *Desire*; whose Captain, John Chudleigh, ruefully confessed that he "could neither catch nor fight" the marauders he had been sent out to suppress. In an affidavit John Masters, seafarer and ship-owner of Dartmouth, swore that between 1612 and 1620 the corsairs robbed him of vessels and merchandise to the value of £1,500, and that he himself had spent twelve months in Algiers as a slave, eventually being ransomed for £200. In all, Dartmouth's total loss from this cause came to £8,000; six vessels being taken so late as 1622, and 130 men borne off in captivity. Yet so ineffective was the guard in the Channel that only one of the many Salee rovers was taken, and that right in the mouth of the Thames. These alien freebooters found strenuous competitors, however, in such native stalwarts as 'Captain' Ned Ward. A petty-officer of the *Lion's Whelp*, he was started on his meteoric career by the intelligence that a gentleman of Petersfield had deemed it wiser, as a known recusant, to sell all his property and put the cash with his plate and jewels, aboard a small 25-ton barque on passage from Portsmouth to Le Havre. Persuading some of his shipmates to join him, Ward obtained leave for the whole party to stay ashore overnight. With the fall of darkness the barque was forcibly seized and taken out to sea. But with daylight the freebooters discovered, to their sulphurous disgust, that the fugitive, having had his suspicions aroused, had sent all his property ashore on the previous afternoon, leaving Ward and his companions nothing but a mess of victuals and what, in their opinion, was an entirely inadequate supply of liquor. But the Rubicon had been crossed; piracy had been committed, and in an English port. The only thing to do was to set out boldly on the course to which they were already committed. Nor was it long before ex-petty-officer Ward had more than solaced himself for his earlier disappointment. With a large-hearted disregard for the nationality of his victims, he played the pirate with such abounding success that he was enabled to retire and establish himself in Tunis. Here he thought it advisable to turn Turk, as a preliminary to building himself an ornate marble palace and setting up as a Pasha, complete with slaves and a *hârim*. From this new vantage point he proceeded to scourge the trade of the Levant as successfully as he had pillaged the commerce of the narrow seas.

Plymouth, as always, furnished a ready market for pirated goods, even the mayor of that all-too-enterprising seaport being strongly suspected of trafficking with a foreign-owned corsair, whose crew of thirty-five included seventeen worthies from Dartmouth and Kingswear. Another local freebooter, Captain Nutt of Torbay, could afford to pay such handsome wages that the men of the King's ships deserted to him in shoals, seeking his service as eagerly as others clamoured for admission to the ships' companies of his equally prosperous rivals, William Parker and Stephen Infold.[1]

*   *   *

The twelve-year truce concluded between Spain and the United Provinces in 1609 served to encourage James even further to indulge his extravagance at the expense of the navy. Money slipped through his fingers like sand. On the occasion of a visit by his brother-in-law, the King of Denmark, for example, he spent a whole subsidy of £453,000 on feasting and drinking; and over the year 1614 half a million was squandered in plays, masques, swilling and gormandising. It followed that the expedients to which he resorted to raise funds—especially the increased scale of Customs dues embodied in his new Book of Rates—speedily embroiled him with Parliament. At the same time his individual unpopularity was intensified when, personally loathing the weed, he sought to tax tobacco out of existence and at the same time fill his own pockets. The poundage rate on the raw leaf was raised from 4d. to 1s. 4d., and that on the manufactured product from 6d. to 1s. 6d. This, of course led to widespread smuggling of the commodity, which speedily increased in scope when James clapped a consolidated tax of 6s. 8d. a pound on tobacco that had already yielded 2d. a pound to the Customs.

Indeed, James was ever resourceful in devising means of replenishing his perennially empty coffers. The failure of an experiment to break the monopoly exercised over the cloth trade by the Merchant-Adventurers, by exporting dyed and 'finished' English cloths—which the Dutch, determined to keep dyeing and 'finishing' in their own hands, refused to accept— led to the King's intervention on behalf of the aforesaid

[1] State Papers, Domestic, X.C.24

Merchant-Adventurers. But the restoration of their privileges cost the Company a cool £50,000 by way of a 'gratification' for the King. The unfortunate outcome of James's earlier attempt to interpose on behalf of Alderman Cockayne and those who had sought to export indifferently dyed and 'finished' cloths to a country that specialised in dyeing and 'finishing', was a steady decline in the sale of 'unfinished' English woollens abroad, a falling off in demand which subsequent war conditions only served to aggravate the more.

The King's straitened means were matched only too faithfully by the country's general want of soundly based prosperity. The greedy, exclusive attitude of the Chartered Companies tended to squeeze out the small, enterprising individual shipper; the activities of the Turkey Company, for example, with its monopoly of trade with the Levant, playing havoc with the private commercial interests of Southampton; while Portsmouth was frankly reported as in "a weak and ruinous condition". Exeter derived little benefit from its exclusive right to trade in West Country cloth with France; Southampton's insistence on its legal title to prohibit all buying and selling within its boundaries, save by its own freemen and those of the Cinque Ports, only served to tighten the noose of medieval monopolism with which it was deliberately strangling a prosperity already close to its final gasp. Dover was reduced to imposing an additional duty of 12*d.* on every packet landed at the port, as the only means of raising the money for the repair of its pier. Everywhere the wool and cloth industries exhibited a sharp recession—they had virtually collapsed in once-prosperous Wiltshire[1]—struggling overseas settlements, such as Virginia, were rather a source of expense than profit, while the Portuguese were half a century ahead of their English rivals in India, as were the Hollanders in the Dutch East Indies.

An analysis of the country's shipping in 1616 revealed that, apart from the East India and Turkey Companies' craft, and certain vessels plying to Virginia and Bermuda, there were 20 ships trading to Italy, mostly in herrings, 20 to Portugal and Andalusia, 60 craft plying, respectively, to Holland and to Bordeaux, 30 to Dantzic and Königsberg, and 5 to Norway.

[1] *The Wiltshire Woollen Industry*, G. D. Ramsay.

In addition, there were some 250 fishing vessels voyaging to the Newfoundland fishing grounds, and about 400 colliers, only a few of which, however, were ocean-going. For the most part the cargoes of coal were broken out in London, for transhipment in vessels from Bremen, Emden, and the United Provinces.

The decline in the country's general prosperity is witnessed by the fact that whereas in 1613 there was a favourable balance of trade of £346,283 17s. 10d., by 1622 there was an adverse balance of £298,878 7s. 2d.

A Commission on trade, which had already rendered an interim report, was established as a permanency; its functions anticipating those subsequently performed by the Board of Trade and Plantations.

By 1616 it had become clear that Philip and the Emperor Ferdinand II were preparing for a war in defence of the Holy Roman Empire. In a forlorn attempt to impress the Spaniards with the naval resources at his command and to ease his burden of debt, James released Raleigh from confinement and sent him, at the venturer's own expense, in search of a gold mine reported to exist in Orinoco.

Despite the fact that his son-in-law, the Elector Frederick, was amongst the first victims of the strife in central Europe which led to the thirty years of carnage committed in the name of religion, the Protestant English King's policy committed him to an inactivity which permitted free passage through 'his' narrow seas to Spanish mercenaries intent on the slaughter of all Protestants on whom they could lay their hands. For it was James's hope to arrange a marriage between his son Charles and the Infanta of Spain, whose wedding portion would come in remarkably handy. That the project was extremely unpopular with a large proportion of his subjects and, if successful, would inevitably lead to war with the Dutch, were considerations to which he scarce gave a thought. So eager was he to propitiate the Spanish Court, indeed, that, when Raleigh returned from a venture which, in its failure, had not only cost him his son's life but—owing to James's thoughtless blabbing to Philip's Ambassador, Gondomar—had led to a clash between English seamen and the Dons, the last great Elizabethan seaman was incontinently condemned to the block. It was a dastardly sacrifice to a cringing policy from which the whole country recoiled in horror, and for which the shipmen never forgave the man by whose orders it had been carried out.

One consequence of the flight of English subjects from an increasingly hostile United Provinces was the arrival in the home country of a little band of religious and political 'separatists'—for in the early seventeenth century the one involved the other—whose intention was to strike out and form a new habitat for themselves on the other side of the Atlantic. The Virginia Company being willing to sponsor them, the 50-ton *Speedwell* and the graceful 183-ton *Mayflower* were purchased at a cost—together with a small trading stock—of £1,700. At Southampton 120 emigrants embarked in each ship; but the two craft were no sooner at sea than Captain Reynolds, the master of the former, complained of the leakiness of his barque, and both vessels put into Dartmouth for repairs. These effected, the passage was resumed, but "only a hundred leagues beyond the land's end" the unseaworthy ships had to put about and seek refuge in Plymouth. Here the harassed voyagers found temporary refuge in a barn which later years were to turn into a flourishing distillery. But despite the excellent timbers furnished by the firm of Hawker,[1] the *Speedwell* could not be rendered seaworthy. So it was alone that, on September 6th, 1620, the *Mayflower*, having on board 100 passengers and "freighted with the destinies of a continent, loosed from Plymouth and, with the wind east-north-east and a fine small gale", put out to sea on one of the most momentous voyages in all recorded history.

James's fidelity to his current *mignon en titre* although intense was never lasting. Mansell had been succeeded by the profligate rip Robert Carr. He in turn was superseded by George Villiers— Court gossip averred for having tactlessly wiped his mouth after having been kissed by the King. Ennobled and eventually created the Duke of Buckingham, 'Steenie' was selected to accompany Prince Charles to Spain as the principal negotiator of the hoped-for marriage settlement. As it transpired, however, the terms Philip demanded, including as they did complete

[1] A descendant of this family, Colonel John Hawker, was the first American Consul in Plymouth, serving in that capacity from 1792 to 1795 and from 1801 to 1812. Another descendant, Captain James Hawker, R.N., was one of Nelson's Captains. The timbers of the *Mayflower* were eventually built into the barn in the Quaker settlement at Jordans, Buckinghamshire.

liberty of worship for English Catholics, were such as even James dared not accede to; while the slights and indignities to which Charles and his companion had been subjected during the course of the *pourparlers* brought Buckingham home in such a towering, blustering rage that war with Spain was virtually ineludible.

Doubtless James would have preferred a land war for the recovery of the Palatinate, but a hasty alliance with Louis XIII —which embodied arrangements for the marriage of the Heir to the Throne to Princess Henrietta Maria—perforce turned his thoughts to a consideration of his own naval resources. For little support could be anticipated from France, where Richelieu's efforts to revive the country's maritime might had yet to be put in train. A report on the fleet was hastily prepared which, even after three modifications of the original text, revealed a state of affairs as scandalous as they were alarming. As a result, Mansell was promptly "kicked upstairs" and the worn-out, aged Howard of Effingham beguiled into relinquishing his post of Lord Admiral. In his place 'Steenie' was appointed to the single-handed control of the Navy, with the new and exalted title of Lord High Admiral of England.

Although Buckingham was not unfashionable enough to reject a bribe of £10,000 from the East India Company for permission for their fleet to sail by a given day[1]; where the interests of the country as a whole were concerned his patriotism was not to be impugned; and he was a fairly competent administrator. But the neglects and omissions of Mansell's long years of maladministration were not to be made good by a well-meaning amateur in a matter of months. For when Captain Christian, of the relatively new *Bonaventure*, wrote of "the weak, I may say truly miserable state of this ship", with its rotten gear and hopelessly landlubbery crew, his report epitomised the sorry state into which the whole of the country's Navy had been allowed to degenerate. Buckingham wrought wonders in the short time at his command; but as one of the wisest of our naval historians has gravely emphasised, "Ships might be replaced and open peculation checked, but the deeper wounds of spirit and discipline caused by fourteen years of licence . . . were not so readily healed."[2]

[1] And another £10,000 *doceur* from their gains at the capture of Ormuz.
[2] Oppenheim, *op. cit.*

The immediate trouble was that Buckingham's ambitions outran his capabilities. But he had got the bit between his teeth, and even the death of James, in the March of 1625, was not allowed to interfere with the preparations for his hare-brained attempt to reproduce Drake's shattering descent on Cadiz.

When the enterprise was finally set in motion, in a fleet of over a hundred vessels only nine were King's ships; most of them wearing the sails and running gear that had seen service in the Armada year. Among the indifferent auxiliary merchant craft the dearth of competent Sea-Officers and pilots led to innumerable collisions and departures from sailing orders[1]; while the soldiery embarked to undertake the projected land operations were the most unhandy of raw recruits, unpractised with their weapons and entirely wanting in discipline; facts that were duly noted by the youthful son of a bluff but impoverished Devonshire squire, George Monck by name, who had shipped with the expedition to escape the pressing attentions of the local sheriff's officer. As was only to be expected, the venture to Cadiz ended in humiliating failure. Furthermore, since Parliament had refused the King tonnage and poundage save on terms he found unacceptable, and offered a subsidy for the war so inadequate that Charles had indignantly refused it, there was no money to pay off the men on their return to Portsmouth. So they were held aboard ship, half starved, and the victims of a pestilence which, despite the local inhabitants' pharisaical refusal to have anything to do with the ailing, spread so quickly that the town "was like to perish".

Fortunately, the Spanish marine was in no condition to stage an attempt at invasion; for the coastal defences—manned by no more than a corporal's guard—had fallen into disgraceful decay. In Sandgate fort there remained but a single gun; while the men in Dover's Black Bulwark looked on helplessly while a Dutch ship was pillaged in the harbour, since they lacked the necessary weapons with which to intervene.

With England openly at war with Spain, it was scarcely a propitious moment in which to become embroiled with France.

[1] This despite the fact that in 1621 it had been decreed that no one should hold the office of master or pilot without being certified as competent by Trinity House. Naval Officers who aspired to command were also required to submit themselves to examination by the same authority.

But Louis had not only retained seven English ships on temporary loan for service "against whomsoever except the King of Great Britain", but sought to employ them to overpower the Huguenot garrison holding out in Rochelle. To this mission neither the Vice-Admiral, Sir John Pennington,[1] nor his ships' companies would assent, and at Dieppe the vessels had been taken over by Gallic crews; the English shipmen returning to England. Further provocation was offered when a number of harmless English merchant craft were held in Gallic ports. Some gesture of self-assertion on Charles's part was obviously called for, and plans were made to send an expedition to succour the Rochelle Huguenots. With some wisdom, however, the Rochellese declined English intervention; and since a stroke against France was still considered necessary, it was determined to stage a descent on the Ile de Rhé. But such was the dearth of competent Sea-Officers that for want of a better leader the command of the venture was taken over by Buckingham himself. What was overlooked was, that whereas the run-down of a navy can be brought about in the matter of a twelvemonth, it takes years to restore it to a proper state of discipline and robust fighting efficiency. No hasty reimposition of Fish Days, no offer of a subsidy for shipbuilding, not even pension schemes, an improved scale of rations, and an increase in the seaman's wages to 20s. a month (about 14s nett[2]), could make good the defects begotten of the recent period of stagnation, corruption and neglect. With the venture finally launched, the delays it experienced in beating its way down Channel in the teeth of persistently unfavourable winds, only postponed the disaster it eventually encountered. Nor did better fortune attend a subsequent venture under the Earl of Danby; and in consequence trade with the Protestants of Montauban, Nismes and Montpelier came to a virtual standstill.

However patriotic and well-intentioned his sentiments, few men in the country had aroused more animosity than Buckingham, and on his return to Portsmouth he fell a victim to the knife of John Felton, an ex-Naval Officer smarting under a

[1] He had been Second-in-Command to Raleigh in the Orinoco expedition.

[2] There was a compulsory weekly contribution of 4d. "for the preacher", and 2d. for the barber, with 6d. a month going to the Chatham Chest.

sense of personal grievance. Instead of appointing a successor to his erstwhile favourite, the King took the unusual step of putting the post of Lord High Admiral into commission; and such small fleet as kept the sea was administered by the existent Board of Navy Commissioners.

In the terrible years that followed England—with scarce a dozen ships exceeding 200 tons sailing from the great port of London—could hardly claim to take rank as a maritime Power; while no fiscal expedients could disguise the fact that trade was not only in visible decline, but found itself increasingly the victim of the corsairs who roamed the narrow seas virtually without let or hindrance. Between 1609 and 1616 Algerine freebooters alone had overwhelmed 466 English craft and en-slaved every survivor amongst their crews. Early in 1625 Plymouth had written to complain that over the previous twelvemonth a thousand of its shipmen had been captured by sea-rovers, of whom 200 had been sold into bondage; while 27 vessels had been lost in the first few days of January.[1] So alarmed had been the authorities at Trinity House by the general lawlessness prevailing that they had given orders for the Lizard light to be extinguished, since "it helped to conduct pyrates". After a squadron of French privateers had impudently sailed in to loot the warlike stores laid up along the coast, a similar course was taken with the light at Dungeness which Sir Edward Howard had been licensed to erect in 1615, and the cost of which he had recouped by levying a toll of 1d. a ton on all shipping passing within sight of the pharos. But these precau-tions, presumably, had constituted no more than a minor handi-cap to Captain John Nutt of Lympstone on the Exe, whose long career in these waters had rendered him a scourge more to be dreaded even than the worst of the Algerines.

Matters had been bad enough at the opening of Charles's reign, but with the failure of Mansell's half-hearted punitive expedition to Algiers, North African freebooters continued to course the lower reaches of the Thames as boldly as they lay Portsmouth under contribution and filled their row-benches with men snatched from every haven along the Channel coast.[2] The final humiliation came when a handful of King's ships was

---

[1] *The Scourge of Christendom*, Lieutenant-Colonel R. L. Playfair.
[2] *The Navy under the Early Stuarts*, C. D. Penn.

forced to turn tail by a squadron of alien privateers. Upon such widespread activities as these the belated issue of Letters of Marque and Reprisal could effect virtually nothing. With King James's ban on privateering the English shipman had been deprived of that school of sea-warfare in which he had learned to give so formidable an account of himself. Equally, with the exception of shipmasters of the East India Company, the mercantile marine appeared completely to have forgotten that the only chance of real safety lay in sailing in well-disciplined, mutually-supporting convoy.

In the prevailing circumstances—with Richelieu maintaining three squadrons in constant readiness for action, the Dutch ever eager to fly to arms in support of their commercial policy, and Spain still of some nuisance value—Charles's resolve to build a strong and numerous fleet is as readily to be understood as his enactment forbidding English shipwrights and naval artificers to pass overseas into foreign service. His main trouble, of course, was to find the means to pay for the armament he desired. With his father's heavy debts to meet as well as his own, and a Parliament that denied him supplies save on terms that his whole upbringing and outlook impelled him to spurn, the expedients to which he resorted to raise the necessary money ranged from the pledging of the Crown jewels to the sale abroad of 610 superb iron cannon for the substantial sum of £300,000. His next step was to demand their traditional ship service from certain of the ports,[1] and call upon the coastal towns and areas to render the ship money it had been customary for them to pay since before the Conquest, and which, so late as Elizabeth's day, had been forthcoming without a murmur.

It was, however, when the King, bolstered up by the "general opinion" of twelve Judges and the arguments adduced from Selden's *Mare Clausum*, set out to extend the scope of the ship money impost to inland towns and districts that he found himself confronted with an opposition to the absolutism he sought to wield by virtue of the Royal prerogative, which had been crystallising since the days of his father. It was not so much the nature of the tax itself to which objection could be made, for

---

[1] Thus Portsmouth was called upon to furnish one ship of 900 tons, manned by 350 seamen and gunners, one of 800 tons, with 260 men, four each of 500 tons, with 200 men, and one of 300 tons with 150 men.

obviously the Navy, as a national and not merely a local asset, had the right to look for support from nation-wide and not purely regional funds. Neither could the burden of the impost be regarded as particularly onerous, since with a calculated yield of £207,000 on the existent acreage of England and Wales, the dues amounted to no more than £1 on every 174,447 acres.[1] It was simply that the King had imposed the tax without reference to Parliament and for what many of its members deemed to be the wrong object. Had Charles's policy favoured the Dutch and the Elector Palatine rather than Spain and Austria, such men as the Earl of Warwick, John Hampden, Pym and Cartwright well might have regarded the moment unpropitious for the declaration of their anti-monarchical sentiments. As it was, Parliament found that its brittle dignity had been outraged; and 'ship money' became the stick with which any legal pedant or frothing anti-monarchist could belabour the individual who epitomised a system of government of which he elected to disapprove. The real tragedy lay in the fact that the King's belief that he was always in the right was as adamantine as his opponents' conviction that they were never in the wrong, and that neither side was prepared to concede anything to that faculty for compromise which, in the fullness of time, was to become the Englishman's salient characteristic.

One accusation that even his most rancorous enemy could not, with justice, hurl against the King was that he applied such ship money as he contrived to raise to any other purpose than that for which it was intended. With the funds at his disposal he built some of the finest warships ever to take the sea, including Phineas Pett's masterpiece, the magnificent three-decker ship of the line, the 1,740-ton *Sovereign of the Seas*. Armed in all with 144 guns, ranging from swivels and small "murdering pieces" up to 46- and 60-pounders, and proudly wearing the (old) Union Flag, exclusive to the Navy, at her sprit-topmast,[2] she was richly gilt and boasted a 'great lanthorn' in which ten people could stand upright. Less suited, maybe, for the suppression of Dunkirk corsairs than for a full-dress battle action,

[1] *Six Centuries of Work and Wages*, J. E. Thorald Rogers.
[2] Merchant vessels wore the Cross of St. George or the Cross of St. Andrew, according to whether they were English or Scottish. Shortly after, the warship took to wearing the Cross of St. George in addition to the Union Flag.

she was none the less the perfect flagship for a fleet that was slowly—all too slowly—taking shape. Its organisation was to be in Red, White and Blue squadrons, in that order of precedence; and when the capture of the two famous Dunkirk privateers, the *Swan* and the *Nicodemus*, revealed to English shipwrights the secret of frigate construction, a revolution in ship design was eagerly adopted which was destined to exert an influence on the development of English sea-warfare whose importance it would be impossible to exaggerate. A good start had been made and ship money began to justify itself practically if not legally. The Barbary pirates who in the summer of 1637 had made a most successful raid on the south-west coast, were drastically dealt with by a squadron commanded by Captain William Rainborough. The Dutch were temporarily so impressed with Britain's growing maritime strength that they grudgingly parted with £30,000 for permission to finish their summer fishing in waters which had always given grounds for dispute. But Hollander resentment quickly mounted against "a slothful and prodigal people" who had demanded payment "for a mere passage along the coast of England"[1]; and presently—having carefully chosen a moment when the King was preoccupied with war on the Scottish border—they struck.

By an arrangement concluded between Charles and Philip IV, reinforcements passing through the narrow seas to the gateway of the Spanish Netherlands were escorted by the handful of ships which represented such of the ship-money fleet as had been completed. Thus it came about that while the ship money abolitionist, John Hampden, fulminated about *Magna Carta* and the *De Tallagio* Statute of Edward I, a convoy of Spanish transports, attended by twelve British warships, came up Channel and cast anchor in the Downs. There, in defiance of all known maritime law, the ill-armed Spaniards were first blockaded and then smitten like a thunderbolt by Maaten Tromp, at the head of a hundred Dutch men-of-war. Battered and set ablaze, twenty of the transports were driven ashore between Deal and Walmer, several more surrendering, and many being burnt to the water-line by the fire-ships loosed among them. Throughout the whole ghastly massacre a jubilant crowd of spectators on the cliffs cheered on the Dutchmen wildly. The probability that

[1] *The Interest of Holland*, J. De Witt.

their Hollander co-religionists would prove a greater menace to
their peace and prosperity than ever the hated Spanish Papists
had been, was a consideration that never so much as entered
their heads.

Too few and too weak to intervene, the British craft stood by
helplessly while seventy out of seventy-seven Spanish hulls were
either made captive or destroyed.

For want of the means to build a fleet strong enough to give
it protection, an English anchorage had been turned into a
slaughter-house; and to celebrate the event the Long Parliament met and promptly proceeded to declare the exaction of
tonnage and poundage and the imposition of ship money to be
illegal.

CHAPTER XIII

The Rivals

"There is a limit at which forbearance ceases to be a virtue."

EDMUND BURKE

A FLEET can survive the setback inflicted upon it by an enemy so long as it continues to enjoy the nation's confidence and is itself possessed of a morale strong enough to avenge the discomfiture it has suffered.

After its humiliating experience in the Downs, the embryo ship-money fleet could boast neither the one nor the other. Nor did it rejoice in a leader of the quality to restore it to discipline and self-confidence. In the outcome, the demands of the King's war with a rebellious Scotland removed so many vessels from the Channel Guard that with virtually no opposition to overcome, Barbary pirates were again free to raid the narrow seas and carry off some sixty men and women from the neighbourhood of Penzance. At the same time a squadron of 24 Dunkirker privateers, with the tacit approval of the Spanish authorities, systematically pillaged the Kent and Sussex shores; such Naval vessels as were patrolling local waters being forbidden to interfere with their activities. For Charles was still hoping for Spanish funds and troops to aid him in his struggle with an antagonistic Parliament and the anti-monarchist Puritan-*cum*-Presbyterian element amongst his subjects, determined—as a platform from which to demand further restrictions—to insist upon a sweeping abridgement of the Royal Prerogative.

Upon ascending the Throne Charles had solemnly affirmed: "We have no other intention but by our government to honour Him by Whom Kings reign and to procure the good of our people, and for this end we preserve the right and authority wherewith God has entrusted us." It was a declaration, however outmoded by the temper of the times, that was perfectly honest

266

and sincere. Charles's concern for the welfare of his people and his belief in his Divine Right, as their Sovereign, to rule them for their own good, was as unquestioning as the rejection of such pretensions by a large proportion of his subjects. To authenticate the 'divinity' of his position, the King, perforce, needed the blessing of the Church—a Church, headed by "that little meddling hocus-pocus", Archbishop Laud, which a large proportion of his people opposed with that explosive rancour which appears to be reserved for disagreement on matters of religion. Fuel was added to the fire of sectarian intemperance by the mass of subversive Calvinistic literature smuggled into the country by 'owlers'[1] indifferent to the nature of their contraband cargoes so long as they showed a profit.

A tussle between obscurantists sooner or later has to resort to the sword; thus when King Charles set up his Standard at Nottingham in the August of 1642, the strife which ensued was not a conflict between an autocratic Monarch, supported by a feudal aristocracy, and a new, pushing bourgeoisie, but a struggle between irreconcilable social, political and religious ideologies. This was made abundantly clear when the main body of the Crown fleet went over to a Parliament more lavish than the Sovereign in its promises—and, as time was to demonstrate, even less punctual in their redemption; a fact not without considerable influence in subsequent events.

So far as the divided loyalty of the Navy was concerned, Charles, to a considerable degree, had been the victim of the very scrupulousness with which he had applied the ship-money to the purpose for which it had been exacted. For with Parliament refusing to meet the navy's wage bill, it would have been no more than a venial offence to deflect some of the funds raised to construct ships to the payment of the men who built and sailed them. At the outset of the reign charges—including those involved in the cost of living—were generally high. The expense of maintaining 10 of the King's ships and 10 auxiliary armed merchant craft in the narrow seas for a twelvemonth therefore worked out at over £57,000; and this at a time when there was an outstanding debt of £100,000 for arrears of pay. Indeed, many of the shipmen and dockyard workers had not drawn a

---

[1] 'Owler' as a colloquial term for the smuggler was just coming into common use.

penny piece for nigh on eighteen months. Had there been a little less of Gerard Christmas's gilt plastered on the *Sovereign of the Seas*' elaborate scrollwork and a little more silver in the men's pockets, it is highly unlikely that the King's sailors would have turned against him; although as the son of the man who had sent Raleigh to the block, the initial prejudice he had to overcome was far from negligible. As matters fell out, Parliament found itself in control of the dockyards and possessed of sufficient sea-power [1] to discourage any attempt by sympathetic Monarchs overseas to send aid to a cause for which all hereditary rulers were bound to feel the liveliest concern. None of them, however, was in a position to translate concern into action. Richelieu had built up the Gallic Navy to a strength of 100 warships, backed by admirable port facilities and ample storehouses. But the Cardinal was dying, and policy stepped aside to attend his deathbed. Spain was in irreversible decline; John IV of Portugal had only just scrambled back onto the Throne, while the Dutch regarded their neighbours' domestic quarrels as a heaven-sent opportunity to accelerate the pace of their own overseas expansion.

With the outbreak of hostilities Northumberland, the Lord High Admiral, was succeeded in effective command by the Parliamentary sympathiser, Robert Rich, Earl of Warwick. It was by Warwick's orders that five ships were available to help in Sir William Waller's reduction of Royalist Portsmouth, and ready to intercept a couple of vessels bringing bullion and powder to the Cavaliers. But it was Warwick's Vice-Admiral, William Batten, who snapped up the Royalist *Bonaventure* and *Swallow*, and the frigate *Robert*. Then, "being alone in the *Constant Reformation* off Beachy, he met with the Vice-Admiral of Holland and four great ships more, and, although they suffered him to shoot divers shot at them before they would strike, yet when they saw his resolution they lowered topsails and did homage".[2] In the May of 1647 a Swedish fleet was compelled to render similar homage; Batten coming to the support of

[1] At the outbreak of hostilities the Navy consisted of 82 sail. The Parliamentary Party found itself immediately possessed of 32 vessels, of which 16 were armed merchantmen. Captures and ships re-equipped and re-commissioned speedily added to this total (*Social England*, Vol. IV, W. Laird Clowes; Penn, *op. cit.*).

[2] *Report of the Commissioners of the Navy.*

Captain Owen of the *Henrietta Maria*, who had gallantly tackled the alien squadron single-handed.

Batten—who "swore merrily" and was "near as broad as he was long"—was also extremely active in the West; where, in a predominantly Royalist Devon and Cornwall, Dartmouth, Lyme and Plymouth remained enclaves of intractable Roundhead resistance. It might have been a very different story had the Crown Navy, over the immediate past, been able to protect the Western coast from the depredations of the swarm of Algerine, Biscayan and Dunkirker pirates who had haunted it. As it was, the general attitude was one of sullen resentment of a Government that had so signally failed in its task of guardianship. Thus when a Royalist contingent under Prince Maurice marched from Bristol to subdue rebellion in the West, Dartmouth immediately set about strengthening its defences; guns and munitions being provided by the local merchants and shipowners out of their private funds. It called for a month's close siege to overcome the township's stout resistance; operations being conducted in consistently vile weather, which led to much sickness, and to many desertions from the forces of investment.

Further west, with the approach of Hopton's army of 'Malignants', Thomas Ceely, Plymouth's mayor, promptly seized the castle and St. Nicholas island, and made every preparation to withstand a siege; although the Parliamentary vessels off the town contributed indifferently to the subsequent fighting, "surveying the scene but doing little to help the issues". It was Batten who contrived to throw in aid to the defence; as he had earlier come to the rescue of Melcombe Regis and Weymouth. He took an equally active part in the operations launched by Fairfax to recover Dartmouth; while the Isle of Portland and the castle surrendered to him in the April of 1646.[1] In due course Batten permanently identified himself with the West by contributing £500 of his own money towards the erection of a fort at Plymouth, known originally as Batten's Tower, and subsequently as Mount Batten.

Portsmouth having earlier been brought under Parliamentary control, another enterprising Officer, Captain Richard Swanley, turned his attention to Southampton. Having dealt with the

[1] *Sailors of the Civil War and Protectorate*, Sir Charles Firth.

forts at Southampton Water and stopped the flow of provisions from the Isle of Wight into the town itself, he was enabled speedily to bring it to submission.

Chichester, inspired by the example of Sir Edward Ford, the Royalist Sheriff of the County, closed its gates and, with very meagre stores of food and munitions, held out stoutly for eight days. When Sir William Waller's numerically superior forces at length got possession of the city, Protestant zeal took delight in thoroughly despoiling the Cathedral, seizing the ornaments and consecrated plate, smashing the organ and the stained glass windows, and everywhere wreaking such wanton damage that, in the words of the contemporary Dean, Bruno Ryves, "they left not so much as a cushion for the pulpit".

The loss of so many ports and havens—including the head-port of London—naturally had the effect of depriving the King of much desperately needed revenue, in the form of Customs dues.

With the anti-monarchist party's Council of State steadily increasing the number of vessels on patrol in the Channel, there was little reason to doubt the Parliamentary navy's ability to 'keep the ring' and confine the issue to a straightforward land fight between Cavalier and Roundhead.

Normally, nothing can be more destructive of a nation's commerce than civil strife. But in England's case the conflict between King and Parliament initially inflicted remarkably little injury on the country's trade as a whole. The Parliamentarians held the principal cloth-making districts, and other forces were at work tending to the development of the various branches of British industry, which compensated for the damage done to them by the incidence of warfare. Certainly Russia held aloof in contemptuous disapproval of an upstart republican regime, and Antwerp was still in a sorry state of decay. But there was plenty of business to be done in Amsterdam and Lübeck, as in Denmark and Portugal; the last-named having concluded a treaty with England in 1642 which legislated for free commerce between the two countries.

In general, money wages had risen, although Puritanism, by abolishing holidays, discountenancing amusements of all kinds, and frowning on all forms of relaxation, could indulge its natural bent for money-grubbing by insisting that longer hours should be worked and greater application given to the work itself. The abnormally steep rise in the cost of living had been checked in the early part of Charles's reign; and it was, paradoxically enough, precisely those mercantile classes which had advanced in wealth and importance through the rise in prices and now found their prosperity checked, that played the chief part in opposing the King.

The real menace to the country's commercial well-being lay with the supremacy in the carrying trade, as in the traffic with the Spice Islands, that the Dutch took every opportunity of consolidating. Against the numerous vessels of the mercantile marine wearing the United Provinces' flag that plied in Eastern waters, even the East India Company's 15,000 tons of shipping compared unfavourably. Moreover, the banks of Amsterdam and Rotterdam had established a mechanism of credit and exchange far ahead of anything known in England, which meant that finance was never wanting to support the industry, thrift and commercial aptitude with which the Hollanders were so generously endowed. Preoccupied with her own internecine struggle, England had no time to assess the magnitude of the progress made by her most enterprising and unscrupulous rival.

*   *   *

In the March of 1646 Charles Prince of Wales escaped from England to take temporary refuge in the Scillies. Thence he moved on to Jersey; where his desperate, impoverished state did not deter him from indulging in a youthful liaison with a Welsh gentlewoman, Lucy Walter, the "brown, beautiful, bold but insipid slut" with whose willing aid he sired the son later known to the world as James Duke of Monmouth.

In 1648 certain sporadic activities in the neighbourhood of Maidstone and Colchester inaugurated the second phase of the struggle between a King and a Parliament equally incapable of producing a system of government that could command majority assent. With the renewal of warlike activity, however, Parliament's unfulfilled pledges to its seamen came grimly home to roost. So early as 1643 one disgusted Captain had written of his craft, "Never hath ship been sent to sea as we have, nor used worse than we are; . . . a man would have scarce imagined that a ship could be so badly fitted with necessaries as we have been."[1] Subsequent conditions showing little or no improvement, a considerable proportion of the fleet hoisted the Royal Standard and defiantly set sail for Helvoetsluys. There they were joined by the Prince of Wales and his cousin, Prince Rupert, who took over the command. Shortly after, the gawky fifteen-year-old James Duke of York was reunited with his elder brother, when he escaped across the narrow seas in the unlikely guise of a primping *jeune fille*. As yet, the lad evinced none of those outstanding qualities which, in the fullness of time, were to establish him as one of the country's most distinguished naval administrators. There was a very real accretion of strength, however, when Batten, transferring his alliegance, joined the Royalist forces in company with Captain Joseph Jordan, who brought with him the vessel of which he was the commander, the *Constant Warwick*—the prototype of the frigate that was to exert so profound an influence on naval warfare in the years to come.

It was no easy command for an impetuous cavalryman-turned-sailor to assume, and Rupert "suffered two or three mutinies", in the course of which he was "compelled to throw two or three seamen overboard by the strength of his own arms".[2] Eventually ten ships were made ready for sea and in the August of 1648 set sail for the Downs. Picking up some useful prizes, the flotilla also succeeded temporarily in blockading the mouth of the Thames. It was a stroke more frightening to the Londoners—and particularly the 'great cobs' of the City upon whom Parliament relied so slavishly for support—than anything the Cavaliers had hitherto been able to achieve. With the collapse of the Royalist cause in Kent and Essex, however, and with Cromwell hunting the Scottish loyalists back over the border, the blockading fleet perforce withdrew to Holland.

With the beginning of 1649 the Royalist cause was galvanised into vengeful life by the folly of its enemies in sending Charles I to the block. For "the axe carried the King of England from London to Rupert's headquarters"[3]; while intensifying the sympathy of other rulers to the point where they looked on

[1] Captain Swanley to the Governor of Portsmouth: H. M. C. Welbeck MS.

[2] *History of the Rebellion in England*, Edward Hyde, Lord Clarendon.

[3] Callender, *op. cit.*

indulgently while the Royalist commander sailed from their harbours to prey on that maritime commerce upon which the newly created Republic depended for its subsistence. So grave was the menace threatening the Commonwealth that radical steps had to be taken to countervail it. Following the precedent instituted with Buckingham's assassination, the Council of State put the office of Lord High Admiral into commission; the powers of Admiralty being vested in a committee of three. As a precaution, merchant vessels were ordered to proceed in convoy; while such Officers as failed to protect sea-borne trade with their lives were liable to capital punishment. A system of prize money was introduced whereby half the value of every vessel was allocated to the ship's company that had taken her. The other half went to a fund for the relief of the sick and wounded, and the widows and orphans of those slain. Were the enemy craft sunk, the victors were rewarded by a sum equivalent to the number of her guns multiplied by £20 sterling. Furthermore, the sailor's pay was raised to 19s. a month for Ordinary Seamen and 22s. 6d. for the new rating of Able Seaman; a wage which for some time was paid with wary punctuality. Men brought in by impressment were given 12d. 'prest money' and 1½d. a mile "conduct from the place where they shall be"; a reversion to the 'coat and conduct money' of earlier times. Equally important, the erstwhile pinch-gut dietary of small beer, biscuit, pickled beef and salt pork was enriched by the addition of oatmeal, rice, bacon, butter, cheese, prunes, currants, sugar, treacle, vinegar, and a not illiberal ration of brandy. As Oppenheim drily points out, "Throughout the history of the Navy any improvement in the position in the man-of-war's man is found to bear a direct relationship to the momentary needs of the governing class."

While Colonel Thomas Pride was laboriously trying to purge the corrupt Deptford Victualling Yard of the worst of its irregularities, at Chatham Peter Pett was busily at work building frigates. Limehouse, Wapping, Maldon, Deptford, Chatham, Redriffe (Rotherhithe), Shoreham, Woolwich, Horsleydown, and even the long-neglected stocks of Portsmouth, echoed to the thud of the shipwrights' hammers, as the timber came rolling in from the many forfeited Royalist estates, or was carted, at 5s. a load, from as far afield as the Forest of

Dean. For the prodigal cutting over the past centuries had brought about a serious shortage of oak; and without a proper scheme of re-afforestation the problem of obtaining the necessary supplies was to grow progressively acute. It was not until the days of John Evelyn and his *Sylva, or a Treatise on Forest-trees* that it was brought home to the responsible authorities that timber is a crop.

Of particular importance was the appointment, on February 27th, 1649, of the three "Commissioners for the immediate ordering and commanding the fleet at sea"—Edward Popham, Richard Deane, and the forty-nine-year-old Robert Blake. All three had held command in the Parliamentary army, and both Deane and Popham had seen something of sea fighting, the former being esteemed the most accomplished artillerist in the country. The Bridgwater merchant's son, Robert Blake, on the other hand, had won his reputation purely as a soldier and as an inspired amateur at that. But resolute and able as he had shown himself on land, it was in command of a fleet at sea that his genius for warfare was to find its fullest scope. Incidentally, it is worthy of note that Blake's flagship had been commanded, as the *Victory*, by Hawkins at the time of the Armada, having been launched in 1561 and "altered to the form of a galleon" in 1586. Rebuilt in 1610 and renamed *Prince Royal*, under the Commonwealth the craft underwent another change of name to that of *Resolution*. Once more renamed, as the *Royal Prince*, she was destined to play her part in the "Four Days' Battle" of June 1666.

Blake's primary task was to put an end to Rupert's skilful and costly raids on the Commonwealth's maritime commerce. So successfully did he set to work that the Prince was hunted out of the Portuguese and Spanish havens that had sheltered him and driven to seek refuge in the West Indies. All that was left of the Royalist fleet was the flagship, the *Constant Reformation*, and two smaller craft.

Rupert having been driven from the scene, Blake, with Sir George Ayscue as Second-in-Command, was free to undertake the reduction of the forlorn Royalist outpost in the Scillies. Landing at Tresco, he speedily erected a battery that so effectively commanded Broad and Crow Sounds as to prohibit passage in and out of St. Mary's harbour. Cut off from all hope of reinforcement and supply, Sir John Granville surrendered at discretion; with eight hundred rank and file and "Officers enough to head an army".

The Dissenters who had proclaimed Charles II their King at Scone in 1651 carried their passion for discord and disputation to such inordinate lengths that the 'Black Boy's' foray into England was doomed to disaster even before it set out. On Worcester Field in the early September of that same year the Royalist forces met with such overwhelming defeat that the youthful King was forced to abandon his followers and seek safety in flight. After an odyssey of over forty days, which brought him by way of Bristol and the western counties to within sight of the Channel, he found refuge for himself and his companion, Lord Wilmot, in the home of loyal Colonel Gounter. Enquiries were immediately set on foot to secure a passage overseas. Failing to find an accommodating boat at Emsworth, recourse was made to a certain Mr. Marshall of Chichester, a merchant whose business interests included a steady commerce with France. With his aid, arrangements were finally concluded with Captain Nicholas Tettersal to ship "two gentlemen who had been engaged in a duel and mischief done" safely across the Channel for the sum of £60 down. Embarked on the 34-ton coal-brig *Surprise*, Charles and his companion lay hidden throughout the night. At high water, between seven and eight o'clock the following morning, the brig set sail, steering a westerly course as though making for Poole, the vessel's normal destination. On deck "the dark young gentleman's" skill in navigation quickly won Tettersal's wholehearted admiration. But one thing troubled him sorely. The King's identity having been revealed to him under the pledge of secrecy, he was quite at a loss to explain to his men why it was necessary to alter course. In his perplexity he repaired to his youthful Sovereign and begged his help. With all his effortless charm, Charles turned to the men, ruefully explaining that he and his friend were merchants who had suffered loss and were temporarily flying their debts. This confession was so well received that the King went on to offer the four hands and the ship's boy twenty-five shillings if they would second his endeavours to persuade the Master to set him and his companion ashore in France. A combination of fine natural thirst and

innate sympathy with anyone victimised by Puritan rapacity
brought ready agreement; and Tettersal chimed in with a
remarkably good show of allowing himself to be cozened into
consent. So about five in the afternoon, with the Isle of Wight
still in sight, the brig stood off with a northerly wind for France.
At dawn on Thursday October 16th Charles landed at Fécamp,
after a passage across the narrow seas that all who shared in it
were to remember to the last day of their lives.

In the meantime, a counterfeit 'Black Boy' had made his
appearance in Sandwich, where he relieved the loyalist Peter
Vanderfleet of £100 in gold, "borrowed a good gelding, and
ere long ran away through the haven like the rogue he was".[1]

On Gallic soil the King was safe. But with Portugal, Spain
and the States General grudgingly according recognition to a
grimly arrogant Commonwealth, the Royalist cause, on land
and sea, was temporarily in eclipse.

*   *   *

By 1651 the Commonwealth had resolved itself into a small
and entirely unrepresentative body of men—amongst whom
Oliver Cromwell was the most prominent—who used the Council of State as their executive agent. Like all so-called 'popular'
governments, they were fecklessly extravagant and quite irresponsible about meeting their debts. In addition, they had
waged an extremely expensive war which, over the six-year
period of its greatest intensity, had cost £40,000,000, much of
which sum was still outstanding. But even the extension of
tonnage and poundage and the imposition of many new taxes
failed to meet the continued high rate of expenditure. Money
was raked in by any and every means; by the sale of confiscated
Royalist property, by the compositions forthcoming from political 'delinquents', and by the monthly assessments paid by the
community and by the big trading corporations; which led the
Merchant-Adventurers—who had already parted with £30,000
for the confirmation of their traditional privileges—to double
the 'fines' exacted from their members. These extra-ordinary
sources of revenue eked out the loans from the City, the gold-
smiths, and such wealthy Jews as Menassah Ben Israel, by
which some five and a quarter million pounds were annually

[1] MS. in the possession of William Boys, F.A.S.

screwed out of the country.[1] Yet even with an Administration quite unashamedly living on capital, the Navy debt went on accumulating; while the laggard payment of wages and prize money provoked a constant stream of protest, as it was the cause of widespread hardship and distress.

A modified Navigation Act passed in 1650 had forbidden all trade with those colonies still faithful to the Stuart cause. It was followed by another enactment—that of October 1651—as stringent as any of its predecessors; and this was accompanied by a clear intimation that in future the right of search and the 'Salute of the Flag' would rigorously be exacted.

This maritime legislation was, of course, aimed at the Dutch, whose abounding prosperity had been built, in part at least, by the opportunity to forge ahead which their rival's pre-occupation with the civil war had so generously afforded them. For having captured Cartagena in the West Indies—together with a treasure worth £3,000,000—the Hollanders had followed up the unrequited massacre of Amboyna by commandeering the English factories in Ceram and the neighbouring islands. Dutch privateers had almost put the coasting trade out of existence; English fishermen had been driven from their traditional fishing grounds; while the Dutch had landed on English soil to dry their nets, and offered violence to all who dared to protest their trespass. The final outrage came with the assassination of the British emissary, Dr. Dorislaus,[2] and the insult and abuse heaped upon his successors, Oliver St. John and John Strickland; for which the States General expressed no more than perfunctory regret.

For these and other injuries Cromwell, in the name of the military junta of which he was the spokesman, demanded full apology and immediate compensation to the tune of £1,700,000. (The money would be extremely useful, and an exterior war would serve as a welcome catalyst to transform seething domestic unrest into laudable resentment against a foreign foe.)

The Dutch, individually sleek with prosperity, although burdened with onerous public debts and rent by internecine political animosities, had been without real experience of sea

[1] Under Charles I national revenue had rarely touched and never exceeded one million pounds in the year.
[2] Sometimes given as Doreslaar.

warfare since their truce with Spain of 1609. They were, therefore, far from eager for conflict, and sought by negotiation to
meliorate the stringent measures taken against them. But when
Parliament rescinded the prohibition on privateering for which
the pusillanimous James I had been responsible, and freely
authorised Letters of Marque and Reprisal, the die was as good
as cast.

The spark which set off the explosion was struck by Captain
Antony Young, of the *President*. Cruising off the Start, he encountered a fleet of Dutch 'butter-boxes', escorted by three
men-of-war. Earlier on, Tromp had ostentatiously neglected to
render the traditional salute to Dover Castle, although a shot
had been fired across his bows by way of reminder of "the
antient right of the nation". He had also given his Officers
orders "at all hours to keep ready their guns and firearms". It
followed that all Antony Young's requests that the Dutch
Commodore should conform to custom and render 'the Salute
of the Flag' were scornfully rejected. Without more ado the
British Captain ran out his guns; and having "handsomely
banged away" at his opponent and "given him a bellyful of
it", he had the satisfaction of seeing him haul down his
Colours.

A few days later the fiery Tromp himself, flying his Flag in
the majestic *Brederode*, appeared in the Downs—the scene of
his humiliation of the Spaniards and their British escort in 1639.
He was in command of a squadron of 42 ships, which he coolly
proceeded to exercise in battle-practice, despite Rear-Admiral
Nehemiah Bourne's broad hint that, with Blake in the offing,
the Dutchman's tactful withdrawal from the immediate vicinity
would undoubtedly make for the avoidance of trouble. Eventually it seemed as if Tromp had decided to take Bourne's
temperate council to heart, for he bore away into the open
Channel.[1]

At this moment there arrived on the scene Captain Joris van
Zaanen, with a report of Antony Young's activities of seven
days agone. Thus it fell out that when Blake sailed into Dover
roads at the head of a flotilla of 13 ships, it was to perceive
Tromp and his squadron once more bearing down on the
English shore, and in something suspiciously like battle order.

[1] *Blake, General-at-Sea*, C. D. Curtis.

As the two fleets closed to within musket shot, the Dutch ensign flying defiantly at Tromp's masthead, Blake, to ascertain the Hollander's intentions, loosed three separate shots "at his Flag". The reply was a broadside and a signal, thrown out by the *Brederode*, for the Dutch fleet to engage. As the glass in his stern-walk casements splintered, Blake gruffly commented, "I take it very ill of Tromp that he should take my ship for a bawdy house and break my windows", and as gruffly gave the order to return fire.

For four hours the conflict raged furiously. But for all his opponent's numerical superiority Blake, with the heavier metal at his command, and with the help of a timely reinforcement of eight ships, was more than able to hold his own. Darkness found him in stubborn possession of the scene of action, with two prizes to show for his pains.

After re-fit, Blake set about perfecting his plans to cut all the threads of outward and home-bound Dutch trade; while the Hollander fishing fleet, its protective squadron put out of action, was forced to discard its catch and agree not to trawl the waters into which it had intruded, save under licence. Down Channel, Antony Young was still purposefully on the prowl; while another privateer Captain, the rumbustious John Heaton, of the *Sapphire*, with cheerful impudence adorned his stays, back-stays and shrouds with the Colours and pendants of the Dutch, French, Spanish and Burgundian vessels that had fallen victim to his enterprise.

Obviously committed to a war *à outrance*, the commoner-dictator imperiously exacted that nation-wide tax for the up-keep of the navy which had aroused such purblind opposition when demanded by an autocrat-king—and no reincarnated John Hampden arose to say him nay![1]

Once again the cannon foundries' leaping fires blazed by day and night; at Enfield Lock the new powder mills came swiftly into operation. Every dockyard was calling for more and yet more carpenters and shipwrights—at Portsmouth they were short of the latter by over a score—while Plymouth was in an uproar as the saturnine Captain Hatsell proceeded to make good his promise to bring the crews of the *Monmouth* and *Southampton*

[1] The actual John Hampden had died, in the June of 1643, of wounds taken at Chalgrove Field, near Oxford.

up to full strength by organising a thoroughgoing 'general press'
of the town. There was even talk of impressing seamen from the
colliers—men normally exempt from conscription.

The die was cast, and the Republic was determined, while
ensuring security for the future, to exact just reparation for the
past.

*   *   *

Up to the time of the first Dutch war the prevailing naval
strategy had been for the warships rather to busy themselves
with the destruction of enemy commerce than seek the annihilation of the hostile battle fleet. It was a method of procedure
the Anglo-Dutch conflict was very largely to reverse; commerce-
destruction being left in the main to the privateers. How
thoroughly they performed their task is witnessed by the fact
that in two years they captured or destroyed 700 of the 1,500
prizes taken during the course of the war.

With Blake warily keeping watch on Tromp, Sir George
Ayscue—who earlier had been forced to employ evading tactics
against De Ruiter in the Downs—sallied out from Plymouth to
challenge the Dutchman, who was engaged in shepherding a
convoy down Channel. As action was joined, the respective
fleets were found to be of about equal strength, with several East
Indiamen taking part on either side in a fight as stubborn and
hard-pressed as it was heavy in casualties and damage to
shipping. Smarting under the knowledge that the convoy had
escaped him, but with his squadron too crippled to pursue the
equally battered Dutchmen, Ayscue limped into Plymouth.
Thereafter, his temper was scarcely sweetened by the discovery
that scores of his wounded, refused refuge and attention by the
surly townsfolk, had been dumped into the Castle, hastily
improvised as a hospital

Ayscue had better fortune, however, when he dashed out to
intercept another outward-bound convoy. Engaging with great
élan, the British commander boldly cut adrift from all tradition
by breaking through the enemy line to engage De Ruiter from
to windward. It was a stroke that anticipated Nelson's successful
tactic at Trafalgar by over a century and a half; and but for the
blundering of subordinates, which enabled the bulk of the
convoy to escape, it might have proved equally shattering.

By August Blake was again in the Downs, whence he sailed to deal summarily with a Gallic flotilla on passage for the relief of Dunkirk. In so doing the British General-at-Sea missed the main Dutch armament, under De Ruiter and Cornelius De Witt, as it swept down Channel; driving half a dozen merchantmen ashore between Folkestone and Hythe, and passing so close in-shore that De Witt's flagship came under fire from the guns in Sandgate Castle. It was on September 28th that De Ruiter and De Witt, on their return sweep of the narrow seas, encountered Blake, William Penn and Nehemiah Bourne in the shoal waters of the Kentish Knock, a sandbank a few miles to the north and east of the North Foreland. Numerically the fleets were about equal, although Blake had the superior weight of metal. Against this must be set the fact that De Witt enjoyed the advantage of position; for to win the weather gage the English were forced to manœuvre in shoal water. This imposed a dangerous handicap on their larger vessels of deep draught, and more than one was grounded in the course of the action. With their shallower keels the Dutch ships could back and fill without risk; but in the event this liberty of action brought them little or no profit. Failing to close sufficiently to board and enter, they got by far the worse of the gun duel into which the action developed. With the loss of four ships, De Witt seized on darkness to seek the refuge of his own shallow home waters, where Blake was precluded from pursuing him.

Thereafter, as the weather steadily worsened, a number of the bigger craft—according to contemporary custom—were laid up in ordinary for the winter; the balance of the fleet, on the rash insistence of the Council of State, being scattered in separate squadrons at the several ports.

In the last week of November a watcher in Margate steeple sighted Tromp making his way down Channel with a fleet that he put at a hundred sail, warships and armed merchantmen. Blake, cruising in Dover roads, could muster about forty vessels, of which, as with his opponent, a large proportion was of merchant craft.[1] But without a moment's hesitation he determined to attack.

The Dutch were proceeding in three parallel lines, each

[1] According to Gardiner, Blake ultimately concentrated 45 sail to Tromp's 85 (*First Dutch War*, S. R. Gardiner).

column headed by its leader—Tromp, De Ruiter and Jan Evertzen. Blake's aim was to concentrate his small striking force on the dangerous triple head and by destroying the three centres of direction and control, throw the remaining mass of the enemy shipping into a state of confusion, of which he could then proceed to take full advantage. It was a bold plan courageously carried out by Blake himself and his Second-in-Command, the pugnacious, hard-headed, tobacco-chewing veteran, George Monck. Indeed, the assault might well have succeeded had the auxiliary merchantmen—of which many of the masters may have been part-owners [1]—exhibited less anxiety for the safety of their hulls and a better stomach for fighting. But with many of them turning tail, the British suffered a decisive beating. It was left to Blake to try and rescue, single-handed, two of the prizes that had fallen to the Hollanders, and he only desisted from the attempt when his masts went by the board. Fortunately, Thames-mouth offered him a refuge, whither the Dutchmen could not pursue him for want of a pilot skilled enough to negotiate the King's Deep channel, the only means of approach. As an alternative, Tromp landed 800 men to pillage Kent and Sussex, raiders who "drove away abundance of cattle and sheep and plundered divers houses". [2] The Dutch had undoubtedly had the best of the encounter, and the legend speedily came into being that Tromp had triced a broom to his masthead as a symbol of his intention to sweep the English from the sea.

On the morrow of this setback Blake, with great dignity, offered to resign his command. But a contrite Administration, harshly confronted with the consequences of its own unenlightened meddling, promised to do whatever he directed if only he would remain in office. The General-at-Sea was at last in a position to make his own terms.

To begin with, he demanded, and received, permission personally to take that disciplinary action against anyone guilty of dereliction of duty—such as the recreant masters of the

[1] This is no more than surmise, based upon inherent probability. The archives of Trinity House have no record of the particulars of these merchant vessels, or of the manner in which their ownership was distributed. It is only possible, therefore, to argue from effect back to cause to try and arrive at the reason for this uncharacteristic timidity.

[2] *Moderate Intelligencer*, December 8th, 1652.

merchantmen in the recent encounter off the Ness—which had hitherto been regarded as a 'droit of Admiralty'. As in the past, his Captains would deal with lesser offences; but if there were to be any more Augean stables in need of cleaning, Blake was determined to deal with them himself.

To clarify the whole state of affairs a code of laws was drawn up, known as the 'Articles of War'. They were designed to govern the lives and activities of all those serving as naval servants of the State. On paper they were sufficiently draconic, one-third of the thirty-nine articles carrying the death penalty without alternative, another third including it as a permissible award. In practice, the degree of severity with which the regulations were administered was largely determined by the character of the individual in command. In any case the delin-quent stood a considerably better chance of obtaining justice at the hands of one of the new courts of war than if he had remained at the mercy of the old traditional 'laws and customs of the sea'. None the less, the promulgation of these 'Articles of War' was very shortly followed by the first recorded instance of 'Flogging round the fleet'; when "William Hancock, car-penter's mate of the *Hound*", was tried and found guilty of "drunkenness, swearing and uncleanliness". He was con-demned "to be cashiered, to receive ten lashes with the whip by the side of each flagship present, with a paper in his hat stating his crime; a drum beating at the boat's head; and when within the platform at Portsmouth to be towed at the boat's stern to Gosport"[1]. Blasphemers had a hole bored through the tongue with a red-hot spike; mutineers received thirty lashes, or were condemned to stand for two hours with a halter about the neck and the right hand nailed to the mainmast. The lashes were laid on by the Bo'sun's mate, wielding that Cromwellian innovation, the cat-with-nine-tails.

To balance the tightening up of discipline there was an increase in the pay of the Able Seaman to 24s. a month; with a bonus of a month's wage for every Officer and man who served a full half-year[2]. All plunder in a prize, on or above the level of the gun-deck, was an additional perquisite of the foremast

[1] Cal. S.P. Dom. 1653–4.
[2] Blake was remunerated at the rate of £3 a day, his Vice-Admiral at £2, and his Rear-Admiral at £1.

hands[1]. Despite all these allurements, the known delays over the payment of wages and prize money made it extremely hard to come by the 16,000 shipmen required by the Fleet. When the Mayor of Southampton received an order to furnish 100 men—if necessary, by use of the press—he produced a beggarly list of 21, with the specious explanation that owing to the lack of trade and the few ships in port, mariners were not to be had. Sandwich's Warrant for 400 able-bodied seamen brought in 80 protesting landsmen. Of Ramsgate's quota of 80 A.B.'s not one half put in an appearance. The West was drained so dry of capable seafarers that both commerce and the fishing industry suffered severely for want of them. In the outcome a number of the 'New Model' soldiery were sent afloat, to perform the duties subsequently to become associated with the Marines.

In the meantime Blake and his coadjutors were building up what can only be termed a 'New Model' Navy; a navy made up exclusively of vessels built specifically to take the pounding of contemporary artillery, and designed primarily as floating gun-platforms—in short, *war*ships. With the States General in command of 150 sail, Blake's target was a minimum of 200. But even at the speedy rate of contemporary construction, ships took time to build. So it was with little over fifty craft that Blake, supported by Monck, Deane and Penn, set sail from Thames-mouth to waylay Tromp in the early February of 1653. For intelligence had come that the Dutchman was homeward bound in command of an armada of 150 vessels; two-thirds of which, it was reported, were packed with highly valuable freight.[2]

The rival armaments made contact off Portland; Blake in the *Triumph*, supported by about 30 vessels, fighting back grimly under the fury of the first massed onslaught; as Monck, commanding the White squadron to leeward, sought doggedly to claw his way into the vortex of the battle. Aboard the flagship casualties were heavy, the Captain, Andrew Ball, the master,

[1] This sometimes worked out seriously to the detriment of the owners of an English merchantman recaptured from the enemy, who well might undergo greater loss at the hands of the rescuer than from the original captor.

[2] A conservative estimate puts Tromp's fleet at 75 men-of-war, 1 fireship, and 5 smaller vessels, escorting some 150 armed merchantmen. Blake had about 70 craft by the time action was joined.

Broadbridge, and Sparrow, the Admiral's Secretary, all being struck down, together with a hundred men out of the ship's company of three hundred and fifty. Blake himself was badly wounded in the left thigh, but returned on deck the moment the injury had been bandaged, "nor was out of his place all the time of service".

With both Monck and Penn resolutely serving their guns an even heavier toll was taken of the Dutchmen; the English pounding away to try and hull their opponents, whose own fire was more directed at the masts and rigging. With nightfall Blake could plume himself on the fact that he had repulsed the attack of a force far more numerous than his own; and with daylight the fight was vigorously resumed. By Sunday morning the Dutchman's shot was giving out and he was hard put to it to safeguard his wallowing merchantmen from the swift-sailing frigates Blake had loosed against them.

As darkness fell Tromp skilfully gained the sanctuary of Cape Griz Nez; and owing to the danger of the many damaged English ships of deeper draught being carried to leeward by the ebb tide, the pursuit had reluctantly to be abandoned.

The Dutch loss amounted to 76 vessels, 19 warships and 57 merchant craft; with between two and three thousand killed and wounded, and one thousand five hundred prisoners. With revolting unctuousness the *Mercurius Politicus* of February 22nd reported that, "All the men-of-war who are taken are much dyed with blood, their masts and tackle being moiled with brains, hair and pieces of skull, dreadful sights though glorious as being a signal token of the Lord's goodness to this nation." The British success had been won at a cost of twelve hundred slain or injured, and five vessels badly knocked about, "with masts maimed, guns dismantled" and "mightily torn". Portsmouth was so crowded with wounded that many of the sufferers had to be transferred to Gosport, Dover, Deal, Weymouth and Sandwich. A fund was opened for the widows and orphans and for the injured themselves, to which Dover promptly subscribed £500. Doctors were sent down from the metropolis to aid those already on the spot; beds were cleared to accommodate the wounded in the London hospitals, and a special Emergency Hospital was opened for them in Deal. From the very first a wonderful example of self-sacrifice was set by

Elizabeth Alkin, more familiarly known as 'Parliament Joan'. Tireless and unseeking, so great was her concern for her stricken charges that, with her government grant exhausted, she emptied her own slender purse rather than let them go wanting.[1] Such was the price of a victory which restored England's naval prestige and once again endowed her shipmen with command of the narrow seas.

It had been so straggling, inchoate and ill-disciplined an encounter, however, that Blake, Monck and Penn sat down to formulate an operational doctrine upon which the conduct of future sea battles should be based. The outcome of their deliberations was the issue of the *Instructions for the better Ordering of the Fleet in Fighting*; a set of precepts which embodied a real attempt to develop the principle of attack in close-hauled line ahead. The governing Article ran:

"(3) As soon as they shall see the General engage . . . then each squadron shall take the best advantage they can to engage with the enemy next unto them; and in order hereunto all the ships of every squadron shall endeavour to keep in line with their chief. . . ."

It was not always possible, however, to impose a specific tactical gambit on an enemy with his own ideas of the way in which the game should be played. So there was little of the close-hauled line ahead in the action of June 1653, when Monck, off the Gabbard Shoal—the most northerly and easterly of the banks off the mouth of the Thames—encountered Tromp returning from the bombardment of a defiant Dover. The action which ensued took the form of a game of long bowls—an artillery duel at fairly extensive range, in which the heavier British ordnance soon established a superiority of fire. Monck, chewing stolidly on his quid, remained quite unperturbed even when the Dutch innovation of chain-shot cut the unfortunate Richard Deane to pieces right at his side. When the vessels already engaged were joined by an additional squadron under Blake, the British force was brought up to a strength with which the Dutch could not contend. With six of his vessels sunk, two blown up, and thirteen captured, Tromp sullenly drew off and took refuge within the Weilings sandbanks.

[1] One shilling a day was allowed for board, lodging and medical attention for the English, and sixpence a day for the Dutch.

For a month after the encounter Blake and his coadjutor maintained a close blockade of the Dutch coast, capturing many prizes, including eight Baltic merchant craft crammed with a cargo of 380 guns for delivery at Amsterdam.

In a final encounter between Monck and his doughty Hollander opponent, Tromp was slain by a stray musket ball; and the Dutch began to weaken just when victory might have been within their grasp. Their retreating craft were sternly pursued by Monck, who issued the order that the enemy vessels must be sunk rather than taken. It had been a furious tussle, fought throughout in veritable line of squadrons; and with the Dutch defeat and the loss of their most brilliant commander, the hour had struck.

By the April of 1564 the Treaty of Westminster had brought the war to an end. The Dutch consented to acknowledge the right of England to the sovereignty of the narrow seas and agreed to pass through the Straits of Dover only after receiving permission. The East India Company, the Baltic traders, and the heirs of those who had suffered at Amboyna, were all compensated with fair liberality; and as a final gesture, gold chains and medals were voted by Parliament to Blake, Monck, Lawson and Penn.[1] The fact that England was no longer 'in Coventry' was demonstrated by the conclusion of treaties with Denmark, Sweden and Portugal—all within the year.

Under the brilliant direction of Colbert, the French had made a useful contribution to the war against the Dutch, taking Dunkirk, which, together with the fort at Mardyke, was subsequently handed over to British occupation. With the Hollanders temporarily reduced to impotence, Blake was set free to castigate the Spaniards and read the Algerine sea-rovers so sharp a lesson that for a considerable time the narrow seas were rid of their piratical activities. This was the last service this bonnie fighter was to render the land of his birth; for he died—worn out but still in harness, as he would have wished—as his homing vessel opened Plymouth Sound.

[1] This was not the first distribution of medals. Parliament had authorised their issue to all Officers and men who had fought at Dunbar in 1650. Even earlier, medals had been bestowed on her Gentlemen Pensioners by Queen Mary in recognition of their loyal service at the time of the Wyatt rebellion in 1554.

In the homeland for which Blake had striven so steadfastly, however, all was very far from well. A great many of those who had supported first the Parliament and then the Protectorate had committed the traditional mistake of confusing revolution with liberty. They had lived to discover that all their freedom meant was licence to submit to an arbitrary master, supported by a handful of prosing left-wing 'Saints' with a very pretty taste in self-righteous tyranny. Under their repressive sway not only had individual liberty been monstrously invaded, but the general prosperity had been seriously affected by the reluctance of the European monarchies to traffic with a coven of regicides; by rising prices; by depreciation in the value of money, and by a general recession of trade. The prohibition of wool exports may a little have helped the native cloth industry, but the loss to the Customs occasioned by the lapse of the tax on exported wool was by no means made good by the increase in the impost on incoming wines. Equally, the new fiscal device of an 'Excise' on home-brewed ale and beer, meeting with considerable 'customer resistance', entirely failed to yield what had been expected of it. The only foreign goods exempt from what was virtually a contemporary purchase tax were corn, bullion, victuals, arms, ammunition and ordnance. Time had been when the first and last of these had been profitable exports. It was the Navy, of course, which constituted the heaviest drain on the country's resources. For the financial year ending on September 29th, 1657, for example, the total public income amounted to £1,050,000. Of this £809,000 was assigned to the Sea Service, already encumbered with debts to the tune of £506,000.[1] There is a nemesis awaiting the man or the government which persists in regarding capital as income; and in England's case the gap between revenue and expenditure could hardly be made good by such sums as might accrue from the fines levelled on shipmen and fish porters under the ordinance forbidding "profane cursing and swearing"! With his wages and prize money long in arrears the first-named had every excuse for freely indulging in both.

Having earlier denounced the practice, the Government was ultimately forced to 'farm' the Customs; and thus "the Great

[1] The figures are those given in Oppenheim's *Administration of the Royal Navy*.

Revolt, which at its outset was marked by bitter persecution of revenue-farmers, may be said to have expired amidst requests for tenders".[1]

Many folk, in despair of conditions improving at home, realised what property they could and set out to make a new life for themselves on the great, largely unpenetrated continent of America. Among them was John Washington from North-amptonshire, the grandfather of the boy who was to be the first inhabitant of the White House in the capital to which he gave his name.

As has frequently been demonstrated, the English never for long consent to be hectored and rounded-up; that is a little too un-English a procedure for a people sufficiently law-abiding to resent being law-ridden. So with Cromwell's death in 1658— "damned to eternal fame"—the rickety edifice of government he had erected tottered towards inevitable collapse.

Then on a sunlit afternoon in the May of 1660 the debonair King Charles II—after a meal of "ungarnished sailor's victuals, pease and pork, and boiled beef"—ended his dreary exile as he stepped ashore at Dover, to a roar of cheering, the pealing of bells, and the thunder of the welcoming guns. Monck, who, after all, had started out a Royalist, was waiting to make offer of his sword. Blake's old subordinate, Sir Edward Montagu, full of those second thoughts which had suddenly become so fashionable, was in close attendance[2]; while the rear was brought up by the Admiral's Secretary, Mr. Samuel Pepys— not too proud to carry "a dog the King loved", but a little anxious because "the King had forgotten to teach him company manners".

"A Monarchy laid aside at the expense of so much blood, returned without the shedding of a single drop". Merrie Eng-land, the *Anglia plena jocis* of Henry of Huntingdon, was herself again.

[1] *The King's Customs*, Harry Atton and Henry Hurst Holland.
[2] Monck was shortly to be created Earl of Albemarle; Montagu was to become the first Earl of Sandwich.

CHAPTER XIV

Trident in Jeopardy

"There is not so lawful or commendable a jealousy in the world as an Englishman's of the growing greatness of any Prince at sea."

KING CHARLES II

KING CHARLES II was recalled from poverty-stricken exile to take up the reins of government in a land whose Exchequer held exactly £11 2s. 10d.

The envoys to The Hague conveying the invitation for the King's return had been accompanied by a deputation of London citizens bearing a trunk containing £10,000 as a gift for their Sovereign. It was a welcome boon, but compared with the mountain of debt which formed the salient feature of Charles's inheritance, it amounted to very little. Charles I had left outstanding liabilities amounting to £530,000, for which his successor accepted full responsibility; as he did for the Lord Protector's many unsettled obligations, which included an outlay of £19,303 for his funeral; with the possible exception of the Coronation of George IV, the most garishly ostentatious State ceremony in the country's history.

The cost of Cromwell's 'trophy' of Dunkirk was £130,000 a year; the upkeep of the Army demanded £55,000 a month, that of the Navy for a similar period, £180,000.[1] Investigation revealed that despite a decade of unexampled taxation and unbridled pillage, the debits left unsettled by the Commonwealth totalled £1,888,352, of which the Navy debt accounted for £1,250,000; wages alone being in arrear to the tune of £354,000.

Through its reckless mishandling by Charles's predecessors, the royal revenue had seriously diminished. Yet there were scores of legitimate claims on his consideration it would have

[1] House of Commons Journals, VII, 627-31.

been ungrateful and impolitic for the King to ignore. Royalists' lands had been confiscated by the Parliament and lost to their original owners; Royalists' jewels and plate had been sold or melted down to help support the cause. During the dark days of the interregnum loyal subjects had rendered devoted personal service to the Monarch which he was sincerely anxious to requite.

Amongst those who had risked liberty and life for the King's sake, Captain Nicholas Tettersal took the most original course of recalling himself to the Sovereign's memory, by anchoring his 34-ton *Surprise* in the Thames off Whitehall, where Charles could not fail to see him whenever he walked abroad in the Privy Garden. The hint was not lost on a Monarch whose lazy eye missed nothing. Tettersal was awarded a Captain's Commission in the Navy, with a pension of £100 a year, while the *Surprise* was taken on the Navy List under her new name of *Royal Escape*, and given a complement of "Ten men and no guns".

Unfortunately, other and equally legitimate claims on the King's benevolence were not so easy to adjust equitably. Charles had been voted a Parliamentary grant of £1,200,000 to cover all the expenses for which the Sovereign remained responsible, but of this sum no more than £70,000 was forthcoming.[1] This unsatisfactory state of affairs clearly reflected the sorry financial condition to which the country as a whole had been reduced. Prior to the abrupt dismissal of the Long Parliament the general prosperity enjoyed by all classes had been made abundantly manifest by the refusal of an offer of £900,000 for the farm of the Customs and Excise for one year. But by 1654 an acute observer could write, "Who has seen it [London] in the King's time, and looked upon it now, would discern a great change in it"[2]; and from 1654 onwards the descent into the abyss of financial chaos took on a veritably Gadarene precipitancy. The Restoration first halted and then reversed the process; but it was a long, steep climb back to prosperity; for throughout the twelve years it took to get the wheels of industry

[1] Compare this with the £700,000 *per annum* voted, and paid out, to George II, which additional sums—from the Prince of Wales's grant and the overplus of the Sinking Fund—brought to a total of £900,000 *p.a.*
[2] Thurloe, State Papers, II.

turning properly, the gap between revenue and expenditure
was never less than £400,000, while interest rates stood at 6 per
cent, as against 4 to 5 per cent charged in Holland.[1] At the outset, therefore, retrenchment was imperative. But when the
reduction of the bitterly unpopular Army to a handful of
Household Troops was followed by economies designed to
diminish the Navy debt, the fact was overlooked that even as
things stood the country's first line of defence, as Mr. Pepys
dejectedly recorded, was "in a very sad condition".

It was the *Royal* Navy now, by special decree; although
paradoxically enough, the cost of its upkeep was at the mercy
of a Parliamentary vote. It followed that the sums allocated
in response to the Sovereign's application for funds were rarely,
if ever, adequate to meet the requirements of the Service.

As Lord High Admiral, James Duke of York headed a Navy
Board of seven, of which four members—including the comely,
good-natured Sir William Penn and the more mature Sir
William Batten, paunchy and rubicund of face, as became a
stout trencherman and sworn enemy of empty flagons—were
experienced seamen. The Clerk of the Acts was youthful
Samuel Pepys, scholar of Magdalene College, Cambridge, and
kinsman and protégé of the newly created Earl of Sandwich. A
man of unwearying diligence and outstanding administrative
ability, Pepys was speedily to prove himself, in Monck's
generous phrase, "the right hand of the Navy".

To revise and endorse the Commonwealth *Articles of War* and
Fighting Instructions was the Board's first and obvious step. But
they faced a far more difficult task when it came to fitting out
for duty at sea the most serviceable of the 135 warships, of all
rates,[2] taken over from the Protectorate. For such was the
dearth of money that "the credit of the [Navy] office", as
Pepys glumly recorded, "is brought so low that none will sell
anything without our personal security given for same". The
ships' chandlers refused to supply any more tallow or candles
'on charge'; the Barber-Surgeons' bill for filling medicine chests,
totalling £1,496 6s. 10d., was still outstanding; and when the
Queen Mother crossed the Channel to visit her son there was

---

[1] In France the rate stood at 7 per cent, in Spain 10 to 12 per cent, in
Turkey 20 per cent, and in Italy 3 per cent.
[2] Totalling about 25,000 tons.

not enough powder in the warships' magazines to fire a Royal Salute.

In the Victualling Yards Pride's purge had proved far less effective than on the occasion when he had so summarily metamorphosed the Long into the Rump Parliament. He had, of course, a good deal of rotten wood to clear away; for even Mr. Pepys—like Hawkins before him—was not above accepting a modest *douceur* if, as he vigorously protested, he could pocket it "without wrong to the King's Service". There were others, however, who were less scrupulous. It was not so much that the provisions issued were poor in quality as that they were sadly deficient in quantity. The outlay on 'gratifications' given in return for the award of victualling contracts could only be made good by deliberately overlooked shortages.[1] The same want of integrity characterised the dockyards, where every sort of petty embezzlement was indulged in; and, as one clerk of the cheque repined, "Our people's hands are so inured to stealing, that if the sawyers leave any work in the pits uncut, it's a hazard whether they find it in the morning". To guard against the perpetual theft of articles for re-sale, the Lord High Admiral gave orders for all possible equipment to be marked with a broad arrow[2]; while as an additional precaution an especial mode of manufacture was adopted for the Navy's sails, pennants and rope; the last-named having coloured threads woven into the strands to distinguish it from all other cordage. This widespread pilfering was, of course, the outcome of uncertainty as to their payment on the part of the men who were expected to toil from 5.30 a.m. till 6.30 p.m. from March to September and from daylight to dusk for the remaining months of the year. Nominally, this represented a remarkably long day with the nose to the grindstone. Actually, ample time off was allowed for breakfast, and the dinner break was a generous hour and a half. There was the additional inducement of an annual nine-day holiday with pay, with the option of a further four days vacation at half-pay. In general, discipline in the yards left little

[1] S. P. Dom. Charles II, CCXXXV, 136.
[2] A similar device was adopted by Henry Sidney, Earl of Romsey, on his appointment as Master-General of the Ordnance, in 1693; the pheon, or broad arrow, forming part of his armorial bearings. In the days of Richard I the symbol had been used by the King's ale-takers, to mark up beer that had been brewed to the required strength.

to be desired, since any misconduct that could be interpreted as mutinous was visited with the dreaded penalty of service with the fleet at sea. Most serious trouble of all was the unconscionable delay in the payment of the seamen's and dock-labourers' wages; while their distribution when a little money became available was bedevilled by all the opportunities for chicane presented by 'false musters' and the issue of 'dead pay'; which last was disbursed on a scale far more lavish than ever was legislated for in the regulations.

Chronic shortage of money, however, did not discourage the Navy Board from instituting several useful reforms. Ships were given a fixed 'establishment' of men according to their rate. Flag Officers were instructed to take precedence according to the Squadron—Red, White or Blue—in which they served; and they wore a flag at sea denoting their rank. In action, the White Squadron took the van; the Red Squadron, under the commanding Admiral, the post of honour in the centre; while the Blue Squadron brought up the rear. Officers holding Admiral's rank were also allocated a sum of 'table money', to enable them to entertain when in a foreign port, and generally uphold the dignity of their position. 'Plate money' was another perquisite eventually granted to Officers authorised to carry passengers, jewels, or specie, under Royal Warrant. For it had been realised at long last, that under certain conditions bullion and plate were commodities it could be profitable to export.

In due course the appointment of a Surgeon-General was supported by the promulgation of a scale of gratuities for those injured while on service. As finally determined, the allowances ranged from "present relief" at the rate of £13 6s. 8d. and "as much settled as an annual pension for his lifetime" for the man who lost two legs, down to £4 "for an eye lost". Lesser injuries were compensated "according to the chirurgeon's discretion". Dependants of those killed in action qualified for a pension based on the rate of pay drawn by the deceased during his service; and arrangements were made to care for the totally disabled.

The sick and injured were distributed amongst the existent hospitals, and when accommodation in these was exhausted they were billeted "upon private persons at the King's expense; fire, candle, linen, medicaments, and all things necessary" being provided under the auspices of a local agent; as were the services of "a physician (if need be) and chirurgeon and nurses".

An especial Commission attended to the award of gratuities to "the widows, children, and impotent persons of such as shall be slain in his Majesty's service at sea". But it was not until 1673 that a regular scale was established on which these gratuities were to be distributed. It was finally determined that the widows of men slain in the line of duty should be granted a sum equal to eleven months of their late husband's pay, with an additional third for each orphan unwed at the time of the father's death. If the deceased left no widow, the bounty went to his mother, provided that she herself was a widow, in poor circumstances, and over fifty years of age. The bounty to a child was allowed to accumulate until it was of an age to be apprenticed.

Well-intentioned as undoubtedly they were, all too often these measures foundered on the adamantine rock of finance. In 1665, for example, during the course of the Dutch War, John Evelyn wrote that he had 5,000 sick, wounded, and prisoners dying for want of care and shelter.

Equally, perpetual shortage of funds crippled the efforts made to improve a dietary which, as all responsible officials recognised, had hitherto been quite inadequate to maintain the English shipman in health and vigour. For as Pepys was himself at pains to point out, "Englishmen, and more especially seamen, love their bellies above everything else, and therefore . . . to make any abatement from them in the quantity or agreeableness of the victuals, is to discourage and provoke them in the tenderest point, and will sooner render them disgusted with the King's service than any one other hardship that can be put on them"—an expansion of Howard of Effingham's shrewd comment, "Nothing doth displease the seaman more than sour beer."

Unfortunately, a combination of financial stringency on the part of the Navy Board and shameless malpractice on that of the victualling contractor[1]—"resolved to save himself in the uncertainty of his payment by the greatness of his price"—frequently reduced the mariner's alimentation far below the proper

---

[1] Of whom one soured commander remarked that until a few of them had been hanged on land nobody would thrive at sea.

level of subsistence. As it stood, the table worked out in 1667 left little to be desired, each man being entitled to:

> "One pound averdupois of good, clean, sweet, sound, well-bolted with a horse cloth, well-baked, and well-conditioned biscuit; one gallon, wine measure, of beer; two pounds averdupois of beef killed and made up with salt in England,[1] of a well-fed ox, for Sundays, Mondays, Tuesdays and Thursdays, or instead of beef, for two of these days one pound averdupois of bacon, or salted English pork, of a well-fed hog, and a pint of pease (Winchester measure) therewith; and for Wednesdays, Fridays and Saturdays, every man, besides the aforesaid allowance of bread and beer, to have by the day the eighth part of a full-size North Sea cod of 24 inches long, or the sixth part of a haberdine 22 inches long, or a quarter part of the same if but 16 inches long; or a pound averdupois of a well-savoured Poor John, together with two ounces of butter, and four ounces of Suffolk cheese, or two thirds of that weight of Cheshire."

This was adequate diet enough, but it was rarely maintained at the full, either when subsistence was managed by a Victualling Commission 'on account'—when the State kept the business in its own hands—or by the issue of contracts, under the over-all supervision of a Surveyor-General of Victualling, with subordinate Surveyors in each port. Far too often, indeed, it was a case of 'bare Navy', the maritime equivalent to the soldier's 'hard-tack'; and the new term of 'banyan days' soon crept in to describe a period stretching from sunrise to sunset during which there had been no issue either of meat or fish.[2]

Pay rates were also raised, although disbursement frequently lagged many dreary months behind the date when payment had fallen due. On paper, however, the Ordinary Seaman rated 19s. a month, the A.B. 24s., the Gromets (now apprentices) 14s. 3d., and the Ship's Boys 9s. 6d. Master-gunners, Bo'suns and Carpenters qualified for from £2 to £4 a month according to the rate of the ship in which they served. Officers' pay ranged from the £3 (rising to £4 per diem) for an Admiral, down

---

[1] There was a great prejudice against Irish beef, which was said to be "very unwholesome, as well as lean, and rots our men".

[2] A lighter diet, which included wine in lieu of beer, flour, raisins and olive oil, was devised for ships serving in the Mediterranean.

to a shilling or two a day for those aspirants for Commissioned rank who were content to make a start as 'Captain's servants'. In 1672 the principle of granting pensions upon superannuation on the score of age was first given recognition, and in the year following it was extended to include Officers inactivated by wounds taken at sea; a benefit further expanded, in the same year, to include "Volunteers borne by particular order of the Lord High Admiral", and "the Officers of the land soldiers serving on board any of his Majesty's ships, both to their own relief in case of wounds, and their widows and orphans in case of death".

Warrants issued by the Crown gave dignity and added authority to such petty officers as the Master—trained, after 1675, at Christ's Hospital and Trinity House—the Gunner, the Bo'sun, the Carpenter and the Purser. Youths of good family were encouraged to adopt the Navy as a calling by entering the Service as 'King's Letter Boys'. Enrolled at not more than sixteen years of age and rated in turn as Ordinary and Able Seamen, they went to sea literally to learn the ropes—and much else of which an embryo Officer was required to inform himself. After continuing afloat as a Midshipman until the age of twenty, the aspirant proceeded to the Tower of London to be orally examined. If found sufficiently knowledgeable in the duties of his profession he was passed as qualified to receive a Lieutenant's appointment. The 'King's Letter Boys', of course, appeared on the ship's books in addition to those youngsters entered under the heading of 'Captain's nominations'.

Finally, in a belated effort to remedy the continued shortage of timber, in 1668 an Act [1] was passed for enclosing and planting with oak trees a waste area of 11,000 acres in the Forest of Dean.

If more was intended than was actually accomplished, it was not for want of royal sympathy and support, for no one took a deeper interest than the 'Black Boy' in all to do with the sea and ships. Charles had gained his practical knowledge of seamanship —which Nick Tettersal never ceased to extol—as a penniless exile in Jersey; and his love of all things aquatic even extended to the boisterous, hard-swearing Thames watermen, a close-knit fraternity whom he termed his nursery of seamen. Quite early in his reign the King wrote to his cherished sister Henriette

[1] 20. Car. II, Stat. I, Cap. 3.

that he was "newly returned from seeing some of my ships that lie in the Hope ready to go to sea". In the same year he again took up his pen to describe how he had contracted a chill through removing his wig and waistcoat while visiting the fleet at Chatham "in great heat". Later still, his loyal subjects in Sandwich observed him skilfully threading his way through the Goodwins to drop anchor in the Downs. In the July of 1671 he embarked at Portsmouth for a "divertisement by water", the object of which was to inspect the new citadel at Plymouth. In the cutter-rigged *Cleveland* Charles completed the first long-distance yachting trip on record; although on the return passage he was wise enough to put in at Dartmouth and proceed thence by road, rather than attempt Portland race in a head wind, with the lee shore of Chesil beach looming ominously abeam.

But even in naval matters it behoved the newly-crowned Monarch, like Agag, to tread delicately. At the mercy of a Parliament which, after the first fine careless rapture, proved as unwilling to subsidise short-term needs as it was unready to support long-term measures, the King was driven to conduct affairs by a series of improvisations and expedients. Moreover, it was impossible to leave out of calculation the bilious anti-royalist sentiment which in certain parts of the country still seethed and plotted. Plymouth had scowled at the envoy bearing the ratification of the treaty with Spain, not because he had brought peace, but because his country had concluded it with a Royal Administration. When the King's prospective bride, Catherine of Braganza, crossed the narrow seas she was landed at Portsmouth and not at Southampton, as had originally been intended. For only the previous year a *cache* of illicit arms had been seized by the authorities and a number of malcontent sectaries clapped into gaol, and the town was still regarded as 'unreliable'. When Charles, in consideration of a Gallic down-payment of two million *livres* and the promise of a further million within two years, rid himself of the incubus of Dunkirk —with an anchorage too shallow for the contemporary big ship, and strategically of no value without the support of Calais— there were angry murmurs from those who saw in the deal a base betrayal of Cromwellian imperialism.

On the other hand, the effect on the prosperity of the ports

of the acquisition of Tangier and Bombay—part of Catherine
of Braganza's dowry—was almost immediate. For possession
of the former materially helped trade expansion in the Mediterranean; while the latter furnished a rival centre of commerce
in the heart of a territory hitherto dominated by the Dutch.
The barometer of the country's industry started on a steady
climb upward; and while more associations—such as the
Hudson's Bay Company [1]—sought incorporation as Chartered
Companies, the progressively successful activities of the 'interlopers' ensured a growing measure of free trade—or more
precisely, freedom to trade. In effect, monopoly was on the
decline, and the movement towards *laissez faire* gained considerable momentum in what was steadily approximating to a
'mixed economy'.

The East India Company directors were soon busily engaged
in constructing a small wet dock at Blackwall for fitting out
their vessels after launching from the slips in their adjacent
shipyard.[2] All about it flowed the vessels engaged in the brisk
coasting trade—exclusive to English craft—which brought to
the Thames-side wharves tin, pilchards and china clay from
Cornwall, serge and hides from Exeter, malt from Arundel, and
fresh fish from Rye, Deal, Folkestone and the Isle of Thanet;
while sea coal came to the London Pool in 300–400-ton
colliers from the North. Poole, Weymouth and Exeter boasted
over a thousand tons of coastal shipping apiece; while even
hard-hit Southampton acted as an entrepôt for the malt, cheese,
currants, hops, oatmeal, timber, leather, cottons, and wearing
apparel destined for the Channel Islands. The only drawback
was that with the Islands themselves not yet in a position to
export much in the way of marketable wares, far too many
return passages had to be made with empty holds. Even Cowes
shipped some 250 cargoes coastwise annually [3]; only Portsmouth,
as primarily a naval base, failed to compete to any serious extent
with the busy traffic which elsewhere threaded the coastal waters.
Furthermore, the men of the coasting vessels were virtually
immune from the virulent scurvy and deadly calentures which

---

[1] The Hudson's Bay Company received its Royal Charter in 1670.
[2] Subsequently incorporated in the Brunswick dock, which in turn was
absorbed in the East India dock.
[3] Rising to over 400 by 1687.

were the bane of the ocean-going shipmen; for the first of which there was as yet no reliable remedy, let alone an efficacious prophylactic.[1]

For the first eleven years of the Restoration the Customs were 'farmed'. Estimated to bring in an annual £400,000, the actual yield for 1661 was £361,356. For the next four years it averaged £507,774, and would have reached an appreciably higher figure had it not been for the barefaced frauds perpetrated by the Navy Officers, who so overcrowded their holds with goods intended for private trade that "they had no room to throw by their chests and other cumbersome things upon occasion of Fight".[2] But since "the system of assessment and collection was slovenly and imperfect, and the preventive regulations were erratically administered",[3] attempts to cheat the Customs were not confined to the Navy. At Plymouth a positive feud raged between the Customs' officials and the mayor and corporation. On one occasion, indeed, the exchange of high words was followed by blows. This was the mayor's opportunity: naming the Customs' men the aggressors, he clapped them into cells till the goods in dispute could be disposed of and whisked out of sight. Nor was Plymouth singular —save in the lengths to which it was prepared to go—in this glaring defiance of authority.

*   *   *

There were few elements amongst the British people with cause to favour the Dutch. "The trade of the world is too small for both of us", as one blunt old tarpaulin captain put it to Mr. Pepys, "so one of us must go down." Thus it was largely at the behest of "the great cobs of Lombard Street" that the King consented to stiffen the *Act for the Encouragement and Increase of Shipping and Navigation* promulgated in the first year of his reign. Charles's acquiescence in their plea was all the more easily secured since he had not forgotten the readiness with which the States General had complied with the Commonwealth's demand for his own expulsion from Holland; while his sympathies

---

[1] Scurvy was no new affliction, Richard Hawkyns having recorded that in twenty years' ocean-going experience he had seen no less than 10,000 men fall victim to the scourge.

[2] *Discourses of the Navy*, John Hollond.

[3] Atton and Holland, *op. cit.*

were entirely on the side of those Orange relatives of his who had been excluded from power.

In essence, the enactment of 1660 was the traditional Navigation Act in slightly amended form. It was subsequently bolstered up by the appointment of a Surveyor of the Act of Navigation, empowered to keep a register of all English shipping; for which there was a rebate on Customs dues for new craft built up to certain specifications, the main proviso being the inclusion of gun-ports for a minimum of thirty cannon. The Act was also fortified by an absolute ban on the export of live sheep, wool fells, wool, woollen yarn, and fuller's earth, under pain of forfeiture of the goods themselves and the ship in which they were freighted. The only exception to the rule—that of 12 Car. II, c. 32—was made in favour of the Channel Islands, which were permitted to import 3,300 tods[1] of unkemed wool annually, to provide the raw material for their new stocking industry, soon to reap both fame and fortune. In effect, as De Witt ruefully commented in his *Interest of Holland*, "The English settled their rates of Customs and convoy-money so well, to favour their own people as much as possible, and to burden all masters of foreign ships and merchants, that it is to be feared the English merchants may in time bereave the Dutch of much of their trade."

With the effects of the Navigation Act being acutely experienced and fiercely resented, with the mounting challenge to Dutch supremacy in India, on the Guinea Coast, and in North America—where New Amsterdam had been recaptured and renamed New York—with the widespread issue of Letters of Marque and Reprisal and the seizure of Hollander shipping, and with the King's insistence on the 'Salute of the Flag', an open declaration of war could only be a matter of time.

In a highly explosive atmosphere the French were given ample excuse to strengthen their support of the Dutch when an English frigate intercepted the *St. Pierre de Rouen* in mid-Channel and insisted on taking the craft into Dover 'for search' —a term which was extended to include the removal of all the ship's gear and cargo, as a preliminary to torturing the crew in an endeavour to extract the confession that they were carrying

---

[1] The tod was stabilised at 32 lb.

contraband of war to Holland. Charles was furious when the incident was reported to him by the French Ambassador; the frigate Captain was cashiered and a number of the crew flogged round the fleet. But the damage had been done, and the King confronted a coalition in which the Dutch had every reason to anticipate active Gallic participation. In the event, it was circumspect to a degree.

In a conflict that was plainly destined to be fought out in naval terms, it was the British fleet that succeeded in putting to sea first; the Duke of York, in the April of 1665, appearing off the Texel, where he captured a number of Smyrna merchant-men,[1] homeward bound, and vainly summoned the enemy armament to come out and fight. Want of provisions impelling the British to seek their home ports, the Dutch emerged to snap up nine merchant vessels laden with naval stores from Hamburg, which they came up with off the Dogger.

Aroused by events to a belated sense of its obligations, Parliament hastily voted £2,500,000 for the prosecution of the war,[2] and for the upkeep of the 108 warships and 14 fireships which constituted the Fleet; against which the Dutch could oppose 103 ships of war and 11 fireships.

With the British craft back from the Texel for refit, and as many of the quondam Officers of Blake's Roundhead fleet cheerfully set aside their political prejudices to take up commands in the Royal Navy, De Ruiter made his appearance in the narrow seas at the head of a numerous fleet; a sight which set Southampton to the hasty erection of breastworks. But the Dutchman's real aim was the shipping at Portsmouth; and when an assault on this threatened to prove altogether too risky, he contented himself by demonstrating off Southsea Castle ere putting about and making for open water. In February Mr. Pepys had been fluttered by a rumour that Lord Sandwich was in contact with the Dutch "on the backside of the Goodwin". But it was not until June 3rd that the rival fleets made contact about forty miles off Lowestoft; with York, Rupert and Sand-

---

[1] One was laden with a cargo worth £20,000.

[2] The sum was raised by a general assessment of the population, including the clergy, hitherto self-taxed in convocation. In reward the clerics were endowed with the right to vote in Parliamentary elections. It was intended that the expenditure of the two and a half millions should be spread over two and a half years.

wich heading an armament of just over 100 ships.[1] They were confronted by a fleet of equal strength, commanded by the ex-cavalryman, Opdam van Wassenaar.

The Dutchman had peremptory orders to fight, but with very little discretion as to how and when. York was equally deter-mined to force the issue, and manœuvred freely to press home his attack. With guns a-roar so loudly that the sound of the firing could be heard in Dover, the death of a subordinate Dutch commander threw his crew into so shameful a panic that they seized command of their vessel and carried her out of action. It was an example only too speedily followed by thirteen other craft, the whole van giving way. Opdam tried vainly to close the gap in his line; but in a desperate attempt to grapple the British flagship, his own craft blew up, and he perished with most of his ship's company.

As four of the Dutch craft ran foul of one another, a fireship launched against them set them blazing; and the whole enemy armament, in considerable confusion, drew off under cover of a squadron commanded by Cornelis Tromp, son of Blake's old adversary in the days of the Commonwealth.

After sixteen hours of close fighting Dutch losses totalled 18 vessels taken and 14 sunk,[2] with 2,000 prisoners in British hands. At one stage in the conflict the British 40-gun *Charity* had fallen into enemy clutches. But such had been the anxiety of her captors to clear the scene of action that they turned her adrift, as they had earlier consigned her wounded to an open boat. Some of the less seriously injured contriving to scramble back aboard the deserted craft, she was brought safely back to her moorings by a crew only a little less crippled than she was herself.

The Duke of York—who had displayed great coolness and courage throughout the fight—had won an undoubted victory. But critics were not wanting to maintain that a little less manœuvring and a good deal more close fighting would have paid him better. Since it was impossible for the King to ignore such criticism without laying himself open to the charge of fraternal partiality, the Duke and his principal lieutenant, Sandwich, were quietly replaced by Prince Rupert and the veteran George Monck.

[1] 96 men-of-war, 4 fireships, and tenders.
[2] Mr. Pepys, however, insists on 24 sunk.

It was Sandwich, however, who took a strong squadron to Bergen, where he sent in Vice-Admiral Sir Thomas Tyddemann, with 20 ships, to attack 50 Dutch East Indiamen, lying snugly under the harbour guns. With an off-shore wind to contend with, the intruders were speedily in difficulties, their fireships being rendered useless by the contrary direction of the breeze. It was obvious madness to continue with an action so patently abortive, and Sandwich drew off, having lost some of his most reliable subordinate leaders during the course of the fight.

Preparations for further activity were sadly handicapped by the outbreak of the Great Plague. Raging in London, it was introduced into Southampton by a child evacuee from the metropolis, and quickly took fierce hold. With terrifying speed the pestilence spread to Deal, Dover and Sandwich. Neither was Chatham immune from the scourge; which placed a heavy responsibility on the modest naval establishment at Sheerness, where an excellent anchorage was only serviceable so long as the British retained command of the Channel.

Somehow a fleet was fitted out to take up winter station at the Nore. But it failed to intervene when an enemy armament indulged itself in a demonstration off the Thames, and then went on to bombard Margate, "breaking chimneys and maiming most of the vessels in the harbour".

The French had exhibited singularly little eagerness to fulfil their treaty obligation to come to the Hollanders' support. But the significance of their pledge to intervene is not to be measured by the fact that Louis's Admiral, de Beaufort, neither made junction with De Ruiter nor fired a single shot. For in the 'Four Days' Battle', which began on June 1st in the waters between the North Foreland and Dunkirk and ended in the mouth of the Thames, Rupert was out of the fight for many crucial hours, having been detached to deal with a hypothetical Gallic threat which only materialised after a French squadron had joined up with the Dutch armament in Dunkirk itself.

Left to his own devices, Monck set forth in search of his enemy, whom he brought to bay in the narrow gut between Dunkirk and the Downs. Signalling to engage forthwith, the outnumbered British commander bore down on his foe in such admirable formation as to impel a Gallic onlooker to comment,

"Never was a line drawn straighter than the line drawn by the English ships. They fight like a line of cavalry handled according to rule." Massing on the hostile van, Monck boldly seized the initiative, and for a time the very audacity of his attack brought it prosperity. But the ebb and flow of the fight had brought the British into dangerous shoal water, and Monck was forced to put about. The action degenerated into a general *mêlée* as the Hollanders promptly fell on his weakened rear with their own strong centre and rear, handling it roughly. Monck was forced to retreat to the shelter of the English coast, having lost a number of ships and men.

At this juncture the tough old sea-fighter was joined by Rupert and a reinforcement of undamaged ships. Without a moment's hesitation he returned to the attack, breaking the Dutch line from to leeward, but failing to penetrate the second. From the confused fighting that ensued it was De Ruiter who drew off first; with Monck chewing stolidly on his quid, automatically hitching up his breeches, and cursing the 'butterboxes' for turning tail. Yet notwithstanding the retreat of the Dutch, with the loss of many men, Monck could claim no more than a Pyrrhic victory. The enemy had been despoiled of five war-vessels and several fireships; but Monck's own losses in major craft had amounted to ten, including Sir George Ayscue's Armada veteran, the 90-gun *Royal Prince*, which had gone aground on the Galloper Shoal, thereafter being captured by the Dutch and burned. "She was like a castle in the sea", reported Sir Thomas Clifford, "and I believe the best ship that ever was built in the world to endure battering, but she is gone, and this is an ill subject to be long upon." The last link with the brave days of Drake and Hawkins had been severed; and the balance of the fleet limped home to refit. John Evelyn, inspecting the battle-worn vessels where they lay awaiting repair in Medway, frankly wrote of them as "miserably shattered . . . appearing rather so many wrecks and hulks, so cruelly had the Dutch mangled us". There was, indeed, truth as well as malice in King Louis's comment that the English really were beat, for he knew no people in the world who would endure beating three days together but the English.

One of the battle casualties had been the veteran tarpaulin Captain Sir Christopher Myngs. As Pepys and Sir William

Coventry left the church after the venerated old sea-dog's funeral they were accosted by "a dozen able, lusty, proper men", who earnestly besought permission to fit out a fireship and set off straightway to "do that that shall show our memory of our dead commander, and our revenge".

They had not long to wait, for within two months the fleets were again at sea. On July 23rd Monck sallied out to challenge the Dutch armament of 73 line-of-battle ships, 26 frigates, and some 20 light craft, which had been holding the very gateway of the Thames. Between them, Monck and Rupert deployed 87 fighting craft and a flotilla of fireships; 15 frigates having been left behind for sheer want of crews to man them, so fearful had been the toll of pestilence.

Assembling at the Nore, the fleet, headed by the *Royal Charles*, worked out into King's Channel, helped by a racing ebb. De Ruiter, who had been waiting off the Naze, stood out to sea; and with first light on St. James's Day the drums and trumpets were sounding fiercely to battle. A sudden storm delayed the moment of contact, incidentally destroying one of Monck's first-rates, the *Jersey*, struck by lightning. When at last action was joined, Monck massed on the enemy van. There was no great attempt to manœuvre, gun replied feverishly to gun; the rolling echo of their thunder being heard by anxious strollers in St. James's Park. As with a much later tussle, it was "a damned pounding match"; and the Dutch were the first to wince away. But by clever sailing De Ruiter eluded the trap that Monck sought to spring on him and made all speed for the shelter of home waters.

During the pursuit Rupert sent his own little sloop, the *Fan-Fan*, freshly off the stocks, to engage with no less an opponent than De Ruiter himself. For an hour she harried the great flagship like a game little terrier snapping at a bull's heels. Working in so close that the Dutch could not bring their pieces to bear, she banged away resolutely with her own small guns "to the amusement of the English, and indignation of the Dutch to see their Admiral so chased".

Monck undoubtedly enjoyed the better of the encounter, and was free to blockade the enemy coast, make prize of many homebound merchantmen, and keep the vast Dutch fishing fleet in ruinous idleness. On August 8th he even penetrated behind the island of Terschelling, to burn at their anchors 160 merchantmen—including several great East Indiamen—while a shore party under Sir Robert Holmes plundered the warehouses and put the island town of Brandaris to the torch. All in all, 'Holmes' bonfire', as it was termed, wrought damage to the tune of a million sterling. This feat accomplished, in dire need of provisioning and overhaul, the victorious fleet returned to its home ports.

*   *   *

Both the English and the Dutch fleets were at sea during the late summer and autumn, as were de Beaufort's squadrons. But typical Channel gales frustrated every attempt to get into action. With the coming of winter the possibility of negotiating a settlement with the Dutch persuaded the Administration, in view of the prevailing want of money, to fall back on a purely defensive policy rather than attempt the formidable task of restoring the fleet to a proper war footing. It was not that Parliament—had it done its duty—would have been unable to find the needful funds, despite the heavy loss of revenue consequent on the disorganisation of the coal industry and coasting trade, the earliest victims of Dutch privateersmen. As the contemporary economist, Sir Josiah Child, wrote in his *Brief Observations Concerning Trade*, "There were more men to be found on the Exchange worth £10,000 than in 1651 were worth £1,000"; a submission substantiated by Sir Charles Petrie's comment that "England has rarely been so prosperous as under Charles IInd."[1] But Cromwell's ruthless methods of extorting taxation at the sword's point had gone by the board with the Restoration; and "the people, closing their eyes to the needs of the Navy, spent their money with contentment on themselves".[2] They would not even honour the debt to the seamen for services rendered. Paid with 'tickets' which if negotiable at all, could only be encashed at ruinous discount, the disgruntled veterans of the 'Four Days' Battle' and St. James's Day, after demonstrating vainly in the streets, went over

[1] Revenue from the postal services, no less than from the Customs, reflects the condition of a country's prosperity; at this period it averaged well over £21,000 a year.

[2] Callender, *op. cit.*

to the Dutch in shoals. In consequence, first the big ships and then the second- and third-rates were laid up in ordinary; while to man the few frigates in trim to keep the sea, the press-gangs could only scrape together a meagre harvest of "loose and unknown persons" caught up haphazard from the highways and byways. For the tremendous drain on Navy personnel occasioned by the recent pestilence, by desertion, or by the secession of large numbers of seamen to the merchant service—where they were reasonably sure of their pay and victuals—had in no way been offset by the formation, in the October of 1664, of the Lord High Admiral's Maritime Regiment,[1] the lineal forebears of the Royal Marines. Indeed, owing to the chronic shortage of man-power, even work on the projected fortifications, the corner-stone of the new 'defensive policy', lagged deplorably. At Garrison Point, Sheerness, for example, the contractor's average muster amounted to no more than ten able-bodied labourers. Not that anyone was seriously perturbed, for even if negotiations for a peace treaty with the States General did hang fire rather ominously, at least a show of reconciliation had been brought about with France.

This did not, however, deter a certain Captain La Roche, in command of a couple of Gallic men-of-war, from scouring the narrow seas in search of prizes. As the *Sainte Marie* of Ostend was lying peacefully in Torbay her master saw the Frenchman bearing purposefully down on him. Distrusting the newcomer's intentions, the merchant skipper took refuge within the harbour of Torquay, making fast to the quayside itself. As an additional precaution, he landed his guns, munitions, sails and tackle, giving them into a local townsman's keeping. But impudently disregarding the fact that the *Sainte Marie* was technically under the protection of the English Sovereign, La Roche landed an armed party which seized the ship and forcefully removed all its gear from its temporary custodian's premises. This done, the Frenchman set sail and cleared the bay. A few days later he was guilty of a similar outrage, when he swooped into Cowes Roads to snatch a chaloupe from its moorings, right under the shadow of the castle.

King Charles at once protested to Louis of France; in the meantime sending Sir Thomas Allin to search out La Roche,

[1] Called the Yellow Regiment from the colour of their coats.

force him to surrender his prisoners and restore the *Sainte Marie*
and the chaloupe to their respective owners. Since Louis had
already been requested to deal with the matter, he indignantly
protested at his brother-monarch's summary handling of
affairs; and Mr. Pepys nervously opined, "Everybody do think
a war will follow; and then in what case we shall be for money,
nobody knows."

But whatever Louis's ulterior intentions, they were anticipated by the Dutch. Fearful of a Gallic invasion of the Netherlands,[1] they were determined to pursue a struggle from which
Louis had agreed not to withdraw without his ally's consent.
For the States General were shrewd enough to foresee that real
peace between France and England could lead to nothing but
an alliance between them, with the Hollanders as their predestined adversaries.

So it fell out that in the early hours of June 7th De Ruiter
made his way inside the Gunfleet Sand with 66 ships of war;
the renegade British shipmen amongst their crews yelling, "We
did heretofore fight for tickets; now we fight for dollars!" By
the 10th the half-finished defensive works at Sheerness had been
blown up, together with a substantial dump of naval stores, and
the chain across the Medway at Upnor cleared out of the way.
Disregarding the fact that he had been forced to burn several
of his vessels that had been grounded and stubbornly refused to
be worked free, Rear-Admiral van Ghent, in command of the
van, continued up-stream in the face of such scattered fire as
could be brought to bear. Together with his subordinate, John
De Brakel, he seized over two score vessels, including several
warships; while from the poop of the stately *Royal Charles* a
'butter-box' trumpeter insolently sounded off the derisive ditty
Joan's Placket Is Torn. As flames roared destruction to the *Royal
James*, *Royal Oak* and *Loyal London*—and while Captain Natha-
niell Darrell and a handful of Marines and artillerymen
resolutely beat off another Hollander attack on Landguard
Fort, in the Harwich estuary—De Ruiter roused out his towing
lines and coolly bore away the captured *Royal Charles*—the
proudest ship that ever left an English dockyard, and the very
symbol of Monarchy restored.

[1] Louis based his claim to the Spanish Netherlands on his marriage to
Maria Theresa, daughter of Philip IV of Spain.

Chatham was in an uproar as Monck arrived post-haste to organise some sort of defence for the vessels lying unmanned and unrigged in Gillingham Reach, under threat from a landing party of 800, led by the apostate Colonel Dolman, once an Officer in the Commonwealth Army.

London's bewilderment at these unprecedented events quickly yielded to panic, as the fear spread that the next favourable tide would bring the enemy forces to the assault of the capital itself. As the King and the Duke of York personally superintended the erection of field works on either side of the river and saw to the sinking of a line of vessels to block the waterway at Blackwall, there was a run on the goldsmith-bankers and a hurried flight of the more craven-hearted. Even Mr. Pepys busied himself in dispersing his worldly possessions so that, in the event of the Hollanders arriving in the metropolis, "something might be saved". To add to the general alarm and despondency a fanatic Quaker, naked save for a wisp of loincloth, prowled the streets with a cauldron of live coals on his head, calling on all and sundry to "Repent!" As the orders went out to mobilise the Trained Bands and organise a *levée en masse*, certain of the more wantwit even went to the length of demanding an immediate reassembly of Parliament— the very body whose misguided policy had brought the nation to such peril.

The general panic, however, subsided as quickly as it had arisen; with London and the bigger ports not a whit less eager to strike back than courageous little Deal, where "the common people and almost all other ran mad to get at the Dutch". But the Hollanders, lacking a land force to exploit their naval successes, put about and made for home. The French, to whom the invasion of England at this moment would have presented few difficulties, preferred to embark on the conquest of the Spanish Netherlands. The Dutch, faced with this threat to their land frontiers, hastily brought their quarrel with the Restoration Government to a close with the Peace of Breda; hopeful that the English would realise that French domination of the Rhine Delta embodied as great a threat to the people of the island realm as to their late enemies. As the outcome of certain broad hints on these lines, in the January of 1668 Charles concluded a defensive alliance with the States General, which *inter alia* saw a considerable relaxation of the Navigation Act in favour of the Dutch.

Peace with the Dutch left England the undisputed master of the expanding American colonies, and a maritime Power which—so long as it was careful not to lower its guard—was not lightly to be challenged. Such failures as the Navy Board had been guilty of throughout the recent struggle were attributable less to York and his coadjutors than to the ineludible effects of the Plague, and to a Parliament which had failed to vote anything like adequate supplies. Charles had bluntly informed his 'faithful Commons', "No part of those moneys you gave me for the war have been diverted to other uses, but on the contrary, besides all those supplies, a very great sum hath been raised out of my standing revenue and credit, and a very great debt contracted." Even so, Pepys's extremely modest aim to pay the foremast hands "once a year at furthest" had not been realised; while the joint efforts of the Clerk of the Acts and his fellow-diarist, John Evelyn, to found hospitals at Chatham and Rochester for the care of the many sick and wounded had also faltered for want of the necessary funds to subsidise them. Small wonder that the harassed King morosely confided to Lady Jerningham, "The more you stir a man of politics, the more he stinks."

Hampered as it might be, however, there were a few significant reforms the Navy Board could bring about. To ensure that a reasonable number of experienced Naval Officers, surplus to peace-time requirements, would instantly be available in time of war, arrangements were made to put certain Admirals, Vice-Admirals and Captains of flagships on half-pay when not employed at sea. The immortal pity was that financial considerations would not permit the extension of this boom to all ranks and ratings. But at least it had been recognised that developing battle-practice demanded a professionalism in the Royal Navy that could only be founded on continuity of service. In principle, at least, duty in the King's ships had ceased to be a part-time activity and become a whole-time vocation.

Doubtless it was also thought that a little uncompromising professionalism would serve to check the mischief wrought by many of the "young gentlemen Captains", whose inattention to their duties and youthful inability to carry the responsibility of command was so deplored by Mr. Pepys, and in speaking of whom Monck was reported by his outspoken wife to have "cried mightily out", while longing for "the old plain sea-captains that served with him formerly".

*   *   *

If there was one thing the English people dreaded more than Dutch commercial rivalry, it was a return to the Roman Catholic thrall, which with Spain no longer an international menace, was chiefly associated in the public mind with the Court of Louis XIV. Charles, of course, was free under the Constitution to pursue his own foreign policy. But if he were not to risk once more "going on his travels", the reaction of public opinion to the designs he initiated had to be taken seriously into account. It was necessary for him, therefore, to adopt a particularly lonely and sinuous course if his hopes of anything like an enduring *rapprochement* with France were to be fulfilled. Yet it had to be recognised that were France and England simultaneously to woo the States General, Gallic blandishments would undoubtedly prevail; and instead of a defensive Anglo-Dutch coalition there would arise a greatly strengthened combination of Gaul and Hollander, with England's utter destruction as their joint interest. For Colbert's spade work was bearing fruit in the form of a French marine which would add appreciably to the ability of the States General to wage war at sea.[1] In the immediate circumstances—although few but the King had the wit to realise it—the only sound policy was to follow the example of Elizabeth and Cromwell, and make an alliance with our enemy's bitterest foe.

Working through the skilled intermediation of his sister Henriette, Charles concluded a secret treaty with Louis—signed at Dover on May 22nd, 1670, by his confidential representatives, Arlington and Clifford—by the terms of which England's Sovereign was to receive an immediate subsidy of £150,000 "to aid him in announcing his conversion" to Rome. A further £225,000 a year was to be forthcoming so long as war with the

---

[1] In 1661 France possessed 30 war vessels, of which only 3 were ships of the line. When Colbert died in 1683 the total was 169 vessels, of which 12 were line-of-battle ships of the first class, armed with from 74 to 120 guns; while 50,000 mariners were registered in the *Inscription Maritime*.

Dutch was steadfastly maintained. Charles was further to assist the French King to make good his claim to the Spanish succession; while the interests of the Prince of Orange were to be given primary consideration.

Clifford, for one, had every belief in the sincerity of the King's professed desire to be reconciled to Rome; but since neither Charles nor Louis evinced the slightest inclination either to bruit the matter abroad or press it to a conclusion, it is to be doubted if they attached the same importance to this proviso as to the more mundane articles of the agreement. What is unquestionable is, that of the first instalment of his subsidy, amounting to £84,700, Charles paid £76,000 straight into the Navy Board's coffers. Furthermore, on the question of over-all command in the forthcoming contest, the King was adamant. "My Captains", he blandly informed Colbert de Croissy, the French Ambassador to the Court of St. James, "know the seas surrounding these islands, and the methods of fighting the Dutch, far better than those commanding the French ships possibly could. Moreover", he added proudly, "it is the custom of the English to have command at sea, and if I were to order the commander of my fleet under pain of death to obey foreigners, he would not do it."

*   *   *

Hostilities against the Dutch reopened without any formal declaration of war, when Sir Robert Holmes was given orders of some moral obliquity, committing him to waylay the homeward bound Dutch Smyrna fleet. Lying off the Isle of Wight with a mere eight ships, the British found themselves confronted by an armada of sixty-six merchant craft, of which twenty-four were fully armed, escorted by six men-of-war. Nothing daunted, Holmes attacked straightaway, and a stubborn fight continued all day. With a reinforcement of four ships, Holmes was able to sink one enemy warship and capture three others; but the valuable merchantmen contrived to make good their escape.

The Dutch being unable to prevent a junction between the British ships and a fleet proudly organised by Colbert,[1] the combined force, numbering, with fireships, some ninety craft,

[1] Prior to the outbreak of hostilities Colbert had not boggled at hiring the very best Dutch shipwrights to help complete his armament.

sailed eastward from the Gunfleet to bring the Hollanders to action. Contrary winds so delayed the armament, however, that it was forced to put into Sole Bay to water. From this anchorage William Batten, writing to Joseph Williamson, Keeper of His Majesty's Papers of State, affirmed, "I was yesterday aboard the *Prince* and saw the Duke,[1] . . . never did I see so brave a fleet before, nor the world neither from the days of Noah, I believe. He told me a scout had come in that had discovered the Dutch fleet twelve leagues off." With the news Sandwich urged the Duke to weigh at once, but for some reason the Lord High Admiral delayed. To while away the time of waiting debonair Lord Buckhurst turned to versifying:

> To all you ladies now on land
>   We men at sea indite,
> But first would have you understand
>   How hard it is to write.
> Our paper, pen and ink, and we
>   Roll up and down our ships at sea.
>
> Should foggy Opdam chance to know
>   Our sad and dismal story,
> The Dutch should scorn so weak a foe
>   And quit their fort at Goree:
> For what resistance can they find
>   From men who've left their hearts behind?

During the night the wind changed, putting the English armament on a lee shore; and the Dutch, having got the weather gage, sailed in to the attack; the scouts *Infant* and *Spy*, running for the anchorage and firing their guns to warn the fleet, inadvertently acting as pilots for the enemy.

York, with his fleet embayed and scattered, at once gave the orders to weigh. Many vessels were forced to cut their cables, and a good deal of confusion arose out of the hasty scramble to put to sea. The French immediately took the opportunity to cast on the port tack and stood off to the South[2]; while the English, taking the starboard tack, steered East, thus dividing

---

[1] York had taken over the command again with the death of Monck in the January of 1670.

[2] Evidence is not wanting that Louis had instructed his Admiral to spare his ships as much as possible.

the armament at the very outset. All were under full sail by 5.30 a.m., with a falling wind.

Sandwich in the *Royal James* took the lead, and his ship fired the first shot of the day, at the leading vessel of Van Ghent's squadron. For his part De Ruiter deliberately sought out the Duke of York in the *Prince*; while Admiral Bankert gave chase to the French. A hot, scrambling action ensued, during which York was twice forced to shift his flag, first to the *St. Michael* and then to the *London*. It was noticeable throughout the entire struggle that Captain John Churchill—the future Duke of Marlborough—in command of a detachment of the Yellow Regiment, displayed a coolness and courage the equal of that exhibited by York himself.

With the fleet well out to sea, Sir John Narborough, aboard the *Prince*, set down in his log, "Calm as a milk bowl, and none to get up to help us." A little later a note made by Van de Velde recorded, "The Erle of Sandwich was boarded by Van Brackle across the bow and so fast that the Erle could not get cler [clear] of him unless he cut his bowsprit by the board, but after a long Dispute the Erle of Sandwich Received much Damage; having five hundred men killed and wounded, he got cler." [1] But the *Royal James* catching fire, was soon a roaring fountain of flame; Sandwich being forced to leap into the sea, which subsequently rendered up his grossly swollen carcase with its George Star and heavily-ringed fingers all a-glitter with diamonds.

The struggle lasted until 6 p.m., when the Hollanders drew off in a rising fog; De Ruiter openly affirming that he had never seen a battle so terrible and so long. No English prize was taken by the Dutch, but York's captures included the 52-gun *Joshua* and the 48-ton *Staveren*. Another Dutch vessel was sunk and one blown up. But apart from Sandwich, the English losses included the redoubtable Sir Fretchville Hollis. On balance, however, the advantage of the day had lain with York, as the contemporary poet recognised:

> *They battered without let or stay*
> *Until the evening of that day;*
> *'Twas then the Dutchmen ran away—*
> *The Duke had beat them tightly.*

[1] The note was written on one of Van de Velde's sketches of the action.

The day following the French rejoined, virtually uninjured. It is impossible not to reflect that had they earlier put in an appearance on the scene, they would have done little but add to the confusion.

Before the next campaign could open the provisions of the Test Act had removed the Duke of York from the command, which passed to Prince Rupert. The King himself exercised many of the functions of Lord High Admiral; but despite his best exertions, stoutly supported by those of Mr. Secretary Pepys, the fleet that took the seas was, in Rupert's biting phrase, "merely huddled out". Provisions were in as short supply as men, despite a bounty scheme to encourage recruiting, which achieved as little success as the attempt to revive a proper register for seamen. The indeterminate encounters which followed were only notable for the superb skill with which De Ruiter frustrated Rupert's every attempt to lift Schomberg's army from its camp at Yarmouth and land it on Dutch soil, to combine with Louis's forces massed on the Rhine, and the continuing tepidity of the French when it came to battle-fighting. In what proved the final encounter, off the Texel, Gallic failure to respond to Rupert's signals to engage wrung from that exasperated veteran the angry comment, "Had they but borne down on the enemy, I must have routed them; it was the greatest and plainest opportunity ever lost at sea." Colbert had furnished his country with a magnificent fleet; but battles are not won by ships, but by the men who fight them. As Ardant du Picq so rightly insisted, "*L'homme est l'instrument premier des combats.*"

The Schoonveldt battles had pretty clearly demonstrated that both sides were worn out; and in the period of inactivity that followed both Charles and his people were given time to realise that their true interests did not lie with a nation whose fleet only attended the scene of action "to see if the British Navy earned its pay". Furthermore, a war-weary Holland had undergone a political convulsion which had brought to power the English King's own nephew, William of Orange; a constitutional change which altered the whole complexion of affairs. Charles, who was fully alive to the fact that a King's only morality is the welfare of his people, blandly jettisoned the Anglo-Gallic alliance by signing the Peace of London of February 9th, 1674; by the terms of which the 'Salute of the

Flag' from Cape Finisterre to "the middle point of the land Van Staten in Norway" was freely conceded and the supremacy of the English in the narrow seas specifically acknowledged. New York, which the Dutch had recaptured, was restored to the English Crown, and there was a token indemnity of 800,000 patacoons—the equivalent of some £200,000.

The end of the war found the Navy deeply in debt; with £31,600 owing for dockyard wages alone, and other liabilities on a similar scale. Many of the dockyard men, indeed, were encouraged to find work elsewhere, while still being credited with pay in the place of their official employment. Pepys' desk was littered with such complaints as that the *Swan* had been delayed at Plymouth "from the unwillingness of the tradesmen to trust his Majesty further", or that "the brewer at Portsmouth doth absolutely declare that he will not provide any beer for the *Rupert* and *Centurion* till he is better assured of his payment than now is".

Yet by some means or other the King had managed to establish Greenwich Observatory, where John Flamsteed, England's first Astronomer Royal, could continue his labours to perfect the science of navigation. In addition he was instrumental in founding the Nautical Almanac.

Occasion was also taken to organise the Chaplains' Department, it being decreed that "no persons shall be entertained as chaplains on board his Majesty's ships but such as shall be approved by the Lord Bishop of London". His Lordship's sense of discrimination must have been somewhat easy-going, however, since a certain Henry Teonge was appointed to one of the King's ships—the *Assistance*—the better to enable him to escape his creditors. In sharp contrast to a later Chaplain, Edward Mangin, who at the end of a few weeks "bid adieu to the numerous and (to me) insupportable vexations of a naval life", Teonge positively revelled in his job. "No life at the shore being comparable with that at sea", he confided to his *Diary*, "where we have good meat and drink provided for us, and good company, and good divertisements, without the least care, sorrow or trouble." It was a verdict, however, in which the average foremast hand, in his loose canvas 'drawers' and thrummed 'Monmouth' cap, would have found it difficult to concur.

By 1677 relations with France had grown so strained that a

rupture was considered imminent; and the preparations made in England were given the name of 'the Sham War'—the 'Phoney War' of the period. Fortunately, Parliamentary alarm was sufficiently lively to enable the Navy Board to begin the construction of thirty new vessels; with Samuel Pepys defending the measure in Parliament—in which he now sat as the Member for Castle Rising—in one of the most cogent orations in which his brother legislators had ever been indulged.

The Peace of Nymwegan put an end to the Franco-Dutch war; but by this time the Navy's building programme was well in hand.

A wild accusation that he had been concerned in Titus Oates' and Henry Teonge's trumped-up 'Popish Plot' temporarily removed Pepys from office[1]; drove York from England, and left naval affairs at the mercy of a Commission of Seven, all of them Members of Parliament and most of them Whig opponents of the Sovereign. "No King", Pepys indignantly commented, "ever did so unaccountable thing to oblige his people by, as to dissolve a Commission of the Admiralty then in his own hand, who best understood the business of the sea of any prince the world ever had, and things never better done, and put it into the hands which he knew were wholly ignorant." Being indeed 'wholly ignorant', the Commission's blunderings even further disorganised the dockyards; permitted the reserve of stores to dwindle—or be made away with—and allowed the ships in harbour to fall into disgraceful disrepair. Indeed, under the Commission of Seven the nation was endowed with a less reliable fleet than at any other time during the reign.[2]

Things reached such a pass that in 1684 the Commission of Seven was abolished; the office of Lord High Admiral, for the second time, being executed by the King, with the covert advice and assistance of his brother, 'Dismal Jimmie'. For the post of Secretary there was only one possible nominee, and Mr. Pepys returned joyfully to the labours that none other could carry out with such zeal and capability. But it was not until the brief reign of James II that the Navy returned to full strength and efficiency.

[1] He was committed to the Tower on the Speaker's Warrant.
[2] In addition to all else, the important Naval station of Tangier was evacuated in 1683.

Under wartime conditions commerce had inevitably suffered —from loss of markets as from the activities of privateers and freebooters; although the Act of 1664[1] rendered a shipmaster liable for damages and for what would now be termed the loss of his 'ticket', if he surrendered his ship without a fight. For one of the Barbary pirates' most wily practices had been to return their own goods to the master and crew of a craft that had put up no resistance, retaining only the wares freighted by the merchant-consignors. On the whole, however, the damage to trade had not been too grave.[2] The East India Company had between 25 and 30 sail of strong, stout ships always in commission, about 40,000 tons of shipping were employed in the Guinea and American trade, while there was a modest but steady traffic with the Mediterranean ports, Russia, Denmark, Sweden and the Baltic. Due to the popularity of French wines, brandy, silks, hats and linen, these imports had long been a drain on the country's resources. But an adverse balance of trade with France which in 1668 had stood at £2,132,864, by 1683 had been reduced to £1,250,000, owing in a considerable degree to the increase in silk manufacture in England. The production of cloth had been encouraged by every conceivable means, it even being forbidden, by an Act of 1666, to bury a corpse in "any shirt, or shift, or sheet, made or mingled with flax, hemp, silk, hair, gold or silver, or other than what shall be made of wool only, upon forfeiture of £5 to the poor of the parish".[3] But the strict interdict on the export of wool in any shape or form other than finished cloth put an enormous premium on the raw material being smuggled overseas. This applied particularly to the Romney Marsh area, where the owlers were always busy. For despite the fact that the King had endowed the Cinque Ports with a new Charter, reaffirming all their ancient rights and privileges, the havens had fallen into a sorry state of decay; with the result that for many men

[1] 16 Car. II, Stat. I, Cap. VI.
[2] Sir William Petty made the following estimate:

English (merchant) shipping	300,000	tons
United Provinces	900,000	,,
France	100,000	,,
Hamburg, Dantzic, Denmark and Sweden	250,000	,,
Spain, Portugal and Italy	250,000	

[3] 18 Car. II, Stat. I, Cap. IV.

smuggling offered far too attractive an alternative to more laborious but less remunerative toil, for the risks attendant on running contraband to be given serious considerations. So great was the loss occasioned by this illicit traffic that in 1674 orders were given for the organisation of a seagoing Preventive Service to cope with the owlers on their own element. At the outset the *Margate Smack* (Master, Peter Knight), the *Gravesend Smack* (Master, Thomas Symonds), and the *Queenborough Smack* (Master, Nicholas Badcock) were hired for this purpose and manned with crews consisting of the Master, five hands and a boy.

From the Slough of Despond which had been the Common-wealth and Protectorate, the country had been put back on to the highroad to domestic peace and advancing prosperity—and this very largely owing to the untiring efforts of that 'Black Boy' who, whatever his personal defects of character, had put the welfare of the land above all other aims. He had fought a long and wearying rearguard action to preserve some remnants of the royal authority, but he had always been prepared to concede a little more to the clamour for 'popular' government when urbane tenacity would no longer serve the ends for which he strove. As he lived, so he died; for on that cold, bitter February morning of 1685 the King's tenacious spirit fought its last courageous fight, till at length he was brought to express his sorrow "to be so long in dying". A little before noon, as this strange, wise, enigmatic man lapsed into unconsciousness, London's river was at full flood; with the stout warships and stately East Indiamen he had so dearly loved all ready to slip their cables and take passage through those narrow seas whose dominion he had sought so steadfastly to maintain.

CHAPTER XV

'Treasons, Stratagems, and Spoils'

"The tools to him who can handle them."
THOMAS CARLYLE

THE Reformation of Henry VIII was political, the outcome of England's determination to throw off the yoke of foreign domination. With its assumption of a religious character, tolerance flew out of the window as bigotry came in at the door. Charles II, who had always protested that "he would be easy, and have all men about him easy too", had sponsored a Declaration of Indulgence which had sought to endow both Catholics and Dissenters with liberty of conscience. But a similar Declaration of James II—a professed Catholic—was scarcely credited as being worth the paper on which it was written. The soil of bigotry had been too prodigally enriched with the humus of past antagonisms. Apart from all else, the King was known to be assiduously cultivating the powerful Catholic Court of Louis the Sun King. France was already dominant on the European mainland, and its emissaries were so cunningly deployed in North America that the "plantations"—as the British settlements on the eastern seaboard were termed—were hemmed in until they appeared "like an intrusive alien fringe on a continent otherwise French".[1] The removal of the ban on Gallic imports, engineered by James, might be grudgingly approved. But the welcome given to the flood of hapless refugees from sectarian oppression which followed on the revocation of the Edict of Nantes, only served to emphasise the distrust and detestation in which the French were held by a very considerable proportion of the population.

Kingship expresses itself better in personality than in brains. Charles II had possessed both, but had been careful to conceal

---

[1] Callender, *op. cit.*

the brains behind an engaging affectation of indolence. James's personality was cold and unendearing, while his otherwise admirable brain had been addled by a sectarian obsession that was little short of pathological. His real genius lay in naval administration, as was again made evident. For one of his first acts as Sovereign was to designate Sir Phineas Pett, of the famous shipbuilding family, Resident Commissioner for Chatham and Sheerness, the centre of contemporary naval activity. He followed this useful step by appointing a Special Commission, headed by the naval architect, Sir Antony Deane, and Sir John Narborough, the hero of the war with the Algerines, to undertake a thorough regeneration of the country's Sea-Service.

The liabilities of the Navy Office on the Lady Day of 1686 stood at £171,836. Having regard for the strain on resources imposed by the two Dutch wars, this was a remarkable reduction on the £1,277,161 owing twenty years earlier. In addition, the Commission rendered it possible for the Treasurer of the Navy to pay off a further £305,806, in settlement of sundry unsecured debts incurred during the reign of Charles II. Whereafter, tunnage rates on wines, spirits and vinegar were raised to provide funds against "weighty and important occasions"— i.e. the regular upkeep and repair of the Navy's vessels to ready them for any emergency.

The price of neglect in this particular had been made only too manifest in the case of the 30 ships constructed to the new design worked out by Antony Deane after his inspection of the French *Superbe* at Portsmouth at the time of the Third Dutch War. Complaint that the rapid deterioration of Deane's shapely H.M.S. *Harwich* and the other second- and third-rates built under the Act of 1677 was attributable to their having been put together with "doted and decayed English timber" met a spirited reply from Mr. Secretary Pepys.[1] Boldly championing "East country plank", he acidly pointed out that "the plain omission of the necessary and ordinary precautions for the preserving of newly-built ships—lack of graving and bringing into dock, neglect to air and clean the holds "till I have with my own hands gathered toadstools growing in the most considerable of them, as big as my fist"—furnished reason enough for the craft's mouldering and unseaworthy condition.

[1] Pepys had been promoted to the Secretaryship of the Navy Board in 1673.

The Commission's work was both so speedy and so thorough that the 1688 Navy List revealed that, exclusive of fireships and yachts, there were 105 vessels in service, as compared with the 135 in existence at the time of the Restoration; many of the newer vessels being sheathed below the water-line with lead. Moreover, with thirty fewer vessels than had been available in 1660, James's fleet boasted far greater fighting power, being stronger in third- and fourth-rates, while including the first bomb-vessel to throw shells, and nine first-rates, as against the Commonwealth's three; with crews totalling 22,000. The final tribute to the Commission's good work came with the report of the Parliamentary Committee of 1692, which recorded that 'the ships built, rebuilt and repaired by the Commissioners were fully and well performed . . . with great exactness, sufficiency, and frugality of expense, in the managery and conduct thereof".[1]

It was at the King's suggestion that all ships' Captains were instructed to keep a log of proceedings throughout their respective voyages; while Pepys's "Tables for the Gunning and Manning of the Whole Fleet", devised in 1677, were confirmed and adopted. The survey of the Thames ordered by Charles II having revealed that the depth of the waterway had decreased by four feet, an effort was made to dredge some of the more important reaches; while an attempt to improve the navigation of the Medway was put in hand, to ensure the easier passage of timber and naval stores to Gillingham. To encourage shipbuilding for the coasting trade, and with the additional aim of discouraging foreign competition, a duty of 5s. a ton was imposed on all coal freighted in foreign bottoms. Half of this levy went to the Chatham Chest and the balance to charities operated for the benefit of the mercantile marine by Trinity House. In general, merchant tonnage was nearly double what it had been in 1666; and further to stimulate the activities of the mercantile marine "Commissioners for Promoting the Trade of the Kingdom" were appointed in 1688. The forerunner of the modern Board of Trade, the Commission was speedily transformed into a Permanent Committee, with Parliamentary representation. Tobacco growing having been

---

[1] In 1660 naval tonnage had totalled 62,594 tons; by 1688 it had increased to 101,032 tons.

forbidden in England, the importation of the leaf from the plantations, like that of sugar from the West Indies, yielded a useful and steadily increasing Customs revenue. In effect, despite resurgent Hollander competition, trade was healthy enough for the average nett contribution from the Customs to exceed £555,000.

James's efforts to regenerate his marine and infuse a little much-needed discipline into its personnel naturally took time to bear fruit. In the interim the Dutch were the principal victims of renewed activity on the part of the Algerine corsairs; for where Hollander vessels were concerned English folk of all classes and sectarian sympathies were cheerfully prepared to condone the freebooters' activities. Not only did many of the pirate ships refit unhindered in Channel ports, but some thirty Dutch craft were sold to buyers in English harbours. James's warships turned a blind eye on these proceedings, and 'no questions asked".

For that matter the Navy had no eyes for the three vessels that stole into the famous cobb at Lyme, to decant the Duke of Monmouth, come to restore liberty of conscience to England—and maybe snatch a crown for himself in the process. The self-styled 'Protestant Defender' based his pretension to the Throne on the allegation that his royal sire had contracted a secret marriage with Lucy Walter which only the stern demands of policy had persuaded him to disavow. But, generally speaking, such appeal as he exerted went little beyond a patchy recognition of him as the Champion of Dissent and the sworn enemy of Catholicism.

Exiled from the English Court, Monmouth had for some time been living in Zeeland, and in close touch, of course, with his Orange relatives. Indeed, it was Prince William who, at one period, had urged the Duke to repair to the Imperial camp in Hungary, where war was raging against the infidel Turk. Monmouth's thoughts, however, had already turned to a descent on England; a project from which William made no attempt to deter him even if he did not privily connive in it.

The success with which Monmouth eluded the British Navy deserted him, however, almost as soon as he unfurled his blue Standard on the Castle Field at Taunton. With the news of the Duke's landing and his progress through the West at the head of a rabble of enthusiastic but militarily untutored followers, James and his Parliament were prompt to take action. Orange William's unblushing offer to head the troops mustered for the suppression of the rebellion was declined with no more than perfunctory acknowledgment. With £400,000 authorised as an 'extraordinary expenditure', that was a task which James preferred to consign to more trustworthy hands; and the Dutchman consoled himself by reinforcing the 'fifth column' he had installed to work in his interest, at the time of his first visit to England in 1670.[1] He could afford to wait while an English broadsword—or a headsman's axe—did the work he had originally assigned to a Turkish scimitar.

In England an Act had hurriedly been passed making it a treasonable offence to "bring the Person or Government of the Sovereign into contempt". Thereafter, a strong force was sent into the West under the Earl of Feversham, and the Stadtholder was curtly requested to return the six regiments of volunteers—three English and three Scottish—temporarily on service with the Dutch. It was a request with which 'Orange Billy' made no hesitation in complying. For he was confident that, given sufficient rope, James would hang himself in the process of ridding his would-be supplanter of a rival.

The rout of Monmouth's rustic following at Sedgemoor was followed by James's incredible blunder in condemning the Pretender to the scaffold; his final letter of appeal having been intercepted and suppressed by the Earl of Sunderland, the blindly trusted counsellor, who was already trimming his sails to suit the imminent change of wind. Alive, Monmouth would have proved an innocuously popular and infinitely less dangerous focus for romantic Protestant dreams than the resourceful William, despite the Dutchman's handicap in belonging to a detested race with which the country had recently been at war. With the pinchbeck 'King Monmouth' dead, the Whigs had to find another 'Protestant Defender' sufficiently reliable—yet conveniently ductile—to float them back to power on the popular wave of anti-Romanism still in ferment. It is a measure

---

[1] It was under the general control of a certain Colonel Lambert, who was closely in touch with the 'Devonshire faction', made up of James's bitterest opponents, the Earls of Devonshire, Danby, and Shrewsbury, Lord Lumley and Edward Russell (subsequently Earl of Orford).

of their own complacence as of their fatuous misreading of his shifty, machiavellian character, that their choice should have fallen on the Prince of Orange.

Distrust of France being as deep-rooted as the fear of Papistry, James's pro-Gallic policy speedily proceeded to alienate those supporters who had rallied to him at the time of the Monmouth rebellion less because they favoured the Romanism their Sovereign openly professed than because they detested the aggressive proletarianism upon which the rising had been founded.

Matters were brought to a head by the birth of a son to James, in whom the succession of a Papist King to England's Throne would be assured. With great celerity, many who earlier had exhorted Parliament to penalise all those who would "bring the person or Government of the Sovereign into contempt", sent an invitation to William of Orange to take such steps as would secure the right to the succession of his wife— Mary, James's elder daughter by his first marriage. The actual message was carried overseas by Admiral Arthur Herbert, somewhat melodramatically disguised as an Ordinary Seaman. A perfervid Whig, Herbert was subsequently rewarded for this particular exploit by elevation to the Viscounty of Torrington.

William paused in his covert preparations for invasion only long enough to indite a letter congratulating James on the birth of an heir. It was a missive characterised by a quality of hypo-critical dissimulation remarkable even in an age wherein agile *attendistes* had come to regard unswerving loyalty as an in-genuous and palpably unprofitable affectation. James was in no way deceived by this epistolary Judas kiss; and he was fully on the alert when, headed by the frigate *Brill*, the Orange force put out from Helvoetsluys—only to be blown back by a violent tempest from the west. The same wind could easily have carried the vacillating George Legge, Earl of Dartmouth, to destroy the Dutch armament in its harbour as Drake had annihilated the Spaniards in Cadiz. But Dartmouth disregarded Pepys's sage advice to "get to sea off the Dutch coast" on the feeble excuse that to miss the Dutch, owing to a possible change of wind, would be to leave the country unguarded. The wind *did* change, so by November 1st a strong easterly breeze was hustling Orange William's fleet of 61 warships and 200 transports briskly down

Channel. As it went through the Straits the armada was seen to extend to within a league of Dover on one side and Calais on the other. The same strong 'Protestant' wind nailed the 21 vessels of the British fleet to their anchorage at the Nore; while Dartmouth employed himself by writing fatuously to assure the King, "Your statesmen may take a nap and recover, and the women sleep in their beds." [1]

William's armada was safely out of reach even as this piece of balderdash was being penned. Unmolested, he made his landfall at Brixham; and then the wind veered capriciously to the south-west, forcing such of Dartmouth's vessels as had set out in half-hearted pursuit of the Dutchman to put in to Spithead.

Not that James's rival would have had much to fear from Dartmouth, in any event; for the Fleet Admiral was as much under the thumb of his Second-in-Command, the Orange partisan, Sir Samuel Strickland, as the unfortunate James himself was at the mercy of the treacherous advice given him by Sunderland. In any case the virus of politics had infected the Navy, which was largely Whig in sympathy, and entirely forgetful of the wise council of that sturdy Commonwealth and Restoration Admiral, Sir John Lawson, that "the Service has nothing to do with political dismissions or speculative opinions concerning government, its first and only object ought to be to serve the country".

William's welcome by the inhabitants of Brixham was singularly lacking in warmth. But the invader who heads a dependable army of 15,000 can afford to dispense with ebullitions of popular approval; and as London rang with the subversive doggerel ditty *Lillibulero*, the Dutchman headed purposefully for the capital; where hundreds of his proclamations had been run off and stacked ready for distribution.

It was a time of confusion, wavering loyalties and painful indecision, in which no man exhibited a more fatal irresolution than James himself. In earlier days Condé had stoutly affirmed that "in the matter of courage in a man, he desired to see nothing better than the Duke of York". In command throughout the Lowestoft battle of 1665, he had remained on deck for eighteen hours, perfectly calm and in full control of himself and

[1] Dartmouth wrote from the Gunfleet Shoal, a notoriously ill road in an easterly wind.

of the situation, even when spattered with the blood of those shot down at his side.[1] Yet in the greatest crisis of his life he temporised and procrastinated, feverishly begging advice from true man and traitor alike. At length the King set out to challenge the would-be usurper in the field; for there were strong hopes that Dartmouth would be able to blockade Orange William's fleet and cut off supplies. But a fiercely westerly gale springing up, the British vessels were unable to put out from Portsmouth—even had their crews been willing to sail them. And this is extremely doubtful, for Prince William's 'fifth column' had been tremendously busy spreading alarmist rumours. At Sandwich, for example, a number of shipmen went to the Town Major, Captain Stokes, to demand permission to put the place in a state of defence against "the wild Irish", alleged to be on the march from Gravesend. With a fresh *canard* that the French were about to land in the bay, the men took the law into their own hands, seizing Deal, Walmer and Dover castles—but certainly not in the King's name.[2]

Deserted by both the daughters of his earlier marriage, by his erstwhile adherents, Grafton, John Churchill, Clarendon's son, Cornbury, and George of Denmark, the husband of Princess Anne, and with the sentry under his own Whitehall windows absentmindedly whistling the rebel ditty *Lillibulero*, the unhappy James at last took refuge in flight; having first ensured that the Queen and the Prince of Wales were safely out of the country. Detained and plundered by a mob of fishermen at Sheppey, the refugee's final departure was made under the covert surveillance of William's Dutch Guards. For 'Orange Billy' was far too crafty to commit the political folly of martyrising the man he had succeeded in ousting. It was from Sir Richard Head's riverside house at Rochester that loyal Captain Trevannion conducted his fugitive Sovereign to a smack lying off Sheerness; and in this humble craft he crossed the narrow seas to land at Ambleteuse. It was Christmas Day.

Through its insensate resolve to gain a *political* hold over the land through the agency of the most ductile of its sons, the

---

[1] While in exile James had fought with rare courage and distinction for the Spaniards at the battle of the Dunes, and by them had been appointed Army Commander and High Admiral of Spain.

[2] Records of Sandwich.

Catholic Church had put a noose about its neck which a Whig junta had thrust into the hands of Orange William so that he might pull it tight.

Not the least of contemporary tragedies was, that with James's flight to France, Samuel Pepys's splendid and ungrudging labour for the Sea-Service he loved so truly and so well came to its untimely end.

Thus it fell out that on January 22nd, 1689, a special Commission proffered the warped, asthmatical little Hollander, not Prince Consortship, as might have been expected, but an outright share of England's historic Throne. This was all the more extraordinary in view of the fact that, as Stadtholder, he had demonstrably proved his inability to rule even the Dutch.[1] That William evinced no reluctance in accepting the offer goes without saying; and the best excuse for his assumption of boots a good deal too big for him is to be found in his laudable desire to confront Louis of France with a combination of the two States most vitally concerned in preserving the freedom of Antwerp, the Scheldt, and 'the English Sea'.

*　　　*　　　*

With the achievement of a moiety of his ambition, William found himself in control of that British sea-power to which he looked to implement the other half of his desire—the defeat of France through maritime supremacy.

Colbert had given the French a fleet which, with 221 vessels, outnumbered the British armament by 113 craft. It required all Dutch William's powers of persuasion, however, to convince the many Parliamentarians with shipping interests that the best way in which maritime commerce could be protected was by substantially increasing the number of its Naval guardians. Yet even with the British fleet's total brought up to 174 vessels— supplemented by elements of the Dutch marine—Louis was able without serious interference to support James's attempt to reconquer his kingdom by way of Scotland and Ireland, with French troops and Jacobite auxiliaries. Colbert's efforts to make France a maritime power as well as a land-power may have been largely artificial, but in Torrington's crippled hands the

---

[1] Amsterdam was notoriously an *imperium in imperio*, pursuing its individual way with scant regard for the wishes of the House of Orange.

British fleet in home waters was quite incapable of exposing the fraud. For however ill it consorted with his 'Continental' strategy, William was forced personally to seek out James in Ireland; withdrawing some of his best ships, under one of his most accomplished Admirals, Sir Clowdisley Shovel,[1] from the defence of the Channel. Other valuable craft, under Killigrew, were engaged in what proved an unsuccessful attempt to blockade the Gallic fleet in Toulon. It followed that when the combined Brest and Toulon fleets entered the Channel over 70 strong, Torrington could muster no more than 30 sail with which to oppose them.

The British Admiral's plan was, in his own imperishable phrase, to "keep his fleet in being", playing for time until Killigrew and Shovel could speed to his aid. But the Gallo-Jacobite plot to force the Thames and seize the Queen and the principal Ministers had thrown the authorities into such a panic that Torrington was peremptorily ordered to seek out the 'invasion fleet' and at all costs destroy it. In the circumstances, and despite his mental reservations, he could only comply with his instructions.

The French fleet had sailed on June 13th, while Torrington lay off the Isle of Wight—with not a single ship scouting to the west of St. Helen's Head. By the 23rd the enterprising De Tourville was off St. Alban's Head, and only then did the Fleet Admiral become aware of the enemy strength. By the 25th the French had made the Isle of Wight, with the English falling back steadily to eastwards.

When the rival armadas made contact off Beachy Head, Torrington's one advantage lay in the fact that, in almost a flat calm, he had such of the weather-gage as there was. Determined to maintain a strategic defensive, he so far obeyed orders as to launch a tactical offensive. Massing on the enemy rear squadron with the last half of his line, his advance half deliberately hugged the wind, refusing to come to action; a manœuvre by which the line was deliberately broken. The aim was to strike one strong disruptive blow ere drawing off to "keep the fleet in being". Unhappily, as the outcome of Orange William's pre-occupation with his Army, the naval strength and consequence

---

[1] Shovel was a man of humble birth who had "come up through the hawse-hole", rising, by sheer merit, from cabin boy to Admiral.

of the Dutch fighting marine had sharply deteriorated. The weak Holland flotilla that belatedly joined Torrington was, therefore, not only unsure of itself, but lacked all idea of the general battle plan, as it was entirely unfamiliar with British signalling methods.[1] Foolishly allotted to a position in the van, it became embroiled with a good half of the enemy vessels, by which it was outweighed and 'doubled'.[2] The Dutch were rescued from the murderous *mêlée* that ensued by Torrington's ingenious order for all his vessels to drop anchor with sail set; the wind and the ebb tide carrying the 'doubling' French craft back through the shattered Hollanders, who were thus extricated. Destroying a round dozen of his damaged ships lest they should fall into the enemy's hands, Torrington withdrew to the shelter of Thames-mouth; removing the buoys the better to baffle de Tourville's somewhat sluggish pursuit. In the flagship the shot garlands had not been disturbed; Sir Ralph Delaval's squadron having borne the brunt of such fighting as was seen by the British; with Anne Chamberlayne, sister to Captain Edward Chamberlayne of the *Griffin*, courageously refusing to go below till the issue of the day had been determined.[3]

Baffled by the dangerous shoals of the Goodwins, de Tourville put about and headed down Channel. At Teignmouth a landing party, meeting with little resistance—the local defence forces having mustered too far off, at Haldon Hill—ruthlessly pillaged houses and the church ere putting the township to the torch.[4] Shaldon and St. Nicholas, on the other side of the river, also suffered grievously; but the Plymouth Trained Bands, behind their newly erected earthworks, were not called upon to prove their quality. In the face of rapidly worsening weather de Tourville made for his home port.

Torrington had at least contrived to keep his fleet in being; but he was immediately apprehended on William's orders, subjected to trial by Court Martial and—the findings of his

---

[1] So little standing did the contemporary Dutch Admirals possess that at the council table they sat below junior English Captains.

[2] i.e. the French wore round the Dutch line until it came under cross fire.

[3] The lady lived to marry and become the mother of a distinguished Naval Officer. Incidentally, another woman, known as Yorkshire Nan, served in Torrington's fleet as a Carpenter's Mate.

[4] There is still a French Street in Teignmouth.

brother-Officers, who acquitted him, being set aside—dismissed from his country's service. In the bitterness of retirement there was ample leisure in which to wonder if that hurried trip across to the Continent, disguised as an Ordinary Seaman, had really been worth while.

The year 1691 was notable for a desperate conflict between the Gallic *Superbe* and the *Kent*, acting as escort to a convoy of Plymouth merchantmen. It was a fiercely fought little action, in which the Frenchmen were eventually forced to strike their flag; four hundred prisoners being landed at Plymouth. The year following saw further Gallo-Jacobite plans for invasion hopelessly disrupted when de Tourville's armada was surprised near Cap Barfleur under similar conditions to those which had hampered Torrington off Beachy Head. Commanding a fleet more powerful than that of his opponent, Admiral Russell took a heavy toll of his adversaries, scattering the French ships to all points of the compass. A few days later de Tourville's flagship the *Soleil Royal*, together with two other battleships, was destroyed off Cherbourg by the enterprising Delaval. The campaign was crowned by Sir George Rooke's annihilation of no less than 12 battleships in the fortified harbour of La Hogue; with the unhappy James and his would-be army of invasion the helpless spectators of the ruin of all their hopes. Fortune frowned, however, in the year following, when Sir George Rooke, escorting a huge convoy with his 23 ships of war, was set upon by de Tourville in great strength. In the running fight that ensued the British Admiral lost 80 merchant craft and 21 warships. This heavy toll was all the more disheartening in view of the exceedingly serious losses that had been sustained by the British mercantile marine during the course of the war. For a report laid before Parliament revealed that in two years the French had captured or sunk 3,000 sail of Dutch or English trading vessels, large and small, as against a mere 67 taken from the enemy. Having by far the greater commerce, England, of course, offered many opportunities to the privateers out of St. Malo and Bayonne—enterprising and courageous men such as Captain Chibau, the wily Duconte, d'Etchépare, Hiriat and Péré, who had plundered and sunk almost at will.[1] The fact that French losses had been on so modest a scale was almost

[1] *Les Corsairs sous l'Ancien Régime*, E. Ducéré.

entirely attributable to the lack of scruple which permitted the Dutch freely to freight Gallic wares. For without the slightest warrant in international law, they claimed that "Enemy goods were not enemy goods when they were transported in neutral vessels, since the character of the ship determined the character of the goods"—an extraordinary line of reasoning for a people to adopt who were not neutrals at all but ostensible allies.

There could be no immediate recovery, however, from a victory so decisive as that of La Hogue; and in tribute to so signal a piece of good fortune William converted the Royal Palace at Greenwich into a Hospital for "the relief and support of seamen . . . who by reason of wounds or other disabilities shall be incapable of further service at sea and unable to sustain themselves". But although the monthly coppers were deducted from every merchant seaman's wage as a contribution to the Sixpenny Chest which had been founded for the upkeep of the institution, only those mariners who had been injured while on voluntary or impressed service with the Royal Navy qualified for admission. In any case, the fund was constantly 'milked' by those officials responsible for its administration. However, despite much peculation and maladministration, accommodation was eventually provided for 2,710 pensioners.[1]

Of equal moment, in a professional sense, was the revision of the Fighting Instructions, for which responsibility was assumed by Admiral Edward Russell. Designed to eliminate the 'informalism' of the Beach Head battle, such was their rigidity that many Officers-commanding, in the years ahead, were to find their enterprise and initiative seriously cramped by the ultra-formalism they embodied.

In 1694 a temporary law, to encourage shipbuilding, allowed a rebate of one-tenth part of the tonnage and poundage, for the first three voyages, on all three-decker vessels of not less than 450 tons, armed with a minimum of 32 cannon. It was a concession that continued in operation for the ensuing ten years.

An Act of 1696[2] directed that a register should be compiled of the 30,000 mariners, fishermen, Thames watermen,

---

[1] Greenwich supplemented a small hospital earlier established by the authorities at Chatham; its first Treasurer being the diarist, John Evelyn.

[2] 7–8 Guil. III, Stat. I, Cap. 2.

12*

lightermen, keelmen, bargemen, and the like, of ages between eighteen and fifty, with a record of their respective places of residence. In return for an annual bounty of 40s. the registered man was required to supplement the Royal Navy crews when called upon to do so. Registration entitled him to double the amount of prize money to that awarded the unregistered sea-man, and priority of entry into Greenwich Hospital. As an alternative to the detested system of impressment the experiment was persisted in until the ninth year of the reign of Queen Anne, when its proven failure to keep the ranks up to strength necessitated a reversion to the press.

All in all, however, Orange William's preoccupation with 'Continental' strategy, with its concomitant demand for priority of consideration for the Army, tended towards the Navy's progressive neglect. Symptomatic of this trend was the fact that even while work was progressing on the new dry and wet docks at Portsmouth and on Plymouth's new dockyard on the Hamoaze, the 1689 debt of £75,000 for yard wages, in less than three years was allowed to increase to £116,500. It still stood at £107,000 so late as 1693, and showed no immediate prospect of being wiped out. And this despite an onerous poll tax, an increase in the salt poundage, and heavy Customs and Excise duties on wine, brandy, coffee, chocolate, tea, spices, tobacco, ale, and even coconuts.[1] Preferences, however, were gladly given on sugar and tobacco from the West Indies and the plantations by the new Board of Trade, as anxious to foster a growing market for British manufactured goods as it was to develop a fresh and intensely valuable source of raw materials. Thanks to the openings for trade to be found in the colonies, by 1699 exports were bringing in over £6,000,000; with the excess of exports over imports standing at over £4,000,000.

Officially, all trade with France had ceased, although in actual fact it persisted in spite of all efforts to cut it off. With an absolute ban on the export of wool, there was an incessant two-way trade in contraband; liquor, tobacco and other luxuries being smuggled in from France in exchange for the wool so eagerly in request on the Continent. In Rotterdam alone

---

[1] In 1689 one of the first charges on the Customs was the sum of £600,000 by way of a 'thank-offering' to the United Provinces for having under-written Orange William's bid for England's Throne.

nineteen vessels were seen on one day all of which were known to have run illicit cargoes for eventual transfer to French buyers. The Chichester delta and the Cinque Ports' littoral swarmed with well-armed and determined smugglers; and it was through their agency that the innumerable Jacobite secret agents passed to and fro between England and the exiled James's pinchbeck Court at Saint Germain. Romney Marsh was particularly favoured as a reasonably safe point of embarkation: Farmer Hunt's lonely steadings, on the seaward side of Romney, offering overnight shelter for any stealthy traveller prepared to pay the exorbitant charge of a guinea a day for accommodation that was only a little less exiguous than the menu. The Romney route, with its short sea trip to Boulogne or Ambleteuse in William Gill's swift lugger, was one often taken by Birkenhead, the most reliable emissary in King James's service; and it was not unknown to the sinister Simpson, alias Jones, who ranked as the 'arch spy' in Orange William's pay.

Not only Romney but the whole area hummed with the busy traffic of these Jacobite fly-by-nights; "whose heads", as one of the more sober of their number despairingly protested, "were filled with chimeras and noise and nonsense". The fact that the land of their birth was in arms against the country which provocatively gave shelter to their exiled Sovereign troubled them not a whit. They were far too busy hating the Dutchman to have any enmity left over for Louis of France. And meanwhile the Marsh prospered.

The cessation of all legitimate trade between France and the Kent, Sussex and Dorsetshire havens rendered it necessary for the salaries of the local Customs men to be met out of the dues collected in the headport of London. It was a very different story, however, at Portsmouth and Plymouth, where the Searchers and Tide-waiters earned every penny of their pay, coping with the persistent smuggling by Naval Officers, particularly in bullion and coin, and in East India goods picked up in Holland. Warships were so overladen with contraband as to be unsafe in action; while the Captain of the frigate *Stirling Castle* trafficked so heavily in uncustomed goods that he had to be put under arrest, as his ship lay top-heavy in the Sound. One evil result of this practice was that vessels put to sea deficient in stores, their place having been taken by illicit cargoes. When a

Fighting Service descends to politics, it invariably does so at the expense of its integrity.

*   *   *

In spite of his obsession with land-warfare, William possessed small skill in generalship; and it was only the dogged determination of his troops that served to extricate him from the setbacks of Steenkirk and Landen, and gave him possession of the fortified town of Namur. Fighting had been so hard that by 1697 both the French and the English were in need of a breathing space, which was duly afforded them by the Treaty of Ryswick.

The peace that followed was short-lived. But at least it afforded an opportunity for Orange William and the Whig junta that had elevated him so precipitously to the Throne to assess the relationship which had developed between them. As an unblushing *arriviste* the Dutchman's outlook could be sufficiently summed up in the precept *si finis lacitus, media sunt lacita.* Having assumed the purple, he was determined to rule, however much he appeared to concede to his supporters' demand that the legislative body should control the Executive, and that Parliament should undergo election every three years. For the moment a compromise was found in a Privy Council chosen from members of Parliament, a small committee of which became the King's Cabinet.

It was not long before this Cabinet decisively asserted its authority. Faced with debts totalling £21,500,000, to William's ill-concealed chagrin it peremptorily cut down the Army—whose numbers stood at 87,000—by refusing to recommend supplies for a Standing Force of more than 7,000. Retrenchment on the Fighting Services is always popular in England; but beyond this one reduction in expenditure economy halted; the huge National Debt being funded, so that its increasing burden could be passed on to posterity to deal with as best it might. By-product of this exercise in financial skulduggery was the foundation of the Bank of England, with its

> *Blest paper credit, last and best supply*
> *That lends corruption lighter wings to fly.*

One consequence of the prevailing heavy scale of taxation

and the mood of financial irresponsibility it induced, was a growing craze for lotteries and for highly speculative investments, whose commercial soundness was in inverse ratio to the extravagant promises of high profits and quick returns dangled before the dazzled eyes of the greedy and the credulous.

Amongst this welter of wild-cat schemes, however, a small but substantial body of Tory investors took the opportunity to found the General East India Company as a rival to the older Association, which was largely Whig-supported.

With little money in the public till the Navy suffered very much the same neglect as the Army; although the year 1700 saw the first appearance of an official Navy List—or to describe it more accurately, the first Seniority List; while the earliest survey of the coasts of Britain was undertaken under the supervision of Captain Greenville Collins. At the same time the Thames-side shipyards became familiar with the booming presence of the fabulous Peter the Great. Installed at Deptford, and fortified by a vast cellarful of brandy, sherrysac, aquavit, Rhenish and schnapps, the Russian despot bent his very considerable intelligence to the task of penetrating the secret of the English shipwrights' especial skill. Lured by Muscovite gold, many of the native master-craftsmen accompanied the Tsar on his return to his native land; and with their aid he was presently to endow his people with their first recognisable fighting marine.

On Eddystone Rock in the mouth of Plymouth Sound the authorities of Trinity House completed the erection of a lighthouse. It was the work of Henry Winstanley, a noted builder of ornamental fountains; and those few voyagers whose travels had taken them to the Far East were agreed that it resembled nothing so much as a Japanese pagoda.

The September of 1701 saw the renewal of the Grand Alliance of Britain, the United Provinces, Spain, Savoy and the Emperor of Germany, by which the most recent conflict with France had been waged. In bringing this about William barely anticipated the news of the exiled James's death and the formal recognition of his son as the rightful King of England by Louis of France; a step which in itself was tantamount to a declaration of war. As it stood, the issue was not affected either way when the Dutchman's hack *Sorrel*, stumbling over a molehill at

Hampton Court, threw his rider, fracturing his collar-bone and inflicting other injuries from which he died on Sunday, March 8th, 1702.[1] Before his death, however, William persistently urged the advisability of an Act of Union with Scotland; with the Protestant Succession assured once and for all by a definite Act of Settlement.

The gathering war clouds found Britain with registered tonnage totalling 3,281 ships, of all sorts and sizes, manned by 27,196 mariners, and armed with 5,660 guns. Not a few of the Navy vessels, however, which had been laid up in ordinary, were in a sorry state of neglect, having been allotted no proper care and maintenance parties. A report from Chatham voiced the complaint that "a Great Shippe hath lately been without so much as one man on board, only a Woman or two, who, by the way, are Dangerous". This remonstrance eventually brought about the establishment of guard ships in every port, and not before they were wanted. For it was far from unknown for dockyard hangers-on and their women folk surreptitiously to set to work by night to break up craft lying in ordinary, in order to supply themselves with cheap fuel.

For many years Sweden and the other Northern countries had enjoyed a virtual monopoly in the supply of ships' stores; and with war imminent they put on the screw by greatly increasing their prices and, in Sweden's case, by insisting that native wares should be freighted exclusively in native ships. The English authorities, not relishing their unaccustomed role as the victims of some other nation's Navigation Act, very wisely turned to the plantations to fulfil the requirements that had hitherto been catered for elsewhere. Ship's timber, masts and yards, tar and pitch at £4 a ton, rosin and turpentine at £3 a ton, water-rotted hemp at £6 a ton, and all other manner of marine stores, were purchased in enormous quantity. With an annual demand for over 1,000 lasts of tar, and other wares in proportion, the Navy Board gladly sent £10,000 across the Atlantic to help get the industry on its feet, while a bounty was awarded to the tar and pitch manufacturers for all the goods they shipped to the homeland. Merchant fleets of 150 vessels at

[1] This gave rise to the Jacobite toast "To the little gentleman in black velvet"—the mole over whose mound William's horse had pecked, with such far-reaching results.

a time left Virginia for England; and there were many other ships sailing from the Sugar Islands of the Caribbean. For the British 'tar' was not the only one to have made delighted acquaintance with rumbullion; and the spirit itself, like the molasses from which it was distilled, was in steadily increasing demand. In Mr. Edward Lloyd's snug coffee house—removed from Tower Street to more spacious premises in Lombard Street, in 1692—there was a constant coming and going of pursy ship-owners, gnarled sea-captains, and anxious underwriters, all crowding to scan the intelligence of distant vessels and incoming cargoes displayed on the single sheet of print that made up *Lloyd's News*.

In A.D. 1700 Charles of Spain died without direct heir. This afforded Louis of France the opportunity to foist his nephew, Philip of Anjou, on to the vacant Throne. With this threat of Gallic hegemony in Europe, England had no option but to declare war. With the resumption of hostilities in the May of 1702, a conflict which had been started to ensure the exclusion of the Stuarts from the Throne of England and had been continued to aid the Hollanders, developed into a struggle to determine the balance of power in Western Europe.

The war in support of the Austrian claimant took a very different course, however, to that pursued by its immediate predecessor. Louis of France was in no mind to challenge the command of the sea the British exercised in their own home waters. The Channel coast, therefore, became a base from which Marlborough's redcoats were ferried, without the slightest molestation, to those battlefields of the Low Countries whereon they were destined to win such imperishable glory. It was to the selfsame island base that the battered warships returned to revictual and re-fit after Rooke's resounding victory in Vigo Bay; where the capture of 28 bulging Spanish treasure ships was reminiscent of the palmy days of Drake. With Britain's treaty of alliance with Portugal, the French marine was content to wage a fitful *guerre de course* by means of its privateers; and there can be no question that their activities reaped a rich reward. So early as 1692 the famous corsair Jean Bart had successfully scoured the seas, taking more than a hundred prizes into St. Malo within a twelvemonth; and his triumphal career was long continued. Du Guay Trouin, a privateer captain at eighteen, after enjoying an amazing run of luck, found himself confronted with odds of five to one, and was forced to yield, being taken captive into Plymouth. Effecting his escape with the aid of a local wench who had fallen victim to his *beaux yeux*, he immediately put to sea to resume his commerce raiding. By 1704 he was in command of the 74-gun *Jason*, in which craft a British squadron cornered him and fought him to a standstill. He succeeded in making good his escape, however, by taking advantage of a dawn breeze that caught his antagonists with their topsails lowered and their yards braced back too unhandily for speedy trimming. Hervé Dufresne was not only an extremely successful privateer, but was frequently employed by the exiled Jacobites to carry messages between St. Germain and those die-hards in London who habitually drank to "the King over the water".

But the English were not always caught napping. At Plymouth Captain Thomas Hardy,[1] accused in the House of Lords of "brutish obstinacy" and "saucy contempt of remonstrance" in refusing to escort a solitary Canary trader through the chops of the Channel, defiantly put to sea and temporarily cleared the western approaches of prowling privateersmen. A little later the same Officer overtook a number of corsairs sailing in company, blew up one vessel with all hands, and made capture of the other three; one of the craft having merchandise in her holds worth £80,000. Neither were such native practitioners as Stephen Woon and Benjamin Cruse in any way lacking in enterprise, as the contemporary rhyme bears witness:

> *The anchor is up and the harbour chain down,*
> *And the bells ring merrily out from the town;*
> *We shall soon find a Spaniard or Frenchman, they say,*
> *And bring something back to this snug little bay.*

Unfortunately, neither Woon nor Cruse were above combining a little smuggling with their other activities; and having callously slaughtered a Tide-surveyor who interrupted them while running a cargo of brandy, they were condemned to be hanged in chains at Crabtree.

---

[1] Not to be confused, of course, with Nelson's Hardy—Admiral Sir Thomas Masterman Hardy, G.C.B., born at Portisham in Dorset, in 1769.

Further East, the Soundings Squadron furnished protection for any coasting vessels or stragglers from the homeward or outward bound traffic passing over the submerged shelf off the mouth of the Channel, whose waters were too deep for sounding with the lead. Further to regulate the defence of trade, as well as the law of prize, the far-reaching Cruisers and Convoy Act was passed in 1708. It was a comprehensive and highly important measure, which has been re-enacted with the outbreak of every war since that day.

Although the very nature of its duties kept the Soundings Squadron pinned to a monotonous and comfortless task, no one rejoiced more heartily than its ships' companies at the news of Rooke's daring capture of Gibraltar. The key of the Mediterranean had been safely stowed in an English pocket.

The year which saw the death in retirement of Samuel Pepys also witnessed that extraordinary hurricane blowing in from the Atlantic which passed into history as the Great Storm. Speedily whipping itself up to maximum fury, the tempest persisted for seven days from the night of Wednesday, November the 26th. While shattered tiles and chimney pots littered the streets ankle deep, and the lead roofs of churches were rolled up like parchment; while four thousand trees in the New Forest suffered uprooting and over four hundred windmills went down in destruction, the British Mediterranean fleet assembling in the Downs battled desperately for survival. Rear-Admiral Sir Basil Beaumont was among the first to perish, his ship swiftly going aground in 'Trinity Bay', the treacherous 'Abraham's Bosom' of the Goodwins. One after another the labouring warships were cast away—the *Restoration*, the *Stirling Castle*, the *Mary* and the *Northumberland* parting cables to drive helplessly on to the Sands, where many of the crew were left stranded, to await certain death with the next flood tide. A few of the survivors, clinging to any odd bit of flotsam that offered a hold, were brought to safety by the pluck and energy of the Deal 'hovellers', led by the indomitable Simon Prichard and Deal's seafaring mayor, Thomas Powell. It was the last-named who used his authority to sweep aside the objections of the Deal Station Inspector, and commandeer the Revenue cutters which were the only craft that could hope to make the Goodwins and survive; and yeoman service they performed in the work of salvation. In all, Powell and his men rescued two hundred castaways; but the Fleet in the Downs lost 15 vessels, including 4 Third-rates, 4 Fourth-rates, 4 Fifth-rates, and 1 Sixth-rate, and many tenders and small craft, together with 1,500 Officers and men. Even the Navy Yards in the Thames were hapless victims of the tempest's uncontrollable fury; while the Pool was almost emptied of vessels that had cut their cables; one great East Indiaman being cast away at Blackwall. There was an increasing gunfire of distress signals at sea, which claimed a grisly toll of one hundred and sixty merchant craft—hoys, snows, brigs and brigantines—and two hundred colliers. The new lighthouse on the Eddystone disappeared in the wrack, while the *Winchelsea* brig pounded herself to pieces on the rocks whence the warning beacon had so recently shed its light. Since the howling tempest of 1287 the narrow seas had known no storm more fearful. One of the few basins to survive without material injury was the Howland Great Wet Dock, constructed in 1696, and planted with trees as a protection against just such a tempest as it had weathered.[1] Only a few years later the Navy was robbed of one of its sturdiest leaders by another sudden storm that blew up in the Scillies. Homeward bound from his successful assault on Toulon, Sir Clowdisley Shovel came into soundings further north than he had anticipated. While some of his squadron were cast away on the Bishop and Clerk rocks, his flagship, the *Association*, struck the Gilstone, foundering with her full complement of 800 men. Washed ashore, the Admiral's body was rescued from the wreckers who had plundered it and buried it in the sands, and was taken to London.[2] There the erstwhile shoemaker's apprentice was accorded a public funeral in the Abbey; and few men have better deserved the honour.

* * *

The military pact with Portugal had been speedily followed by a commercial agreement—the famous Methuen Treaty—which opened up a highly lucrative market for English woollens, while ensuring imports of excellent wine at a low rate of duty.

[1] It was the nucleus of what became the Surrey Commercial Dock system.

[2] Places of particular ill-repute for the evil work of wrecking included Chesil Beach, Portland, and Chale Bay, Isle of Wight.

Exports were rapidly increased to the tune of £300,000 a year to reach an aggregate of £1,500,000. It was a welcome expansion of revenue at a time when a heavily taxed populace was intoning:

> *Mourn for ten years' war and dismal weather,*
> *And taxes strung like necklaces together,*
> *On salt, malt, paper, cider, lights and leather.*

So early as 1662 Dartmouth had developed a snug trade in wine with Portugal, and with the conclusion of the Methuen Treaty this greatly increased; nor was Southampton entirely left out of this welcome development of commerce with Lisbon and Oporto. The ratification of the Act of Union had done something to stimulate trade between Scotland and her southern neighbour; while the 'interlopers' experienced something of a setback by the amalgamation of the rival East India Companies under an agreement that left two distinct Courts of Directors, but bound them not to trade on separate account.

England's preoccupation with overseas war, and the absence of many of her warships in distant waters, was, of course, an open invitation to the more hot-headed Jacobites to attempt an invasion whose aim would be to seize the Throne in the name of the youthful 'James III'. With Gallic support, the venture was put in motion in the March of 1708; Louis being only too ready to foment a civil tumult that would impel the withdrawal of British troops from Flanders.

Mustered at Dunkirk under the command of the jovial Chevalier de Forbin, five battleships and twenty frigates found accommodation for twelve battalions of troops, under the immediate orders of the Maréchal de Matignon. At this juncture, however, the Pretender elected to develop an attack of measles. Nothing dismayed, de Forbin insisted on putting to sea, thus adding considerably to the wretched James's miseries. A queasy sailor at the best of times, his thoughts as he lay prostrated with *mal-de-mer* must frequently have dwelt on that royal ancestor[1] of his to whom 'a peppercorn rent' was rendered by a tenant whose sole liability was "to hold the King's head during Channel crossings".

The alarm created throughout the country by the news of the

[1] Henry II.

Pretender's sailing was partially allayed when General Cado-
gan, Marlborough's Second-in-Command, hurried back from
the Low Countries at the head of twelve battalions. In any case
Sir George Byng was closing on the Gallic armament in
superior force. At the sight of his topsails Forbin promptly
put about and ran for home; and in the chase that followed
the French were penalised by the loss of one vessel, ere reaching
the safety of Dunkirk.

With the Tories' Parliamentary triumph of 1710, and despite
Marlborough's political downfall, the end of the war was in
sight. Peace was concluded by the Treaty of Utrecht, of March
1713; which unreservedly ceded the naval base of Gibraltar to
the British, and opened up the Caribbean to trade by the South
Sea Company; which, formed in 1711, had speedily qualified
for privileged consideration by loaning the Government a cool
£10,000,000. But the proposed terms of the Treaty of Commerce and Navigation with the French were so bitterly assailed,
as damaging to the profitable trade with Portugal, that the
more concessionary clauses had to be revised. At the same time
a guarantee was extracted from Louis that the fortifications of
Dunkirk and Mardyke should be dismantled and "never be
restored or rebuilt on any pretence whatever".

In the July of 1714 poor bloated 'Brandy Nan' was stricken
by a fit of apoplexy, and her death followed on the first day of
August. The Act of Settlement had arbitrarily secured the
succession of George Louis, son of Ernest Augustus, Elector of
Hanover, and Sophia, the granddaughter of James I. So on
September 18th this peculiarly unsavoury Brunswicker was set
ashore at Greenwich. Immediately the Customs authorities,
with a magnificently objective fidelity to duty, demanded full
payment on his dutiable goods; while the royal baggage was
removed, under seal, to Whitehall, where "the three senior
land-surveyors attended to examine it". As a precautionary
measure, the River Guard was strengthened "to prevent the
running of goods on his Majesty's arrival".

It was a somewhat different mood from that prevailing on
Dover sands on that May afternoon of 1660!

CHAPTER XVI

'Hanover Jacks'[1]

"He that commandeth at sea is at great liberty, and
may take as much or as little of war as he will."

FRANCIS BACON

THE Treaty of Utrecht of 1713, while terminating the War of
the Spanish Succession, left England saddled with King
George's patrimony of Hanover, a petty State situated in the
heart of Europe's traditional cockpit. The responsibility—
which was destined to continue for one hundred and twenty-
three years—was partially offset by the fact that control of
Hanover gave indirect domination over the whole coast from
Denmark to Holland, including the ports of the Elbe, the Weser
and the Ems, a factor of considerable importance in Britain's
fixed design to maintain a balance of power in Western
Europe.

The Whigs' installation of a puppet King, utterly dependent
upon their support, in place of the Stuart claimant favoured by
the Jacobites and many of the Tory opposition, constituted a
triumph for 'Dutch Billy's' aristocracy of the counting house,
and those families whose fortunes had been founded, in the days
of the Reformation, on the loot of the Church.[2] Rank materialists
to a man, they were entirely wanting in the Elizabethan
sense of adventuring, and preferred to chew the cud of a prosperity that their sedulous pursuit of trade or their industrious
acquisition of place and the perquisites that went with

[1] The actual 'Hanover Jacks' were small coins, privately minted, and not
unlike the contemporary tradesman's token, which celebrated the departure
of the unpopular Duke of Cumberland to Hanover. Instead of folk con-
signing their *bêtes noirs* to Jericho they exhorted them to "Go to Hanover!"
[2] The old nobility, whose fiefs had been the reward of military prowess,
had been decimated by the Crusades, and had virtually committed suicide
in the Wars of the Roses. By 1485 less than thirty peers survived, some of
them mere babes in arms.

it could be relied upon to consolidate. For under the prevailing system of Cabinet government, bribery had been so rationalised as virtually to have become respectable. The only commodity without a market was integrity: the only crime was to be poor. Everywhere the property-owning classes—the 'Squires of 'Change Alley'—had been seized with a febrile, incontinent urge to snatch easy money by feverish speculation in any and every wildcat scheme that plausibility could trick out with a promise of huge profits and quick returns. Companies were floated whose purpose ranged from the development of Puckle's Machine-gun to the importation of walnut trees from Virginia [1]; from a proposal to turn salt water into fresh and extract gold from the sands of the seashore, to a design for the introduction of outsize jackasses from Spain to improve the native breed of mules. Of them all, the only schemes to achieve lasting prosperity were those which led to the establishment of the tinplate industry in Monmouthshire, and the plan to expand marine insurance which ultimately saw its inclusion in the operations of the London and Royal Exchange Assurance Company.

Possibly it was the prosperity enjoyed by those fortunate enough to possess shares in the East India, the Hudson's Bay or the new South Sea Company which aroused such an inordinate hunger for pelf. For tyro as it might be, the South Sea association had already got a second great ship a-building, which had tactfully been named the *Royal George*. With the East India Company the chief anxiety was to maintain a monopoly constantly threatened by the interlopers, both British and foreign. [2] In support of their persistently dog-in-the-manger attitude, the Court of Directors could always point to the example set by the Board of Trade and Plantations which while limiting all traffic between America and the homeland to British or colonial-built ships, exerted every endeavour to preserve the colonies themselves as a consumer market exclusive to British exports, while continuing as the source of raw materials for disposal solely to British purchasers. Cloth-manufacture was discouraged since, with the loss of the Swedish market on the accession of George I, English manufacturers had suffered a sharp decline in profits, which they hoped to make good by increasing sales to

[1] Capitalised, on paper, at £2,000,000.
[2] A 'pirate' Dutch East India Company was formed in 1722.

the colonies.[1] Iron-smelting was sternly frowned upon even at a time when Britain was annually importing 20,000 tons of the raw material from Sweden at the penal cost of £240,000—the ironmasters thereafter devastating the ship's timber-producing glades of Stafford, Worcester, Hereford, Gloucester and Salop for cord-wood to feed their furnaces. It was idle for the colonists to protest that their own shipbuilding industry was crippled, their cultivation hampered and their comfort inhibited by reason of the high cost of imported nails, iron for ploughshares and pots and pans, leather for shoes and cloth for garments. With incredible short-sightedness, they were expected to rest content to accept costly wares from outside sources, and keep the looms and ironworks and ports of England busy and prosperous, as a *quid pro quo* for the military protection the motherland afforded them. Nor were matters bettered when the Charter colonies—some at their own request—passed under the Crown. For out of the entanglement of constitutional questions with matters of trade grew the quarrel which was destined to flare into the unhappy open strife of 1775.

There were also many complaints from the Caribbean Islands, whence many valuable cargoes of sugar, rum and molasses, destined for the wharves of London's river, were pirated and borne away to the buccaneers' lair of Tortuga.

An era devoted to what passes for 'peace' so long as it brings 'plenty', is invariably characterised by a recklessly short-sighted neglect of the Armed Forces—as the period of Whig supremacy all too clearly demonstrated. Had there not been a large number of salaried officials dependent on the Navy, it would have been entirely forgotten and left to languish without funds. Even as it was, expenditure on the fleet soon sank to less than half the sum authorised in 1714; while such vessels as left the stocks were so crude and slovenly in design that one Admiral caustically remarked that they must have been "manufactured by the mile and cut off in chunks when required". And this at a time of steady expansion of empire, and at a moment when Louis XIV was bending every energy to enlarge and improve

---

[1] Sweden regarded George I as a sworn enemy; and some of the West Country cloth-manufacturers went so far as to refuse payment of any further taxes unless there were a new Parliament and the restoration of the old amicable relationship with the Scandinavian countries.

both his fighting and his mercantile marine. Furthermore, the rigid scale of dimensions laid down by the Navy Board barred all progress in design, which exhibited no advance until well past the middle of the century. Vessels were slow, crank, cramped, over-gunned, and so deficient in bearing forward that their pitching in bad weather gravely endangered the masts. On the other hand, the introduction of such frigates as the 600-ton, 28-gun *Cerberus* and the 650-ton, 32-gun *Thames* led in due course to the construction of 1,000-ton, 36-gun craft that were both powerful and speedy.

There were no frigates of this quality available, however, to head off the two survivors of the battered Spanish flotilla, carrying arms and money for the support of the Jacobite uprising which—after all-too-lengthy warning of its imminence—faltered into action in the summer of 1715. Encouraged by Alberoni, the Spanish Prime Minister, and in hopes of active support from France, the Pretender's Standard was raised in Scotland by the Earl of Mar. The Duke of Ormonde had been entrusted with the organisation of revolt in the West Country, where it was hoped to whip hostility to the Hanoverian Monarch into active support for the Stuart claimant to the Throne. Alarm for his personal safety, however, persuaded Ormonde to take flight for France by what was becoming the traditional escape route by way of Shoreham; and the revolt in the West fizzled out. In any event, Jacobite prospects had suffered a grievous blow by the death of Louis XIV. For his successor was a minor, and the enthusiasm of the Regent, the Duc d'Orléans, for the cause of Prince James Francis Edward was tepid in the extreme. In the Highlands Mar, "after he had drawn the sword, did not know in what manner to proceed"[1]; and by the time the Pretender—evading the warships sent to detain him—made his appearance on Scottish soil, sheer bungling had thrown away whatever chances of success the insurrection may initially have possessed.

Hopes of a Stuart restoration were further dashed when Orléans succeeded in concluding a treaty with the British Government which had the effect of firmly establishing him in

[1] This was the verdict pronounced by James's natural son, that extremely capable military commander the Marshal Duke of Berwick; vide *Mémoires du Maréchal de Berwick*, Vol. II.

power. This pact, to which Holland acceded in the January of 1717, ensured a period of almost unbroken peace in Western Europe which lasted for the ensuing quarter of a century.

In the steady swell of prosperity which characterised this halcyon interlude the Channel's headport easily held its place as the prime centre of the country's commerce. In the Upper Pool, over 1,750 craft of varying tonnage were allowed to moor in an area designed to hold just over 500. For apart from foreign visitants, the number of vessels between 15 and 750 tons bearing the Port of London's registration came to 1,417. Small wonder that London's was by far the greatest contribution to an annual revenue from the Customs which comfortably exceeded £1,350,000; and this despite the fact that the fiscal system was an unholy jumble, with no line of clear-cut principle between the Customs and Excise. Notwithstanding this vexation, the yearly turnover of the East India Company passed the £2,000,000 mark; with a 'drawback' at the Customs of £400,000 on merchandise for re-exportation. Competing for storage with the tea and other Company wares, were the sugar, the ginger, indigo, cotton, molasses, spices, mahogany and logwood from the West Indies—the first-named selling at 32s. to 35s. a hundredweight as against the old price of £4 and £5 a hundredweight charged by the Portuguese.[1] Naval stores, salt, hemp, lumber, tobacco—up to 60,000 hogsheads a year, at an average of 600 lb. to the hogshead—rice, sugar and rum from America, with the increasing intake of the Hudson's Bay Company's peltry, represented a gross turnover of over £1,000,000 a year, on which the gain was certainly not less than £180,000.

The exports most in demand were woollens and linens, with finished silk and silk thread competing lustily with their older rivals[2]. The successful experiments of Jethro Tull and 'Turnip' Townshend[3] in the cultivation of root crops now enabled breeders to carry a far greater head of stock through the winter; and more stock meant not only more food for home consumption, but more hides for export. Herrings and mackerel, caught at Hastings, Poole and Shoreham, with pilchards netted further

[1] Boyer's *Political State of Great Britain*, Vol. V.
[2] John Lombe, the half-brother of the prominent mercer, Sir Thomas Lombe, had contrived to ferret out the Italians' closely-guarded secret of silk thread manufacture.
[3] Charles, 2nd Viscount Townshend (1676–1738).

west, still found a ready market in Germany and the Mediterranean; while the 'ships' husbands' and ships' chandlers of Exeter, Dartmouth and Poole had their work cut out to cope with the demands of the whaling fleet, for which these havens served as bases. Poole also enjoyed a thriving trade in the export of pipe-clay to the West Indies, where it played a part in sugar refining. Other consignments were sent to Bristol, for the manufacture of tobacco pipes.

*   *   *

Funding the public debt had, of course, greatly increased the scale of taxation, and in the process very appreciably added to the burden of Customs and Excise dues. But the luxury of yesterday becomes the necessity of today; men had accustomed themselves to indulge in wine, spirits and tobacco as freely as womenfolk partook of tea, chocolate and coffee; and they were as little inclined to do without these amenities as they were prepared to pay the extravagant prices that reflected the heavy scale of contemporary imposts. For a very large proportion of the population the problem was solved by the purchase of contraband wares, which the owler bought so cheaply abroad that he could reap a handsome profit on sales that sharply undercut the current market price at home.

Right along the Channel coast from the South Foreland to Marazion the smugglers set the men of the Preventive Service at defiance, duping the Riding Officers ashore as successfully as they eluded the Revenue cutters at sea. Time and again a boat from Looe or neighbouring Polperro would return from Roscoff with £1,000 worth of contraband aboard; and to "receive her the smith left his forge, the husbandman his plough, even the women and children turning out to assist in the unlawful traffic and receive their share of the proceeds".[1] Deal smugglers, in their flat-bottomed 'huvvles', would cache their wares 'in the cellar'—in other words, they sank and buoyed them in the Goodwins, whence they could be retrieved as convenience prescribed. "Brandy for the parson and 'baccy for the clerk" was "found in the outhouse at daybreak and paid for at the back door that night". Nor was the trade by any means a one-way traffic. In the Romney Marsh area wool,

[1] Dr. Jonah Couch.

already made up in neat bales, was run down to the shore by whole pack trains, for illicit shipment abroad. And this despite the Act which decreed that no one living within fifteen miles of the coast should purchase wool without giving bond and offering sureties; and the presence in the district of 299 Riding Officers and Surveyors and four heavily armed Revenue cutters, headed by Captain John Edwards in the *Rye*, on constant patrol between the North Foreland and the Isle of Wight.

One of the most ruthless bands to set the forces of law and order at defiance was the Hawkhurst gang, which operated in the Chichester area, with headquarters at Rye's *Mermaid* tavern. When one of their cargoes of tea had been captured and taken to Poole Custom House, the leader of the gang, Thomas Kingsmill, headed a night attack for its recovery. But he had been seen and recognised, and the word went round that Galley, a Customs officer, and a shoemaker named Chater were prepared to give evidence of identification. The two men were run down by the gang, lashed to a couple of horses and dragged away to be flogged. Galley died under the lash, his body being buried, upright, in a hole. Chater, with his face brutally mutilated, was forced to throw himself, noosed, into a well; great stones being hurled on top of his strangled body to hide it from sight.

So great was the smuggling carried out by the personnel of the homeward-bound East Indiamen that it became the practice for the Revenue officers from Deal to board the craft in the Downs. In this way Captain Thwaites, of the *E. I. Carnarvon*, for one, was caught trying to smuggle in 800 pieces of silk and 1,500 lb. of tea. Similar complaints were made with regard to the Post Office packets plying out of Dover and Falmouth; and feelings ran high between the officials of the Customs House and the 'mandarins' of the General Post Office in Lombard Street —a state of affairs in no way bettered by the exposure of long-standing connivance on the part of a number of Customs officials in the very practices they were employed to suppress.

The smugglers' preference in the way of craft was for a square-rigged vessel up to 100 tons, with a single mast, main-sail, two headsails and square topsail set forward of the mast on a yard. This type of boat was extremely manœuvrable and could be handled with fewer men, and therefore at less expense,

than a lugger of similar size. It followed that the Revenue
officials hired smacks or built sloop-rigged cutters for them
selves—craft such as the *Swift*, whose 'beat' included Poole
Portland, and Jack-in-the-Basket, off the entrance to Lyming
ton harbour. Of similar type was the *Success*, which cruised
between Portland and Spithead, and the hired 'yachts' *Hurs*
and *Calshot* operating in the Southampton area.

For its Commanders, Mates and Deputed Mariners th
Revenue Service had to rely, of course, on individuals who i
they themselves had not turned to owling, were lifelong ac
quaintances of the men they had to hunt down; a state o
affairs that frequently subjected the hunters' sense of duty t
the severest test. The conditions of their service were harsh
lacking in all comfort, for they lived in cramped, constantl
wet quarters, in sight of the land but with little shore leave—
and with the threat of transfer to the Navy, in the event o
misconduct, as a distinctly negative encouragement to th
conscientious fulfilment of their duties.

Empowered to demand the support of the Navy or Arm
should circumstances require it, they were chary of seekin
outside assistance since that involved sharing out the rewar
for a successful capture with those they had called to their aid.
For a seized cargo was promptly sold, and half the valu
having been put aside as "the King's share", the remainder
after the deduction of expenses, was distributed *pro rata* amon
the captors, whatever their particular Service. Since the highes
salary a Preventive man could attain was £150 a year, his wa
obviously a case of payment by results.

Ill-remunerated as it might be, however, the Revenue Servic
toiled with rare devotion to carry out its ungrateful duties. Bu
the owlers were far more numerous and in many respect
infinitely better organised. Moreover, instead of every han
being against them, the majority were ready, however privily
to lend them aid. Since smuggled brandy could be purchase
at a third the duty rate, and tea and tobacco at something unde
half, the vendor of a contraband cargo never lacked for friend
in need. At Poole, for example, when a Collector and thre

---

[1] A captured smuggling boat would be sawn into three pieces and the
broken up. In exceptional circumstances she might be taken over by th
Revenue Service.

Riding Officers came upon four men standing guard over an illicit cargo cached in a chine, the representatives of the law were immediately set upon by a mob that seemed to materialise out of the ground. Badly beaten up and tightly bound, they had the mortification of witnessing their assailants make off with the goods in such an orderly manner that it was obvious that the whole run had been most skilfully planned and organised.

The owlers had their own pet legal representatives to come to their aid when they got into trouble; the most notorious being a certain Andrew Norton, an erstwhile clerk of the solicitor to the Customs. Furthermore, their most ardent champions were "the clergy and churchwardens of the parishes where they resided, who invariably gave them a good character".[1]

It was calculated that up to twenty thousand individuals were concerned one way and another in the owlers' activities. Some idea of the loss of revenue their operations involved may be gauged from the fact that one smuggler alone—'Captain' Joseph Cockburn—running five boats regularly between Boulogne and the Kent and Sussex coastline, imported an average of six tons of tea and 2,000 half-ankers [2] of spirits *a week*. At a minimum, this represented a hebdomadal loss to the Revenue of £3,000.

Even the coasting vessels, between ports, were not above surreptitiously slipping across to Jersey or Guernsey, to pick up a few bales of tobacco or tubs of spirits.

Navigation in home waters had been appreciably aided by the introduction of many new lights along the coast. The lanthorn established by Charles I on the North Foreland—erected on the roof of a half-timbered farmhouse—had been restored after its destruction by fire in 1683; and the Upnor beacon shone forth bravely. A lightship at the Nore was balanced by another at the Dudgeon. Further west, the beacon was repaired at Dungeness, a pharos set up at Portland, and a floating light installed on the Skerries, the deep bank of sand and shingle stretching four miles along the sea bottom, close to the land, in Start Bay. Three years after the destruction of Winstanley's Eddystone lighthouse in the great storm of November 1703, John Rudyerd had set about the task of replacing it. Work on

---

[1] *Chronicles of the Customs*, W. D. Chester.
[2] An anker was the equivalent to ten wine gallons.

the new edifice had been in progress when war with France
had broken out; and an enemy privateer had promptly raided
the rock and borne away the party of artisans at work on the
lighthouse walls. On news of this exploit reaching his ears,
Louis of France had insisted on the captives' immediate restoration to liberty, with all their possessions. "Although I am at
war with England," he had loftily pronounced, "I am not at
war with humanity"; and the men had been sent back to carry
on with their humanitarian labours.

Lights and buoys, of course, meant little to the owlers, who
pursued their highly lucrative activities in waters with which
they had been familiar all their working lives. Even the most
prosperous of them, however, experienced a falling off in trade
with the bursting of the 'South Sea Bubble'—the financial
crash which, almost overnight, hurled thousands of reckless
speculators from the heights of delusive prosperity to the depths
of ruin. For the victims of their own insensate folly there was
small comfort to be derived from the fact that France was undergoing a financial earthquake of equally staggering dimensions.

Conditions being what they were, it was inevitable that the
hopes of the Dissenters and the fears of 'Change Alley should
have combined to elevate to power the singularly apposite
figure of Sir Robert Walpole. One of the strangest political
horse-copers ever to have attained high office, he was a true
man of the times which brought him to prominence, and probably the only individual with the necessary combination of
patriotism and lack of scruple to ride the contemporary whirlwind and direct the prevailing storm.

*   *   *

Relations between Britain and Spain had been strained even
prior to Alberoni's support of the Jacobite rising of the '15. In
1718 a state of war between the two countries had led to a
Spanish attempt to recover Gibraltar, which superior British
naval might had experienced no difficulty in frustrating. Thereafter, the peace patched up in 1721 had constantly been exacer-
bated by complaints of heavy-handed Spanish interference with
British traders in the Caribbean, who were accused—not
entirely without warrant—of consistently smuggling contraband
into local ports where they were debarred from conducting

legitimate trade. Matters came to a head when the master-
mariner Robert Jenkins, summoned to the Bar of the House of
Commons, produced a desiccated object, carefully wrapped in
cotton wool, which he affirmed was the ear sliced from his head
by a Spanish *guarda costa*. Whatever the truth of the story,[1]
public opinion was so incensed that Walpole had to defer to
popular clamour and formally declare war.

With a conflict destined to be almost exclusively conducted
by naval forces operating in remote waters, there was nothing
to disturb the even flow of commerce through the narrow seas;
no reason to suspend the official survey of England's coastline
and headlands, undertaken under Parliamentary sanction.[2] At
Portsmouth the curriculum of the newly-established Naval
Academy, for the instruction of what, during the Restoration,
had been known as 'King's Letter Boys', aimed at endowing
aspirants for a Commission with a sound nautical training
before they went to sea. The course of instruction included
demonstration of the use of the new quadrant devised by John
Hadley, and exposition of the principles advanced in Captain
Daniel Newhouse's *Whole Art of Navigation*.

The "sons of noblemen and gentlemen" of the Academy had
not, of course, entirely superseded the youths who entered the
service under the heading of 'Captain's servant'. There were,
indeed, a number of lads falling in this category in the five
vessels that sailed from Portsmouth with Commodore George
Anson, for the voyage in which he set out to emulate Drake's
great feat of circumnavigation of 1577–1580.

It was to 'Pompey'[3] that the news first came of Admiral
Vernon's order to the fleet in the West Indies, directing that the
generous daily tot of rum should be diluted in the proportion
of a quart of water to a half-pint of spirits, to which sugar and
the juice of fresh limes could be added to taste. Since Vernon's
ancient boat-cloak of grogram[4] had already earned him the
sobriquet of 'Old Grog', the palatable jorum he recommended
soon acquired that name of grog by which it has ever since been
known.[5]

---

[1] It is equally possible that he lost it when condemned, on one occasion,
to the pillory.
[2] 14 Geo. II, Stat. 1, Cap. 39.   [3] The sailor's name for Portsmouth.
[4] A coarse, weather-resistant material made of silk and mohair.
[5] The British seaman soon acquired the nickname of 'Limey' with

Vernon's initial success against the Spaniards at Porto Bello was followed by the failure of the ill-contrived amphibious operation against Cartagena. But tragic blundering in the Caribbean was soon thrust into the limbo of forgetfulness by Britain's intervention in the War of the Austrian Succession. With the death of the Emperor Charles VII the French, with a sharply acquisitive eye on Antwerp, had been prompt to lend their support to the male Pretender to the Imperial Throne. Intent on maintaining a more equable balance of power, Britain had been equally speedy in ranging herself on the side of the Empress Maria Theresa. The focus of British maritime power was in the Mediterranean; with the Channel ports serving as bases for both sea and land operations at very long remove.

Thirty years of neglect, however, found the fleet deficient in many vital particulars, not the least important being the want of sufficient frigates. In the widespread shipbuilding that was immediately embarked upon Buckler's Hard—almost idle since the days of Henry V—once again became the scene of feverish activity, under the inspiration of John Duke of Montagu. With Wyatt and Company responsible for the work, the 24-gun *Surprise* was the first of a long line of stoutly constructed sloops, frigates and ships of the line that took the water beneath the little village, whose double row of cottages was widely separated by enormous stacks of seasoning timber. By the end of the century, when control had passed to the celebrated firm of Adams, the yards found employment for as many as 4,000 workmen coming in from villages all up and down the Beaulieu river.[1]

Buckler's Hard was known for its refreshing freedom from peculation; which is more than can be said for Deptford; where as a precautionary measure the yardsmen had been formed into a rather unhandy regiment of Sea Fencibles. Within its limitations, the move was timely, since the French, in the hope of further embarrassing the British Administration, chose the moment to help the Jacobites in staging another bid for power, this time on behalf of the Young Pretender, Prince Charles Edward.

American mariners, who themselves were invariably furnished with anti-scorbutics in the shape of fresh fruit and vegetables.

[1] Amongst other vessels constructed at Buckler's Hard was the famous *Agamemnon*.

In the February of 1744 an attempt to tranship a Gallo-Jacobite force from Dunkirk to the Thames estuary had failed completely when a typical Channel storm had driven eleven of the armed troopships ashore before they had been given a chance to try conclusions with Sir John Norris and the fleet awaiting them in the Downs.

Following the Pyrrhic victory of the French forces at Fontenoy, however, the need for reinforcements so stripped the homeland of troops—not more than 8,000 being left in the depots—that the Pretender resolved to embark on a further attempt to snatch the Throne, during the absence of George II in Hanover.

It was on July 9th that Captain Piercy Brett, cruising in the 58-gun *Lion*, sighted two suspicious-looking vessels off the Lizard, and gave chase. In the fierce encounter that ensued the *Lion* completely disabled the 64-gun *Elizabeth*, the larger of the two craft, but was herself so crippled that the other ship, the *Du Teilly*,[1] got away unscathed.[2] Aboard her was Bonnie Prince Charlie; and in due course a very sea-sick Pretender was safely landed in Scotland, and raised the Standard of revolt.

It was fully anticipated that if any real success attended the Jacobite uprising, the French would come to its aid with the 30,000 troops concentrated between Dunkirk and Boulogne. Fortunately, Anson, posted to the Admiralty after his voyage of circumnavigation, appointed Vernon to command in the Channel. Concentrating his bigger ships in the western approaches, with his more mobile craft 'Old Grog' proceeded to maintain unremitting watch on the French coast from his commanding position in the Downs. With the owlers furnishing him—at a price!—with up-to-date intelligence, and the privateers *York*, *Carlisle* and *Eagle* very ably supplementing his inadequate forces, the Admiral was able to muzzle any move on the part of the French even when the Jacobite success at Prestonpans gave the Duc de Richelieu his cue for action.

Coolly gathering in two out of the six ships on passage with money and munitions for the rebels, Vernon remained confident that the strong northeasterly wind would confine the

---

[1] Sometimes referred to as *La Doutelle*.

[2] The ferocity of the encounter is witnessed by the fact that on board the *Lion* 55 men were killed and 107 wounded, including Captain Brett, while casualties in the *Elizabeth* amounted to 54 slain and 140 injured (*Naval and Military Memoirs of Great Britain*, Robert Beatson).

French to port. He was further cheered by the news that additional supplies in the *San Zorioco* from Corunna and the *San Pedro* out of Santander had been snapped up by privateers in the western approaches.

With the Pretender at Derby, and London in a panic, British privateers were still dealing summarily with stragglers from the invasion fleet assembling at Boulogne—seventeen fishing shallops laden with stores being driven ashore near Calais in one raid alone. Even when the Admiralty, infuriated by Vernon's brusquerie and independence, replaced him by Vice-Admiral William Martin, the latter made no change in his predecessor's admirable dispositions, which continued to stifle any Gallic attempts to emerge in force.

With the Pretender's retreat from Derby, and his subsequent flight to France in the privateer *Bellona*, the Jacobite *gasconnade* was over; its lack of Gallic support being entirely attributable to the alertness and strategic good sense of the irascible but remarkably efficient Admiral in command in the narrow seas.

Public morale was further restored by news that a handful of American Provincial troops, acting in conjunction with Commodore Peter Warren, R.N., had succeeded in capturing Louisbourg, which the French had long regarded as the key to the St. Lawrence, and therefore of Canada itself.

As a follow-up to the suppression of the Jacobite rising, an expedition was organised for an amphibious attack on L'Orient, where a raid on the garrison and the stores and vessels of the French East India Company would not only inflict considerable material damage, but relieve pressure on the Allied troops in Flanders.

Unfortunately, the Officer commanding, General Sinclair, had been furnished with no information with regard to his objective, the opposition he might be expected to encounter, or the nature of the terrain over which he was to operate; and his request to the egregious Duke of Newcastle for a map of Brittany was met by the belated delivery of a chart of Gascony. Perhaps even worse was the lack of any contemporary doctrine for the combined operation of sea and land forces, nor any ruling as to who should be entrusted with the over-all command.

Setting forth from St. Helen's on August 5th, the expedition of sixty sail was speedily forced back by contrary winds, and it was not until September 14th that the flotilla fetched the French coast, in the teeth of an unhelpful off-shore wind.

With great difficulty and under a persistent harassing fire from the L'Orient garrison and a number of peasant *franc-tireurs*, the main body of the troops was got ashore; and the town was invested in due form. Sinclair, having foolishly rejected a Gallic offer to surrender "with the honours of war", found his own situation deteriorating so rapidly that no option was left but to re-embark before worsening weather conditions rendered such a process out of the question. Having "broken a few windows with English guineas", as one sardonic critic expressed it, the expedition—after a somewhat aimless raid on the Quiberon peninsula—returned to England; some of the scattered vessels having narrowly escaped shipwreck on the cruel rocks of the Ile de Groix.

*   *   *

Anson's tenure at the Admiralty witnessed several reformations and innovations of considerable importance; not the least of which was to put the Corps of Marines on a permanent footing.

Up to the time of the establishment of the Seniority List in 1693 the Naval Officer enjoyed no continuity of service or rank, which were his only during the period of a ship's commissioning —two or three years. The Seniority List had established a certain number of the older Officers permanently in their respective ranks, and endowed them with a right to certain scales of remuneration when not actively employed. By 1747 the plethora of Admirals and senior Captains was blocking promotion so seriously that a number of them were transferred to certain entirely apocryphal posts in what was sometimes referred to as the 'Yellow Squadron', but which, despite the fact that the principle of superannuation had no official recognition, was nothing more nor less than a camouflaged Retired List.

Fighting Instructions, slightly modified by Sir George Rooke in 1703, like the *Articles of War*, were given conscientious overhaul by Anson; many of Vernon's innovations being quietly incorporated in the *Additional Instructions* for which the Admiralty assumed the responsibility. Despite their recasting, however, as a fighting code the revised *Instructions* were still far too formalist and inflexible.

Hitherto, Naval Officers had been arrayed in no standard pattern uniform. A committee of executive or deck Officers therefore forwarded a petition to the Admiralty submitting that some form of standardised dress could only be regarded as "useful and necessary for the Commissioned Officers, as well as agreeable to the practice of other nations". The memorial was favourably received, although there was considerable difference of opinion as to the colour and pattern of the garb to be adopted. Happily, the matter was determined by the King himself. According to a statement by the Hon. John Forbes, this Admiral on being summoned to attend the Duke of Bedford,[1] was "Introduced into an apartement surrounded with various dresses, and his opinion was asked as to the most appropriate. The Admiral said red and blue, or blue and red, as these were our national colours. 'No,' replied his Grace, 'the King has determined otherwise, for, having seen my Duchess riding in the Park in a habit of blue faced with white, the dress took the fancy of His Majesty, who has appointed it the uniform of the Royal Navy.' " So blue, white and gold it was.

The Warrant Officers and Lower Deck, however, were not to qualify for a uniform for many a year to come; although a certain uniformity of dress was the outcome of those 'slops' which, "to avoyde nastie beastlynesse by disease and unwholesome ill smells in every ship", were issued, on charge, from the vessel's slop chest. The foremast hand, therefore, could easily be distinguished by his three-cornered hat or thrummed cap, his striped cotton shirt topped by a gay bandana neckerchief, his short kersey coat and wide breeches flapping above woollen stockings and shoes of neat's leather, garnished with sparkling brass buckles, and the curved hanger swinging at his side.

With a fleet of nigh on a hundred vessels to control, the deck Officers of the East India Company were not behindhand in adopting a uniform very similar to that worn by their comrades in the Senior Service. With even better opportunities for private trading than were enjoyed by the employees of the Turkey Company and the reorganised Royal Africa Company, the East India men were well paid, admirably found, and enjoyed

[1] The contemporary First Lord of the Admiralty.

the benefit of a pension scheme, known as the Poplar Fund, which covered misadventure as well as superannuation.[1]

The hazards of the sea, however, were common to all; and weather conditions in the Channel in the late 'forties and early 'fifties were particularly capricious and severe. In 1748 the *Hope of Amsterdam* was driven on to the treacherous Chesil Bank; with the local population, aflame with greed, frantically scrabbling amongst the shingle, and even in the reedy Fleet stream that runs parallel to the beach, for the £50,000 of gold that had formed part of the castaway's cargo. In 1753 another great storm swept seven vessels ashore at the Isle of Wight, including the *Adrienne* of Bordeaux, laden with wine, a Boston ship freighted with oil and turpentine, the *Friendship*, her holds full of tobacco, the *Sven Hoolm* of Copenhagen, the *Semnel* of Cork, and a brigantine out of Poole, in ballast. Beachcombers, as usual, were quickly on the spot to reap the harvest of disaster. But despite their industry the half-yearly seizures of Wilkinson, the Collector at Cowes, included 3,023 lb. of tobacco; his Tide-surveyor, Godwin, contributing another 2,422 lb.

Sennen Cove, just north of Land's End, had always been a perilous place for shipping; and in 1753 it nearly broke its own record for 1693, of seventy vessels cast away—sometimes through the nefandous activities of wreckers—within the twelvemonth. There was little need for the hypocritical Cornishmen and Scillonians to voice their accustomed prayer: "We pray Thee, O Lord, not that wrecks should happen, but that if any wrecks *should* happen, Thou wilt guide them to our shores for the benefit of the poor inhabitants."

* * *

The Peace of Aix-la-Chapelle, of 1748, did no more than afford an opportunity for recuperation to a France and an England intent on that expansion of empire which could only be achieved at the expense of the rival competitor. By 1756, therefore, hostilities had again broken out, with Austria now ranged on the side of Britain's enemies.

Once again, maritime interest was centred in the Mediterranean; although at the outset the homeland base was rather

---

[1] From the foremast hand's £2 5s. 0d. to the Commander's £10 0s. 0d. a month, the Company's scale of pay was easily the highest available.

the scene of lethargic improvisation than alert preparedness for war—despite the Navy's possession of 270 warships, of an aggregate of 280,969 tons. The efforts of the press gangs to man the fleet were supplemented in some measure when Jonas Hanway—who had already evoked the enmity of the hackney coachmen by seeking to popularise the umbrella—founded the Marine Society, with the object of assisting destitute boys and training them for a life at sea. Some went to the Navy, some to the Mercantile Marine, and the remainder to the coasting trade. All in all, their fate could be favourably compared with that of the youths apprenticed to the skippers of the fishing fleet, where life was anything but a bed of roses. Crabbe's picture of the fate endured by a lad aboard a trawler is no exercise in poetic rant:

> Pinched, beaten, cold, kicked, threatened and abused;
> His efforts punished and his food refused;
> Awake tormented—soon aroused from sleep;
> Struck if he wept—and yet compelled to weep;
> The trembling boy dropt down and strove to pray,
> Received a blow and trembling, turned away.[1]

One skipper of a smack, angered at the way his supper had been prepared, held his wretched apprentice's hands in a pan of boiling fat until they were cooked. Another, infuriated by chance mention of the word rabbits—to the superstitious the bringers of high winds and foul weather—towed the unfortunate lad who had spoken of them astern in the cod-end of a trawl net 'to teach him a lesson'. It was a lesson he did not survive.

There were a number of Marine Society boys with Charles Saunders's and 'Wry-necked Dick' Boscawen's flotillas at the recapture of Louisbourg[2] and the successful investment of Quebec; the prologue to the final expulsion of the French from Canada. With ships and men engaged from 'Pompey' and the West, even this distant conquest was indissolubly linked with the Channel ports on which it had been based.

The Channel havens' more immediate concern with the

---

[1] *Peter Grimes*, George Crabbe.
[2] By the Treaty of Aix-la-Chapelle Louisbourg had been exchanged for Antwerp, to the comprehensible indignation of the American colonists, resentful that their conquest should be used as a pawn in the game of European politics.

course of the war, however, was to furnish the springboard for two diversionary raids on the enemy coast. The first, to St. Malo and Cherbourg, had the misfortune to be encumbered with the ineffable Lord George Sackville as Second-in-Command; and the whole enterprise proved to be just another exercise in "breaking windows with English guineas". A subsequent venture in the same area was best summed up in the contemporary rhyme:

> *We went, we saw, were seen, like Valiant Men*
> *Sailed up the Bay, and then—sailed home again.*

The design of that new luminary, William Pitt, to "win America by victory in Europe" was more than vindicated by the Army's sparkling victories at Minden, Emsdorff and Warburg. In the Mediterranean, however, Minorca—with the exception of a single fortress—had been seized by the French. Admiral John Byng, sent out to restore the situation without being furnished with any land forces, siege train, or store ships, achieved the sort of semi-success which only served to emphasise the Administration's heinous shortcomings. Recalled in an atmosphere of carefully contrived disgrace, he was court-martialled and shot—because Newcastle, the responsible Minister, ought to have been hanged. To screen his own sins of omission and commission the politician has never scrupled to seek a scapegoat in one or other of the Services.

Only a little earlier Admiral Mathews had been disgraced for doing just sufficient to make it plain that the Administration had done nowhere near enough. The responsible Minister was saved, and the Navy lost a competent commander.

In effect, it was a period in which departmental inefficiency, favouritism and the vicious propensity to 'play politics' in making sea appointments, were steadily poisoning a Service in which the very thought of jobbery and political partisanship should at all times be anathema.

PART THREE

The Years of Peril

"Britannia needs no bulwarks,
  No towers along the steep,
  Her march is o'er the mountain waves,
  Her home is on the deep."

THOMAS CAMPBELL

"England, this ancient structure, cemented with blood, is an incredibly delicate and exquisite mechanism, held together lightly by imponderable elements of credit and prestige, experience and skill, written and unwritten law, codes and habits—this remarkable and artistic thing, the British Empire, part empire and part commonwealth, is the only world-wide organisation in existence, the world equaliser and holder of the equilibrium, the only world-wide stabilising force for law and order on this planet."

DOROTHY THOMPSON

CHAPTER XVII

The Island Base

"The wise ancients did not praise the ship parting
with flying Colours from the port, but only that brave
sailer which came back with torn sheets and battered
sides, stript of her banners, but having ridden out the
storm."

RALPH WALDO EMERSON

LIKE a number of his predecessors, George III inherited a
full-scale war; another round in the age-old struggle with
France to establish those outlets for overseas trade which are
the corner-stones of empire.

Following Boscawen's victory at Lagos and Hawke's daring
swoop amidst the treacherous reefs and shoals of Quiberon bay,
to smash the battle-fleet earmarked for England's conquest, the
strangling blockade of the enemy coast was grimly and steadfastly maintained.

To relieve pressure on the troops in the principal theatre of
war, another amphibian expedition was organised early in 1761,
for an attempt on the garrison of Belleisle, off the coast of
Brittany; the whole enterprise being placed under the command
of Commodore Augustus Keppel.

Leaving Spithead on March 29th, the armament reached its
objective by April 7th, there to discover that every advantage
had been taken of the rocky and precipitous nature of the coast
to place the island in a perfect state of defence. Not content with
this, however, the Governor, M. de St. Croix, persuaded the
ladies of the garrison to swell the apparent strength of his forces
by donning uniform and parading along the cliff-top; and as
one chronicler enthusiastically reported, "Such was the
patriotism of these daughters of France that those who had no
horses rode on cows."

Undeterred by this martial display, the phlegmatic British

redcoats were landed under cover of the warships' guns. Owing to the steepness of the ground, however, it was found impossible for the main body to scale the heights, only 60 Grenadiers reaching the top of the cliffs, where they were overpowered after a desperate resistance.

Keppel almost despaired of victory; but a second attempt to assail the works proved successful enough to drive the enemy back into the citadel of Le Palais. Failing reinforcement from the mainland, it could be only a matter of time before this last stronghold submitted; and a heavy mortar fire having reduced the garrison's artillery to silence, St. Croix wisely surrendered to save unnecessary bloodshed. At a cost of some 700 killed and wounded, Belleisle was secured as "a place of refreshment" for the fleet engaged in the weary work of blockading the enemy coast.

It was to the Island base, however, that the battered, storm-tossed ships returned whenever the rare opportunity arose for an overhaul and refit. Even with a Navy debt approaching £3,600,000, enough money was found to improve the facilities for dealing with them and their crews. The foundations were laid for the Royal Naval Hospital in Stonehouse, and the Marines were moved to new barracks from their cramped and insanitary quarters in Plymouth's ancient Barbican. A welcoming beacon to the returning mariners was Smeaton's new lighthouse, which had replaced Rudyerd's Eddystone tower after its destruction by fire on a night of 1756. The docks and fortifications at Chatham, Portsmouth and Plymouth were all enlarged and strengthened; although little was done to check the widespread corruption and peculation which characterised the administrative staff no less than the dockyard 'mateys'. An attempt to introduce piece work and some sort of system of payment by results was promptly met by a strike; and firm measures had to be taken to restore working conditions to something approaching order. At Dover the Sisyphean labour of dredging the harbour was steadily pursued; while a convulsion of the sea-bed having again rendered Rye haven approachable the authorities of Winchelsea were stimulated into constructing a cut channel of sufficient depth to permit vessels up to 300 tons to penetrate to their long-neglected harbour. With this, the local fishing industry took on a new lease of life, although its renascence was no more than temporary. There is no lasting retort to the malignant working of the easterly drift.

The demand for the 70,000 personnel to man the Fleet had been met, in some sort, by the limitation of wages in the mercantile marine—save with the East Indiamen—to 35s. a month, as against the 60s. a month offered by the Navy, plus a bounty on attestation.[1] There was also the chance of extremely handsome prize money; the capture of the *Hermione* by two sloops of war, for example, having involved the distribution of £519,164 10s. 0d., of which comforting sum every Ordinary Seaman, engaged in the action, qualified for £485 5s. 4d.

The Sick and Hurt Office had been reorganised as early as 1740; Campbell's sextant and Harrison's chronometer were added to the aids to navigation; the Astronomer Royal, Dr. Nevil Maskylene, was at work on the production of the first comprehensive Nautical Almanac; Cole's chain pump was under test; while the experiment of coppering the ship's bottom was just over the horizon, as was Dr. Lind's apparatus for the production of fresh from salt water.

During the earlier years of the war the carrying trade had suffered severely. But when the convoy system got smoothly under way, freighting progressively revived. Although the vessels employed were fewer in number, they were of bigger construction and far greater holding capacity.

There were still privateers actively seeking their prey throughout the whole length and breadth of the narrow seas, and of these perhaps the most notable was the *Vengeance* of St. Malo. It was this 36-gun vessel, manned with a crew of 400, that won the long and savage duel with Captain Death's 26-gun *Terrible*. Encountering each other at the mouth of the Channel, the two craft swiftly closed, the Frenchman ranging up on the port quarter to deliver a destructive diagonal blast of small shot across his opponent's deck that wreaked tremendous slaughter. The English Captain replied with a broadside of grape and round-shot, and a murderous exchange of fire at close range speedily piled up casualties. It was the small-arm men in the Frenchman's top that decided the issue of the day; for Death

[1] The Government bounty rose from 30s to £3 a head for an A.B., with £2 as the reward of an O.S. and £1 for a landsman. London and certain other of the bigger cities offered additional bounties ranging from £1 to £2 a head.

was struck down, and nearly a third of his crew killed or injured. The only Officer remaining on his feet had no option but to strike his Colours and the *Terrible* was taken to St. Malo in charge of a prize crew.

Scarcely better fortune attended the meteoric career of the 28-gun *Antigallican* under the command of William Foster. The first prize he brought into Plymouth was the 14-gun *Maria Theresa*, which was well enough for a start. His next capture was the French-Indiaman, the *Duc de Penthièvre*, with a cargo worth £300,000. Having to run before a gale, Foster, together with his prize, perforce took shelter in Cadiz. It was then that he learned something of the tortuosity of Spanish legal procedure; for despite the sworn testimony of Foster's Gallic prisoners, the local Governor set to work to demonstrate that the *Duc de Penthièvre* had been captured in *Spanish* territorial waters! A guard was put on both vessels, and possession being nine points of the law, Foster never succeeded in making good his claim to the French-Indiaman, and was fortunate—at very long last—to regain control of his own *Antigallican*.

In the circumstances it is not altogether to be wondered at that the best of the British privateers—men such as the famous Fortunatus Wright—preferred to operate in more distant waters, leaving the Frenchmen to lord it in those narrow seas where there was always a handy home port for them to run into with their prizes. Some of the smaller and more lightly-armed Gallic privateers made a point of lying in wait for the grain ships plying in increasing number to and fro across the Channel. For England—to her everlasting peril!—had become a grain-importing country: a state of affairs that underwent no remedy when the Peace of Paris, of 1763, brought the Seven Years' War to a close.

The decline in agriculture was, of course, part of the price paid for the increasing rate at which the countryside was being emptied of men and women to serve the fast-growing needs of industry.

Despite obstruction on the part of the workers called upon to handle them, the introduction of the steam engine and the spinning jenny gave an enormous impetus to industrial production; and although wool sold at no more than half its previous price, the aggregate was far greater, while the output of cotton goods was steadily on the increase. An enormous demand for pipe clay arose with the inauguration of the new chinaware industry—which by 1785 was to find employment for 20,000 workers. Its success owed almost everything to the drive and initiative of the progressive self-made industrialist, Josiah Wedgwood. A member of the Society of Friends, or Quakers, he formed one of a highly interlocking fraternity bound together by the nexus of intermarriage, which in the Charles Lloyds, the Galtons, the Reynolds of Coalbrookdale, the Barclays, the Hoares, and the allied Buxtons and Hanburys of the Evangelical Clapham Sect, founded a new industrial dynasty in which banking was the willing servant of the new concept of mass production. The ramifications of their manifold activities ranged from the manufacture of gun barrels—an odd pursuit for a Quaker!—to the purchase of a brewery; from the wholesale acquisition of barrel staves to the bulk shipment, coastwise, of china clay from the Cornish havens of Par and Fowey. Even the ships of the Newfoundland fishery, instead of lying idle in the off-months, were recruited to transport raw materials and finished goods; and "scarcely a vessel sailed from any port of Great Britain without carrying less or more of their universally useful articles".[1] Ubiquitous as they were, the Quakers' interests were even extended to include marine insurance. For it was very largely at their instance that the rule was established which decreed that the owner of an unseaworthy vessel not only lost the insurance on it, but was liable to the shippers of freight for any loss incurred "through negligence or the insufficiency of his ship".[2]

With a Customs revenue, in 1774, of £2,567,769 and a favourable balance of trade amounting to £12,810,610, the country's prospects of complete recovery from the financial strains of the recent war were sufficiently encouraging. Relations with the American colonies, however, were the cause of ever-increasing anxiety.

The colonists had given freely of their men and money to help remove the Gallic threat from their northern border[3];

---

[1] Macpherson, *op. cit.*

[2] *Vide* the verdict in a trial held at the Guildhall in 1763 (*Annual Register*).

[3] One early money grant from the colonies had been so liberal that Parliament had returned £200,000 of it.

they were prepared to concede that with a National Debt of
£138,000,000—incurred, in part, on their behalf—the Mother
Country was justified in looking to the colonies for a proportionate contribution to the general expenses of the war. It was
the heavy-handed, dictatorial manner in which the King's
advisers set about exacting what should, and would, have been
freely offered, that aroused their resentment and fostered the
spirit of resistance.

Pitt having elected to become an effigy in his own lifetime,
in 1761 his Administration yielded place to Bute and the party
of the 'King's friends'; men whose loyalty to what they conceived to be the Sovereign's interests was as unwavering as their
methods of furthering them were indubitably unsound. In
nothing were their activities more mischievous than in their
handling of the colonists. Desperate for money, they arbitrarily
clamped a Stamp duty[1] on "all legal or commercial writings or
contracts, pamphlets, newspapers, advertisements, almanacks,
cards and dice", that was as vexatious as it was fiscally unrewarding. The colonists' response was to ban the legitimate
import of all British goods; which led in its turn to such a
congestion of merchandise in the homeland warehouses, and to
such a multiplication of unfulfilled obligations between merchants and manufacturers—with bankruptcies running to 525
on the year—that the Stamp duty legislation was grudgingly
rescinded. Even so, its repeal was accompanied by a pettishly
provoking Act[2] which expressly asserted that British legislative
authority extended to the American colonies and to the
American peoples, "as subjects, in all cases whatsoever".
Doubtless Parliament was acting within its constitutional rights;
but some principles are all the better for being implied rather
than defined.

For their part, the colonists made it perfectly clear that while
they were quite ready, through their respective Governors, to
negotiate with the Sovereign with regard to supplies, it was
impossible to accept the principle of taxation by Parliament
without representation on its benches. The legal quibble that
technically the plantations were within the Manor of Greenwich,

---

[1] Stamp duties had been unavailingly advocated by Martin Bladen so
early as 1726, and rejected by Walpole in 1739.
[2] 6 Geo. III, Stat. 1, Cap. 12.

and that the colonists were therefore represented by the
Honourable Member for Kent, only served to aggravate the
spirit of resentment already aroused by the obduracy with
which British exporters persisted in operating a commercial
monopoly that sought to perpetuate the most grasping features
of an outmoded medieval trading system.

As yet, however, there was no general desire to sever the ties
with the Motherland. "We have never heard anyone, drunk or
sober", affirmed Dr. Benjamin Franklin, "wish for separation."
Certainly at the outset the demand for independence was confined to the *sotto voce* mutterings of a few malcontents such as the
conspiratorial Samuel Adams, the shifty, sottish Tom Paine,
James Innes, the firebrand professor of William and Mary
College, and the histrionic Patrick Henry—all failures in their
respective ways: and frustrated ambition is like a wounded
animal, and equally dangerous.

The simmering unrest—at its most turbulent in and around
the storm centre of Boston—was brought to a head when the
East India Company, hard pressed for revenue, sought to dump
a large consignment of tea on a resistant New England. For
the Ministry of Lord North was little more than a façade by
which needy mercantilism was furnished with a plausible front.
The colonists, who preferred tea smuggled into the country
without liability to tax, promptly threw a consignment of the
Company's leaf, worth £18,000, into Boston harbour; perhaps
the most costly brew of this dubious beverage in the whole of
history.

From that point the situation degenerated with such ominous
rapidity that the march to Lexington and "the shot that echoed
round the world" were almost an inevitability. The tragedy
was that the quarrel was not a straightforward issue between
plain right and patent wrong, but between half-right and half-
wrong; with men of British stock lamentably deficient in the
normal British genius for compromise at the very moment when
its cool, unflustered application might well have composed a
problem that only hotheads found insoluble.

*   *   *

With a state of war supervening between the colonists and
the Motherland, the American leaders' official ban on the

importation of British goods was largely counterbalanced by the wholesale shipment of these forbidden wares from English ports to the Dutch or Danish possessions in the Caribbean, whence they were carried to the American havens under the colonial or a neutral flag. Owling also played its vigorous part in supplying needs the colonists had no hesitation in satisfying, so long as the transaction contributed nothing to British fiscal revenue. "English goods were smuggled through Nova Scotia, and goods were purchased by American agents from England even before the vessels had started. One ship sailed directly to Boston, where its cargo was disposed of at a profit of 270 per cent. . . . Boston shopkeepers labelled their French goods English, for the demand was only for English goods." [1] Under cover of freighting stores to the reinforced British Army in North America, a number of merchants shipped mixed cargoes of merchandise for disposal amongst the colonists, who evinced no hesitation in purchasing this obvious contraband. All in all, the wharves of Thames-side and the Channel ports had rarely seen busier days.

The reverse traffic, in the form of American tobacco [2] and other commodities, was shipped to the West Indian Islands— particularly the Dutch settlement of St. Eustatius—whence the wares found their way to the Continent; where the owlers made large purchases to be smuggled across the Channel. By 1781 some 5,131,000 lb. of tobacco reached England by the 'round-about route'; a further 6,255,000 lb. being taken as prize of war. A French loan having been negotiated for the purchase of arms, munitions and uniforms, Henry Laurens arrived in Holland charged by the Continental Congress to secure all that was required. He immediately placed a large order with his intermediaries for English cloth, to the explosive chagrin of the French authorities who had taken it for granted that their subsidy would be expended on Gallic wares. But Laurens blandly pointed out that the colonial forces required the best, and that since English cloth *was* the best, English cloth was what he proposed to buy.

The British Administration's problem was to sustain a sufficiently powerful Army over lines of communication that

[1] *The Imperial Commonwealth*, A. P. Poley.
[2] At this period the average import of American tobacco was 55,900,000 lb., of which 44,820,000 were re-exported.

stretched across 3,000 miles of sea. With France content, for the nonce, to strike at her ancient enemy from behind America's shield, the problem of guarding these lines of communication along their whole length did not immediately arise. But the probability that France, with a Navy that had never been more powerful or better found, would sooner or later exchange covert for open hostility demanded a precautionary strengthening of the Fleet that set the Press at work to scour even the rookeries and byways for the necessary men. In London alone over 800 individuals of all sorts and conditions were impressed within a few weeks, while homeward-bound craft were boarded in the Downs and their crews remorselessly fleeced of their better elements. The 'Lord Mayor's Men', youths of good family rounded up in City bawdy houses or other questionable haunts, and given the choice between disgracing their relatives by appearing in the Magistrate's court and service with the Navy, were hustled off to await posting in the hulks moored in the Thames. Transportation to Australia had removed the convicts who had hitherto been engaged in lifting ballast from the river, and their verminous floating prisons had been taken over by the Navy; although Execution Dock, hard-by Wapping-in-the-Wose, remained a 'point of departure' for the convicted pirate and certain other classes of maritime felon.

To release more men for the Navy an Act[1] was passed permitting merchant craft to sail with foreign seamen forming up to three-fourths of their crews; a sweeping modification of the maritime legislation of which the economist, Adam Smith, had averred that "as defence is of much more importance than opulence, the Act of Navigation is, perhaps, the wisest of all the commercial regulations of England".

With the Press casting its net far and wide, all classes of the community were represented in the resultant catch; including a number of individuals with just sufficient education to gird at the squalid, brutalising conditions under which they were forced to serve. For although something had been done to improve the hard lot of the Lieutenants and certain half-pay Captains, the men of the Lower Deck lived under a harsh, oppressive discipline, on indifferent food, and in surroundings that had deteriorated rather than improved since the heyday

[1] 16 Geo. III. Stat. I, Cap. 20.

of the Elizabethan shipman. Admiral Vernon's championship of the foremast hand's many and legitimate grievances had achieved no alleviation of them, and had served no better purpose than to cover his own name with entirely unwarranted odium. Thanks to the good sense of one or two exceptional commanders, the Fleet was not entirely without its 'happy ships', wherein the men could be assured of just treatment, and the sick were indulged in clean bedding, "a nightcap, and a glass of wine from the Captain's table". But they were very much the exception. A spirit of rankling discontent was far more general; and mutinies, such as those aboard the *Chesterfield*, the *Bounty* and the *Hermione*, were a clear indication of the urgent need for reform. Desertions were so numerous that the Customs House officials were especially charged to keep a sharp look out for runaways.

In general, overseas commerce made a fairly quick recovery from the depression which had overtaken it prior to and at the outset of the struggle. For apart from the wholesale traffic in contraband, furnishing the Expeditionary Force with its requirements proved quite as profitable as shipping supplies to the colonists. Individual centres here and there, however, were hard hit. There was considerable distress in the Isle of Wight, for example, where rice from the plantations had hitherto been screened, re-packed and re-shipped to Holland. Both London and Southampton experienced a falling off of legitimate trade; but Poole continued to freight china clay to the Sugar Islands almost without interruption. The activities of the daring and skilful privateers out of Boston and Marblehead, on the other hand, soon wrought such havoc with legitimate British merchant traffic in North American waters that for the first time on record shippers found it wiser to lade their goods in craft enjoying the protection afforded by a neutral flag.

As the scope of the conflict widened, Channel shipping had to run the gauntlet of the privateers organised and commissioned by Silas Deane and Benjamin Franklin, and based on the more-than-benevolently neutral ports of France. Easily the most notorious of these sea-wolves was Gustavus Conyngham, whose capture of the *Prince of Orange* and several other vessels led to the farce of his formal arrest by a Gallic Administration not yet prepared to come out into the open as England's declared antagonist.

None the less, a covert Gallic attempt had been made to disrupt the smooth functioning of the Navy's base organisation when the secret agent, Mathurin Danet, succeeded in firing Portsmouth dockyard. Plymouth's apprehensions were allayed, however, by news of the incendiary's arrest. A little later, another stroke against the Navy's installations in 'Pompey' was undertaken by the American sympathiser James Aitkin, alias 'John the Painter'.

In the first instance, Aitkin approached Silas Deane, *en poste* in France, with a plan to fire the dockyard with a combustible embodying an elementary time-fuse, in the shape of a measured length of candle in a box packed at the base with tinder. Deane was sufficiently impressed with the proposal to promise that, in the event of success, he would do all in his power to further Aitkin's cherished desire to secure a Commission in the Continental Army.

It was on Thursday, December 5th, 1776, that 'John the Painter' succeeded in penetrating Portsmouth dockyard, after surviving a stiff interrogation by a couple of local employees. Planting his infernal machine between the 1,000-foot ropewalk and some adjacent sheds, he made good his escape; and from the neighbouring heights of Portsdown had the gratification of looking down on a very satisfactory blaze.

With the news of Portsmouth's near-catastrophe, Plymouth was again thrown into a state of vigilant watchfulness. For it seemed certain that, inspired by his earlier success, Aitkin would be bound to stage an attempt on the Western port. Such fears were not falsified by events, for in due course 'John the Painter' made his way to Plymouth, and succeeded in gaining access to Government property. The vigilance of the guards, however, frustrated his attempt to fire the storehouses, and a general alarm was raised. With the aid of a rope ladder the intruder managed to scale the dockyard wall and again made good his escape.

For a time Aitkin wandered somewhat aimlessly about the countryside. Eventually, with his money all expended, hunger drove him to robbery; the village constable raised the hue and cry, and with the hunted man's apprehension the passport given him by Silas Deane served to establish his identity as the much-wanted fire-raiser.

Aitkin came up for trial at the Winchester Assizes of March, 1777, and was duly condemned to death. A gallows, sixty feet high, was erected at Portsmouth dockyard gates, and there the sentence was carried into effect; the incendiary's carcase subsequently being suspended in chains at Blockhouse Fort, "so that all going in or out of the harbour should be reminded of his fate".

*   *   *

With Britain and the colonists embroiled in open strife, France lost little time in sending the best of her secret agents across the narrow seas to secure the latest intelligence as to England's state of preparedness—or the reverse. The most experienced of these spies was the Comte de Parades, whose particular objective was the Channel's fixed defences. His reports were both shrewd and comprehensive, and were sent safely back across *La Manche* through the agency of a well-bribed smuggler.

Some idea of the adroitness with which he set about his task may be gauged from the fact that he persuaded an obliging Serjeant of the Guard to take him on an extended tour of Plymouth's Citadel!

Had the responsible official, D'Orvilliers, only taken his agent's reports *au pied de la lettre*, Admiral Byron's ill-found and ill-manned fleet would have been trapped when it set out from Portsmouth, bound for America; but the opportunity was missed. Parades eventually returned to France, and in a personal interview so impressed his views on Sartine, the Minister of Marine, that it was resolved at the first favourable opportunity to mount a full-scale assault on Plymouth and the West Country.

That moment came when the consequences of Lord Germain's[1] criminous neglect to inform General Howe of the supporting role he was expected to play in 'Gentleman Johnny' Burgoyne's advance on Albany, came grimly home to roost. For the British failure at Saratoga encouraged the French in the

[1] Lord George Sackville had changed his name to Germain on coming into a fortune. Unfortunately, he was unable at the same time to exchange a congenital ineptitude and pusillanimity for a reasonable ability to discharge the duties of his office as Minister for the Colonies and War.

fond belief that British enfeeblement now rendered it safe for
the unconvincing mask of neutrality to be cast aside in favour
of open hostility.

With eleven of the line away on the North American station
Admiral Keppel could find no more than thirty vessels—of
which he swore that "only six ships were fit to meet a seaman's
eye"—with which to oppose D'Orvilliers off Ushant on July
27th, 1778. In the contest that ensued the British Commander
was denied anything more than a Pyrrhic victory, largely owing
to the inability, or reluctance, of Sir Hugh Palliser, with the
rear divisions, to interpret and obey his superior's signals. It was
a want of apprehension that can be attributed as much to the
'politics' which bedevilled the contemporary Navy as to any
particular obscurity in the methods of communication then in
service. It led to Palliser's application for a Court Martial on
his superior Officer which was likewise as much a stroke of
political vindictiveness as an attempt to clear his own good
name; as the widespread approbation which greeted Keppel's
ultimate vindication only too clearly demonstrated.

But with the Navy under the control of the 4th Earl of Sandwich—boon companion of the rakehelly John Wilkes, and the
contemptible 'Jemmy Twitcher' of Gay's *Beggar's Opera*—corruption, jobbery and political nepotism had so rotted Service
morale, that several senior commanders refused sea appointments so long as the Admiralty was under the sway of one
esteemed

> *Too infamous to have a friend,*
> *Too bad for bad men to commend.*

As in the venal days of 'Steenie' Villiers, "large sums of
money were appropriated for the repair of ships that were
rotting in harbour and never had a penny spent on them.
Estimates were falsified, ships were counted twice in the Weekly
Progress Lists, and ships were put into commission to 'gratify'
political supporters when there was no intention of fitting them
out for active service." [1]

Thus it came about that with Spain allying herself with
France, a Franco-Spanish fleet of sixty-six vessels appeared off
Plymouth, with no finger raised to bar its progress. Not since the

---

[1] *The British Navy in Adversity*, Admiral Sir William James.

days of the Spanish Armada had England appeared to stand
in greater peril. Dropping anchor in Cawsand Bay, however,
the armament seemed as little inclined for action as the crepitant
Sir Charles Hardy and the handful of British warships hovering
circumspectly on the horizon.

As it transpired, the Spaniards had been so late at their
rendezvous that the Gallic fleet had become weakened by
disease and shortness of provisions to that degree that it was
forced to put about; leaving the 50,000 'invasion' troops
waiting at Havre with no other course than to retrace their
steps. "For some days past", wrote the Commissioner at Plymouth, "I put the question to myself—shall I, Paul Durry, or
Jack D'Orvilliers, set fire to the dockyard?"[1] Fortunately, the
question was never put to the issue.

With a state of Armed Neutrality declared by Russia, Denmark, Prussia, the Emperor, and Sweden, it was clear that
policy would presently range the Dutch on the side of England's
enemies. Meanwhile, a Hollander merchant fleet, escorted by a
number of warships under Admiral Byland, was hailed by
Commodore Fielding off Portland, and the request to examine
the merchantmen thrown out in the usual way. Permission
being refused, Fielding sent off his boats, which were immediately fired on by the Dutch. The Commodore's response was
to put a shot across the Hollander Admiral's bows, and Byland
replied with a broadside. The British crews returned the
compliment with every gun that could be brought to bear; and
without more ado the Dutchman hauled down his Colours. All
the merchant craft carrying naval stores were then taken into
possession; Byland accompanying them as far as Spithead
before slinking off without further word of protest or explanation.

Holland's actual declaration of war, while scarcely involving
the battle fleet in home waters, gave a great impetus to privateering. A swarm of corsairs made the narrow seas their happy
hunting ground; and the Falmouth and Southampton packets
—stout 200-ton brigs, whose orders were to flee if they could,
fight if they had to, and sink their mails if in imminent danger
of capture—had many stern chases. But when it came to running out the guns, they invariably gave as good as they got.

[1] Sandwich Papers, III, 67.

The French privateer Captain Leveillé, in the *Vengeance*, did not baulk, indeed, at attacking the transport *Coldstream* when in the act of taking out a body of 75 soldiers as reinforcements for the Fleet. Manœuvring so as to position himself between the land and the prey he had marked down, Leveillé wasted no time in an exchange of gunfire, but laid his opponent aboard. Lashing the *Coldstream's* bowsprit to his own rigging, he gave the word for his swivels to sweep the other vessel's deck with small shot, aimed at the huddle of seamen and redcoats crowding under the poop. Before the smoke of the discharge had cleared, the privateersmen swarmed over the *Coldstream's* bulwarks and fell on their opponents, slashing out right and left. The fight lasted a bare quarter of an hour before the English Colours were struck, with casualties out of all proportion to the duration of the struggle.[1]

With France a declared belligerent, Franklin was at full liberty openly to add his privateers to those already in operation in the narrow seas. Captain Lambert Wickes, after a meteoric career in which he captured a number of vessels including the King's packet *Swallow*, out of Falmouth for Lisbon, had perished when his ship the *Reprisal* had been wrecked on the coast of Newfoundland. Conyngham and another privateer, Captain William Hodge, were still available, however; and there were other willing tools for the master-hand to manipulate. So it was not long before Franklin, in the name of the American Congress, had commissioned the 120-ton, 16-gun cutter, the *Black Prince*[2]—owned by John and Charles Torris of Dunkirk—with a crew made up of erstwhile smugglers, for the most part hailing from Ireland. Although effective control was in the hands of the owlers' leader, Luke Ryan, discretion prompted the appointment of the Boston ship-master Stephen Marchant to the ostensible command.

On her first course in the English Channel the privateer snapped up a Portuguese brig and a Danish craft, which were taken into Calais. To Ryan's intense disgust, however, the local Admiralty Court ruled that neither vessel was legitimate prize, and ordered their release.

---

[1] Ducéré, *op. cit.*
[2] As the *Friendship* the craft had previously been engaged in smuggling ventures to the Irish coast.

No better fortune attended the *Black Prince*'s second venture, when she overhauled a Dutch West Indiaman armed with enough heavy metal to have blown the privateer out of the water had she not sheered off with a great air of minding her own business. A brush with one of the cutters guarding a convoy of coasters proved the quality of the *Black Prince*'s guns; and proceeding down Channel she took her first prize—the brig *Blessing*—under the lee of Land's End. In quick succession the *Liberty*, the *Sally*, the *Hampton*, the sloop *Elizabeth*, the *Three Sisters*, and the *Orange Tree*, were added to the initial capture, and an eighth prize in the shape of the brig *Goodwill* rounded off an exceedingly profitable four-and-twenty hours.

But it is one thing to take prizes, and quite another to get them safely into port; and owing to the vigilance of Captain George Farmer in command of the frigate *Quebec*, six of Ryan's captures were re-taken and carried into Guernsey, together with their prize crews.

In commissioning the *Black Prince* Franklin had been imbued with the humanitarian aim of securing as many prisoners as possible, for exchange with the American captives held in the Mill Prison at Plymouth and the Forton Detention Barracks at Portsmouth. But the hold of the *Black Prince* had capacity for no more than thirty-five to forty; any men taken in excess of this number being permitted to give sea-paroles, or ransom themselves by signing a bill drawn in favour of John Torris of Dunkirk. With the *Quebec* having taken the twenty-one men forming the prize crews put aboard his captures by Ryan, the cause which Franklin had so much at heart was not appreciably advanced; while Ryan's difficulty in finding replacements to man the *Black Prince* was far from inconsiderable.

Prospects were sufficiently encouraging, however, for the privateer to be re-graved for another cruise. This opened auspiciously with the capture of two brigs and a sloop, so close inshore off the Land's End that the exploit was witnessed from the cliffs. In all, thirteen vessels were taken, most of them being ransomed; and the *Black Prince* returned to Morlaix accompanied solely by the valuable prize *Dublin Trader*, and with no more than eleven prisoners and eleven ransomers between hatches.

It was not a great harvest; but Franklin, learning something of the consternation the operations of his lone wolf had caused along the Cornish littoral, in due course commissioned the *Black Princess* and the *Fearnot* to carry on the work begun by Ryan. For a time their *chevauchées* were the cause of serious loss, a total of 114 British vessels of all descriptions being burned, scuttled, ransomed, or sent in to Gallic ports as prizes. It was only the flagrant violation of neutral vessels and the legalistic wrangle over Franklin's right to issue American commissions to French-owned privateers, that put a period to activities which had called the Admiralty's defensive measures into considerable contempt, caused indignant consternation among the shipowners, and sent marine insurance rates soaring.

* * *

Criticism of inadequate defence measures in the narrow seas was not without some justification. But the relief of beleaguered Gibraltar, first by Rodney and later by Darby, were feats that combined admirable organisation at the Channel's ports of departure with a dogged determination to get through on the part of the respective Admirals concerned. With equal resolution, Hyde Parker had warded off an attack by the Dutch on a flotilla of over 100 merchantmen making for the Island base with naval stores from the Baltic.

Many of the seamen engaged in these activities were East India Company men, the Court of Directors having placed 6,000 of their employees at the Navy's disposal, together with the three 74-gun vessels *Bombay Castle*, *Ganges* and *Carnatic*.

In 1781, at one time and another, there were several inconclusive encounters between De Grasse, Rodney, and Kempenfelt. The last-named—one of the keenest and most thoughtful men to devote his life to the Service—sailed from Plymouth to prevent the junction of strong elements from the hostile fleets, but found himself so grossly outnumbered that he dared not risk bringing on a general action. He chose rather to lie in wait to cut off the convoy for which the French were furnishing the escort. As the enemy van and centre stood on serenely, he bore up in line of battle ahead, engaging the rear with his van and cutting off fifteen sail of merchantmen, and so punishing the four battleships that had been detailed for their protection that they sank with the majority of their crews. Despite the harassing tactics of the French frigates that had hastened to the scene, and a strong head wind, he brought his prizes safely into Plymouth; turning 1,000 prisoners over to the guardships.

In one of Rodney's clashes with De Grasse, so fiercely was the action fought that the British Admiral only just succeeded in making Cawsand Bay in his sinking battleship. In the long run, however, Rodney had the satisfaction of soundly thrashing his opponents, capturing the proud *Ville de Paris* and his old anta-gonist himself.

Good work was also done, especially against the gadfly privateers, by Captain Edward Thompson. Like his con-temporary, 'Gentleman Johnny' Burgoyne, Thompson was something of a dramatist; and when his refurbished version of Shadwell's *Fair Quaker of Deal* was staged at Plymouth the men of his devoted crew stormed the gallery, demanding to be ad-mitted without charge, since they claimed that they were "welcome to anything that belonged to their Captain". Thompson, hearing the hub-bub, gave orders for the whole crew to be admitted at his personal charge. Learning of this and espying their popular Captain in the stage box, the men cheered him again and again, winding up with a spirited rendering of *The Topsail Shivers in the Wind*, a ditty that Thompson himself had composed and taught them. Whereafter, not a single man was late in returning from shore leave; for Thompson's *Hyaena* was one of the 'happy ships' that furnished the exception to the general rule, his ship's company signing on with him again and again.

The whole Service suffered a grievous blow with the loss of the *Royal George*, built in 1756 and regarded in her heyday as "the paragon of beauty and the *ne plus ultra* of perfection in the science of marine architecture". Lying at Spithead, her water-cock was found to be defective, and it was necessary to heel the ship in order to carry out the needful repairs. To do this the guns on the port side were run out and those on the starboard side brought right in amidships. All her lower ports were open, and the breeze had whipped up one of those short, steep seas so typical of the locality. In the circumstances the list was too great for safety, but before any steps could be taken to right the craft she heeled suddenly, bringing the full weight of her guns against the lee side. The strain was too much for her time-worn timbers and a great part of her side fell out bodily. She sank with

amazing rapidity, taking down with her some 800 souls—for as
was customary in port, "there were a great many women
aboard." With the rest perished Rear-Admiral Richard Kempenfelt. He left the legacy of an imperishable memory, and a
new Signal Book which "was not hieroglyphics but language;
not puzzles, but speech".[1]

It was with Kempenfelt's new Signal Book in hand that
'Black Dick' Howe outwitted the French and Spaniards once
more to re-victual and reinforce hard-pressed Gibraltar, in the
October of 1782.

Save in very rare circumstances, success at sea—even on the
scale of Rodney's victory over De Grasse in the battle of 'the
Saints'—cannot ensure the defeat of an opponent unless there
is corresponding achievement on the part of the land forces,
whose invariable task it is to drive the stiff bolt of victory home
in its socket.

With the Earl of Cornwallis's surrender at Yorktown, therefore, the time had come for the Americans to counter the risk of
exchanging rejected British suzerainty for outright Gallic hegemony,[2] by encouraging suggestions for a negotiated settlement
with the Court of St. James.

The outcome was the Peace of Paris, signed in the January
of 1783; an important clause in which ensured that no discrimination would operate against 'natural'—i.e. non-manu-
factured—goods from the United States which were to be
admitted to British ports on payment of similar duties to those
charged on wares imported from the remaining British possessions in America.

Seven years of war had, of course, severely strained British
financial resources. Despite swingeing taxation—an increase of
5 per cent on all former duties, upon all goods imported and
exported, an additional £8 8s. a tun on French and £4 4s. on
all other wines, which brought the total dues to £38 10s. and
£18 10s. respectively; a further 4d. tax on a pound of tobacco
and 8d. on a pound of snuff; and with Excise duties on perry and

[1] Callender, op. cit.
[2] So early as the Spring of 1777 the French Court was debating a scheme
for Washington's ultimate supersession by the crafty, feverishly ambitious
Comte de Broglie. As Viceroy for His Most Christian Majesty Louis XVI,
Broglie was to rule the whole of North America from the Atlantic to the
Pacific coasts, and including a Canada finally purged of the British.

cider raised to 16s. 8d. a hogshead—the National Debt had climbed to £240,000,000. Although wages had risen, so had the cost of living. Bread, having soared to 1s. 5d. a pound loaf, had settled at 1s. ¾d.; the price of meat ranged from 3½d. to 5d. a pound [1]; while so deleterious was the traffic in counterfeit tea— made up of the leaves of sloe, elder and ash, or the exhausted leaves from the teapot re-crisped on hot plates and recoloured with a solution of copper—that a fine of £5 was imposed on anyone found in possession of a pound's weight of the evil stuff. [2]

On the other hand, trade returns, which in 1781 had shown an adverse balance of £1,390,567, by the end of 1783 had swung back to a favourable balance of £1,559,259.

The expansion of empire in the North American continent had summarily been halted. But wealth came pouring in across the narrow seas with every ship that wore 'John Company's' flag; while in India itself the skill and resource of Warren Hastings was carving out another Empire to take the place of the lost domains that folly and misunderstanding had so wilfully forgone.

[1] *Six Centuries of Work and Wages*, J. E. Thorold Rogers.
[2] Over 78,000 lb. of this counterfeit tea changed hands in a twelvemonth.

CHAPTER XVIII

The Wooden Walls

"Upon the shivering and breaking of a great State
and Empire you may be sure to have war."

FRANCIS BACON

BRITAIN's extraordinary quality of resilience has rarely been more vigorously in evidence than throughout the years immediately following the conclusion of the pact signed at Versailles in 1783.

It was generally, if ruefully, acknowledged that America had been lost because Britain's sea-power had been unequal to the task laid upon it. The fact was inescapable that on more than one occasion her Naval leaders had suffered defeat and humiliation at the hands of enemies who "had overborne them on the field they called their own—the Sea"[1]; although in the peace treaty with Holland, England's dominance in the Channel was specifically acknowledged. So far as the stripling United States were concerned, while regret was inevitable for the loss of an embryo empire, the more imaginative—and philosophical—could derive a certain wry comfort from the consideration that the conflict between the colonial peoples and the Motherland had, in its way, been a tribute to the thoroughness with which the offspring had been imbued with the parental spirit of liberty.

So, irrational as it might be, the country's mood was buoyant and optimistic. If 'John Company'—with £923,000 owing to the Customs—was distinctly in the doldrums and forced to borrow from the Government, open trade with North America was reviving; and since British merchandise had no longer to seek the protection of a neutral flag, there was a boom in ship-building. Small industries were springing up, heavy industry

[1] *The Influence of Sea Power on the French Revolution and Empire*, Captain A. T. Mahan, U.S. Navy.

expanding. In 1782, for example, there had been 194 cotton mills in operation. Five years later the total had risen to 543. Raw cotton had originally come from Demerara, Brazil and the Indies, but by 1791 America was supplying all British needs.

To encourage the fishing industry an annual bounty—to run for seven years—was paid on all decked vessels of 15 tons burden and over, built in native shipyards after January 1st, 1780, in return for the regular landing of four barrels of fish for every ton of burden. By 1786 a limited treaty of trade and navigation had been concluded with France; although a whole range of British goods—particularly woollens—continued for some time to be denied entry into Gallic ports. It was only when the duty on French wines was lowered to the scale charged on those from Portugal,[1] that British textiles and other wares were freely admitted on payment of a 12 per cent duty. The embargo on fabrics in which silk was introduced defined the limits within which the youthful Pitt's modest experiment in free trade was allowed to operate.

It was one of the first endeavours of the new Prime Minister to rationalise the welter of obstruction and confusion in which Customs and Excise legislation had long been plunged. The outmoded and vexatious 'Alien's duty' and the 1 per cent additional 'Mediterranean tax' were repealed, denizens and aliens becoming liable for similar charges. With barely a third of the tea consumed in England paying duty, it was no more than elementary wisdom to lower the impost on the leaf so that the best Hyson could be bought at 4s. 11d. a pound, and ordinary Bohea at 1s. 7d.—which represented a reduction of tax from 119 per cent to 12½ per cent on the value of the commodity.

By consolidating the various branches of the Customs,[2] the whole system of inspection and collection was tautened up and simplified; although the shady practices and outright malfeasance of some of the Customs officials themselves remained a cause for grave anxiety.

Even with a reorganised Customs Service, however, the traffic in contraband tea, wines, spirits, tobacco, and other dutiable wares—including bullion—persisted on so colossal a scale as to defraud the Treasury of much of the revenue

---

[1] Thus lowering the impost from £35 14s. 0d. to £17 17s. per tun.
[2] By Act of 23 Geo. III, Stat. I, Cap. 13.

required by the State to meet its obligations; and remedial measures were not easy to devise.

The general Merchant Shipping Acts of 1773 and 1786[1] had not only ensured that all British-owned vessels should be measured according to a standard scale and registered in the owner's name, but made certain that the ship's manifest, signed both by the Master and the Customs officials, should disclose full details of the cargo freighted. Furthermore, the powers of Revenue and Excise officers to seize horses and carts engaged in smuggling were reaffirmed, as was the Act[2] authorising the detention of all vessels, having tea, wines, brandy, or tobacco aboard, found 'hovering' within two leagues of the coast. Another enactment,[3] to deal with owlers who sought to pass themselves off as privateers, had come into operation in 1782; and two years later it was decreed that all "luggers, shallops or wherries . . . built with clench-work,[4] whose length exceeds three feet and a half for every foot in breadth, or carrying above two carriage guns, not exceeding four-pounders, and two muskets for every ten men", should be liable to forfeiture. Any official acting collusively with the owlers was subject to instant dismissal and a fine of £500; a like sum being the penalty for offering a bribe to any representative of the law. As an additional safeguard, it was decreed that East Indiamen should no longer "come up the channels of the Thames", but drop anchor in Long Reach; that no tobacco should be imported in vessels of under 70 tons burden, or in packages of less than 450 lb. dead weight.[5] Since it was calculated that some 13,000 packs of wool were smuggled to the Continent annually, sheep shearing within five miles of the coast was forbidden, save under the supervision of a Revenue officer; and the export of wool—with the exception of an annual 6,600 tods for the Channel Islands' stocking industry—was again strictly forbidden.

Yet even with the search for craft of illegal build or with too many rowlocks, pursued in all creeks, bays, rivers, inlets and builders' yards—a mission the Revenue man of Southampton carried out with particular conscientiousness—smuggling went forward on an ever-increasing scale.

[1] 13 Geo. III, Stat. I, Cap. 64, and 26 Geo. III, Stat. I, Cap. 40.
[2] 19 Geo. III, Stat. I, Cap. 69.   [3] 22 Geo. III, Stat. I, Cap. 21.
[4] i.e. clinker-built.   [5] 25 Geo. III, Stat. I, Cap. 81.

14+

Violence, however, although still frequently resorted to, had been supplemented by cunning; and there was no device too strange for the guileful owler to employ in the hope of hood-winking the sharp eyes of the Revenue men.

Vessels were constructed with false keels, hollowed out to hold contraband; while it was a common practice to rove a rope through the keel by which casks of spirits could be towed under water. Tobacco was rolled up in balls with a clay skin made to look like a potato. Boat fenders were constructed of tightly compressed tobacco with an outer covering of rope. Indifferent brandy, which had been cleared for transhipment to another English haven, would be exchanged at sea for first-class liquor, and then broken out at the port of discharge under the original cocket. Returning colliers—for coal was a regular export—pilot boats and corn ships all trafficked busily in contraband; the mere 1,100 men of the Revenue Service being far too few to cope with their multifarious activities.

Many of the owlers had retained the weapons they had acquired during the war; and so strongly were they armed that William Arnold, the Collector at Cowes, glumly reported, "the Revenue cruisers are not able to contend with them. It is no unusual thing", he continued, "for them to land their goods in open day under the protection of their guns, sometimes in sight of the Revenue cutters, whom they will not suffer to come near, or board them." On occasion, smaller smuggling craft proceeded in convoy under the protection of the larger boats!

The situation was not improved by the shortage of revenue cutters, one of the best of which, the *Swan*—a contract vessel of Cowes, and the forerunner of many later *Swans*—was lost between Hurst and the Needles, during a gale that raged in the mid-November of 1783. With their faster, more heavily armed craft, men such as George Hewson and Richard Combes, or 'Black Jack' Wenham of Hastings, consistently set the forces of law and order at defiance, reaping rich profits with every successful venture. The scope of the owlers' activities can be gauged by a run made at Christchurch, when two large lugsail craft landed tea and spirits whose removal demanded fifty waggons and just under 300 pack ponies. With contraband of this value under hatches, the owlers would fight to the last to resist capture. The 100-ton *Kite* of Folkestone, for example, was sighted in Sandown bay by the Portsmouth Revenue cutter and the Excise cutter from Cowes. Although already two to one, the Preventive men signalled a nearby Naval vessel to bear a hand; and the three craft speedily closed the owler. Taking to their boats, the smugglers put in to Shanklin bay and made good their escape. On boarding the *Kite*, the Revenue officers found three of the crew lying desperately wounded in the fo'c'sle, but no sign of contraband. For the run had been completed on the previous night, after a battle-royal with a Revenue cutter, which had eventually been fought off, having first inflicted casualties so severe that the three men found aboard the owler were handed over to medical care only just in time to save their lives.

Revenue officers who faithfully tried to do their duty were frequently the victims of vile ill-treatment; one particularly zealous individual, on being run to earth, having his tongue cut out and his ears sliced off—one of the latter being nailed to a post outside the local Corn Exchange. As the Collector at Penzance wrathfully summed it up: "The insolence of some of the smuglers (*sic*) and wreckers in this neighbourhood has run to such a height that tho' our officers have from time to time secured severall Hogsheads, it has by force been taken from them [again] and the officers forced to save their lives."[1]

The task confronting the men of the Preventive Service was never easy, and it was at its most frustrating, perhaps, in Sussex. For the political interest of the county was controlled by the Dukes of Newcastle and Richmond; and however notorious their activity as owlers, it would never have done to commit any of the ducal supporters to prison or the plantations!

Such were the consequences of a fiscal system whose exorbitant exactions Adam Smith and other contemporary economists never ceased to condemn.

*   *   *

The most notable feature of the post-war scene was the steady advance of Russia both in the Baltic and the Black Sea. Indeed, it was an open question whether the Muscovites might not come to vie with France and Austria for influence on the Scheldt.

The whole situation in Holland and the Low Countries

[1] Treasury Books,

underwent violent metamorphosis, however, with the political upheaval in France which, from a doctrinaire revolution fomented by a handful of pettifogging provincial lawyers, swiftly developed into an orgy of malicious class-persecution and indiscriminate blood-letting. With the almost rapturous instability by which the French have invariably been characterised, "several million savages impelled into action by a few thousand muddled thinkers" [1] proceeded to demonstrate with what astounding comprehensiveness they could organise disorganisation.

With the judicial murder of Louis XVI the remaining European monarchs proceeded to close their ranks against a rabid assault on the established order and everything that time had deemed worthy of survival. Austria was the first to take up arms, to be followed closely by Prussia; although a shortsighted economy had so fecklessly pared the British military establishment that with hostilities in train on the French border, a mere 1,800 of all ranks was the best contribution that Pitt's Administration could make to the armies of the 1st Coalition.

Fortunately, the Royal Navy was in a good deal better case; for although the sums allocated to the Fleet and its shore establishments had been far from extravagant, under Pitt's stern eye they had been honestly and judiciously laid out. Moreover, the Navy Yards had not been affected by the disastrous fire that broke out on the boat-builder's premises at Cockhill in Radcliff, which spread to some of 'John Company's' nearby premises, and ultimately burned down many wharves and not far short of 500 houses.

In general the Navy dockyards were well stocked, and their accommodation had been enlarged. The Admiralty Lists showed a total of 366 vessels available for service—including seven first-rates—with an aggregate of 391,743 tons; and manned by 45,000 Officers, seamen and Marines. The trouble was that wastage in the Navy still presented an almost insoluble problem. The life of the man-o'-wars-man was "poor, nasty, brutish and short". As Nelson himself was constrained to confess, "the seaman is finished at forty-five, double-ruptured, raw with scurvy, and racked with agonising pains after each meal"; and the demand for replacements was unending.

[1] *La Révolution*, Henri Hippolyte Adolphe Taine.

Immediate efforts were made to build up on the hard core of reliable professionals, and a proclamation recalled all seamen in foreign service [1] and forbade further engagements under an alien flag. The customary bounties were offered by the Admiralty, and the additional premiums found by London and the big cities, having started at sums ranging from two to ten guineas, as the war progressed reached as high as thirty guineas for a thoroughly experienced seaman. Even so, it was speedily found necessary to pass the Quota Act,[2] by which the several shires and counties of England and Wales were required to contribute a definite number of men proportionate to their respective populations—from Kent's 440 to Radnorshire's modest 26.[3] With Howe, Jervis, Hood, Duncan, Collingwood, Saumarez and Nelson, there was no dearth of war-tested leaders; although the quality of some of the Officers of lesser note left a good deal to be desired. Neither had jobbery been entirely banished, when Lord Rodney could ensure the promotion of his son John from the rank of Midshipman to that of Post-Captain in one month and four days! All in all, however, it was an experienced naval force, if inclined to conservatism in its methods.

It was a very different story with the Gallic Navy, hitherto the especial preserve of the French nobility. For under the conditions of snarling, blood-thirsty insubordination bred by the revolution, the wholesale dismissal or obscene slaughter of many of the distinguished veterans of the war years soon denuded the Fleet of three-quarters of its old corps of Officers. Such of the more ductile of them as were prepared to try and do their duty amidst the chaos brought about by the crews' aggressive demands for complete egalitarianism, were supplemented by promoted merchant skippers entirely unversed in the principles of naval warfare, and equally at the mercy of the Lower Deck soviets established in every ship.

If there is one thing that cannot be run by committee it is a man-of-war. So with the Fleet reduced to impotence by want of discipline and skilled direction, and with the flow of naval

[1] The Russian Navy had secured the temporary services of a number of Scottish Officers and other foreigners, including the celebrated John Paul Jones, erstwhile privateersman in the American service.
[2] 35 Geo. III, Stat. I, Cap. 5.
[3] On April 28th, 1795, the Act was extended to Scotland.

stores from the Baltic dammed up by the vigilance of the British warships in the Channel, Gallic activities at sea were reduced to industrious commerce raiding by a swarm of remarkably daring and successful privateers. The Admiralty sought to equalise matters by the liberal grant of Letters of Marque. Between 1793 and 1815 some 10,000 of these warrants were issued; and although over that selfsame period the British lost some 11,000 craft to the enemy sea-rovers, while making no more than 1,000 captures, in the process the French mercantile marine was swept from the face of the waters. So numerous were the Island vessels engaged in commerce, indeed, that according to Mahan's estimate, the loss inflicted by enemy privateers "did not exceed two and a half per cent, and probably fell below two per cent of the total volume of British trade".[1]

The British privateers were supported by a number of frigates, of which the *Diamond* was amongst the most notable. For her Commanding Officer was the redoubtable Sir William Sidney Smith, who had already distinguished himself during the British occupation of Toulon. In the Channel he was equally prepared to reconnoitre Brest harbour with his vessel very flimsily disguised, or tackle, single-handed, a couple of enemy warships sheltering under the fortress guns of La Hogue. For a year and more he ran a very brisk course up and down the narrow seas, until, having captured a privateer off Havre, a strong influx of the tide carried the *Diamond* and her prize far up the Seine; where the Britishers were made captive after a bitter struggle against ever-increasing odds.

In Sidney Smith, however, the French had caught a Tartar. It is, indeed, very possible that his immediate gaolers were little less delighted than their prisoner himself when—at the third attempt—he succeeded in making good his escape—to thwart Napoleon Bonaparte in front of Acre and, in so doing, give world history an entirely new direction.

In contrast to the inanition of the Gallic Navy, the Republican forces in Holland and the Low Countries experienced no difficulty in hustling back the heterogeneous armies of the 1st Coalition and throwing them into inextricable confusion. For they were made up of Austrians who "never opened a

---

[1] Mahan, *op. cit.*, Vol. II, p. 206.

despatch until they had emptied the bottle", Prussians less concerned with the task in hand than with their share in the imminent partition of Poland, and a handful of British whose activities were completely stultified by the blundering interference of perhaps the most cretinous bungler ever to disgrace the office of Minister for War.[1]

With the Coalition obviously disintegrating, the British were forced to retreat through Hanover and Holland, in a bitter winter of snow and ice; which permitted the French Hussar Colonel, Louis Joseph Lahure, to capture a fleet of store ships, frozen up in the neighbourhood of the Texel, with a mixed force of Cavalry and *Chasseurs Tirailleurs*. From Bremen the remnants of the British Expeditionary Force—including the youthful Arthur Wellesley—were borne away to safety by the ubiquitous vessels of the Royal Navy.

The command of the narrow seas had devolved on Lord Howe, a veteran of the War of Independence, a man of proven worth and ability, but getting on in years and inclined to be set in his ways. His primary task was to keep open the trade routes through the Channel's Western approaches. In discharging this responsibility Howe tended to keep his forces too close to his Portsmouth base. For in the unlikely—but still possible—event of the French battle-fleet emerging from its harbours, Torbay or, worse still, Spithead, were too remote, with the prevailing wind, to permit of a speedy concentration of the heavy line-of-battle ships far enough to the westward. Instead of being challenged instantly, the enemy would have to be hunted for, and well might prove dangerously elusive. Matters were not bettered with the institution of Roebuck's visual telegraph linking, by a series of relay stations, firstly London and Deal, and then London and Portsmouth. For the tendency was for Whitehall to pin the Admiral-Commanding to the place where he could be communicated with at the maximum of contemporary speed. And the well-intentioned but rarely well-informed interference by higher authority with the decisions of the experienced man on the spot is more often attended by disaster than success.

---

[1] Henry Dundas, a Scottish lawyer. Ultimately transferred to the Admiralty, he was impeached for malversation of public funds, and disappeared—all too belatedly—from the political scene.

The communications system, as such, was considerably amplified by the establishment, in 1795, of the first Coast Signalling Stations. Extending ultimately to Plymouth, these installations furnished a valuable means of passing intelligence along the whole of the Channel coastline.[1]

A constant responsibility with the warships in the narrow seas was the 'rummaging' of neutral vessels for contraband of war. Much merchandise from the French West Indian islands was freighted in neutral craft, many of them flying the Stars and Stripes. Between the November of 1793 and the March of 1794 some 600 American vessels with contraband of war between hatches were brought into the Channel ports; and it was only the desire to avoid a rupture with the United States which led to a certain relaxation of the Right of Search and Confiscation. To avoid the delay involved in a port search, many craft were 'rummaged' at sea, being given a certificate of clearance if found to be laden with goods which did not come in any of the prohibited categories.[2]

The first sally of the French battle-fleet was occasioned by the need to protect an incoming convoy of 130 merchant craft laden with desperately needed grain. Howe, who had been reluctant to expose his heavy ships to the tempestuous weather by blockading the enemy fleet in its harbours, hurried out to seek it in the open waters. His hope was to engage and destroy the hostile warships while the grain convoy was rounded up by a small force under Admiral Montague. The outcome was a four days' running fight with Villaret-Joyeuse's forces, in which Howe signalised "the Glorious 1st of June" by inflicting a good deal more punishment than he received. But the vital convoy made port in perfect safety. It was generally agreed that 'Black Dick' had fought the enemy battle-fleet to a standstill with his usual gallantry. But perhaps the last word on the value of his activities was uttered by the Isle of Wight Customs official, William Arnold, when he observed, "Lord Howe was unlucky in not capturing all the French fleet, and he is rather

[1] The Signal Stations at Brixham (Torbay) and New Romney (East Bay, Dungeness) had standing orders to report all arrivals and departures of shipping direct to the Admiralty, by means of the telegraph as well as by daily letter.

[2] These certificates were similar to the 'Navicerts' utilised in the wars of 1914–18 and 1939–45.

unpopular about it, tho' I believe he did all he could to take them.[1] But they had the heels of him, and John Bull always judges by consequences."

From Howe's June engagement till the end of 1796 naval interest centred in the Mediterranean. But with Spain forced into unwilling alliance with France, for lack of proper bases, Britain's hold on the waters east of Gibraltar was inevitably paralysed. With the accession of strength given it by possession of the Dutch and Spanish armaments, triumphant Jacobinism determined on a triple assault on its most implacable enemy. Like many desperate men before and since, the Gallic leaders were convinced that superiority of numbers would more than atone for lack of experience. The menace—perhaps the most terrible by which the country had ever been confronted—was lifted when, on February 14th, 1797, Sir John Jervis tore the Spanish wing of the assault to shreds at the battle of Cape St. Vincent.

"A victory is very essential to England at this moment," he had murmured to himself, as his well-tried fleet had closed the enemy. And victory in generous measure had been the outcome of the encounter; with Nelson defying the rigid conventions of the *Fighting Instructions* by swinging out of the line to precipitate himself across the path of seven of the would-be fugitives.

Few victories have been more timely than that of 'Old Jarvie's Valentine'.[2] For amongst other things, it helped to attune men's minds to the unprejudiced consideration of the rights and wrongs of the mutiny in the ships assembled at Spithead.

'The Breeze at Spithead' did not spring up without warning. It had long been recognised that the men had a number of very real and legitimate grievances; and from time to time there had been isolated outbreaks—such as that in the *Invincible* in 1780, and more recently in the *Culloden*[3]—which should have embodied their own warning. The extremely orderly 'sit-down-strike' at Spithead observed exemplary discipline; but the

---

[1] i.e. the grain convoy.

[2] Jervis was created Earl of St. Vincent; Nelson promoted from Commodore to Rear-Admiral, and created a Knight of the Bath.

[3] And see *ante*, p. 376. Captain Talbot's frigate *Eurydice* did not join in the mutiny at Spithead, but *Eurydice* was a particularly 'happy ship'.

14*

perfectly respectful refusal to cast off moorings—"unless the enemy were known to be at sea"—was based on a firm demand for prompt payment, an increase in wages to offset the depreciation in the value of money,[1] and a definite improvement in the scale and quality of victualling. In the first instance, however, the Admiralty's grudging concessions aroused so much resentment and distrust that it called for the personal intervention of the tremendously popular 'Black Dick' to persuade the men to return to their duty.

With a semi-literate ringleader in the person of Richard Parker, the subsequent mutiny at the Nore took on much more of a political complexion. It was only with the ships moored at Thames-mouth and with those that joined up with them from the fleet under Duncan, that had been blockading the Dutch, that the seeds of revolution which had turned France into a nightmare of anarchy, bid fair to germinate. "Parker and his fellow-ruffians were the *sans-culottes* of the Fleet",[2] and stern measures had to be adopted to bring their miserable dupes to their senses. The ten frigates moored in the Lower Hope, and manned by employees of Trinity House, stood by to frustrate any attempt by Parker and his associates to take the Nore squadrons over to the enemy. As an additional precaution, the Corporation removed the seamarks in the estuary; while the lightship newly moored at North Sand Head on the Goodwins temporarily doused its beam.

Duncan's comment that "the quota men have been at the bottom of this," goes far to explain the genesis of the 'Floating Republic' which collapsed like a pricked bubble when Parker and twenty-nine of his closest supporters were swung from the yardarm. But the spirit of insubordination undoubtedly lingered on in the Channel Fleet until St. Vincent, in 1800, brought a little of his 'Mediterranean discipline' to it and stamped it out once and for all. Yet such is the sailor's paradoxical nature that even at the mutiny's height the King's birthday had been celebrated with the customary salute and

---

[1] Pitt's subsidies to his allies had so drained away the country's gold reserves that paper money had come into circulation in 1797, with the inevitable consequences.

[2] Callender, *op. cit.* Parker was a typical 'sea-lawyer', who had been imprisoned for debt after his discharge from the Navy as a Midshipman.

expressions of loyalty; while at Portsmouth all the vessels had voluntarily been 'dressed overall' to impress the visiting Prince of Württemberg! "Who but Englishmen would have made a tour of State to show a foreign visitor their fleet in full mutiny? Or who but English sailors in mutiny would have turned out to salute the touring dignitaries?"[1]

The Spanish prong of the Gallic naval offensive having been put out of action by 'Old Jarvie's Valentine', it was left to Admiral Duncan, at the battle of Camperdown, to deal as faithfully with the Dutch. The Hollanders had lost the opportunity to catch Duncan at a disadvantage during the time of the Nore mutiny; and when de Winter did make his appearance the Scotsman fell upon him with such fury that the ensuing *mêlée* developed into one of the fiercest actions ever fought. Duncan, with no more than a skeleton force of doubtful loyalty, had ably sustained the blockade of the Dutch harbours; and his capture of two-thirds of de Winter's fleet was a fitting end to the first round of the grim struggle against Revolutionary France.

Jacobin armies might triumph wherever they fought, but at sea the British Navy reigned supreme.

*   *   *

In the hopes of reanimating the Coalition, Nelson was sent to the Mediterranean to lend what aid he could to the Austrians; whose appetite for subsidies had again prevailed over a natural disposition to temporise rather than fight. Fortunately, when it came to bolstering up shaky allies, Britain, as the depot for the whole of anti-Jacobin Europe, could boast a commerce that had rarely been more flourishing. In any case, subsidies to allies mostly came home to roost in the form of purchase-money for English goods. Furthermore, being in the position entirely to prohibit the direct admission of all tropical products to the Continent, the re-exportation of them, together with her native wares, became the prime source of the country's staggering prosperity. For that matter, so steady a stream of British merchandise found its way surreptitiously into France that the Directory desperately, but vainly, ordered the seizure of all

[1] *The Floating Republic*, G. E. Mainwaring and B. Dobrée. Württemberg was in England to marry the Princess Royal, and visited Portsmouth to receive the freedom of the City.

wares coming from across the narrow seas. As under the elder Pitt, "Commerce was united to and made to grow by war."[1] American wares, imported annually to the value of $67,000,000, were invariably given an escort for the last lap of the inward passage; and a Convoy Act laid it down that any British Master sailing unescorted without official permission rendered himself liable to a fine up to £1,500, and the loss of his insurance policies. Customs officials were under orders to refuse clearance to any vessels—other than coasters and the well-armed craft of the Hudson's Bay and East India Companies—until the Master had given bail not to sail save in convoy. Once the system was in full operation, insurance rates on many cargoes dropped to 6d. a ton.

With all the busy commerce that characterised Thames-side and the Channel ports, petty theft assumed such proportions that the Act of 1762, requiring all bum-boats to be registered, and rendering all those convicted of trafficking in stolen goods liable to transportation, was quite inadequate to deal with the scourge. Amongst the most inveterate pilferers were the ships' mates, who vigorously asserted their right to "the sweepings of the hold"—i.e. to such part of the cargo as had dropped out of its packaging; and they saw to it that there was no lack of 'sweepings'! In addition to the loss occasioned by this nefarious practice, it was estimated that goods to the value of £460,000 were annually made away with by the swarming wharf-rats.[2]

To cope with a situation that was rapidly getting out of hand a Marine Police Force was instituted in the July of 1798, with Headquarters at Wapping New Stairs. With a judicial department, surveyors, watermen and marine guards, the Service also employed 820 approved 'lumpers' for discharging vessels under the superintendence of police officers and 80 sworn-in 'master-lumpers'. In addition, there were 220 ships' constables, paid by the owners of the vessels employing them; as were the official 'lumpers'. In all, a force of 1,200 waged a progressively successful war with the 11,000 petty thieves whose depredations had hitherto occasioned an annual loss to the Customs revenue alone of close on £50,000.

---

[1] Mahan, *op. cit.*

[2] *Treatise on the Commerce and Police of the River Thames*, J. Colquhoun. Losses of tackle, apparel and stores from vessels lying in the Thames basin came to another £45,000 a year.

Something of the busy traffic passing to and fro across the narrow seas must have been observed by Napoleon Bonaparte when, in company with Kléber and Desaix, he made a survey of the French Channel coast to gauge the possibilities of staging a full-scale invasion of the Island-Kingdom. The prospects were sufficiently discouraging to turn his thoughts to easier conquests in the East. But his subjugation of Egypt was stultified by Nelson's shattering victory in the battle of the Nile; while the urge to follow in the footsteps of Alexander the Great and achieve hegemony in the "fabulous Ind" was permanently thwarted by Ahmed Djezzer Pasha, Governor of Acre, and his coadjutors, the *émigré* Engineer Officer, Phélippeaux, and the ubiquitous Sidney Smith.

The shot-torn prizes from Nelson's victory in Aboukir Bay had scarcely come to their moorings in Plymouth harbour before it became apparent that the descent of an Anglo-Russian force on Holland had achieved a good deal less than had been expected. It was true that the remnants of the Dutch Navy had been captured. But the land forces had withdrawn under a convention that brought the Muscovite *Cornichons*[1] to lap up the oil in the Channel havens' street lamps as though it were vintage wine. Their performance in Holland had badly betrayed their allies, and in considerable disgrace they were hustled back to their Motherland. Pitt's policy of "nibbling at the rind of France"—a typical politician's half-measure—had scarcely paid dividends.

In Central Europe, however, the armies of the Republic were themselves suffering serious setback; and the whole of France was in a turmoil of disorder. The *coup d'état* of *Brumaire 18* which elevated Napoleon to the rank of First Consul, was followed by peace feelers which, after the defection of Russia, the defeat of Austria, the Armed Neutrality proclaimed by the Northern Powers, and the stinging *riposte* by the British Navy at Copenhagen, led to the Peace of Amiens—a peace, in Sheridan's imperishable phrase, "which every man ought to be glad of, but no man can be proud of".

*　　　*　　　*

[1] The Russians were so dubbed by the French, since in their faded green greatcoats they looked uncommonly like pickled gherkins.

It was George III, whose occasional flashes of wisdom were even more startling than his more frequent departures into dementia, who described the pact signed in the March of 1802 as "an experimental peace, nothing more". Unfortunately, his Ministers took it *au grand sérieux*, and proceeded to dismantle the whole apparatus of defence with criminal precipitancy. The Regular Army was reduced to little more than a corporal's guard, the Auxiliary Forces largely disbanded. Nor did the dangerous run-down halt there. From his post in Whitehall Lord St. Vincent had brought the Fleet to an admirable state of discipline, and effected many striking and useful reforms in the Augean stable of the Navy yards. But, sharing the myopic belief that the Peace had really put an end to Napoleonic ambitions, he had gone on to discharge 40,000 hardy, experienced seamen, cut his resources in line-of-battle ships by half, disband the Sea Fencibles, and 'put on the beach' a large number of trustworthy, thoroughly battle-tested Officers.[1]

It is true that the National Debt stood at £530,000,000; that there had been serious resentment when Pitt had increased the duties on sugar and coffee, extended the scope of the Stamp duty, and re-introduced in more stringent form the Income Tax first devised in 1435. But with a favourable trade balance of £12,500,000 to set against the First Consul's inadvertent admission that France had "entirely lost its commerce and in a large degree had exhausted its pecuniary resources", England should certainly have been better prepared, both at sea and on the land, when the inevitable rupture came and the two countries once more found themselves at war.

One of the most serious consequences of the fatuous belief in Napoleon's protestations of peace was, that it left him in possession of the southern half of the Rhine delta. With Antwerp "a dagger pointing straight at England's heart",[2] the temptation to bring *perfide Albion* to utter subjection by invasion and conquest was not to be resisted. What the brilliant field-commander initially refused to recognise was that without dominion over the Channel and its Western approaches the

---

[1] Napoleon had retained half a million men under arms, a total which could be doubled in a matter of weeks.

[2] At St. Helena the Emperor confessed that his fate would have been very different could he have brought himself to leave Antwerp alone.

transportation of the necessary troops could never be a practical proposition.

To confine the enemy ships to their harbours—thereby pinning Napoleon's land forces to a shoreline lapped by waves they had no means of crossing—a fleet, under Nelson, mounted guard over Toulon, while another, under 'Blue-water Billy' Cornwallis, closely blockaded Brest; with detached squadrons at Ferrol and Rochefort. Saumarez lurked by the Channel Islands, and a squadron from Keith's North Sea fleet blocked the Dutch ports, while another kept constant watch and ward in the Downs. As Napoleon's *barraque*, or Advanced Head-quarters, was swiftly assembled on the *Tour d'Odre*, overlooking Boulogne, St. Vincent confidently affirmed, "I don't say they cannot come, I only say they cannot come by sea."

With his Naval Adviser, Admiral Bruix, close at hand, Napoleon—self-created Emperor after May 18th, 1804—was within easy reach of his subordinate commanders, Soult, Davout, Marmont, Lannes, and fiery rufus-headed Michel Ney, and the many cantonments of the *Armée d'Angleterre*. Snugged down everywhere along a line from Brest to Ostend, a force of 190,000 Horse, Foot and Artillery was supported by a horde of auxiliaries and camp followers, including a corps of *Guides Interprètes* and no less than 1,760 *Cantinières*. Parades and inspections, trial embarkations and debarkations in such of the scheduled prames, sloops, gunboats, caiques and pinnaces as had been completed, were varied in the case of Bessières' *vieux grognards* of the Guard, with swimming lessons—"So that some of them will be able to get back, anyway", as the onlookers cynically commented. For month after month the same monotonous routine was sedulously pursued, until everyone wearied even of the novelty of rowing instruction.

For nervy, restless Frenchmen, it was a weary time of waiting, despite the rather jejune concert parties organised for the troops' entertainment by the indefatigable Soult and Marmont.[1] Boulogne, like Calais, was little more than a fishing village, with room for no more than a tithe of the men who sought the sparse amenities offered by its *cafés* and *bistros*; and the inter-minable games of loto and *paire-impaire* very quickly palled.

---

[1] Soult *would* insist on censoring the turns, and succeeded in eliminating the sparkle from most of them.

Even the ready embraces of Magdelaine la Picarde, alias 'Madam Forty-thousand-men', were not for everybody, although she strove to refuse no man in uniform, and even welcomed Eugène Vidocq, once he had exchanged the fustian garb of a police spy for the brave blue jacket of a privateer. Tedious delay was little compensated by the knowledge that the Emperor had already approved the medal, with the mendacious inscription "Struck at London", by which the conquest of England was to be commemorated.

Across the narrow seas British counter-measures had quickly taken shape. The defences of London's river and the Channel coast had been strengthened by the installation of extra floating batteries and the erection of seventy-four Martello towers,[1] thirty feet high and armed with a swivel gun and two howitzers. The Royal Military Canal was cut from Hythe to Rye, completely isolating Romney Marsh; since it was rumoured that the 'Corsican Ogre' was inclined to favour Dungeness as a landing point, and had even landed, in the unlikely guise of a British sailor, to reconnoitre the position in person. Recruiting for the foolishly depleted Regular Army went forward steadily and the Auxiliary Forces were hastily re-embodied. At Shorncliffe Camp John Moore was training a picked body of Riflemen and Light Infantry by methods that were to render both instructor and disciples justly famous. A special 'invasion camp' was assembled at Coxheath, near Maidstone. Warning beacons of a minimum of eight waggon loads of timber with three to four barrels of tar were erected, as night alarm signals, at all suitable points. Orders were given for all windows facing the sea to be obscured at dusk, and for pedestrians' lanterns to be carefully masked once dark had fallen.

Evacuation of the coastal areas, should the necessity arise, was to be under the supervision of the clergy. Cattle were to be driven inland; and a 'scorched earth' policy would account for all ungarnered crops and such consumable stores as might otherwise prove of value to the enemy. To ensure that the roads would not be blocked to military traffic by fleeing refugees, pioneer contingents of from 25 to 70 men, equipped with axes, spades and billhooks, were organised to clear, or obstruct, the

[1] Named after the Corsican fort captured in Mortella (Myrtle) Bay in 1794, and costing £7,000 apiece to erect.

highways as circumstances might dictate. Engineer officers were detailed to supervise the erection of road blocks, *chevaux-de-frize* and abatis, and ensure that the man-traps, landmines, and caltrops were disposed of to best advantage. A special corps of guides stood ready to act as local pathfinders.

Slipping to and fro across the Channel, the owlers blandly trafficked in 'intelligence', which they sold impartially to either side.

In Dover's snug taverns, as seasoned tipplers downed the potent admixture of small beer, brandy, sugar and lemon that went by the name of a 'Sir Clowdisley',[1] rumour was busy with the story of 'Old Boney's' intention to send over a task force on enormous rafts, bristling with cannon and driven by windmills erected on their decks; and with the more nervously inclined the incidence of 'raft weather'—i.e. when the wind blew steadily but gently from the south-east—was the cause of certain irrepressible tinglings of alarm. Another persistent *canard* was summed up in the mocking rhyme:

> For their Officers and baggage in balloons are to come over,
> And Bonaparte drop in his camp just this side of Dover . . .
> A hundred thousand men for him to lose is no more than a trifle,
> He's determined to invade, old England for to rifle.
> Although the Kings of Europe crawl to him for alliance,
> Britannia's sons alone will bid the Corsican defiance.

One preoccupation that the Navy well might have been spared was imposed upon them by the King's inveterate habit of repairing to Weymouth for the sea bathing. It was a predilection which necessitated the presence of a guardian squadron in the bay to ensure that his Majesty's dip in the briny—to the strains of *God Save the King* from an attendant band of musicians —should be enjoyed in perfect security, in the event of any hostile cutting-out party entertaining thoughts of making him their prisoner.

The general situation was not appreciably affected by the arrival in England of the American inventor, Robert Fulton, after his failure to impress Napoleon with the possibilities of his submersible warcraft, the *Nautilus*. It is unquestionable that the 200-ton *Dorothea* was successfully blown up off Walmer roads

---

[1] In commemoration of the Naval hero, Admiral Sir Clowdisley Shovel.

by the American's ingenious device of the torpedo. But official Naval reactions were summed up when 'Old Jarvie' impatiently pronounced, "Pitt is the greatest fool that ever existed, to encourage a mode of war which they who command the seas do not want, and which, if successful, would deprive them of it."

In the circumstances, and from a short-term point of view, that was a verdict not easily to be gainsaid.

In any case it was not to new-fangled contraptions such as torpedoes that people looked to keep "the proud foot of the conqueror" from their native soil. It was to the storm-tossed ships of the blockading fleet, imprisoning the enemy in his ports. Week after week and month after month, year in and year out, they kept their unwinking vigil "come hell and high water". Salt-rimed, with tattered sails, sprung spars and leaking timbers, they hung on until Collingwood, in the aptly-named *Venerable*, was fain to confess, "Our ships are so worn down that they are like post horses at a general election. We have been sailing for the last six months with only a sheet of copper between us and eternity."

On a diet of salt beef, maggoty biscuit and stagnant water, the crews were so cruelly worked that some of the hands became afflicted with ulcers, and had to be landed and cured with vegetables, milk, and "the smell of the earth". Yet as the Naval Préfect at Brest ruefully admitted, "*Les Anglais sont constamment sur nos côtes.*" Mahan was guilty of no exaggeration when he affirmed that it was only "that far-off line of storm-beaten ships, on which the eyes of the Grand Army never looked, . . . which stood between Napoleon and the dominion of the world".

*　　　*　　　*

With Pitt cautiously erecting yet another Coalition, the prevailing deadlock was broken by the escape of the Gallic squadrons from their respective harbours of Rochefort, Cadiz and Toulon, to disappear no man knew whither. But the *Armée d'Angleterre* was already striking its tents to march away and splinter the very foundations of the 3rd Coalition by the shattering victory of Austerlitz; whose thunder almost drowned the echo of the guns which had brought victory—and death—to Nelson, at Trafalgar.

Yet however valorously Napoleon might thrash about Central Europe, piling up victory at Jena and Friedland, coming to an understanding with the Tsar, and threatening to coerce Denmark, the stranglehold of the British blockade was squeezing the life out of an exhausted France. The Emperor's retaliatory stroke was to declare a counter-blockade of the British Isles, and close all Continental markets to British wares. Almost overnight, a legion of port officials sealed off every mainland haven from the Gulf of Finland to the Dardanelles.

Britain's counter-measure took the form of Orders in Council which declared a blockade of all the ports and harbours from which British vessels had been excluded. As a concession to neutrals, they were permitted to carry goods to ports controlled by the Emperor on condition that they first visited a British harbour and there paid the agreed dues for a licence to trade. Napoleon promptly struck back with the Milan decrees, declaring that all vessels plying under a British licence were confiscate to France.

At the same time, privateering was intensified in the hope of wiping out the commerce shuttling to and fro between Britain's overseas possessions and her home ports. The *Sans Souci* of St. Malo, with a crew of 106 men "drawn from the dregs of all nations", effected many profitable captures till she was brought to book by the *Andromache*, which ran her aboard when in the act of pillaging her latest victim. The *Intrépide* sought to evade capture by sailing under false Colours—more often than not American. She was eventually challenged, off the Scillies, by the Revenue cutter *Hind*, and brought to submission after an exceptionally vicious exchange of shot.

There were, of course, periods when, through relaxed vigilance, the French enjoyed an enheartening run of luck; as when a correspondent wrote indignantly to the Admiralty Secretary, John Wilson Croker:

"We had the mortification of seeing two colliers captured the other evening, close under the North Foreland, when not a single cruiser was in sight, except one in Margate Roads. *See if there is not a Lieutenant Leach commanding the 'Cracker' gun-brig, and if that gun-brig is not on the Foreland station. This gentleman, I understand, has a house at Birchington where he usually sleeps, and for this purpose Margate Roads is a very convenient place for his vessel to*

lie in. The Admiral must be remarkably good-natured to grant him this indulgence, so advantageous to the enemy's privateers. [1]

Fortunately, the majority of cruiser captains were both alert and enterprising. The privateer *Le Frontier*, for example, caught a Tartar when she hailed the *Doric*, so far as appearances went a relatively harmless East Indiaman, whose crew appeared so passive that the Frenchman approached prepared for uncontested surrender. The privateer had just ranged alongside when the screens hiding the swivel guns went down with a crash, and a body of Marines leaped from concealment to add their musketry to such a blast of fire across *Le Frontier*'s deck that her Captain could not haul down his Colours too expeditiously.

This precursor of the 'Q-ship' device was again successfully practised by the 74-gun *Plantagenet* when chased by the *Atalante*: and the Channel ports were soon swarming with privateers surprised and captured by the same ingenious ruse.

When the French attempted to turn the tables by disguising a well-armed privateer as a harmless-looking merchantman, the *Swallow* of Plymouth was nearly caught in the trap. Contriving to fight her way free, however, she staggered into port; to pass the warning that the more innocent a stranger-craft might appear, the more dangerous she well might prove to be.

The only craft that sailed the narrow seas immune from interference was the cartel ship that crossed, once a week, from Plymouth to Morlaix. Aboard her were the commissioners responsible for the welfare of the prisoners of war, both French and English; hapless creatures who relied upon these intermediaries for the delivery of their mail and an occasional dole of money.

The strain imposed by blockade and counter-blockade was intensified for the Island people when a state of war was declared by the United States. The operation of the British Orders in Council had inevitably proved costly and provoking to American commerce; and the forcible removal to the lower deck of one of King George's warships of British mariners serving under the Stars and Stripes had frequently been accompanied by the impressment of protesting American seamen. [2]

[1] Mr. (afterwards Sir John) Barrow to Mr. Croker, July 18th, 1810.
[2] British records put the number of American seamen—volunteers and pressed men—serving aboard vessels of the Royal Navy at 3,300. The U.S.

But the tragedy lay in the fact that the announcement of the British Government's suspension of the offending Orders in Council, of June 16th, 1812, had not reached Washington before "Mr. Madison's War"[1] had been declared on June 18th. In the circumstances it was not without irony that it had been the crippling pressure of the Royal Navy which had so reduced Napoleon's resources as to compel him to part with the million square miles of Louisiana to the United States Government for the relatively trifling sum of $15,000,000—a large part of which was found by British bankers.

War with America was an additional burden to a people already almost overborne, but for all that still in far better case than their mortal enemy. Unfortunately, at the very moment when the British effort should have been concentrated, the Government's ineradicable passion for wasting 'operations of detachment' had again asserted itself in the abortive expedition to the Isle of Walcheren. Vaguely conceived and dilatory in execution, its fatal want of impetus had been epitomised in the contemporary lampoon on the respective military and naval commanders:

> Great Chatham,[2] with his sabre drawn
> Stands waiting for Sir Richard Strachan;
> Sir Richard, longing to be at 'em,
> Stands waiting for the Earl of Chatham.

But while Chatham had dawdled in his garden, twelve miles from the front, admiring the two turtles destined to grace his dinner table,[3] typhoid, dysentery and ague had done the work the enemy found it almost unnecessary to further. With a mere 2,000 casualties, but a sick list of 11,500, the dispirited survivors of the Expeditionary Force had been withdrawn to Hampshire and the Isle of Wight. Of all the participants in this sorry venture only the men of the Preventive Service, responsible for the small-boat work, had emerged with unsullied credit.

State Department "had a docket of over 6,500 alleged cases when war began" (*The United States Navy*, Caroll Storrs Alden and Allan Westcott).

[1] As it was termed in Boston, where war with England was bitterly deplored, since France had seized 558 American vessels as against 389 taken by the British.

[2] The elder brother of William Pitt the Younger, in command of the troops detailed for the venture.

[3] See the Diary of General William Doytt, edited by R. W. Jeffery.

Fortunately, operations in the Iberian Peninsula, being under the direction of a far more dynamic leader in the person of the future Duke of Wellington, prospered steadily; with the Royal Navy maintaining his *rubios* with the same calm efficiency as they supported the *guerrillas* strung along the enemy's highly vulnerable lines of communication. For Spain had revolted against the intolerable restraints imposed upon her; and when Russia refused any longer to conform to restrictions that had closed her ports to all normal commerce, the hour of crisis was at hand. With the 'Spanish ulcer' already draining his resources in the West, Napoleon's plunge into the illimitable wastes of Muscovy was an open invitation to catastrophe.

With the snow-filled road across the plains from Moscow a long winding sheet for corpses, the Emperor desperately sought to reorganise and achieve recovery. But the sea-power which for so long had hemmed him in, could as easily transport and maintain the swarm of opponents that drove at him from every side. Thus the inevitable moment came when, with his armies beaten to the ground, the Little Corporal was forced to exchange the splendours of the Tuileries for an *opera-bouffe* kingdom on the sterile rock of Elba.

Unhurriedly the Congress of Vienna assembled to reshape a world in sore need of the most careful political osteopathy. A queer hush settled over Europe as, for the first time in a decade, the guns fell silent. Hesitantly, creaking a little resentfully from their long disuse, the wheels of ordinary, everyday existence slowly began to turn.

Peace with the United States encouraged the reopening of trade relations of vital importance to both countries. Hungry Europe turned eagerly to England for the consumer goods it had so long and so painfully been denied. The Preventive Water Guard, instituted in 1809, as part of the coast-watch, was freed from its war-time duties and at liberty to lend its aid to the Revenue Officers in their eternal warfare with the smugglers. At Portsmouth the old Naval Academy had blossomed out into the Royal Naval College, with the register of students increased to seventy. Swiftly and surely the prisoners at Plymouth, Forton and Porchester, and in the hulks in Portsmouth harbour, were transported across the narrow seas to their homes in France; while the man swinging an open lantern on the sea-front was no longer subject to detention and a swingeing fine.

Then, like a clap of thunder, came the news that 'Corporal Violette' had escaped from Elba, landed at Fréjus, and was heading for the capital, gathering his legions about him as he advanced.

Once again the Channel ports teemed with activity, as Horse, Foot, and Artillery, men, animals, guns, caissons, ammunition waggons, farriers' forges, mess-carts and forage were hurled across the narrow seas; and an allied force was speedily mustered to oppose the 'Corsican Ogre' who had again appeared to menace the world's short-lived tranquillity.

On the rain-soaked field of Waterloo the threat was finally dissipated, as the sun pierced through the sodden clouds to glint on the steel of British bayonets, and Wellington gave the word, "The whole line will advance!"

It was on July 15th that Napoleon surrendered to Captain Maitland aboard the *Bellerophon*—perhaps the vessel that had seen more hard service in England's cause than any other warship in the Fleet. Calling at Torbay on July 24th, within three days the veteran craft had dropped anchor in Plymouth Sound; where the multitudes eager to catch a glimpse of the fallen eagle were so numerous that "many shore boats were rammed, while periodical discharge of blank cartridge was necessary to keep the sightseers from infringing the defined limits—one hundred yards from the *Bellerophon*".

Moving restlessly from one gangway to another, the captive's gaze was not for the milling onlookers crowding to stare at him, as at some caged wild beast. It was for the red earth and soft green hills of unconquered England, and the battered warships lying so quietly at their moorings . . . the wooden walls that all his genius and all his might had been powerless to overcome.

CHAPTER XIX

The Great Transition

> "We must learn to recognise in the development of
> human destinies the play of the contingent and the
> unforeseen."
>
> H. A. L. FISHER

THE main achievement of the Congress of Vienna was to endow
Western Europe with half a century of freedom from major
wars. Prosperity, however, was not in its gift, and many things
conspired to retard its reappearance.

Conquest cannot be made to repay the cost of large-scale
warfare; and Britain, the principal opponent of Bonapartism,
had incurred the heaviest bill with that most relentless of all
creditors—victory. Pitt's long-sustained policy of 'ships and
subsidies' had saddled a population of approximately fourteen
million [1] with a fiscal burden which in 1815 totalled £74,500,000,
including a charge of £32,500,000 on a National Debt of
£860,000,000.[2] Income tax stood at 2s. in the £, and indirect
taxation had increased the cost of a whole range of everyday
commodities, from bread and salt to boots and shoes. In all,
some 1,425 articles were subject to Customs and Excise dues;
and it was not until 1882 that successive reforms reduced the
total to about a dozen.

In the circumstances it was extremely difficult for industry to
make the transition from war to peace production and build up
anything but a precarious equilibrium. Woollen exports, for
example—now very largely fabricated from *imported* yarn!—
were valued at just over £9,000,000 in 1815, but by 1826 the
returns had dwindled to one half that sum. In the same period
cotton exports fell by a quarter, and leather by a third. The
Gallic Treasury had been drained of gold so that Napoleon's
armies could march to Moscow in greatcoats made in Yorkshire

[1] By 1832 it had risen to about twenty-four million.
[2] *The Industrial and Commercial History of England*, J. E. Thorold Rogers.

and boots made in Northampton; but June 18th, 1815, had written off this source of income once and for all. Trade with the United States was curtailed when the need to foster their own struggling industries impelled the American authorities to erect a tariff wall which excluded many of the wares hitherto freely imported. The high rates of interest offered on foreign loans drained away a substantial amount of the capital badly needed for the long-term expansion of home industries. At the same time too exuberant hopes of an immediate boom in trade led to reckless over-production, subsidised by small, under-capitalised private banks. Anticipations not being realised, the ensuing slump led to much redundancy of labour and to sixty banking corporations closing their doors within six weeks.[1] The drift to the towns—at the grave expense of agriculture—had bred a large but mainly unskilled industrial population, as preoccupied with its grievances as the new race of petit-bourgeois employers were governed by the resolve to extort the maximum of work for the minimum of wages. Since the craftsman was at a discount in the new era of mass-production, the old medieval master–workman relationship had hardened into a tussle to determine who should get the better of the other. There was, in consequence, no feeling of confidence between the man who took the risks and the man who took the wages; and the workers, endowed in 1825 with the freedom of combination, failed to realise that strikes in favour of wage advances in times of prosperity are more likely to prove successful than strikes against wage reductions in times of trade contraction. Since the new factory-commerce was very largely in the hands of men who, in an industrial sense, had "come up through the hawse-hole", in a great many instances the class-origins of employer and employee were too akin to foster anything but mutual distrust. It was an innate antagonism whose bitterness has yet to be extirpated from industrial relationships.

With a large number of unemployed, the administration of Poor Law relief was cumbersome, extremely costly, generally depressive of wage rates, and calculated to affront even the most elementary sense of human dignity.[2] The best that can be

---

[1] Poley, *op cit.*

[2] In 1832 the sum spent on Poor Law relief was £7,000,000, and it was not until five years later that it dropped below £4,000,000.

said of such remedial measures as the corn laws—designed to stabilise the price of bread—is that for a time they staved off slightly more injury than they occasioned. The employment of child labour, under scandalous conditions of servitude, was far more reprobated by aristocratic social reformers, such as the 7th Earl of Shaftesbury, than deplored by proletarian parents, who argued that they had a perfect right to "do what they liked with their own".[1]

The East India Company was forced to abandon its monopoly of trade; and it was clear that the continuance of this *imperium in imperio* could not persist indefinitely, although it was not until 1873 that 'John Company's' independent existence was extinguished.

Britain, in effect, was undergoing her first experience of the consequential difference between fighting a 'total' war and waging a war of limited objectives and liabilities. In the circumstances it was no more than in the natural order of things that the Channel ports, which had been so vitally concerned in the prosecution of the recent conflict, should be the first to feel the pinch of stultifying post-war conditions. "Othello's occupation gone" must be plaint of any community that has thriven on the artificial demands of a nation in arms.

Thus Plymouth, with all traffic in prizes and their cargoes at an end, sought rather vainly to revive its fishing industry and to create employment by improving the facilities of Sutton Pool and the Catwater, and constructing a breakwater. Since there was a ban on the export of tin, copper, deals and preserved fish, there was remarkably little to freight in return for the imports of wine, spirits and tobacco that still arrived from overseas.

Falmouth was more fortunately circumstanced, since both grain ships and the postal packets made the Cornish haven their port of call; and there were great hopes of capturing the bulk of the expanding Western oceanic freight and passenger trade. Par shipped Cornish clay exclusively, in coasters bound up-Channel and beyond; while Bideford acted as the central tobacco market for the West. Portland's quarries, worked by convict labour, yielded a building stone that was in constant demand; while the sea-bathing so enthusiastically recommended by Dr. Russell of Lewes had turned Brighton and many other

[1] Poley, *op. cit.* J. E. Thorold Rogers.

watering places into fashionable holiday resorts, where a parasitical native population battened on an ever-increasing swarm of visitors. London, of course, still drew the bulk of the Channel trade. But the congestion in the area of the handsome new Customs House[1] had been little diminished by the construction, by the West India merchants, of a series of enclosed wet docks in the neighbourhood of Blackwall and Limehouse Hole, with a deep-water canal across the miniature peninsula of the Isle of Dogs—a project first mooted in 1799. Further accommodation was provided by the opening of the London Dock Company's range of basins at Wapping; with warehousing that included space for 24,000 hogsheads of tobacco. The Howland Great Wet Dock had changed hands in 1806, and was currently used for North European timber, deals, tar and corn. Other docks, built or building on the river's southern bank, passed eventually under the control of the Surrey Commercial Docks Company. Even so, London's river invariably gave the impression of being uncomfortably crowded, with the characteristic 'spritty-barges' threading their way through the swarm of coasters and colliers, while the local ogglers[2] hurled lurid abuse at the deep-water seamen of the Blackwall frigates, or paused in their work to cheer the graceful tea-clippers, racing to be the first to discharge their eagerly awaited cargoes.

The approaches to Thames-mouth had been greatly improved when the installation of a lightship in the Gull Stream in 1809 had robbed the Goodwins of some of their terrors. Indeed, the day was not far distant when certain adventurous sportsmen, decorously arrayed in silk hats and frock coats, would sally out at low tide to play a cricket match on a temporarily exposed stretch of the sands—with the topmasts of the many sunken vessels as the only witnesses of their temerity.[3]

A favourite hovering ground for pilots was off the Sunk

[1] The Elizabethan Customs House was destroyed in the Great Fire. Rebuilt by Wren, it again went up in flames. Ripley undertook its reconstruction, his work undergoing certain alterations in the late eighteenth century. The main structure of the present edifice was completed in 1817.

[2] In Norman-French the watermen who navigated their craft through the tide race that ran through the many arches of old London Bridge were known as *effleurs*. The term became corrupted to 'ogglers'; a name by which the Thames Police are still known.

[3] A cricket match was played on the Goodwins so recently as the August of 1954.

lightship, and amongst their other rendezvous was Dungeness Point and a stretch of relatively sheltered water between the Needles and Anvil Point.[1]

*   *   *

In the same way that utopias flourish in chaos, politicians in crises, and physicians in pestilence, smugglers are never so prosperous as in times of fiscal extortion. The immediate post-war years, therefore, saw their activity at its height; and this despite the expansion of the Preventive Service made possible by the recruitment of a number of the Officers and men paid off by the Navy.

In the February of 1827, for example, Lieutenant Digby surprised eighty owlers on the beach of Devil's Gap at Rotting-dean, in the act of signalling a vessel hovering off the coast. Knocked down with a bludgeon and overpowered, the un-fortunate Officer was beaten into insensibility and then cal-lously tossed aside while the run was landed. It was not until months later that his chief assailants, May and Palmer, were tracked down and brought up for sentence at Horsham Assizes. In 1829 the London barge *Alfred* was caught by the revenue cutter *Vigilant* off Birchington in the act of picking up no less than 1,045 tubs of spirits, which had been sunk and buoyed, and subsequently brought to the surface with the aid of a 'creeping-iron'—a five-pronged hook with a long shank, which was trailed along the seabed till it caught the ropes fastening the tubs of spirits together.

A huge run went through in the March of 1829, between Jew's Gut and Ness Point; the smuggled goods being brought inland through Lydd in twelve carts, with an escort of eighty well-armed owlers. In the June of the same year a substantial run of half-ankers of spirits took place near Eastbourne, the illicit cargo being brazenly loaded into waggons at high noon. In October a *chasse-marée* was seen hovering off Arundel. Challenged and boarded by men of H.M.S. *Chameleon*, she was found to contain nothing dutiable; although suspicions were aroused by the fact that her boat was missing. This was sub-sequently found lying derelict on the foreshore; for the run

[1] The whole business of pilotage was finally rationalised by the Pilot Act of 1913.

had already been accomplished, 200 tubs of spirits having been landed, which the Frenchmen had obligingly helped to carry inland.

In the early December of 1829 the Preventive men arrived at Rye's Cliffend just as a large number of bales and tubs were being loaded into carts. Armed with 'bats'—long staves, wielded with both hands—the owlers went straight into action. In the sanguinary fight that ensued, four of the Revenue hands were brought low, a number of the smugglers wounded and one slain. But the run went through, the goods being distributed amongst the 'duffers'—large-scale middlemen, who would take as much as 1,000 lb. of tea and 100 tubs of spirits at a time.

This defiant state of lawlessness was little affected by the transfer of control of the Revenue cutters to the Admiralty; although the establishment of the Coastguard in 1856 helped materially to curb the owlers' activities. But it was the steady drop in the open market price of a number of commodities hitherto supplied almost exclusively by the contraband-runners that brought about smuggling's decline.[1] This welcome fall in the cost of living was the outcome of the tentative adoption of a number of free trade measures, with the consequent abolition of the Navigation Acts and the abandonment of the British claim to 'possession' of the narrow seas; an opening up of commerce that reaped at least a transient reward.

An innovation of the greatest possible value to all those who sailed the narrow seas was the institution, in 1824, of the Voluntary Lifeboat Service, sponsored by Colonel Sir William Hillary and Thomas Wilson, one of the Members of Parliament for the City of London. Supported by private subscriptions, the Service was manned almost exclusively by fisherfolk; and there was no tempest too fierce to daunt the life-savers in their noble work of rescue. Intent on rendering aid to the heavily laden *Iron Crown*, for example, the *England's Glory* made her way clean across the Goodwins, to run out kedge anchors to help the stranded brig heave herself off the sandbanks. Walmer, Deal and Kingsdown lifeboats enjoyed a reputation for devoted service it was impossible to outmatch; one Deal lifeboat

---

[1] Owling, of course, has never been entirely eliminated. In 1953, for example, there were 24,167 seizures of smuggled goods in United Kingdom ports and waters.

Coxswain of later days, William ('Bonnie') Adams, helping directly in the succour of 321 lives, and the preservation of fourteen ships.

None the less the narrow seas continued to exact a grim toll of life and property. In 1824 the 95-ton Ordnance sloop *Ebenezer*, carrying stores, was driven towards the hungry jaws of Chesil Bank, and death for all aboard appeared inevitable. But before the ship could strike, a huge wave picked her up and hurled her on to the summit of the shelf. Shaken but thankful to be alive, the crew promptly decanted themselves and trailed their way across the shifting shingle into Portland. A few years later a fleet of ten vessels was caught off the Bank in so towering a sea that nine of the craft were dashed to pieces. The tenth—a vessel of 500 tons—was carried right over the Bank into the stream beyond, suffering little material damage beyond certain badly sprung timbers. The *Pride of the Sea* beat herself to shards on the rocks of the Yellow Ridge off Shanklin; the lugger *Reform* was lost in going to the aid of a ship in distress off the South Sand Head of the Goodwins; the *Walmer Castle*, caught in the deadly tidal race off Dunnose Point, went down with all aboard. Cornwall's churchyards are thick with memorials to those who have perished off her perilous coast; St. Keverne's monuments recalling the loss of the Officers and men of the VII Hussars, drowned in the transport *Despatch*, and the crew of the S.S. *Mohegan*, wrecked on those jagged Manacle rocks which, all through the years, have conspired with the angry waters to claim so many helpless victims.

* * *

With the end of the war in 1815 the British Navy had 606 vessels in commission, manned by 130,127 Officers and men. This as compared with the 37,283 shipmen sailing in foreign trade, the 35,970 engaged in the coasting trade, and the 14,628 employed in the fishing industry.[1] Reductions in Naval personnel were, of course, inevitable. But in the event they were carried out on so sweeping a scale—except amongst the senior Officers, who clung grimly to any appointments they could contrive for themselves—that forty years later the Naval manpower immediately available for the Crimean War totalled a

[1] The totals are those given by the Assistant Registrar General of Shipping.

mere 45,000. It was not only a diminished Navy, but a Navy which long remained faithful to the atmosphere and traditions of the eighteenth century. The Lower Deck still doubled out to the call for "All hands to dance and skylark", and to work off the effect of too many potations of 'Pale Death'[1] by a game of leap-frog—much as they had limbered up on the morning of Trafalgar. Indeed, in spite of the successful attempt of William IV to limit the term of the impressed seamen's service with the Navy to five years, the harsh treatment of the man before the mast in one of H.M. ships had undergone little amelioration. Flogging remained the corrective even for relatively trivial offences[2]; with drunkenness punished in the traditional way, by lashing the delinquent to the forerigging and pouring salt water down his throat with the aid of a funnel "until it passed right through him". But the chief drawback so far as the Lower Deck was concerned was all lack of continuity of engagement. Hands were paid off and turned adrift at the end of each commission; and it was even held that should a vessel suffer shipwreck, that in itself was sufficient to terminate a man's contract of service.

It was not, indeed, until 1853 that the manning of the Navy was put on a proper footing by the introduction of the Continuous Service Scheme, with its opportunities for permanent employment and its accompanying right to ascending scales of pay, gratuities for good conduct, and a pension after the completion of a certain number of years of unblemished devotion to duty. At the same time impressment, which in 1835 had been limited to occasions of "grave national emergency", was abolished altogether; the hope that better pay and prospects would bring in all the men required being fully justified by events. In effect, the creation of a professional long service Navy, down to the lowest rating, had become an obvious necessity, since the skill of the merchant seaman was inadequate to the demands of a Fighting Marine whose problems promised to become progressively more technical. Professionalism was further recognised in 1857 by the adoption of a Lower Deck uniform, and the disappearance of the old slop chest and its

---

[1] Rum.

[2] It has to be borne in mind that the list of grievances for which the Spithead and Nore mutineers sought remedy did not include flogging.

medley of more or less standardised habiliments. It was with
considerable regret, however, that the crews of the Captains'
gigs shed the picturesque individual garb by which so many of
them had been distinguished—such as the blue and white
striped guernseys of the men of the *Blazer*, the acorn and oak
leaf ornamented jean collars of the *Royal Oak* oarsmen, and the
replicas of the scarlet uniform worn by the winners of Doggett's
Coat and Badge which had been the particular pride of the
Vernon's barge crew. At the same time Regulations laid it down
that all Naval personnel should be either clean-shaven or fully
bearded; Queen Victoria having expressed the august opinion
that "moustaches have rather a soldier-like appearance".

The Royal Naval College, after being centred in H.M.S.
Illustrious, had been removed to H.M.S. *Britannia* in 1859; the
craft being transferred from Portland to Dartmouth in 1863.
The construction of the Dartmouth instructional shore establishment followed in 1896; and here the youthful embryo of a
Naval Officer combined an ordinary education with instruction
in the techniques of his chosen calling—from the mysteries of
knotting and splicing to the workings of the compass and the
improved methods of signalling.

The institution of an 'Active' and 'Retired' list for Officers
helped materially to accelerate the flow of promotion.

The Corps of Marines, which had passed under Admiralty
control in 1755, had long been regarded by the Navy as its own
particular progeny. In 1802 St. Vincent had publicly affirmed:
"I never knew an appeal to their courage that did not more
than realise my expectations"; and their steadfast devotion to
duty—particularly at the time of the Spithead and Nore
mutinies—had been recognised by the award of the prefix
'Royal'.

The post-war Navy had not been entirely without active
service experience. In 1827 it had helped to deliver Greece
from oppression by its intervention in the battle of Navarino.
In 1833 a British fleet had swept away a would-be usurper to
establish the youthful Queen of Portugal on her Throne. But
they had been encounters fought on traditional eighteenth-
century lines; and thereafter the Service had been inclined to
lapse into stagnation, oblivious to the portents of an age of
maritime revolution.

For steam had come to navigation's aid, and by endowing ships with freedom to move at choice, had robbed the winds of their ancient lordship.[1]

The steam engine, invented in 1769, had been applied to river craft before the French Revolution. In the year of Waterloo a sea-going tug proceeded from Greenock to London under her own steam-power. On passage, she called at Portsmouth, where the novel spectacle she presented broke up a Court Martial sitting in H.M.S. *Gladiator*. As a young Officer, Admiral Raigersfeld recorded the appearance of a "steamboat . . . almost daily steaming up and about the Hamoaze to draw the attention of the population to the invention"; although he contemptuously dismissed the idea of "its ever being put into competition with line of battleships . . . as one broadside would annihilate such presumption".[2]

This opinion was certainly shared by Melville, the contemporary First Lord of the Admiralty, who in 1828 had pontificated, "Steam is calculated to strike a fatal blow at the Empire." The real trouble was that a hostile warship could strike a fatal blow at the frail paddle wheels by which the vessel was driven through the water. These cumbersome excrescences, moreover, would have seriously restricted the number of guns in the broadside. The Navy's first experiment with the new device, therefore, went no further than the purchase of a few steam-powered tugs.[3]

The invention of the steam-driven screw propeller put a very different complexion on affairs; and when the screw-fitted *Rattler* and the paddle-equipped *Alecto* were lashed stern to stern and ordered to go right ahead, the former emerged so easy a winner in the ensuing tug-of-war that steam was grudgingly accepted by the Navy as an auxiliary to sail.

Steam posed another problem for the Fighting Marine, since it became necessary to replace the staff of civilian mechanics, sent by the manufacturers to install and 'work' their steam

[1] A memorial in St. Margaret's Church, Westminster, pays tribute to James Rumsay, honoured by the State of West Virginia as the inventor of the steamboat. He died on the Christmas Eve of 1792. Fulton's *Demologos* can advance substantial claim to have been the first steam-driven warship.

[2] *The Life of a Sea Officer*, Jeffrey Baron de Raigersfeld.

[3] The famous picture of the *Fighting Temeraire* depicts the use to which steam was first put by the Navy.

engines, with the appropriate Naval Engineer Officers and engine-room ratings; amenable to that Naval Discipline Act which, in 1866, had taken the place of the erstwhile Articles of War. The assimilation of the 'Black Squad' into the general pattern of the Navy was not unattended with difficulties; but in due course they earned the acceptance and respect to which their sterling qualities entitled them.

Improvements in ordnance were the next to demand attention; and when the Russians' new 'shell gun' blew the Turkish fleet out of the water at Sinope, the contest was joined between metal-piercing missiles and protective armour; with steel replacing iron in warships' construction; and the Bessemer process for hardening steel as much a friend to the attack as to the defence. The former soon regained the advantage, however, with the invention of the breech-block and the novel system of rifling the gun-barrel. Improvements in motive power, fabric, weapons, and their propellants were bringing about changes as revolutionary as those which had accompanied the introduction of gunpowder and the gun-deck in the days of 'Henry Tydder'.

In the Declaration of Paris of 1856 it was agreed to refrain from employing privateers in time of war; a proviso which occasioned some very long faces amongst the old-timers of the Channel ports![1] It was further decreed that a blockade, to receive recognition as such in International Law, must be "effective"—a shrewd hit at Britain, who had, on occasion, been content to "declare" a state of blockade without physically enforcing it.

In the years following the Crimea, however, there was a sharp deterioration in Anglo-French relations; with Admiral Aube's rumbling threats, in the event of war, to bombard defenceless watering places and sink British merchant shipping at sight, backed up by the launching of the ironclad *Gloire*. Britain's response was to embody the Naval Coast Volunteers and to commission a private shipyard to construct the 9,000-ton *Warrior*, an iron-hulled, exclusively steam-driven craft, protected by 4·5-inch side-armour. It was an innovation which brought the exceptional skill and experience of the great

---

[1] The United States reserved the right to employ privateers at will, in the belief that by so doing she would be spared the necessity of maintaining large standing Naval forces.

merchant-shipbuilding industry to the service of the Royal Navy; whose dockyards thereafter were, in the main, utilised as maintenance bases.

In 1847 the French scientist Sobrero, seeking a remedy for headaches, had evolved the propulsive agent nitro-glycerine. Then in 1868 a certain Alfred Nobel produced a violent explosive which he named dynamite. Entertaining the fatuous belief that the stuff would be employed exclusively as "the agent of peace, helping the miner, blasting quarries, tearing holes out of mountains so that the railway engineer will be more easily able to link people with people", no one was more genuinely if naively astonished than the inventor when it was adopted by every War Department that could lay hands on it. A powerful propellant had taken its place in the armoury that obviously called for more resistant fixed defences, including those of the battleship. As protective armour was thickened, so in turn ordnance was made more powerful; Armstrong's built-up gun and Whitworth's armour-piercing projectile maintaining the great gun as the primary weapon of naval combat; with the torpedo and the mine playing their potent subsidiary roles.

Thoroughly awakened from the torpor in which they had been sunk throughout the first half of the century, the responsible British authorities announced their intention of adopting a "Two-Power Standard" by which the Royal Navy was to be kept at a strength to match the combined might of the next two most powerful maritime nations. The timely publication of Captain A. T. Mahan's powerful and illuminating work *The Influence of Sea-Power on History, 1660–1783*, greatly stimulated interest in naval problems and led many folk to *think* about their Navy and Mercantile marine instead of just taking them for granted. But in no country did the work create a deeper impression than in the Germany of Kaiser Wilhelm II.

Some years earlier Bismarck had given the solemn warning, "I fear that the German, that landlubber, will one day try to launch out on the water, and that would be the worst of follies." But his admonition had wilfully been disregarded. Prestige, a growing sense of nationhood and a restless desire for self-assertion, aggravated Germany's tumescent urge to challenge the Naval might that had serenely maintained the *Pax Britannica*, impartially protected international trade in every quarter of the globe, and in the process spared the United States the trouble of implementing her foreign policy by giving reality to the Monroe doctrine for her.[1]

Right up to the late 'eighties the Kaiser had spoken with real fervour of an Anglo-German understanding; England had responded by exchanging Heligoland for the Reich Protectorates of Zanzibar, Witu and Somaliland, on the understanding that the first-named should be utilised solely as "a refuge for fishermen".[2] It was a mood of amicability that was speedily dissipated when Lord Salisbury let it be known that Germany's *Drang nach Osten* and aspirations towards "a place in the sun" were too excessive to be acceptable. Joseph Chamberlain's efforts to arrive at a compromise were frustrated by the Kaiser's growing distrust and petulance, Chancellor von Bülow's intransigence, and the immutable hostility of the Reichstag.

So early as 1805 Professor Arnold Heeren of Göttingen had prophesied that "a united Germany will strive to master Europe"; and unity had come with the ceremony in the Versailles Hall of Mirrors, of January 1871, which established William I as Emperor of Germany. Just under three decades later "the fatal concentrations of capital, the fatal expansions of bourgeois imperialism were forcing an insatiable and militarist empire into a collision with a satiated and civilian one; ... and at the root of Anglo-German rivalry as it grew out of the 'eighties and increased in intensity, there lay the germinating enmities of industry and commerce".[3]

For despite temporary slumps in the late 'seventies, mid-'eighties and early 'nineties, England was thriving as never before in its history. The turnover in foreign trade, which in 1800 had totalled £80,000,000, by 1900 had reached the figure of £1,467,000,000; while 'invisible assets', in the form of interest on foreign loans and investments, represented another form of income whose aggregate bordered on the fabulous. Lloyd's and marine insurance were almost synonymous terms;

[1] "For years", declared John Quincey Adams, "America has been a cock-boat in the wake of the British man-of-war".
[2] It was immediately fortified on passing into German possession.
[3] *Victoria's Heir*, George Dangerfield.

while the country's iron and steel, engineering and ship-building industries, its manufactories, its banking facilities, and its reserves of capital represented a great body of wealth without parallel throughout the globe. And not only was the Island Realm the world's workshop and emporium, but the pick of the carrying trade was at its command for the asking.

In many respects, of course, it was more the era of the ship-owner, the banker and the speculator than of the industrialist—who was beginning to live in mortal dread of giving offence to the progressively more capricious customer. Such were the fruits of reversing the old policy of utilising national power to foster commerce. Under Free Trade Britain's unbalanced economy became vulnerable all over the globe. For Free Trade can only be made to work satisfactorily if it is reciprocal; and in far too many instances it was found that the foreigner had adopted the fiscal strategy that Britain herself had practised for over four centuries. Only the unrivalled enterprise of British pioneers succeeded in opening up new markets to replace the old ones that had ceased to be of service; and there is a limit to the number of fresh outlets that even the most enterprising can discover.

Moreover, the country was failing to keep its means of production up to date. Plant which had been the *dernier cri* twenty years previously had come to look remarkably jaded and *démodé*; while exports frequently found themselves confronted with un-yielding tariff walls, erected to nourish products fabricated by brand-new British machinery inconsequentially sold to foreign purchasers the better to enable them to transform themselves into formidable trade rivals. On the surface, however, it seemed that all was for the best in this best of all possible worlds. A network of railways facilitated the transport of passengers and goods; and in the process restored prosperity to many a coastal haven that had languished for generations prior to the coming of the 'Iron Horse'. Southampton, for one, with its shorter railway journey to London, had stolen the Western oceanic trade from Falmouth, and in the process had blossomed out into a city whose £140,000 tidal dock, its enclosed dock, and its £60,000 graving dock were soon seen to be barely adequate for the flow of commerce and passenger traffic crowding up its waterway. By 1880 the city had attained fourth place amongst

English ports; in the year following its population—standing at 46,960 in 1861—had risen to 100,866, and the increase had steadily continued. Plymouth had also revived with the coming of the railway; and many of the Navy's steam trials took place in local waters. Dartmouth was chosen as the port of call for the Cape and Natal Steamship Company, and in addition built up a useful bunkering trade. To serve these and other revitalised havens, a British Mercantile Marine, safeguarded by the Merchant Shipping Act of 1876—with its Plimsoll mark, amongst other things, to guard against overloading—had won a reputation for skilful seamanship and reliability second to none. For all that, the trend was for the wealth accumulated when Britain was 'the world's workshop' to be exported to support foreign loans and investments. Slowly but surely, John Bull was exchanging the role of manufacturer for that of moneylender.

For all her lack of equipoise, in covetous German eyes Britain loomed up as the greatest aggregation of undefended loot the world had ever seen. The only thing that gave pause to surging Teutonic ambitions to despoil it was the thought of Britain's Navy. But that could first be equalled and then outmatched; and so heavy a building programme was scheduled that the Tsar of Russia, alarmed at the threatening arms race, proposed an international conference to consider the advisability of limiting naval construction. All that came out of the convention was the appointment of Admiral von Tirpitz to command the Fleet authorised by the Reich Navy Law of 1898, and the cutting of the Kiel Canal to link the Baltic with the 'German Ocean'.

In the situation that confronted him, Lord Salisbury's point of view remained unaltered—that the Triple Alliance of Germany, Austria and Italy was sufficiently balanced by the Dual Alliance of France and the enigmatic Russian colossus; with England uncommitted to either side, and therefore free, should the necessity arise, to lend her might to the weaker. It was the traditional policy which had been successfully pursued in the days of Philip of Spain, of Louis XIV, and of Napoleon. Salisbury's hand was forced, however, by King Edward, whose resentment of most things Germanic, engendered by the ultra-Teutonic upbringing inflicted on him by those twin pedants,

Baron Stockmar and the Prince Consort, scarcely predisposed him to favour a brash, bombastic nephew who postured on Germany's Throne like the tenor in a Wagnerian melodrama. Repelled by *sauerkraut*, the King had swung to the other extreme, ostentatiously to favour *sole bonne femme*. The *Entente Cordiale* which was the outcome of this obstinate predilection had the effect of aligning the British with a nation they had helped to defeat in 1856 and an ancient, oft-vanquished enemy the Germans had also trounced "to the last gaiter button" in 1871.

With the British Navy League vigorously seeking to outsoar its Teutonic counterpart in its advocacy of a 'big Navy' policy, Admiral Sir John Fisher was appointed to the Admiralty—taking up his duties, appropriately enough, on the anniversary of Trafalgar.

With his advent a wide divergence of opinion developed between the new First Sea Lord and Admiral Beresford as to the best way in which Britain's naval lead could be maintained. In the teeth of constant opposition, the ebullient 'Jacky' sponsored many innovations in an endeavour to turn the Fleet into the most powerful, swift and flexible fighting force on the high seas. The 12-inch gun was replaced by the 13·5 [1]; the mine was developed, and great attention was paid to improving the submarine, despite Admiral Sir Arthur Wilson's indignant description of this instrument of the warfare of the future as "underhand, unfair, and damned un-English". Nor was the portent of Louis Blériot's pioneer flight across the Channel lost on the more farsighted.

Oblivious to Beresford's scornful references to "Fisher's toys", the First Sea Lord scrapped dozens of craft he declared to be "too weak to fight and too slow to run away". Then in the *Dreadnought* he produced a vessel that patently outclassed all previous battleships, British as well as German, and rendered the Kiel Canal inoperable till it had been widened to take ironclads of the *König* class, which constituted Germany's reply to the high-speed all-big-gun warcraft.[2]

It was Fisher's aim to incorporate the Channel and Atlantic

[1] Until the Fisher era the War Office was responsible for the provision of ships' guns, the Navy having no Ordnance Department.
[2] The widening process was not completed until 1914.

fleets into a 'Home Fleet' to be stationed permanently in the North Sea. "Our only probable enemy", he insisted, "is Germany. Germany keeps her whole Fleet always concentrated within a few hours of England. We must, therefore, keep a fleet twice as powerful concentrated within a few hours of Germany." To this aim he remained constant, reinforced in his resolve by the knowledge that the Admiralty's scheme to build an enclosed harbour at Dover—work on which was completed in 1907[1]—had greatly strengthened the means of defending the vulnerable Straits.

In 1909 the House of Commons was informed that Germany was building warships so fast that unless the British Government accelerated its Naval programme, by April 1912 the Kaiser might well possess 21 *Dreadnoughts* to England's 20. For the coming of the *Dreadnought* type of vessel had put the two countries on an equality so far as the future capital ship was concerned. Fisher therefore firmly pressed not for six, but for eight new *Dreadnoughts* in the current building programme; and the public took up the demand with the cry, "We want eight, and we won't wait." Eight of these mighty vessels were therefore put on the stocks; while Percy Scott's insistence on more and more gunnery practice to ensure ever-increasing accuracy, involved an expenditure of ammunition that must have made Elizabeth Tudor turn uneasily in her grave!

Speed, firepower, stoutness of fabric, superiority of numbers, and all the supplementary help that could be forthcoming from a well-organised Royal Naval Reserve and Royal Naval Volunteer Reserve—they would all be wanted, and at no distant date. For despite Lloyd George's cretinous assurance that "In the matter of external affairs, the sky has never been more perfectly blue",[2] the sands were fast running out. It only needed a spark to explode the European powder-barrel; and that spark was forthcoming when a hare-brained chauvinist put a revolver bullet into the Arch-Duke Franz Ferdinand, Heir to the double Throne of Austria–Hungary.

Austria was resolved to crush the assassin's homeland of Serbia, despite Russia's avowed intention to support her fellow-

[1] Work on this project had begun in 1897, the year prior to the passage of the first German Navy Act.
[2] In a speech at a City dinner on July 17th, 1914.

Slavs. With Austria committed and Italy equivocating, the principal partner in the Triple Alliance had no hesitation as to his own course of action. Possessed of the strongest Army in Europe, with ample and immediately available reserves, and with a Fleet which had long drunk to *Der Tag* when it would challenge British might at sea, the gage was flung down when, in accordance with the long-matured Schlieffen Plan, the field-grey columns marched into neutral Belgium.

Britain's nebulous 'conversations' with France had committed her to all the obligations of an alliance without any perceptible compensatory advantages. Yet however divided the Cabinet might be on the issue of peace and war, the German Chancellor's dismissal of the 1839 Treaty guaranteeing Belgium's neutrality as a mere "scrap of paper" aroused immediate and widespread public indignation.[1]

With war a virtual certainty, the preliminary measures planned by the War Office and Admiralty were quietly put in train. Instead of Grand Manœuvres in the North Sea as in previous years a test mobilisation, announced in the previous Spring, had fortuitously concentrated the Navy in full strength at Portland; and there the ships and men were held despite previous arrangements for their dispersal on July 27th. As the German Naval Attaché telegraphed to Berlin on July 28th, ". . . the British Fleet is preparing for all eventualities. . . . 1st Fleet is assembled at Portland. The battleship *Bellerophon* which was proceeding to Gibraltar for refit has been recalled. The ships of the 2nd Fleet are at their bases; they are all fully manned. . . . Ships of the 2nd and 3rd Fleets have coaled, completed with ammunition and supplies. In consequence of the training of reservists, just completed, latter can be manned more quickly than usual. The destroyer and patrol flotillas and the submarines are either at or *en route* for their stations. . . . All ships and squadrons have orders to remain ready for sea. . . ."

With Germany's rejection of the British ultimatum demanding the prompt withdrawal of the invading forces from all

[1] This was an early triumph for popular propaganda, since the Treaty had long since been invalidated by the construction of a ring of forts about Antwerp, which had been specifically designated "solely a port of commerce".

15*

neutral territory, the only agency which could preserve the British Isles from the fate which was already overtaking Belgium and Northern France had moved to its war stations. From Scapa Flow down through the narrow seas and on to Land's End and the vital Western Approaches, the grim grey ships were stripped and—ready.

CHAPTER XX

'Look to Your Moat'

"L'Angleterre est une île."
JULES MICHELET

FROM time immemorial a Navy's prime object, in time of conflict, has been to seek out and destroy the enemy wherever he might be found. It was not until the Dutch wars of the seventeenth century that it began to be fully appreciated that the destruction of an antagonist's seaborne communications and commerce is equally as important as the annihilation of his fighting fleet. Nothing demonstrated this fact more clearly than the experience of the Napoleonic wars, when the conjunction of a close blockade and the wholesale capture of the French mercantile marine reduced the 'Corsican Ogre' to impotence.

By 1914, however, the incidence of the torpedo and the mine had rendered close blockade inoperable, as they had outdated the International Law bearing on the subject. Under contemporary conditions, long-range surveillance was the most that could successfully be attempted.

In all her wars with the Spaniards, Dutch and French, Britain's plan of operations had pivoted on the narrow seas. But with Germany the opponent the emphasis shifted from what had become the subsidiary theatre of the Channel to the North Sea; where the German fleet was based on harbours as well-found and well-guarded as the improvised British havens were lacking in all but the most elementary facilities.

From Scapa Flow the Grand Fleet, while affording some protection for the unfortified East Coast, exercised a remote *military* blockade by its ability to pin the German High Sea Fleet to its harbours or challenge it should it emerge from them. At the same time an attempt was made to institute the *commercial* blockade of the Reich by stationing warships in certain 'cruising grounds' in the North Sea and the Channel's western approaches, with the object of barring the entry of contraband of war into any German port. To these measures the enemy's reply could only take the form of interference with the Allies' maritime trade by means of the submarine and the far-ranging commerce raider.

With the German drive through Belgium, attention again focused on the Channel; so recently traversed by the British Expeditionary Force without the loss of a single man or gun. While forestalling any enemy attempt to enter the Straits, the Allies' obvious strategy was to exploit their dominion in the narrow seas by launching a blow against the right flank of the advancing German army. But for this it was necessary to make the fullest use of Antwerp as a base. Yet even had Britain possessed the needful troops for such a stroke, two governing factors rendered the port as good as inaccessible. The same sandbanks that had taken such grim toll of the Spanish Armada debarred the modern battleship from approaching the Belgian coast; while impetuous denunciations of Germany's "rape of Belgium" could scarcely be followed by British violation of Dutch territorial waters through forcing the water-gate of the Scheldt.

Since no consideration had been given to the possibility of a German advance along the coast, at the outbreak of the war the Dover flotilla had been administered from Harwich. But with the Belgians rapidly falling back from the Dyle river line, a Dover Command was hastily constituted, with Rear-Admiral Hon. Horace Hood at its head. Some extremely venerable destroyers were supported by the cruiser *Attentive* and the monitors *Severn*, *Mersey* and *Humber*; while Lieutenant-Commander Rigg started work on an anti-mine defence with four old trawlers, which stank to high heaven, having come straight from their fishing grounds after jettisoning their malodorous cargo over the side.

With the collapse of the Dyle river defences a small contingent of Royal Marines and Naval ratings was sent to try to hold off the enemy advance while the Belgians extricated themselves from the Antwerp enclave, and the main Franco-British forces struggled to extend their line northwards. With the fall of the city, however, the *feldgraus* pushed on to occupy

Zeebrugge and Ostend, their resolute advance not being arrested till it reached the line Dixmude–Nieuport.

From daybreak on October 18th till nightfall on November 7th the British warships gave unceasing support to the operations on land, often in difficult weather, and under a return fire that inflicted considerable damage and a number of casualties. With both sides digging-in, it was demonstrated yet once again that naval gunfire, although extremely effective against troops and transport in motion, ceases to be of much substantial value once the enemy has gone to earth, and is also in a position to reply with mobile artillery.

With Zeebrugge and Ostend in hostile hands the necessity to seal the Straits was urgent. But that was not a process which could be completed overnight, and in the interim there was little to impede the passage of submarines through the Narrows. Indeed *unterseebooten* which had so speedily avenged Admiral Beatty's victory in the Heligoland Bight, by sinking the cruisers *Hogue*, *Cressy* and *Aboukir*, lost no time in sending the aircraft carrier *Hermes* to join them. In October, when a submarine was reported off Cherbourg with another in the vicinity of the Isle of Wight, the Admiralty was forced to re-route the troopships bearing the Canadian Expeditionary Force, so that the men were debarked at Plymouth instead of Southampton, as had originally been intended. For many a loyal 'Canuck' the first glimpse of the Old Country he had come to defend was of the Sound and Drake's Island, and the red hills of Devon.

*   *   *

With the outbreak of the war the Allies could call on some 24,000,000 tons of merchant shipping, or 58 per cent of the world's mercantile marine.[1] Between them, the Austro-Germans could muster 6,200,000 tons, or 14·7 per cent; the neutrals some 13,000,000 tons, or 27·3 per cent.

The chief points of ingress for German imports were Roumania, Italy, Switzerland, Holland, Denmark and Sweden; goods destined for the last three having to pass through the 'cruising grounds' in the North Sea or Western Approaches. Those coming up-Channel would inevitably find themselves

[1] British and Dominion merchant craft of 100 tons gross and over aggregated 20,524,000 tons.

subject to any control organisation the authorities elected to establish at the toll-gate of the Narrows.

Developments during the years subsequent to the Declaration of Paris had emphasised legislation's perennial dilemma—how to reconcile precedent with ever-changing conditions. The regulations governing contraband of war agreed upon in 1856 had speedily revealed so many imperfections that in 1909 the Declaration of London had sought to clarify a state of affairs as imprecise as it promised to be fruitful in disagreement. In the process, however, Britain's offer—in return for a guarantee to abolish privateering—to forgo her traditional claim to confiscate enemy property found in neutral vessels, met with such violent protest, both within and without Parliament, that the proposed legislation was duly vetoed by the House of Lords. None the less, to make confusion worse confounded, the provisions embodied in the moribund Declaration of London made a somewhat apologetic appearance in the official Prize Manual; a publication that was still in circulation with the outbreak of hostilities in 1914.

In effect, with conflict actually raging, the law with regard both to blockade and contraband of war was so nebulous, badly antiquated, and generally inapplicable to contemporary conditions, that such obvious war potential as raw cotton, rubber, and metallic ores—to name no more—were theoretically not subject to forfeiture.

This was a matter of considerable strategic importance. For during the period 1910–13 Germany's imports for home consumption averaged some £510,000,000. Her exports—many of which were founded on alien raw materials—averaged £445,000,000.[1] Furthermore, it was estimated that nearly 70 per cent of the imports (by value) and 60 per cent of the exports were seaborne. Since a heavy proportion of these imports reached the Fatherland in foreign bottoms, it was clear that if control of neutral shipping could follow the elimination of the German mercantile marine, the whole structure of the Reich economy would be gravely, even fatally, imperilled. With nothing in the way of International Law to serve as a guide to conduct save a welter of unresolved legal pedantries, the British authorities resolved to follow an empirical course,

[1] *The Allied Blockade of Germany 1914–1916*, Dr. Marion Siney.

designed gradually to tighten the hold on the enemy's commerce —contraband and non-contraband—while seeking to avoid all measures calculated to affront neutralist susceptibilities.

At the outset pressure was brought to bear with a relatively light hand; Germans travelling in neutral vessels, for example, were permitted to proceed on their way unmolested; while ships were 'rummaged' at sea, whenever possible, thus avoiding the delay and expense involved in that "deviation of course" which a port search inevitably entailed.

Ironically enough, it was the Germans themselves who enabled the British to put on the screw, by announcing their intention of mining the approaches to all ports of arrival and departure made use of by British troops. When two Danish vessels were blown up by mines that could only have been laid surreptitiously by submarine or an enemy vessel wearing a neutral flag, a good deal less was heard about the inconvenience attendant on repairing to a port for 'rummaging'; a procedure which in earlier days would have occasioned considerable protest.

With the principal Examination Station established at Ramsgate,[1] shipping awaiting clearance by the Naval boarding parties and the trained 'rummagers' of the Customs Service was mustered in the Downs—sometimes to the number of a hundred and twenty-five vessels at a time.[2]

Naturally, the concentration of so vulnerable a mass of tonnage within two hours' top-speed steaming of the nearest enemy base called for the strongest defensive measures that could be devised out of the extremely limited resources available. By the time that Rear-Admiral Bacon took over the Dover Command in the April of 1915, in addition to the *Attentive* and the original three monitors, he had been reinforced by the 6th Flotilla, consisting of 12 pre-1906 'Tribal' class destroyers and 12 so-called "30-knotters" of the vintage of 1897–8.[3] Later and very welcome arrivals were three relatively up-to-date flotilla leaders. In addition, there was a drifter force, charged with

[1] There was a subsidiary Examination Service at Falmouth, empowered to issue certificates to vessels cleared at this port.

[2] From January to July 1915, some 2,466 vessels arrived in neutral ports in the North Sea, of which 2,132 had submitted to search in the Downs.

[3] Needless to say that by 1914 the alleged 30-knotters could not do more than 20–25 knots at the utmost.

net-laying and patrol, which eventually totalled 132 craft. A trawler force was constantly at work sweeping for mines amidst the sluicing tides, and mostly in misty or tempestuous weather. Not the least of its responsibilities was to help the drifters maintain a net-defence for the shipping congregated in the Downs, and to clear the war channel leading from Folkestone gate to the sanctuary behind the Goodwins. The whole of this swept traffic line was divided into sections, to each of which two trawlers were permanently assigned; and occasions were far from infrequent when the traffic channel had to be swept twice a day. The minimum of trawlers to carry out sweeping properly, over an area of approximately 4,000 square miles, was 66; and the duration of the patrol for each crew of a skipper and six deck hands was four days and four nights. At the outset the drifters and the trawlers went entirely unarmed, and it was some time before the men in the former were doled out with a rifle or a small gun, or the hands in the latter acquired a stock of depth charges and a wireless telegraphy set. The trawlers and drifters, although commanded by R.N. or R.N.R. Officers, were manned exclusively by fisherfolk; and their wearisome, unending work was absolutely invaluable. Well may Admiral Sir Charles Saunders have warned the House of Commons in 1774, "Give up the fishery and you lose your breed of seamen."

The highly assorted armament of the Cinderella Dover Command, which by the Spring of 1915 totalled some 400 craft, included a few old C-class submarines,[1] Motor Launches for light patrol work, Paddle-boats—the "shilling sicks" pleasure steamers of happier days—for work in shallow waters where the trawlers would have gone aground, Trinity House vessels, three Yachts, Coastal Motor Boats that were part seaplane, part boat and part torpedo, and the Armed Boarding Craft of the Examination Service. With Dunkirk retained as an Advanced Headquarters, the French were able to contribute four medium and eight small destroyers of an antiquity to match that of the British 30-knotters. It was left to the Royal Navy, however, to keep the approaches to Boulogne and Calais clear and sweep the channel to Dunkirk—which the Germans never attacked from the sea, although it was well within their power to launch an assault on it in strength. For in addition to the formidable

---

[1] Two E-class submarines were borrowed for a brief period.

force of submarines based on Zeebrugge and Ostend, there were never less than a dozen, and sometimes as many as two and twenty powerful modern destroyers available for raids into the thinly-defended Narrows; over which constantly passed those sinews of war required to sustain the B.E.F. that continually grew in numbers as in demands.

The Command also benefited from an increasing volume of support from the Royal Naval Air Service, although the force had been given little time to develop from its primitive beginnings in 1911. As it had fallen out, however, the first R.N.A.S. air station had been established in the nearby Isle of Sheppey; and with another installation at Dunkirk, aircraft were soon working in close co-operation with the seaborne patrols; a dozen Farmans and Avros being maintained at Dover's Guston Road aerodrome, and another twelve at St. Pol. Work was well in hand on stations for heavier-than-air craft at Capel and Pole-gate; and the seaplane[1] carrier *Riviera* was attached for duty with the command. The W/T sets were far from efficient, however, and for armament the pilot nursed a rifle or shot-gun on his knees!

*　　　　*　　　　*

Admiral Bacon's primary concern was to establish a cross-Channel net-barrage from the Goodwins to Dunkirk, and to screen the shipping in the Downs. In all, some thirteen and a half miles of mine-nets were drifted and constantly patrolled. The arrival of monitors armed with 12-inch guns added weight to the bombardment maintained, in anything like suitable weather, on the batteries the Germans had established along the coast from Middelkerke to Westende.[2] Naval installations in Zeebrugge and Ostend were also brought under fire, the work being aided by the kite-balloon ship and by 'spotter' 'planes from Dunkirk.

The Germans were indefatigable mine-layers, often sowing new minefields at the rate of one in every four days; and with races, rips, contending tides, and evil weather to swirl it out of alignment the net-barrage let through more than one submarine to prey on shipping in the Channel. Mines claimed the P. and

[1] F.B.A. boats and W and T's.
[2] Ultimately the coast was defended by 80 heavy guns.

O. vessel *Maloja* and the Hospital Ship *Anglia*, which went down hard-by No. 8 buoy, off Dover's Copt Point, a few of the wounded being saved by the torpedo boat *Ure*. The trawler *Falmouth III* also struck a mine and sank on top of the *Anglia*. The steam packet *Sussex*, crowded with passengers, was torpedoed in the same area as had seen the sinking of the *Anglia*; and such travellers as were saved owed their lives to the magnificent work of Lieutenant-Commander Perceval of the *Afridi*, who placed his destroyer right alongside the sinking craft, handling her superbly until the task of rescue had been completed. The Hospital Ship *Asturias* was attacked off Havre, the trawler *Dagon* fell victim to a torpedo, while the Gallic vessel *Etoile Polaise* was mined near the South Goodwin lightship. A minefield off the Folkestone gate—as often renewed as it was swept—claimed the S.S. *Shenandoah* and the S.S. *Othello II*, while the S.S. *Volscian* struck a mine near the Sunk lightship, and the torpedo-boat *Gurkha* was holed off Beachy Head. The paddle mine-sweepers introduced in mid-1915, although of much shallower draft than the trawlers, were no more immune from trouble than their bigger brethren. The P.M.S. *Montrose* struck a mine off Gravelines and sank in fifty seconds, with a loss of twelve lives. The *Nepaulin*, the *Redcar* and the *Kempton* were all mined, while the *Albion* was one of the few vessels to be hit from the air. None of these losses created so profound and terrible an impression, however, as the sinking of the *Lusitania*[1] in the Atlantic approaches in the early May of 1915—a blunder as cold-blooded in its execution as it was far-reaching in its consequences.

The *unterseebooten* did not have it all their own way, however. In the March of 1915 the destroyer *Viking* was on patrol when Sub-Lieutenant Frank Younghusband spotted a submarine half a mile distant, and the British craft hurled itself at the enemy full tilt, firing her foremost 4-inch gun. With only seconds to spare, the U-boat crash-dived, leaving the *Viking* to cruise hopefully in the area of the encounter. While thus engaged a torpedo was launched at her, but it ran badly and missed. Sweeps were got out and the zone thoroughly combed, the *unterseeboot*'s periscope being glimpsed from time to time.

[1] A small craft, also named *Lusitania*, was mined when seeking to render aid to the sinking hospital ship *Anglia*.

Suddenly the sweep of one of *Viking*'s companion destroyers caught in an obstruction and was exploded. In a swirl of foam the submarine rose slowly to the surface, to come under the concentrated fire of the assembled destroyers. A shell struck the U-boat's conning tower just as her Captain emerged with both hands raised in token of surrender. Boats were hastily called away and the crew of the submarine brought off, prior to taking the U-boat in tow. But the Germans had opened the sea-cocks, and with a lurch the prize upended and sank in sixteen fathoms of water. But by nightfall her crew was under hatches in the British submarines' parent ship, *Arrogant*.

The guns installed in the Tirpitz and Hindenburg batteries on the coast outranged the 12-inch weapons in the monitors by 17,000 yards. But the shoots were continued under the cover of a smoke screen, with portable tripods dropped on to the sea-bed from which the fall of shot could be seen and reported. The organisation of one of these bombardments called for quite elaborate planning, so that the monitors from the Swin rendezvoused punctually with the destroyers, drifters and tripod ships off the Kentish Knock, as a preliminary to the whole armament steering for the North Hinder lightship and the enemy coastline.

Apart from the hope of denying Ostend and Zeebrugge to the U-boats and thus committing them to a 350-mile journey north-about to reach the Channel,[1] these bombardments helped to encourage speculation as to a possible amphibious landing in support of a major offensive on the Western Front. Admiral Bacon was, indeed, charged with the preparation of a plan to put a strong military force ashore on the Belgian coast, to join hands with another body of troops driving north from Ypres. But with land operations making little progress and the erection of yet another enemy battery at Knocke, the project was allowed to languish.

In return for several vicious air raids on Dunkirk, Zeebrugge was subjected to intensified bombing, directed against the dock area in the hope of making the destroyer force put to sea. The ruse was successful, and the G.88 was sunk by a torpedo launched from one of the lurking C.M.B.'s.

Meanwhile every effort was made to maintain the barrage off

[1] With no Zeebrugge and Ostend to fall back on, the *unterseebooten* would have had to base themselves on the Elbe.

the Belgian coast and complete a combined mine and net-barrage from Folkestone to Griz Nez. This work was well in hand by the third week in April 1916; and during the course of the operation a seaplane was brought down and a submarine, which had fouled the nets, was destroyed by depth charge. Another U-boat was caught in the nets drifted by the appro-priately named *Gleaner of the Sea*, while a submerged explosion could be interpreted as the end of a third *unterseeboot*. The drifter *Clovis Bank*, on the other hand, lost direction and blew up on the mines just laid by the trawlers; while a British sea-plane underwent the unique experience of being shot down by the gun in a U-boat! Three subsequent underwater explosions implied further 'kills' in the minefield.

The only sound tactics for a force thrown on the defensive, such as the Germans at Zeebrugge, is to take every oppor-tunity to thrust home a punishing sortie. As a highly important Naval base Portsmouth, of course, was a standing invitation to enemy enterprise, but it enjoyed almost complete immunity from off-shore interference throughout the whole period of the war. Only once—on the night of September 25th, 1916—did a Zeppelin appear in the skies over the town. Dropping four bombs—one of which fell perilously near to Nelson's *Victory*—the airship passed serenely on its way, well out of range of the anti-aircraft guns yapping so industriously below. So far as hostile action at sea was concerned, it was not until the night of October 26th–27th, 1916, that the enemy destroyers staged their first raid into the narrow seas. With one division of six craft steaming for Griz Nez, another of equal number headed for Dover. The 'Tribals' on routine 'rest' in Dover's ever-turbulent harbour were immediately ordered forth, and the boats guard-ing the Downs were instructed to weigh and move out to meet any attack directed against the shipping in the anchorage. The first serious casualty was the old 30-knotter *Flirt*, which had been with the drifters in the eastern area of the Channel. Turning on her searchlight to go to the aid of a damaged drifter, she was pounced upon by two enemy destroyers, riddled with shot and sunk. Taking full advantage of the ele-ment of surprise, the Germans contrived to down 6 drifters and 1 trawler, and inflict damage on 3 more drifters, with a loss of 45 Officers and men killed and 1 Officer and 9 men captured and borne away. The Griz Nez force overhauled and sank the empty transport *Queen*; and although the hostile vessels promptly turned tail as soon as the 'Tribals' put in an appearance, their Parthian shots inflicted considerable damage on the *Amazon* and the *Nubian*.

Having lost her prow, *Nubian* was taken in tow, but parted her cables, and drifted on to the chalk reef jutting out from the South Foreland. After riding out two gales, she was brought into Dover; and the *Zulu* having been denuded of her stern by a mine, the two segments were joined to make a perfectly sound destroyer that was promptly named the *Zubian*!

The Germans' initial foray had scored quite a notable little success, but their hope had been to catch and sink a crowded trooper or bulging leave boat. But these crossed the narrow seas only by daylight and with a strong destroyer escort; 2,500,000 men passing through Southampton alone between August 4th, 1914, and December 24th, 1916.

There was a second tip-and-run raid on November 23rd, which reaped a remarkably scanty reward, slight damage being inflicted on the drifter *Acceptable* before the enemy destroyers turned tail and made for their base.

To be successful a destroyer action requires to be rammed home with the undeviating thrust of a cavalry charge. The Germans invariably exhibited a caution that robbed their forays into the Channel of half their potential effect; for as Admiral Fisher had long since pointed out, "Moderation in war is imbecility."

*   *   *

In all wars it is extremely difficult to convince neutralist commercial circles that the conflict is not being waged exclusively for their financial benefit. Negotiations over the flow of seaborne trade in and out of Holland and Scandinavia were both difficult and delicate. Eventually a *modus operandi* was worked out that had for its background the arresting consideration that Britain could always withhold essential supplies of coal from any non-belligerent unprepared to make reasonable concessions to her demands. So far as their own commercial latitudinarians were concerned, the British authorities drew up Statutory Lists of individuals and companies in neutral countries, to trade with whom was to court the severest penalties.

The United States, with her traditional advocacy of un-inhibited freedom of the seas—at any rate for vessels wearing the Stars and Stripes—exhibited considerable reluctance to accept restrictions similar to those imposed by her Federal Government during the War between the States. For the sweet reasonableness of measures of restraint always becomes suspect when the role of belligerent has been exchanged for that of neutral.

A great point was made of the fact that Britain's own seaborne trade with the non-belligerents had greatly increased. But as Whitehall gently pointed out—so had America's; cotton exports to neutral countries alone having gone up from $5,000,000 for the period June 1913 to June 1914 to over $60,000,000 for the corresponding period for 1914–15,[1] while general commerce with Holland and the Scandinavian countries had more than doubled.

This particular point of dispute was solved in a manner best calculated to appeal to the American cotton tycoons, when Britain arranged to buy up the current cotton crop by means of a loan floated in New York.

Obviously, at this stage, there could be no such thing as total prohibition of trade with the neutrals. A certain amount of commerce had therefore been permitted, under licence, with the representatives of enemy firms in neutral countries, on the principle that German gold drained into British coffers helped to weaken the hostile war economy, while preserving post-war markets to British firms. Ultimately, a system of rationing curbed the export of British goods and alien wares "on continuous voyage", in excess of a neutral's normal needs—a sacrifice in turnover that British commercial circles had to accept.

There was still a certain amount of trouble over smuggling. For the more unscrupulous had no hesitation in shipping contraband under a false description; while rubber was hidden in barrels of herrings, medicinal drugs in cheeses, and tin was made up in laths, painted to resemble wood, and mixed in with genuine timber.

[1] Since the Declaration of London had never been ratified, it was meaningless to insist that under its terms raw cotton was not accounted as contraband of war.

It was when the German Government announced its intention of seizing all stocks of corn and flour—thus rendering grain an article of war—that the Asquith Administration found itself in the position to detain all ships of presumed enemy origin, ownership, or destination.[1] It was, admittedly, a measure of reprisal outside the framework of existent, but unrealistic, International Law. But it found its justification in Germany's prior infraction of that selfsame law by the prosecution of her 'intensified' submarine campaign, and by the announcement of her intention to impound all the stocks of grain on which she could lay her hands.

With this unequivocal declaration of Britain's resolve to safeguard her own vital interests, neutrals who hitherto had sworn by the Declaration of Paris when its provisions appeared to sanction their activities, and, alternatively, had solemnly referred to the Declaration of London when that had better suited their convenience, found themselves somewhat drastically short-circuited. It occurred to few of those who made indignant appeal to whichever law they momentarily favoured that *silent leges inter arma*.

In the long run, the British authorities very largely succeeded in persuading neutral Governments to "maintain embargoes that, in practice, were comparable to the Allied contraband lists".[2]

Under the steady, inexorable pressure of the Allies' blockade Germany angrily announced that as from February 1st an *unrestricted* submarine campaign would be waged against all hostile and neutral shipping approaching French or British coastal waters, which in future the *unterseebooten*, without discrimination, would sink at sight.[3]

Increased activity on the part of the U-boats—with the holing of the S.S. *Valacia* off the Eddystone amongst their earlier successes—was accompanied by further destroyer raids into the Narrows. On March 1st one division of enemy boats raided Broadstairs, their gunfire wreaking a certain amount of promiscuous damage. One G-boat of the other division fired a

---

[1] By Order in Council of March 11th, 1915.

[2] Siney, *op. cit.*

[3] It is credibly recorded that Admiral von Tirpitz derived the idea for this campaign from a story by Conan Doyle, entitled *Danger*.

torpedo at H.M.S. *Laverock*, but it failed to explode; and with that the night's activities ended.

Later in March, after a lightning bombardment of Ramsgate,[1] an attempt was made on the patrol line near Calais. In the confused action that ensued, H.M.S. *Paragon* was torpedoed, sinking in ten minutes, with few survivors. *Laforey* and *Llewellyn* going to their sister ship's aid, the last-named was also torpedoed, but managed to make Dover. Close to the North Foreland the enemy destroyers also contrived to sink the S.S. *Greyhound*, and score hits on the drifter *Paramount*.

In these enemy *chevauchées* the Command suffered some hard knocks and experienced many bitter disappointments. But the news of America's entry into the war was an enheartening augury for the future, since it was clear that the U.S. Navy would be ready to lend a hand long before the country's small Regular Army could be expanded and trained for service overseas. In Germany the new development bred a grim determination to force Britain to her knees before American aid could be brought to strengthen her blows on sea and land.

On the night of April 20th, therefore, the fifth destroyer raid was launched, with two out of the six enemy vessels engaged making for Calais. The remaining four steered for the Kentish coast, where the trawler *Sabreur* was hit and Dover reminded by a spray of gunfire that in coastal towns "the inhabitants must expect to get their skin scratched".[2]

Commander Peck in the *Swift* and Commander E. R. G. R. Evans in the *Broke*[3] were patrolling the western end of the barrage. The night was so dark and conditions so suitable for an enemy attack, that everyone was preternaturally strung up and on the alert. As the gun flashes pierced the murk in the direction of Dover, the flotilla leaders increased speed with the intention of cutting off any attempt by the raiders to play havoc with the shipping congregated in the Downs.

It was not long before the enemy were sighted, about seven miles from Dover, steaming swiftly in an easterly direction in line ahead. Both *Swift* and *Broke* closed at their best speed, and

[1] Three houses were hit but there were no casualties.

[2] Mahan, *op. cit.*

[3] *Broke* had been reconstituted after having taken a pretty hard hammering at the battle of Jutland.

opened fire. *Swift*, in the forefront, hammered away briskly as she passed down the enemy line; while Evans, slightly altering course to avoid his leader's wake, held his fire till the director sights on the bridge came on for firing the port foremost torpedo. He then conned the ship so as to be in a position to ram. At the same time the foremost 4-inch guns roared into action, drowning the exultant shout of Despard, the 'Number 1', "We've got her!"

Almost in the same breath the port torpedo reached its mark, striking the G.85 plumb amidships. With the thunderclap of the explosion, Evans put his helm over hard a-port, and swung away to starboard far enough to enable him to turn in on the next G-boat in line. The German craft vainly sought to avoid the impact by putting on a burst of speed, but *Broke* crashed into her port side just abreast of the after funnel. As the destroyer's sturdy prow clove its way into the enemy's flank, above the crunch of buckling plate Evans let out a whoop of "Hurrah! That means two months' leave!"

Steaming at 27 knots, *Broke* virtually put her enemy on her beam ends, while the destroyer's guns, which would bear maximum depression, opened up at point-blank range, echoed by a steady crackle of small-arms fire. On the forecastle Despard piped 'boarders' as some of the Germans clambered up *Broke*'s bow and sought to make the deck. But there was no question of their boarding and entering with any other intention than of surrendering.

There were many casualties up forward, but Midshipman Donald Gyles, R.N.R., although himself wounded by a shell splinter, organised a gun's crew from the survivors, and the fire never slackened for a moment.

Broke was steaming ahead with G.42 firmly impaled on her bow. None the less she tried to torpedo an enemy craft that passed astern of her; but all the controls had been shot away and the tubes failed to respond. The stern of G.42 was sliding further and further into the depths, and eventually *Broke* shook her off and steamed right over her. Evans then tried to ram another enemy vessel, but owing to an explosion in one of the boiler rooms, his craft had lost so much speed that the attempt failed.

Afire amidships and on the bridge, with her steering damaged and her speed reduced to half, *Broke* was glad to welcome H.M.S. *Mentor* alongside to take off her wounded, and accept the aid of two eager tugs to help her limp into Dover, in company with a sister-ship no less worthy of acclaim than the battered veteran of Jutland. Their resolute work had done much to atone for the loss of 6 drifters and the damage done to 3 others and a trawler.

In furtherance of the Germans' fixed design to force an issue, the destroyer raids were supplemented by a good deal more activity in the air. Dunkirk was drenched with bombs again and again.[1] London was twice raided, once in bright sunshine. But of the force of enemy Gothas taking part in these forays, 2 were destroyed and 4 driven down out of control on the first occasion, while in the daylight raid a further 2 were shot down in flames, with 2 more seriously damaged—an undoubted tribute to the interceptor squadron based on Dunkirk.

It was not from the air, however, but from beneath the waves that the deadliest danger threatened. For the toll of the U-boats for the first three months of their unrestricted submarine campaign totalled 1,974,000 tons of Allied and neutral shipping. During April one out of every four vessels sailing from the United Kingdom had been sunk; undiscriminating recruitment had reduced shipbuilding in British yards by something like 75 per cent; while the American construction programme that was to replace vessels faster than they could be sunk had yet to get into its stride. On immediate showing Britain would be starved out of the war before the next harvest, since there was only three weeks' supply of grain in hand.[2]

To help curb this ever-growing menace the old device of the decoy ship had been revived. Battered 'tramps' and other assorted craft whose innocent appearance insouciantly belied the powerful armament they concealed, sought to entice the U-boat's attention. With its approach a 'panic party' would ostentatiously abandon ship, hoping to lure the submarine well within range of the apparently deserted vessel's hidden guns.

---

[1] In all, Dunkirk suffered 214 bombardments from the air or from the sea.
[2] Of the 869,000 total for April, British losses accounted for 545,000 tons. It was the German aim to sink 600,000 tons of shipping a month for five consecutive months.

At the outset the ruse frequently proved successful. Commander Gordon Campbell in the *Farnborough* sank the U-68 in the Atlantic approaches to the Channel; an event somewhat grimly celebrated by one of the hands playing a gramophone record of *Down Among the Dead Men Let Him Lie*.

On a later occasion Campbell was duly torpedoed in the disguised S.S. *Pargust*, whose hard-core ship's company then proceeded to put the *unterseeboot* out of business in four minutes of rapid gunfire.

In all, the Q-ships between them downed a total of eleven submarines; and the U.S. Naval authorities were sufficiently impressed to fit out the *Santee* at Plymouth to act as a decoy. Unfortunately, although this American Q-ship was duly torpedoed, with all the accompaniment of 'panic parties' scuttling from her deck, the U-boat failed to surface, but made off submerged.[1] The Germans, in short, had learned to be extremely wary.

This was amply demonstrated in Campbell's last fight in the 3,000-ton *Dunraven*, which occurred on August 8th, 1917, in the Channel's western approaches. When an enemy submarine was sighted on the starboard beam the usual procedure was carried out; and the 'panic party' having 'abandoned ship' a deliberately ill-aimed return fire replied to the well-directed rounds from the *unterseeboot*'s deck-gun. But an explosion of ammunition and depth charges aboard *Dunraven* so alarmed the U-boat Commander that he gave the order to crash-dive. A second 'decoy party' then left the Q-ship in the hope of persuading the peering Germans that at last their prey was really deserted. The few determined men left aboard settled down to await torpedoing—with ammunition exploding on every side and a fire raging near the main magazine.

But having discharged a 'tin fish' that hit home just abaft the *Dunraven*'s engine room, for an hour or more the U-boat circled cautiously around the doomed vessel; finally submerging when U.S.S. *Nona* came hurrying up to the sound of the firing. For five hours *Dunraven* had stood up to a battering that left her a blazing hulk, and still the *unterseeboot* had not been lured to its destruction.

Very different was the fate of the U.C.-61, stranded in the

[1] *History of the Modern American Navy*, Donald W. Mitchell.

shoals near Wissant, whose partly blown-up hulk was captured with tremendous *brio* by a detachment of Belgian Cavalry![1]

*   *   *

On the Western Front a British assault launched from Arras had been checked; while the much-vaunted offensive directed by General Nivelle had collapsed in such a welter of frustration, wasteful slaughter and pricked vanity that disaffection and outright mutiny amongst the Gallic rank and file ultimately contaminated no less than 258 battalions and 8 artillery regiments. For all practical purposes the self-styled "finest military force in Europe" was out of the war.

With the whole burden of the fighting on British shoulders, Sir Douglas Haig mounted a series of offensives, which he requested the Dover Command to be ready to support with an amphibious landing, in Divisional strength.

Admiral Bacon immediately set to work to develop the plan worked out in 1915; his preparations including the construction of some ingenious pontoons for speedily putting troops ashore, which anticipated, in many respects, the landing craft of later days.[2] But the deadlock which supervened in the third battle of Ypres precluded the idea of carrying this design into immediate effect.

In a land which produced less than three-fifths of its food and no more than 20 per cent of its raw materials, the overriding problem was, of course, the darkening menace of the submarine campaign. For

> *The young disease which shall destroy at length*
> *Grows with its growth and strengthens with its strength.*

and U-boat sinkings were still perilously numerous. The U.S. Admiral William S. Sims, and one or two of the more historically-minded British sea-Officers, were warmly in favour of adopting the convoy system as the only answer to the lurking *unterseeboot*. But their recommendations met with no endorsement from Sir John Jellicoe[3]; the official Admiralty point of

[1] See page 395 for the only other instance of the capture of warships by Cavalry.

[2] They also embodied a modern version of the sliding ramp employed in their landing craft by the tenth-century Byzantines.

[3] Transferred from the command of the Grand Fleet to the post of First Sea Lord in the November of 1916.

view being that "the larger the number of ships forming the convoy, the greater is the chance of a submarine being enabled to attack successfully, the greater is the difficulty in preventing such an attack".[1]

Yet within five months of the circulation of this minute a convoy had arrived safely in port. The immediate trouble lay in the absence of a sufficiency of cruisers, destroyers, aircraft carriers and 'planes—particularly the last-named—to furnish the necessary escorts; part of the price that had to be paid for Fisher's all-big-gun battle fleet. At least it is on record that with the eventual adoption of the convoy system, while 312 vessels were torpedoed while under escort, only two attacks scored any sort of success when the convoy had aerial protection in addition to the cruiser or destroyer screen.[2]

In June, a month that was to disclose total sinkings of 690,000 tons, Sir Douglas Haig recorded of a conference with the First Sea Lord and others, "A most serious and startling situation was disclosed today . . . Admiral Jellicoe stated that owing to the great shortage of shipping, due to German submarines, it would be impossible for Great Britain to continue the war in 1918."[3] Admiral Bacon had already confided to Sir Douglas that the Zeebrugge–Ostend area was of vital importance, since "the Germans command the East end of the Channel from there and threaten England".[4]

It was unquestionable that despite all precautions, the U-boats were streaming freely through the Channel; and Admiral Bacon was urged to work out plans for blocking Zeebrugge and Ostend, while establishing as strong a Belgian Barrage Patrol as more up-to-date resources permitted. At the same time British G.H.Q. started preparations for an offensive designed not only to distract hostile attention from the tottering French, but to take Bruges and the Ostend-Zeebrugge area from the rear.

In a terrain only a few feet above sea level and seamed with an elaborate but fragile drainage system, the meteorological factor was paramount. Careful enquiry having established that fine weather might be anticipated from mid-July to

---

[1] *Vide* an Admiralty minute of January, 1917.
[2] *North Sea Air Station*, C. F. Snowdon Gamble.
[3] *The Private Papers of Sir Douglas Haig*, edited by Robert Blake.
[4] Bacon, *op. cit.*

mid-August, the offensive at Passchendaele was timed to open on July 25th. In the event, the delay occasioned by the dilatory General Antoine and the six French divisions scheduled to mount a holding action on the northern flank, impelled the British to postpone their initial assault until July 31st—the very day the weather broke in a deluge of rain that continued, almost without intermission, for weeks on end.

With the offensive drowned out amidst Passchendaele's reeking swamp, the need to tackle Ostend and Zeebrugge from the sea was only too starkly apparent.

*　　　　*　　　　*

In the December of 1916 Herbert Asquith had been replaced as Premier by David Lloyd George, an individual whose tolerance for his own shortcomings did not extend to those he found it convenient to perceive in others. Shallow, flashy, and obsessed with the desire for quick 'results' that would serve as political window-dressing, his impatience with Admiral Bacon's long-term planning led to his supersession in the Dover Command by Rear-Admiral Sir Roger Keyes.[1]

Keyes immediately set to work to reconstitute the system of Channel defences with several lines of mines at different depths, which were to be patrolled day and night—the whole area being brilliantly illuminated throughout the hours of darkness. As the minefield thickened, the new technique certainly brought results. Before the end of February the U-95, U-109, U.B.-35, U.C.-30 and U.B.-38 had all been sunk. After U-109 failed to return to base orders were given by the German High Command for all ocean-going *unterseebooten* to go north-about.

None the less, a number of submarines managed to sneak into and through the Channel, under cover of a destroyer raid. One of their number even had the audacity to lie off Dover and lob a number of shells into the town. In some desperation Keyes turned to a suggestion to span the Narrows with a series of towers armed with 4-inch guns and searchlights.[2]

The general state of affairs underwent violent reorientation,

[1] Up to the end of Bacon's tenure of command (December 31st, 1917) some 1,200 mines had been destroyed in the Channel; but 63 merchant craft had been lost in addition to 6 destroyers and 38 patrol vessels.

[2] The suggestion was for 10 towers, from the designs furnished by Colonel Gibb, to be installed at a total cost of £1,500,000. The war ended before the scheme could be put into operation.

however, when the collapse of the Imperial Russian Empire released such substantial bodies of German troops that Ludendorff was enabled to stage his March offensive against the thinly-held lines of the British IIIrd and Vth Armies. The initial prosperity that attended the Germans' last desperate thrust presented the Allies with the choice of maintaining touch by jointly retreating southwards to the Loire, or of drawing apart as Pétain prepared to protect Paris and Haig swung back to defend the Channel ports.

Ludendorff's wild gamble was accompanied by a strong destroyer raid on Dunkirk. Scheduled to be kept up at top pitch for an hour, so hot was the reception that greeted it that it lasted exactly ten minutes. And all the time the transports were hurtling across the narrow seas bearing the flood of re-inforcements—hitherto retained on the home front by the Premier's own egregious obstinacy—whose earlier presence on the scene might well have blasted the enemy onset in the earlier stages of its development.[1]

With Ludendorff's over-extended offensive halted, the hour had come to attempt the blocking of the coastal exits which permitted the 30 submarines and 35 torpedo craft based on Bruges to make their way to sea.

After a couple of false starts, in which the enterprise had to be called off on the score of lack of wind to extend the essential smoke screen, the 76 vessels comprising the expedition set off from their various stations, to rendezvous punctually at a point near the North Goodwins.

The plan was for the old cruiser *Vindictive* to grapple herself to Zeebrugge's Mole and deal with the torpedo craft moored alongside it and the batteries at its seaward end; and for the blockships *Thetis, Intrepid* and *Iphigenia* to approach the entrance of the harbour and sink themselves across its mouth. Shore parties from *Vindictive* would meanwhile deal with the seaplane sheds and other installations on the Mole itself; while two old submarines, crammed with explosive, would be jammed under the viaduct linking the Mole and the shore, and there be left to blow up and isolate the scene of action from any hope of reinforcement from the town.

---

[1] In the seven days March 29th to April 4th some 120,000 troops were safely transported across the Channel.

The armada approached its objective in bright moonlight, but the heavy pall of the smoke screen enabled *Vindictive* to get within 300 yards of the Mole extension before coming under fire. Unfortunately, owing to the smoke and the dazzle of star shell *Vindictive* badly overshot her mark, exposing herself thereby to the fire of the shore batteries; a piece of misfortune to which must be attributed the partial failure of the subsequent activities on the Mole. Many casualties were inflicted as the assault force sought to scramble ashore, for the *Vindictive*, from the position she had taken up, was unable to get to grips with the guns on the Mole extension or bring her weapons to bear on the troops protecting them. They were free, therefore, to play havoc with the Marine and Bluejacket storming party, which was pinned down and badly punished.

Meanwhile the three blockships, shepherded by Keyes in the *Warwick*, and with the *Thetis* deliberately drawing the enemy fire, were groping their way through the smother, under an increasing cannonade, to take up position to sink themselves across the mouth of the harbour. *Thetis* grounded, and as *Intrepid* was in danger of swinging into the Channel instead of lying across it, the charges had to be blown while the crew was still aboard. The men took to the boats, and, miraculously enough, there was only one casualty out of a total complement of 87, despite the incessant shelling and the tempest of machine-gun fire. Lieutenant Billyard Leake in *Iphigenia*, having observed that *Intrepid* was very much out of the desired alignment, remained under heavy fire, manœuvring his vessel to fill the gap left exposed. The M.L. commander, standing by to take off *Iphigenia's* crew, subsequently commented, "I thought the damned fellow would never stop juggling with his engines!"

The M.L. 526 and M.L. 282 particularly distinguished themselves in rescuing the crews of the blockships; Lieutenant P. T. Dean of the latter bringing away over 70 of the survivors.

One of the submarines charged with blowing up the viaduct unfortunately parted her tow on the way out. But the crew of the C.3, rejecting the Admiral's advice to abandon their craft short of its objective and let it proceed by gyro steering, rammed it into the viaduct till the bows were well wedged in the girders. The enemy went vigorously into action as Lieutenants Sandford and Howell-Price, with the four hands, scrambled into their skiff and pushed off. Under intense rifle and machine-gun fire, the craft was holed many times, but was still defiantly afloat when the viaduct went up with a roar and a shower of debris and shattered bodies.

The skiff, with three of its occupants wounded, was in a sinking condition, however, by the time rescue loomed up out of the murk in the shape of the picket boat commanded by Sandford's elder brother.

Under a hail of fire that *Vindictive*'s guns could do little to subdue, the demolition parties did their utmost to carry out their respective missions, but casualties had been so heavy that when the Recall sounded much had to be left unaccomplished. With *Vindictive* taken in tow by the Mersey ferry steamer *Daffodil*, and sheltered by a smoke screen laid by the ubiquitous Motor Launches, the battered armada drew off.

If less had been accomplished than high hopes had anticipated, the cause must be found in the excusable error of judgment that had laid *Vindictive* alongside the Mole at a point where she was least able to support the gallant work of the storming and demolition parties. And if the same quasi-unfavourable fortune dogged the attempt to block Ostend, nothing could tarnish or belittle the puissant and selfless devotion to duty that had distinguished the feat of arms by which St. George's Day had been so fittingly commemorated.

*   *   *

The swing of the pendulum in France, which began with the Allied advance of August 8th, was accompanied by distinct evidence that at last the submarine campaign was under control. With American destroyers and submarine chasers added to the British forces in the Channel, it became possible to permit convoys to break up and individual ships to proceed to their ports of discharge without challenging disaster. Plymouth—where two squadrons of submarine chasers were stationed under Captain Lyman A. Cotten, U.S.N.—became happily familiar with the American 'white caps', as did 'Pompey', where the United States authorities had installed a number of shore establishments and a hospital.

Dover experienced a terrible moment in September when a magazine in H.M.S. *Glatton* exploded while the ship was in

16+

harbour. A raging fire made it clear that it would be only a matter of time before the vessel herself blew up, as the after-magazine could not be flooded owing to the blazing oil. The only thing to do was to sink the craft where she lay. She was torpedoed at close range and mercifully sank before her main magazine could explode and wreck the town. Sixty men trapped in the ship were killed or missing and 19 Officers and men were taken off badly injured.

As the Allied thrust eastward gathered impetus, the Dover Command ably supported the advance of the Belgians and the British IInd Army; but every effort was made to spare Ostend and Bruges, which were crowded with civilians. As early as October 17th Admiral Keyes landed at Ostend, where the stranded *Vindictive* was crowded with Belgian children cheering and waving the flags of the Allies with which an enterprising German had furnished them—at a price—before discreetly taking his departure!

The Armistice was celebrated in the Channel ports and waterways with much the same delirium of thankfulness as greeted the news elsewhere. But for all the hysteria and facile laughter, there was sober realisation that once again the land had been given proof that "the vital British policy must always be that the coasts of the enemy are the frontiers of England".[1]

[1] Fisher.

CHAPTER XXI

Mainly Political. The Years of the Locust

"Blessed with victory and peace,
May the heavens rescue the land."
FRANCIS SCOTT KEY

WITH the German High Sea Fleet interned at Scapa Flow and a British Army of Occupation on the Rhine, the business of demobilising the vast host of men brought into the Forces by the demands of 'total' war went jerkily into action. But when a war ends neither the dead nor the living can go home. The slain lie quietly in "some corner of a foreign field"; the living return to something entirely different to the home they knew. With the Service-man filtering back into 'civvy street', there was an un-bridgeable gulf between the cosseted individual who had been extremely well paid to make the gun and the man who had accepted a pittance to wield it in the face of the enemy.

Wars are won not only by men and weapons, but by material reserves and financial credit; and the inroads made on both the last-named had been stupendous. The politician talked *au large* of "making Germany pay till the pips squeaked", but with no very clear idea how this engaging feat was to be accomplished. In the meantime one traditional method of economising—by swingeing reductions in the Fighting Services—was seized upon with such avidity that the 'Geddes axe' sheared away £21,000,000 from the Navy Estimates and denuded the Service of some 35,000 of its remaining long-service Officers and men.

The share-out of a Prize Fund of £15,000,000 went a very little way towards consoling those whose hopes of a career in the Service of their choice had been so summarily shattered.

It was left to the provisions of the Washington Naval Treaty of 1921, however, to reduce Britain's cruiser strength to the danger point and so drastically to scale down the total of her capital ships that she was in no case to defend such Far Eastern possessions as Singapore or honour her bond with Australia and New Zealand.[1]

The *mot d'ordre* circulating in the Ministries was, "There is no possibility of war for at least ten years." But since the same cant-phrase was being chanted with the same unctuous fervour a decade later, it is clear that all responsible thinking on the subject had been replaced by the fond wish that is father to the thought.

In 1921, however, the emasculation of Britain's traditional first line of defence typified the mood of a period too slugged with incessant doses of high-mindedness even to look that strange gift horse, the League of Nations, as carefully and critically in the mouth as its soaring pretensions obviously demanded.[2] Only the coldly practical voice of the Gallic politician, Philippe Berthelot, was raised to dismiss the whole cloud-castle postulation of the League as "a colossal *fumisterie*, a grotesque hoax". In many circles, however, the foundation of this amorphous international areopagus was received with a rapture virtually indistinguishable from hysteria; for the aftermath of war is invariably characterised by a spinsterish rejection of anything even remotely bordering on reality.

The reality where Britain was concerned included a burden of debt to the total of £7,434,949,000, and the loss of some 8,000,000 tons of merchant shipping, with a sacrifice of 15,000 Merchant Service Officers and men.

To make good the wastage suffered by the mercantile marine, British shipyards in 1920 launched new craft to a total of 2,000,000 tons, the largest tonnage ever to be put in the water in a twelvemonth. But the boom was not maintained.

In the 'nineties four-fifths of all the ships built throughout the world had been laid down in Britain. Just prior to the outbreak of hostilities in 1914 the proportion was still 60·6 of the gross tonnage under construction, with foreign orders accounting for 22 per cent of the total. By 1924 the tonnage launched the

---

[1] In 1918 Britain had possessed 42 capital ships, her Navy consisting of 700 warships of all types.

[2] Two thousand five hundred years before President Wilson wrote the League of Nations Charter into the Versailles Peace Treaty, a precisely similar concept had been sponsored by Hsiang Hsu, Premier of the State of Sung. The first experiment won no greater success than was achieved by its several successors.

world over was greater than the pre-war aggregate; but Britain's share was proportionately less. Much of the work had been secured by foreign competitors; for British prices were high, and incessant labour troubles made the date of delivery vexatiously uncertain. From 806 berths fully employed in 1920, the total had fallen to 686 by 1925.[1] Since Britain's export trade in 1924 was about a third less than it had been in 1913, the demand for vessels on the part of native shippers had undergone proportionate decline. There was also an increasing tendency to avoid heavy British taxation by acquiring 'flags of convenience'—i.e. by paying a small licence fee to register the vessel as Liberian or Colombian or Panamanian.

When global trade contracted sharply as the result of the world financial crisis of 1929, British shipbuilding firms, between them, were compelled to close down 160 yards that were no longer capable of maintaining themselves. With 36·1 of the insured workers in the shipbuilding industry idle, some 36·7 of employees in the kindred iron and steel industry were also thrown out of work.

In engineering products British manufacturers were rapidly being overtaken by their German competitors, who had cannily used their country's inflationary period to modernise their plant. Rice-eating Japan and India, with the aid of imported British machinery, could turn out the cheaper lines in cotton goods at a price with which meat-eating Lancashire could not begin to compete: as Lafcadio Hearn had never tired of emphasising, "the East can always under-starve the West". On the other hand, new industries, such as the manufacture of artificial silk, motors, furniture and electrical goods, exhibited reasonable signs of prosperity. But the Iron and Steel Industry required the protection of a 33⅓ per cent import duty on all rival products to bolster up its sagging fortunes.

The greatest falling off in profitable exports—reflected only too faithfully in the carrying trade—was in coal. In 1913 some 287,000,000 tons of coal had been produced, of which 98,000,000 had been exported at substantial profit both to mine owners and to shippers. In the post-war period, even in the peak year of 1937, only 241,000,000 tons of coal were mined, of which

[1] *Britain Between the Wars*, Charles Loch Mowat. *How Strong is Britain?* Count Puckler.

very much less than a third was exported. There were colliers lying idle at their moorings in many of the ports; while the coasting trade was seriously affected by the competition of the railways which, having been taken over by the State, during the war period, were compelled by law to carry commodities at far less than cost, the difference being made good by that perennial milch-cow, the taxpayer.

Between 1863 and the outbreak of the war the country's population had practically doubled, and the greater proportion of the residential increase had located itself on the seaboard. Indeed, nearly fifty per cent of Britain's inhabitants had come to live within fifteen miles of a port; a thickening up of the hinterland-dwellers which, particularly along the Channel coast, did much to counterbalance the loss of the legitimate commerce in which the havens had previously been engaged. Dover and Folkestone, of course, enjoyed a steady cross-Channel traffic; the fisher-folk brought in their sea harvest to all the smaller havens, while Southampton was still the great entry-port for the western oceanic trade. The flow of commerce to the headport of London demanded the construction of the George Vth Dock, the extension of the Tilbury Dock, and the reorganisation of the India and Millwall Docks; work which was carried out under the paternal eye of that Port of London Authority which had become responsible for the administration of the waterway, below Teddington, by the terms of the Port of London Act of 1908.

*　　　　*　　　　*

A marked feature of the immediate post-war years was the tendency to repose a blind trust in that collectivism which Dicey has defined as "faith in the benefit to be derived by the mass of the people by the action or intervention of the State"[1] —than which no process is better calculated to stifle that healthy individualism which constitutes a country's primary asset. This trend was accompanied by an increasing tendency on the part of the trades unions to turn themselves into pressure groups to maintain the high 1914–18 rate of wages, regardless of the prevailing conditions in their respective industries. For their sense of self-importance had been enormously inflated by

[1] *The Law and Public Opinion*, A. V. Dicey (2nd edition, 1914).

the flattery and concessions employed by Lloyd George to keep them on the job throughout the recent conflict. The men's discovery that it is much more difficult to hold 'peace' to ransom than it is to 'cash in' on the calamity of war, sent them purposefully to the polls in the General Election of 1923 to return the first Socialist Government to office, if not to power.[1] If Mr. Ramsay MacDonald and his colleagues failed to realise their supporters' expectations by promptly showering pennies from heaven upon them, at least they ran true to form by immediately inaugurating fresh economies in the Fighting Services. The cruiser building programme was cut from the eight vessels scheduled by the previous Administration to five, and all work was stopped on the harbour and defences of Singapore. Almost at once Plymouth began to feel the chill of under-employment. Dockyard 'maties' were discharged wholesale; and being men whose especial skills were not easy to fit into any other industry, there were soon 10,000 insured local residents out of work.

The economies that so severely flayed Plymouth penalised 'Pompey' on an equal scale.

In Germany where, under the invertebrate Weimar Republic, the mark stood at 22,300 million to the £—thus reducing the savings of the middle and lower classes to something less than the value of a single meal—the way was paved for any adventurer peddling a nostrum for recovery. He duly arrived in the person of the Austrian paper-hanger, Adolph Hitler, who was speedily recognised as a force to be reckoned with, despite the momentary setback he had experienced in his Bavarian *putsch*.

The MacDonald Government remained in office just long enough to disappoint all but its most ardent and obstruent supporters. It was followed by an Administration headed by Mr. Stanley Baldwin, whose chief claim to recognition, to that date, lay in his conduct of the American debt settlement, which had committed Britain to the payment of a rate of interest twice as high as that negotiated by France and eight times higher than that agreed for Italy.

[1] It is reasonable to submit that the majority of 'floating' voters cast their votes *against* the tariff reform with which Mr. Baldwin had been experimenting, rather than *for* 'Labour'.

With an overall majority of 321, Mr. Baldwin could have given the country a period of firm and constructive government. Instead he preferred to

> *Promise, pause, prepare, postpone*
> *And end by leaving things alone;*
> *In short, to earn the people's pay*
> *By doing nothing every day.*

It is true that as against a national income in 1914 of £1,988,000,000, that of 1924 showed a total of £3,887,000,000. But while the cost of living between 1914 and 1924 had risen by 75 per cent, the average increase in industrial wages had been 94 per cent.[1] In consequence, British goods on foreign markets repeatedly found themselves undercut by cheaper wares from Germany and Japan. Moreover, the new light industries did not expand fast enough to compensate for the decline in prosperity suffered by the old-established 'heavy' industries. Nor did a stubborn disregard for the peculiar requirements of foreign markets help to win popularity for British products. Furthermore, the brief but hectic post-war boom had had the effect of dangerously over-expanding production and grossly inflating capital.

It was at this moment of precarious unbalance that organised 'Labour' elected to stage a general strike; the miners' resistance to a wage reduction winning the support of the Trades Union Congress and the 'key' unions it controlled. It was a consolidated attempt by a well-organised minority to impose its will on the unorganised majority of the community; and with picket lines forming in every direction it seemed as if Adam Smith's "nation of shop keepers" had turned into a nation of shop stewards. The attempt to hold the nation to ransom failed because the authorities were as well prepared to deal with the situation as the professional and middle classes were entirely *un*prepared to knuckle under to coercion.

One thing the industrial upheaval had demonstrated past all question—that the modern counterpart of the medieval *burgeis de la gilde* was no longer master in his own house. The wheel had swung full circle; and while it is true that mercantilism is not an entirely estimable institution, it is equally clear that the

[1] Mowat, *op. cit.*

least endearing of its by-products is Demos with a chip on his shoulder.

*   *   *

The period between 1919 and 1930 might aptly be termed the era of conferences—conferences on reparations, conferences on disarmament, conferences on the elimination of war as a means of settling international disputes, *et hoc genus omne*. So far as the value of these international jamborees is concerned, their deliberations were more notable for flabby-minded confusion of thought than for any practical recommendations. Indeed, when the representative of fifty-six nations who, in 1928, had hopefully signed a pact solemnly 'outlawing' war, met again four years later, it was for the purpose of discussing what weapons it would be permissible to employ in any future conflict!

This predilection for inconclusive debate reached its climax with the Locarno conference of 1930. A number of illusory guarantees were given regarding international frontiers, but the real powder barrel—the question of Germany's eastern borders—did not come up for discussion.

As one of the salient after-effects of Locarno, however, the British Navy touched the lowest level it had reached in forty years. For the *Statement on Defence* produced by the Government in the March of 1931 rendered it clear past any peradventure that in the event of war, Britain would be unable to secure her sea communications, to bring in the necessary food and raw materials required to sustain her population and her factories. For the London Treaty of 1930—a direct outcome of the peculiar afflatus characterising Locarno—had effectively prevented Britain from replacing her capital ships or increasing the number of her light craft until the year 1936. A pious resolution condemning the use made by the Germans of the undersea-boat as a commerce destroyer failed to secure Gallic ratification, and therefore never became effective—even on paper.

The whole country was still making desperate efforts to recover from the effects of the financial blizzard which had struck the world in 1929; and one measure of economy was to institute yet another cut in Service pay. The Admiralty were well aware of the hardship this would involve, and were at

16*

great pains to forward a detailed, carefully-written explanation, well in advance, to all Commanders-in-Chief. Captains
were instructed to get their ships' companies together and go
fully into the situation.

Unfortunately, the Commander-in-Chief, Home Fleet, was
sick, and his Staff failed to redirect this important communication to his Second-in-Command, the Flag Officer commanding
the 2nd Battle Cruiser Squadron at Invergordon. The ships'
companies, therefore, received the news of the sacrifices demanded of them without any placatory explanation.

The result was what, in industrial circles, would have been
termed a strike, but which Admiralty Regulations could only
interpret as mutiny. For seditionaries had speedily appeared on
the scene and got avidly at work to encourage any and every
sign of disaffection. Yet the real cause of the seamen's rebellious
mood was not so much the new pay codes in themselves, as the
fact that the news of the cuts arrived like a thunderbolt, by way
of the daily press. In those Channel ports where the situation
was thoroughly gone into by sympathetic Officers, the mess
decks 'groused', as was only to be expected, but there was no
refusal of duty.

Far greater significance than their degree of gravity war-
ranted was attached by foreign observers both to the General
Strike and to the Invergordon 'mutiny'. Interpreting events in
the light of their own hopes, prophets were not wanting to
forecast Britain's progressive enfeeblement and eventual eclipse
as a major Power. This was particularly true of political quid-
nuncs in Germany—where Hitler had been appointed Reich
Chancellor in the January of 1933. Believing disaffection to be
widespread throughout the British Navy, secret hopes for an
early resurgence of the Reich were further stimulated by the
ululations of such muddleheaded bodies as the League of
Nations and Peace Pledge Unions, and the vote passed by the
puling *précieux* or the Oxford Union, that "this House will in
no circumstances fight for its King and country". The German
never has been able to grasp the fact that the froth on the pint
is no indication of the quality of the beer.

With a Disarmament Conference bickering interminably at
Geneva, and with the French Schneider-Creuzot munition
works paying a dividend of 25 per cent and the Czechoslovakian

Skoda works one of 23 per cent, that hollow oracle General Smuts took occasion to assure the Royal Institute of International Affairs that "the expectation of war tomorrow or in the near future is sheer nonsense". Within less than a twelvemonth Hitler had torn up Part V of the Treaty of Versailles and re-introduced conscription, and Berlin had experienced its first A.R.P. exercise.

Less than three months after Hitler's accession to power Sir Horace Rumbold, Britain's Ambassador to Germany, had warned the Foreign Office that the new Reich Chancellor's policy meant war. But no representations regarding infractions of the Versailles Treaty were made either to Berlin or to the League of Nations, as Sir John Simon regarded such a course as "not expedient".[1] This was sheer poltroonery. Britain might be weak, but was not yet so enfeebled that propitiation was her only line of policy.

In the outcome, with a minimum of 550,000 men scheduled for the new Germany army, the rule of force replaced an apocryphal rule of law the Western Powers had consistently shown themselves unwilling to uphold and if necessary to enforce.

It was given to the Italian dictator, Mussolini, to set in train the events which served so bleakly to demonstrate the complete ineffectiveness of so-called "collective security". Having defied the League of Nations by marching into Abyssinia, the 'sanctions' declared, but indifferently applied, against Italy so little affected even her precarious economy that the Duce continued on the course he had set for himself, virtually unhindered.[2]

The Abyssinian crisis having demonstrated the British Navy's alarming state of unpreparedness for action, its war-potentiality was further diminished by the Anglo-German Naval Agreement of June 1935. For by its terms the Germans were free to build up to 35 per cent of the strength of the Royal Navy; in submarines up to 45 per cent, or up to parity "should a situation arise which in their opinion makes it necessary". In effect, Germany's fighting marine was to be new and concentrated, while Britain's was ageing and dispersed. At the

---

[1] *Documents on British Foreign Policy, 1919–1939*, Second Series, Vol. V.

[2] Italy's greatest need was oil, but no 'sanction' applied to this! About 25 per cent of the League members, including Switzerland, who held a key position economically, did not apply the more drastic 'sanctions' at all.

time when Sir Samuel Hoare and Herr von Ribbentrop put their respective signatures to the pact, submarines were already in production in the German yards, where the 'pocket-battleships' *Scharnhorst* and *Gneisenau* were also under construction.[1] If the Locarno Treaty had been violated by the alliance between France and Russia, then the bilateral Anglo-German Naval Agreement threw the dog-eared Versailles Peace Treaty finally into the waste-paper basket.

*   *   *

The early 'thirties had witnessed Britain's slow but reasonably steady recovery of a fair measure of prosperity. With a datum line of 100 for 1929, the index of production for 1936 stood at 118. The total for merchant shipping plying the oceans under the 'Red Duster' stood at 20,000,000 tons[2]; for 'tramp' tonnage had been restored in some measure by the *British Shipping (Assistance) Act* of 1935, with its bold scheme to "scrap and build". The *North Atlantic Shipping Act* of 1934 had furnished timely Government loans, up to £9,500,000, for the construction of vessels for the American run. Out of this development arose the merger of the Cunard and White Star lines, and the resumption of work on the *Queen Mary*, which had long been rusting on the stocks at Clydebank.

At the same time an extremely slow and very reluctant start was made on rearmament; although Sir Eric Phipps' boast to the United States Ambassador in Berlin, that "England has abandoned her disarmament policy of the last fourteen years. She will spend up to £300,000,000 a year now in order to have a greater Army, a bigger Navy and ample air defence",[3] proved to have erred wildly on the side of optimism. Apart from Britain—and exclusive of Germany—the world's faltering faith in the efficacy of the League was reflected in an expenditure on armaments, for the year 1935, of just over £855,360,000.

In Britain, however, public opinion, where it was not apathetic, was perversely against rearmament in any shape or

---

[1] In the *Bismarck* and the *Tirpitz*, laid down under the same building programme, Germany was to possess two battleships swifter and more powerful than any vessel in the fleets of Britain, France and the United States.

[2] It was to fall to 17,500,000 tons by 1937.

[3] *Ambassador Dodd's Diary*, William E. Dodds, Junior.

form. The Army—not to say the Navy—had become unfashion-able, even slightly ridiculous; the 'glamour' of the Air Force was regarded as entirely spurious. The 'revelations' in the 'war' books of cringing neurotics who had obviously been too concerned about their own personal safety and comfort to appreciate the merits of the cause to which they had grudgingly lent their services, appeared to have robbed combat even of the saving grace of courage. Books by ferociously 'pacifist' writers commanded a large reading public; the League of Young Liberals called upon Britain to disarm, "if possible in concert with other nations, otherwise alone". George Lansbury, the Leader of the Socialist Opposition, advised his supporters not to enlist in the Armed Forces; Herbert Morrison, a war-time 'conscientious objector', as chairman of the London County Council refused the use of the L.C.C. schools for meetings of the Cadet Corps. The members of Canon Dick Sheppard's Peace Pledge Union bound themselves not to fight in any circum-stances whatsoever. The Archbishop of York, on the other hand, unblenchingly affirmed that "It may be necessary to have another great and horrible war in order to establish the efficacy of the League of Nations."[1] Hell knows no fury like that of a non-combatant!

It was, in short, an era of noisy cranks and braying defeatists, and Germany made the mistake of believing that they spoke for the whole nation. At the time, however, it was a reasonable enough assumption, since the informed but sober warnings uttered by Winston Churchill were scoffed at and dismissed as so much sabre-rattling fustian.

The General Election of 1935 was accompanied by a private canvass of the electorate in the form of a Peace Ballot; a re-markable example of the lack of scruple inherent in fanatics with an axe to grind. For the queries in the printed question-naire were framed so tendentiously that to answer them in any manner other than the one the promoters intended was vir-tually to be self-branded as a warmonger. At the time the total electorate stood at 28,288,076, of whom 22,001,837 voted for the candidate of their choice. In the Peace Ballot no more than 1,599,165 voters bothered to record their views. This total proved more than sufficient, however, to persuade Mr. Baldwin

---

[1] In a speech on December 6th, 1935.

criminously to minimise Germany's degree of rearmament, and
deliberately to delay Britain's; since he confessed that to take
the contrary course would have made the loss of the election
"from his point of view" a certainty. This was not so much
pusillanimity as sheer stupidity. "At any moment the British
nation would have fallen in behind a Government that told it
the truth. As in 1931 it firmly confronted an unprecedented
financial crisis, so in 1936 it would have faced the necessity of
meeting the danger of war." [1] The whole thing was far too
grave to be prostituted to the level of electioneering tactics, for
as Churchill bluntly and truthfully pointed out, "The responsibility of Ministers for the public safety is absolute and requires
no mandate."

Between 1923 and 1937 Britain had only two Premiers,
Baldwin and MacDonald, who played Box and Cox with their
great office, and ducks and drakes with their country's safety.

Germany had been steadily rearming ever since Hitler had
come to power, and in 1935 Sir John Simon and Anthony Eden
learned from Hitler's own lips that the Reich was already
stronger in the air than the whole of the British Empire. Then,
on March 7th, 1936, the German Fuehrer took the bull by the
horns and reoccupied the Rhineland. It was not too late, as the
German military leaders very well knew, to halt him. His bluff
could have been exposed in the very act of debouching on to
the road to conquest. The German Army was no more than
half-manned, and half-trained; the Poles and the Czechs were
ready to march if France gave the word.

But from a land leprous with Communism and the defeatism
of Leon Blum's 'Popular Front', no such word was forthcoming.
France and England were at loggerheads, moreover, on the
question of Italy and Abyssinia; each waited so long for the
other to make the first decisive move that no such move was
made. The Council of the League of Nations went through the
solemn farce of "condemning" Germany; the French Chamber
abandoned itself to empty histrionics, while Britain forwarded
a formal questionnaire to the Reich—which still awaits an
answer—and valorously proceeded to appoint as Minister for
the Co-ordination of Defence Sir Thomas Inskip, a great
authority on the Book of Common Prayer.

[1] G. Ward Price.

With the outbreak of the Spanish Civil War, the ease with which Hitler supplied General Franco with *matériel* offered sufficient proof—if further proof were needed—of the immense advances made in Germany's preparations for waging war. The Spanish cockpit, moreover, furnished an admirable proving-ground both for German technicians and the war-products rolling off the production lines in German factories. Yet with this elaborate dress rehearsal going forward for all the world to see, Lloyd George, with characteristic irresponsibility, pontifically pronounced, "I tell you, as one who has studied the whole situation, I don't think Hitler is a fool—he is not going to challenge the British Empire by any act of folly."

This was precisely the sort of shallow thinking to appeal not only to the great mass of the people, to whom foreign politics are either a sealed book or a bad joke, but to the new Prime Minister, Mr. Neville Chamberlain. For installing Mr. Neville Chamberlain in Number 10 Downing Street was rather like putting the leadership of a *safari* in charge of a man firmly convinced of the general benevolence of the sabre-toothed tiger. Perfectly capable of dealing with a recalcitrant member of a local Board of Guardians, the new Prime Minister's capacity to comprehend, let alone handle, a blood-boltered *condottieri* born out of his century was altogether inadequate. Obsessed with a hatred of warfare which signally failed to realise that peace without security invariably leads to a war of desperation, he also lacked the acumen to recognise the moment when wise concession degenerates into reprehensible propitiation. Chamberlain, like his chosen adviser, Sir Horace Wilson, had the eye of faith: but the eye of faith, alas, is so often afflicted with a cataract.

Naturally enough, where Hitler was concerned, "increase of appetite had grown by what it fed on"; and with the Rhineland safely in his pocket, his thoughts turned to ensuring *lebensraum* by first engulfing Austria and then annexing that curious arti-fact created by the Treaty of Versailles that went by the name of Czechoslovakia—not so much a country as a collection of dialects, folk tunes and rankling sectional enmities. Bismarck had pointed out that "he who controls Bohemia controls Europe"; and there were enough disgruntled Germans on Czechoslovakia's Sudeten territory to render an excuse for intervention on their behalf a simple matter of high-pressure propaganda.

Mr. Chamberlain's personal intervention in affairs had the effect of throwing the unfortunate Czechs to the wolves—while incidentally jettisoning the potential services of some 40 Czech Army divisions—in return for a "scrap of paper" bearing Hitler's signature. This scribble, the Prime Minister affirmed, with appalling naivety, ensured "peace in our time". And amongst the multiple cypherage of the House of Commons there was only one man to remember Drake's great-hearted call of "Stop him now and stop him ever", and his was the voice of one crying in the wilderness.

Chamberlain's appeasement of the German dictator at Munich has been alleged by his apologists guilefully to have won a twelvemonth in which England could hastily rearm—an England which was alleged to have been rearming since 1935. But at Munich the Prime Minister was playing for "peace in our time", not for a breathing-space to repair the gaps in the country's fighting-strength for which he, as Chancellor of the Exchequer, had largely been responsible. It was only when post-Munich developments rendered it crystal-clear that, unless it argues from strength, appeasement simply doubles the danger it seeks to avoid, that a real but perilously belated attempt was made to put the Fighting Forces in some state of readiness for war.

German rearmament meanwhile was going ahead with re-doubled energy[1]; and when—in the March of 1939—the Prime Minister gave the German Fuehrer a "solemn warning" to mend his ways, Hitler retorted by denouncing the non-aggression pact between Germany and Poland, declaring his intention also to abrogate the Anglo-German treaty.

The rage of a cornered sheep is a terrible thing to behold. But it is as nothing compared to the self-righteous anger of a good man hoaxed and betrayed; and Chamberlain was "a 'good' man in the very worst sense of the term", as Disraeli once said of Gladstone.[2]

[1] Additional submarines were constructed in Spain and Finland.

[2] All things considered, it is not without irony that the country which produced Jefferson, Woodrow Wilson and Franklin Delano Roosevelt should also have sired in Henry Adams the one historian to affirm that "It is always the good men who do the most harm in the world."

Tardily stung to fury, the Prime Minister thundered forth, "Any threat to Polish independence, and His Majesty's Government would feel bound at once to lend the Polish Government all support in their power." Since Poland, in a military sense, was about as accessible as Kamtchatka, this 'guarantee' was more provocative to Germany than helpful to the Poles.

Last-minute hopes of influencing German intentions by securing the support of the Georgian *Kinto* lording it in the Kremlin were shattered with the abrupt announcement of the Russo-German pact. This piece of skulduggery accomplished, German troops were free to pour over the Polish border.

As the British nation went to its action stations, the Navy, with grim memories of the bad days of 1917, must have been particularly cheered to recall Sir Samuel Hoare's airy assurance of 1937,[1] that "Today we are justified in saying that, although we regard the submarine as an extravagant nuisance that ought to be abolished, the submarine itself is no longer a danger to the British Empire."

So easily do the flighty-minded forget the lessons which history furnishes with such unwearying abundance.

[1] In his capacity as First Lord of the Admiralty.

CHAPTER XXII

'The Sea that is the Wall of England'

"... A people, on their beloved land,
Risen, like one man, to combat in the sight
Of a just God for liberty and right."

WILLIAM WORDSWORTH

HISTORY is repetitive to the degree that nations become involved in "the same purposes otherwise conceived, the same problems otherwise approached". In the September of 1939, while the issues at stake closely resembled those which had torn the world apart in 1914, the qualities, if not the incentives, of the principal belligerents had been subtly modulated by trends that had developed in the course of the intervening years. It was, therefore, almost with an air of bravado that a berserk Germany caught up the gage reluctantly thrown down by a cowering France and an England whose faith in its political leaders remained comprehensibly tepid despite the welcome appointment of Winston Churchill to the Admiralty.

In French official circles it was scarcely sought to disguise the fact that the majority of people approached the war very much in the spirit of a bather who exhibits extreme reluctance even to try the water with his toe. In the field the "magnificent French Army" incontinently went to ground in the £600,000,000 death-trap of the Maginot Line; while Britain confronted Germany with naval, military and material resources far inferior to those she had commanded a quarter of a century earlier.

Where the Navy was concerned, the perilous insufficiency in cruiser strength was the chief cause of anxiety, for there was a shortage of six vessels even on the extremely modest building programme agreed in 1925.[1] There was also a grave lack of

---

[1] For years the Admiralty had insisted that 70 cruisers was the minimum required to meet the country's responsibilities. In 1939 there were 58 available.

flotilla craft, for the delivery of the 30 Fleet destroyers and 20 smaller 'Hunt' class vessels on order, like that of the 15 submarines on the stocks, could not be expected for at least a twelvemonth. Little help could be anticipated from the French, for as Paul Reynaud privily confessed, "We are disastrously short of warships; the lack of destroyers is such as to chill the blood." [1]

Germany's building programme, on the other hand, having been framed on the assumption that there would be no war until 1942, had been dangerously overtaken by events; although in the battle-cruisers *Scharnhorst* and *Gneisenau* [2] Hitler possessed two vessels with a greater potential hitting-power and turn of speed than was enjoyed by any craft at the Admiralty's disposal. There was, however, a shortage of flotilla craft, while a total of 57 submarines fell far below the 300 Admiral Doenitz had declared to be the minimum required to blockade Britain into submission. [3] Every effort was being made, therefore, to speed up production, either in Germany itself or in 'friendly' foreign shipyards. All in all, Goering's *Luftwaffe* seemed far more ready for combat than Raeder's half-completed Navy.

In 1914 merchant ships of 100 tons gross and over, plying under the British flag or that of one of the Dominions, had aggregated 20,524,000 tons. By 1929, despite the rise in population and the consequent increase in demand for seaborne commodities, the total had diminished to 20,520,000 tons, of which only 17,500,000 tons represented vessels of 1,600 gross tons and over. This decline could be attributed to high running-costs, the catastrophic fall in coal exports, the larger subsidies enjoyed by foreign ship-owners, and the employment by foreign Governments of certain measures of protection which, in effect, operated like the erstwhile British Navigation Acts in reverse. Moreover, the proportion of tonnage registered in the Dominions had increased by some 80 per cent, while United Kingdom tonnage—the only tonnage over which the British Government could exert control—was about one and a half million gross

---

[1] *Assignment to Catastrophe*, Major-General Sir Edward Spears.
[2] The Germans always referred to them as battleships, but since they more nearly resembled battle-cruisers in speed, they were thus classified by the British Admiralty.
[3] *The Fuehrer Conferences*.

tons less than in 1914.[1] Finally, it was a matter of uneasy speculation as to what extent neutral vessels would continue to ply to British ports now that the submarine menace had been reinforced by the extreme likelihood of aerial bombardment.

Indeed, the effect that aerial bombing would have on port facilities, the speed of ships' turn-round, the pace of transit-shed clearance, and the smooth working of the railway system by which commodities were borne away from the seaboard for distribution inland, posed a peculiarly sinister imponderable.

But whatever else might give cause for anxiety, the Admiralty's defensive measures went smoothly and expeditiously into operation, despite the handicap imposed by the Administration's supine dilatoriness throughout the previous summer. Every light on the Goodwins was promptly extinguished; an up-to-date mine-barrage was laid across the Dover Straits; the Naval Contraband Control sealed both ends of the Downs with guardships, while the nucleus of a Channel Force was mustered in the shape of two fairly old R-class battleships, with attendant cruisers and destroyers, based on Portland. At Portsmouth, Admiral Sir William James could reckon upon the immediate services of the 12th and 16th destroyer flotillas (12 vessels), 5 anti-submarine craft and 8 mine-sweepers; with a further 9 destroyers and a few mine-sweepers at Dover. Portsmouth Command also had 67 trawlers in hand for conversion and another 33 were promptly requisitioned, while nearly 200 yachts and other small craft were sent to the yards to be fitted for anti-submarine and mine-clearance duties. Within its limitations the Home Fleet was alert and efficient; the Reserve Fleet could speedily be commissioned; subject to the bounds imposed by the cruiser shortage, "the traditional and well-proved methods of convoy" could be put into working order at relatively short notice. Furthermore, some 7,000 Officers and men of the Mercantile Marine had been made available to the Royal Navy, and the Royal Naval Volunteer Reserve was ready and willing, and capable of immediate expansion.

From the outset a blockade of Germany was instituted which struck a balance between the full rights Britain claimed as a belligerent and the demands for freedom of commerce protested by the neutrals. There were leaks during the early

[1] *Merchant Shipping and the Demands of War*, C. B. A. Behrens.

months of conflict, of course, and contraband of war undoubtedly got through. None the less, 338,000 tons of forbidden wares were seized during the first six months of hostilities, while 41 enemy merchant craft were sunk or captured, representing an aggregate of 229,891 tons.

So early as August German submarines had been sent to sea to take up their war stations—armed with a new electric torpedo that left no betraying wake. Six of these *unterseebooten*, stationed in the Western Approaches, sank 32 vessels in the first month of the war, including H.M.S. *Courageous*, one of Britain's few aircraft carriers.[1]

At this stage, ships sailing in convoy were fairly immune from attack. Enemy U-boats had not yet learned to seek their prey far out in the Atlantic, and vessels nearing their landfall had a stout ally in Coastal Command, at the sight of whose machines the *unterseebooten* invariably crash-dived. It was the ship not sailing in company that courted destruction. For it was not until early in December that the first 1,000 merchant craft were completed with defensive armament.

Only one U-boat was known to have penetrated the Dover defences, although two blew up on the minefield in October and a third ran aground on the Goodwins. In any event, no attempt was made to interfere with the passage of the British Expeditionary Force, although the use of proximate Channel ports was refused by the French for fear of provoking reprisals from the air. The troopships were therefore committed to the longer and more exposed route to Cherbourg and further west. By September 24th, however, the whole operation had been completed; a Staff Officer laconically reporting to Admiral James, when the last convoy vessels had returned from Brest, "We've been weaned"![2] Some 158,000 troops, with their weapons and stores, had been transported overseas without the loss of a single man or gun.

*   *   *

Unaided even by diversionary activities on the Western

[1] Up to the end of December 1939, 114 British and Allied vessels had been sunk, representing 421,156 tons (*The War at Sea*, Captain S. W. Roskill, R.N.).
[2] *The Portsmouth Letters*, Admiral Sir William James.

Front,[1] Poland was speedily torn to pieces by the German
hyaena, while the Russian wolf hastened across the borders,
with jaws slavering to secure its agreed share of the spoil. With
that inflexible composure with which the onlooker invariably
supports his neighbour's afflictions, Britain entered into what
an American commentator frankly described as the "phoney
war" period; waged with a confetti of pamphlets and with
Labour Party branches all over the country passing anti-war
resolutions, and certain of the flabbier type of publicist hinting
broadly at the desirability of a compromise peace. The only
alarm experienced by the Prime Minister and his immediate
associates was occasioned by the discovery that, until the harvest
had been garnered, no more than three weeks' supply of wheat
remained available for distribution.

The general complacency, however, was not shared by the
Admiralty. For on September 16th the S.S. *City of Paris* had
been damaged by what was obviously a novel type of mine;
and by the end of October this new device had accounted for
19 vessels, with an aggregate of 59,027 tons. Far worse was the
fact that no counter-measures could be taken against the weapon since its exact nature was unknown.[2] In November the
position deteriorated rapidly, with a destroyer sunk and another injured, in addition to the loss of 27 merchant craft
aggregating 120,958 tons. Several other vessels were damaged,
including the cruiser *Belfast* and the mine-layer *Adventure*; and
great difficulty was experienced in safeguarding the passage of
vessels out of Thames-mouth, where only one of the deep-water
channels remained unmined.

On October 23rd, however, two complete mines were recovered off the mudflats of Shoeburyness. A group of experts,
consisting of Lieutenant-Commanders J. G. D. Ouvry and
J. Lewis, Chief Petty Officer Baldwin and Able Seaman Vearn-
combe, immediately set to work to try to dissect them.
Divided into two parties, the Ouvry and Baldwin team initiated each new stage in the stripping down, signalling their

---

[1] The first British battle-casualty did not occur until December 9th.
[2] The British had tried out a version of the magnetic mine during the
1914–18 war, but it had proved unsatisfactory, and further experiment had
been abandoned during "the years of the locust". An effective mine was
produced in the Spring of 1940.

progress to the other pair, so that in the event of the first mine detonating, work could be continued on the one remaining. This display of cool, calculated courage reaped a rich reward, for examination of the cylinder containing the secret of the magnetic mine enabled counter-measures to be put in hand. But the process of demagnetising British tonnage, by winding several turns of electric cable around each hull, was a colossal task, at one time demanding the production of 1,200 miles of wire cable a week.

The magnetic was followed by the acoustic mine, fired by underwater sound emanating from a passing ship. Yet once again the antidote was found and applied as fast as the workshops could turn out the necessary gear. But so great was the volume of work thrown upon its anti-mine department that the Admiralty appealed for the services of several thousand fishermen to strengthen the patrols. As ever, the call for aid met with a ready and cheerful response. By the April of 1940 the original mine-sweeping force of 76 vessels and 2,000 Officers and men had expanded to embody 320 craft and a personnel of 10,500.

*　　　*　　　*

With the outbreak of hostilities the borrowing power vested in the Chancellor of the Exchequer had been increased from £400,000,000 to £800,000,000, while the Bank Rate had been doubled. The drain on hard currency was immediate, the American Legislature's passage of the "Cash and Carry" enactment necessitating a preliminary realisation of dollar resources in the United States which was the precursor of many more to follow. The end of the year showed an excess of imports over exports of £401,212,213,[1] notwithstanding that the inflow of commodities had been restricted by two shortages—of shipping and hard currency. Government borrowing—exclusive of the £73,000,000 represented by small savings and investments in War Loan—swiftly added £280,000,000 to the floating debt.[2] 'Henry Tydder's' favourite maxim, that "war once begun should pay itself", was obviously a good many years out of date!

*　　　*　　　*

[1] *Annual Register.*
[2] *Statistics Relating to the War Effort of the United Kingdom*, Cmd. 6564.

Intent upon securing a base on the flank of the western oceanic sea lanes, while at the same time ensuring protection for the convoys transporting essential iron-ore from Narvik to the Reich, Hitler successfully invaded Denmark and Norway in the early April of 1940. In the absence of proper air cover for their activities, the Allies' efforts to counter this stroke were as ineffective as they were wastefully gallant. Painfully the lesson had been underlined—that domination on the sea is useless unless accompanied by lordship of the skies above it. The only good that emerged from a venture that barely escaped fiasco was the succession of Winston Churchill to the Premiership.

Having seized and retained the initiative, on May 10th Hitler unleashed his *Fall Gelb* against Holland and Belgium, and the Franco-British forces deployed between the Belgian frontier and the abrupt termination of the Maginot Line at Montmédy.[1]

The Dutch were the first victims of a *Blitzkrieg* which, amongst other things, alternated a hail of bombs on defenceless cities with a steady drizzle of parachutists intent on disrupting the Army's flanks and rear. Resistance collapsed in four and a half days; and the British Navy was hard put to it to evacuate Holland's invaluable stock of commercial diamonds, the members of the Royal Family, and the heads of Government.

Further south, Hitler's dive-bombers and swift-moving armoured forces drove so deep a wedge into the Anglo-French defences that by May 20th the British line of supply through Abbeville had been severed. With that, the German advance swung north and raced for the Channel ports.

With incredible folly—in the light of past experience—the B.E.F. had been placed under French command. Thus when it was resolved to try to cut off the far-flung enemy spearhead from its reinforcements, it was left to a few virtually unsupported British elements to make the attempt.

Small local successes were useless, however, in face of the collapse of the French Ist and IXth Armies; and nothing was left to the Anglo-Belgian forces in the north but to continue their retreat. Plans for the seaborne evacuation of the B.E.F. had to be taken into serious consideration.

Fugitives were already streaming from Antwerp, Ostend and

[1] Out of a highly vulnerable frontier of 800 kilometres the Maginot Line afforded static defence for a bare 150.

Zeebrugge—the last-named blocked by the Royal Navy at the second attempt—through channels swept clear, at considerable cost, by a force of British trawlers. By May 20th over 400 fishing boats had left the Belgian and French ports crammed with refugees, to sail down Channel and berth, in many instances, as far west as Brixham and Dartmouth.

In Boulogne, the 20th Guards Brigade [1] and the French 21st Division were swamped by the headlong rush of the enemy. Many survivors, however, were brought away by the supporting destroyers; which often fired over open sights at hostile tanks and armoured cars only a few hundred yards away from their gun-muzzles. [2]

With the determination taken to evacuate as many as possible of the B.E.F., a garrison was hastily thrown into Calais, to delay the enemy advance on the one escape corridor to the sea that still remained open. From Tuesday May 21st to the night of Sunday 27th one battalion of the Royal Tank Regiment and a single brigade of 'Greenjackets' [3] held out against the continuous onslaught of three full-strength Armoured Divisions. Refusing the demand to surrender sent in under a flag of truce on the morning of the 26th, their tenacious holding action made it possible to form a perimeter about Dunkirk from which it was hoped, at the sacrifice of the remainder, to evacuate up to 45,000 troops.

With the conduct of the operation entrusted to the capable hands of Vice-Admiral B. H. Ramsay, a reconnaissance party was immediately despatched to ascertain what embarkation facilities remained available in Dunkirk. They found the waterworks destroyed and the huge oil tanks blazing furiously. Furthermore, out of the 115 acres of dockland the whole of the inner harbour had been reduced to a shambles. The West Mole, however, although badly damaged, could still be made use of; the East Mole, consisting of a pile-supported plank-way barely wide enough for three men to move abreast, was obviously not designed for berthing ships, since the movement of the tide between the piles would render it extremely difficult to bring

[1] The 2nd Irish and 2nd Welsh Guards.

[2] Some 4,360 men were removed from Boulogne, leaving 300 Guardsmen and a few others in German hands.

[3] It consisted of the 1st Queen Victoria Rifles, 1st Rifle Brigade and 2nd/60th Rifles.

vessels snugly alongside. To the east of the town stretched a
ten-mile expanse of shelving beach, which ended at La Panne.

On the night of Saturday 25th, with the B.E.F. already condemned to half-rations, the Belgians on their left obviously
cracking, and the fall of Calais imminent, the authorities could
take comfort from the fact that a large number of wounded,
hospital personnel and base details had already been brought
over to England. At 06.27 on the Sunday morning Admiral
Ramsay authorised the signal which set "Operation Dynamo"
in motion.

Some 129 merchant craft, of varying capacity, were immediately available for the lift; with destroyers, mine-sweepers and
trawlers steadily arriving to replace those lost or docked for
repair. By the southern or shorter passage it was some 55 miles
from the North Goodwins to Dunkirk; and this was the route
tried out by the *Maid of Orleans* and the hospital ships *St. Julian*
and *St. Andrew*. Almost immediately the convoy came under the
fire of guns mounted outside Calais, and while the *Maid of
Orleans* got through to pick up a full load of troops, her sister
ships were forced to turn back. Hard-by, the *Mona's Queen* was
riddled by fire from a Junkers that was eventually shot down;
and a second machine, diving to attack, was set afire and
crashed into the sea. The *Isle of Guernsey* and the *Worthing* were
forced to change course to avoid a duel between a couple of
destroyers and the Calais batteries; while two squadrons of the
R.A.F. gallantly broke up a massed attack on the shipping
channel by Junkers 87's and 88's, covered by a swarm of Mes-
serschmitt 109's. In four hours over a score of enemy bombers
and fighters were shot down for a loss of 7 British machines.
Qualitatively, there was no question of the British airmen's
superiority, although it was painfully clear that it would be
impossible to maintain daylight cover in sufficient strength to
prevent interference with the flow of shipping.

Such was the pattern of an activity that swiftly intensified as
the pace of the evacuation quickened. For with the Belgian
Army's surrender on the left, and the expulsion of the French
from Mardyck, away on the right, the perimeter inevitably
contracted, and more and more men were withdrawn to the
beaches.

In the prevailing circumstances there could be no question

of ignoring the sparse facilities offered by the East Mole. Ships berthed alongside as best they might, with the men scrambling aboard over gangways made of mess tables and benches, or even single planks. Fortunately, the constant assaults of the enemy aircraft were hampered in some degree by the heavy pall of smoke that swung sullenly over the town.

As the men filtered out of the perimeter and swarmed on to the sands, a Brigadier on a borrowed cart-horse rode up and down marshalling them into some sort of order. Another senior Officer was similarly employed, mounted on an antiquated lady's bicycle. Inevitably, some one had found a cricket bat, and stumps having been improvised, the German pilots were regaled with a bird's-eye view of "the mad English" happily indulging in one of their favourite pastimes.

With the fall of Calais, German batteries had been pushed forward to Gravelines and Les Hemmes. This development, taken in conjunction with the incessant assaults from the air, had resulted in the loss of so many personnel ships as to rule out their further employment save at night. Even so, a longer sea-route had to be taken, involving an all-round voyage of 174 miles. It followed that throughout the hours of daylight all attempts at evacuation had to be entrusted to the better armed war-vessels and to small craft of such shallow draft that they could run right in and lift their human cargo directly from the beaches—now becoming dangerously congested and under constant fire.

The vanguard of the little-ship armada was formed of cutters, Hayling Island ferry-boats, Dutch *shuyts*, Naval whalers, Pickford's coasting vessels, yawls and ketches from a score of half-forgotten Kent and Sussex moorings, a firefloat and the "shilling sicks" from London's river, tugs, paddle-boats, Belgian fishing smacks, passenger packets from the Channel Islands and the Isle of Man, cockle boats from Leigh-on-Sea, and drifters with such jaunty names as the *Girl Pamela* and *The Boys*. They were manned by amateur yachtsmen, Naval ratings, longshoremen and fisherfolk; and a large proportion of them lacked even such elementary instruments as compasses and dividers. But nothing daunted them. Under a ceaseless rain of bombs and machine-gun fire, they went right in to bring off the haggard men in khaki who waded out, shoulder-deep in the water, bearing their wounded and clinging tenaciously to the personal weapons with which they were still armed.

Anxious to accelerate the pace of evacuation, the Admiralty cast its net still wider. From a score of boat-builders' sheds or from their moorings on some sleepy, willow-shaded backwater of the Thames, came the weekenders' motor cruisers and pleasure launches. Many of them were fouled-up and unhandy from their 'tween-season hibernation, but they were skippered by men who were not to be baulked of their share in the inspiring task of succour. Mustered at Sheerness, after hasty overhaul they resolutely set a course for the maelstrom of fury and destruction that awaited them just over the horizon. On their eastern flank the scanty force of M.T.B.'s kept vigilant watch and ward to head off the E-boats that sought to add their mischief to that wrought by the Junkers and Messerschmitts circling overhead. Far out of sight of the rescue fleet and the weary survivors clustered on the sand dunes, the pilots of the R.A.F. sought tirelessly to intercept the enemy attacks before they could concentrate on the open beaches and the inviting target of the shipping.

Nor was all the toil and peril and stoical endurance destined to go unrewarded. With Dunkirk under the direct fire of the enemy artillery and despite spells of unhelpful weather, the total of those brought away steadily mounted—50,000 on the 29th, 53,000 on the day following, and 64,000 on the 31st.

Since the French—regardless of their empty vaunt that there would be no surrender—were already cramming into the escape corridor, the obligation to furnish them with shipping to eke out their own inadequate rescue fleet, imposed an additional burden on resources already strained to the uttermost. But somehow the British genius for improvisation found a way out of the dilemma, so that in addition to the Gallic survivors transported in their own vessels, some 30,000 Frenchmen were brought off with the British rearguard.[1] This raised the total of those evacuated between May 20th and June 4th, in British or Allied craft, to 366,162. But a vast mass of heavy weapons and *matériel* had perforce to be abandoned.

The only men of British blood left on what now had become hostile soil were the prisoners in German hands and the devoted

[1] In all, some 123,000 French troops were given refuge in England.

Medical Officers and their subordinates who had drawn lots to determine who should stay behind to tend those of the wounded it had been deemed too dangerous to move.

Deliverance had been made possible by British control of the narrow seas, but the price of succour had been heavy. In all, 42 Naval vessels had been sunk, including 6 British and 3 French destroyers, with 19 British destroyers damaged. Eight Dutch craft had been sent to the bottom, and Merchant Service losses came to 4 large and 65 smaller craft.[1]

It had also to be borne in mind that deliverance, however miraculous, was a lesser thing than victory; although victory in the skies could unquestionably be claimed by the R.A.F., with a score of 394 enemy 'planes destroyed for a loss of 114. In their own element the daring and endurance of the pilots and the quality of the machines they fought gave sure promise of the triumph that awaited them in the days so near at hand.

* * *

In Paris, General Weygand, like Trochu in 1870, announced that he "had a plan". Since it proved to be based upon the fallacious belief that linear defence constituted the right answer to attack in depth, the unfortunate British troops on the south of the Somme were soon in dire need of seaborne evacuation. With 150,000 men distributed over the bases and erstwhile lines of communication, and the 1st Armoured and 51st (Highland) Divisions still in contact with the enemy, the task of extricating them was one of considerable magnitude and difficulty, but an evacuation fleet was promptly sent to Le Havre. The hapless 51st, however, was so tardily released from French Command that it was overrun before it could reach the scheduled embarkation area. Some 1,500 British and French linesmen who had eluded capture were snatched up at Veules-sur-Rose, a few miles further round the coast; and with Marshal Pétain grovelling for armistice terms, over 136,500 British and 12,700 Allied troops were brought away from Cherbourg, Brest, St. Nazaire and La Pallice. Fortunately, the seven U-boats known to be in the western approaches exhibited far less activity than the Naval Command had been given reason to anticipate. Their principal victim was the *Lancastria*, which was

[1] Roskill, *op. cit.*

sunk with the loss of nearly half the 6,000 men she had aboard.

The death-knell of the Third Republic, like that of the Offenbach Empire of 'Napoleon the Little', had been sounded at Sedan. There were men in the land of the highest courage, and integrity, but so pitifully few of them that they could not leaven the whole. With Pétain's abject capitulation the average Britisher's reaction was best summed up in the cheerful comment of Admiral Cunningham's Chief-of-Staff[1]: "Now I know we shall win the war, sir; we have no more allies."

England, left alone to set the Nazis at defiance, still seemed a sanctuary to the harried refugees that continued to swarm across the narrow seas. The *Isle of Sark*, the last passenger ship to leave the Channel Islands, had sailed on July 28th. Over 200 fishing vessels from Cherbourg and beyond had taken refuge in Dartmouth. Southampton Water teemed with every variety of alien craft, from trawlers, hopper-barges and spume-encrusted tugs to a harbour-master's trim launch. In Plymouth, British, Czech, Polish and Canadian troops rubbed shoulders with a bewildered, sullen mob of French *poilus*, amongst whom defeatism and disaffection were spreading fast. The same evil canker was even more prevalent amongst the Officers and men of the Gallic warships in the harbour. When a British Naval detachment arrived to immobilise the vessels, there was a scene of violent opposition, with one of the boarding party killed before the French crews could be rendered harmless. At Portsmouth, which had given refuge to the old battleship, *Courbet*, a destroyer-leader and a mixed armament of *chasseurs*, submarines and mine-sweepers, Admiral James wisely overawed all impulse towards resistance by turning out two battalions of Infantry, 500 Marines, and 1,000 Naval ratings. The French Officers pouted and struck attitudes, but the men seemed indifferent; and the whole business was carried through without overt obstruction.

Then on June 19th, with the first enemy bombs falling on Addington in Surrey,[2] Hitler—with France in his pocket, Russia biding her time, and the rest of Europe cowed—served notice of his immediate intention—to invade and subjugate his one remaining adversary. With somewhat lukewarm assistance

---

[1] Vice-Admiral J. C. Tovey.
[2] Obviously a bad shot for Croydon aerodrome.

from Admiral Raeder, Generals Kleist and Heusinger thereupon settled down to plan *Fall Seelowe*. Its objective was to land
13 Divisions, with 26 to follow, between Margate and Portsmouth. The way was to be opened by a *Schwerpunkt* of at least
60,000 men, whose task it would be to establish a lodgement
area between Folkestone and Brighton.

While Lieutenant-Colonel Dudley Clarke and Captain
Garnons Williams, R.N., audaciously kept the spirit of attack
alive by a tip-and-run Commando raid on enemy installations
near Le Touquet, the Prime Minister and his coadjutors grimly
took stock of the country's slender means of defence. The Navy
could produce about a hundred 4-inch and 12-pounder guns,
disinterred from beneath a mountain of coal in one of the
Royal Dockyards.[1] The saluting gun from Edinburgh Castle—
a successor to 'Mons Meg'—joined forces with a vintage
German 5·9 field piece, raped from a provincial war memorial.
There also came to light a few veteran 9·2 guns and 12-inch
howitzers, and one monster weapon was sent to lurk in a tunnel
near Canterbury. Fifty tanks represented the maximum available, and there was a chronic shortage of engineer's stores, uniforms, equipment, mortars, machine-guns, ammunition and
small-arms. A few shiploads of rifles, hurried across from the
United States, helped to arm a moiety of the Local Defence
Volunteers—or Home Guard, as they were subsequently renamed—a force which had sprung into existence by the hundred thousand almost literally overnight. Attempts to "set the
sea on fire" by means of an adhesive molten liquid were more
successful in starting hair-raising rumours than in attaining
their object, save at rare moments when the shoal-waters were
exceptionally calm.

In the Channel the fact had to be taken into serious consideration that the Germans were now free to base their submarines and surface craft on the French ports of which they had
been quick to take possession. Traffic in the narrow seas was
therefore within a few minutes' flight of hostile airfields; and
the inner patrol of motor craft, organised to warn the Army of
any approach by enemy seaborne forces, could invariably be
located by 'plane and attacked in detail by E-boats working

[1] They were from vessels dismantled under the several disarmament
agreements.

by night. In one such encounter off the Isle of Wight four of the larger patrol vessels were sunk by a sudden burst of fire from a flotilla of *Schnellbooten* that had closed the M.T.B.'s unperceived.

In the circumstances it was enheartening to learn that the American President—who earlier had vetoed the U.S. Navy Department's projected sale to Britain of 20 M.T.B.'s—was prepared to exchange 50 reconditioned destroyers for the lease of certain overseas British bases. For Hitler's order for the total blockade of the British Isles and his threat that all neutral shipping caught in the adjacent waters would be sunk at sight drew disquieting attention to the persistent shortage of M.T.B.'s and escort craft. Losses in merchant ships, due to the activities of the U-boats throughout June, had totalled 260,479 tons, despite the ceaseless activities of Coastal Command, whose machines had flown over a million and a half miles on convoy duty. None the less, over the period January–June Thames-mouth had witnessed the passage of 2,105 coasting ships in 64 convoys outward bound, and incoming vessels to the total of 2,141, in 65 convoys. The "coal-scuttle brigade" regularly swept past the gaunt Maunsell Forts in course of construction in the Thames estuary; as lonely a posting as that of the guardian "pepper-pots" in the eastern approaches to the Solent. Destroyers bustling past the Marines and Gunners marooned in these isolated strong-points would cloak their sympathy in facetious enquiries as to the welfare of "the little Princes in the Tower".

'O.R. 178' was the last major convoy to run the gauntlet in the Channel. For on July 4th enemy aircraft attacked it off Portland, sinking four ships and damaging nine, while E-boats put down another vessel and severely hammered two sister-ships. It was an era characterised by what Admiral Max Horton bitterly described as "complete lack of co-operation between the Air Force and the Naval authorities", and exhibited the perils of divided responsibility at their very worst. By way of extenuation, Fighter Command could plead with some legitimacy that its first responsibility was the defence of Britain; and what that involved was very speedily to be demonstrated.

Much discussion by the German O.K.W.[1] had reached the

---

[1] Armed Forces Supreme Command.

conclusion that no attempt to ferry an invasion force across the Channel should, or could, be attempted until the Royal Air Force had been cleared from the skies. Thus on August 8th the all-out air offensive against Britain went grimly into action over the quiet orchards and spreading hop-fields of Kent; and with eager courage the British and Allied fighter pilots rose in the air to meet the challenge. On the 18th the German Press proclaimed "Conclusive Phase of the War Begun". On the 22nd, while the crucial battle raged overhead, Dover experienced its first shelling from the monster guns installed on and around Cap Griz Nez. By the 24th the *Luftwaffe*'s attacks had been concentrated on the sector airfields covering London. In the city streets or in lonely country lanes the passer-by, turning to gaze skywards,

> *Heard the heavens fill with shouting as there rain'd a ghastly dew*
> *From the nations' airy navies grappling in the central blue.*

Nor was the enemy assault confined to the attempt to knock out Fighter Command. Movement in the narrow seas invited instant attack. On August 8th eight ships in the vicinity of the Isle of Wight were swiftly sent down or damaged beyond repair, and the destroyer *Delight* was dive-bombed off Portland. On the 12th fifty 'planes bombed Portsmouth, destroying the Harbour Station and scoring repeated hits on the Naval Barracks, Whale Island, and the shore establishment H.M.S. *Hornet*.

With the fighter duel *à outrance* in the air, the pace was altogether too fierce to be maintained. August 15th saw 76 enemy machines destroyed and 9 damaged; three days later 71 were shot down and 23 damaged; and when in September the *Luftwaffe* started to launch daylight raids on London, the average score was little less.[1]

In effect, with Goering's failure to achieve the air superiority[2] which was a prerequisite to invasion by land forces, postponement, if not outright abandonment, of *Fall Seelowe* appeared to be inevitable. None the less, on the night of Saturday, September 7th, every remotest unit of England's Armed Forces

---

[1] The figures given are those of the corrected totals, as revealed after the war.

[2] The Luftwaffe's mistake was to switch from military to civilian targets, thus enabling Fighter Command to recover its wind.

17+

hastened to take up its battle stations, as the call went out that the invasion attempt was imminent. Fortunately, it was a clear, balmy night, and when the official word to Stand Down followed early the next morning, even the most rheumaticky Home Guard had taken little hurt from a false alarm that had at least served to test the country's state of readiness.

While the German leaders were reconciling themselves—with no great reluctance in some instances—to the deferment of the invasion project till the Spring of 1941, a sardonic humorist was dressing the window of his Brussels haberdashery with placards advertising "Bathing Suits—For Swimming the Channel"!

In the *Luftwaffe's* continuing raids on London the port area and riverway came in for particularly vicious attention; Tilbury suffering almost as heavy attack as Rotherhithe and the Isle of Dogs. The Surrey Commercial Docks were isolated by a wall of fire when forty-two major conflagrations raged in an area of less than 250 acres. Fire brigades from as far afield as Bristol and Rugby fought beside their London comrades to subdue an unbroken sheet of flame that stretched along the water's edge for 6,500 yards. Rivers of blazing spirit flowed from Rum Quay in the West India Docks, but the dock-master and his staff braved everything to tow away oil-loaded barges to the relative safety of midstream. For 57 nights the Docks were under full-scale assault, and there were constant raids by day. There were many wrecks in Thames-mouth, although the salvage vessels *Yantlet* and *King Lear* always contrived to clear the navigation channels.

Southampton's November ordeal razed the shopping centre to the ground, with 674 properties of one sort and another ablaze at one time. The ancient Bargate alone stood unscathed and defiant amidst the detritus of smouldering rubble; and much destruction was inflicted on the Docks and on aviation works essential to the war effort.

As a Naval base Portsmouth was a constant target; the Town Hall, the Naval Barracks, Clarence Yard and the shore establishment known as H.M.S. *Vernon* all receiving damage; in the midst of which the venerable timbers of Nelson's *Victory* seemed to epitomise the indestructible quality of the city's spirit of resistance.

In the Spring of 1941 came Plymouth's turn. Frequently raided since the July of 1940, between March and April of the following year the city was repeatedly saturated with incendiaries, which served to illuminate the bombers' target perfectly. The Guildhall was burnt to a shell; all save the tower of the church of St. Andrew, whence the townsfolk had streamed to welcome Drake's return from Nombre de Dios, was reduced to a skeleton. The shopping centre was wiped out; the Marines' Barracks, the Naval Hospital and the Royal Dockyard were all badly knocked about, and 20,000 public and private properties were destroyed or seriously damaged. During the height of the raids the leat bracket constructed by Drake to bring water from Lake Burrator to the town was called into requisition to help extinguish the many raging fires; while American Mobile Canteens were amongst the first to render aid to the city that had given shelter to the voyagers of the *Mayflower*.

*   *   *

In the December of 1940 the operations of Coastal Command aircraft and the ships of the Royal Navy were integrated under a unified command; a move which was to exert a far-reaching effect on the campaign against the U-boats.

By June it was only Hitler's incredible folly in invading Russia which served to distract attention from America's helpful "Lend-Lease" legislation and the modification of her Neutrality Act; which came, indeed, at a time when British fortunes seemed to have reached their lowest ebb. For the egregious intervention in Greece and the costly evacuation of Crete that followed had invitingly enfeebled the forces in North Africa, and dissipated resources that well might have saved Singapore; while the submarine war in the Atlantic was exacting a toll of British shipping that clearly threatened disaster.

The staggering blow of Japan's attack on the U.S. Naval Base at Pearl Harbour inevitably brought America to war not only with her Asiatic assailant, but also with Italy and the Reich.

On January 26th, 1942, the first "Lend-Lease" cargo arrived at Southampton, the harbinger of many more shiploads, that kept the twenty-two Trinity House pilots hard at it shepherding vessels up the navigation channel from the Isle of Wight.

The misty weather so characteristic of the narrow seas had often helped to cloak British coastal convoys stealing down the Channel. It was to play a far from negligible part in the February of 1942, when the oft-assailed but still fully operational *Scharnhorst* and *Gneisenau*, together with the heavy cruiser, *Prinz Eugen*, sallied out by night from Brest, intent on slipping through the Narrows to reach the sanctuary of the Weser. Steaming forth from their anchorage at 20.30 hours, along newly-swept channels and under strong air cover and destroyer escort, at the outset the three vessels were so conveniently shrouded in mist as to pass unobserved by any patrolling submarine or aircraft. Their situation was inadvertently bettered by the British authorities' preoccupation with a combined sea-air exercise then in progress, and by the fact that the bulk of the destroyer and M.T.B. forces were engaged elsewhere on convoy escort duties.[1]

Shortly after midnight the mist cleared sufficiently for the shore lights of the Casquets to be visible from the *Scharnhorst*'s bridge,[2] but there was still no indication that the British had become aware of the runaways' presence. Daylight came, bringing strong 'fighter' cover, and still the ships passed on their way unperceived and unmolested.

It was not until the Isle of Wight was nearly abeam that a spotter 'plane flew over the speeding vessels; and with that their commander, Admiral Ciliax, realised that their presence had been discovered and would most certainly be reported. So it was, although almost as little credence was attached to a vaguely-worded signal from a 'plane ambling home after a dull routine patrol off the enemy coast as had been given to earlier 'Intelligence' warnings as to the ships' probable emergence.

It was not until Boulogne was abeam that British M.T.B.'s hove up on the convoy's port bow; with torpedo 'planes also hurrying to intervene. But at 30 knots even a line of ships offers a difficult target, and the M.T.B.'s were driven off by the destroyer escort without having hit home on their quarry. The only hope lay with the aircraft. But without the support of a

---

[1] *Sealion*, the most up-to-date submarine available, had been sent right inside the area used by the German warships for exercises, but had been forced to withdraw to charge batteries.

[2] *The German Side of the Channel Dash*, Captain H. J. Reinicke (former German Navy), United States Naval Institute *Proceedings*, June, 1955.

'fighter' escort, "the torpedo 'planes 'smelled of mothballs'. They were veterans—a flight of old *Swordfish*—and, facing the concentrated fire of every gun on the port side, they pushed their attack through unhesitatingly until all six vanished in the sea and left burning and smoking piles of wreckage and large patches of gasoline as testimony of their gallant death ride. Their torpedoes, dropped at too great a distance, were easily dodged by a short turn together to starboard".[1]

R.A.F. bombers hurried to the scene to take up the fight; but getting to work, as it seemed, without cohesion or settled plan, achieved no greater success than the gallant *Swordfish* pilots. Neither did the big guns at Dover register a hit on their swiftly-moving target; and the only damage the fugitives suffered before reaching port was inflicted by the destroyers from Harwich—at considerable cost to themselves—and by mines laid from the air a few days earlier.

From the British point of view the episode was rich in little but grounds for searching self-examination.

In other respects, despite the constant activity of the *Schnell-booten*, the vigilance and enterprise of the British M.T.B.'s were beginning to establish real dominance in the narrow seas. On the strength of this, Combined Operations Command set to work to plan an experimental raid in force on enemy installations at Dieppe. There had already been a number of small-scale Commando raids—on Guernsey, on a rest centre for *Luftwaffe* pilots at Le Touquet, on St. Nazaire, and on the enemy radar station at Bruneval. But the Dieppe venture was to employ just under 5,000 Canadians, 1,000 Officers and men of the Commandos, and 50 Officers and men of the 1st Ranger Battalion, U.S. Army.

Dieppe lies in the mile-wide gap in the downland made by the entrance to the river D'Arques. Its 1,500 yards of beach, backed by a broad boulevard and a line of heavily fortified hotels and houses, was commanded by powerful batteries at Berneval, to the east, and at Varengeville-Quiberville, on the west. The immobilisation of these 'Goebbels' and 'Hess' defensive positions would be an obvious prelude to the assault of the densely wired-in chain of works covering the beach.

The expedition set out on the night of August 18th/19th. All

[1] Reinicke, *op. cit.*

went well until the Steam Gunboat piloting No. III Commando, on the left, ran into five enemy surface craft, which opened fire at point-blank range. In seven minutes the S.G.B. was a shot-riddled hulk. The landing craft were scattered, and only 3 officers and 17 men of the Commando got ashore. Naturally enough, so small a force could make no impression on the powerful 'Goebbels' defence system, which remained free to bring the full weight of its metal to bear on operations in the centre. Better fortune attended Lord Lovat's No. IV Commando, on the right, which put in a sinewy and successful attack on the immensely strong 'Hess' battery and its garrison. Half a dozen men of the Rangers took part in the assault, and quickly demonstrated the value of their specialised training.[1]

Delayed at the outset, without intelligence of the failure on the left, and having forfeited all element of surprise, the Canadians went in grimly to try to storm their way ashore on the central beach. Under the concentrated fire that met them from behind the sea wall and beat in upon them from the 'Goebbels' flank defences, they fell in swathes. The men fought with the utmost gallantry to make good their lodgement, but as the day advanced it was clear that the warships' support weapons lacked the power to silence the batteries on the east cliff and the headland flanking Pourville beach, which were too well dug-in for the aircraft to get at them. With the attack pinned down, the tide receding, and the enemy bringing up reinforcements, there was no option but to give the order to re-embark. It was deadly work to close the beaches to bring off the survivors, but the crews of the landing craft went in time and time again. At 12.20, when the signal was made "No more evacuation possible", just under 3,000 survivors had been snatched away from the shambles.

A convoy of close on 200 craft set off on the return journey across the Channel, plagued the whole way by aerial assault. The destroyer *Berkeley* had her back broken by a bomb, which killed two Officers and blew Lieutenant-Colonel Hillsinger of the Rangers on to the foredeck; where he sat contemplating the bloody mess where his right foot had been. The foot itself, still

---

[1] Corporal F. Koons, of the Rangers, is credited with having been the first American soldier to bring down a German opponent in the second of the two wars against the Reich.

neatly shod, could be seen floating a few yards from the sinking destroyer. With a curse, the Colonel tore off the left shoe and flung it after the other. "Take the goddam pair," he growled. "New shoes! First time on! What d'you know?"

With A.A. guns blazing and the R.A.F. resolutely breaking up the enemy's aerial assault, the convoy eventually made its landfall. In many respects the venture had proved a costly failure. But a number of valuable lessons had been learned, the heavy price of which the future was unquestionably to justify. The first fruits came with the successful Allied landing in North Africa in November.

*　　*　　*

In the April of 1943 Goebbels gloatingly affirmed, "In the U-boat war we have England by the throat"; and with losses for March alone totalling 627,000 tons of shipping it was plain that the battle of the Atlantic had to be won lest all other efforts should be nullified. By the turn of April there were indications that the work of the Very Long Range aircraft, the escort carriers and the hardworking support groups, had wrought a change. With 69 *unterseebooten* sunk in May, and June losses down to 101,000 tons, it was plain that the tide had turned.

Russia's recovery, the invasion and defeat of Italy, the sinking of the *Scharnhorst*, and the arrival of the first United States Ground Forces in England, all lent emphasis to the fact that the initiative had passed into the Allies' hands. While perfervid Russophils howled for "A Second Front *Now*", without the slightest comprehension that a forced landing in Europe would involve—apart from a tremendously powerful army—a minimum of 5,000 vessels, manned by 125,000 Naval Officers and ratings and 70,000 of the Mercantile Marine, actual plans were going forward to launch just such an operation in the late Spring or early Summer of 1944.

As U.S. 'planes joined in the daylight bombing of Germany, whole areas of the English seaboard were cleared of their inhabitants to furnish battle-practice grounds. The seven-mile stretch of Slapton Sands was the frequent scene of forced landing rehearsals conducted under conditions approximating closely to the real thing; while M.T.B.'s based on Dartmouth guarded the recurrent night exercises off the Devon coast. The Naval College echoed to the bustle of an American Head-quarter Staff; in the haven itself crews were undergoing intensive training in small boat handling and the technique of landing troops and vehicles.

Work on preparing Southampton as an embarkation area had begun so early as 1942; and the docks steadily filled up with landing craft. A trot of 13 buoys to take yet more of them was established in the Hamble river; the Beaulieu river, Buckler's Hard, and a score of nearby creeks and inlets not only offered shelter for L.C.'s, but, like Poole, harboured some of the components of the 1,500,000-ton artificial 'Mulberry' harbour, which it was designed to install off the beach at Arromanches, the point on the Cotentin peninsula chosen for the initial landings. Preparations were also made to lay a pipe-line— 'P.L.U.T.O.'—under the sea to carry petrol direct to the Armies as soon as they had established a lodgement area.

As D-day drew ever nearer, staging accommodation was provided for 53,750 men and 7,070 vehicles in and about Southampton, which soon earned the sobriquet of "the Sausage Machine". Additional camps stretched back as far as Winchester. At the same time Dover and its neighbouring havens were busy with the "cover plan", designed to hoodwink Hitler into the belief that the coming descent on the Normandy beaches was no more than a diversion, and that the main assault was to be delivered in the Pas de Calais area. Dummy support craft filled the harbours till "you could hardly see the water for ships". Vast camps were simulated; empty or non-operational airfields sprouted aircraft and gliders made of plywood; rubber tanks and guns were ostentatiously leaguered in the open; mock-up landing craft were easily to be detected by enemy reconnaissance 'planes in all the waters about Sheppey, Mersea and the Isle of Grain. And in Zurich, Stockholm and Madrid suave British Embassy officials guilefully made 'secret' enquiry for copies of the Michelin map-sheet No. 51—which covers the area of the Pas de Calais.

Then, after an agonising postponement attributable to the malignant caprice of the Channel weather, on the night of June 5/6th the greatest armament that has ever put out from the English shore set forth for the assault on the beaches between Cherbourg and the river Orne—a front extending over sixty miles. Preceded by 117 mine-sweepers to clear "the Spout",[1] 6 battleships, 23 cruisers, 104 destroyers, 4,102 landing craft, 316 coastal and 152 escort vessels, 4 monitors, 324 auxiliary craft, 224 merchant ships, and 1,032 small 'tramps' and blockships, thrust steadily forward across the intervening waters. Scores of M.T.B.'s and M.L.'s were ready to serve as navigational guides or to lay smoke, while others guarded the flanks against possible assault by E-boats out of Le Havre, or by the 76 U-boats that Admiral Doenitz was known to have concentrated in the Biscay ports. Overhead, Allied aircraft were in such overwhelming strength that enemy interference with the invasion fleet was virtually negligible. On the western flank every *unterseeboot* that showed on the surface was pounced upon by the pilots of Coastal Command, while those that tried to get through submerged were mercilessly hunted by the Escort Groups and American P.T. boats under Commander J. D. Bulkely. To strengthen the defence, Captain 'Johnny' Walker's No. II Support Group—which had won imperishable fame in the battle of the Atlantic—was added to the forces previously assigned to the west; and not only sank six U-boats in the first twenty-four hours, but even indulged in a blistering exchange of comments with the Germans guarding the Ushant lighthouse.

The landings, with tremendous support from the Navy's big guns and a blizzard of rocket fire from the tank landing craft, experienced less resistance than had been encountered in the Dieppe raid a couple of years previously. For the success of the "cover plan" had resulted in the retention of reserves further north. Thereafter, despite an anxious moment due to the vagaries of the Channel weather, the build-up went forward steadily and methodically; with 2,000 merchant craft, aggregating 4,000,000 tons, allocated to maintain and expand the forces in the lodgement area. Cherbourg fell on June 27th; and by D-day plus 100 some 2,200,000 men, 450,000 vehicles, and 4,000,000 tons of ammunition and warlike stores had been put ashore.

In turn, Le Havre, Dieppe, Etaples, Boulogne, Calais and

[1] The name given to the channel swept clear for ships on the round trip between England and the Normandy beaches.

Ostend were freed and opened up for the discharge of cargo. Antwerp, miraculously, fell into British hands practically undamaged; although remaining under fire from V1 and V2 weapons. But the task of clearing the enemy out of the Walcheren and Beveland approaches to the port—vexatiously delayed by the abortive airborne operation at Arnhem—involved some particularly desperate fighting. It was not until early in November that a Marine Commando and a Brigade of the 52nd Division succeeded in establishing a bridgehead, in the teeth of strong opposition. Ultimately, support from the veteran "battle-waggon" *Warspite* and a couple of monitors contrived to put all but one hostile battery out of action; and at long last Walcheren was cleared of its surviving garrison. But there still remained seventy miles of channel-way to rid of mines before Antwerp could safely be approached by sea. It proved a long and dangerous task; and the flow of *matériel* was not freely passing over the city's quays till December. The delay in subduing Walcheren and rendering its head-port accessible banished all hope of ending the war in the West in 1944. To give Arnhem precedence over the clearance of the Scheldt had been fatally to put the cart before the horse.

It was not until the following Spring that Antwerp could play its vital part in supporting an offensive destined, in due course, to bring Nazi Germany to her knees.

For a time the E-boats from Hamburg continued to sally forth to challenge the M.T.B.'s and gunboats in the Channel's eastern approaches. But in the last few weeks before Germany's surrender all hostile naval activity had ceased. For all that she was so grievously bruised and battered, drained of her wealth, and mourning the loss of so many of her best and bravest, England once more reigned supreme as mistress of her narrow seas.

*　　*　　*

The days of

> *Peace preserved by fleets and perilous seas*
> *Secure from actual warfare*

are no longer with us. In this age of nuclear-fission projectiles and inter-continental ballistic missiles, Britain could be wrecked, her fields polluted, and her cities reduced to mounds of blasted rubble. But she could not be conquered save by invasion and physical occupation. So long as her people remained unaffected by democracy's fatal tendency to under-nourish the will to resistance, so long as there were survivors left to defend "the sea that is the wall of England", the shores that bound it and the skies above it, "the proud foot of the conqueror" would never spurn our island refuge.

The grey waters of the narrow seas still constitute the lifeline of our commerce and the last ditch of our defence. Physical isolation could still prove our salvation. So long as we retain the skill to traverse those waters in times of peace and the courage to stand to their defence in time of war, they will aid us in the future as faithfully as they served us in the days gone by. "What's past is prologue."

THE END

APPENDIX

The Cinque Ports and 'Members'

IN addition to the Cinque Ports of Hastings, Romney, Hythe, Dover and Sandwich and the two "Antient Towns" of Winchelsea and Rye, the headports' respective 'members' comprised, as corporate members of Hastings, Seaford, Pevensey, Fordwich and Deal; as corporate members of Dover, Folkstone and Faversham; as a corporate member of Romney, Lydd; as a corporate member of Rye, Tenderden. The non-corporate members under Hastings were Bulverhythe, Hydney, Oetit Isham (or Yaham or Higham), Bekesbourn, Grenche (or Grange) and Northeye. Non-corporate members under Sandwich were Reculver, Sarre (or Serre), Stonor (Eastenore), Ramsgate, Walmer and Brightlingsea in Essex. Non-corporate members under Dover were Margate, St. John's, Goresend (now Birchington), Birchington Wood (now Woodchurch), St. Peter's, Kingsdown and Ringwould. Non-corporate members under Romney were Old Romney, Bromehill (now Promehill), Dengemarsh and Orwaldstone. The non-corporate member under Hythe was West Hythe.

Bibliography

A.H.L., Naval Years, 1616–1831
Annual Register, The
Army Quarterly, The
Black Book of the Admiralty, The (ed. Sir Travers Twiss)
British Minor Expeditions (War Office Publication)
British Museum, Additional MSS
Calendars of State Papers, Domestic
Calendars of State Papers, Edward VI
Calendars of State Papers, Mary
Calendars of Treasury Books and Papers
Cambridge Medieval History, Vol. III
Cambridge Modern History, Vols. V and VI
Chapter House Books
Chronique de Normandie (*Duchesna's Hortoriae Normannorum Scriptores
    Antiquae*), Cotton MSS
Domesday Book
Draft Report of the State of the Navy (1608)
Exchequer Warrants for Issues
Gentleman's Magazine
Hatfield Papers, The (Historical MSS. Commission)
Historian's History of the World, 25 vols.
Journals of the House of Commons
Journals of the House of Lords
Journal, Royal United Service Institution
Mariner's Mirror, The
Mémoires des Belles Lettres de Stockholm, 1783
Memoirs of the Royal Society of Copenhagen, Vol. VIII
Moderate Intelligencer, The
Naval and Military Magazine
Naval and Military Sketch Book
Naval Miscellany, 3 vols.
Oak Book of Southampton, 3 vols. (ed. P. Studer)
Pipe Office, Declared Accounts
Port Books of Southampton (Southampton Record Society)
Proceedings, United States Naval Institute
Relation of a Short Survey of 26 Counties, A. (ed. L. G. Wickham
    Legg)

Sandwich Papers, The, 3 vols.
Saxon Chronicle, The
Scheldt, Papers Relating to the Expedition to the, 2 vols. (Admiralty Publication, 1810)
Secretary's Common Letter Book
Spencer Papers (Naval Records Society)
State Papers (Denmark)
State Papers (France)
State Papers (Spain)
State Papers (Venetian)
Statues at Large, 6 vols. (ed. William Hawkins)
Treasury Books
Victoria County Histories: Hampshire, Kent, Devon, Somerset and Sussex

ANON.: Coastwise Trade of the United Kingdom, The, intro. Sir Alfred Read
ANON.: Naval Operations (Official History of the Great War)
ANON.: Portsmouth in the Great War
ARMSTRONG, THOMAS: Dover Harbour
ARNOLD-FOSTER, REAR-ADMIRAL D.: At War with Smugglers
ARTHUR, SIR GEORGE: From Wellington to Wavell
ASSER: Life of Alfred
ATHERLEY-JONES, I. A.: Commerce in War
ATKINSON, C. T.: Anglo-Dutch Wars
ATTON, HENRY, and HOLLAND, HENRY HURST: The King's Customs, 2 vols.
AVESBURY, ROBERT OF: De Gestis Mirabilibus Regis Edwardi Tertii (ed. E. Maunde Thompson, Rolls Series, 1889)

BACON, FRANCIS: History of the Reign of Henry VIII
BACON, ADMIRAL SIR REGINALD: Dover Patrol, The, 2 vols.
BARBOUR, E.: Dutch and English Merchant Shipping in the 17th Century (English Historical Review, Vol. II)
BARNES, JOSHUA: History of Edward III, A
BASSETT-LOWKE, W. J., and HOLLAND, G.: Ships and Men
Battles of the 19th Century, 7 vols. (ed. Major Arthur Griffiths)
BAYNES, E.: Battles of the 19th Century
BEATSON, ROBERT: Naval and Military Memoirs of Great Britain, 6 vols.
BEHRENS, C. B. A.: Merchant Shipping and the Demands of War
BELLOC, HILAIRE: Elizabethan Commentary
BENZE, J. F.: Anglo-Dutch Relations
BERWICK, MARÉCHAL DE: Memoirs, 2 vols.

BINDOFF, S. T.: Tudor England

BIRCH, T.: History of the Royal Society, 4 vols.

BLACKSTONE, SIR WILLIAM: Commentaries on the Laws of England

BLONDEL, ROBERT: Narrative of the Expulsion of the English from Normandy

BONFILS, LAPEYROUSE: *Histoire de la Marine Française*

BOYER, W.: Political State of Great Britain, 5 vols.

BOYS, W.: Collections for a History of Sandwich (Canterbury, 1792)

BRENTANO, LUGO: Introduction to English Guilds

BRETON, WILLIAM LE: *Philippide*

BREWER, JOHN S.: Henry VIII

British Battles on Land and Sea (ed. Field-Marshal Sir Evelyn Wood) 2 vols.

BROOKS, F. W.: The English Naval Forces, 1199–1272

BROWN, P. HUME: History of Scotland

BRUCE, JAMES: Report on the Spanish Armada (State Paper Office, 1798)

BRUT: The, or Chronicles of England (ed. F. W. Brie)

BRYANT, SIR ARTHUR: King Charles II

BRYANT, SIR ARTHUR: Samuel Pepys, 3 vols.

BUCHAN, JOHN: History of the War of 1914–1918

BUNBURY, SIR HENRY: Passages in the Great War with France

BURCHET, PETER: Complete History of the Most Remarkable Transactions at Sea

BURNET, BISHOP GILBERT: History of the Reformation

BURNET, BISHOP: A History of His Own Times

BURROWS, MONTAGUE: History of the Cinque Ports

BUSCH, WILHELM: England under the Tudors

BUTLER, LIEUT.-COL. EWAN, and BRADFORD, MAJOR J. SELBY: Keep the Memory Green

BYRNE, M. ST. CLARE: Elizabethan Life in Town and Country

CAESAR, GAIUS JULIUS: Commentaries

CALENDER, SIR GEOFFREY: The Naval Side of British History

CALENDER, SIR GEOFFREY: The Evolution of Sea Power under the Tudors

CAMDEN, WILLIAM: Britannia

CAMPBELL, REAR-ADMIRAL GORDON: My Mystery Ships

CAMPBELL, JOHN: Lives of the Admirals, 5 vols.

CAPGRAVE, JOHN: Chronicle of England (ed. F. C. Hingerston)

CAPGRAVE, JOHN: *De Illustribus Henricis*

CARTER, GEORGE GOLDSMITH: Forgotten Ports of England

CARTER, GEORGE GOLDSMITH: The Goodwin Sands

17*

CAWSTON, G., and KEANE, A. H.: Early Chartered Companies

CHATTERTON, E. KEBLE: The Auxiliary Patrol

CHATTERTON, E. KEBLE: The Mercantile Marine

CHATTERTON, E. KEBLE: Seamen All

CHATTERTON, E. KEBLE: Q-ships and their Story

CHESNE, DU: William of Poitiers

CHESTER, W. D.: Chronicles of the Customs

CHILD, SIR JOSIAH: Brief Observations Concerning Trade (1688)

Chronicle of Calais, The (ed. John Gough Nichols, Camden Society, 1845–6)

CHUQUET, A.: *La Guerre de la Révolution*

CHURCHILL, WINSTON S.: World Crisis, 1911–18, 2 vols.

CLARK, G. N.: English and Dutch Privateers

CLARK, G. N.: The Wealth of England

CLARKE, BRIGADIER DUDLEY: Seven Assignments

CLOWES, SIR J. LUARD: History of the Royal Navy, 5 vols.

CLOWES, SIR J. LUARD: Maritime Warfare and Commerce

COLLIER, BASIL: The Defence of the United Kingdom

COLQUHOUN, P.: Treatise on the Commerce and Police of the River Thames

CORBETT, SIR JULIAN: Drake and the Tudor Navy, 2 vols.

CORNWALL-JONES, R. J.: The British Merchant Service

CREASY, SIR EDWARD: Fifteen Decisive Battles of the World

CROKER, JOHN WILSON: Correspondence and Diaries

DANGERFIELD, GEORGE: Victoria's Heir

D'AVERNANT, CHARLES: Discourses on the Public Revenue and Trade of England (London, 1698)

DAVID, H. W. C.: England under the Normans and Angevins

DAVIES, REV. J. SILVESTER: A History of Southampton

DEFOE, DANIEL: A Tour Thro' the Whole Island of Great Britain

DESBRIÈRE, E.: *Projets et Tentatives de Débarquement aux Iles Britanniques*

DEVINE, A. D.: Dunkirk

DEVIZES, RICHARD OF: *Tempora Regis Ricardi Primi*

DODDS, WILLIAM E., JNR.: Ambassador Dodds' Diary

DRAPER, THEODORE: The Six Weeks' War

DRINKWATER, JOHN: Mr. Charles, King of England

DUCÉRÉ, E.: *Les Corsairs sous l'Ancien Régime*

DURO, FERNANDEZ: *La Armada Invencible*

DWYER, F. E.: The Elizabethan Sailorman

DYOTT, GENERAL SIR WILLIAM: Diary (ed. R. W. Jeffrey)

EISENHOWER, GENERAL DWIGHT D.: Crusade in Europe

ELLIS, L. F.: The War in France and Flanders

ELMHAM, THOMAS DE: *Vita et Gesta Henrici Quinti Anglorum Regis* (ed. T. Hearne)

ELYOT, SIR THOMAS: The Boke of Gouvenour

EVANS, CAPTAIN E. R. G. R.: Keeping the Seas

EVELYN, JOHN: Diary

FABYAN, ROBERT: The New Chronicles of England and France (ed. Henry Ellis) (London, 1811)

FAYLE, C. E.: The Shipmoney Fleets

FÉVRE, JEAN LE: *Histoire de Charles VI*

FFOULKES, CHARLES: Arms and Armament

FFOULKES, CHARLES: The Gun-Founders of England

FIENNES, C.: Through England on a Side Saddle (ed. Hon. Mrs. Griffiths)

Fighting Instructions, 1530–1816 (ed. Sir Julian S. Corbett)

FIRTH, SIR C. H.: Sailors of the Civil War (Mariner's Mirror, vol. XII, 1926)

FLANNAGAN, REV. THOMAS: British and Irish History

FLEMING, PETER: Invasion 1940

FORTESCUE, HON. SIR JOHN: British Statesmen of the Great War

FORTESCUE, HON. SIR JOHN: A History of the British Army, 13 vols.

FRANK, WOLFGANG: Enemy Submarines

FREEMAN, EDWARD AUGUSTUS: History of the Norman Conquest

FREEMAN, EDWARD AUGUSTUS: William the Conqueror

FROUDE, JAMES ANTONY: A History of England, 12 vols.

FROUDE, JAMES ANTONY: English Seamen

FUGGER BROTHERS, The: Newsletters

FULLER, MAJOR-GENERAL J. F. C.: Armaments and History

FULLER, MAJOR-GENERAL J. F. C.: Decisive Battles

FULLER, MAJOR-GENERAL J. F. C.: The Second World War

GARDINER, S. R., and ATKINSON, C. T.: Papers Relating to the First Dutch War, 6 vols.

GARDINER, S. R.: The First Dutch War

GARDINER, S. R.: The Expedition to Rhé

GAMBLE, C. F. SNOWDON: The Story of the North Sea Air Station

GEORGE, DAVID LLOYD: War Memoirs, 2 vols.

GIDDEN, H. W.: The Charters of Southampton

GLAZECOCK, CAPTAIN W. N.: The Naval Sketch Book

GOLDINGHAM, C. S.: The Navy under Henry VII

GOODWIN, THOMAS: The History of the Reign of Henry V

GRAS, N. S. B.: The Early English Customs System

GRAVES, R., and HODGE, A.: The Long Week-end

GROSE, FRANCIS: Military Antiquities

GROSS, DR. CHARLES: The Gild Merchant

GUERIN, L.: *Histoire de la Marine Contemporaine de France*

GUICHARD, LOUIS: The Naval Blockade, 1914–18 (Mrs. C. R. Turner)

GUILLAUME LE MARÉCHAL: *Histoire* (ed. Paul Meyer)

GUINGAND, MAJOR-GENERAL FRANCIS DE: Operation Victory

HAIG, FIELD-MARSHAL SIR DOUGLAS: The Private Papers (ed. Robert Blake)

HAKLUYT, RICHARD: The Principal Voyages, Trafficks and Discoveries of the English Nation

HALE, JOHN RICHARD: The Great Armada

HALE, JOHN RICHARD: Famous Sea Fights

HAMMOND, R. J.: Food (History of the Second World War, U.K. Civil Series)

HAMPDEN, JOHN: An Eighteenth Century Journal

HANNAY, DAVID: Ships and Men

HARDY, W. J.: Lighthouses

HARGREAVES, MAJOR REGINALD: This Happy Breed

HARRIS, RIFLEMAN: Recollections

HARTMANN, CYRIL HUGHES: Angry Admiral

HARTMANN, CYRIL HUGHES: The King My Brother

HEMINGBURGH, WALTER DE: Chronicle

Henry VIII: Memorials (ed. Sir William Tennant Gairdner)

HIGGINSON, T. W.: The Old English Seamen

HOLINSHED, RAPHAIL: Chronicles of England, Scotland and Ireland

HOLLOND, JOHN: Discourses of the Navy

HOTHAM, ADMIRAL SIR WILLIAM: Private Papers

HUDLESTON, CAPTAIN R.: Coast Signal Stations (Mariner's Mirror, vol. I, No. 7)

HUME, MAJOR MARTIN: Treason and Plot

HURD, SIR ARCHIBALD: A Merchant Fleet at War

HURD, SIR ARCHIBALD: The Merchant Navy

HYDE, EDWARD, EARL OF CLARENDON: History of the Great Rebellion

INNES, ARTHUR D.: England under the Tudors

JACOB, E. F.: Henry V and the Invasion of France

JAL, A.: *Scènes de la Vie Maritime*

JAMES, ADMIRAL SIR WILLIAM: The British Navy in Adversity

JAMES, ADMIRAL SIR WILLIAM: The British Navy in the Second World War

JAMES, ADMIRAL SIR WILLIAM: "Old Oak", John Jervis, Earl of St. Vincent

JAMES, ADMIRAL SIR WILLIAM: The Portsmouth Letters

KEARY, C. F.: Norway and the Norwegians

KEMP, A. J.: Particulars of the Armada and Preparations against Invasion

KEMP, PETER: Mine Were of Trouble

KEMP, COMMANDER P. K.: Fleet Air Arm

KENFIRK, T. D.: A History of the Vikings

KENNEDY, LUDOVIC: Nelson's Band of Brothers

KEYES, VICE-ADMIRAL SIR ROGER: Naval Memoirs, 2 vols.

KINGSFORD, C. L.: Chronicles of London

KNOWLES, BERNARD: Southampton, The Gateway of England

KNYGHTON, HENRY: *Chronicon de Eventibus Angliae*

LAHURE, LIEUT.-COL. JOSEPH: *Souvenirs*

Letters of the English Seamen (ed. E. Hallam Moorhouse)

LEWIS, MICHAEL: The Navy of Britain

LIEBERMANN, F.: *Die Gesetze der Angelsachsen*

LINDSAY, W. S.: A History of Merchant Shipping and Ancient Commerce

LIPSON, E.: The Economic History of England, 3 vols.

LLOYD, CHRISTOPHER: The Nation and the Navy

LOCKHART, SIR ROBERT BRUCE: The Marines Were There

LYON, J.: The History of the Town and Port of Dover (2 vols., Dover, 1513-14)

MACDONNEL, A. G.: Napoleon and His Marshals

MACFADYEAN, J.: Alfred the Great

MACPHERSON, DAVID: The Annals of Commerce, 4 vols. (1805)

MCFARLANE, K. B.: England: The Lancastrian Kings

MADOX, T.: History and Antiquities of the Exchequer

MAHAN, CAPTAIN A. T.: The Influence of Sea Power upon History

MAHAN, CAPTAIN A. T.: The Influence of Sea Power upon the French Revolution and Empire

MAHAN, CAPTAIN A. T.: Types of Naval Officers

MAHAN, CAPTAIN A. T.: The Life of Nelson

MAINWARING, G. E.: The Safeguard of the Sea (1442)

MAINWARING, G. E., and DOBRÉE, BONAMY: The Floating Republic

MAITLAND, W.: History of London (1739)

MALMESBURY, WILLIAM OF: Chronicles of the Kings of England

MASEFIELD, JOHN: Sea Life in Nelson's Time

MASON, A. E. W.: Drake

MATHEW, DAVID: The Naval Heritage
MESURIER, HAVILAND DE: Thoughts on a French Invasion
MITCHELL, DONALD W.: History of the Modern American Navy
MONMOUTH, GEOFFREY OF: The English History
MONSON, SIR WILLIAM: An Account of the Navy, 1585–1641
MONSON, SIR WILLIAM: Naval Tracts (ed. M. Oppenheim)
MONSTRELET, ENGUERRAND DE: Chronicles
MOORE, GENERAL SIR JOHN: Diary (ed. General Sir Frederick Maurice)
MOTLEY, J. R.: Rise of the Dutch Republic
MOWAT, CHARLES LOCH: Britain between the Wars

NASH, E. G.: The Hansa
NEF, PROFESSOR J. N.: The Rise of the British Coal Industry
NEWBOLT, SIR HENRY: Submarine and Anti-Submarine
NICOLAS, SIR NICHOLAS HARRIS: A History of the Royal Navy, 2 vols. (1847)
NORMAN, C. B.: The Corsairs of France

OMAN, CAROLA: Britain against Napoleon
OMAN, CAROLA: Nelson
OMAN, SIR CHARLES: A History of the Art of War in the Middle Ages
OPPENHEIM, M.: The Administration of the Royal Navy
OPPENHEIM, M.: Royal and Merchant Shipping under Elizabeth

PARIS, MATTHEW: *Historia Major*
Paston Letters, The: (ed. J. Gairdner)
PENN, C. D.: The Navy under the Early Stuarts
PENN, GRANVILLE: Memorials of Sir William Penn
PEPYS, SAMUEL: DIARY
PEPYS, SAMUEL: Memoirs of the Royal Navy (ed. J. R. Tanner)
PETIT-DUTAILLES, CHARLES: The Feudal Monarchy in France and England
PETRIE, SIR CHARLES: The Four Georges
PETRIE, SIR CHARLES: Pitt
PETRIE, SIR CHARLES: When Britain Saved Europe
PHILLIPS, C. E. LUCAS: Cockleshell Heroes
PLAYFAIR, R.: The Scourge of Christendom
POLLARD, A. F.: Henry VIII
POOLE, AUSTIN LANE: Domesday Book to Magna Carta
POULIN, THE ABBÉ: *St. Malo, La Cité Corsaire*
POWER, DR. EILEEN: The Medieval Wool Trade
PUCKLER, COUNT: How Strong Is Britain?

RAIGERSFELD, BARON: The Life of a Sea Officer
RAMSAY, G. D.: The Wiltshire Wool Industry
RASMUSSEN, STEEN EILER: London, the Unique City
REED, T. D.: The Battle for Britain in the Fifth Century
RIGORD, and LE BRETON: *De Gestis Philippi Augusti*
ROBERTSON, SIR C. GRANT: England under the Hanoverians
ROBINSON, COMMANDER CHARLES N.: The British Tar in Fact and Fiction
ROBINSON, SIR CHRISTOPHER: *Collectanea Maritima* (London, 1801)
ROGERS, E. THORALD: A History of Agriculture and Prices
ROGERS, E. THORALD: Six Centuries of Work and Wages
ROGERS, STANLEY: Sea Lore
ROSKILL, CAPTAIN S. W.: The War at Sea, 2 vols.
ROUND, J. H.: Feudal England
ROUND, J. H., and OPPENHEIM, M.: The Royal Navy under Elizabeth
ROWSE, A. L.: The England of Elizabeth
ROWSE, A. L.: Tudor Cornwall
RUSSELL, PERCY: Dartmouth
RUSSELL, PETER: Diary (1806–1814)
RUTTER, OWEN: Red Ensign
RYMER, THOMAS: *Foedera*

SALUSBURY, G. T.: Street Life in Medieval England
SALZMAN, E. F.: English Trade in the Middle Ages
SCOTT, LIEUTENANT-COMMANDER P.: The Battle of the Narrow Seas
SELDEN, JOHN: *Analecton Anglo-Britannicon*
SELDEN, JOHN: *Mare Clausum*
SINEY, DR. MARION: The Allied Blockade of Germany, 1914–16
SLATER, BRIGADIER JOHN DURNFORD: Commando
SMITH, ADAM: An Enquiry into the Nature and Causes of the Wealth of Nations
SOUTHEY, ROBERT: Life of Horatio Nelson
SOUTHEY, ROBERT: Lives of the British Admirals
SPEARS, MAJOR-GENERAL SIR EDWARD: Assignment to Catastrophe
SPELMAN, SIR JOHN: Life of King Alfred
Spencer Papers (Navy Records Society)
STONE, J. M.: Mary I, Queen of England
STOW, JOHN: Survey of London and Westminster
STRECCHE, JOHN: Chronicle, 1414–22
STRUTT, JOSEPH: Manners and Customs of the Inhabitants of England, 2 vols.
STRUTT, JOSEPH: Manners and Customs of the Ancient Britons
STUBBS, WILLIAM: Select Charters

TACITUS, GAIUS CORNELIUS: Agricola
TACITUS, GAIUS CORNELIUS: The History
TAINE, HENRI: Le Révolution
TANNER, J. R.: Naval Administration under Charles II and James II
TANNER, J. R.: Naval Preparations of James II
TANNER, J. R.: Samuel Pepys and the Royal Navy
THIERRY, AUGUSTIN: The Norman Conquest
THOMPSON, H. W.: Dieppe at Dawn
THURLOE, JOHN: State Papers
Touching the Adventures of Merchantmen in the Second World
    War (ed. J. L. Kerr)
TOUT, PROFESSOR T. F.: France and England
TRAILL, H. D., and MANN, J. S.: Social England
TREVET, NICOLAS: Annales Sex Regum Angliae
TURNER, SIR JAMES: Pallas Armata (1683)

VEGETIUS, FLAVIUS: De Re Militari
VERGIL, POLYDORE: Anglica Historica
VICKERS, KENNETH H.: England in the Later Middle Ages

WACE, ROBERT: Chronicle of the Norman Conquest from the
    Roman de Rou (Trans. Edgar Taylor)
WALLING, R. A. J.: The Story of Plymouth
WALSINGHAM, THOMAS: Historia Anglicana, 2 vols. (ed. H. T. Riley)
WARD, EDWARD: The Wooden World
WARD, JOHN: The Roman Era in Britain
WEDGWOOD, DR. C. V.: The King's Peace
WHEELER, H. F. B., and BROADLEY, A. M.: Napoleon and the Invasion
    of England
WHITE, JOHN BAKER: The Big Lie
WHITFIELD, HENRY FRANCIS: Plymouth and Devonport in Times of
    War and Peace
WILBRAHAM, ANNE, and DRUMMOND, J. C.: The Englishman's Food
WILLAN, T. S.: The English Coasting Trade, 1600–1750
WILLIAMSON, J. A.: Hawkins of Plymouth
WILLIAMSON, J. A.: The Navy, 1485–1558
WILMOT, CHESTER: Struggle for Europe
WOODFORD, REV. JAMES: Diary
WOODWARD, E. L.: History of England
WORCESTER, FLORENCE OF: Chronicon ex Chronicis
WORDSWORTH, WILLIAM: Poems
WORSLEY, SIR HENRY: History of the Isle of Wight
WRIGHT, T.: Queen Elizabeth and Her Times

Index

(To avoid congestion the names of a number of individuals, ships and places, of lesser importance to the narrative, have been omitted from the Index.)

509